APOLLOS OLD TESTAMENT
COMMENTARY

8

1 & 2 SAMUEL

TITLES IN THIS SERIES

LEVITICUS, Nobuyoshi Kiuchi
DEUTERONOMY, J. G. McConville
1 & 2 SAMUEL, David G. Firth
DANIEL, Ernest Lucas

APOLLOS OLD TESTAMENT
COMMENTARY
8

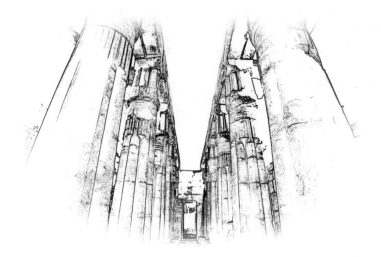

1 & 2 SAMUEL

Series Editors
David W. Baker and Gordon J. Wenham

DAVID G. FIRTH

Apollos
Nottingham, England
—
InterVarsity Press
Downers Grove, Illinois 60515

APOLLOS
An imprint of Inter-Varsity Press
Norton Street, Nottingham NG7 3HR, England
Email: ivp@ivpbooks.com
Website: www.ivpbooks.com

INTERVARSITY PRESS
PO Box 1400, Downers Grove, Illinois 60515, USA
Email: email@ivpress.com
Website: www.ivpress.com

First published 2009

British Library Cataloguing in Publication Data
A catalogue record for this book is available from the British Library.

UK ISBN: 978–1–84474–368–1

Library of Congress Cataloging-in-Publication Data
These data have been requested.

US ISBN: 978–0–8308–2508–0

Set in Sabon 10/12pt
Typeset in Great Britain by CRB Associates, Reepham, Norfolk
Printed and bound in Great Britain by The Cromwell Press Group, Trowbridge, Wiltshire

CONTENTS

For Jonathan, Rhiannon and Benjamin
Learning to sing the Lord's Song in a strange land.

EDITORS' PREFACE

The Apollos Old Testament Commentary takes its name from the Alexandrian Jewish Christian who was able to impart his great learning fervently and powerfully through his teaching (Acts 18:24–25). He ably applied his understanding of past events to his contemporary society. This series seeks to do the same, keeping one foot firmly planted in the universe of the original text and the other in that of the target audience, which is preachers, teachers and students of the Bible. The series editors have selected scholars who are adept in both areas, exhibiting scholarly excellence along with practical insight for application.

Translators need to be at home with the linguistic practices and semantic nuances of both the original and target languages in order to be able to transfer the full impact of the one into the other. Commentators, however, serve as interpreters of the text rather than simply its translators. They also need to adopt a dual stance, though theirs needs to be even more solid and diversely anchored than that of translators. While they also must have the linguistic competence to produce their own excellent translations, they must moreover be fully conversant with the literary conventions, socio-logical and cultural practices, historical background and understanding, and theological perspectives of those who produced the text as well as those whom it concerned. On the other side, they must also understand their own times and culture, able to see where relevance for the original audience is transferable to that of current readers. For this to be accomplished, it is not only necessary to interpret the text; one must also interpret the audience.

Traditionally, commentators have been content to highlight and expound the ancient text. More recently, the need for an anchor in the present day has also become more evident, and this series self-consciously adopts this approach, combining both. Each author analyses the original text through a new translation, textual notes, a discussion of the literary form, structure and background of the passage as well as commenting on elements of its exegesis. A study of the passage's interpretational develop-ment in Scripture and the church concludes each section, serving to bring the passage home to the modern reader. What we intend, therefore, is to provide not only tools of excellence for the academy, but also tools of function for the pulpit.

David W. Baker
Gordon J. Wenham

9

AUTHOR'S PREFACE

The writing of this commentary has been an exciting journey that I have undertaken along with my family since Professor Gordon Wenham's invitation to write it after delivering a paper on Samuel at the Tyndale Fellowship meeting in 2001. Until that time I had seen the Psalms as my primary academic focus, and indeed delivered the paper on Samuel at that conference only because the then secretary of the Old Testament group indicated he already had enough on Psalms and wondered if I had any other research to present. As a result, a paper I had toyed with writing for some time moved from what might be described as my academic hobby to the foreground of my research. The books of Samuel have remained at the centre of my research and writing since that time in what has been a frequently exhilarating process of discovery. Perhaps my greatest surprise was in discovering how much could not be said in a volume of this length, especially since there seem to be more issues to be resolved now than when I began the process.

Many people have accompanied me in this project. Most notably, my family has been with me through it all, including the not altogether incidental fact that midway through we moved from our native Australia to reside in England when I took up my current post at Cliff College. In the foreword to an earlier book I took the apostle Paul's words about love to describe my wife Lynne and her support, noting that she is one who 'always protects, always trusts, always hopes, always perseveres'. I simply need to note that nothing has changed on that front. Our children, Jonathan, Rhiannon and Ben, have also been part of the process, even when they did not know it, and it is appropriate that this book be dedicated to them. Other friends have also contributed. When we left Australia, Castle Hill Baptist Church gave us a gift that enabled me to purchase my own copy of Fokkelman's exhaustive studies, a tool that has been a great help. My head of department at Wesley Institute in Sydney, Dr Jim Harrison, has continued to offer support and encouragement. Thanks are also due to my colleagues here at Cliff College, especially my New Testament colleague Dr Pete Phillips with whom I have had long and fruitful discussions on the role of literary theory in Biblical interpretation and how it applies to Samuel. Mention is also due to Professor George Brooke at the University of Manchester who enabled me to try out some of my ideas in the Erhardt Seminar, and his colleague Dr Adrian Curtis, who kindly gave me a copy of the latest edition of the *Oxford Bible Atlas*, which he had edited. Professor Gordon Wenham has been both a stimulating editor and an encouraging friend, and Philip Duce from IVP has continued to provide support every time we met. No doubt others can be mentioned, but suffice it to say that the support of so many friends is itself a testimony to the grace that is ours as God's community in Jesus Christ, and to which even the solitary experience of writing a commentary can testify.

David G. Firth

ABBREVIATIONS

TEXTUAL

4QFlor	*Florilegium*
11QPs^a	first Psalms scroll found in Qumran, Cave 11
4QSam^a	first Samuel manuscript found in Qumran, Cave 4
4QSam^b	second Samuel manuscript found in Qumran, Cave 4
4QSam^c	third Samuel manuscript found in Qumran, Cave 4
Aram.	Aramaic/Aramaism
Gr.	Greek
Hebr.	Hebrew
LXX	Septuagint
LXX^A	Septuagint as found in Codex Alexandrinus
LXX^B	Septuagint as found in the Codex Vaticanus
LXX^L	Lucianic rescension of the Septuagint
MS(S)	Manuscript(s)
MT	Masoretic Text
Syr	Syriac
Tg(s)	Targum(s)
Vg	Vulgate

HEBREW GRAMMAR

abs.	absolute	K	Kethibh (the written Hebrew text)
art.	article	m.	masculine
const.	construct	ni.	niphal
dat.	dative	pi.	piel
f.	feminine	pl.	plural
hiph.	hiphil	po.	poel
hith.	hithpael	Q	Qere (the Hebrew text to be read out)
hoph.	hophal	sg.	singular
inf.	infinitive		

MISCELLANEOUS

ANE	Ancient Near East(ern)
Ant.	*Jewish Antiquities* (Josephus)
art.	article
AV	Authorized (King James) Version
b. Bat.	*Babylonian Talmud Baba Batra*
ch(s).	chapter(s)
diss.	dissertation
EA	El-Amarna tablets (most easily accessed in William Moran, *The Amarna Letters*, Baltimore: Johns Hopkins University Press, 1992)
ed(s).	edited by; editors(s); edition
Eng.	English
esp.	especially
ESV	English Standard Version
ET	English translation
EVV	English versions
Gilg.	*Gilgamesh*
HB	Hebrew Bible
JB	Jerusalem Bible
in.	inches
lit.	literally
mg.	margin
NASB	New American Standard Bible
NASU	New American Standard Update
NEB	New English Bible
NIV	New International Version
NRSV	New Revised Standard Version
NT	New Testament
OL	Old Latin
OT	Old Testament
REB	Revised English Bible
Pt.	Part
rev.	revised (by)
repr.	reprinted
RSV	Revised Standard Version
v(v).	verse(s)

JOURNALS, REFERENCE WORKS, SERIES

AB	Anchor Bible
AOTC	Apollos Old Testament Commentary
ASTI	*Annual of the Swedish Theological Institute*

AusBR	*Australian Biblical Review*
AUSS	*Andrews University Seminary Studies*
BA	*Biblical Archaeologist*
BAIAS	*Bulletin of the Anglo-Israel Archaeological Society*
BAR	*Biblical Archaeology Review*
BASOR	*Bulletin of the American Schools of Oriental Research*
BDB	F. Brown, S. R. Driver and C. A. Briggs, *A Hebrew and English Lexicon of the Old Testament*, Oxford: Clarendon, 1907
BHS	K. Elliger and W. Rudolph (eds.), *Biblia Hebraica Stuttgartensia*, 2nd ed., Stuttgart: Deutsche Bibelstiftung, 1977
Bib	*Biblica*
BibInt	*Biblical Interpretation*
BK	*Bibel und Kirche*
BN	*Biblische Notizen*
BRev	*Biblical Review*
BSac	*Bibliotheca sacra*
BST	The Bible Speaks Today
BT	*Bible Translator*
BTB	*Biblical Theology Bulletin*
BZ	*Biblische Zeitschrift*
CBC	Cambridge Bible Commentary
CBQ	*Catholic Biblical Quarterly*
CurTM	*Currents in Theology and Mission*
DCH	D. J. A. Clines (ed.), *Dictionary of Classical Hebrew*, 6 vols., Sheffield: Sheffield Phoenix, 1993–2008
DD	*Dor le Dor*
ETL	*Ephemerides theologicae lovanienses*
ETR	*Etudes théologiques et religieuses*
ExpTim	*Expository Times*
FOB	Focus on the Bible
FOTL	Forms of the Old Testament Literature
Fund	*Fundamentum*
GKC	*Gesenius' Hebrew Grammar*, ed. E. Kautzsch, rev. and trans. A. E. Cowley, Oxford: Clarendon, 1910
GTJ	*Grace Theological Journal*
HALOT	L. Koehler and W. Baumgartner, *The Hebrew and Aramaic Lexicon of the Old Testament*, trans. M. E. J. Richardson, 2 vols., Leiden: Brill, 2002
HBT	*Horizons in Biblical Theology*
HS	*Hebrew Studies*
HTR	*Harvard Theological Review*
HTS	*Hervormde Teologiese Studies*
IBS	Interpretation Bible Studies

ICC	International Critical Commentary
IDBSup	*Interpreter's Dictionary of the Bible: Supplementary Volume*, ed. K. Crim, Nashville: Abingdon, 1976
Int	*Interpretation*
ITC	International Theological Commentary
JBL	*Journal of Biblical Literature*
JBQ	*Jewish Bible Quarterly*
JET	*Jahrbuch für Evangelische Theologie*
JETS	*Journal of the Evangelical Theological Society*
JHS	*Journal of the Hebrew Scriptures*
JNES	*Journal of Near Eastern Studies*
JNSL	*Journal of Northwest Semitic Languages*
JSOT	*Journal for the Study of the Old Testament*
KAT	Kommentar zum Alten Testament
NAC	New American Commentary
NCB	New Century Bible
NCBC	New Century Bible Commentary
NEchtB	Neue Echter Bibel
NGTT	*Nederduitse gereformeerde teologiese tydskrif*
NIBCOT	New International Biblical Commentary on the Old Testament
NICOT	New International Commentary on the Old Testament
NIDOTTE	*New International Dictionary of Old Testament Theology and Exegesis*, ed. W. A. VanGemeren, 5 vols., Carlisle: Paternoster; Grand Rapids: Zondervan, 1996
NIVAC	New International Version Application Commentary
NTT	*Norsk Teologisk Tidsskrift*
OTE	*Old Testament Essays*
OTL	Old Testament Library
OTS	*Oudtestamentische Studiën/Old Testament Studies*
OTWSA	Ou-Testamentiese Werkgemeenskap in Suid Afrika
PEQ	*Palestine Exploration Quarterly*
PIBA	*Proceedings of the Irish Biblical Association*
POT	De Prediking van het Oude Testament
Presb	*Presbyterion*
RB	*Revue biblique*
RevExp	*Review and Expositor*
RTL	*Revue théologique de Louvain*
SABJT	*South African Baptist Journal of Theology*
SBLDS	Society of Biblical Literature Dissertation Series
Scr	*Scripture*
ScrB	*Scripture Bulletin*
SHBC	Smyth & Helwys Bible Commentary
SJOT	*Scandinavian Journal of the Old Testament*
SK	*Skrif en Kerk*

TBC	Torch Bible Commentaries
TBT	*The Bible Today*
TK	*Theologie und Kirche*
TMSJ	*The Master's Seminary Journal*
TOTC	Tyndale Old Testament Commentaries
TPBC	The People's Bible Commentary
TWOT	R. L. Harris and G. L. Archer, Jr. (eds.), *Theological Wordbook of the Old Testament*, 2 vols., Chicago: Moody, 1980
TynB	*Tyndale Bulletin*
TZ	*Theologische Zeitschrift*
UF	*Ugarit-Forschungen*
USQR	*Union Seminary Quarterly Review*
VE	*Vox evangelica*
VT	*Vetus Testamentum*
VTSup	Supplements to Vetus Testamentum
WBC	Word Biblical Commentary
WTJ	*Westminster Theological Journal*
ZAW	*Zeitschrift für die alttestamentliche Wissenschaft*

INTRODUCTION

1. GENRE AND PURPOSE

David Jobling (2000) intriguingly asks, 'What, if anything, is 1 Samuel?'
He thus questions the legitimacy of treating Samuel as a coherent text in its
own right, arguing that the canonical division of Joshua–Kings into a series
of discrete books is the outcome of a Masoretic process that divided
existing material rather than recognizing something inherent in it. Jobling's
argument is specific to 1 Samuel alone, but the basic issue stands, especially
given his view that Judg. 2:11 – 1 Sam. 12 and then 1 Sam. 13 – 2 Sam. 7
constitute legitimate objects of study that might more coherently be
described as books than 1 Samuel. Given that the division between 1 and
2 Samuel is artificial (see below, 'Structure'), then Jobling has a reasonable
case, suggesting that attempts to treat 1 Samuel on its own are illegitimate.
But Jobling also raises a larger question about those texts that surround
Samuel and the extent to which they constitute reference points for it. For
Jobling, Joshua–Kings constitute a large block of material that has only
secondarily been broken up. Privileging certain points as beginnings and
endings (and he here has in mind especially Eslinger 1983) creates readings
that might support some groups but undercut others. In short, is it
legitimate to regard Samuel as a coherent block of text? And if we do,
what effect does this have?

The issue of Samuel's relationships is not only tied to Joshua–Judges, but
also to the books of Kings. For many years, scholars have assumed that

1 Kgs 1 – 2 continues the story left off at the end of 2 Sam. 20 (see Fokkelman 1981: 411–430 for a literary integration), so that studies of the so-called Succession Narrative (following Rost 1982) have routinely crossed the canonical divide. Even though it can be argued that 1 Kgs 1 – 2 constitutes a later piece of literature written in full awareness of 2 Sam. 9 – 20 (Keys 1996: 43–70; see 'Form and structure' on 2 Sam. 9), the tradition of the LXX in naming the books of Samuel–Kings as 1 – 4 Kingdoms indicates that those responsible for it believed there was a close link between these texts. The crucial point to make is that a close link makes it legitimate to study Samuel as a discrete text. If Keys is correct (cf. McCarter 1980b), Kings was written in awareness of 2 Sam. 9 – 20, but still as a discrete text. We should also note that both Judges and Samuel conclude with material that is superficially nothing more than appendixes (Judg. 17 – 21 and 2 Sam. 21 – 24), but that, on closer inspection, is more closely integrated to the surrounding material than many have thought (see Klement 2000a: 61–85). The canonical text concludes each book with such material, suggesting it is intended to conclude a section. That is to say, the presence of such conclusions indicates that Judges and Samuel can be treated as discrete units, whereas the absence of anything similar within Samuel suggests that the books of Samuel should be read together and not as separate entities. Joshua–Judges provides important background necessary for interpreting Samuel, while Kings continues its story; but we are still to read Samuel on its own terms.

That we can read Samuel as a discrete text enables consideration of its genre and purpose. Genre labels are something generated by readers to assist in interpretation, but a genre is still chosen by an author as a mechanism for communication (Brown 2007: 140), in particular for communicating the work's central purpose. Modern readers might construct genres differently from ancients, but attention to genre is essential for recognizing a work's purpose.

At a most basic level, we can note that Samuel is a piece of narrative prose recounting the story of monarchy's beginnings in Israel and its ultimate association with David. Several other genres are embedded within this narrative, including poems (e.g. 1 Sam. 2:1–10), prophetic utterances (e.g. 1 Sam. 2:27–36) and parabolic material (e.g. 2 Sam. 12:1–4), while there is also considerable diversity in the type of narrative employed. Although observing that Samuel is a narrative may not take us too far, it is worth noting that narrative prose was not the only option available for recounting monarchy's origins in Israel. One could, for example, create an epic poem that focused solely on the decrees of deity, but Samuel's authors instead chose to tell a story that, although shaped by Yahweh's presence, is still concerned with political events involving historical characters.

If Samuel is about kingship's origins and consolidation under David, can we speak of it as a work of history? From the perspective of history as a modern (or postmodern) discipline, the answer is 'No', because such history is written by analysing identifiable causes (Provan, Long and Longman 2003: 36–43), and appeal to God is excluded. But it is doubtful that any in Israel, or the ANE as a whole, would think like that (Walton 2007: 220–222). Even Ps. 14's observation about the fool who says there is no God is actually concerned with someone who acts as if Yahweh is not active in life, suggesting that folly is denying Yahweh's involvement in the world rather than genuine atheism. Even Qoheleth, for all his uncertainty about exactly what God does, cannot bring himself to separate God from daily life (e.g. Eccl. 8:17). So within an ancient frame of reference it is certainly arguable that Samuel is written with a historical intent, although much of it is written in a manner different from modern patterns (see Whybray 1968: 11–19). That historical intent is apparent from how Samuel describes events foundational for later Israelite readers, events that helped to explain their identity. Kingship and the Davidic covenant were vital features for national life, and yet the challenge of the major powers of the first millennium BC constantly questioned their place.

As a work with historical intent, Samuel offers a testimony to explain these issues, a testimony that interprets that history. As with any testimony, because it generates problems it must be probed as to its concerns and reliability, though these are not generally incapable of resolution (Provan, Long and Longman 2003: 193–238; cf. Tsumura 2007: 23–32). But it is important to stress that it is not offering a complete history of the period. Such a history would need to consider many issues that simply do not arise in Samuel, which instead chooses to tell its story through three central characters, *Samuel*, *Saul* and *David*. These three are linked in Yahweh's purposes, so one can assert that Yahweh is the book's central figure. This is true even in long stretches of text that barely mention him (e.g. 2 Sam. 9 – 20), because explicit theological interpretations are given at crucial points (e.g. 2 Sam. 11:27; 17:14). Moreover, the narrative often modifies its order of presentation of events from their historical chronology (see below, 'Key literary devices') to accentuate the theological concerns. Whatever we might say about Samuel's historical intent, it is also a work of theology. Kingship's story is not interpreted as something deriving from political and military forces. Instead, it is ineluctably tied to Yahweh's relationship with Israel, a relationship that reaches a new level in the establishment of the Davidic covenant (2 Sam. 7:1–17; 23:1–7). Hence only a narrow strand of Israel's history from this period is discussed, because only that which contributes to an understanding of Israel's relationship to Yahweh through kingship is relevant. It is perhaps because of this overriding theological concern that attempts to decide whether sections like 2 Sam. 9 – 20 are either pro- or anti-Solomon have reached an impasse, because they are not so much for or against a particular individual (Gunn 1978: 25) as concerned to declare Yahweh's justice (Brueggemann 1985: 44).

Yet attention to genre and purpose must still deal with the fact that Samuel is a carefully, indeed artistically, created whole. Narrative studies in the HB since Alter (1981) have emphasized the skill with which these stories are told, and Long (1994: 86–87) has shown that such skill is employed in texts with historical intent. Although referring only to 2 Sam. 2 – 20, Gunn's argument (1978: 85–111) that we are presented with a work of serious entertainment is appropriate to the whole of Samuel. It should be seen as artistry operating within the framework outlined above, as a theological assessment of certain historical data (see Martin 1984a). But it is important that this is not a dry recounting of events. The narrative is meant to grip those who hear and read it, and attention to the narrative skill employed is a vital interpretative element, since it is through the narrative's artistry that the theological themes are developed. Knowing that Yahweh had acted for his people was not merely a set of facts to be passed on. The theological excitement this generated must also have held the interest of those who encountered it, which is why such narrative artistry was required. This highlights a crucial hermeneutical issue for interpreting Samuel, which is that if artistry is crucial for communicating the message, then exegesis cannot simply examine that to which the text refers (vital as that is), but must also attend to the techniques employed in that telling. Access to a good atlas is vital for situating the events narrated here in the physical world, but the text must also be examined for its techniques and forms, since these interpret what is recounted.

2. COMPOSITION

2.1. Authorship

Consideration of Samuel's date and authorship must begin from the basic datum of the text's anonymity. A Talmudic tradition (*b. Bat.* 14b, 15a) associates it with Samuel, Nathan and Gad, presumably depending on 1 Chr. 29:22. But it is doubtful that the Chronicler claims they were Samuel's authors, merely that they had compiled important source materials on David. Since Samuel's death is recorded in 1 Sam. 25:1, it is unlikely that the title indicates authorship, and association with Nathan and Gad is more to do with wanting to name the author than something demonstrable from the text.

Following the apparent triumph of documentary analysis of the Pentateuch, it was for a time fashionable to trace these sources through the Former Prophets. The impetus for this came from Wellhausen's division of parts of 1 Samuel into pro- and anti-monarchic sources that were ultimately identified with his Pentateuchal sources J and E. Such a view was still suggested by Eissfeldt, who added an L source (1965: 275), but this approach was largely overcome by Noth's (1981; German original 1943) suggestion that Samuel was part of a unified piece created in the exile by an author he called the Deuteronomistic Historian. Although the

Deuteronomistic History's exact nature continues to be debated, this remains the dominant critical mode for reading Samuel, understanding it as created in and addressed to the exile. The success of this approach is evident in the title of the series of works by Robert Polzin (1980, 1989, 1993) where he seems simply to use the term 'Deuteronomist' to refer to the author. Yet the ubiquity of such language masks the deep divisions in what is understood by the term. Noth understood the Deuteronomistic History to be a unified work, created in the exile, but American scholars (following Cross 1973: 217–289; cf. Nelson 1981) have posited two stages of composition, the first at the time of Josiah and then a second in the exile. Complicating matters is the school associated with Smend (2000; see Dietrich 1972; Veijola 1975), which posits a basic text (DtrH) that has been variously supplemented by legal (or nomistic, DtrN) and prophetic (DtrP) sources.

This is not the place for a detailed assessment of the theory of a Deuteronomistic History (see Auld 2004: 16–21 for an excellent summary; yet note Noll's case against the hypothesis, 2007: 312–318), but it is worth noting that Noth regarded much of Samuel as essentially reproducing older source materials available to the Historian (1981: 54–57). On this approach, the Deuteronomistic Historian is a compiler of existing material to which small supplements have been added. One could find ways of reconciling this with the approaches of Cross and Smend, but this is distinctly different from Polzin (1989, 1993; cf. Green 2003b), who appears to regard the Deuteronomist as a creative author rather than a compiler of traditions. The concept of a creative author, though not tied to the concept of a Deuteronomistic Historian, has also been advanced in Fokkelman's massive analysis of Samuel (1981, 1986, 1990, 1993). Although Polzin speaks of the Deuteronomist, his work, along with Green's, is conceptually closer to Fokkelman. The question for authorship is then whether we are dealing with a creative author or a compiler of earlier traditions. But if we are dealing with an author, is this author actually Deuteronomistic in outlook? Noth (1981: 9) anticipated this issue, and argued that the Deuteronomistic Historian was a creative author who planned out the entire work, though this sits in some tension with his views on the material in Samuel.

A unifying feature of most of these approaches (Fokkelman eschews such issues) is that they regard the exile as the pivotal point for Samuel's composition, albeit in different ways. But this was challenged by Campbell (1986), who has argued that much of 1 Sam. 1:1 – 2 Kgs 10:28 belongs to a document (which he calls the Prophetic Record) originating among northern prophetic circles in the latter part of the ninth century BC (1986: 1). His recent commentaries on Samuel (2003, 2005) have enabled a full-length exploration of the proposal without significant modification (2003: 319–331), though he then suggests ways in which this was ultimately incorporated into the Deuteronomistic History (2003: 221–338). Campbell acknowledges the existence of sources in this Prophetic Record, but his principal concern is to demonstrate the work's existence. Although ultimately integrated into the Deuteronomistic History as an exilic work, its primary setting is considerably closer to the time of David. In addition, Tsumura (2007: 29–31) has pointed to linguistic data suggestive of an earlier date, though the value of his observations depends upon Campbell's framework, since they might otherwise be regarded as archaisms rather than evidence of the text's age. But seen as a supplement to Campbell's work, it provides a strong case for much of the book's originating far earlier than the exile.

Read this way, Samuel can be interpreted as the work of a creative author engaging with earlier sources, the development of some of which is the focus of Adam (2007), though he does not work from Campbell's perspective. If one regards Deuteronomy as a product of the time of Josiah, then a ninth-century setting for much of the material prevents one from calling it 'Deuteronomistic', since it would predate Deuteronomy. But McConville has challenged such a setting for Deuteronomy (2002: 33–36), arguing that at least the core of Deuteronomy comes from the pre-monarchic period. If McConville is correct, and his case seems sound, then there is no reason to assume that the so-called Prophetic Record could not therefore be Deuteronomistic in outlook. If so, then much that is typically described as 'Deuteronomistic' may simply be idiomatic of a reasonable cross-section of educated Israel across several centuries.

I have so far avoided the question of what it means to say that something is Deuteronomistic, but this issue cannot be set aside. Noll (2007: 317) suggests a text is Deuteronomistic if it employs words and phrases derived from Deuteronomy and affirms its ideology. Noll uses this model to argue for a much later date for these texts, but does not engage Campbell's evidence. Such an approach seems to underlie Weinfeld's widely influential list of Deuteronomic terms and phrases (1972: 320–365). But the list's problem is that many of them are not actually in Deuteronomy. Indeed, in his first section on the struggle against idolatry he lists eighteen items, but gives no examples for nine of them in Deuteronomy. There are conceptual links, but this is not the same as a semantic or textual one. Moreover, even within the subset of terms and phrases occurring in both Deuteronomy and the Deuteronomistic History, it is remarkable that references to Samuel are so sparse. This is not to deny the presence of points of important linguistic contact between Samuel and Deuteronomy, but these are mostly clustered around 1 Sam. 7, 8, 12, 15 and 2 Sam. 7. That is to say, there are significant points within Samuel where a close relationship with Deuteronomy is evident, but for much of the book reference to the Deuteronomists need be no more than a convention.

Graham Auld (2004: 189) has noted something similar, and proposes that we read backwards from Kings to Deuteronomy, so the Former Prophets, and especially Kings, are the primary influence and Deuteronomy the result.

This approach builds on his earlier synoptic work on Kings and Chronicles (Auld 1994) and from which he argued that their synoptic material derived from a common source he later came to call 'The Book of Two Houses' rather than, as has been commonly assumed, because Chronicles borrows from Kings. Discussion on the relationship between Kings and Chronicles is irrelevant here, though there are significant synoptic portions between 2 Samuel and Chronicles (e.g. 2 Sam. 6 and 1 Chr. 13; 2 Sam. 7 and 1 Chr. 17), so the matters he raises do impact our interpretation of Samuel. On that matter, although Auld resists the charge, it still seems that Ockham's razor is against him and we should not multiply sources unnecessarily, especially if Campbell's case for the Prophetic Record is sound, since it implies that the material existed considerably before the Persian period, which is the earliest possible date for Chronicles. Accordingly, Chronicles is treated here as a later text employing Samuel so that its value for interpretation is largely textual. The primacy of Kings in relation to Deuteronomy is a different issue, because it recognizes the linguistic links between them. Yet Kings seems to have been written in awareness of Samuel. For example, it can be argued (see 'Form and structure' on 2 Sam. 9) that 1 Kgs 1 – 2 is a later text written from the knowledge of 2 Sam. 9 – 20. But we have also noted that certain portions of Samuel do show a strong awareness of Deuteronomy. If so, then the traditional solution is the best. Samuel was written with some knowledge of Deuteronomy and Kings with some of Samuel. Deuteronomy therefore predates Samuel, and Samuel Kings. But the evidence indicates that Deuteronomy became more influential at the time of the final composition of Kings, something consistent with Josiah's reforms (2 Kgs 22:8 – 23:27), as well as Deuteronomy's apparent influence on Jeremiah (McConville 1993: 173–181).

Further consideration of the so-called Deuteronomistic material in Samuel suggests that it does not necessarily reflect the latest literary strata in the book. For example, 1 Sam. 28 shows awareness of 1 Sam. 15, especially given that the sin which leads to Saul's death is divination, a sin already indicated in 1 Sam. 15:23, where his ultimate rejection is announced. The language of *ḥerem* (devotion to destruction) in 1 Sam. 15 has overtones in Deut. 20, fulfilling Noll's criterion for a text's being Deuteronomistic. But if the Deuteronomistic material is the closing layer, then we would not expect 1 Sam. 28 to be aware of it, because although it comes later in Samuel, it would be an earlier text in terms of composition. Yet the links between the chapters are clear, and 1 Sam. 28 does seem to refer to 1 Sam. 15. One can account for this through a complex process of Deuteronomistic redaction (so Foresti 1984: 133–136), but such a process creates a situation where elements are declared Deuteronomistic to support the hypothesis even though there is nothing otherwise Deuteronomistic about them. But if we dispense with the hypothesis that Samuel is in the first place a Deuteronomistic composition, then there is no need to do this. Indeed, the Accession Narrative (1 Sam. 27 – 2 Sam. 1) shows extensive intertextual links across the whole of Samuel (Firth 2007: 75–80), both looking back to earlier portions to which it acts as a conclusion and preparing for what follows. Similarly, Avioz (2005b: 43–68) has shown that there are extensive allusions to 2 Sam. 7 across large sections of Samuel. If so, then we need to consider Samuel's composition in a more unified way, an approach not dissimilar to Fokkelman's.

In conclusion, it is appropriate to note the presence of Deuteronomistic material and themes, but there is no need to regard the Deuteronomists as Samuel's authors. The book's literary coherence (see below, 'Key literary devices' and 'Structure') along with the way that different sections of the book interact all suggest that Samuel is a planned composition. It certainly draws on sources (some of which may themselves have been worked over at earlier stages), but our ability to trace these earlier levels is limited by the fact that we have them only in the form in which Samuel presents them. Although this work has subsequently been drafted into a larger work that can reasonably be called a Deuteronomistic History, it has not changed the book's fundamental character. In that sense, we can agree with Noth that the Historians took over this material largely as it came to them, but we also need to draw on the narrative-centred insights Fokkelman developed and appreciate Samuel as a text in its own right. In short, the book was composed by a creative author who drew on earlier material but still composed freely from it. In turn, this book was drafted into a longer history, but perhaps one that recognized the material in Samuel as complete but to which the later material in Kings was added to complete the story, though drawing on its own range of sources. We may not be able to identify this creative author, but we can appreciate the skill with which the story is told.

2.2. Sources

Although Samuel is a creative composition, it has drawn on a range of sources. As noted, these sources were for a time identified with the putative ones behind the Pentateuch, but this is no longer the case. Far more dominant is the grouping of sources developed in Rost's (1982; German original 1926) influential work on the so-called Succession Narrative. It would be a mistake to attribute the identification of this source grouping to him alone, because they were discussed in earlier scholarship. But just as Wellhausen drew together a range of earlier discussion to provide what was then the definitive study of Pentateuchal sources, Rost provided the comprehensive study that seemed for some time to have carried the field in the study of Samuel's sources. Although other materials were identified, the three key sources were an Ark Narrative, a History of David's Rise and a Succession Narrative. Although all three labels continue to be used, confidence in their existence has fallen in recent years.

The Ark Narrative is held to be approximately 1 Sam. 4:1b – 7:1 plus 2 Sam. 6, a stretch of text that continues to generate studies (Campbell 1975; Miller and Roberts 1977; Brueggemann 2002). Rost (1982: 33) deletes some portions, though this does not change the text's fundamental character. According to Rost, the Ark Narrative was distinctive from the text around it but internally complete, ultimately explaining how the ark of the covenant came to Jerusalem (1982: 34). It is certainly true that 1 Sam. 4:1b – 7:1 represents a distinctive narrative unit in which Samuel's own absence is something of a surprise, since 4:1a emphasized his importance as a prophet. Similarly, the structure of 2 Sam. 5:17 – 8:14 allows for essentially discrete elements, such as 2 Sam. 6, to be placed together without attempting to join them. However, although it is not unreasonable to posit the existence of a source concerned with the ark (also mentioned in 1 Sam. 3:3; 14:18), there is some difficulty with the idea that our current text reproduces that source. In particular, Rost's theory requires the ark's arrival in Jerusalem to be the source's goal, but it is more likely that 2 Sam. 6 is a separate piece written in full awareness of 1 Sam. 4:1b – 7:1 than its continuation (see 'Form and structure', 2 Sam. 6). Likewise, although 1 Sam. 4:1b – 7:1 has several independent elements, it can be shown to depend upon several elements from 1 Sam. 2 – 3 (see 'Form and structure', 1 Sam. 4:1b–22). Hence, although it is likely that a source concerned with the ark was available and was probably quite ancient, the material is integrated into the book as a whole, so the source itself cannot be recovered.

A second key source is the so-called History of David's Rise. This source is only tangential to Rost's concerns, but prepares for his major focus on the so-called Succession Narrative. Unlike the Ark Narrative, the boundaries of this source are less clearly defined, but discussion of it roughly spans 1 Sam. 16 – 2 Sam. 5. One can say 'roughly' only because some have proposed including 1 Sam. 15 at the beginning, while the ending has been stretched to cover 2 Sam. 7, or at least some form of it (see the summary in Gordon 1984: 61–63). On the other hand, Gunn has argued that the story of David traditionally regarded as the Succession Narrative actually begins in either 2:8 or 2:12 (1978: 66–68). This uncertainty over the source's boundaries is perhaps one reason why it has not generated the same level of interest as the other two, though Grønbaek analysed it (1971), and Adam recently examined the possible development of some parts of it (2007). As with the Ark Narrative, it is certainly possible to note certain themes that hold the section together, most notably Yahweh's presence with David and his refusal to grasp power. But whether this is enough to posit a separate source is doubtful. Both the Ark and Succession Narratives, even if we decide we do not have such sources accessible, have the virtue of offering more or less coherent narratives. Yet apart from the Accession Narrative (which is not a source; see Firth 2007: 81) the History of David's Rise tells a range of stories. Moreover, it can be demonstrated that the Accession Narrative contains allusions that depend upon parts of

Samuel across the traditional source divisions (Firth 2007: 75–80), as well as other allusions with its more proximate chapters. As with the Ark Narrative, we have to conclude that although source materials concerned with David's time while fleeing from Saul in Judah (1 Sam. 18 – 26) and among the Philistines (1 Sam. 27 – 2 Sam. 1) can be plausibly posited, we cannot trace it back to a single identifiable source. Further, the significant questions about the boundaries of the History of David's Rise probably indicate the presence of multiple sources rather than a single piece, but again the whole has been integrated such that the individual sources cannot now be identified.

Rost's most influential proposal, and the one that formed the heart of his book, was the Succession Narrative. One outcome from the disputes about the boundaries of the History of David's Rise is that its exact boundaries are also disputed. Rost famously worked back from the putative conclusion in 1 Kgs 1 – 2 through the narrative's main body that was more or less 2 Sam. 9 – 20, to which he also added 2 Sam. 6:16, 20–23, 7:11b and 16 (1982: 87), but general discussion of the Succession Narrative since then has tended to use the label as a shorthand for 2 Sam. 9 – 20 and 1 Kgs 1 – 2. The difficulty of a narrative beginning abruptly with 2 Sam. 9 is an issue that has never been entirely resolved, though Rost's own proposals have not persuaded many. But if Gunn's proposal that the story of King David begins in 2 Sam. 2:8 or 2:12 is correct (1978: 66–68), then we are dealing with a very different text. His proposal has the advantage of seeing 2 Samuel as a more integrated whole, though it fails to deal with the text's key structural elements. Carlson also highlights ways in which 2 Sam. 9 is tightly integrated into its current setting (1964: 131–139), though still recognizing that a new element in the narrative is initiated there. But Keys not only rejects the idea that 2 Sam. 9 initiates a new and continuous narrative (1996: 72–81), she argues at some length that 1 Kgs 1 – 2 belongs to a separate literary tradition, one aware of 2 Sam. 10 – 20, but building on it for different reasons (Keys 1996: 54–70; cf. McCarter 1981: 361–362). Keys's case for removing 2 Sam. 9 is less persuasive, but once it is recognized that we are dealing with material that has been carefully integrated into Samuel, then the process of identifying sources becomes less secure. This material is bounded by a pair of balancing chiasms in 2 Sam. 5:17 – 8:14 and 21 – 24 with lists of David's officers joining the segments (8:15–17; 20:23–26; see Firth 2001), so it again becomes possible to see that although a source or sources containing information about David's court and the rebellions against him is a plausible postulate, that source cannot be reconstructed on the basis of the present text, because of its level of integration into Samuel as a whole. This has the ancillary benefit of acknowledging that much of the Succession Narrative shows very little interest in the question of succession, for which reason the label Court Narrative is preferable (see also 'Form and structure' on 2 Sam. 9), while also appreciating that the so-called Samuel

Appendix (2 Sam. 21 – 24) is not a miscellany but rather an intentional conclusion to the whole of the book (Klement 2000a: 247–249).

That there are significant difficulties with the now traditional source analysis does not mean Samuel was written without any sources, something apparent in those segments of text most clearly Deuteronomistic in character. But one reason why it is difficult to disentangle these sources is that they may already have been incorporated into Campbell's (1986) Prophetic Record from those close to Elisha in the ninth century. Campbell excludes 2 Sam. 9 – 24 from the Record, but does include large sections of Samuel up to that point, though with concerns at certain points (such as excluding the Ark Narrative; Campbell 1986: 65–82). Campbell's criteria for this date and location are sound, since there are clear similarities in Saul, David and Jehu's anointings (see 'Form and structure', 1 Sam. 9:1 – 10:16; 2 Kgs 9:1–13). Coupled with the possibility that the material underlying the Court Narrative may derive from the time of Solomon (Seiler 1998: 319–321) and that lying behind the story of the ark from even earlier, it becomes probable that Samuel's main building blocks were all available by the ninth century. McCarter (1980a: 18–23) proposes something similar, dating it to the late eighth century, but does not take into account the links with Jehu that point to the ninth century. Nevertheless, Campbell's analysis can still be faulted for being too tied to Rost's source analysis, especially when one notes that the so-called Ark Narrative is more thoroughly integrated than he allows. Hence, although it is highly probable that a Prophetic Record was produced in the ninth century, that source too has been carefully integrated into the whole of Samuel, which explains why Campbell has to wrestle with whether or not certain texts should be included in his source. Moreover, this Record must have drawn on earlier traditions associated with the sanctuary at Shiloh, Samuel's ministry, Saul's story, David in his wilderness and Philistine periods and David's time as king. But the crucial point is that these were available by the ninth century, a date consonant with the reference in 1 Sam. 27:6 to Ziklag belonging to the kings of Judah since David.

One source that has not received large-scale examination yet that seems to be retained in its original form is the collection of poetic texts found across Samuel, and especially the four longer poems in 1 Sam. 2:1–10; 2 Sam. 1:17–27; 22:1–51 and 23:1–7. Examination of each of these poems indicates that they are quite ancient, but with important links between them. Most notable is that each centres on the theme of kingship and within some shared vocabulary includes *māšiaḥ*, normally translated as 'anointed', but which takes on a special resonance within a poem about kingship. Since 2 Sam. 22:1–51 and 23:1–7 constitute a matched pair within the Samuel Conclusion that must be treated together as a single block, it means that a wider range of shared vocabulary can be noted, especially that associated with military equipment, while the root *gbr* is also prominent (see 'Form and structure' on 2 Sam. 22). The extent of these relationships suggests that these poems constituted a collection concerned with kingship and military matters, which predated both Samuel and Psalms (where 2 Sam. 22 occurs as Ps. 18). Adam (2001: 145–203) has analysed the place of Ps. 18 and 2 Sam. 22 within the redactional history of both Psalms and Samuel, but his focus within Samuel on the narrative tradition means he has not paid sufficient attention to the relationship between the major poems. Although each poem is clearly distinct, each also creates an interpretative framework for the narratives around it. In particular, Hannah's Song (1 Sam. 2:1–10), with its emphasis on how Yahweh transforms fortunes by raising the weak and bringing down the powerful while also anticipating the coming of kingship, sets out the whole book's major themes, while David's two closing songs (2 Sam. 22:1–51 and 23:1–7) meditate on the fact that a king can be successful only when he understands Yahweh's authority. This balances Hannah's Song, making clear how some can remain in power, though David himself also came from a position of relative weakness. These blocks of song pivot around the lament over Saul and Jonathan (2 Sam. 1:17–27), which reflects on their glories from the perspective of Saul's ultimate failure and its implications. The one who sought to retain power lost it, brought down by Yahweh, so David's only hope was to hold lightly to power. This combination of close integration into the book's narrative structure (the two closing poems are also the centre of the Samuel Conclusion's chiasm), shared themes and vocabulary and probable antiquity all suggest that these Royal War Songs (for want of a label, though given that 2 Sam. 1:17–27 is drawn from the Book of Jashar, all four may have been part of that ancient book) constitute one, if not the oldest, source behind the text that we now have.

2.3. Date

From the discussion of authorship and sources it becomes possible to make some observations about the probable date of composition. Much discussion of date has centred on the observation in 1 Sam. 27:6 that Ziklag belonged to the kings of Judah 'to this day'. The exact significance of the phrase 'to this day' within the so-called Deuteronomistic History is a matter of debate (Geoghegan 2003), though it generally refers to a pre-exilic setting. Despite Geoghegan's efforts, one cannot always assign it to the Deuteronomists, and with 1 Sam. 27:6, Geoghegan's case (2003: 221) depends almost entirely on his argument for other occurrences being Deuteronomistic. While some occurrences in Kings probably are, we should not impose a Deuteronomistic uniformity on to the whole of the Former Prophets. The absence of internal evidence makes it unnecessary to assign the phrase to the Deuteronomists and insist it is exilic, though in fact Geoghegan (2003: 225) believes it points to a pre-exilic edition of the Deuteronomistic History, possibly from before Josiah. But Tsumura

(2007: 32) notes that the phrase would have been meaningful within a couple of generations of David, and certainly from the time of either Abijam or Asa in Judah (1 Kgs 15:1, 9) in the ninth century. The phrase probably requires the division of the Kingdoms (1 Kgs 12:16–24), and is otherwise pre-exilic, but leaves a fairly large window for dating the book.

This observation squares with those made about the sources underlying the book. Although the now common division was shown to be doubtful, it can be seen that there were sources concerned with the traditions at Shiloh, the ark, the origins of the monarchy, Saul's reign and rejection and David's reign and his problems. The Royal War Songs, the oldest of these, collects four poems, each of which can plausibly be dated to the tenth century. The other sources are difficult to trace with confidence because they appear to have been worked into a Prophetic Record in the ninth century, around the time of Jehu. The presence of Deuteronomistic material in Samuel does not require a late dating, since it is integrated into the text, and Deuteronomy itself may be earlier than many critics have suggested. In short, it is possible that the source materials were gathered by the time of the Prophetic Record in the ninth century, though not yet compiled completely in their current form. However, the ninth century, and the time of Jehu (c. 842–814) in particular, constitutes the earliest point at which the book could have been written.

A latest date is more difficult to identify. However, if we are correct in seeing 1 Kgs 1 – 2 as separate material reflecting back on Samuel, then it would seem that there was a fairly early point at which dialogue with the text began. Care must be taken with this because it too is part of Campbell's proposed Prophetic Record (Campbell 1986: 83), though it should be noted again that Campbell doubts that 2 Sam. 9 – 20 was a part of that source. If this assumption is correct, then the Prophetic Record contains texts aware of 2 Sam. 9 – 20, but the Prophetic Record itself has not included them. My own view of the Prophetic Record is somewhat more fluid, but, if nothing else, it demonstrates that by the late ninth century there was already a degree of interaction taking place with a text that at least began to resemble our books of Samuel.

Beyond this point we are forced to guess rather more. Samuel's distinctive nature with its extended narratives about Saul and David, whereas Kings treats its subjects much more briefly, strongly suggests a work complete before Kings, and certainly before the exile. But how much earlier than the exile it was completed cannot be resolved with certainty. At best we can guess that the finished text might have been written when questions about the authority of David's house were being raised, and for this several times are possible. We can rule out the time of Rehoboam, simply because it would not leave enough time for 1 Sam. 27:6 to be meaningful or for the Prophetic Record to have formed, but the threats to Judah under Hezekiah (2 Kgs 18 – 20) and Josiah (2 Kgs 22:1 – 23:30) may constitute possible settings. Both of these kings reigned when Judah was seriously threatened by outside powers and the power of David's house was weakened and questions were perhaps being raised about the validity of policies centred on faith in Yahweh. One can easily enough point to texts in both Isaiah (e.g. Isa. 7) and Jeremiah (e.g. Jer. 7, 26) to indicate that these issues were prominent around the time of both these kings. Of the two, preference should probably be given to Hezekiah (late eighth century) because the later the text is written up the less reason there is to retain as much detail as there is about Saul's reign. The text is clearly pro-David, but Saul could easily have been diminished in much the same way as occurs in Chronicles (1 Chr. 10). That so much is retained suggests the final composition was when Saulide tradition was still a strong feature of local memory and some forces might have remained loyal to his family. Further, a text completed by the time of Hezekiah would enable later writers to have an established model on which to draw, which would be important at the time of Josiah. Yet if the final write-up is a careful composition that draws together well-known material that could not be extensively reshaped since its form was well known but without reproducing all of it exactly (since specific sources other than the Royal War Songs are not identifiable), then a later date in the time of Josiah is still possible.

2.4. Key literary devices

2.4.1. Narrative chronology

In noting that Samuel shows evidence of carefully planned composition, the book's use of narrative techniques has been noted. The major aspects of Hebrew narrative style are well documented with copious reference to Samuel (Alter 1981; Sternberg 1985; Bar-Efrat 1989), so there is no need to comment on the areas of plot, dialogue, scene, narrator and point of view beyond noting that attention to each is a vital component when interpreting these narratives. Rather, we need to consider those aspects used in specific ways and that point to some of Samuel's particular stylistic elements. In particular, we note here that Samuel employs sophisticated techniques in playing with narrative chronology.

Narrative chronology can broadly fit into one of three categories, though in reality individual texts will tend towards one or the other rather than being restricted entirely to one. It can be chronological, achronological or dischronological. A *chronological* narrative recounts its story from start to finish so that the representation of the story conforms to its chronological sequence, and is usually presented linearly, though the linear structure might also work from end to beginning as famously used by Orson Welles in *Citizen Kane*. One can tell a story within a chronological structure but still delay the narration of elements within it, as for example in Jon. 4:2, where Jonah's complaint refers to a statement he has earlier made to Yahweh that is chronologically between Jon. 1:1 and 1:2. But this is still a chronological narrative. Most narratives within Samuel are constructed on this pattern, working from beginning to end, though at times the narrator complicates the order within the narration both to clarify and intrigue. For example, 1 Sam. 26 contains the second story of David's not killing Saul. It is narrated linearly, beginning with the report David received of Saul's arrival in his area and concluding when he and Saul separate. However, in 26:12, only after David and Abishai have successfully entered Saul's camp, evaded three thousand choice men to reach the central entrenchment where Saul and Abner are sleeping and even have time to discuss whether Abishai should kill Saul, does the narrator inform us that Yahweh has caused a deep sleep to come on Saul's camp. This must have happened before 26:7, but, to generate interest, the narrator refrains from mentioning it.

More complex work with a chronological narrative occurs through the synchronization of multiple narratives. In 1 Sam. 21:2 [ET 21:1] – 22:23 we have a complex of stories related to David's flight from Saul, starting with his visit to the sanctuary at Nob where he encounters Ahimelech the priest. Within the encounter with Ahimelech (1 Sam. 21:2–10 [ET 21:1–9]) we are introduced to Doeg the Edomite (1 Sam. 21:8 [ET 21:7]), who is detained before Yahweh. David subsequently moves on from Nob to Gath, Adullam, Moab and then back to the south of Judah at Hereth (1 Sam. 21:11 [ET 21:10] – 22:5). Yet, having followed David to these various points, the narrative returns to Saul at Gibeah in 1 Sam. 22:5. Saul complains about conspiracies against him and is informed by Doeg of David's actions at Nob, resulting in Saul's ordering the slaughter of the priests when he decides they are part of the conspiracy. The events at Gibeah must have followed David's visit to Nob reasonably closely, thus preceding at least some of David's journey to the Philistines and Moab. But because the narrator wants to create a synchronism between the two, preparing for Saul's attempts to track David down in the Judean wilderness, this mode of chronology is employed. The narrative is chronological and linear for both David and Saul, but the reader must make the connections between them from the clues provided.

Purely *achronological* narration is insignificant in Samuel. As a model, it refers to placing narratives in a proximate relationship to one another but without any necessary chronological relationship between them. However, *dischronologized* narrative, where a set of complete narratives are placed in a relationship to one another that is not chronological but where there continue to be markers of chronology, does occur. The crucial point that distinguishes these from chronological narratives and the ways in which they can play with the order of recount is that we are now dealing with the relationship between complete narratives rather than plays on chronology

within a narrative. However, achronological narratives and dischronologized narratives stand in a continuum with one another, while these
two together stand in a continuum with chronological narratives. Within
Samuel, one can say that the book's narrative is chronological, but
segments within it are dischronologized relative to other segments, and
that components within these will be achronological.

At points the level of dischronologization within Samuel tends towards
achronology. For example, the narratives in the Samuel Conclusion
(2 Sam. 21 – 24) are placed in such a way that it is difficult to know their
exact relationship. This is especially the case with the warrior accounts
(2 Sam. 21:15–22; 23:8–39), while the citations given for David's mighty
men in 23:8–23 stand in no particular relationship to one another and are
thus achronological. These are sample stories, and there is no necessary
chronological order among them. However, they are placed within a
collection of stories which overall give enough hints that we can place them
within the broad movement of David's story, at least in terms of whether
they are early or late in his career. The goal of both 2 Sam. 5:18 – 8:14 and
21 – 24 is to provide a dischronologized selection of accounts from David's
life that assess the whole of his career, and it is a fact that enough
chronological clues are left behind to enable this to happen (Firth 2001).
Similarly, the opening stories of David (1 Sam. 16 – 17) are dischronologized (see 'Form and structure' on 1 Sam. 16:1–13) because of the desire
to present information about David's rise in a way that parallels Saul to
indicate the former's superior qualifications for being king (Firth 2005d).

Perhaps the most complex example of how Samuel plays with narrative
chronology is found in the Accession Narrative (1 Sam. 27 – 2 Sam. 1; see
Firth 2007). Here, the narration plays with both dischronologization and
synchronisms. The dischronologization allows the narrative to move
through unresolved climaxes first for David and then for Saul. Chronologically, it is clear that 1 Sam. 28 follows 1 Sam. 29, as is evident from the
geographical markers. The dischronologization enables the unresolved
climaxes to relate to one another (see Fokkelman 1986: 555–557), while
also synchronizing David and Saul's experiences (see the chart in Fokkelman
1986: 594) so that the chronology is recoverable. This ability to play with
the reader's chronological expectations, often subverting them for larger
goals, provides evidence for the book's compositional artistry.

2.4.2. Modes of narration

As well as skilfully varying chronology, Samuel also displays considerable
skill in its employment of different modes of narration, moving between
paratactic and hypotactic narration. *Paratactic narration*, sometimes called
episodic narration (see Ska 1990: 12) occurs where the logical and temporal
links between narratives are unexpressed, whereas in *hypotactic narration*

they are expressed. In other words, paratactic narration represents a series of independent narrative pieces where no specific logical or temporal links are provided, whereas hypotactic narration represents points where each narrative builds on what has gone before and into what follows. This distinction provides a helpful tool in analysing narrative modes, though they can sometimes blur into one another.

Most of Samuel's narration is paratactic, but hypotactic narration does occur. For example, Saul's fall and rejection come in two stories (1 Sam. 13, 15) centred on a third narrative concerned with his folly in battle as opposed to Jonathan's skill (1 Sam. 14). One can conclude that the events of 1 Sam. 15 are later than those of 1 Sam. 13, but this is not actually specified. 1 Sam. 13 and 15 are complete in themselves, but their logical and temporal links are never made specific. On the other hand, 1 Sam. 14 is clearly continuing the events in 1 Sam. 13, even though its principal content is distinct. 1 Sam. 13 and 14 stand in a hypotactic relationship to one another, but in a paratactic relationship to 1 Sam. 15. But it is the movement between narrative modes that helps us to understand the tragedy of 1 Sam. 14. Jonathan was introduced in 1 Sam. 13:2, though his relationship to Saul is specified only after Saul has lost the right of succession (1 Sam. 13:14). Yet after this we see Jonathan's skill and Saul's folly in 1 Sam. 14, so it becomes a meditation on what might have been had Jonathan succeeded his father. The hypotactic juxtaposition of this with 1 Sam. 15 then enables the narrator to explore this tragedy in greater depth. The skill in the narrative's construction goes beyond this when we note that 1 Sam. 28, though out of proximate relation to 1 Sam. 15, deliberately creates hypotactic links with it so that this narrative functions in a hypotactic relationship to both 1 Sam. 15 and 1 Sam. 27 – 2 Sam. 1.

One notable aspect of Samuel's narrative mode is how it gradually moves towards longer stretches of hypotactic narrative. The first significant block of hypotactic narration comes in the ark's story (1 Sam. 4:1b – 7:1), with paratactic narration then dominant (though not exclusive) until the Accession Narrative in 1 Sam. 27 – 2 Sam. 1. The story of David's final move to the throne and then the first assessment of the totality of his reign return to paratactic narration in 2 Sam. 2 – 8, before the extended stretch of hypotactic narration in 2 Sam. 9 – 20, though this is made up of two hypotactic narratives (2 Sam. 9 – 12, 13 – 20) placed in a paratactic relationship. Although these extended narrative blocks have sometimes been treated as evidence for recoverable sources, we have already seen that this is impossible. What we should note instead is that varying modes of narration intersect with the book's play with chronology both to engage readers' interest and to highlight crucial themes. Paratactic narration enables the exploration of themes through the proximate placement of narratives, while hypotactic narration is employed where a particular theme needs to be explored in some depth.

2.4.3. Repetition

A final element to note here is how Samuel employs repetition to achieve a variety of effects (Kent 2008: 143–219). That repetition in various forms is a crucial element of the narrative tradition of the OT has long been recognized, though the standard taxonomies of repetition (e.g. Alter 1981: 95–96) do not fully address the issue, simply because the levels and functions of repetition in Samuel are so diverse. But this very diversity as well as its extent across the book require attention, though only the briefest summary is possible here.

At a microtextual level, repetition approaches the forms of parallelism well known in Hebrew poetry. This is evident in 1 Sam. 5:1–4, where the captured ark is taken to Ashdod. Vv. 1–2 are virtually identical, except that v. 2 adds the additional information that the ark was taken to Dagon's temple. This additional information resolves a question posed by v. 1, since Ashdod was not the most obvious Philistine destination for the ark after its capture at Ebenezer. Likewise, the opening of vv. 3–4 is almost identical, except that in v. 3 Dagon's status as fallen is ambiguous, whereas in v. 4 the additional elements demonstrate his total defeat before Yahweh's ark. These repetitions are designed to evoke a response from readers seeking clarification about the precise nature of events, with the repetition resolving tensions. Repetition can thus be employed both to evoke interest and to provide clarification.

Repetition can also involve the careful repetition of key words and phrases, though its significance may be deferred for some time. For example, in David's visit to Nob the word 'hand' (*yād*) is carefully spread through the passage (1 Sam. 21:2–10 [ET 21:1–9]), including points where it seems redundant. Yet the repetition is important for Saul's subsequent actions against Nob in 1 Sam. 22:6–19, where it again becomes prominent. Equally skilful are the diverse uses of *mlṭ* (from 'escape' to 'slip away') in 1 Sam. 19. The repetitions prepare readers for its polyvalence when Jonathan speaks to Saul in 20:29, where he intends 'slip away', but Saul can interpret his speech as meaning 'escape'. Other repetitions take longer to reach their pay-off. In 1 Sam. 15:22–23 Samuel compares Saul's rebellion to divination, the import of which becomes apparent only in 1 Sam. 28:8, where Saul asks the spirit mistress at Endor to practise divination for him and bring up Samuel. Indeed, 1 Sam. 28 is full of careful connections with earlier parts of Samuel. For example, the robe (*mĕʿîl*) is a carefully developed trademark for Samuel in 1 Sam. 2:19 and 15:27, these earlier references coming together to identify Samuel in 28:14. Likewise, Joab's violence is marked by stabbing people to death in the belly (*ḥōmeš*; 2 Sam. 3:27; 20:10), but his two killings are paralleled by Abner's killing of his brother Asahel (2 Sam. 2:23) and Ish-bosheth's murder (4:6). The word does not appear outside 2 Samuel and its repeats thus encourage readers to interpret each killing in the light of the others, especially since it is not technically required at any point.

Other repetitions take on larger-scale blocks of text. For example, in 1 Sam. 18 – 19 we find a diptych where each panel (chs. 18 and 19 respectively) parallels the other quite closely, except that in ch. 18 Saul's attempts on David's life are covert, but overt in ch. 19. More extensive repetitions occur in 1 Sam. 24 and 26 with the two accounts of David's not killing Saul. Although much critical discussion here has been concerned with determining which is original on the assumption that they are doublets, the view argued here (see 'Form and structure' on each chapter) is that there is an intentional development between them, especially seen in that 1 Sam. 24 contains an unsought opportunity to kill Saul, whereas 1 Sam. 26 is one that David created but used to demonstrate to his men the inappropriateness of using violence to claim the throne. This theme is interpreted through 1 Sam. 25, where Abigail's intervention prevents David from employing violence against Nabal. Similarly, the two accounts of Saul's death (1 Sam. 31; 2 Sam. 1:1–16) are not doublets but a mechanism for exploring his death's implications from different angles. Such repetitions thus function on the larger scale much as the microtextual example of 1 Sam. 5:1–4, with the repetition explaining issues not addressed when the theme is first introduced. Examples of repetition can be multiplied, as for example the thematic links in 1 Sam. 1 – 7 and their exploration of the rise of kingship and Yahweh's independent reign (see Firth 2005a), but enough has been said to demonstrate that attention to narrative repetition is vital for Samuel's interpretation.

3. STRUCTURE

Consideration of Samuel's sources and narrative techniques points to the importance of assessing the structure of the work as a whole, since this too demonstrates its overall integrity. The two most important studies in this regard are the related works of Koorevaar (1997) and Klement (2000a: 61–159), though Martin (1984b) offered an earlier study that tried, not altogether convincingly, to structure the book around the fertility principal. Although Koorevaar's appeared first, it builds on Klement's doctoral thesis, so the two offer a similar (though not identical) perspective on the book's structure. Klement's main concern is how the Conclusion (2 Sam. 21 – 24) relates to the rest of Samuel, and he takes its chiastic structure (see 'Form and structure' on 2 Sam. 21:1–14) as a model for the rest of the book, where he finds a series of chiasms that build into each other and for which the Samuel Conclusion functions as a crucial summary (see the summary in 2000a: 157–159). Koorevaar's study complements Klement's in that he is concerned to examine formal criteria, especially through leadership (1997: 64), as opposed to Klement, who is concerned with matters of literary content (Koorevaar 1997: 75–80). As a result, Koorevaar identifies a chiastic structure for the whole of Samuel (1997: 72), pivoting around 1 Sam. 8 – 14 as the high point for Samuel and Saul, and David's high point in 1 Sam. 15 – 2 Sam. 8.

Although chiasm is undoubtedly a crucial element in Samuel, one wonders whether these studies prove as much as they claim, especially since one can reasonably suggest that the theological implications claimed by Koorevaar (1997: 74–75) can be identified without recourse to an extensive chiasm. In addition, the difference in length in Koorevaar's components makes it difficult to recognize them within a chiasm unless one is looking for one. It is also doubtful that either of their studies gives sufficient weight to the fact that David is only someone approaching the throne until 2 Sam. 1, but is king from that point on (Firth 2007: 64–68). But granting these weaknesses, their basic insights remain sound. In particular, Klement (2000a: 157) has noted the important part played by the Royal War Songs in the work's structure, and that Hannah's Song sets in train the main issues explored in the book through raising the weak and bringing down the powerful. These themes are balanced by David's reflections in 22:1 – 23:7, where he understands that as king he retains power only because of Yahweh's greater authority. Because 2 Sam. 1:17–27 is the point where a transition of power becomes possible, his lament over Saul and Jonathan becomes the pivot for the book as a whole.

It becomes evident on the basis of the placement of the Royal War Songs and their role within the narrative that we need to consider Samuel as a coherent whole. But attention to the book's structure ought to consider not only the text's boundaries, important as they are, but other structural elements within it. Although Klement and Koorevaar place too much stress on chiasm, there are points where it is important. In particular, 2 Sam. 5:17 – 8:14 and 21 – 24 provide a pair of balanced chiasms dealing with similar themes, exploring David as both a public and a private figure. These chiasms represent dischronologized narratives from all his career that seek to assess him positively, and to limit any negative assessment of him made on the basis of the single narrative of failure in 2 Sam. 9 – 20 (Firth 2001). Thus extended structural considerations enable us to consider the book's message.

But these elements are integrated into a range of structural elements, employing the key narrative techniques noted above. Moreover, the structural components are carefully integrated and may play more than one part. For example, 1 Sam. 16 – 2 Sam. 1 contains a long rivalry story between David and Saul that is followed in 2 Sam. 2 – 4 with a short rivalry story between David and Ish-bosheth. Similarly, 2 Sam. 13 – 19 recounts a long rebellion story, while 2 Sam. 20 is a short one. So these textual segments mirror one another. But the short rivalry story also introduces elements, notably the technique of killing by striking the belly (2 Sam. 2:23; 3:27), that recur in the short rebellion story (2 Sam. 20:10). Thus the narrative integrates structural elements, leading readers to re-examine elements previously thought to be understood and so reassess earlier conclusions. This is particularly evident in the motif of a man having a sexual relationship with someone else's wife, a theme introduced almost in passing in 2 Sam. 3:7–10, the significance of which is developed through 11:1–5, 12:8–10 and then 16:20–23. Structural techniques within Samuel provide textual boundaries marking segments within the text, yet also provide a technique for assessing elements within the narrative, forcing readers to reassess what has already been read. But throughout, the theme of kingship first flagged in Hannah's Song and developed in the other Royal War Songs remains central.

4. TEXT

By common consent, Samuel's text poses more than its fair share of difficulties, and the MT is frequently emended by reference to LXX and, more recently, the three Samuel fragments from Cave 4 at Qumran (4QSam$^{a, b, c}$). Reasons for this are not hard to find, and can be seen for example in the extended introduction to 1 Sam. 11:1 found in 4QSam^a (see NRSV) or the significantly shorter text of 1 Sam. 17:1 – 18:16 represented in some editions of the LXX. In addition, where we have synoptic portions shared with 1 Chronicles there are points where it is unclear whether the Chronicler is reproducing a different source text or making editorial adjustments related to that book's concerns. Perhaps the most celebrated example of this occurs in 2 Sam. 21:19 and 1 Chr. 20:5 on the question of whether Elhanan slew Goliath or Goliath's brother Lahmi, something of great importance for the interpretation of 1 Sam. 17.

The text-critical questions cannot be solved solely by comparing the various traditions. This becomes apparent when we realize that appeal to the LXX frequently means appeal to one of its recensions, so that we need to distinguish between the Lucianic recension (LXX^L), Codex Alexandrinus (LXX^A) or Codex Vaticanus (LXX^B). Care is also needed with LXX simply because of its own text-critical issues, though this is not unique to Samuel. Although these texts have enough in common to regard them as representing the LXX text, their own variations are enough to show that within the LXX a tradition of editorial adjustment was taking place that requires considerable care.

The discovery of the Samuel fragments in Cave 4 at Qumran have certainly opened up textual questions, since they provide a much older Hebrew text than was previously available, being roughly a thousand years older than Codex Leningrad, the MS which the main printed editions of the MT (*BHS*) continue to reproduce. Of the three, 4QSam^a is easily the most important, with portions covering sections of 1 Sam. 1 – 12, 14 – 15, 17,

24 – 28, 30 – 31, 2 Sam. 2 – 8, 10 – 16, 18 – 24 (see Ulrich 1978: 271), though the longest continuous segment of text is 2 Sam. 22:30–51, with most being considerably shorter, often only a handful of verses. A restored version of the MS, which employed a method for determining the content of the text not necessarily extant, was published by Fincke (2001) and has been used as the basis for assessing 4QSam[a] in this commentary, though because of the system employed it must be cross-checked with secondary sources that have had access to the completed MS. 4QSam[b] (representing 1 Sam. 16:1–11; 19:10–17; 21:3–10; 23:7–17) and 4QSam[c] (1 Sam. 25:30–32; 2 Sam. 14:7–21; 14:22 – 15:15) offer considerably less, but are still important ancient sources. However, although these are all older MSS, it is clear that they have their own difficulties and errors (Gordon 1986: 64), meaning that one cannot simply accept their readings wholesale.

The approach I have taken here is to work with the MT as the basic vehicle for recovering the text (following Childs 1979: 103–106, though assuming an *Urtext* can be recovered), and to compare it with LXX and the Qumran MSS (and other versions where necessary). It is not the case that one compares the MT only when it has some difficulties, since its own coherence can mask errors, but it remains our primary witness to the Hebrew text. What becomes evident from this approach is that both LXX and 4QSam[a] often offer evidence not so much of a different text as a different recension, as can be seen from Walters's (1988) study of 1 Sam. 1. So, unless there is an obvious error in the MT, one cannot thereby claim these other traditions as a basis for emending the MT. Pisano's painstaking research (1984) has also demonstrated the MT's general reliability (1984: 283–287), though one cannot automatically assume it is correct, since there are points where one needs to follow the evidence of the other MS traditions. For example, there seems to have been a long haplography in the MT at 1 Sam. 13:15 that can be reconstructed on the basis of LXX. Yet the longer (and more difficult) reading of the MT is preferable in 1 Sam. 17, the shorter reading of LXX[B] indicating an attempt to resolve the MT's difficulties (see 'Form and structure' at 1 Sam. 17). But this does not mean that one automatically accepts the MT just because the general trend supports it. Staying with 1 Sam. 17, both internal structural evidence and the combined witness of LXX, 4QSam[a] and Josephus lead to the conclusion that Goliath's height was four cubits and a span, not MT's six cubits and a span. Similarly, comparison with 1 Chr. 20:5 at 2 Sam. 21:19 suggests that Chronicles is more original, since one can explain the form of Samuel's text on the basis of a mechanical error there. At other points, one must be careful to note that what seem like mechanical errors might represent different forms of spelling (Tsumura 1999). Therefore, although the MT is far from perfect, it may be more reliable than has often been assumed, and is not to be emended too quickly, but without granting it a quasi-canonical status.

5. PLACE IN CANON

Samuel's canonical status is not seriously questioned, and both Jewish and Christian traditions continue to honour it. Within the Christian tradition, this is clear from the NT and the Church Fathers. Although 1 Samuel is quoted only once in the NT (Acts 13:22, citing 1 Sam. 13:14), and 2 Samuel four times (Rom. 15:9, citing 2 Sam. 22:50; 2 Cor. 6:18, citing 2 Sam. 7:8, 14; and Heb. 1:5, citing 2 Sam. 7:14), there is an extensive range of allusions to both books, most notably to Hannah's Song (1 Sam. 2:1–10) in Mary's Magnificat (Luke 1:46–55). Beyond the NT, 1 Clement twice cites 1 Samuel, quoting 13:14 at 1 Clement 18.1, and 2:7 at 59.3, and there are allusions to Samuel in other parts of the Apostolic Fathers. The significance of allusions can be difficult to assess, but an examination of the direct quotations indicates that apart from 1 Clement 59.3, messianic concerns direct the use of the text, though the interpretation of 2 Cor. 6:18 is contested. 1 Clement 59.3's use of 1 Sam. 2:7, part of Hannah's Song, comes within a liturgical conclusion that draws on a range of biblical texts to celebrate God's power to create new life and provide hope for the weak. The strong preference for a messianic reading of Samuel is unsurprising given that Jesus' descent from David was a central theme in early Christian preaching (e.g. Rom. 1:1–5). But Samuel was not simply a mine of messianic proof texts, and the allusions to it indicate that it was a treasured part of the church's Scripture from the beginning.

Although Jewish and Christian traditions continue to value Samuel, they do so rather differently because of the differences in how each constructs the canon. The Jewish tradition divides the canon into three groups, Torah (usually, but inadequately, 'Law'), Nebiim (Prophets) and Ketubim (Writings). There is a diminishing level of authority moving through the divisions, but Samuel is placed within the Prophets, and in particular in the Former Prophets, which consists of Joshua, Judges, Samuel and Kings. The Christian tradition has generally followed LXX's order (via the Vg) and includes Samuel within a collection broadly regarded as historical books. Included within this group are all the Former Prophets, plus Ruth, Chronicles, Ezra–Nehemiah and Esther. Any structure for the canon will highlight certain elements not stressed in others. The Jewish tradition, by placing Samuel within the Prophets, stresses its dependence upon the Torah, but also its prophetic nature. Although prophecy ought not to be equated with prediction but rather understood as a word from God (though this may include prediction), it is arguable that the NT's preferred messianic mode of reading Samuel fits well with this. On the other hand, the Christian tradition of reading Samuel within the history books highlights its role as a witness to Israel's story and is perhaps reflected in the continued attempts to read the Former Prophets as a Deuteronomistic History. We should not therefore privilege one approach over the other but recognize that each provides a hermeneutical insight to be explored as one reads the book.

6. CENTRAL THEMES

6.1. The reign of God

Kingship lies at the heart of Samuel. However, although it relates the story of Israel's first two real kings (Abimelech, Judg. 9, controlled only a limited area around Shechem), it places their story within the context of Yahweh's larger reign. This is a vital concern because it means that whatever authority is ceded to the king is mediated through Yahweh, and is therefore subservient to him. In particular, Samuel stresses Yahweh's authority as one not dependent upon human kingship but who still chooses to operate within its framework.

An element that stresses Yahweh's reign is the reversal-of-fortunes motif. Though perhaps not quite as all-encompassing as Martin suggests (1984d), it is still woven into the whole book. It is announced in Hannah's Song, in particular in 1 Sam. 2:4–8. Here Hannah reflects on Yahweh's ability to raise the poor and bring down the powerful, a reflection appropriate to her own situation, but which then introduces this dominant theme. After Hannah, the theme of the reversal of fortunes is explored through Eli and his sons, Hophni and Phinehas. They stand in a position of authority because of their role as priests in the Shiloh sanctuary, but it is authority that Hophni and Phinehas abuse (1 Sam. 2:11–17, 22), abuse to which Eli responds only ineffectually (2:22–25). Yet, in responding to Hannah's prayer, Yahweh grants her a son, Samuel, who serves at the sanctuary (2:18–20; 3:1–18). Although only young, he is contrasted with Eli's sons. In response to the abuse by Eli's family, there are two accounts of Yahweh announcing the end of the family's position of authority (2:27–36; 3:10–14), announcements that largely overlap, though with some developments (Firth 2005a: 6–10). The family's end is then narrated through the story of the ark's capture and return (1 Sam. 4:1b – 7:1), but by placing this narrative after the predictions of the family's end it is shown that Yahweh has brought them down. Yet the reversal of fortunes is not merely bringing down the powerful. Hannah's Song also celebrates the triumph of the weak, and within the same narrative block (1 Sam. 1 – 3) we also see Samuel arrive as a significant figure, the lad who is the answer to his mother's prayer and through whom Yahweh's authority comes to be mediated.

Eli's story becomes the paradigm against which Saul's story is to be read. Saul begins from relatively humble roots, though his family's status (1 Sam. 9:1) suggests he is not poor. But he is chosen by Yahweh and brought to power to deliver and restrain Israel (1 Sam. 9:16–17). Much to his own surprise, Saul is raised to power, but once there does not submit fully to Yahweh's authority, with the result that Yahweh rejects him (1 Sam. 13, 15) and chooses instead to work with David (1 Sam. 16:1–13). The motif of the reversal of fortunes is much more drawn out in their case, but it is clear that Saul's death is told with deliberate reference to Eli's (Firth 2007: 78–79), especially in that both die with their sons on the one day in accordance with a prophetic announcement. Hannah's Song announces that Yahweh raises the weak and brings down the mighty (1 Sam. 2:4–8), and Saul experiences both. However, Saul's story, especially in the light of his double rejection, particularly indicates that those who cling to power are brought down. Thus during Saul's decline David twice refuses to claim power through violence (1 Sam. 24, 26), waiting instead for Yahweh to bring about Saul's end (1 Sam. 26:10). David is raised to power from weakness because he does not claim power for himself, but true to the constitution of 1 Sam. 12 and its emphasis on Yahweh's reign David is not finally brought down himself because he sees that the final authority belongs to Yahweh (2 Sam. 15:25–26). David teeters on the brink of the reversal of fortunes, but is spared because he accepts Yahweh's right to discipline him.

Yahweh's reign is also expressed by the fact that kingship does not take him by surprise. A key issue for the book is to recount how kingship comes about, kingship that is often regarded as Yahweh's concession rather than his choice (McCarter 1980: 19). But just as there are two points where Eli is rejected, so also there are two points where kingship is announced in advance of its request in 1 Sam. 8:4–5. Given the prominence of Hannah's Song in establishing the book's key themes, it is no surprise to note that the song ends by referring to what Yahweh will do with and through his king (1 Sam. 2:10). The announcement of the fall of Eli's house by the man of God also refers to Yahweh's anointed (2:35), a term given a specifically royal interpretation by Hannah. The implication of these passages is that kingship is Yahweh's design for the next stage in Israel's life. When we read the request that comes, the issue is what sort of king Israel will have, because the flaw with the model requested is that it denies Yahweh's kingship over the nation (1 Sam. 8:7). The request's flaw is evident as it unfolds because it wants a king to lead the nation in battle (1 Sam. 8:20), even though both the story of the ark's return (1 Sam. 4:1b – 7:1) and the victory at Mizpah (1 Sam. 7:2–11) demonstrate that Yahweh achieves victory without human assistance (see Firth 2005a: 12–15). Yahweh's kingship is clear, but the book stresses that he chooses to mediate his authority through his king.

Even where Yahweh has his chosen king, he retains authority over him. Although Yahweh promises David that he will establish his throne (2 Sam. 7:11b–16), he makes it clear that David's descendants cannot treat the promise as a blank cheque to do as they wish. All human authority exists under Yahweh's reign, a theme that comes to further prominence in David's closing songs (2 Sam. 22:1 – 23:7). Apart from Yahweh, Israel's kings have no authority.

6.2. Kingship

Given the primacy of the origins of Israel's kingship, it is no surprise to note that the nature of kingship is a central theme in Samuel. Human kingship, however, is always seen in terms of Yahweh's kingship, and cannot be interpreted independently of it. In particular, human kingship is one manifestation (but only one) of Yahweh's reign, since human kings always stand under Yahweh's authority.

The issue of kingship arises initially in Hannah's Song (2:10) and the message of the man of God to Eli (2:35). In these passages it is clear that the king is under Yahweh's authority, since in both he is Yahweh's anointed. Legitimate kingship is initiated by and belongs to Yahweh, and this is why conflict is generated in 1 Sam. 8 – 12 over the appropriateness of Saul's rise. Although the difficulties are often discussed in source-critical terms (see 'Form and structure' on 1 Sam. 8, 12), it is better to read the text as a coherent expression in which the narrator's own voice is not found in the voice of any one character but through the juxtaposition of the narrative's different voices (Eslinger 1983: 117), though Yahweh's own voice does provide a key for interpretation. Read this way, the issue is the type of king Israel is to have, because the elders' request is for a king who is like the nations (8:5), that is to say, who has the level of authority found in nations around Israel. But Yahweh will give them a king like the nations, that is to say, Israel can have the same structural system of government (monarchy), but not a monarch who is like the nations in terms of personal authority. In effect, the narrator explores monarchy's rise through an intentional ambiguity latent in the initial request. No one, including Samuel himself, fully understands this, and it is then worked through in the subsequent narrative where Saul loses some donkeys but finds a kingdom (1 Sam. 9:1 – 10:16), is recognized by lot (1 Sam. 10:17–27) and finally demonstrates the possibility of reigning (1 Sam. 11:1–11), though kingship itself must first be renewed (1 Sam. 11:12 – 12:25) before the system can be finalized. In particular, we must take the language of renewal (1 Sam. 11:14–15) seriously because it sets the context for Samuel's speech in 1 Sam. 12, which effectively declares a constitution, insisting that although Israel's request for a monarch is sinful in its initiation, yet a workable model is available if both king and people submit to Yahweh. This was hinted at when Samuel announced kingship's responsibilities in 10:25, but is made explicit in 1 Sam. 12.

But Saul will not succeed, and is rejected in two stages in 1 Sam. 13:8–14 and 1 Sam. 15. It is important that this is recounted after 1 Sam. 12's constitutional declarations, because this demonstrates that Saul is not destined to fail (against Gunn 1980a: 65), but rather that he cannot resolve the ambiguities inherent in his rise, so that David is ultimately Yahweh's anointed, the one to whom both 1 Sam. 2:10 and 2:35 look. David's rise is recounted in a long conflict narrative with Saul (1 Sam. 16 – 2 Sam. 1) and then a short conflict narrative with Ish-bosheth (2 Sam. 2 – 4). The tension in the long conflict narrative is that both Saul and David are Yahweh's anointed, though this enables the narrator to explore what this status should mean by contrasting them. In particular, Saul gradually becomes more like the king Samuel warned about in 1 Sam. 8:10–18, while David (though far from perfect) demonstrates that Yahweh's anointed has to wait upon Yahweh and that the kingdom cannot be gained by force (1 Sam. 24 – 26). Only after Ish-bosheth's death does David finally gain all Israel's throne, and it is notable that this is done by means of a covenant before Yahweh (2 Sam. 5:3). This effectively takes further the notion of a constitution developed in 1 Sam. 12, so that there is a regulated relationship between king and people.

The high point of the theology of kingship is undoubtedly 2 Sam. 7:1–17, where the Davidic covenant is established (Firth 2005b; P. R. Williamson 2007: 121), a covenant confirmed in David's last words (2 Sam. 23:1–7). Although it is frequently treated as something almost separate from the rest of Samuel, Avioz has shown (2005b: 43–68) that there are important allusions to it throughout the book, both preparatory (in 1 Sam. 13, 20, 25) and reflecting back on to it (in 2 Sam. 11 – 12; 23:1–7). Yahweh's election of David is thus pivotal. Yet David is far from unblemished, and 2 Sam. 11 – 12 and the punishment narratives in 2 Sam. 13 – 20 demonstrate this. But David differs from Saul in one crucial aspect: he accepts Yahweh's right to judge and discipline him, whereas Saul resists these actions. It is this, and the positive overall portrayal of David in 2 Sam. 5:17 – 8:14 and 21 – 24, that enables him to be the model monarch of Kings. Even there David's faults do not go unnoticed (1 Kgs 15:4–5), but it is acknowledged that David sees worship and a reign submitted to Yahweh as essential. It is this model for kingship, a model that is positive for the future rather than the negative model many have assumed dominates the so-called Deuteronomistic History (for a positive view of kingship in these books, see Gerbrandt 1986) that lies at the heart of Samuel. Kings reign under Yahweh's authority, and demonstrate their acceptance of this in their commitment to authentic worship as both a public and a private act.

6.3. Prophetic authority

That kingship functions under Yahweh's overarching reign raises the question of how kings know Yahweh's will and so reign under him. Curiously, although the initial request for a monarch alludes to the kingship law in Deut. 17:14–20, there are no specific reflections in Samuel concerned with the enthroned king making his own copy of the Torah, presumably meaning something approaching Deuteronomy itself rather than the Pentateuch as a whole. This is especially intriguing if Torah's primacy is integral to Deuteronomy's kingship law (McConville 2002: 295). However, the law in Deuteronomy is concerned to stress that the king's knowledge of the Torah is a mechanism for ensuring that the king revere Yahweh and not be lifted above his compatriots. Given the king's role in establishing justice this may also be an element, but the Torah is not the means by which the king is guided into Yahweh's will to submit to him. As such, this theme's absence is not as surprising as it may seem. One can certainly find points where David's actions as king are consistent with Torah, but there is no direct reflection on its guidance in Samuel. Rather, Yahweh's will is primarily made known to the king by valid prophets so that kings, and indeed all leaders, can conform to it.

The importance of prophetic figures is indicated from the outset. Although Hannah is never referred to by any of the OT's prophetic labels, her Song (1 Sam. 2:1–10) is clearly treated as a prophetic utterance (Klement 2000a: 112–113). Her message about Yahweh's power sets in train the book's main themes, themes that receive further reflection in the other Royal War Songs. Hannah's Song is paired within the opening narratives with the declaration of the man of God who announced the fall of Eli's house in 1 Sam. 2:27–36. Where Hannah does not receive a prophetic label, this anonymous man is known only by his prophetic label. His message to Eli both confirms Hannah's Song and lays the foundations for Samuel's prophetic ministry, which is established in 1 Sam. 3:1–18. Samuel is initiated into a prophetic ministry at a time when Yahweh's word is scarce (1 Sam. 3:1), though it is abundant by the chapter's end where Samuel's first message (1 Sam. 3:10–14) largely matches that of the man of God, confirming the fall of Eli's house. The authority of Samuel's message and its reliability are stressed in 3:19 – 4:1a, but the story of the ark's capture in 1 Sam. 4 also demonstrates this as well as the authority of the man of God, since the end of Eli's family is an integral element within both their messages. Neither the man of God nor Samuel is active within 1 Sam. 4:1b – 7:1, but their message hangs over the whole of it. In short, the prophets' authority is shown by the fact that Yahweh ensures that their message comes to pass.

Having established the prophets' importance, the narrative also shows that when prophets act outside their area of authority (as a vehicle for Yahweh's message), they have no authority. To some extent, this is evident in 1 Sam. 7:2–11, where Yahweh effectively sidesteps Samuel when defeating the Philistines, but it becomes much clearer in 1 Sam. 8:1–3, where Samuel appoints his sons to act as judges, though they are as corrupt as Eli's sons before him. This triggers the request for kingship, and there is a sense in which Samuel's somewhat testy response to it is presented more as his own hurt pride than anything else (1 Sam. 8:7). Yet if Yahweh has announced that he is moving towards kingship (1 Sam. 2:10, 35), then Samuel has no basis to appoint his own sons to a judicial position. Just as kings could transgress their proper role and place, so also prophets could claim authority not rightly theirs. As a prophet, Samuel had authority when he brought Yahweh's word, but he could not move into a quasi-monarchic role by establishing his own dynasty. Even before a king has been appointed, there is thus a hint of the importance of separating powers so that the king exercises civil authority, though Yahweh through his prophets has the final say.

The primacy of prophetic ministry is well illustrated through Saul's rise and rejection. Once Yahweh convinces Samuel that a monarch is to be appointed (1 Sam. 8:22), the various stages enabling this are controlled by prophetic action. Samuel first anoints Saul in response to an earlier message from Yahweh (1 Sam. 10:1) and then gathers the people to Mizpah for Saul's public election (1 Sam. 10:20–24) as well as to declare the duties of kingship (1 Sam. 10:25). Even when Saul seemingly proves himself in delivering Jabesh Gilead (1 Sam. 11:1–11), Samuel again assembles the people at Gilgal to renew the kingship (1 Sam. 11:14–15), the content of which is delivered through his speech in 1 Sam. 12. Each step in Saul's rise occurs under prophetic direction, with Samuel's acting as Yahweh's mouthpiece in declaring what is right to king and people. This process continues through Saul's rejection in 1 Sam. 13 – 15. First, Saul fails to wait the seven days Samuel stipulated for a sacrifice at 10:8 and so loses the right of dynasty (1 Sam. 13:8–14), and then loses his claim to the throne after keeping some of the spoil from Amalek for a sacrifice (1 Sam. 15:26). A post-mortem Samuel even gets to announce Saul's death (1 Sam. 28:17–19). In all these cases the prophet's role is to declare Yahweh's will, that the king may obey it. Saul's failure is that he does not accept this and instead resists Yahweh's will as revealed through the prophet.

Prophetic authority is also vital in David's story. Like Saul, David is anointed by Samuel at Yahweh's direction (1 Sam. 16:1–13), though Samuel plays a relatively small role in the balance of David's story save for when David flees to him at Ramah when escaping from Saul in 1 Sam. 19:18–24. But two other prophets are active in David's career, and they too direct him by declaring Yahweh's word. Gad is the less prominent of the two, first appearing at 1 Sam. 22:5 when directing David to leave his stronghold (presumably in Moab) to return to Judah, and then returning in 2 Sam. 24:11–14, 18–19 to rebuke David over his census. Since David asks him about the possibility of building a temple for Yahweh (2 Sam. 7:1–3), Nathan is the better-known figure, who brings back instead Yahweh's announcement that he will build a house for David (2 Sam. 7:4–17). Nathan also confronts David following the king's assault on Uriah and his ultimate murder in 2 Sam. 11, and announces Yahweh's punishment on David (2 Sam. 12:1–15a), later indicating Yahweh's love for Solomon (2 Sam. 12:24–25). What distinguishes David is that he accepts the prophet's authority to declare Yahweh's will, even when it is a word of punishment.

Yahweh guides the king in other ways, notably through the ephod and Urim and Thummim. Saul receives guidance concerning the source of sin in the camp in 1 Sam. 14:36–46, though the narrative's ironic tone makes clear that it is not the guidance he desires. Later, following the murder of the priests at Nob, Saul is denied access to this resource when Abiathar brings it to David (1 Sam. 23:6). David uses it to escape from Keilah (1 Sam. 23:9–12) and later, in 1 Sam. 30:7–8, to decide whether to pursue the raiding Amalekites. However, a distinction must be drawn between this guidance, which reflects decisions concerning immediate situations, and the guidance given by prophets. Although there is obvious overlap, prophetic guidance is initiated by Yahweh to establish policy patterns for his king, whereas guidance received through Urim and Thummim and ephod respond to the king's request in a specific situation. Yahweh guides his king through both, but it is specifically through the prophet that Yahweh's reign as Israel's primary authority is demonstrated. Kingship is within Yahweh's plan, but it can function only under Yahweh's authority, and this authority is mediated through authentic prophetic figures who declare Yahweh's message to his people and king. Acceptance of this was the litmus test of any Israelite leader's authenticity. Nevertheless, it is perhaps in part because Yahweh's guidance for his king was through both prophet and priest that the NT makes clear that Jesus is prophet, priest and king.

TEXT AND COMMENTARY

1 SAMUEL 1:1 – 2:10

Translation

[1]And there was a man from Ramathaim, a Zuphite, from the hill country of Ephraim, and his name was Elkanah ben Jeroham ben Elihu ben Tohu ben Ziph, an Ephrathite. [2]And he had two wives; the name of the first was Hannah and the second was Peninnah. Now Peninnah had children, but Hannah had no children. [3]And that man went up from his city every year to worship and to sacrifice to Yahweh of hosts in Shiloh. And the two sons of Eli, Hophni and Phinehas, were the priests to Yahweh there. [4]And it happened on the day when Elkanah sacrificed that he gave portions to his wife, Peninnah, and her sons and daughters, [5]but to Hannah he gave one special portion because he loved her and Yahweh had closed her womb. [6]And her adversary vexed her greatly to the point of thundering because Yahweh had closed up her womb. [7]And thus it would happen year by year, as often she went up to the house of Yahweh, thus she vexed her, and she would weep and not eat. [8]And Elkanah her husband would say to her, 'Hannah, why are you weeping? And why are you not eating? And why is your heart grieved? Am I not worth more to you than ten sons?'

[9]And Hannah rose up after eating and drinking in Shiloh, and Eli the priest was sitting on his throne beside the doorpost in the temple of Yahweh. [10]And she was bitter of soul, and prayed to Yahweh and wept bitterly. [11]And she made a vow and said, 'Yahweh of hosts, if you shall truly see the affliction of your maidservant,

and remember me and not forget your maidservant, but give to your maidservant a descendant, then I shall give him to Yahweh all the days of his life, and a razor will not come up upon his head.' [12]And as she kept on praying before Yahweh, Eli observed her mouth. [13]And Hannah was speaking within her heart; her lips moved, but no sound was heard, so Eli thought she was drunk. [14]And Eli said to her, 'How long will you make yourself drunk? Take away your wine from upon you.' [15]But Hannah answered and said, 'No, my lord, I am a determined woman; I have drunk no wine or strong drink, but I have poured out my soul before Yahweh. [16]Do not regard your maidservant as a daughter of Belial, for from the abundance of my complaint and my vexation have I spoken until now.' [17]And Eli answered and said, 'Go in peace. And may the God of Israel grant you the request that you have asked of him.' [18]And she said, 'Let your maidservant find favour in your eyes.' And the woman went on her way, and her face was no longer sad.

[19]And they rose early in the morning and worshipped before Yahweh, then returned and came to their house at Ramah. Then Elkanah knew Hannah his wife and Yahweh remembered her. [20]And it happened at the turning of the days that Hannah conceived and she gave birth to a son, and she named him Samuel because 'I asked for him from Yahweh.' [21]And the man Elkanah went up along with all his house to make his annual sacrifice and vow, [22]but Hannah did not go up because she said to her husband, 'After the boy is weaned I shall take the lad up and he will appear before Yahweh and will remain there for ever.' [23]And Elkanah her husband said to her, 'Do what is right in your eyes; stay until you have weaned him. Only may Yahweh establish his word.' And the woman stayed and nursed her son until she weaned him. [24]Then she took him up with her when she had weaned him with three bulls, an ephah of flour and a skin of wine, and she brought him to the house of Yahweh at Shiloh. And the lad was young. [25]And they slaughtered the bulls and brought the lad to Eli. [26]And she said, 'O my lord. As your soul lives, my lord, I am the woman who stood with you here praying to Yahweh. [27]For this lad I prayed, and Yahweh gave me the request that I asked from him. [28]And also I have dedicated him to Yahweh; all the days that he lives is he dedicated.' And he worshipped Yahweh there.

[2:1]And Hannah prayed and said,

'My heart rejoices in Yahweh,
    my horn is lifted high in Yahweh.
My mouth boasts over my enemies,
    because I rejoice in your victory.
[2]There is no holy one like Yahweh
    because there is no one besides you
    and there is no rock like our God.
[3]Do not multiply your speaking haughty things,
    or let arrogance come from your mouth,
  for Yahweh is a God of knowledge,
    and actions are weighed by him.
[4]The bows of the mighty are broken,
    but those who stumble gird on strength.

⁵Those who were satisfied with bread have hired themselves out,
  but the hungry do so no longer,
the barren has borne seven
  but she with many sons is forlorn.
⁶Yahweh kills and brings to life,
  he brings down to Sheol and raises up.
⁷Yahweh makes poor and rich,
  he makes low and he exalts.
⁸He raises the poor from the dust,
  he lifts the needy from the ash heap
to seat them with princes
  and inherit a glorious throne.
For the pillars of the earth are Yahweh's
  and he has set the world upon them.
⁹The feet of his holy ones will he keep,
  but the wicked in darkness shall be silenced,
for not by power does one prevail.
¹⁰ Those who contend with Yahweh will be shattered,
from heaven shall he thunder against them.
  Yahweh will judge the ends of the earth,
and give strength to his king,
  he will exalt the horn of his anointed.'

Notes on the text

1:1. The *wayyĕhî 'îš 'eḥād* is similar to Judg. 13:2, but evidence from LXX is insufficient to follow McCarter (1980a: 51) and emend. With Driver (1913: 1) read *ṣûpî* for *ṣûpîm*, the mem occurring from dittography.

5. The meaning of *'appayim* is unclear. *DCH* suggests one side (half) of a portion, though the Tg suggests a special portion. Since the *kî* clause provides a positive reason for this action, *DCH* is doubtful. LXX is problematic. D. C. van Zyl (1993) argues from comparative studies that it may refer to an old religious practice where the nose was given as a sign of favour. Though speculative, it explains the Tg, which may represent the oldest exegesis of this phrase. It is preferable to NIV, which follows Peshitta with 'double portion'.

6. *harrĕ'imâ* normally refers to 'thunder', not 'irritation' (NIV, NRSV). The irritation is that which leads to Hannah's crying out in rage and frustration. Dagesh in the resh is unusual.

7. *ya'ăśeh* is awkward since the second half of the verse refers to Peninnah, not Elkanah. Klein (1983: 2) emends to a f. verb, but it is retained as impersonal (GKC §144b).

10. With many MSS, read *'el yhwh* for *'al yhwh*.

11. LXX and 4QSam^a attest a longer reading, making explicit Samuel's status as a Nazirite. With Walters (1988) these indicate different narrative traditions, and are not a basis for emendation.

15. Against Driver (1913: 14), *qěšat rûaḥ* does not mean 'obstinate', so reversion to LXX is unnecessary: it is determination that is emphasized (see Muraoka 1996).

16. 'Daughter of Belial'. The etymology of 'Belial' is unclear (perhaps a combination of 'not' and 'profit'), but is a standard term for someone of doubtful moral character (e.g. Judg. 19:22; 20:13), and Eli's sons will be called 'sons of Belial' (2:12).

18. LXX adds a cultic meal before Hannah's departure. However, MT is coherent, highlighting Walters's (1988) thesis that the LXX represents a different narrative tradition. *ûpāneyhā lō' hāyû lāh 'ōd* is peculiar; lit. 'and her face was not to her again'; but none of the alternatives offers any advantage. In context, it is perhaps an idiomatic way of saying she was no longer downcast.

23. The suffix on *dibrô* is unexpected since there is no previous reference to a word from Yahweh. McCarter (1980a: 56) among others follows LXX 'your word', though also following the wider LXX phraseology, unlike NEB. However, it is difficult to see how LXX could have given rise to MT, and vice versa. Walters (1988: 385–387) shows that recourse to LXX at this point creates a text that never previously existed. It is the unexpectedness of this statement that highlights its point.

24–25. 'Three bulls' is commonly emended to 'a three-year-old bull' (e.g. NRSV), but the sg. in 1:25 is a collective (Ratner 1987; cf. Gen. 15:10), while the unusual word order can be paralleled (1 Sam. 25:2). The last phrase of v. 24, lit. 'the lad was a lad', is difficult, but recourse to LXX on grounds of haplography is unnecessary since the word *na'ar* is simply repeated (see Walters 1988: 403–404; though his solution seems inappropriate). Since *na'ar* becomes a key term, it is probably a deliberate emphasis of what will become a central motif. Age, not a change of role (contra Eslinger 1985: 89), is stressed.

2:2. 'Because there is no one besides you' (*kî 'ên biltekā*) is not in LXX or 4QSam[a] (Lewis 1994: 28 omits it). The range of variants is large, but without a clearly better reading. MT may be maintained. The disputed line breaks the parallelism, so foregrounding it (Eslinger 1985: 107).

3. With many MSS, reading *lô* for *lō'*.

5. *ûrě'ēbîm ḥādēllû 'ad* has long been regarded as problematic. A verb *ḥdl* II, 'to grow plump', has been suggested, but Lewis (1985) shows this is inappropriate. The line can be interpreted as it stands.

8–9. LXX and 4QSam[a] differ considerably from MT. Although similar, they are not identical, with expansions and omissions (see Lewis 1994: 37–38). The expansions draw heavily from Jer. 9:22–23 and are probably a gloss. The omissions are more difficult. These emphasize the blessing bestowed on those who keep their vows. MT is preferred on internal grounds: Hannah's story has a different narrative structure in LXX and 4QSam[a], and the song has been shaped by those concerns (see Bartelmus 1987: 23–24, though for different reasons).

Form and structure

In beginning a story, a narrator must decide where to begin. This is a complex process because events seldom have neat beginnings and endings, but are made up of different events woven into a larger experience. Intriguingly, this narrative of kingship's rise does not begin with the powerful. Instead, it begins with a relatively obscure family and their experience of worship, though drawing on familiar themes such as the favoured wife's being barren and Yahweh's acting to provide a son. It echoes the stories of Sarah (Gen. 12 – 21), Rachel and Leah (Gen. 29 – 30) and the wife of Manoah (Judg. 13:2–7). The theme continues into the NT with the birth story of John the Baptist (Luke 1:5–25, 57–66; see Jarrell 2002: 3–18). There are variations that prevent us from reading these narratives as simple replications since each is carefully placed within its narrative framework. Nevertheless, this background shapes readers' expectations because they anticipate that Yahweh will provide a son. Telling a story to evoke an expectation of Yahweh's involvement indicates that this family's circumstances are more interesting than they might seem. The variations are related to kingship's beginning, a theme hinted at in frequent allusions to the name of Israel's first king, Saul (although he never actually appears), and explicit in Hannah's concluding reference to 'Yahweh's anointed' in 2:10. Before we come to monarchy itself, we need to be introduced to Samuel and understand why he is so pivotal for the wider narrative. The beginnings of kingship lie in Yahweh's gracious gift of a son to a woman whose womb he had previously closed (see Brueggemann 1992: 234). However painful the move towards monarchy will be, it is still Yahweh's initiative.

Monarchy's rise inevitably meant the fall of another; in this case the priestly family of Eli. One had to supersede the other, an outcome hinted at in the closing chapters of Judges, with their repeated reference to the absence of a king (17:6; 18:1; 19:1; 21:25). Thus we read this story within Samuel, but also as a part of the larger narrative that has suggested that monarchy is the way forward for Israel. The problems this shift faces become apparent when one considers the 'royal' presentation of Eli as one who sits on a 'throne' and administers a *hêkal*, a term meaning either 'temple' or 'palace'. Thus we are prepared for a possible struggle between Eli's pseudo-monarchy (see Polzin 1989: 23–24) and that which comes to birth with Samuel.

Critical discussion has long focused on Hannah's Song, usually concluding that it is a secondary intrusion (e.g. Stoebe 1973: 106). More recent scholarship has tended to regard it as an intentional element in the opening chapters (Watts 1992: 19–40), though Miscall's (1986: 15) dissent should be noted, while Becker-Spörl (1992) treats the song as an independent artefact. Klement (2000a: 112–113) has argued that Hannah's Song functions within the narrative as a prophetic text, so its traditional expressions take on a new role, a reading that opens fresh possibilities. Taken with its boundary-marking function (see 'Introduction', 'Structure'), it is apparent that Hannah's Song functions to shape readers' perceptions of Yahweh's activity in both its immediate context and the whole of Samuel. Yahweh brings hope to those who cannot bring hope to themselves, because he reigns. Hannah's story, and especially her song, testifies to God's reign as well as providing a grid through which to read what follows.

Comment

Narrative introduction: 1:1–8

1. As is traditional, the narrative initially focuses upon the leading man of the story, although Elkanah himself plays a relatively minor role in the story as a whole. Like Manoah (Judg. 13:2) we expect him to play a major role, but the text subverts this. Elkanah comes from an Ephraimite town called Ramathaim (Ramah in 1:19). Not previously mentioned in the Bible (Ramah in Josh. 18:25 is too far south); it is most likely modern Rentis (Arimathea in the NT [Matt. 27:57]), about 15 miles east of Joppa. Like the two closing stories of Judges (chs. 17 – 21) it places us in the hill country of Ephraim, an area noted for the chaos that came when there was no king. Such a loaded geographical marker automatically raises a question: Is this also to be a story of corruption, chaos and violence? But, unlike the Levites in Judg. 17 – 21, Elkanah is a model of piety. 1 Chr. 6:11–13 (EVV 6:27–29) places him within a Levitical family (see Driver 1913: 4–5 on some difficulties), but this narrator is not interested in highlighting any Levitical background. As Eslinger (1985: 66) notes, this is a thoroughly ordinary genealogy, mentioning no one who is prominent elsewhere. The one through whom the monarchy begins is one of the humble who will be raised just as Hannah's Song indicates (2:6–8).

2. Elkanah had two wives, Hannah and Peninnah. Although monogamy was more common, wealthier citizens practised polygamy, and the story indicates that Elkanah was comparatively wealthy. Hannah ('Favour' or 'Attractive') was the first wife, while Peninnah ('Fruitful' or 'Fecund') was the second. We are told Hannah had no children, while Peninnah did – perhaps the reason Elkanah had two wives. But this provides the context for conflict to exist between the wives since Hannah's status was undermined by her childlessness.

3. The family's annual worship practice prepared for the events of one particular year. Although the focus shifts from Elkanah to Hannah, there is an intrusion anticipating the next chapter through the introduction of Eli's sons Hophni and Phinehas, although they play no role in this chapter. The family's worship is not associated with the three main pilgrim festivals

(Deut. 16:1–17), so this is probably a private practice (though see Young-blood 1992: 571 and Gnuse 1984: 184 for possible festivals). The sacrifices are presumably peace offerings (Lev. 3), offerings consumed by the offeror before Yahweh as an act of fellowship. This is the first time the divine name 'Yahweh of hosts' is used in the Bible, though it subsequently becomes a major title. There is considerable discussion about its significance (see Klein 1983: 7), but the narrative assumes it was a well-accepted epithet. It is used with great regularity in Samuel, both with reference to the ark (1 Sam. 4:4), and David's reign (2 Sam. 5:10). What is striking is that its uses are clustered in three blocks, each associated with a period of transition, but not elsewhere. It occurs three times in 1 Sam. 1 – 4 (1:3; 1:11; 4:4), twice in chs. 15 – 17 (15:2; 17:45) and six times in 2 Sam. 5 – 7 (5:10; 6:2; 6:18; 7:8; 7:26; 7:27). 1 Sam. 1 – 4 tells how control of worship shifts from Eli's family, the second block concerns the shift from Saul to David, while the third is concerned with the shift of worship and administration to Jerusalem. Where the first block concerns a transition in cultic leadership and the second in political leadership, the third block brings these elements together. The sanctuary was then at Shiloh, modern Seilun (Bimson 1995: 281–282), a town in Ephraim about 25 miles north of Jerusalem. What is described here is not a location for the tabernacle, but a building of some sort, and in v. 9 it is called a 'temple'. According to Jer. 7:1–15, 26:6–9 (cf. Ps. 78:60), there had been a sanctuary at Shiloh that had been destroyed. It is more than a tent, though 2 Sam. 7 suggests it was not too grand. Perhaps we are to imagine a temporary building that contained the ark (3:3).

4–8. The typical events of their worship are now described. Although beginning with Elkanah and his offering, the focus moves to the relation-ship between Hannah and Peninnah. This is achieved by beginning with Elkanah's practice of giving a portion of the sacrificial meal to Peninnah and her sons, plus a special portion to Hannah (see 'Notes'). The narrative goes further, and stresses Elkanah's love for Hannah, a love not undone by the fact that 'Yahweh had closed her womb' in spite of the importance placed on children within a marriage. The observation that 'Yahweh had closed her womb' is noteworthy. The typical expression is that a woman was 'barren' (e.g. Gen. 11:30), so Hannah's condition is thus differentiated from other barren women. This is similar to many complaint psalms, where Yahweh is both the cause of the problem and the one who can bring resolution (e.g. Ps. 88). Hannah's experience provides a narrative context against which those psalms can be read (see A. H. van Zyl 1984). Elkanah's actions exacerbate the conflict between his wives. Similar relationships between a first wife and a fertile second one are not unknown (e.g. Gen. 16, 21). Hannah suffers under the tongue of Peninnah (described as her adversary), because she pushes Hannah to the point of crying out with rage, notwithstanding Elkanah's concern for her. We are then again told that Yahweh had closed Hannah's womb (1:7). Worship is a paradox for Hannah: she comes to worship the God who has caused her vexation, yet her vexation is increased by her adversary. Her husband's attempts at consolation appear to offer little. Elkanah expresses his love to Hannah in spite of her condition, but his attempts appear egocentric (Amit 1994) and ineffective, though the phraseology may be idiomatic (Baldwin 1988: 52; cf. Ruth 4:15). Hannah has become the narrative's point of focus as one trapped in vexation and the emptiness of childlessness in a world in which a woman's worth was largely determined by how many children she had.

Hannah's prayer and vow: 1:9–18

9. The narrative's main action now occurs as Hannah goes to the sanctuary to pray, moving from customary behaviour to specific events. While there, Eli observes her as he sits on his throne by the temple's doorpost (possibly a royal allusion; see 1 Kgs 7:5). Hannah thus breaks the patterns that govern her experience. Instead of being vexed, she eats, drinks and rises to go to the temple. The language about Eli is striking because of its use of royal language. The word *hêkal* can describe either a temple or a palace. As a priest, we naturally translate the word as 'temple', but the association of palace and temple is not easily separated in the ancient world, especially when we note that Eli sits upon a 'throne' (*kissē*). Eli's priestly role is freighted with royal overtones, preparing for the negative evaluation that becomes explicit in 2:27–36 and 3:16–18. Eli sits and watches, whereas Hannah seeks Yahweh.

10–11. Hannah's torment is apparent from the language describing her: it is in bitterness of soul and with tears that she prays. Making the break to come and pray does not mean the pain has been left behind. Hannah vows that if Yahweh gives her a son, then the child will be dedicated to him. There are similarities between Samuel and Samson in that neither was to have his hair cut; but, unlike Samson (Judg. 13:5), Samuel is never specifically identified as a Nazirite (but see 'Notes'), and abstinence from wine and other forms of alcohol (Num. 6:3) is not included here. People normally made the Nazirite vow themselves (Num. 6:1–2) rather than having it made for them, and these vows were usually temporary (see Acts 18:18; 21:23). Cartledge (1989: 411–415) suggests there were originally two classes of Nazirites, permanent (see Amos 2:11–12) and temporary, the temporary vow reflecting a later development. But Samson was exceptional (see Num. 6:1–21), though not necessarily unique. The important point is that the child will be dedicated to Yahweh; the vow is the means by which she pleads with Yahweh for a son.

12–14. Although the content of the request and vow is outlined in v. 11, this was an extended time of prayer, and there is a shift in focus to consider Eli's response to Hannah. The contrast is marked. Hannah multiplies her prayers whereas Eli, like a priestly peeping Tom, watches her pray. Eli sees her lips moving but hears no sound and assumes she is drunk. This anticipates his later lack of awareness because, although he is the priest, he cannot recognize sincere and devout prayer. His response is to rebuke Hannah, telling her to put away her wine. Other than Hannah's silence, no reason for Eli's assessment is offered. Yet his rebuke is stunning, especially since he makes no effort to confirm his interpretation by speaking to Hannah. His opening 'How long' (a reversal of the complaint psalms shaping Hannah's prayer [see Ps. 6:4; Hab. 2:6]) is both an accusation and a judgment, insisting that she remove her wine. Eli watches Hannah's lips, but does not understand her.

15–16. Hannah rejects this identification, disavowing any drunkenness, and in her first recorded words specifically asks that she not be considered a 'daughter of Belial', a highly derogatory label (see 'Notes'). In what is surely an intended irony, given that his sons will be known as 'sons of Belial' (2:12), Eli can see only worthlessness in those distant from himself. Instead, Hannah points to her anguish and grief, requesting recognition as someone determined to bring her petition before Yahweh and thus passionate in prayer. It is a polite response that denies Eli's premise.

17. In response, Eli blesses Hannah, though without apology. The blessing is an indirect prayer, 'may the God of Israel give you your request', where the priestly voice is added to that of the petitioner, and encourages Hannah. A key element of the blessing is the introduction of the root *š'l* (×2 in v. 17), a root that increases in prominence in the rest of this chapter (1:20, 27 [×2], 28 [×2]). This root, also the base of Saul's name, most commonly means 'to ask' or 'enquire' (Judg. 5:25; 1 Kgs 3:10; Ps. 122:6; Jon. 4:8), though the hiphil can mean 'to lend' in dedication (see 1:28). This has led many to suggest that this story is Saul's nativity, not Samuel's (e.g. McCarter 1980a: 63), but this neglects the story's function. It is the beginning of monarchy, and in one sense the narrator intends allusions to Saul to be recognized. But the narrative involves a reversal of expectations. Readers familiar with the tradition expect to begin with Saul, but we actually begin with an otherwise insignificant family from Ephraim. Monarchy does not begin with a request for a king but with Yahweh's actions on behalf of a childless woman (see Polzin 1989: 25–26). Allusion to Saul reminds readers of their expectations but reshapes them, a process that is even more important when we recognize that an overriding purpose of Samuel is to justify David as Yahweh's king (Klement 2000a: 252).

18. Hannah accepts Eli's blessing, though retaining polite forms of address to him. In speaking of herself as a 'maidservant', Hannah uses a different term from that used in v. 16. There she used the word *'āmâ*, but this time she uses *šipḥâ* (cf. 1 Sam. 25:24–41; 2 Sam. 14:6–19). Although translated similarly, *šipḥâ* may represent a more humble position (Chisholm 1998: 42–43). Hannah's request is that she might find grace in Eli's eyes, not Yahweh's, perhaps because she believes this to be more difficult. This segment is closed by a second account of Hannah's going and eating, forming an inclusion with v. 9, but this time she is not downcast. There is no material change in her circumstances but, like the complaint psalms, the priestly blessing appears to provide the necessary reassurance (e.g. Ps. 13; see Kim 1984).

Fulfilment of the vow: 1:19–28

19–20. The narrative pace now picks up, describing Samuel's birth and dedication. Indeed, the birth account is almost matter of fact. After worshipping together, the family returned to Ramah, about 19 miles west of Shiloh. Once there, Hannah fell pregnant, not only because Elkanah 'knew' his wife, but specifically because Yahweh remembered her (cf. Gen. 30:22). This birth was not simply the result of normal marital relations; Yahweh's actions are what matter. Thus Hannah conceived and gave birth to a son, naming him Samuel on the grounds that she had 'asked' Yahweh for him. However, the name relates to this by paronomasia, sound play, not by etymology. The three consonants of 'ask' (*š–'–l*) occur in this order in the name Samuel, but are closer to the name Saul. As with many OT naming stories, the name does not depend on an etymology but an association of sounds.

21–23. Hannah remained with the child for subsequent trips to Shiloh, staying with him until he was weaned. By noting this through dialogue, the narrator demonstrates that Hannah initiated this, though with Elkanah's agreement, even though Elkanah initially assumed Hannah would travel with the household. Hannah's increased autonomy is shown; though in an ancient society she could never be entirely independent of her husband. The increase in dialogue is an important narrative device, preparing us for Hannah's Song as the point at which dialogue is both thanksgiving and commentary on these events. Elkanah is said to intend to fulfil 'his vow', a puzzling comment because up to this point we have reference only to Hannah's vow (1:11). Evans (2000: 17; cf. Gordon 1986: 77) suggests Hannah and Elkanah may each have made a vow. Num. 30:6–15 allowed a husband to override his wife's vow when he heard of it, though it would otherwise stand. Although Elkanah was an acquiescent husband, he still had this right, so it is possible Hannah's vow became his (Hertzberg 1964: 28). If so, it seems Elkanah assumed that Hannah's vow was also his and intended to hand Samuel over immediately. Hannah's refusal to follow this pattern demonstrates her autonomy, because it is finally her vow, even if Elkanah has accepted it. Hannah retains control of her vow, insisting she will take the 'lad' when he is weaned. It seems that children were not weaned until they were about three years old (see 2 Maccabees 7.27), which would be consistent with events here. Hannah is not stalling because of maternal instincts (Eslinger 1985: 87) since the vow included no time-table. Elkanah agrees, expressing the hope that Yahweh will confirm his word, something that becomes an important feature of Samuel's ministry (3:19 – 4:1a). The narrative is full of allusion to coming events, though there has not yet been an explicit 'word of God' to which Elkanah refers other than Eli's blessing and Hannah's vow.

24–28. After Samuel was weaned, Hannah took him to the sanctuary, where he was to remain. Where the previous visit focused on Elkanah's concerns, this visit is concerned with Hannah and her actions at Shiloh with Samuel (indeed, it is never stated that Elkanah was present), including a range of sacrifices (see 'Notes'). These are significant, though the items sacrificed would have matched their home area's produce (Meyers 1995: 82). Although the closing words of v. 24 are awkward (see 'Notes'), they foreground the word 'lad' (*na'ar*), a term prominent in the next two chapters. What appears to be emphasized is Samuel's age, as a child just beyond suckling. Both the sacrifice and Samuel are brought to Eli together, showing Hannah's fulfilment of her vow. Hannah confirms this to Eli when she identifies herself and indicates that she is fulfilling her vow. Direct speech allows Hannah's words to provide a summation of the story so far. Hannah stresses the reality of Yahweh's response to her prayer: it was for this lad that she had prayed, and Yahweh had given him to her. There is again emphasis on the root *š'l* (to ask) in Hannah's statement that Yahweh had given her 'the request I requested of him'. Again, the language alludes to Saul without mentioning him directly. Yahweh had answered Hannah's prayer, bringing joy into a childless life, and Hannah responds by fulfilling her vow. Her closing statement evokes Saul even more since 'he is dedicated to Yahweh' could be 'He is Saul – for Yahweh'. Allusion is made to Saul only to reject him since the reader knows that the child is Samuel. Monarchy does not begin with Saul, but with this son of a woman whose womb Yahweh had closed; so the power of God is shown through one who was otherwise powerless. The narrative ends in worship, worship that prepares for Hannah's song of thanksgiving.

Hannah's Song: 2:1–10

1–3. Hannah's Song is pivotal for the narrative, though standing outside the main events. The narrative has gradually moved towards speech to provide a theological commentary on events, and that climaxes here as we see Yahweh as the one who works for the poor and oppressed. Hannah's story is an application of this truth, a theme that resonates through the rest of Samuel. This song is an important pause in the narrative, a moment of taking theological stock before going on. The song is similar to hymns in the psalter, though elements of the individual thanksgiving are present. The complaint psalms typically vow that praise will be given once Yahweh has acted, so Hannah's thanksgiving is expected since her prayer was answered (see Miller 1994: 237–238). It is possible that this adapts an existing psalm; however, the key issue remains the song's function within the narrative and not a presumed original status (but see Klein 1983: 15–19). It is notable that the text insists Hannah 'prayed and said'. Prayer is an important motif throughout the story, and prayer (rather than the more specific thanksgiving) continues to be the focus here. Hannah's Song is a prayer that initially focuses on what Yahweh has done in changing her situation. Indeed, the dominant motif is that Yahweh has changed Hannah's situation so that instead of barrenness she now experiences joy. The language of v. 1 reflects that of a victory psalm, but, instead of overcoming a military enemy, it is now victory over Peninnah (1:6). Instead of being put down by Peninnah, Hannah rejoices in the salvation that Yahweh wrought through the birth of her son. Yet there is also an important link between Hannah's experience and that of the coming king in that Hannah celebrates the fact that Yahweh will raise the 'horn' (a symbol for power) of the king just as he has raised hers (2:1, 10). Even the powerful need to be raised by Yahweh: it is not by their own might that they prevail. David's closing reflections (2 Sam. 22:2; 23:3) on these themes indicates their importance in the literary design of the whole of Samuel. Because Yahweh has granted Hannah such favour, it is only natural that she rejoices in him. This comes to a special focus in v. 2, which affirms Yahweh's incomparability. A number of psalms employ the technique of testimony (e.g. Pss 30, 34, 73; see Firth 1999: 440–454), usually with a bifurcation in address in which pl. verbs are used to address the community. Although testimony is addressed to God, the psalmist also addresses the congregation and those who read the text, urging them to learn from the testimony offered. These texts insist that the experience of the one who prays is not unique, but rather representative of something more typical. V. 3, though part of the song's opening (note the finite verbs rather than the participles that gradually dominate), applies this to the rest of the community, though it is particularly relevant to Peninnah. Hannah had experienced the vexation of her speech, and she is now among those warned against the use of such words. Hannah knows that Yahweh is defined by knowledge, and nothing escapes his scrutiny. For a warrior king, these words may well have found meaning in an enemy's defeat, but for Hannah they take on a special significance within her story.

4–5. A description of Yahweh's characteristic actions is now presented, though they also apply to Hannah's experiences. Vv. 4–5 consist of three polar opposites that speak of the reversal of fortunes, with the powerless delivered and the powerful brought low. Structurally the first two reversals prepare us for the third, which is particular to Hannah. In vv. 4–5a the first line of the reversal considers the situation of the powerful before turning to the powerless, whereas in v. 5b the reversal begins with the barren woman who is contrasted with the one with many sons. Because this is a general pattern of divine activity, explicit congruence with Hannah's situation is not required, though that the sequence climaxes with one who is barren indicates that this song has been deliberately placed here, even if we do not know of Hannah having seven children (according to 2:21 she had five).

6–8. Yahweh is explicitly named as the one who has brought these reversals. These do not just happen; they are Yahweh's actions for the weak and the poor. Yahweh's care of the weak and the poor is stressed, a theme grounded in creation (Ps. 96:7–13), and though Hannah was not financially poor she suffered with the poor in her inability to have children. Yahweh is thus the source of life, but also the source of death, though this needs to be seen in the context of his aim of giving life to all. This recitation of Yahweh's acts is not offered solely as Hannah's own doxological outpouring. The community is summoned to join in praise, while also preparing for the reference to the king. Authority belongs to Yahweh, and the king's status is always determined by his relationship to him. The foundation for this is seen in the closing lines of v. 8, which focuses on Yahweh's role as creator, which is what enables him to be involved in such an active and positive manner.

9–10. The song is now brought to its conclusion. In a sense the final line of v. 9 sums up the whole song: one does not prevail by one's own power but rather through Yahweh's presence. This is established by another antithesis, so that v. 9 closes off the series introduced in vv. 4–5. Where the final verb in that series indicated a completed action, these verbs are imperfect. Although these could have a future, and perhaps eschatological, orientation (Youngblood 1992: 581), the creation context suggests they describe how Yahweh continually acts for his holy ones, though without excluding an eschatological implication. The contrast between the 'holy ones' and 'wicked' here indicates that the poor and weak for whom Yahweh works are also those who have dedicated themselves to him (e.g. Pss 30:5; 31:24; 32:6; 37:28; 85:9; 97:10; 149:1, 5, 9). Hannah's Song indicates that Yahweh acts for those who devote themselves to him. The song points to a counter-intuitive reality, which is that power is not the means of prevailing. The weak who rely on Yahweh are those who prevail. This, then, is why v. 10 triumphantly asserts that Yahweh's enemies will be defeated and that he will give power to his king. The God who sends thunder from heaven (see 7:10) is the one who overcomes all foes, because all creation is under his power. Again, creation themes are woven into the song of a woman who has only belatedly been able to fulfil the creation mandate to be fruitful and have children (Gen. 1:28). The climax of this is revealed in the last two lines of the song: Yahweh will judge the ends of the earth, but he will do so through his king, exalting the 'horn' of his anointed. At this stage, we do not know who the king will be, but Judg. 17 – 21 has prepared readers for the likelihood of kingship. By introducing this theme, Hannah's Song provides a subtle indication that the narrative is moving towards kingship. Israel's request for a king in 8:5 will not take Yahweh by surprise, because kingship is indicated here. But Israel knows that their king cannot be like those of the surrounding nations, because

Yahweh's king must understand the paradox that real authority comes from yielding power to Yahweh. Hannah's situation has thus become a paradigm through which we read Samuel, remembering that power belongs to Yahweh alone and that seeking power is the way to lose it (see Mark 8:35).

Explanation

This narrative works at two levels, though they ultimately work through one another. First, it is the story of how Yahweh acts to answer a woman's prayer and her faithfulness in fulfilling the vow she made to him. Hannah is presented as an exemplary woman of faith. Hope for the weak continues to lie with Yahweh alone. Such a message has significance for all who know themselves as the weak. Hannah lived in a world in which a woman's worth was seen in terms of motherhood. Without children, and in spite of Elkanah's remarks, she was on the margins of society and powerless to change that situation herself. Even when she went to the temple, praying with such passion that Eli thought she was drunk, she remained powerless. The reason for this lies in the phrase twice used to describe her situation: Yahweh had closed her womb (1:5–6). Hannah's world was one in which Yahweh was both the oppressor and the one who brings life and hope. We could imagine the words of Hannah's prayer (something like Ps. 6), though they are not recorded for us. We do not need to know words, only the passion with which they were prayed, a passion that led to Hannah's offering to dedicate the son she wanted to Yahweh. It is the offer of a woman with nothing to give who can only offer to return what she has not yet received. It is a story of God's grace in granting that child, honouring Hannah's vow that she in turn honoured when she brought Samuel and presented him to Eli. Thus Hannah praises God with passion, celebrating his activities on her behalf. God works against the powerful, the abusers; he works for his holy ones. Instead of the pursuit of power, Hannah's story and song suggest a different way forward for God's people, where hope lies in submission to the reign of God, trusting in him as the one who brings about the reversals for which the poor cry.

But this is also a story preparing for the move to kingship, and it deliberately includes elements we recognize at a second reading as being a part of this. These events point beyond themselves to the greater purposes of God. Hannah is a woman whose womb Yahweh has closed; yet he responds to her impassioned cry with a son. Samuel is not the first king, however much the narrative plays with Saul's name, but kingship will finally come through him. We do not know here how this works out, but Hannah's Song, with its triumphant closing reference to Yahweh's anointed, prepares for the king. We are reminded that the small stories of faithful families are themselves woven into the greater purposes of God for his people. The astonishing affirmation here is that the kingdom of Israel does not begin with the request for a king. It begins with Yahweh's response to the cry of a childless woman, because Yahweh gives life and Yahweh exalts. These themes will be worked out in the rest of Samuel, climaxing in their reaffirmation in David's songs (2 Sam. 22:1 – 23:7).

We cannot leave this story with David, for Hannah's Song is the basis for another great biblical song from an unusual mother in Luke 1:46–55. Mary was not barren, and God had not closed her womb, for Mary's disgrace came from the fact that she was to have a baby. But as Mary sings, she evokes the imagery of Hannah's Song, seeing her situation as another example of the great reversals of fortune of which Hannah sang. God's decision to act through the weak and powerless did not end with the accession of a king to the throne of Israel. It continued on so that Mary could see herself within the themes Hannah had announced. God remains the champion of the poor and the weak who cry to him, he still brings down the mighty and exalts the poor. For Mary, the anointed one took on a new significance because of her role as the mother of Jesus. As Luke makes clear, these themes climax with Jesus' death on the cross. God's mercy is thus shown to those who fear him, and God's power is made perfect in weakness. It is this theme Paul recognizes in his own ministry: where the 'super-apostles' boast of their prowess, Paul knows that strength comes only in weakness (2 Cor. 12:1–10), that only those who do not seek power can be exalted by God. There is no guarantee that the humble will always be exalted (martyrs down through the centuries prove that), but God's ultimate work is with those who submit themselves to him and recognize his reign.

1 SAMUEL 2:11–36

Translation

[11]Then Elkanah went home to Ramah, and the lad ministered to Yahweh before Eli the priest.

[12]The sons of Eli were sons of Belial; they did not know Yahweh. [13]The custom of the priests with the people was that whenever someone was offering a sacrifice the priest's lad would come while the meat was boiling with a three-pronged fork in his hand, [14]and thrust it into the pan, kettle, cauldron or pot and all that the fork brought up the priest would take for himself. Thus they did in Shiloh to all the Israelites who came there. [15]Also, before the fat was burned the priest's lad would come and say to the sacrificer, 'Give meat for the priest to roast. He will not take boiled meat from you, only fresh.' [16]If the man said, 'Let them burn the fat first, then take what you desire,' he would say, 'You must give it to him now, otherwise I shall take it by force.' [17]So the sin of the lads was great before Yahweh, because the men treated Yahweh's offering with contempt.

¹⁸But Samuel was ministering before Yahweh, the lad wearing a linen ephod. ¹⁹His mother would make him a small robe and bring it up to him each year when she came up with her husband to offer the annual sacrifice. ²⁰Eli would bless Elkanah and his wife and say, 'May Yahweh grant you seed from this woman in place of the petition she dedicated to Yahweh.' Then they would return home. ²¹Indeed, Yahweh visited Hannah and she conceived and bore three sons and two daughters. But the lad Samuel grew up before Yahweh.

²²Now Eli was very old, and he heard about everything his sons were doing to all Israel and how they lay with the women who served at the entrance to the Tent of Meeting. ²³He said to them, 'Why do you do these things? I hear of your evil deeds from all these people. ²⁴No, my sons, it is not a good report I hear Yahweh's people spreading. ²⁵If one sins against another, then God will arbitrate for him. But if one sins against Yahweh, who will intercede for him?' But they did not listen to the voice of their father because it was Yahweh's pleasure to put them to death. ²⁶But the lad Samuel was continually growing in stature and favour with Yahweh and the people.

²⁷A man of God came to Eli and said to him, 'Thus has Yahweh said, "Did I indeed reveal myself to your father's house when they were in Egypt as slaves to the house of Pharaoh, ²⁸and choose him from all the tribes of Israel to be my priest, to go up to my altar, to offer incense and to wear the ephod before me? Indeed, I gave the house of your father every offering made by fire from the children of Israel. ²⁹Why do you scorn my altar and my offerings that I commanded for my dwelling? And you have honoured your sons more than me to make yourself fat from all the best of all the offerings of Israel my people! ³⁰Therefore," declares Yahweh, the God of Israel, "I affirmed that your house and the house of your father would walk before me for ever. But now," declares Yahweh, "far be it from me! Those who honour me I will honour, but those who despise me will be disdained. ³¹Behold, the days are coming when I shall cut off your strength and the strength of your father's house so there will be none who grow old in your house, ³²and you will see distress on account of iniquity in all the good done for Israel, but no one will ever again be old in your house. ³³Everyone I do not cut off from before my altar will only be spared to wear out your eyes to make your heart grieve, and all the multitude of your house shall die by the sword of men. ³⁴And this will be the sign that will come to your two sons, to Hophni and Phinehas: the two of them shall die on the one day! ³⁵And I shall raise up for myself a trustworthy priest; he will do what is in my heart and mind. I shall build him a trustworthy house, and he shall go before my anointed for ever. ³⁶All who are left in your house shall come to prostrate themselves before him for a wage of silver or a loaf of bread, and say, 'Please attach me to one of the priests so as to eat a morsel of bread.' " ' '

Notes on the text

11. LXX is often followed and Hannah made the subject of the verb. Though Hannah was the central character, the journeys to Shiloh were family events, and Elkanah's return includes the whole family and correction to Hannah as the subject is more likely. The term *na'ar* is used for Samuel, as foreshadowed in 1:22, 24, 25 and 27. However, there is ambiguity in this chapter where this term variously refers to Samuel (2:11, 18, 21, 26), Hophni and Phineas's servant (2:13, 15) or Hophni and Phineas (2:17). The translation 'lad' is used throughout to highlight the ambiguity.

14. LXX has three items in the list, and 4QSam^a two. McCarter (1980a: 79) prefers the shorter list, but it is possible scribes might abbreviate seemingly redundant items. Also, the closing letters of the first word in MT are the same as those of the closing item, but LXX and 4QSam^a have a different opening item, so a range of scribal tendencies is attested. MT is retained.

20. Reading *šā'ul* for *šā'al* (dedicated). This construction is rare (Driver 1913: 32), but creates a meaningful text with only a pointing change.

22. 4QSam^a and LXX^B do not mention the serving women. This is the only reference to the Tent of Meeting (Exod. 33:7) in the narrative, which otherwise mentions a temple. It may be from a different source, though this does not require its excision (so Smith 1899: 20).

25. This may be an instance where *'ĕlōhîm* (normally, 'God') means 'judges' in the sense of those appointed by God to act on his behalf (see NIV mg.), possibly also in Pss 82:1, 6; 138:1; Exod. 21:6; 22:8–9. Ps. 45:7 is probably another example of this derived usage, referring to the king. Since the parallelism of the statement links *'ĕlōhîm* with Yahweh, a translation of 'God' is maintained, though it seems likely that the intent is that God act through a human judge. The parallelism is extended through the distinction in meaning between the pi. and hith. of *pll*.

28. Ordinarily, the verb *nś'* means 'to bear', though the verb is so used in 1 Sam. 14:3 (possibly 14:18, if LXX is correct) and 22:18. The ephod in 22:18 is linen, and a garment is implied, as in Exod. 25:7; 28:4, 6; 29:5; 35:9; 1 Sam. 2:18 and 2 Sam. 6:14 (= 1 Chr. 15:27). Usually, it is a priestly garment, but 2 Sam. 6:14 suggests it was not purely priestly. Other texts refer to the ephod as a means for determining Yahweh's will, suggesting a carried device (1 Sam. 23:6; 30:7; Gideon's idol-ephod [Judg. 8:27] is of a different class). A consistent interpretation might be that it was a linen chest-piece laid over the normal clothing, with the inlaid stones (Exod. 28:6–12) as an integral part of its role in determining Yahweh's will (see BDB). Hence it was both worn and borne.

27. Restoring *'ăbādîm* (slaves) on the basis of 4QSam^a and LXX. MT requires a noun before *lĕbêt par'ōh*, and the loss of *'ăbādîm* on the basis of homoioteleuton is probable.

29. *mā'ôn* (dwelling) is undeniably awkward, but no satisfactory solution has been offered (Gordon 1986: 86). A terminal *yod* could have been omitted for the reading offered above, though the absence of a preposition makes for a rough text. 4QSam^a and LXX have smoother texts, but MT is retained as more difficult.

31. LXX (followed by McCarter 1980a: 88) reads *sperma*, vocalized as *zera'* instead of MT's *zĕrōa'* ('strength'; lit. 'arm'), a reading possible through defective spelling. But MT makes more sense in context. The balance of the oracle does not promise an absence of descendants but of any who would reach old age.

32. With Eslinger (1985: 133) *mā'ôn* is repointed *me'awôn* (account of iniquity). The current reading occurs by interference from v. 29.

33. LXX has 'his eyes' and 'his heart' (*nepeš* here refers to one's inner being, better represented by 'heart' than 'soul'), but since the judgment is directed at Eli, MT is maintained. However, with 4QSam[a] and LXX, add *bĕḥereb* before *'ănāšîm*.

Form and structure

This passage functions as a pivot within 1 Sam. 1 – 3, concluding Samuel's birth narrative and preparing for coming events. It concludes Samuel's birth narrative by offering insights into his life in Shiloh, stressing the fulfilment of Hannah's vow. A second level of conclusion is offered by interleaving Samuel's story with that of Eli's sons. They never interact, but the structure forces a comparison (see Garsiel 1983: 35–41). Though the narrator's perception of the children of both families is made clear, judgments are not provided for their parents (see Polzin 1989: 39–40). This moves the comparison between Eli and Hannah on a generation, showing that the parents' patterns continue in their children. Apart from mention of their death (4:4, 11, 17, 19, 21), Eli's sons receive no prominence beyond this point.

The passage's pivotal function is clear from the concluding reference to Yahweh's anointed (2:35). This motif also concluded 1:1 – 2:10, so the opening segments of Samuel conclude with this same climax. Both references occur in prophetic speech, though this time it is delivered by a 'man of God'. Many assume these references were added to an older Shiloh tradition, usually through a Deuteronomistic redaction (Stoebe 1973: 107–108) since reference to Yahweh's anointed would have been meaningless in Eli's day. However, the whole of chs. 1 – 2 represent a carefully balanced selection of materials that contrast and extend one another, so excision of references to kingship is unwarranted. There are clearly a range of sources present, but the text stands as a whole (see Rendtorff 1993: 142–145; contra Brettler 1997: 604–611). Monarchy's arrival and its relationship to these families connect these narratives, both as an account of the families and a preparation for kingship.

This passage looks forward and back, though the backward look prepares for the plot's advancement. So this chapter's climax both announces Yahweh's anointed and declares that Eli's family will no longer occupy the priesthood (2:27–36), in spite of Yahweh's prior oath (see Loader 2000: 496–503). This theme recurs in 3:11–14. There are two references to kingship, and there are two references to the destruction of Eli's family, though the climax of ch. 3 rests on Eli's acceptance of this. The climax pattern of chs. 1 – 3 can thus be noted:

1:1 – 2:10	2:11 – 36	3:1 – 4:1a
Joy at Samuel's birth	Destruction of house of Eli	Destruction of house of Eli
Origins of monarchy	Origins of monarchy	Vindication of Samuel

These interleaved motifs drive home the main themes: Israel was moving towards monarchy, and Samuel, not Eli, was central in Yahweh's purposes in achieving it. The absence of plot of which Fokkelman (1993: 114) speaks is actually a function of the narrative. The plot is not formulated in classical terms but is developed through the comparisons, ultimately climaxing in the announcement of the end of Eli's family and the move towards a new structure that includes both a faithful priest and Yahweh's anointed.

Comment

Life at the sanctuary: 2:11–21

11. Hannah gradually fades from the story, preparing for the interleaving of Samuel, Eli and his sons. We do not hear that Hannah returned to Ramah, but only of Elkanah's returning. Hannah is not named again until 2:21, though she is active in 2:18–20. Hannah's removal directs attention back to her song, and it becomes the prism through which we read what follows. After Elkanah's departure, Samuel stays with Eli at Shiloh, ministering before Yahweh under Eli. Samuel's work is undefined, though clearly priestly. Strictly, Samuel is too young to be a 'lad', but the word is used because of the play on its meaning in 2:11–20 (see 'Notes').

12. The narrative aims to show the failures of Eli and his sons by contrasting them with Samuel. Samuel is portrayed positively in that he is not like Eli's sons, though direct comment is made in 2:26. Expressly positive characterization is developed from ch. 3, which stresses the effectiveness of his prophetic ministry. Eli's sons were introduced previously without characterization (1:3), but are now called 'sons of Belial'. This phrase is idiomatic of one who is worthless and neglects Yahweh. Hannah denied she was a 'daughter of Belial' (1:16), but by making a direct comment the narrator leaves no room for doubt about Eli's sons. It is also said they 'did not know Yahweh'. As priests this cannot mean that they did not know about Yahweh; it must mean that they did not have a relationship with him. This is consistent with 3:7, which uses the same idiom (see Gordon 1986: 81–82).

13–14. It is not entirely clear whether these verses describe a deviation from accepted procedure, or what should have been done (McCarter 1980a: 77; cf. NEB). The former seems more probable as there is no indication elsewhere that these actions were acceptable. But what was the custom (*mišpāṭ*) of Hophni and Phinehas, and does the text describe one sin (Youngblood 1992: 584; cf. NIV) or two (Smith 1899: 18; cf. NRSV, ESV)? The law required the priest to receive the fat and the liver, along with other parts (Lev. 7:34; Deut. 18:3) but these priests were not satisfied with this. Instead, they would send a servant (*na'ar*) with a three-pronged fork, examples of which have been found at Gezer (Youngblood 1992: 585). The servant would place the fork into meat being boiled, claiming whatever was on the fork as the priest's share. This would bring up a substantial amount of meat, so McCarter's observation (1980a: 85) that the amount gained would be 'modest' seems inappropriate. This pattern of behaviour refuses to accept Yahweh's provision and claims more for themselves while denying worshippers their portion (Fokkelman 1993: 119).

15–16. This custom is linked to vv. 15–16 by the conjunction *gam* (also). Although it can be a copulative, it can also intensify (GKC §153), a sense more probable here. So, it seems best to see a second sin described here, albeit linked to the previous example. There it was assumed the meat was being boiled, but in this instance the meat is being prepared, allowing the servant to insist that the worshipper give raw meat, not what has been boiled, because of the preference for roasted meat. It is not just the strong-arm tactics that are deemed inappropriate, but also that this takes place before the fat has been burned. Lev. 7:31 requires the fat to be burned first, but the priests are both claiming excess meat and ignoring Yahweh's prior claim. Thus the priests both claim an excessive portion and take it before it has been offered.

17. The narrator comments that this was a great sin because of their attitude to the offering. This comment balances the observation in v. 12, demonstrating what it meant to say Hophni and Phinehas were 'sons of Belial'. Up to this point, Samuel or their servant was called a 'lad' (*na'ar*), but here the priests are called this. Hertzberg (1964: 35) observes that this is not to excuse them, but rather is a way of belittling them. Their linguistic demotion prepares for their greater demotion by the chapter's end.

18–19. A contrast is offered through Samuel. Resuming the language of v. 11, he is presented as a lad (*na'ar*) ministering before Yahweh and wearing the linen ephod, probably a form of priestly dress. That Samuel is a lad indicates he has not achieved the maturity that occurs after his call in ch. 3, after which he is no longer a *na'ar*. Through the linguistic demotion of Eli's sons, Samuel is their social equal, though his exemplary behaviour contrasts with theirs. Apart from the ephod, his clothing was annually supplemented by a robe (*mě'îl*) made for him by his mother and delivered when the family came for their sacrifice. Hannah gives and Samuel receives, whereas Eli's sons take. Interestingly, the focus in v. 19 is on Hannah's activity in worship, stressing that she comes up to worship.

20–21. Hannah previously begged Eli to look favourably upon her; now he routinely blesses Elkanah and 'his wife'. Eli's blessing is primarily directed to Elkanah, but is expressed through Hannah. Thus Yahweh is said to 'visit' Hannah so she conceives three sons and two daughters. Samuel has been presented at the sanctuary and Hannah is granted fecundity. Crucially, Samuel continues to grow in Yahweh's presence. Though still a lad, Yahweh has another purpose for him.

Eli's attempted intervention: 2:22–26

22. The narrative focus returns to Eli and his sons through Eli's attempt to discipline them. Readers know this comes somewhat late, a point confirmed by the announcement that 'Eli was very old'. Curiously, Eli responds to a report he has heard rather than observing his sons' behaviour. Hannah needed to inform Eli of her prayer's passion, and others inform him about his sons since their abuse of sacrificial procedure somehow avoided Eli's notice. Eli's blindness is not introduced until 3:2, and it is only that his eyes had 'begun to grow dim', so this is not offered as an excuse. This report not only covered the sacrificial abuses, but also sexual misconduct with women serving at the sanctuary (referred to as 'the Tent of Meeting'), though it is clearly only a summary.

23–26. A common technique in these chapters is to move towards direct speech. Eli does not directly rebuke his sons but poses a pair of questions that bracket his disappointment at what has been reported. Any rebuke is only implied, and the direction of Eli's questions can also be understood as concern at what might be lost if this behaviour continues. The first question assumes the correctness of the reports he has heard, and simply asks the sons for a reason for their behaviour, though the narrator never allows the sons to respond. Eli's disappointment is expressed in v. 24, though it is still not a direct rebuke. Rather, in a classic understatement, he observes that the spreading report is not good. The decisive point from Eli's perspective is reached in v. 25: if one sins against another human, God can arbitrate a resolution. This is because God stands outside the dispute and is therefore impartial. But this is not the case when one sins against Yahweh since there is no one who is above and beyond the dispute, and it is clear that the sins of Hophni and Phinehas are against Yahweh. Their actions were sins against worshippers, but their activity was a sin against Yahweh. As Fokkelman notes (1993: 132), Eli effectively told his sons their case was beyond hope. It is unsurprising to discover that his questioning was ineffective, and his sons did not change their behaviour. Nevertheless, it still comes as a shock to be told it was Yahweh's pleasure to put them to death. It is not that God derives pleasure from the death of the wicked, but rather that the path they had chosen was the path of death (Birch 1998: 987). Hannah's Song works itself out, because it is Yahweh who kills, and Yahweh who brings to life (2:6). In contrast, Samuel grows in the areas where Eli's sons are failing.

The word of the man of God: 2:27–36

27–29. Into this context, a man of God comes to bring Yahweh's word, a word announcing Yahweh's judgment on Eli and his family. Where Eli's family had received a revelation from Yahweh while in Egypt as Pharaoh's slaves, as sanctuary priests they needed someone to come and speak. A 'man of God' was a prophetic figure who lived on the boundaries of Israel's social existence (Petersen 1981: 40–50), so a liminal figure was required to speak the truth to those at the centre (see 1 Kgs 13). Yahweh speaks for the first time in Samuel, and his message is one of judgment. The oracle is formed on the basis of a set of questions centred on a direct statement of Yahweh's provision. The initial question is intriguing in that one would commonly expect a question phrased in this way to have a negative answer (functioning as a denial [see Smith 1899: 24]). However, this form of question can also express the conviction that what follows is well known (GKC §150e; also 1 Sam. 20:37, among other examples). The question thus highlights shared information. So the man of God emphasizes known points, hearkening back to Aaron's experience in Egypt. Within this process their family was called to service at the altar, so the question invites Eli to agree, and thus be drawn into the oracle. The second question can then announce the problem on the basis of shared assumptions about a family's election to the priesthood, which is that those chosen to serve are responsible for cultic purity. As a question it refrains from a direct accusation. Instead, it asks Eli (and family – the verb is pl.) to justify their actions as priests since they had disqualified themselves from their role because they had scorned (lit. 'kicked'; see Deut. 32:15) the offerings. The second half of the question shifts to the sg. to focus on Eli's role. He was not a participant in his sons' abuses, but neither had he stopped them. Instead, he honoured them more than Yahweh, an announcement (introducing the root *kbd* ['honour' or 'heavy']), which becomes very important in chs. 4 – 6) because he had shared with the whole family in the abuse of the sacrificial system. Eli's ineffectiveness in rebuking his sons is highlighted, as is the certainty of Yahweh's judgment.

30–34. The man of God shifts from rhetorical questions to direct announcement of judgment. It is solemn, marked by the double use of the formula 'declares Yahweh' in v. 30 and the divine epithet 'Yahweh, God of Israel'. The judgment announced in vv. 30–36. makes clear that Eli's family forfeit their privileged role, their actions effectively nullifying Yahweh's promise. Although the Aaronic priesthood was perpetual, the family of Eli is removed because it still required that serving priests understand the priority of Yahweh's glory. The second half of v. 30 might almost quote a proverb, though one that makes use of the root *kbd* ('heavy' or 'honour'), which is here compared with *qll* ('light' or 'trifling'; hence 'disdained'). Priesthood is taken from Aaron's family, but a new line is chosen. In David's time this was that of Zadok, while under Solomon, Abiathar, the last of the Elides, was removed from all priestly work (1 Kgs 2:35). The point is not the family's obliteration, but its quarantine from Yahweh's blessing, with none left who grow old. In v. 33 the focus returns to Eli's experience, with his family's removal causing untold grief. There will be some left at the altar, but even they will cause grief, perhaps because of the certainty of violent death and the loss of the family's status. The deaths of Hophni and Phinehas on one day are the sign that the other events described will take place.

35–36. The removal of the Elides creates space for a faithful priest defined as one who acts in accordance with God's will, indicating that the priestly role was never viewed solely in ceremonial terms. Yahweh promises to build a sure house, a dynasty, for this priest, a promise preparing for the similar terminology in 2 Sam. 7:11. This priest will stand before Yahweh's anointed (the king), even though there has not yet been a formal move towards kingship. Kingship is coming, and a faithful priest-hood is an essential component of its structure. Eli's family is excluded from this, and the oracle concludes with the devastating picture of family members begging from the faithful priest, living out another element of Hannah's Song (2:5). No identity of the faithful priest is declared. Eslinger (1985: 135–137) argues that it must be Samuel, though this reading has to face the failure of Samuel's sons (1 Sam. 8:1–3). A classical reading (see Smith 1899: 23) is that this refers to the Zadokites who took on the role (1 Kgs 2:27), displacing Abiathar. But this leaves the meaning of the oracle unclear to the reader, a problem compounded if 1 Kgs 2:27–46 is not from the same source as this part of Samuel. Although it is not an intrinsic difficulty, such a reading generally assumes that the oracle is prophecy after the event. The constant references to Samuel, and his establishment as a prophet in the next chapter, encourages a reading that includes him. Keil and Delitzsch (1956: 38–40) suggest multiple fulfilments, an approach that has literary coherence, but which seems harmonistic. A simpler solution lies in a parallel with Deut. 18:18, which uses the hiph. of *qwm* to refer to the establishment of a prophet, though in fact it is a succession of prophets (see McConville 2002: 303). A succession of priests, each of whom is required to be faithful, is thus indicated. Such a succession begins with Samuel, but reaches its climax with Zadok.

Explanation

Like 1:1 – 2:10, this narrative also works at two levels. In one sense, it is the account of how one family departs from what is expected from priests, and the outcome of such behaviour. Eli, now an old man, is unable or unwilling to control his sons, and thus brings the whole of the sanctuary at Shiloh into dishonour. More than this, Yahweh is dishonoured through their activities. Yahweh acts against this breach of his honour. His activities are focused on Samuel, a lad serving under Eli's direction, whose character is the opposite of Eli's sons. Samuel will initiate a new approach to priesthood because Yahweh seeks a faithful priest, not someone who uses the role for self-serving activity. Thus the contrast between Samuel and Eli's sons works through until we come to the oracle from the man of God, which announces that Eli's family will lose their status and an alternative line (probably beginning with Samuel) will commence. The family discovers that Yahweh acts against those who claim the right to abuse religious power by removing all power from them since those who serve Yahweh must have their goals shaped by Yahweh's. This pattern is not unique to the OT. In Acts 8 Peter rejects the attempt of Simon Magus to purchase the power of the Holy Spirit, because he sees a motivation other than a desire to glorify God (Acts 8:14–24). Those who claim to serve God must honour him above all else, which is why Yahweh removes Eli's family, even as he promises he will raise up others who will be faithful.

But to read this narrative on that level alone is to see Yahweh only as reactive. Yet this narrative also points to Yahweh as an initiator. The mystery of this is that Yahweh initiates through the actions of people like Hannah who cry out in prayer and a lad like Samuel who at this stage is unaware of his destiny. This initiation is seen in how this narrative builds towards its climactic announcement of a faithful priest who will serve before Yahweh's anointed. Before we knew of the Elide corruption we knew from Hannah's Song that the story is moving towards kingship, and in particular to one who will be Yahweh's anointed, a status that implies kingship under his control. We are not given any indication of who that king will be, though any subsequent reading of these verses knows it is ultimately David. But the king's identity is not a matter of priority at this stage. Rather, it is a matter of recognizing that Yahweh is changing the social structure; so, although the request for a king might initially look like rebellion by the people, it ultimately conforms to Yahweh's purposes. But one of the mysteries of Samuel is that it always allows participating humans to be fully free in their activities, so even Yahweh's 'pleasure' in putting Eli's sons to death must be seen in response to their denying him honour. There is a close relationship between these two elements that should not be lost through overemphasis upon divine causality or human responsibility. Thus the narrative insists that even the seemingly chaotic events at Shiloh stand within a process initiated by Yahweh whereby kingship will reach Israel, and even the elders' surprising request for a king (1 Sam. 8:4) is not such a surprise after all.

1 SAMUEL 3:1 – 4:1a

Translation

[1]The lad Samuel was ministering to Yahweh before Eli; and the word of Yahweh was scarce in those days; visions were not common. [2]Now it happened at that time that Eli was lying down at his place, and his eyes had begun to dim; he was not able to see. [3]The lamp of God had not yet gone out and Samuel was lying down in the temple of Yahweh, which is where the ark of God was.

[4]Then Yahweh called to Samuel, and he said, 'Here I am.' [5]He ran to Eli and said, 'Here I am, for you called me.' But he said, 'I did not call you. Go back. Lie down.' So he went and lay down. [6]And Yahweh called again 'Samuel,' and Samuel rose and went to Eli and said, 'Here I am, for you called me.' But he said, 'I did not call you, my son. Go back. Lie down.' [7]Samuel did not yet know Yahweh, and the word of Yahweh was not yet revealed to him. [8]Yahweh again called Samuel a third time, and Samuel got up and went to Eli and said, 'Here I am, for you called me.' But Eli discerned that Yahweh was calling the lad. [9]So Eli said to Samuel, 'Go, lie down, and if he calls you, you shall say, "Speak, Yahweh, because your servant hears."' So Samuel went and lay down in his place.

[10]Yahweh came and stood and called as before, 'Samuel! Samuel!' And Samuel said, 'Speak, because your servant hears.' [11]And Yahweh said to Samuel, 'Behold, I am doing something in Israel that will make both ears of whoever hears it tingle. [12]On that day I shall fulfil against Eli all that I have said concerning his house, from beginning to end. [13]I have declared to him that I am judging his house for ever on account of the iniquity that he knew, because his sons were cursing the Awesome One and he did not restrain them. [14]Therefore, I swore to the house of Eli, the iniquity of the house of Eli will not be atoned for by sacrifice and offering for ever.'

[15]Samuel lay down until morning; then he opened the doors of the house of Yahweh. Samuel was afraid to report the vision to Eli, [16]but Eli called Samuel and said, 'Samuel, my son.' And he said, 'Here I am.' [17]He said, 'What was the word he spoke to you? Do not hide it from me. Thus may God do to you, and more, if you hide anything from me from every word he spoke to you. [18]So Samuel reported to him all the words and did not hide anything from him. Then he said, 'It is Yahweh. May he do what seems good to him.'

[19]And Samuel grew and Yahweh was with him. He did not permit anything he said to fail. [20]And all Israel, from Dan to Beersheba, knew that Samuel was attested as a prophet for Yahweh. [21]Yahweh continued to appear at Shiloh, because Yahweh revealed himself to Samuel at Shiloh by the word of Yahweh.

[4:1a]Thus the word of Samuel came to all Israel.

Notes on the text

3:1. The last clause of this verse is not easily translated. *yāqār* generally means 'precious' (Isa. 28:16; Prov. 1:13; 3:15), but lexica mostly offer 'rare' for this occurrence. The rendering 'scarce' brings these elements together since that which is scarce (and wanted) is valuable. Watson (1985: 90) points to the Akkadian *parāṣu*, 'to lie', as a possible parallel and explanation of the unusual *niprāṣ* (common). The root *prṣ* most commonly means 'to break through', but the meaning of 'to spread about' is attested in 2 Chr. 31:5, and possibly 1 Sam. 28:23, 2 Sam. 13:25, 27, 2 Kgs 5:23, though 'prevail' or 'urge' might be preferred there. If Watson is correct, 'lying visions' were rare, but this seems counter to the narrative flow. Although the linguistic evidence is not strong, 'spread about' seems the best option.

7. Repoint *yd'* (know) as an imperfect (see GKC §107c).

13. Most (e.g. Stoebe 1973: 122; cf. NRSV, ESV, NIV mg.) prefer LXX, bolstered by the *tiqqune sopherim* (deliberate changes supposedly wrought by the scribes to protect God's honour) and emend *lāhem* (Awesome One) to *'ĕlōhîm* since the phrase is difficult to construe (though cf. AV, 'made themselves vile'; similarly, NIV). But Althann (1984: 28–29) demonstrates plausible Ugaritic interference with *lhm*, a byform of *l'm*, just as the main verb, the hapax legomenon *khh* II is a byform of *k'h*. As a stative participle, it is a reference to God as 'the Awesome One'. This overcomes the problem that elsewhere the pi. of *qll* is always construed with the accusative of the person cursed.

15. McCarter (1980a: 86) and Klein (1983: 29) prefer the longer LXX reading, where Samuel gets up before opening the doors. But this appears to paraphrase a terse text; MT stands.

16. With a number of MSS, reading *'el* (to) for MT *'et*.

17. These curses seem to require a sign act indicating an action that will be performed against the speaker since the 'thus' stands forbiddingly incomplete. A similar form of imprecation occurs in Ruth 1:17, 1 Kgs 2:23 and 2 Kgs 6:31 (apart from seven in Samuel), so no emendation is necessary.

19. Stoebe (1973: 126) highlights the fact that the pronominal suffix on *dĕbārāyw* (anything he said) is ambiguous, possibly referring to Yahweh or Samuel. But Claasen (1980: 6) has demonstrated that the reference must be to Samuel, though Yahweh acts on his behalf.

Form and structure

This chapter begins to tie together the strands developed so far. It is already clear that Samuel is a significant figure for subsequent events, as is evident in his role as the answer to Hannah's prayer and the contrast of ch. 2. One might assume that he would be a Nazirite (1:11) or priest (2:35). But neither role is emphasized, though Samuel will fulfil some priestly roles. That Samuel was both a Nazirite (of sorts) and a priestly figure is important, highlighting the variety of roles he played. But his role as a prophet is of decisive interest. As a prophet he discerned Yahweh's will to anoint Israel's first kings, combining a prophetic ministry with national leadership. Since nothing so far points to this, the narrative of Samuel's prophetic call is recorded emphasizing why all Israel knew Yahweh's prophet.

Although it recounts the origin of Samuel's prophetic ministry, the story does not conform to the classic structure of the call narrative (Habel 1965). Gnuse (1984: 140–152) argues it is closer to auditory message dream reports (it occurs at a sanctuary and focuses on what is heard; dreams focus on what is seen [Gen. 40:9–11, 16–17; 41:1–7] or what is seen and heard [Gen. 28:12–15]) that occur across the ANE, critiquing attempts to link it to call narratives (1984: 134–140). However, care is necessary because dream interpretation was regarded as a lower form of divination, meaning there are not many dream reports. Also it is called a 'vision', and not a 'dream'; the difference generally being that visions are experienced while awake, though the distinction is not absolute. Though this text is not precisely a call narrative, the similarities with ANE sources cannot deny it because this clearly is the beginning of Samuel's prophetic ministry. The purpose of the message Samuel receives is to establish his status as Yahweh's prophet, a call that is authenticated in the outworking of his message. The narrative is thus a hybrid, representing elements of both the call narrative and the auditory message dream; Fokkelman's (1993: 193) warning against the Procrustean bed of rigid form criticism should be heeded.

This chapter confirms the message of the man of God in 2:27–36 through the message given to Samuel, creating a climax to the whole of chs. 1 – 3. As noted (see 'Form and structure' on 2:11–36), chs. 1 – 3 use two key themes that pivot around 2:27–36. Hannah's Song (2:1–10) and the man of God's announcement (2:27–36) conclude with reference to monarchy, stressing that Yahweh recognizes monarchy before it comes about (Firth 2005b: 4–6). But this points to the second issue: leadership has hitherto been through judges (which 4:18 indicates was one of Eli's roles) and priests. Kingship required a change in the nation's leadership structures. But 2:27–36 not only confirms monarchy's coming; it also announces the fall of Eli's house. The confirmatory announcement of the fall of their house is provided through the message that establishes Samuel as a prophet (3:11–14). The narrator then comments that the word of Yahweh continued to come to Samuel and that Yahweh ensured it did not fail (3:19–21), and that this word was brought to Israel (4:1a). The focus thus shifts from the announcement of Yahweh's word to the way it works itself out in Israel's experience (see Spina 1991: 59–61).

A number of structural devices are employed that complement one another (see Watson 1985: 90–93 and Wicke 1986: 256–258). An important feature is the ring structure where 3:1 and 3:21 – 4:1a counterbalance each other (Fokkelman 1993: 158). This structure shows how the narrative moves from a shortage of Yahweh's word to an abundance, all of which is centred on the person of Samuel. This is also achieved through the choice of vocabulary. Wicke (1986: 258) points out that 'word' (*dābār*) occurs in 3:1 and then not again until Samuel is about to know Yahweh in 3:7. After this it occurs fourteen times, reinforcing the abundance of Yahweh's provision. Thus 3:7 represents an important shift in Samuel's experience, because from this point he knows Yahweh, and is thus equipped for his roles.

Comment

Narrative introduction: 3:1–3

1. The introduction provides the interpretative framework to understand events. Two key elements here are the place of Samuel and the scarcity of Yahweh's word. Samuel is still a lad (*na'ar*) working under Eli. This may indicate these events are close to those of the previous chapter, though no chronological markers are provided. An exact definition of his role is not given, though he is perhaps Eli's apprentice, being initiated into Yahweh's work, but Eli is not called 'priest'. This omission hints at the fulfilment of the man of God's word (2:27–36), because priestly language is no longer appropriate for Eli. However, it is a difficult time to work because of the rarity (see 'Notes') of both Yahweh's word and revelatory visions. This narrative relates how Yahweh removed this scarcity as an outpouring of revelation bypassed Eli and came to a lad who did not yet know Yahweh.

2–3. Eli is pictured as lying down in his place, presumably a room attached to the sanctuary, though separate from the sanctuary proper. Eli's frailty is stressed through his failing eyesight, a theme that climaxes at 4:15 when his blindness is reported. But his lack of physical sight also points to his inability to perceive Yahweh's activity. The events occur before the lamp of God is put out. Exod. 27:20–21 indicates the sanctuary lamp was lit from twilight to dawn, indicating Samuel's encounter with Yahweh was nocturnal. Samuel's presence in the temple overnight may suggest he is participating in an incubation ritual to receive information from Yahweh. Depending on how they are read, certain psalms (e.g. Ps. 3) may show the practice in Israel, but the evidence is inferential. Since the narrative is careful to indicate Samuel does not yet know Yahweh, such a conclusion seems improbable. Rather, Samuel is tending the lamp that accompanies the ark, and so sleeps in the sanctuary. Nevertheless, he is in a place where encounters with Yahweh are possible.

Samuel's call: 3:4–9

4–6. The main narrative movement now begins as Yahweh calls Samuel, initiating his prophetic role. This is vital because Yahweh will identify his king through Samuel. During the night Yahweh speaks to Samuel, and Samuel responds almost unknowingly, 'Here I am,' a phrase evoking Abraham's encounter with God in Gen. 22. Samuel then runs to Eli to ask why he has called, because he assumes Eli is the one calling. Eli's response after denying that he has called Samuel is terse, just two imperatives, 'Go back. Lie down.' The pattern is repeated in v. 6, though with some variations (see Fokkelman 1993: 165). On the second occasion, Yahweh calls Samuel only once, Samuel walks to Eli instead of running, and responds 'Here I am' to Eli, before insisting that Eli has indeed called him. Eli's response is identical, but by slowing the narrative a degree of suspense is built, while the sense of exasperation on both sides is emphasized. Readers know it is Yahweh who calls, but neither Samuel nor Eli has yet realized this.

3–7. The narrator now comments directly, indicating Samuel does not yet know Yahweh. By placing the comment before Yahweh's third call of Samuel, the denouement is delayed while also explaining why Samuel does not know that Yahweh is calling him. The phrase must be understood in the light of the parallel description of Eli's sons in 2:12. There it referred to them as those who did not have a personal experience of Yahweh. But there is a slight change in terminology that indicates a different future for Samuel. Samuel does not yet know Yahweh, implying he subsequently will. He is thus distinguished from Eli's sons, although he is like them still in lacking personal experience of Yahweh. But Samuel's future is one where he knows Yahweh and speaks for him.

8–9. The third encounter repeats the essentials from the second apart from noting that this is the third time Yahweh speaks, and its lack of direct speech from Yahweh. A shift occurs as Eli perceives the source of the voice: Yahweh is calling the lad. Eli must discern this since Samuel does not yet know Yahweh. Eli's answer does not guarantee that Yahweh will call, but he provides Samuel with a mechanism for response if he does. His instructions provide Samuel with words to confirm that it is Yahweh, placing Samuel in the position of his obedient servant. This enables Samuel to move from ignorance to knowing Yahweh. Eli's instructions enable Samuel to hear Yahweh's word, which 3:7 indicated will be revealed to him.

Yahweh's word to Samuel: 3:10–18

10. The possibility Eli recognized becomes reality as Yahweh again calls to Samuel. Yahweh's presence is described in more detail as he comes and stands beside Samuel. Yahweh calls Samuel twice, perhaps hinting at greater urgency, but also setting this occurrence apart from the previous ones. Apart from the vocative 'Yahweh', Samuel's answer is identical with that provided by Eli. This may hint that Samuel is unsure of who is speaking, but is probably a simple narrative variation.

11–14. Only now does Yahweh outline his purposes to Samuel, largely repeating the man of God's message in 2:27–36. The repetition is important since it is the mechanism by which the main themes are reinforced. Yahweh is about to act against Eli in accord with the previous message. This will shock all who hear, since they regard the priests' position as inviolable. The image of the 'tingling ears' is a stock metaphor, and always indicates bad news (2 Kgs 21:12; Jer. 19:3). What is emphasized is that Yahweh will see the process through to completion, carrying out all that has previously been announced. Eli's house will be judged for ever because of the wickedness of Eli's sons and Eli's failure to discipline them. We are never told of direct sin on Eli's part (Birch 1998: 993); that is always from his sons. But there is some tension caused by Yahweh's statement in v. 13 since according to 2:23–25 Eli has spoken to his sons about their actions, though he has not actually stopped them. Eslinger (1985: 152–153) thus suggests that Yahweh is not being truthful with Samuel, that Samuel is a pawn in a game Yahweh is playing to bring about the downfall of Eli's house so he can replace them with someone more malleable. But Yahweh's statement indicates that their actions include their cursing 'the Awesome One' (a divine title), something going beyond the issues addressed by Eli. Arguably, their whole life is blasphemous, but Eli's lack of action remains. Where this message exceeds its predecessor is by excluding any hope of atonement, something emphasized by the use of an oath. Klein (1983: 33) notes the appropriateness of their punishment: they covet gifts and offerings for themselves, so these can now not be effective for them. Also theirs is deliberate sin not covered by the priestly system, which emphasizes its effectiveness against unintentional sin (Lev. 5:14, 17). That said, the repetition from 2:27–36 indicates the emphasis is less upon the message's content and more upon Samuel's prophetic inauguration.

15–18. After receiving the message, Samuel lies in his place until morning before opening the sanctuary doors, indicating the opening of access to the sanctuary to all, and perhaps the opening of God's word to all (Janzen 1983; but see Evans 2000: 30). Yahweh's word has been revealed to Samuel, but the temple remains accessible to all. It is unsurprising that Samuel is afraid to tell Eli the content of the revelation, which is here called a 'vision' (*mar'â*, as opposed to *ḥāzôn* in v. 1) to Eli. But in a neat irony, Eli calls Samuel just as Yahweh has and Samuel responds as he has in the night, except that this time it is Eli calling. Eli solemnly directs him to recount the message and to omit nothing, something that will have been a strong temptation given Samuel's fear. Eli is certain it is Yahweh who calls Samuel and there will be a message for him, even though such messages were then rare. As such, he wants to be sure he receives the full message, perhaps suspecting the message to Samuel will continue that of the man of God. Eli counters Samuel's reticence with a curse that will be pronounced if Samuel does not fully recount Yahweh's message. The content of the curse is not explicit since the reference of the 'this' is unstated, though it is undoubtedly a significant threat. A modern example may be someone drawing their finger across their throat as they speak, though Smith (1899: 29) suggests that the reference may be to the slaying of an animal, implying that the same thing will be done to one breaking the oath. Thus the message is recounted and Eli accepts Yahweh's judgment upon him and his family (note David's similar response in 2 Sam. 15:25–26). Eli may not think that what Yahweh is about to do is good, but acknowledges he has no means to resist, especially since this message confirms the earlier one.

Narrative conclusion: 3:19 – 4:1a

3:19–20. With the main event recounted, we now have direct comments from the narrator indicating the narrative's main thrust is to demonstrate Samuel's initiation into the role of Yahweh's prophet. No longer are we concerned with Samuel as a lad. Henceforth we encounter him as an adult who variously exercises the roles of priest and judge, though primarily prophet. But the decisive statement is made in v. 19 as evidence that the condition of 3:7 no longer applies: Yahweh is with Samuel, and does not permit (lit.) 'any of his words to fall to the ground'. This same idiom occurs in Josh. 21:45 and 23:14, where it indicates that none of Yahweh's promises concerning occupation of the land has failed. It affirms the reliability of Samuel's message, confirming him as a prophet who is to be trusted (see Deut. 18:22). Samuel speaks Yahweh's message, and the scarcity of Yahweh's word has been overcome. This is significant for the whole nation, with 'Dan to Beersheba' being a standard means of describing the country from north to south (1 Kgs 4:26). The event with Eli begins Samuel's prophetic ministry, a ministry recognized by the whole nation because of Yahweh's presence with him. Samuel is thus attested (*ne'ĕmān*; see 2:35) as Yahweh's prophet. Samuel is a faithful prophet, something the community recognizes, with the use of similar wording linking his role as a faithful prophet back to that of the faithful priest.

3:21 – 4:1a. The note in v. 21 stresses that Yahweh continued to reveal himself to Samuel at Shiloh. It was not a one-off experience but a consistent element in Samuel's experience. Where Yahweh's word had been scarce it was now abundantly available as Samuel ministered at Shiloh. But this word was not revealed to everyone. Rather, the word came through Samuel and came through him to the whole nation. But how that word would resolve itself depended upon the resolution of Samuel's message to Eli, and it is to that which the narrative now turns. Although Samuel is absent from the whole of 4:1b – 7:1, that narrative is the outworking of his message (and that of 2:27–36).

Explanation

It is easy to read this chapter only as the religious awakening of a young boy, something consistent with 3:8–21 when Samuel comes to know Yahweh. But to stay there is to distort the narrative's central aim, which is to establish Samuel's credentials for the nation as an attested prophet. This attestation prepares for the change in national leadership that becomes a reality when the oracles against Eli and his family are fulfilled in ch. 4. This change could be recognized by all because Yahweh was with Samuel, preparing for his decisive role in the development of monarchy as Yahweh's spokesman and the one who anoints kings.

The process by which the change of leadership occurs is important, because it demonstrates Yahweh's commitment to complete transformation. As well as the change in leadership the scarcity of Yahweh's word with which the chapter began (3:1) has become abundant by its conclusion (3:19–21). Yahweh's word is the central means by which the leadership change can occur. Reasons for the initial scarcity are not given, and it is perhaps surprising in the light of the word recounted in 2:27–36, though that this word was unusual is emphasized 3:1. Although it is never made explicit, conditions at the sanctuary under Eli may be an implied reason for the scarcity (see Amos 8:11–12).

The narrative also highlights the rejection of Eli's house. Through Samuel, Yahweh rejects them because of their failure to honour him. Samuel is the faithful priest who initially replaces this family, though more importantly he is the vehicle by which Yahweh's displeasure with their abuse of power at his sanctuary is made clear. Eli declines in importance as Samuel rises through the chapter. This is seen most markedly either side of the point when Samuel receives Yahweh's word. Before that he was personally ignorant of Yahweh, dependent upon Eli to guide him in all things, even to the extent of requiring an appropriate response to Yahweh when he appeared to him. But once Samuel knows Yahweh and has received his word, Eli is placed in a lesser position than Samuel. What Samuel now announces, Eli must accept, even though it signals the end of his family's priority and power.

Therefore, although this is the account of Samuel's initial experience of Yahweh and the origin of his prophetic ministry, it must be seen in terms of Yahweh's initiative and activity for his people. Yahweh is revealed as opposing religious authority, even that acting in his name, which because of its corruption prevents his people from expressing their relationship to him. On the other hand, it emphasizes Yahweh's commitment to the creation of a leadership structure that is faithful to him, leadership validated by a real relationship with him and that announces his word. Yahweh brings transformation for his people, transformation in the revealing of his word, so we move from scarcity to abundance and through this transformation in the provision of leadership that points back to him by faithfully proclaiming his word. Samuel is the one through whom this ultimately happens, yet it happens through Samuel because of the initiative of Yahweh that reaches back to his birth. But Samuel's leadership is transitional since 2:10 and 2:35–36 have indicated that kingship is coming. Yahweh acts to bring transformation for his people, but the process is dynamic, responding to Israel's condition, even as it points to Yahweh's freedom as his people's sovereign.

1 SAMUEL 4:1b–22

Translation

[1b]Israel went out to battle against the Philistines. They camped at Ebenezer and the Philistines camped at Aphek. [2]The Philistines arrayed themselves to confront Israel. When the battle was spread, Israel was defeated before the Philistines, who struck down about four thousand men on the battlefield. [3]When the people came to the camp, the elders of Israel said, 'Why has Yahweh defeated us today before the Philistines? Let us bring to ourselves the ark of the covenant of Yahweh from Shiloh that it may come into our midst and save us from the power of our enemies.' [4]So the people sent to Shiloh and brought from there the ark of the covenant of Yahweh of Armies, who sits between the cherubim. And the two sons of Eli, Hophni and Phinehas, were there with the ark of the covenant of God.

[5]As the ark of the covenant of Yahweh was brought into the camp, all Israel raised a great shout, and the ground shook. [6]When the Philistines heard the sound of the shout, they said, 'What is the meaning of this great shout in the Hebrews' camp?' When they learned that the ark of the covenant of Yahweh had entered the camp, [7]the Philistines were afraid, for they said, 'A god has come to the camp.' And they said, 'Woe to us, because nothing like this has happened before. [8]Woe to us! Who will deliver us from the hand of these great gods? These are the gods who struck down Egypt with all kinds of plagues in the wilderness. [9]Take courage and be men, O Philistines, lest you serve the Hebrews as they have served you; be men and fight!' [10]So the Philistines battled and Israel was defeated and fled, everyone to their own tent. The slaughter was very great, and thirty thousand foot soldiers fell from Israel. [11]The ark of God was taken and the two sons of Eli, Hophni and Phinehas, died.

[12]A man from Benjamin ran from the battle line and entered Shiloh that day; his clothes were torn and dirt was on his head. [13]When he came in, Eli was sitting on his throne beside the road watching closely because his heart trembled because of the ark of God. The man entered the city to report and the whole city cried out. [14]When Eli heard the sound of the cry, he said, 'What is the meaning of this tumult?' Then the man hurried and came and reported to Eli. [15]Eli was ninety-eight, and his eyes were set and he could not see. [16]The man said to Eli, 'I am the one who has come from the ranks; I fled the ranks today.' Then he said, 'What is the message, my son?' [17]The messenger responded, 'Israel fled before the Philistines,

and there has also been a great defeat among the people. Also your two sons, Hophni and Phinehas, have died, and the ark of God has been taken.' [18]When he mentioned the ark of God, Eli fell from the throne backwards by the side of the gate and his neck was broken and he died, because he was an old and heavy man. He had judged Israel for forty years.

[19]His daughter-in-law, the wife of Phinehas, was pregnant and about to give birth. When she heard the news of the ark of God's capture and the death of her father-in-law and husband, she bowed and gave birth because her labour pains came upon her. [20]As she was about to die the women attending her said, 'Do not be afraid, for you have given birth to a son.' But she did not answer or pay attention. [21]She named the lad Ichabod, saying, 'The glory has gone from Israel,' because the ark of God was captured and because of her father-in-law and husband. [22]She said, 'The glory has gone from Israel, because the ark of God is captured.'

Notes on the text

1b. An opening sentence about Eli's family and a chronological note is found in LXX (supported by McCarter 1980a: 103), but reads more like a scribal aside.

2. MT *watittōš* is awkward. *ntš* normally means 'abandon', but 'spread' could be a derived meaning since the battle was uncontrolled, and thus spread out.

7–8. Although *'ĕlōhîm* can have a sg. meaning, the Philistines are portrayed as speaking of a plurality of gods because of the pl. adjectives in v. 8. The sg. verb in v. 7 could suggest they believed the ark represented one of Israel's gods.

9. The description of Israel as 'Hebrews' represents a play on words between 'Hebrews' (*'ibrîm*) and the verb 'to serve' (*'ābad*).

13. Eli's seat is called a *kissē'* (see 1:9), contributing to his quasi-royal presentation. That Eli is beside the road is understood from Q. McCarter (1980a: 111) follows the LXX and suggests he is on top of the gate. However, MT is preferable. The same issues recur in 4:18.

14–15. LXX appears to be a conflation of different readings. Klein (1983: 38) defends the MT.

16. The repetition in the man's speech is odd, and has led to attempts at abbreviation (e.g. McCarter 1980a: 112). But both lines are in LXX, and it may be a narrative technique that shows the man stuttering (Alter 1999: 24), perhaps after an exhausting run.

17. Normally, *mĕbaśśēr* refers to someone bearing good news. This is the one point in the narrative treating the ark as f.; 2 Chr. 8:11 is the only other occurrence. Against Fokkelman (1993: 574), this is evidence of the messenger's broken speech.

19. LXX suggests Eli judged Israel for twenty years.

Form and structure

This chapter begins a narrative (running through to 7:1) both discrete from the preceding accounts and yet paradoxically integral to it. It continues the focus on Eli's family, recounting the deaths of Eli, his sons and daughter-in-law, yet also reports the birth of his grandson Ichabod. The narrative thus confirms the message of the man of God in 2:27–36 and Samuel's authority to announce Yahweh's word. It confirms 4:1a – Samuel's word has come to the nation through its demonstration in Eli's family. Continuity with the past sets the agenda for what follows.

Yet the whole of 4:1b – 7:1 is largely separate from what has gone before. Although Eli's family are mentioned, Samuel is not, and the central concern is with the ark, though apart from 3:3, the ark has played no role in the narrative so far. Hence this is the beginning of the narrative of the ark's capture and return, and is frequently known as the Ark Narrative (see 'Introduction', 'Composition', 'Sources'). The narrative's boundaries are disputed (see Campbell 1975 and Miller and Roberts 1977 for the alternatives), and many scholars continue to see 2 Sam. 6 as the original conclusion. However, see 'Form and structure' there for reasons why it should be seen as separate. One effect of this is that the ark narrative is frequently studied as a separate story, in much the same manner as the so-called Succession Narrative of 2 Sam. 9 – 20 and 1 Kgs 1 – 2.

We should, however, note the links with the earlier chapters (see Willis 1971: 297–301; Gitay 1992: 222–224). Even if redactional, they are still important for the finished text. In particular we should note that the man of God's prophecy in 2:27–36 is worked out when Hophni and Phinehas die on the one day (2:34). This also confirms the word given by Yahweh to Samuel (3:11–14); Samuel is thus absent from these chapters only to the extent that he is not a direct actor. The message that establishes his prophetic credentials is a subtext active throughout this chapter. There are also links to the following narratives, especially in the way chs. 4 and 8 both show human attempts to usurp Yahweh's reign (see Eslinger 1985: 57–60). This suggests we should read 4:1b – 7:1 as a bifurcated narrative, where the narrator has two separate narrative strands, but leaves one aside until the completion of the other since its completion is essential to what follows (see Ska 1990: 9–12). This level of integration suggests that the final text needs to be our focus in order to appreciate the narrator's skill.

This chapter is thus the start of a longer narrative, but one that has its own integrity, as well as contributing to the story of the ark. It rounds off the story of Eli's family but sets this within a larger context where Yahweh's authority is verbally acknowledged but does not shape behaviour. Drawing on exodus motifs (see 'Form and structure' on 5:1 – 7:1), it shows that both Israel and the Philistines know about Yahweh's power, and the Philistines even know the meaning of the exodus, although they do not have the facts straight. Functionally, therefore, both Israel and the

Philistines are in a position similar to Eli's sons and Samuel before his encounter with Yahweh: they know *about* Yahweh but do not *know* Yahweh. For the Philistines, this means they believe they must fight with greater vigour on the assumption that Yahweh can be defeated. As becomes apparent in the subsequent narrative, this belief is fundamentally flawed, but the flaws are not apparent to them yet. For Israel the problem is that they misunderstand their election, and although they ask why Yahweh has defeated them (4:3) they never enquire if sin may be the issue. Instead, by drawing in the ark they attempt to convert a normal border dispute into a Yahweh war. The ark was certainly present at previous examples of this (Josh. 6), but the point was that it was to be initiated by Yahweh, not the people. Human attempts to initiate Yahweh war was an inversion of Yahweh's authority. Israel and the Philistines both mirror the individual experiences of Eli's sons at the national level, but the deaths in Eli's family indicate that Yahweh's authority remains. The interface of the family story and those of the nations is thus vital to the narrative's theme.

Comment

The Ark's capture: 4:1b–11

1b–2. War with the Philistines is unexpected. Although mentioned in the book of Judges (Judg. 3:31, especially with Samson, Judg. 13 – 16), there is nothing here that prepares for the conflict. This may indicate that an original introduction to the ark narrative has been omitted because the conflict's cause is of no interest to the narrator. However, the Philistines become the archetypal enemy of Israel throughout the early monarchy until their defeat by David in 2 Sam. 5:17–25. They appear to have settled on the southern coastal plain about the same time as Israel entered the land, generating natural conflict over control of the region. Amos 9:7 indicates that Israel believed them to have come from the region of Crete (Caphtor), something consistent with the view of Egyptian sources that regard them as one of the Sea Peoples, marauders from the Aegean. The Bible consistently portrays them as living on the southern coastal plain of Palestine, with their power base built on their pentapolis of Ashdod, Ashkelon, Ekron, Gath and Gaza. Although Gen. 20 and 26 describe Abraham and Isaac interacting with Philistines, they differ from those described in Samuel, having a king and living in the region of Gerar, about 10 miles south-east of Gaza. They are probably ethnically different, but the label is used because of their location (Hoerth, Mattingly and Yamauchi 1994: 237–238). Because the battle's cause is of no interest, the account simply describes the arrival of the participants. The Israelite camp is called Ebenezer, though this name is given later (1 Sam. 7:12), but is employed as that known to later generations. Ebenezer is probably Izbet Sartah, an

Israelite site occupied until about 1,000 BC, roughly 2 miles from Aphek. Several sites bore the name Aphek (fortress), with this one slightly east of Tel-Aviv (see Bimson 1995: 28), on the headwaters of the Yarkon River. This is about 25 miles north of the most northerly Philistine town, Ekron, so they have pushed well into Israel. Since the Philistines indicate they believe the Israelites are currently subject to them (4:9), this situation is entirely believable. V. 2 then describes the initial encounter, where Israel is defeated and about four 'thousand' die. It is a defeat, but an orderly one, since the Israelite casualties are on the field of battle, in contrast to the second defeat, where the Israelite troops flee. The number of Israelite casualties may be understood as describing four military units known as 'thousands' rather than a literal number (see J. W. Wenham 1967), in which case they would have been considerably smaller. This makes more sense of the subsequent casualty reports, though the loss of four units would still be highly significant.

3–4. Following on from the accounts in Judges, there are two surprising omissions here. No judge is raised up by Yahweh as a deliverer and no reason is given for the defeat. The absence of a judge is overcome by reference to Eli as having 'judged' Israel in 4:18, though the analogy with Judges suggests this is the beginning of a period of oppression. Ps. 78:56–66, which reflects on the whole of the ark narrative, suggests idolatry as the reason for the defeat (Ps. 78:56–58), but this narrative refrains from doing so, being more concerned with the two prophetic words against Eli and his family. These reasons are not contradictory, but each text reflects its own central concerns. In response, Israel's elders do not entertain the possibility that the Philistines may have defeated them, and their question is only about why Yahweh has defeated them. It is not a political or military defeat that they discuss; it is a theological issue. However, rather than waiting for Yahweh's reply, they demonstrate hubris in deciding to bring the ark more than 20 miles from Shiloh to the battle site. The speed of their action suggests the initial question was rhetorical rather than a genuine attempt to enquire of God. The possibility of sin is not entertained, though the events of chs. 1 – 3 suggest it as an issue. Instead, they expect Yahweh should fight for them. The gravity of their decision is emphasized by the full title given to the ark on its arrival. Not only is it the 'ark of the covenant', but it also belongs to 'Yahweh Sabaoth' (Cf. 'Comment' on 1:3), which is compounded by the qualifying phrase 'who sits between the cherubim', thus referring to the mercy seat. Two central themes about the ark are drawn together; it is both a cultic item and an essential element in Yahweh wars (see Gordon 1986: 94). Israel believed that the ark's presence guaranteed victory. Israel sought to make a Yahweh war, even though a Yahweh war must be initiated by Yahweh. Although the elders know it is Yahweh who must fight for them, v. 3 presumes that the ark will save the people because of the presumed control this brings over Yahweh, compelling his action. The ominous link with the preceding chapters is seen in that Hophni and Phinehas were those responsible for the ark and were with it when it arrived at Aphek, hinting already at a possible fulfilment of 2:34.

5–9. The introduction has indicated the main line of the plot, though it also raises an important question: Can Israel control Yahweh through the ark? The ark's presence in the Israelite camp generates conflicting sets of emotions. The Israelites let out an excited battle cry (*tĕrû'â* in Josh. 6:5, 20 is associated with a Yahweh war involving the ark), making the ground shake. Israel believes it has initiated a Yahweh war, and the shout is the final element. But the Philistines hear the cry with concern, and though they misconstrue Israel's history in polytheistic rather than monotheistic terms, they interpret the cry in terms of the exodus, foreshadowing an important theme that runs through 5:1 – 7:1. Paradoxically, it is the Philistines who know the traditions of the exodus, and that the Hebrew deity is not one with whom they can trifle! Their immediate concern is with the possibility that they may now have to serve Israel. The other part of the Philistine response is to confront their fears, and to encourage bravery in the face of a seemingly insurmountable opposition (though see Eslinger 1985: 171). The Philistines expect defeat, but will not simply surrender. Both sides thus anticipate an Israelite victory.

10–11. Instead of victory, we now read of Israel's defeat. The ark has not brought Israel victory. In fact, the defeat is heavier, with thirty 'thousands' killed (on 'thousands', see 'Comment' on v. 2). The battle account is brief because the narrator's concern is with the people's attitude towards Yahweh rather than the battle itself. Nevertheless, the structure of v. 10 is striking. The Philistines are active: it is they who wage war. But the passive verbal form is used for Israel; it is not that the Philistines defeat Israel but that Israel is defeated, the implication being that it is Yahweh who has done so. Moreover, the verb used (*ngp*) is associated with the plague narratives in Exodus (Exod. 7:27 [ET 8:2]; 12:23, 27). The Philistines feared the God of the exodus, but Israel discovered his power in a total rout. Moreover, the ark was captured, and in fulfilment of 2:34 (cf. 3:12), Hophni and Phinehas die on the same day. Instead of a glorious victory, hubris brings its inevitable result. Israel cannot control Yahweh, and trying to do so through the covenant is folly, though folly consistent with what Yahweh has previously announced. This is the irony that lies at the centre of this part of the narrative. Attempts to control Yahweh merely make clearer his control. The price Israel pay is great, though the numbers killed indicate that the nation's sins go well beyond Hophni and Phinehas (see Campbell 1979: 35). The sins of the leaders affect the whole people, just as was the case in the wilderness (Num. 16). Through her attempt to control Yahweh, Israel finds herself in the same situation as when in the wilderness or even that of Pharaoh in the exodus. Israel experiences a reverse exodus, something consistent with the covenant curses (Lev. 26:17; Deut. 28:25), because she insists on the ways in which Yahweh acts on her behalf.

Eli's death: 4:12–18

12–13. The ark's capture and Hophni and Phinehas' deaths are the trigger for a number of other events, each dependant upon what has gone before, each linked back to 2:27–36 and 3:11–14. The first of these is Eli's death. The narrative is sparse, recounting the journey of one Benjaminite soldier, who flees over 20 miles west to Shiloh. The soldier comes as one in mourning, as is evident from his torn clothing and the dust on his hair. Eli is by the road, keeping watch because of his concern about the ark, though given his blindness (3:2) he needs others to watch for its return. An important issue relates to the cause of Eli's fear. Eslinger (1985: 177) conflates the interpretations of Campbell (1979: 37) and Davies (1977: 12), so that Eli is afraid of both the ark's loss and its possible effect on his sons because of their sin. But this is improbable. Although Davies correctly notes that the verb *ḥrd* means to 'tremble from fear' (cf. Ezra 10:3), the earlier portrayal of Eli showed him as prepared to accept Yahweh's decision (3:18), rendering this interpretation unlikely (see Alter 1999: 24; Bergen 1996: 93). It is the ark's presence in battle that worries Eli, though whether his concern is the ark's loss or that it may act against Israel is not stated. The soldier's initial report is to the town rather than Eli, so Eli can only respond to the noise he hears. This time the people cry to God for action (cf. Judg. 3:9, 15; 1 Sam. 7:8; Jer. 11:11; though the next such cry will be uttered by the Philistines in 5:10!). If Kaufmann (1988) is correct in defending a northern site at Shiloh for the sanctuary, then it naturally reaches the town first.

14–17. When Eli hears noise from the town, he wants to know what it means. Fortunately, the messenger hurries to report to him. Before his report is given, we are told of Eli's age and blindness (cf. 1 Kgs 14:4), information necessary to interpret what follows, since the man's appearance should indicate Israel's defeat, though it also serves to retard the action. Indeed, even after mentioning in v. 14 that the man 'told' Eli, the report is not given until v. 16. Because Eli could not see properly, he has to ask about what was obvious to anyone with normal sight, though both the question and many details of the answer foreshadow the report of the Amalekite to David in 2 Sam. 1:4–10. Thus the man reports that he has fled from the battle, leading to Eli's request for additional information. At this point the man is called a messenger (*mĕbaśśēr*), practically the only time in the OT where the term refers to someone bearing bad news. The report is terse, highlighting what we already know from v. 11, with the emphasis upon the ark's fate. The report is given in terse, nearly broken, statements that suggest someone struggling to speak after running a distance close to the modern marathon. The report moves from the man's situation, to Israel's flight, to the nation's defeat, through to the death of Eli's sons, and finally to the ark's capture. The messenger does not claim that the Philistines have defeated Israel, leaving open the possibility that Yahweh acted against them. From Eli's point of view, the report moves from his most distant concerns to that which is most important, so placement of the ark's capture at the end of the sentence stresses its importance.

18. In response to the ark's capture, and not the death of his sons, Eli falls from his throne and dies from a broken neck. His weight is too great for him to survive, though there is a play on the root *kbd*, which can mean both 'heavy' and 'glorious', preparing for a play that runs through the balance of the ark's story (cf. 5:11). No direct connection is made with 2:27–36 (Birch 1998: 1002), though the sign of the death of Eli's sons on the one day has been fulfilled. Curiously, there is then a notice that Eli 'judged' Israel for forty years. Eli has a wider role than just what is described here, though we have no indication that he was a charismatic or military leader. But the end of his leadership creates the setting where Samuel can come to the fore. Although unmentioned in 4:1b – 7:1, he remains constantly in the background.

Ichabod: 4:19–22

19–20. The closing vignette provides a poignant glimpse into the effect of the deaths of Eli and his sons with the account of Ichabod's birth. As with Eli, the primary emphasis is on Phinehas' wife's response to the ark's capture. Although the deaths of her husband and father-in-law are linked to it, the priority of the ark's loss is indicated by its initial mention. The woman is unnamed because the emphasis is on her son. The tragic news triggers a difficult premature labour, and the woman is on the point of death after her son's delivery, when her female attendants seek to encourage her with the news of her son.

21–22. The child is named Ichabod (presumably, just before her death, though it is not narrated), because with the death of her husband and father-in-law and the ark's capture, she believes the glory has gone from Israel. The derivation of the name is unclear. The *chabod* component means 'glory', but the prefix's meaning is uncertain, though it seems to have a negative connotation. The point is clear even if the philology is not, and it is made specific in v. 22. Although v. 21 may suggest that it is both the deaths in her family and the ark's capture that represent the problem, her speech in v. 22 stresses the ark's centrality. The use of the word 'exile' in v. 22 would be redolent in meaning for those who read this story later. There is irony in her closing words, for God's glory has not departed with the ark, but rested heavily on Eli and Israel.

Explanation

With this chapter we both begin the Ark Narrative and complete the introductory material of chs. 1 – 3. Although many regard the narrative as originally independent, it is well integrated into its context. Thus it concludes the announcements made in 2:27–36, yet looks to the future, since the hope of monarchy remains. But this chapter also introduces a new theme: Yahweh cannot be manipulated by his people; his sovereignty remains and cannot be avoided.

We must recognize that this is part of a larger narrative unit that extends through to 7:1, though it is distinctive enough to consider it in its own terms. Here the narrator has skilfully brought together the themes of the ark's capture, Eli's death and Ichabod's birth to highlight the futility of attempting to manipulate God. God cannot be placed under the control of his people, even if they try through covenantal means. The witness of Samuel is that God is in every way sovereign, and his people must recognize his authority. The chapter is a warning to all subsequent generations of the outcome of a failure to recognize this. It stands with the Jephthah narrative (Judg. 10:6 – 12:7) in warning against such an approach to God. Modern readers may feel they are unlikely to make such a mistake, but perhaps should consider the way so many church meetings make decisions that God is subsequently summoned to bless to realize that this is not necessarily the case (see Davis 2000: 41–44).

This tragedy needs to be understood against the backdrop of the exodus since there are intentional echoes of it. But special care is needed on this point. Birch (1998: 1003) points out that it is the Philistines who recognize the association with the exodus, suggesting that in so doing they encourage those who read the text to bring to mind their own recollection of it. Thus he suggests there is a positive message of hope here in the God who gives life in the face of death. One cannot disagree with such a statement as an overall reflection on the biblical message, but this reading runs counter to the text's structure. Although the Philistines recognize the exodus themes, it is still Israel who receive Yahweh's judgment. Phinehas' wife may be wrong to imagine the glory has left Israel because the ark has gone, but she understands that Yahweh is not acting for Israel as he did in the exodus. If anything, there is an element of anti-exodus here, because Israel experiences Yahweh's power as the Egyptians did in the exodus, or at best as do those who rebel in the wilderness. The traditions of the exodus are a source of nourishment to God's people, but they are not to be recalled without some understanding of where we are meant to stand in relationship to God any more than the Lord's Supper is to be taken without consideration of our relationship to Christ and his church (1 Cor. 11:17–34).

Finally, we should recognize the ways this chapter shows God's word working itself out. Within this, Eli's family, and Israel as a whole, imagine themselves to be working out their own purposes in their decision about the ark. Yet the reality is very different. God's purposes in relationship to Eli's family have been announced twice, and 4:1a insists that Samuel's word, which we recognize as Yahweh's, comes to all Israel. There is an important tension that must be retained. The text never indicates that Eli's family or the nation are somehow puppets that can do only what Yahweh announces through his prophet. Their actions are always at their own initiative. But still they achieve what has been announced, so that even their rebellion serves God's purposes. The modern tendency is to stress one side of this tension to the exclusion of the other, but the text resists this. Even as it warns against trying to manipulate God and of being on the wrong side of the values of the exodus, it continues to assure us of the certain fulfilment of God's word.

1 SAMUEL 5:1 – 7:1

Translation

[1]The Philistines took the ark of the covenant and brought it from Ebenezer to Ashdod. [2]Then the Philistines took the ark of the covenant and brought it into Dagon's temple, and placed it beside Dagon. [3]When the people of Ashdod rose early the next day, behold, Dagon was fallen over face downward before the ark of Yahweh, so they took Dagon and returned him to his place. [4]When they rose early the next morning, behold, Dagon was fallen over face downward on the ground before the ark of Yahweh and Dagon's head and his two hands were cut off on the threshold; only the body of Dagon remained. [5]Therefore, the priests of Dagon and all who enter the temple of Dagon do not tread upon the threshold of Dagon in Ashdod to this day.

[6]The hand of Yahweh was heavy upon the people of Ashdod and he ravaged them, and he struck them with tumours, both Ashdod and its district. [7]When the men of Ashdod saw the situation, they said, 'The ark of the God of Israel must not remain with us, because his hand has been severe against us and against Dagon our god.' [8]So they sent and assembled all the Philistine rulers and said, 'What shall we do with the ark of the God of Israel?' They said, 'Let the ark of the God of Israel be moved to Gath.' So they moved the ark of the God of Israel.

[9]After they moved it, the hand of Yahweh was against that city, causing very great panic, and he struck the inhabitants of that city, both small and great, and tumours broke out on them. [10]So they sent the ark of God to Ekron, but as the ark of God was entering Ekron the people of Ekron cried out, 'They have moved the ark of the God of Israel to kill us and our people.' [11]They sent and assembled all the Philistine rulers and said, 'Send away the ark of the God of Israel and let it return to its place and not kill us and our people.' For a deadly panic had come upon every city – the hand of God was very heavy there. [12]The men who did not die were struck with tumours and the city's outcry went up to heaven.

[6:1]The ark of Yahweh was in the Philistines' fields for seven months. [2]Then the Philistines summoned the priests and the diviners and said, 'What shall we do to the ark of Yahweh? Tell us with what we can return it to its place.' [3]They said, 'When returning the ark of the God of Israel, do not send it back empty, but you shall surely send him a reparation offering. Then you shall be healed and it shall be known to you why his hand has not been lifted from you.' ⁴And they said, 'What is the reparation offering that we should return to him?' They responded, 'Five gold tumours and five gold mice, according to the number of Philistine rulers, because the one plague has afflicted all of you and your lords. ⁵And you shall make images of your tumours and images of your mice that are destroying the land and give glory to the God of Israel. Perhaps he will lighten his hand from upon you, your gods and your land. ⁶Why do you harden your hearts as Egypt and Pharaoh hardened their hearts? When he had dealt severely with them, did they not send them out and they went? ⁷And now, take and prepare a new cart and two milk cows which have not had a yoke upon them. You shall hitch the cows to the cart, but bring their calves that follow them home. ⁸Then take the ark of Yahweh and place it on the cart, and the golden objects you are returning to him as a reparation offering place them in a box beside it. So you will send it and it will go ⁹and you shall watch. If it goes up the border road of Beth Shemesh, then he has brought this great suffering on us, but, if not, we shall know his hand has not struck us; it has happened to us by chance.'

¹⁰The men did so and took two milk cows and hitched them to the cart and shut up their calves at home. ¹¹They placed the ark of Yahweh on the cart along with the box and the gold mice and the images of their tumours, ¹²and the cows went straight on the road to Beth Shemesh, lowing as they went along. They did not turn aside to the right or to the left, and the Philistine lords were going along behind them until the border of Beth Shemesh. ¹³As the people of Beth Shemesh were harvesting wheat in the valley they looked up and saw the ark and rejoiced at what they saw. ¹⁴The cart came to the field of Joshua of Beth Shemesh and stopped there. A large stone was there, and they cut up the wood of the cart and offered up the cows as a burnt offering to Yahweh.

¹⁵The Levites brought down the ark of Yahweh and the box with the golden objects in it and placed them on the great stone, and the men of Beth Shemesh offered up burnt offerings and made sacrifices to Yahweh that day. ¹⁶When the five Philistine lords saw this, they returned to Ekron that day.

¹⁷These are the gold tumours the Philistines returned as a reparation offering to Yahweh – one each for Ashdod, Gaza, Ashkelon, Gath and Ekron ¹⁸and the number of the golden mice accorded with the number of the Philistine cities belonging to the five lords, both walled cities and unwalled villages. The great stone where they set the ark of Yahweh is a witness to this day in the field of Joshua of Beth Shemesh.

¹⁹But he struck the men of Beth Shemesh because they looked on the ark of Yahweh – he struck seventy men and the people mourned because Yahweh had struck the people a great blow. ²⁰The men of Beth Shemesh said, 'Who is able to stand before Yahweh, this holy God? To whom shall he go away from us?' ²¹So they sent messengers to the residents of Kiriath Jearim saying, 'The Philistines returned the ark of Yahweh to us. Come down, take it up to yourselves.'

⁷:¹So the men of Kiriath Jearim came, took up the ark of Yahweh and brought it to the house of Abinadab on the hill. And they consecrated Eleazar his son to keep the ark of Yahweh.

Notes on the text

5:2. McCarter (1980a: 118) and Klein (1983: 47) prefer LXX[L], where the ark is not directly named; but the repetition in naming the ark cautions against such a reading.

4–5. The translation of *miptān* is disputed. BDB and *DCH*'s 'threshold' is preferable to *HALOT*'s (see REB) 'platform' since priests are unlikely to tread on the platform. As Gordon (1986: 99) notes, it cannot mean 'platform' at Zeph. 1:9 since one would hardly leap over the platform; while 'threshold' is preferable in Ezek. 9:3; 10:4, 18; 47:1. The end of v. 4 is difficult; lit. 'only Dagon was left upon it'. LXX suggests a missing word before Dagon since it refers to Dagon's spine (*rachis*). Tg reads *gwpyh*, suggesting *gēw* (back) rather than LXX's more specific reading. Dagon is face down, the 'back' is what can be seen, so 'body' can be assumed.

6. LXX is longer, introducing mice not represented in MT until 6:4 (similarly, Josephus, *Ant.* 6.3). The principal of *lectio brevior* supports MT, as does LXX's association of the mice (rats?) with ships, although Ashdod is not coastal. For K *'plym* (tumours) Q suggests *ṭḥrym*, generally translated 'haemorrhoids'. The latter occurs at 6:11, 17. Q may represent a polite form (Smith 1899: 41), so these terms are probably synonyms. A haemorrhoidal interpretation of the epidemic is rejected (see Wilkinson 1977: 138).

8. The speaker near the verse end is unclear. LXX provides a subject for the verb through the residents of Gath, but they are not said to have come. MT's Philistine rulers are preferable. Also, the speech in LXX is quite different from MT, so LXX offers a different textual tradition. But 'Gath' is awkward. The simplest solution is probably that a he-locale dropped out after Gath, which is placed in an emphatic position.

9. For MT *'ōtô* read with 4QSam[a] *gth*. MT represents a corrupted abbreviation, requiring restoration of *tēn kibtōn* from LXX[L].

10–11. The closing pronominal suffixes are sg. (my), but pl. (us) in meaning. The intent may be distributive (GKC §145m).

6:3. Despite awkwardness of MT, *nôda'* is retained in preference to 4QSam[a] and LXX (Miller and Roberts 1977: 53). The Philistine leaders have asked for knowledge and are now shown how to receive that knowledge.

4. The introduction of mice is surprising since they are previously unmentioned. The reference is absent in 4QSam[a] and LXX (see 'Notes' on 5:6). Against McCarter (1980a: 129), there is no contradiction with 6:17–18 since the five chief Philistine cities include their surrounding villages.

5. Following McCarter (1980a: 134). *'ûlay* is stronger than English 'perhaps', indicating an anticipated but uncertain outcome.

18. With a few Hebrew MSS, read *'eben* for *'ābēl*. Similarly, LXX. Revocalize *'ad*, *'ēd*, 'witness' (see Driver 1913: 85).

19. The number struck varies in the tradition. MT's 'seventy men, fifty thousand men' is hard to defend on historical and grammatical grounds. Josephus (*Ant.* 6.1.4) has seventy, though the major textual witnesses retain the fifty thousand (Fouts 1992). It is best to regard the large number as a gloss. More awkward is the identity of those struck. REB (also NRSV) follows LXX[B] to make it 'the sons of Jeconiah' (along with other variances). McCarter (1980a: 131) conjectures that 'sons of Jeconiah' should be 'sons of the priests', but there is little to be said for this. Since Yahweh subsequently strikes all of the men of Beth Shemesh, MT is preferred as more awkward grammatically but narratively more consistent.

Form and structure

Israel's defeat give the Philistines what seems a great prize: the ark. It dominates the narrative, being mentioned twenty-five times in thirty-four verses. The Philistines learn about Yahweh through the ark, knowledge perceived in how the ark is gradually named. Indeed, it highlights an exodus typology employed such that this becomes the account of the ark's exodus:

ark of the covenant	5:1, 2
ark of the God of Israel	5:7, 8 (×3), 10, 11; 6:3
ark of God	5:10 (×2)
ark of Yahweh	5:3, 4; 6:1, 2, 8, 11, 15, 18, 19, 21; 7:1 (×2)
The ark	5:9

From the Philistine perspective, there is little difference between 'ark of God' and 'ark of the God of Israel'. Both expressions simply clarify that the ark does not belong to Dagon but rather to Israel's God. The narrative is placed within a Philistine setting, but draws readers into the Philistine experience by using their terminology. Although the specifically Israelite terms 'ark of the covenant' and 'ark of Yahweh' are used in 5:1–4, they occur in straight narration, not in material reflecting a Philistine orientation.

Initial Philistine speech concerning the ark is generic: the Philistines do not name the God who acts, though the narrator insists it was the 'hand of Yahweh' (5:6, 9). The Philistines personalize the ark and imagine it acts against them (5:7), but this is portrayed as their obtuseness to Yahweh's presence and power because the ark is not captured so much as temporarily exiled. Through it, Yahweh shows his power by allusion to the exodus. Indeed, the experience of the inhabitants of Ekron parallels that of the Egyptians during the exodus as they suffer plague and then cry out for deliverance (Exod. 11:6; 12:30). The turning point in Philistine speech occurs at 6:2, where they first use the name 'Yahweh' when questioning their priests and diviners. Indeed, in response to a second question they make reference to the 'plague' (*maggēpâ*) that has struck, a prominent term in both the exodus (Exod. 9:14) and wilderness traditions (Num. 14:27; 17:13–15) that was also used by the messenger who reported the ark's capture to Eli (1 Sam. 4:17). The Philistine priests evoke the exodus to explain why they should make reparation and not become hard-hearted like Pharaoh (Exod. 5:2). Structuring the Philistine speech in this way enables readers to follow their discovery of the identity of Yahweh as the God of Israel in the context of the ark's exodus. Yahweh achieves the ark's return without human involvement. This may be why the themes of the 'hand' and 'glory' of Yahweh (note the plays on the root *kbd*) are so prominent. Yahweh achieves his purposes, and those who respond to his glory do so by recognizing his holiness (see Stirrup 2000: 95–100).

Comment

The ark in Dagon's temple: 5:1–5

1–2. A key element in many belief systems was that when national armies fought, there was a simultaneous combat among the gods, with the victorious god's army also winning. Israel's monotheism theoretically precluded such a belief, though echoes of divine combat are found in a number of places (e.g. Pss 106:7, 9, 22; 136:13; Isa. 50:2). The short narrative of the ark in Dagon's temple is an example of such a combat, though it is placed within a narrative that knows of no other God than Yahweh. Here the aniconic Yahweh overcomes the Philistine deity Dagon by overcoming his image. Although Campbell denies the presence of humour here (1975: 88), there appears to be a satirical edge, so black humour is not precluded. Dagon is shown to be powerless in spite of Philistine pretensions to the contrary. The ark is initially brought by the Philistines from Ebenezer (4:1) to Ashdod, a central Philistine city about 20 miles north-east of Gaza, and approximately 40 miles south-west of the battle. The reason for this journey (which bypasses Ekron; see Firth 2003) is to take the ark to Dagon's temple. Older interpreters regarded Dagon as a fish deity (deriving the name from *dāg* (fish), defended by Holter (1989), but the current tendency is to regard him as a fertility god (from *dāgān*, 'wheat, grain'; see Orel 1998: 427–428). Other biblical references (Judg. 16:23 and 1 Chr. 10:10) provide only passing mention of the name, and there is also a paucity of Ugaritic information (Wiggins 1993). Since older Akkadian sources mention a deity by this name, it is probable that Dagon was an East-Semitic deity adopted in the west. As a Semitic deity, Dagon cannot have been a native god for the non-Semitic Philistines, but must have been adopted by them (see Delcor 1964: 144–148). A crucial point is the contrast between the size of Dagon's image and the ark. Since the idol fell over and reached the threshold, it would have been set against a wall opposite the entrance and have been higher than the building was wide (Orel 1998: 428). The comparatively small ark is brought as a trophy of victory, pointing to Dagon's victory (see Miller and Roberts 1977: 43–44). But the narrative undermines this perception of victory, demonstrating the centrality of the Israelite question of 4:3.

3–4. The story's humour comes to the fore as Ashdod's residents rise early the next morning to come to Dagon's temple. Since Yahweh's representative item was brought to Dagon's temple, worship there was appropriate, perhaps a feast similar to when Samson was captured (Judg. 16:23–27). But when they enter the temple, they find Dagon lying face down on the ground. As Gordon (1986: 92) observes, Dagon has been turned into Humpty-Dumpty before the ark. Presenting Dagon as fallen hints at the idol-polemic in Isa. 40 – 55, though Dagon apparently lacked the nails to keep him in place (Isa. 41:7). The repetition of Dagon's fall is important because there is ambiguity about the initial fall's interpretation. The participle *nōpēl* can mean something has accidentally fallen (Exod. 21:23), that it has fallen dead (Deut. 22:4) or that someone has fallen prostrate in obeisance (Esth. 7:8). The participle is never used of someone falling before a deity, but fits the verb's semantic range (Gen. 17:17; Job 1:20). The Philistines do not know which interpretation is correct. They cannot know if Dagon is worshipping Yahweh or has been killed by him. The careful repetitions in v. 4 provide an answer. Rising early, the Philistines discover Dagon lying before the ark of Yahweh with Dagon's head and hands cut off and lying on the threshold, indicating complete defeat (see Zwickel 1994: 244–249 for ANE parallels). Although beheading is common (17:51), removal of the hands is not unknown (Judg. 8:6). Dagon is thus powerless since the hand was a symbol for power (Judg. 6:13; Jer. 12:7). Dagon does not lie before Yahweh's ark in obeisance (against Hertzberg 1964: 54; Fokkelman 1993: 253–255), nor from an accident that could have been resolved with some well-placed nails. Dagon is utterly defeated. All that is left are the idol's remains. The possibility that Dagon has defeated Yahweh is excluded, and all that remains is the question of 4:3: Why has Yahweh defeated Israel?

5. This aetiology delays the plot's resolution, though also heightening the irony. Dagon is no longer a recognizable god, but the Philistines revere his temple by not treading on the threshold. Thresholds, and especially temple thresholds (Zeph. 1:4–9), were viewed as entry points into the underworld and treated with care (Wiggins 1993: 271). That Dagon is face down indicates he has begun the journey into the underworld, making this threshold especially dangerous, which is why those entering the temple do not tread on it. This practice endured 'to this day', a phrase indicating that the final narrator is not contemporary to them, though perhaps not too far removed in time (Campbell 1975: 251–252; according to Shea 1990c, we may possess a brief contemporary account).

Yahweh's heavy hand: 5:6–12

6. Dagon's hands are cut off, but Yahweh's hand is 'heavy' upon Ashdod and its surrounding regions, something Ashdodites recognize in their statements about Dagon. Yahweh's hand is mentioned four times through this section (5:6, 7, 9, 11), emphasizing Yahweh's power as opposed to the nullified Dagon. Yahweh's hand being 'heavy' plays on the root *kbd*, which variously means 'to be heavy' (or 'harden') or 'to be glorious'. Israel's glory (*kbd*) has been exiled, but Yahweh's hand is heavy (*kbd*) on the Philistines. Yahweh's ravaging of the Ashdodites indicates he leaves them with nothing significant apart from their tumours. The identification of their illness is unclear. Josephus calls it dysentery (*Ant.* 6.1.1), but without medical precision. There is also a change of terminology (see 'Notes'). That MT does not associate the affliction with mice weakens without disproving the common suggestion that the illness was bubonic plague. What should be discounted is the view that the illness was haemorrhoids (against Geyer 1981: 296) since they would not produce the fatalities here (Wilkinson 1977: 138). The Hebrew *ʿŏpālîm* suggests a swelling, though we cannot be more precise. Bubonic plague produces acute swellings, and reference to swellings (5:12) fits this, but a definite diagnosis is impossible. If it was not bubonic plague, then it had a similar effect, though the text's concern is to emphasize Yahweh as its source.

7. The Philistines interpret their affliction as evidence of Dagon's defeat, ignoring the evidence of 5:3–4. Instead, they announce that the ark of the God of Israel cannot remain in their city because Yahweh's hand is heavy on both them and Dagon. There is a shift in vocabulary here. When the narrator speaks of Yahweh's heavy hand, the verb *kbd* is used, but the Philistines use *qšh*, 'burdensome' (Deut. 15:18; 1 Kgs 12:4). The Philistines see Dagon's powerlessness, but do not yet see Yahweh's glory, though they see the symbol of Israel's God working, since the deity's power is available through its representation. This is faulty theology, but the narrator allows the Philistines to voice matters in their own terms.

8. Resolution of the Ashdodite problem involved gathering five Philistine rulers. This designation is a standard one in the OT, with one from each of Ashdod, Ekron, Gath, Gaza and Ashkelon. The title used (*seren*) appears only in the pl., and only to describe them. The word is not Semitic, and is possibly related to a word borrowed into Greek as *tyrannos* (*IDBSup*, 667). However, the title functions in much the same way as does 'Pharaoh', a standard title for a group of rulers. The Ashdodites summoned these rulers to resolve their difficulty. Their question is blunt: 'What shall we do with the ark of the God of Israel?' Dagon is no help, and the ark is causing considerable distress, so a new location is needed. Although the text is problematic (see 'Notes'), it is probable that we have only the leader's decision and no voluntary action by the people of Gath. Once the decision is made, the ark is moved to the town. The site of Gath is disputed (Bimson

1995: 140; see 'Comment' on 21:11 [ET 21:10]), though is of no significance for this narrative. The wheel has now turned. In 4:3 the Israelites wondered why Yahweh had acted against them. Now the Philistines wrestle with how to handle Yahweh's representative in their midst.

9–10. With the basic pattern established, the narrator telescopes the process so that Gath's experience can be passed over quickly to come to Ekron (probably modern Tel Miqne). But escalation is still involved. Yahweh's hand was heavy against Ashdod (5:6), but in Gath it produces 'very great panic', and as it enters Ekron the inhabitants are convinced that, since the ark's presence brings certain death, it is a deliberate action against them. Gath also experiences an eruption of tumours, with the additional note that the whole population is afflicted. This is too much for the inhabitants of Ekron, whose cry is reminiscent of that of the Israelites in Egypt (Exod. 2:23), except here Yahweh is acting against them (cf. Shiloh in 4:13). Where the movement of a captured trophy of another deity normally announces victory, it is now painfully clear to the Philistines that it announces defeat.

11–12. The pattern of repetitions continues as the opening words of v. 11 replicate almost exactly those of v. 8. The message of the Ekronites to the Philistine rulers is direct: the ark of the God of Israel must be sent away. Their reasoning is simple: the ark has caused death among them, so the only way to stop this is its return. In this way the deadly terror (cf. Exod. 12:29–32) will be removed. The effect of this is seen in v. 12 with the statement that even those who do not die are struck with tumours, evoking the earlier defeat of Israel (4:2), but which also suggests that, in spite of the Philistine bravado in 4:9, Yahweh is overcome neither by human strength nor by Dagon.

The ark's return: 6:1–18

1–2. The chronological note indicates that the Philistines possess the ark for seven months, a period sometimes said to be equivalent to the seven days of the first plague in Egypt (Exod. 7:25; Klein 1983: 56). Although probably a round number, it is probable that the ark was present for such a period, but without precluding an exodus echo, especially in a text rich in such allusions. This timescale allows for the Ekronite desperation to have some significance. The actions described in v. 2 are those of both the Philistine rulers and the people in general. They summon the priests and diviners to determine the appropriate response. 'Priests' (*kōhănîm*) is a standard term in the OT, but 'diviners' (*qōsĕmîm*) represent a group prohibited within Israel (Deut. 18:10–14; Ezek. 13:23), though one acknowledged as existing among the nations (Num. 23:23). The Philistines seek a religious answer since Dagon's defeat has created this problem. The question is the first time the name 'Yahweh' occurs in Philistine mouths in this narrative, a crucial turning point for them (see 'Form and structure').

The question initially repeats that of the Ashdodites save for the divine name, crucially adding a request for information about what should be returned with the ark (cf. Mic. 6:6; Keil and Delitzsch 1956: 61–62). Worshippers expect to enter a deity's presence with an offering (Exod. 23:15), so the question is a natural one. As worshippers of a defeated deity, the Philistines seek the means to restore their relationship with Yahweh, the one they now name.

3. The answer almost quotes the question, but reverts to the generic 'God of Israel' before asserting that the ark cannot be returned without an offering. The terminology suggests the Philistines wish to acknowledge their own sin in doubting Yahweh's authority and reign. As Klein (1983: 56) suggests, the requirement is for reparations rather than the priestly sense of the transfer of guilt on to a substitute (Lev. 5; 6:10; cf. Num. 5:8), which is why the offering is made to Yahweh rather than the Israelites. It is now that the Philistines begin differentiating between Yahweh and the ark. They now know that it is the unseen God, not the ark, who really matters (Fokkelman 1993: 265–267). Miller and Roberts parallel this with the Hittite prayer of Mursilis (1977: 53–54), indicating that this type of behaviour is culturally explicable. The Philistines seek confirmation – if Yahweh accepts their offering, the land will be healed and they will know Yahweh's hand afflicted them (similarly, Youngblood 1992: 604).

4–6. A second question follows logically: What should this offering contain? The answer given poses a number of questions. The first part is clear enough. There are five Philistine cities and rulers, the offering must cover each of them, and that offering will restore the Philistines. But the qualifying phrases are problematic. They are to return five gold tumours and five gold mice because there has been 'one plague'. The term for 'plague' repeats that from 4:17 (again evoking the exodus), so the Philistines acknowledge that they are in the position of the Egyptians. But why 'one plague' if the offering is tumours *and* mice? Even if the affliction was bubonic plague, it would not explain the link between the mice and the illness as one plague since the association between rats and bubonic plague is a comparatively modern one, and *'akbôr* elsewhere means 'mouse' and not 'rat' (Lev. 11:5; Isa. 66:17). V. 5, however, notes that mice are destroying the land, so both this and the tumours are regarded as one plague. The solution is probably to accept that the plague is the illness (Geyer 1981: 293–297), but the priests and diviners also address an additional problem of mice in their fields. That the plague is only the illness seems clear from its association with the ark. But if Dagon is a grain deity, then mice ravaging the crops indicate the need to appease Yahweh on this issue as well. This does not resolve the question of what five gold tumours might have looked like, though given the close association with what is actually experienced, Margalith's (1983: 340) attempt at linking the 'tumours' with Apollo (the plague god) is unnecessary. What is indicated is how these offerings would be effective. Why should Yahweh be interested in them, especially since a mouse was an unclean animal? Yet that Yahweh accepts the offering should not pose a major problem since here the giver's attitude is more important than the gift, as through them the Philistines give Yahweh glory (*kābôd*; cf. 5:6). They expect that Yahweh will now lighten his hand upon them. The plays on *kbd* continue in v. 6, where the pi. means 'harden' in another allusion to the exodus. When Yahweh overcame Pharaoh (see Exod. 10:2), he had no choice but to send Israel away, so it made good sense to send the ark before it caused more problems.

7–9. Proper procedure was needed for the ark's return, especially if it was to prove that Yahweh had acted against the Philistines. The process needed both to return the ark and resolve the theological question. The method chosen sought to place difficulties in the process, so overcoming them provided the necessary proof. The method apparently reflects local custom, and like the offering shows no knowledge of normal Yahweh worship. Cows were chosen that had never been yoked and whose calves still followed them. They would not normally respond positively to the yoke, while the removal of their calves was a significant barrier. However, this also meant that neither they nor the cart had previously been used, making them particularly suitable for the process if Yahweh was acting against them (Num. 19:2; Deut. 21:3–4). Only a strong overriding force would lead the cows to deliver the ark, and if it happened, then those things accompanying it should be suitable for such a role (Gordon 1986: 101–102). The cart allowed the ark to be returned, along with the golden tumours and mice, the latter placed in a box on the cart. With everything prepared, the test was simple. If the cart went to Beth Shemesh (probably then the border town), the Philistines would know it had been Yahweh. Beth Shemesh is identified as Tell er-Rumeilleh, about 16 miles west of Jerusalem, a site indicating significant settlement at the time of these events (Bimson 1995: 72). Although the Philistines retain the option that it is all chance, the narrator uses their final comment to insist it is Yahweh who was active.

10–12. The narrative speeds up, and there is no attention to the construction of the cart or the box. Instead, the narrator affirms that the procedure is carried out: the cows are gathered, their calves separated from them and then they are hitched to the cart. Apart from the fact that it is a rather noisy journey, the cows go straight to Beth Shemesh, with the Philistine rulers following. In this way, they can confirm it has been Yahweh, and the possibility of chance is thus removed. Ahlström (1984: 144) suggests Beth Shemesh was ruled by the Philistines rather than the Israelites at this time, but this runs counter to the fact that the ark's arrival at Beth Shemesh is held to have proved that it was Yahweh acting against the Philistines.

13–14. A shift in perspective occurs, and, instead of following the Philistine leaders, events are seen through the eyes of the inhabitants of Beth Shemesh. The ark arrives there during the wheat harvest in May–June. The harvesters are in the fields, probably in the Sorek valley, which runs to the north of Beth Shemesh and was the natural route from Philistine territory. Their rejoicing at seeing the ark contrasts with what has happened so far since it previously brought expressions of dread (4:8–10; 5:10), but is understandable given the importance of the ark as a symbol of Yahweh's presence. The point of the ark's arrival is noted at the field of a resident named Joshua. The great stone that marked the spot is said to 'be there to this day' (see Geoghegan 2003), indicating that the site continued to be remembered for some time. The proof of Yahweh's involvement is clear and all criteria of the Philistine test are satisfied. The correctness of the Philistine decision to send cows and a cart appropriate for sacrifice is borne out by the fact that the inhabitants of Beth Shemesh did break up the cart and offer the cows as burnt offerings to Yahweh.

15. The narrative could be complete here, which is why v. 15 is often thought to be a later addition. But repetition is important, and functions to clarify events, as in the two accounts of Dagon's falling before the ark (5:3–4). So it is better to treat this verse as an integral part of the narrative, where the flow is briefly broken to introduce material preventing any misunderstanding of what had happened. One could assume the Beth Shemeshites had mishandled the ark in bringing it down from the cart, and that the sacrifices were unacceptable, so the narrator prevents this interpretation. Beth Shemesh was a Levitical town (Josh. 21:16), so the presence of Levites is not unexpected, and the narrator now clarifies that it was Levites who removed the ark and the box with its offerings before resuming the account of the sacrifices (both burnt offerings and other more general sacrifices). Likewise, the great stone was not an impromptu altar, but the site for placing the ark and the box.

16–18. The narrative now returns to the Philisitines. The test has been passed and the Philistine rulers know it. Having seen the ark's arrival and the joyous Israelite sacrifices, the Philistine rulers return to Ekron, the ark's last location on Philistine territory. From here on the Philistines are ignored. Since the test has been passed, there is no need to hear a final Philistine report. All that is needed is a summary of the Philistine offering, confirming that there was one tumour and one mouse for each Philistine town. The mice also covered the villages, apparently being experienced in farming towns (against Smith 1899: 47). However, the number returned is still only five since the villages are associated with the main towns. That the mice are not directly related to the 'one plague' (6:4) but are an additional expedient is indicated by the fact that only the gold tumours are regarded as a reparation offering. The great stone (see 'Notes') in Joshua's field attests this.

The ark back in Israel: 6:19 – 7:1

6:19–20. That the label 'Ark Narrative' is not entirely appropriate becomes apparent in these verses. Rather, the narrative as a whole emphasizes Yahweh's glory and holiness, emphasized through the ark. The issue is

Israel's willingness to operate on Yahweh's terms. Israel could not use the ark to force Yahweh's hand (4:3–11). Yet the ark's absence had not taught Israel this lesson. The narrative could end at 6:18, but that is appropriate only if the story is about the ark's return. Yet the larger narrative of chs. 1 – 7 indicates that Israel's problems were more profound than that. Hence it is necessary to show that Israel after the ark's exodus were not significantly different from what they were before. The problem here is that Yahweh struck down seventy of the men of Beth Shemesh because they looked into the ark. According to Num. 4:20, even the Levite clan charged with responsibility for the holy things could not look into them, so the outcome here is not in itself shocking except for the number involved. Israel could be struck in the same way as the Philistines, with language evoking the earlier battle account (4:2), the Philistine perception of the exodus (4:8) and the outbreak of the plague against the Philistines (5:7, 9, 12). When Israel ignores Yahweh's holiness, the ark's presence is a matter of grave danger (Birch 1998: 1012). The key is the question the Beth Shemeshites pose, 'Who is able to stand before Yahweh, this holy God?' The Beth Shemeshites are in the same position as the Philistines. They are not struck by plague, but understand their relationship to Yahweh and the ark in the same terms. This question serves to balance that of 4:3, so the whole narrative is bounded by key interpretative questions, except now they want the ark removed.

6:21 – 7:1. The second half of the question in v. 20 asked about where the ark could be taken. The Beth Shemeshites offered the ark to Kiriath Jearim, though they were economical with the truth. Kiriath Jearim is usually identified as Tell el'Azhar, about 8 miles west of Jerusalem, and the only Gibeonite city to have an Israelite population (Blenkinsopp 1969: 146–147). It means 'City of the Forest', and Gordon (1986: 104) indicates that its association with the ark may be celebrated in the reference to the 'fields of the forest' in Ps. 132:6. No attempt was made to remove the ark to Shiloh, perhaps indicating that no valid priesthood remained there. No response from the inhabitants of Kiriath Jearim is indicated. Instead, the narrative simply reports their coming to Beth Shemesh and taking the ark there. It was then installed in the house of Abinidab, whose son Eleazar was consecrated as a priest for it. The holiness of Yahweh that had so distressed the Beth Shemeshites is not a problem here, indicating that the ark's treatment was acceptable. None can stand before the holiness of Yahweh if they do not recognize the danger it poses, but it is still possible to live with this dangerous holiness. The narrative closes by indicating that Yahweh could express his sovereignty over the Philistines without losing his authority over Israel.

Explanation

The ark's capture and exile of Yahweh's 'glory' in ch. 4 set up the narrative for the events that unfold here. Within the context of ANE theology, ch. 4

could be read as the story of Yahweh's defeat by the Philistine gods. But the narrator refrained from mentioning them because this is precisely what is not intended. Instead, Israel's question in 4:3 dominates.

That Yahweh routed Israel is apparent from the events in 5:1–5. Here, the ark was brought to the temple of Dagon to function as a trophy for Dagon and remind Philistine worshippers of the greatness of their god in regard to Yahweh. The surprise for the Philistines was not only that the idol of Dagon fell over, but that Yahweh effectively 'killed' Dagon. If there was any doubt that the leading question was why Yahweh had routed Israel, then this should remove it. The narrator portrays this from the Philistine perspective as they experience it as a shock. But worse was waiting as Yahweh struck wherever the ark went with a deadly affliction. There are regular allusions to the exodus, so the Philistines parallel the Egyptians. Consistently we are told that Yahweh's hand was heavy against the Philistines. The ark's movement is then a parody of a victory tour through the Philistine territory showing Yahweh's freedom to act. Yahweh is greater than Philistine gods and can act as freely in their territory as he does within Israel.

A strain of dark humour runs through these chapters, continuing through the ark's return as the Philistine leadership responded to their people's call to remove the ark. Exodus imagery comes to the fore in 6:1–9, where arrangements are made for the ark's return, arrangements dependent upon advice from Philistine priests and diviners, people who would not normally know Yahweh's will. Their advice is almost completely against the law; instead of properly consecrated Levites, it is returned on a cart with unacceptable reparation offerings since mice and tumours were unclean. These men do not know Yahweh's requirements, yet they recognize that the Philistines stand in the same danger as Egypt during the exodus. Like all great humour, this cuts both ways. Israel laughs at their folly in imagining that these processes would be acceptable, yet it was these religious professionals of another deity who understood what Yahweh was doing. Israel's corrupt priesthood is ridiculed in the mirror of the folly of the Philistine priests and diviners. It is the Philistines, and not Israel, who come truly to know Yahweh through this.

The ark's return continues to demonstrate Yahweh's authority as the cart, with two untrained cows acting against maternal instinct, went straight to the border town of Beth Shemesh. It was met with rejoicing by the locals, but also confirmed to the Philistines that all was Yahweh's work. God's glory was seen among the Philistines, and God's glory is welcomed back to Israel with joy. In contrast to the Philistines, the narrative is at pains to show that the Israelites did initially follow proper practice. But it did not last. Although the exact nature of 6:19 is obscure, we are suddenly brought face to face with Israel's pain as Yahweh killed seventy men for failing to recognize the ark's holiness. This was not the

Philistine problem, but confronted by it Israel also sought to remove the ark. In doing so, a key question is posed at 6:20: Who can stand before Yahweh? The answer is nobody, yet everybody. God's holiness is both blessing and danger, depending on how it is treated. The ark could not be sent from Israel, so an alternative had to be found within Israel. This was Kiriath Jearim and the ark stayed there for twenty years with a properly consecrated keeper. People can stand before Yahweh, but his holiness must be understood.

It is common to refer to 1 Sam. 4:1b – 7:1 as the 'Ark Narrative', an appropriate descriptive title. However, the story is only incidentally about the ark. It is really about Yahweh's freedom. Yahweh can overcome the Philistines without human involvement. The story insists that Yahweh is absolutely sovereign, but that if Israel stands in a proper relationship to him, they can have security. What matters is not human power, but the God who reigns over all. This theme is taken up in terms of Israel's kings in Ps. 2, a theme the NT redirects to Jesus in Acts 4:25–26. Thus the wider biblical witness seeks to make the same point: God remains absolutely free and yet all nations must recognize his reign and respond to his holiness.

1 SAMUEL 7:2-17

Translation

[2]From the time the ark was lodged at Kiriath Jearim many days passed – twenty years – and the whole house of Israel lamented after Yahweh. [3]Samuel said to the whole house of Israel, 'If with your whole heart you are returning to Yahweh, remove the foreign gods and Ashtaroth from your midst. Fix your hearts on Yahweh and serve him only, and he shall deliver you from the hand of the Philistines.' [4]So the people of Israel removed the Baalim and the Ashtaroth and served Yahweh alone.

[5]Samuel said, 'Gather all Israel to Mizpah and I shall intercede on your behalf with Yahweh.' [6]So they gathered to Mizpah and drew water and poured it out before Yahweh and fasted on that day and said there, 'We have sinned against Yahweh.' Then Samuel judged the people of Israel at Mizpah. [7]The Philistines heard that the people of Israel had assembled at Mizpah, and the Philistine rulers went up against Israel. When the people of Israel heard, they were afraid of the Philistines. [8]And the people of Israel said to Samuel, 'Do not cease from crying out to Yahweh our God for us, that he may save us from the hand of the Philistines.' [9]Samuel took a milk lamb and offered it as a whole burnt offering to Yahweh. Samuel cried out to Yahweh on behalf of Israel, and Yahweh answered him. [10]As Samuel was offering up the burnt offering the Philistines were drawing near for battle with Israel. But Yahweh thundered with a great sound on that day against the Philistines and confused them and they were defeated before Israel. [11]So the men of

Israel came out from Mizpah and pursued the Philistines and struck them down as far as below Beth Car.

¹²Samuel took a stone and set it up between Mizpah and Shen and named it Ebenezer. And he said, 'Thus far has Yahweh helped us.' ¹³So the Philistines were subdued and did not continue to enter Israel's borders. The hand of Yahweh was against the Philistines all the days of Samuel. ¹⁴The cities the Philistines had taken from Israel were returned, from Ekron to Gath, and Israel delivered its border from the hand of the Philistines. So there was peace between Israel and the Amorites.

¹⁵Samuel judged Israel all the days of his life. ¹⁶He went year by year on a circuit to Bethel and Gilgal and Mizpah. So he judged Israel in all these places. ¹⁷Then he returned to Ramah because his home was there, and there he judged Israel. He built an altar to Yahweh there.

Notes on the text

2. The verb *nhh* elsewhere occurs in only Mic. 2:4, Ezek. 32:18, both in qal. The ni. is an awkward hapax legomenon, but the variance in the LXX cautions against using it as the basis for emendation.

3. LXX has Asherim instead of Ashtaroth. 4QSam^a supports MT.

5. MT reads *hammiṣpātâ*, which may be 'to the lookout' rather than a named place. See v. 7.

6. LXX's additional 'upon the ground' concerning the water is an explanatory expansion.

8. LXX has 'your God'. MT is retained as *lectio difficilior*.

12. On the basis of LXX (and others), McCarter (1980a: 142) supports a reading of 'Jeshanah', a town on the Judean–Israelite border (see 2 Chr. 13:19). But this seems to be the wrong direction, so the otherwise unknown Shen should stand. Since this is lit. 'the tooth' it may refer to some distinctive physical feature rather than an identifiable site.

16. The closing *'ēt kôl hamměqômôt* is awkward. LXX adds *en* (in), but is probably only making sense of the phrase.

Form and structure

The previous six chapters have brought Israel to a crossroads that the nation needs to cross. The opening three chapters recounted Samuel's birth, highlighting that he is Yahweh's messenger. Although he fulfils some priestly functions, his priestly role is not stressed. Likewise, apart from his mother's vow, we would not know he might be a Nazirite. But the prophetic ministry established for him in ch. 3 was vital for the whole of his story. Eli, however, had been the nation's judge, and thus its human leader. But his death along with his sons in ch. 4 robbed the nation of its judge. Eli was probably closer to the minor judges since he is not shown leading the nation in war, and his role was probably more administrative. Nevertheless, the lack of a human leader as a vehicle for Yahweh is notable, and no one has risen to take on this role.

At the same time, 4:1 – 7:1 stressed Yahweh's freedom and that his power cannot be controlled by Israel. Rather, they had to submit to his will and align themselves with his purposes. The Philistines, the external power that had been such a threat to the nation, were shown to be powerless before Yahweh, even when he had permitted them to overcome Israel. Defeat for Israel did not mean defeat for Yahweh, but it did mean his power would be shown by alternative means. This is seen in that the Philistines felt constrained to return the ark because of the plagues.

Thus two issues have been raised: Yahweh has shown he is capable of independently overcoming the Philistines, but has not adopted a human figure to act as his vehicle in Israel. The office of judge (if we may speak in such terms) is vacant, but was the traditional means by which Yahweh's rule was demonstrated. This chapter brings these elements together, indicating that Samuel is both a prophet and also the judge through whom Yahweh's reign is demonstrated. Samuel is thus paralleled with Deborah since she too was a prophet and a judge (Judg. 4:4; see Garsiel 1983: 55). The close literary relationship this demonstrates with the preceding narratives (note the motif of the Yahweh's hand in v. 13, alluding to 5:1 – 7:1) makes it essential that we consider the text in its present form, notwithstanding the possible redactional history (see Boecker 1969: 93–98; Birch 1976: 20–21). This creates a further tension in that the book's opening chapters created expectation of a king, the point towards which Judg. 17 – 21 built. This tension will be explored in chs. 8 – 12. What we need to know first is that Yahweh's rule can be established with Samuel as a judge and that the Philistines can therefore be defeated. Yahweh is still Israel's king, and the coming move to human kingship needs to be seen in that light.

As presented, 7:2–17 is an essentially coherent narrative, though the presence of what appears to be some doubling in vv. 2–6, where we may have two separate accounts of the one gathering, has suggested to some the presence of different sources. The common conclusion is that the Deuteronomistic Historian composed vv. 2–3 to highlight the main themes here (so Klein 1983: 66). But as the chapter stands, vv. 5–14 describe the events of an Israelite gathering interrupted by a Philistine raid, while vv. 15–17 are a narrative appendix, showing that Samuel had taken on the role of judge left vacant by Eli's death. The important point is that Samuel has not only demonstrated his status as a judge, but has also effected reconciliation between Yahweh and Israel (Fokkelman 1993: 294), though this reconciliation will be questioned in the next chapter.

Comment

National repentance: 7:2–4

2. The narrative begins properly here, though the function of the chrono-logical note is less than clear, and it cannot be easily integrated into the overall chronology of Joshua–Kings. Nevertheless, its immediate function within the narrative movement of 1 Sam. 1 – 7 is apparent. At the end of ch. 3 Samuel was a lad (*na'ar*). Sufficient time had to pass for his status as Yahweh's authentic prophet to be confirmed so he could then lead the nation. The difficulties in determining the overall chronology of Joshua–Kings should not blind us to the possibility of local chronological references, especially since it is possible that the periods mentioned in Judges may be concurrent rather than consecutive. It is difficult to conceive of the whole nation lamenting after Yahweh for twenty years since Samuel needs to instruct them to remove their foreign gods. So the intent is probably to suggest that their lamentation was the result of the period.

3–4. Samuel's speech uses traditionally Deuteronomistic language, employing phrases like 'all your heart' and referring to the Baalim and Ashtaroth, the archetypal Canaanite deities that were a snare to Israel. But the language is not merely conventional (Stoebe 1973: 172). Samuel insists that Israel needs to remove these foreign gods if they are to know deliverance by Yahweh from the Philistines. Samuel's call echoes Judg. 10:6–16, terminology that associates Samuel with the judges. Where the people's repentance there was a half-hearted attempt to manipulate Yahweh, here it is as an authoritative call from Samuel who is thus both prophet and judge. As was typical of the judges, a political crisis evokes a theological response. However, it is first made clear that there was genuine repentance where the foreign gods, the Baalim and Ashtaroth were removed. The language of v. 4 carefully echoes that of v. 3, so what Samuel summoned is shown to have been done. Thus Samuel speaks as a prophet and acts as a judge.

The gathering at Mizpah and battle with the Philistines: 7:5–14

5. With the general setting established, the narrative moves to its central action. This takes place in three stages: a further account of the national gathering, the raid by the Philistines and their defeat, and the establishment of the stone Ebenezer. Although vv. 5–6 may describe the same assembly as that in vv. 3–4, the text suggests that Samuel initiated a further assembly at Mizpah (possibly a hill north of Jerusalem in the area of Benjamin, but the site is disputed) to formalize the agreement made in the previous verses. It was not a spontaneous gathering, but one initiated by Samuel. Hence he began to act like a judge by summoning the people in preparation for military activity. But Samuel will not permit military action that takes place outside Yahweh's will, which is why he indicates he will also take on a priestly role and intercede for the nation. In Samuel so far only Hannah has prayed (1:10, 12; 2:1), while Eli pondered its possibility (2:25). Samuel's actions thus mark him out as distinctive in his priestly role.

6. While at Mizpah, the people drew water and poured it out before Yahweh. The meaning of this rite is uncertain, and there are no precise parallels (though see McCarter 1980a: 144 and David's rite in 2 Sam. 23:16–17). However, it functions as a sacrifice to Yahweh, and is linked to the nation's fasting and confession of sin. Given the rejection of Canaanite worship, it may be an attempt to indicate that life belongs to Yahweh. In this way, the people are shown as separating themselves from both food and water, and entirely trusting Yahweh, something given greater clarity in their confession of sin. No divine response is recorded, though it is noted that Samuel judged Israel. Unlike the earlier judges, no specific period is specified, because a period of peace has not yet been established. Samuel as judge, however, is a sign that things may be improving for Israel.

7–9. Hearing that the Israelites have assembled at Mizpah, the Philistines see the opportunity to reinforce their hold over the Israelite territory, and their coming strikes fear into the Israelites. In spite of Samuel's assurances, there is no expectation that repentance will lead to national deliverance. Hence the people request Samuel to be diligent in crying out to Yahweh on their behalf, something that was his intent in inviting the people that he might intercede for them. The people do not wish to cry out themselves, so Samuel is a prophet like Moses since there were also instances when Moses interceded for the people after they had sinned (Exod. 33:12–16; Num. 14:13–19). More importantly, there is a clear expectation that, as happened during the exodus, Yahweh will respond to the people's cry to him. Within this process of intercession, Samuel also offers a whole sacrifice, a milk lamb perhaps being one that only just meets the eight-day minimum age (Exod. 22:30; Lev. 22:27). This is not to convince Yahweh to act but is a testimony of the people's commitment to his service. Yahweh responds to this, though the means is not initially stated.

10–11. The importance of Yahweh's response is stressed by v. 10, which indicates that it was as Samuel was making the offering that the Philistines approached for battle. This was a desperate situation since the Philistines were in battle array but Israel was not. Israel's fear was not matched by preparedness for warfare. But Yahweh comes to the fore, and responds with thunder, causing the confusion and subsequent rout of the Philistines. Hannah's Song celebrated Yahweh as the one who thundered and overcame his foes (2:10; though see 1:6), and what was previously announced as possible is here a reality. Moreover, what Israel's cry could not achieve in 4:6 Yahweh now achieves (see Eslinger 1985: 241). The terminology of the confusion is drawn from Yahweh war texts such as Josh. 10, where it is notable that some form of astral event is associated with the victory. The point is that the victory belongs to Yahweh alone: it was achieved neither by Samuel as a military leader, nor through any king. It is Yahweh whom the nation need, and they in faithfulness simply need to follow him as their king. This is emphasized by their success in overcoming the enemy over some distance, though the location of Beth Car is unknown. Even the role of the judge is marginalized as Samuel does not actually lead the nation in battle. Political structures are less important than theological ones.

12–14. With the Philistines overcome the Israelite assembly is reconvened between Mizpah and Shen, where Samuel establishes a stele as a memorial to the victory. The stone is named Ebenezer, 'Stone of Help'. The name was mentioned in 4:1, though there it was ironic since Israel found no help. It is not that the stone has provided the help, but it points instead to Yahweh's help in overcoming the Philistines. This point is made clear by Samuel's statement 'Thus far has Yahweh helped us.' The stone is more than a physical marker; it points to what Yahweh has done so far in Israel, though without making promises for the future. That needs to be resolved in the coming chapters. Beyond this, the Philistine threat was subdued and they did not continue to enter Israel's territory. Just as Yahweh's hand was active in 4:1 – 7:1, we are now assured it continued to act. However, the exact sense of this claim needs some care, because it is apparent from the period of the reign of Saul that the Philistines were far from a spent force, and much of his reign was while Samuel was alive. Most likely, therefore, 'all the days of Samuel' does not refer to the whole of his life but to the period when he acted as judge without a king. But as a subdued people the Philistines return the towns they previously captured. Israel's borders are restored because Yahweh has acted.

Samuel as judge: 7:15–17

15. The section ends with a brief summary of Samuel's ministry as a judge, stressing that this continued throughout his life. The subsequent narratives will take place in the context of kingship, so the possibility of tension is introduced. The relative merits of judges and kings have not yet been resolved, though in a sense the importance of Samuel as a judge (as opposed to prophet and priest) has been diminished.

16–17. Although it was as a period of military need that led Samuel to act as a judge, the role described here is administrative, the judge travelling a circuit each year. Yahweh is the nation's leader, so Samuel's other roles take precedence. The towns described are all within a day's walk of his home at Ramah, so his role as a judge was somewhat limited. He functioned as a local judge while also judging the whole nation. This was not separated from his priestly role, because he also built an altar at Ramah, a single fixed sanctuary not yet having been chosen by Yahweh.

But even in his success, the narrative raises questions about the need for human military leaders.

Explanation

In moving Israel across the crossroads so that there was again a judge to mediate Yahweh's reign, this passage prepares for the tensions that follow when the nation moves towards the appointment of a king. We have been expecting such an appointment since 2:10, but this chapter makes the fundamental point that Yahweh's reign is all Israel needs, provided they remain faithful to him. It is not a king but Yahweh that is needed. Nevertheless, something more tangible will soon be requested.

Before that point is reached the chapter points to a wider theological framework within which all human leadership in Israel needs to be appreciated. Samuel fills the role of judge, succeeding Eli, though since this was a charismatic position there was no necessity that it be filled. But there is a subtle diminution of the role. Previously, judges had been raised up by Yahweh in response to a specific crisis (Judg. 2:16; 3:9), but here Samuel is already in place before the crisis is described, even though it is clearly extant. More importantly, the status of the judges was demonstrated by the way they led Israel into battle against the oppressor. But Samuel is not said to have followed this pattern. The victory is won, but at no time is Samuel said to have engaged in the battle. Samuel is neither the deliverer, nor the one through whom deliverance is wrought. Instead, deliverance is brought about directly by Yahweh, and the people are then able to follow through on this. As a judge, Samuel operates only at an administrative level, and then largely within a limited geographic context. In fact, it is his priestly and prophetic roles that are more effective. Thus a significant theological context is established that in itself also points to a possible crisis: Yahweh is Israel's king, and yet Yahweh is also the one moving the nation towards kingship. That is why the theological framework is so important. Samuel as priest and prophet acts as an intermediary, one who announces Yahweh's word to the nation and also intercedes on their behalf. Yahweh is king, the one who leads the nation in battle, and Samuel is the one through whom he deals with his people. What they need to do is remain faithful to him and recognize that he indeed has been their help, their Ebenezer.

1 SAMUEL 8

Translation

[1]When Samuel grew old, he appointed his sons as judges for Israel. [2]The name of his firstborn son was Joel, and the name of his second Abijah; they were judges in

Beersheba. ³But his sons did not walk in his ways; they turned aside after dishonest gain, accepted bribes and perverted justice.

⁴All the elders of Israel gathered themselves, and came to Samuel at Ramah ⁵and said to him, 'Behold, you are old, and your sons do not walk in your ways. Now, appoint a king for us to judge us like all the nations.' ⁶But it displeased Samuel when they said, 'Give us a king to judge us,' so Samuel interceded with Yahweh. ⁷And Yahweh said to Samuel, 'Listen to the voice of the people, to all that they said to you, for they have not rejected you. It is me they have rejected as king over them. ⁸According to all they have done from the day I brought them up out of Egypt even to this day, they have forsaken me and served other gods. Thus they are also doing to you. ⁹But now, listen to their voice. However, you shall surely testify against them, and declare to them the "justice" of the king who will reign over them.'

¹⁰Then Samuel reported all the words of Yahweh to the people who were asking for a king from him. ¹¹He said, 'This will be the "justice" of the king who will reign over you: he will take your sons to himself and appoint them for himself among his chariots and horsemen, and they shall run before his chariots. ¹²He will appoint for himself commanders of thousands and commanders of fifties, and some to plough his field and to reap his harvest and to make his implements of war and equipment for his chariots. ¹³He will take your daughters to be perfumers, cooks and bakers. ¹⁴He will take the best of your fields, vineyards and olive groves and give them to his attendants. ¹⁵He will claim a tenth of your seed and vineyards and give it to his officials and attendants. ¹⁶He will take the best of your male and female slaves and young men, and your asses and put them to his work. ¹⁷He will take a tenth of your flock and you will be his slaves. ¹⁸And you will cry out on that day because of your king whom you have chosen for yourselves – but Yahweh will not answer you on that day.'

¹⁹But the people refused to listen to the voice of Samuel, and they said, 'No – a king shall indeed be over us. ²⁰And we shall be like all the nations. Our king will judge us and go forth before us and fight our battles.' ²¹When Samuel heard all the people's words, he repeated them in Yahweh's hearing. ²²Yahweh said to Samuel, 'Listen to their voice, and give them a king.' Then Samuel said to the men of Israel, 'Go, each one to his city.'

Notes on the text

3. With Q and a number of MSS, the pl. 'ways' is read. See v. 5.

8. LXX's *moi* is probably an explanatory expansion (against McCarter 1980a: 155; cf. Stoebe 1973: 182). Harris's proposal (1981) is interesting, but depends on an unnecessary reading of the narrative (cf. Fokkelman 1993: 341).

12. LXX and Syr show (different) variations conforming the numerical pattern to that of Deut. 1:15. MT is more likely precisely because it does vary. McCarter (1980a: 155) supports a longer reading from LXX^L that includes gathering of grapes, but this seems to conflate MT and LXX^B. 4QSamᵃ appears to support MT.

15. *sārîs* (official) is traditionally 'eunuch' (see BDB). However, it is unlikely that eunuchs operated as officials in Israel (Lev. 22:24; Deut. 23:2). Although the root may mean 'emasculate', and eunuchs were employed in some courts, they are here senior court officials. See *TWOT* 2:635.

16. LXX has 'cattle' in place of 'young men'. Although this makes for an easier transition to asses and is a phonologically explicable confusion between *ḥ* and *q* (though see Driver 1913: 69; the pl. of *bqr* is doubtful), MT is retained as the more difficult reading.

19. The common confusion between *lō'* and *lô* is reflected here in the textual traditions. *lō'* is read as asseverative, which combined with *kî 'im*, indicates the force of the request.

Form and structure

The tensions lying in the background of the previous chapter come to the fore as Samuel's sons are no more effective than Eli's in continuing their father's ministry. Samuel to some extent opens the door for a request for a monarchy through his decision to appoint his sons as judges. Nevertheless, we now come to the decisive movement towards monarchy that has been building since the opening chapters. What is surprising is that it comes through a request from the people. From the perspective of Deut. 17:14–20, which deals with the law of the king and lies in the background, it was a natural expectation that the people would request a king. Yet the statement in 2:35 may intimate that monarchy would result from a divine initiative. However, it is a request from the elders of Israel that finally leads to this move.

This brings us to the major debate about the interpretation of these chapters. Here Samuel is very critical of monarchy, a theme that recurs in his speech in ch. 12; his comments in 10:17–27 are similar. But 9:1 – 10:16 and ch. 11 seem favourable. Older approaches, following Wellhausen, tended to resolve these issues by positing different sources, some of which were positive to kingship and some opposed (see Birch 1976: 21–29; Boecker 1969: 1–9; Schüngel-Straumann 1981: 198). But this grossly oversimplified the problem, because whatever sources were available, it seems clear from the finished book that Yahweh did not absolutely oppose that kingship, and would later enter into a covenant relationship with David centred on kingship (2 Sam. 7:1–17; 23:6). Although 1 Sam. 7 showed Yahweh as Israel's true king, 2:10 and 2:34–35 indicate that Yahweh was moving towards monarchy. We have to reckon with the narrator's intention in the finished text. This means accepting the reality of the tensions as reflecting what took place at the time, while accepting that in Yahweh's inscrutable grace he would grant the people their king. Differing viewpoints needed to be articulated, but it is ultimately the narrator's voice that we heed (Eslinger 1983: 68), and that voice is not necessarily equated with the characters'. Samuel may have opposed kingship as proposed by the people, but it is not necessarily the case that the narrator opposes kingship as such (see Eslinger 1985: 259–262; Polzin 1989: 85–88). The larger question may be what type of monarchy was acceptable, and it is there that Samuel and the people differ. In resolving this dilemma, Yahweh supports neither Samuel nor the people, even as he accedes to their requests. Yahweh is giving his people a new model of government that will continue to reflect his purposes and aims. There were competing claims about government, and it was Yahweh's task to adjudicate such that his overarching purposes were fulfilled. This chapter is the prologue to that move (Gunn 1980a: 59), so it does not resolve all the issues within it.

The chapter's movement is defined by its main narrative sections. What is less apparent is how so much is also built around the different senses of the root *špṭ* (see Leuchter 2005: 554), which occurs in vv. 1, 2, 3, 5, 6, 9, 11, 20. The root is basically about justice or judgment, but it also has derived senses concerned with conduct. A related play on words revolves around the different senses of the root *šm'*, which variously means 'hear' or 'obey'. These wordplays are difficult to reproduce in translation, and the major versions compromise to some extent. Nevertheless, the semantic range of these roots is significant for the narrative's plot, and the ambiguities with which it plays, as well as for determining the narrator's voice.

Comment

Samuel's sons: 8:1–3

1–2. Ch. 7 closed with Samuel acting as the nation's judge and leading it in worship. This theme is taken up, but moves along a number of years. Samuel is now an old man, though he remains relatively active for some time. Nevertheless, he initiates something new and unexpected (see Nihan 1998: 28–29) by appointing his sons as judges in Israel, though they are active only in Beersheba, traditionally the southernmost point of the nation. Josephus (*Ant.* 6.32), refers to a tradition that had one son in Bethel, though the basis for this is uncertain. This is the first step towards dynastic succession, although Samuel's sons fulfil only the legal role and do not act as military leaders. Indeed, within the period of Israel's occupation of the land they are the first males to be described by the noun 'judge' (see Judg. 4:4), all the previous judges having been described through the verb: they had 'judged' Israel. This shift in terminology may be significant since previous judges had been raised up by Yahweh, something not said of Samuel's sons. Joel and Abijah's names are indicative of Samuel's own piety: Joel means, 'Yahweh is God', while Abijah means, 'My Father is Yahweh'.

3. Samuel's sons are like Eli's, and their actions are the opposite of what is expected of a judge in Israel. The way of the father is not the way of the son, a recurring motif in Judges and the early chapters of Samuel. In pursuing unjust gain, taking bribes and perverting justice they act in the way that later generates sharp prophetic critique, as well as breaking the law (Exod. 23:6–7; Deut. 16:18–20; cf. Amos 2:6–8). Eli did not discipline his sons, but there is no comment on Samuel (unless it is in his appointing them to so remote an area), principally because the dominant concern is to show how their appointment and behaviour led to the request for a king.

A king requested: 8:4–9

4–5. Samuel's appointment of his sons and their subsequent failure triggered the request for a king. The request came from the elders who assembled to see Samuel at Ramah. That they were elders suggests that they were landowners since only landowners could be elders. Samuel is not negotiating with the 'common people' but with the nearest that ancient Israel had to a landed gentry. Israel was not meant to be a stratified society, but it seems likely that stratification developed fairly early. The phrasing of the request is striking. They ask for a king that he might 'judge' them, which was the role Samuel sought for his sons. By phrasing their request in this way (the language of royal rule is introduced by Yahweh) they make it seem that they are seeking an institutionalization of the judge. This is consistent with what Samuel has done in appointing his sons as judges, though it raises questions about Samuel himself. Samuel, they point out, can no longer fulfil this role, and his sons are a bitter disappointment; hence Samuel needs to appoint someone to initiate an alternative dynasty. This request is filled with ambiguities. Is Samuel approached because he is Yahweh's prophet, or because Samuel can appoint his sons in dynastic succession (see Edelman 1991: 39)? What does it mean that this king should judge them 'like all the nations'? Are they requesting a model of government with a king as human head of state, the pattern followed in the nations, or are they asking for a human ruler with the same authority as the surrounding nations? Arguably, in view of their latter reference to the king leading them in battle, it is this latter model, though this is not made explicit. But the ambiguities inherent in the request open up the tensions explored here.

6. Such a change would not enjoy universal support, and the suggestion was unsatisfactory to Samuel, who represented an older, more traditional view of Israelite society. As in ch. 7, Samuel interceded with Yahweh. The content of this prayer is not provided, and we have to assume it was a summation of events so far. Nevertheless, we have no access to the prayer because it is not the prayer's content that is important (unlike 2 Sam. 7:18–29). What matters is Yahweh's response, which begins the process of adjudication between Samuel and the elders, though the process of intercession demonstrates Samuel's integrity.

7–9. Yahweh's response is as remarkable as the elders' request. He listens to the request, though recognizing that the deeper issue is not their rejection of Samuel but of himself. Yahweh is the nation's real king, but the elders' request rejects this. What Samuel experiences in his own rejection is akin to what Yahweh has experienced through the nation's continued rebelliousness since the exodus, rebellion that particularly includes going after other gods, so seeking a king is seen in these terms. Hence Samuel is to testify about the king's justice in his rule. The use of legal language here is deliberate. Although *mišpaṭ* can mean 'pattern of conduct' as an extension of its basic meaning of 'justice, judgment', the use of the emphatic form of 'testify' in v. 9 indicates that the forensic sense is present. A profound irony is explored since the king's role in Deut. 17:14–20 was to ensure justice. Yet here we see ways in which the model of monarchy requested generates oppression by seeking to negate Yahweh's authority. Samuel's testimony is against the elders for seeking this model as one where Yahweh's authority is usurped and put into the hands of a king and ultimately a dynasty. Samuel must still listen to the people, though at this stage it is unclear that he should 'obey' their request (see 'Form and structure'). He is to hear their request, and describe its implications as a humanly initiated model of government.

The king's justice: 8:10–18

10. Accepting Yahweh's directive, Samuel recounted the king's 'justice' to the elders. Again we note that he is not speaking to all the people but only those who requested a king. We should not imagine a gap between the introduction of Samuel's speech and what is recounted in the following verses, as if they represent Samuel's addition to Yahweh's message (see Miscall 1986: 49). Rather, this verse is a solemn assertion that what follows is indeed Yahweh's words, a point that is distinct from the fact that they are requesting (*hašō'ǎlîm*, punning Saul's name) a king from Samuel, not Yahweh.

11–18. In describing the king's 'justice', the dominant word is 'take', the verb occurring in vv. 11, 13, 14 and 16. The king will take the people's sons and daughters and force them to serve his ends in army and court (see Mendelsohn 1956). Samuel is still addressing the elite since the concerns he raises are those specific to the economically powerful who imagine that they have the most to gain through a king's appointment. It would be expected that sons of prominent families would become the commanders of army units, though the roles assigned to the daughters are less attractive.

Maintaining a standing army and court is costly, especially in maintaining loyalty, so Samuel notes that the king will take land from the citizenry and assign it to his attendants. And the land the king will take is the best, not what the elders might voluntarily yield. In addition, the king will claim the best of the male and female slaves along with a tenth of all the land's produce. Samuel insists that kingship is taxing, and a great deal will be lost. Further, in referring to 'the king you have chosen' Samuel distances himself from the people's decision to request a king. Thus he concludes that when the people cry out to this king they have chosen, Yahweh will not answer them. The king will not be Yahweh's representative if they want something the same as the nations, and they cannot expect his beneficence since the king's service is idolatrous (Garsiel 1983: 66).

The request reaffirmed: 8:19–22

19–20. In spite of Samuel's speech, the people still want a king. At v. 19 the broader term 'the people' is used rather than 'elders', suggesting that the elders' request had grass-roots support. But whoever is present, they are emphatic, and although Samuel has listened to them, they will not listen to him; they want a king to reign over them. Again, they affirm that this will make them like the nations, in that their king will 'judge' them, though they also desire the king to lead them into battle. Yet both ch. 7 and the account of the ark have proved this unnecessary.

21–22. Though the people do not listen to Samuel, he continues to listen to them. Samuel's response is not described, though he again engages in prayer. Yahweh's response is to direct Samuel to appoint a king, so that only now does listening become obedience. This shift is crucial, because it means Yahweh takes the initiative in appointing the king (Fokkelman 1993: 354). Rather than being the elders' medium for the establishment of their monarchy, Samuel is to be the one through whom Yahweh will establish his. The model of kingship Yahweh wants for Israel cannot be what Samuel has described. What is vital is that Yahweh has claimed the initiative, even though we do not know how this will be played out, as the narrative ends with Samuel dismissing the people.

Explanation

This remains one of the most difficult chapters in the book to interpret. The key to resolving this tension is to understand the ambiguity inherent in the elders' request, Samuel's actions and Yahweh's response. It is in the interplay of these positions that the narrator constructs the account, though as the prologue to a longer tale of monarchy's beginning we do not see a complete resolution. Samuel, in the appointment of his sons, opens the way for a dynastic approach to government. This then creates circumstances where the elders can approach him and request a king, though a king who will act as a formalized judge. The language of being 'like the nations' evokes Deut. 17:14–20, and so cloaks their request with apparent legitimacy. Samuel is concerned that they have rejected him, and has sensed that his judgeship is questioned, but the directly theological interpretation of the request comes only through Samuel's prayer. Here we see that the elders' request is fundamentally a new idolatry, an attempt to establish a model of government that supplants Yahweh's authority with that of a king. Samuel's speech about the justice of the king is not therefore a description of what monarchy was meant to be in Israel, but rather what it would be if the elders achieved their intention. Only after the people as a whole reject Samuel's position and insist on a king does Yahweh initiate his own move towards kingship. The chapter ends with conflicting possibilities about the type of king that will come. Will it be the model towards which Yahweh has been moving, or will it be that of the elders? What is certain is that Yahweh has reclaimed the initiative, placing government back under his reign, since it is no longer to be the people's choice of king, but Yahweh's. Kingship remains Yahweh's intent, but the momentum towards it needed to be wrested back.

The chapter continues to warn against seeking security where that security is not wholly dependent upon faith in God. The fundamental sin here was to look for an external source of security, a temptation not restricted to the time of Samuel (see Matt. 6:25–34). It leaves open the possibility that God's people may seek to move in the same direction as God, but for the wrong reason and thus have their own purposes reshaped even as the purpose itself is achieved. Seeking the right thing for the wrong reason is a particularly subtle form of sin. Working through such situations has its own inherent ambiguity, which is why retaining the chapter's ambiguities is crucial.

1 SAMUEL 9:1 - 10:16

Translation

[1]There was a man from Benjamin named Kish, the son of Abiel, the son of Zeror, the son of Becorath, the son of Aphiah, a Benjaminite, a man of wealth. [2]He had a son named Saul, young and handsome, and there was not another man from the Israelites who was better looking than him; from his shoulders upwards he was taller than all the people. [3]The donkeys of Kish, the father of Saul, were lost, so Kish said to Saul his son, 'Take one of the lads with you, arise, go, seek the donkeys.' [4]Then he passed through the hill country of Ephraim and the land of Shalisha, but they did not find them. Then they passed through the land of Shaalim, but they were not there, so he passed through the land of Benjamin, but they did not find them.

⁵When they entered the land of Zuph, Saul said to his lad who was with him, 'Come, let us return, lest my father ceases being concerned for the donkeys and becomes anxious for us.' ⁶But he said to him, 'Behold, a man of God is in this city, and the man is held in honour – all that he says comes true. So now, let us go there, perhaps he will declare our way that we might go upon it.' ⁷But Saul said to his lad, 'Behold, if we go, then what can we bring the man? The bread is gone from our bags, and there is no present to bring the man of God. What have we got?' ⁸The lad answered Saul again, 'Behold, a quarter of a shekel of silver is found in my hand, and I shall give it to the man of God that he may declare our way to us.' ⁹(Formerly in Israel, a man who was going to enquire of God would say, 'Come, let us go to the seer,' because the prophet of today was formerly called a seer.) ¹⁰Saul said to his lad, 'Well said – come, let us go.' And they went to the city where the man of God was.

¹¹As they were going up the ascent to the city, they found some girls coming out to draw water, and said to them, 'Is the seer here?' ¹²They answered, 'Yes. Behold, he is just ahead of you. Hurry now, for he has come to the city today because there is a sacrifice today for the people at the high place. ¹³When you enter the city you will find him before he goes up to the high place to eat. The people will not eat until he comes, because he must bless the sacrifice. Afterwards, those invited shall eat. Now, go up, for you shall find him immediately.' ¹⁴And they went up to the city, and as they were entering the city, behold, Samuel was coming out towards them on his way up to the high place.

¹⁵Yahweh had revealed to Samuel one day before Saul came, ¹⁶'About this time tomorrow I shall send to you a man from the land of Benjamin, and you shall anoint him as leader over my people Israel. He will save my people from the hand of the Philistines because I have seen my people's affliction because their cry has come to me.' ¹⁷When Samuel saw Saul, Yahweh told him, 'Behold, the man of whom I spoke to you. This one will restrain my people.' ¹⁸Saul approached Samuel in the midst of the gate, and he said to him, 'Please tell me, where is the seer's house?' ¹⁹Samuel answered Saul, 'I am the seer. Go up before me to the high place and you shall eat with me today, and I shall send you on in the morning and declare to you all that is in your heart. ²⁰As concerns your donkeys that have been missing for three days, do not concern yourself about them since they have been found. But for whom is all that is desirable in Israel? Is it not for you and your entire father's house?' ²¹Saul answered, 'Am I not of Benjamin, from the smallest of Israel's tribes, and my clan is the humblest of all the clans of the tribe of Benjamin. So why do you speak to me in this way?'

²²But Samuel took Saul and his lad and brought them to the hall, and gave them a place at the head of those who had been invited – about thirty persons. ²³Samuel said to the cook, 'Bring the portion I gave you, concerning which I said to you "Set it aside."' ²⁴And the cook took up the leg and what was on it, and set it before Saul. Samuel said, 'Behold, here is what was left for you. Eat, for this was kept for you until the appointed time, since it was said, "I have invited the people."' So Saul ate with Samuel.

²⁵When they came down from the high place to the city, they laid a bed for Saul on the roof and he lay down to sleep. ²⁶They rose early as dawn was breaking, and

Samuel called to Saul on the roof, saying, 'Rise, and I shall send you on.' So Saul rose and both he and Samuel went out to the street. [27]As they were going down to the edge of the city Samuel said to Saul, 'Tell the lad that he may pass over before us and when he has passed over, then stay here yourself for a while, and I shall make known to you God's word.'

[10:1]Then Samuel took a flask of oil and poured it upon his head and kissed him and said, 'Has not Yahweh anointed you to be leader over his inheritance? [2]When you depart from me today, you will find two men by Rachel's tomb in the territory of Benjamin at Zelzah, and they will say to you, "The donkeys you went to seek are found. And behold, your father has abandoned any worry about the donkeys but is concerned about you, saying, 'What shall I do about my son?' " [3]Then you shall pass on from there further, and you shall come to the oak of Tabor. Three men going up to God at Bethel will find you there. One of them will be carrying three kids, one three loaves of bread, and one a skin of wine. [4]They shall greet you and shall give you two loaves of bread, which you shall accept from their hand. [5]After this, you shall come to Gibeath Elohim where there is a Philistine garrison. As soon as you enter the city you will meet a band of prophets coming down from the high place with a harp, tambourine, flute and lyre and they will be prophesying. [6]And the Spirit of Yahweh will rush upon you and you shall prophesy with them; and you shall become another man. [7]So when these signs have happened to you, do whatever your hand finds to do, because God is with you. [8]Then go down before me to Gilgal, and behold, I am coming to you to offer up burnt offerings and to sacrifice peace offerings. You shall wait seven days until I come to you and I shall make known to you what you are to do.'

[9]When he turned his back to go from Samuel, God changed his heart, and all these signs came about on one day. [10]When they reached Gibeah, behold, a band of prophets met him, and the Spirit of God rushed upon him and he prophesied in their midst. [11]When everyone who knew him before saw him prophesying with the prophets, the people said to one another, 'What has happened to the son of Kish? Is Saul also among the prophets?' [12]And a man from there answered and said, 'And who is their father?' Therefore, it became a proverb, 'Is Saul also among the prophets?'

[13]When he ceased prophesying, he came to the high place. [14]Saul's uncle said to him and to his lad, 'Where did you go?' And he said, 'To seek the donkeys. But when we saw that they were not to be found we went to Samuel.' [15]So Saul's uncle said, 'Please tell me what Samuel said to you?' [16]So Saul said to his uncle, 'He told us plainly that the donkeys were found.' But concerning the kingdom of which Samuel had spoken, he did not tell him anything.

Notes on the text

9:2. *tōb* may mean either 'morally good' or 'handsome'. In spite of Hunter's (1991) arguments that this represents intentional ambiguity, the following lines indicate that appearance is the point at issue.

4. The confusion between sg. and pl. verbs in this verse has left a trail of confusion through the MS tradition, with an array of readings, all of which harmonize them one way or the other (see *BHS*). The agreement between 4QSam^a and the majority of MT MSS suggests that we should retain the more rugged reading and regard the others as natural attempts at harmonization. Driver (1913: 69) points to parallels in Num. 13:22 and 33:7, though he also regards these texts as defective. Variation between expected use of sg. and pl. is a feature of this narrative.

12. A number of scholars follow Wellhausen (e.g. Driver 1913: 72; McCarter 1980a: 169; Klein 1983: 82) in reconstructing the Hebrew with reference to LXX's *kata prosōpon hymōn* to have a regular set of plurals throughout. But 4QSam^a generally agrees with MT, so MT should be retained.

16. Following LXX's *epi tēn tapeinōsin*. This may suggest an original *'ny*, and could have been missed by a scribe who went straight to *'my* by haplography. See Fincke's reconstruction of 4QSam^a at this point (2001: 16).

17. The translation 'rule' (e.g. NIV, NRSV; cf. BDB) for *'ṣr* is unlikely since it means this nowhere else. In its forty-six occurrences it always means either 'to restrain' (e.g. Gen. 16:2), 'to retain' or 'hold' (e.g. 2 Chr. 22:9; Job 12:15), or 'to close up' (e.g. Gen. 20:18; Jer. 20:9). It refers to a force applied to prevent another action. McCarter (1980a: 179) offers 'muster', but Gordon (1986: 115) is rightly dubious. Arguably, attempts to offer a positive reading of Saul's role here are determined by the assumption that this is a pro-monarchic narrative. The verb's ambiguity should be retained.

20. *ḥemdâ* refers to the object of desire. Hence a more likely reading is not that the nation's desire is fixed on Saul (NIV, NRSV), but that whatever is desirable within the nation belongs to Saul.

24. There is a bewildering array of variants here (see *BHS*, with more in 4QSam^a), stemming from its rather abrupt and rough character. Provided one assumes Samuel speaks in the second half of the verse, remaining the subject of *wayyô'mer* by ellipsis (the 'cook' as the immediate antecedent), then the MT is intelligible, and the variants are attempts at making a rough text smooth. Van der Jagt (1996) argues from anthropology that the leg given to Saul was the right hind leg, so what was 'on it' was the fat. Though plausible, the text does not make this clear, though a special portion is intended.

25. MT is lit. 'And they came down from the high place [to] the city and he spoke with Saul on the roof.' MT is defective, and LXX is followed.

26. A good case can also be made for following LXX. However, the major issue is the interchange between sg. and pl., and this (see vv. 4, 12) interchange is a feature of this narrative.

10:1. LXX records a longer text, indicating Saul is to be Israel's deliverer, and the following events will be the signs that demonstrate his new status. Although widely supported as original (e.g. Klein 1983: 83, NRSV, ESV), it is suspiciously harmonistic in terms of the following signs (see Stoebe 1973: 197). The narrative is careful to minimize and ambiguate Saul's role, and the addition is contrary to this.

10. Reading *miśśām* with LXX rather than MT *śām*.

13. The common emendation, proposed by Wellhausen, of changing *bāmâ* to *bêt* is unnecessary (see Na'aman 1992: 641).

Form and structure

We now reach the point of kingship's initiation within Israel, though it is a tale with some oddities, such as the missing donkeys and the curious fact that the word 'king' (*melek*) never appears. The nearest it comes is in the closing verse, where Saul refrains from mentioning the kingdom to his uncle (10:16). Saul will be anointed, something anticipated since ch. 2, but anointed as *nāgîd*, a term of imprecise meaning, but with enough breadth (see *NIDOTTE* 3:20) to cover tribal (2 Chr. 19:11), royal, military (1 Chr. 13:1) and priestly leadership (2 Chr. 31:12). Although much of the evidence of linguistic range comes from later than the time of Saul, it seems the term is intentionally ambiguous. Certainly, 'crown prince' is too precise (against Lipinski 1974). Saul's exact status is not made clear to him, although ch. 8 has already shown there is to be a move towards kingship. Indeed, there are a number of points of deliberate ambiguity within this narrative. The word 'king' will again be used in 10:19 and 24, though in the former it is simply Samuel's quoting the people's words back at them, while 10:24 is the people's acclamation of Saul. Curiously, at no point in kingship's initiation is Yahweh said to have appointed Saul as king, a striking omission considering this is a part of Samuel's supposedly pro-monarchic section (though see 15:1).

Yet the kingdom is clearly the matter at hand, and the restraint employed needs to be understood in terms of the text's final shape, not its tradition history. The reading offered here suggests Saul's anointing is anticipatory (Bettenzoli 1986a: 229 prefers provisional), part of a process that will recur with David, where there is a private anointing, public acceptance and military demonstration (see Humphreys 1980: 18–27; Edelman 1991: 28–36). This can be listed, as in the table below:

	Saul	*David*
Private anointing	1 Sam. 10:1–8	1 Sam. 16:1–13
Public acceptance	1 Sam. 10:17–27	2 Sam. 5:1–5
Military demonstration	1 Sam. 11	1 Sam. 17

The order of events is different, but that is necessitated by David and Saul's comparative status. That is to say, the absence of the term 'king' is explained by the fact that the private anointing initiated by Yahweh is not completed until the public declaration of the choice in 10:17–24, while this choice is publicly demonstrated by ch. 11. Saul is not informed fully until the point of public acceptance, so we do not have a double tradition of Saul's election, but a single one that moves in stages to the point where the kingdom is established.

This helps to clarify the issue of the supposed pro- and anti-monarchic sources (see Rudman 2000: 528–529). Such sources may have existed (and this section has been subject to analysis of its internal development; see Birch 1976: 29–35; Na'aman 1992: 640–642), reflecting the tensions that must have been felt within Israel, but the coherence of the final form of chs. 8 – 12 should be noted (Long 1994). There is no opposition to the king's appointment in chs. 9 – 11, because ch. 8 ended with Yahweh's announcement that Samuel was to appoint a king. Process must be followed through to its conclusion. Only once that is done can we return to the critique of kingship evident in ch. 8 through Samuel's concluding speech. Nevertheless, elements of critique still surface, notably the satirical way Saul is presented (he seeks lost donkeys and finds a kingdom, and his lad knows more than he does), while dark allusions to his background are also present (K. I. Cohen 1994; Garsiel 1990: 84).

Comment

Saul seeking some donkeys: 9:1–14

1–2. The narrative's opening is a surprise. Ch. 8 ended ambiguously, with Yahweh's directing Samuel to appoint a king but Samuel's only sending the people home. We expect that Samuel will initiate the process by which this appointment will happen. So when we begin with a genealogy centred on Kish, who is either a 'wealthy man' or a 'man of valour' (*ḥayil* could be taken either way; a double entendre is possible), we suspect we have found our man. A lengthy genealogy is appropriate to someone of importance, yet it will be Kish's son Saul who will be of interest, though this becomes apparent only in v. 2. Nevertheless, we seemingly have a suitable candidate for leadership. But there are worrying hints in the presentation. In particular, there are allusions to Judg. 19 – 21. There, too, we encounter men from Benjamin who are 'men of valour' (20:44–46), but they have resisted the nation. Moreover, Kish, and therefore Saul, must be descended from the rather suspect marital process described in Judg. 21, which involved both deception and kidnapping. Although the language about Saul may be entirely conventional, there is enough to suggest concern.

3–4. But the theme of national leadership is not initially developed. Instead, we focus on the fact that Kish's donkeys have escaped and that Saul and his 'lad' were sent to find them. Saul's companion is most likely a servant, though not a slave, and one of the story's central features is that he is more resourceful than Saul. The search for the donkeys is ultimately fruitless, even though an extensive search is undertaken. The narrative goes out of its way to emphasize the distance travelled, although most of the places mentioned cannot be identified with certainty. Nevertheless, travel from Benjamin to Ephraim and back again is certainly a significant journey. There is the possibility of an implied criticism of Saul. Kings were supposed to 'shepherd' their people, but Saul cannot do so even for some large animals that will eventually find their own way home (Bergen 1996: 121).

5–6. Their arrival in the land of Zuph changes the narrative focus. Here Saul acts as a responsible son and suggests they return home. But the lad knows of a 'man of God' in a nearby town (never named), and that his word is inevitably effective. Readers know that this is the territory of Samuel's family (1:1), while the effectiveness of his word recalls 3:19–20. But the narrator is careful only to reveal information from Saul's perspective, which is why Samuel's name is not revealed until v. 14. Given the authority of this man of God, the young man suggests they should seek clarification about their journey from him.

7–10. Saul is not easily persuaded, especially since he knows they lack the resources available to pay the anticipated fee. The custom of an Israelite prophet charging for directions is not otherwise attested (but see Balaam in Num. 22:7), and may have been a donation rather than a fixed sum. However, the young man has a quarter of a shekel in silver (a little over one gram, this being before coinage) and is prepared to use this, though there is no indication that payment was made. Saul is notably less resourceful than his servant, leading Gordon to make a comparison with Jeeves and Wooster (1986: 113). V. 9 sits a little oddly in context: the reference to the former custom of calling a prophet a 'seer' does not fit directly since there have been no previous references to a 'seer' or a 'prophet' in Samuel (see Fenton 1997 for a possible solution), though it does prepare us for the fact that in vv. 11–19 the man of God is called a seer. But with his lad's assurance, Saul agreed to see the man of God.

10–14. As they approached the town, they were met by a group of young women coming out to draw water. This was normally done in the evening, suggesting the day was well advanced. The account's form fits with a biblical-type scene that typically leads to a betrothal (Gen. 24:15–50; 29:9–20; Exod. 2:16–22; Alter 1981: 181), but the narrator introduces this element only to subvert it, because this does not happen. The town's water supply would have been in the valley, with the town itself situated on the hill. Since it also had a 'high place', it seems there was an area above the town as well as below it on the hill, though with the anonymity of the city, the exact layout is uncertain. When they met these young women, Saul and his companion enquired about the seer's location. Their answer was effusive, offering considerably more information than requested. The presence of a high place does not appear to cause any embarrassment, perhaps because there was not yet 'the one place' that Yahweh would choose (see Deut. 12:5), so there could still be freedom concerning locations of worship. This high place must have been an established shrine, because Saul eats in the hall there with thirty guests, indicating a substantial structure. Saul and his companion have some time, because the town must wait for the seer to bless the sacrifice; though in this we have a preparatory allusion to what Saul will fail to do in ch. 13. Only as they approach the town do they see the man of God. Keeping to the technique of allowing us to see only as Saul does, only now do we confirm that this man of God coming towards them is Samuel, though the text is deliberately ambiguous about whether Samuel is coming to meet them or is simply heading towards them.

Samuel encounters Saul: 9:15–24

15–16. Although the encounter with Samuel occurred in an unexpected manner, the rest of the narrative is more traditional. It begins with a flashback to a message whispered by Yahweh to Samuel (lit. Yahweh 'uncovered Samuel's ear'; see 8:21) that Yahweh was sending Saul, and Samuel was to anoint him as leader (carefully avoiding the word 'king'; see 'Form and structure'). In doing so, we recognize that the events so far have not been merely fortuitous, but a real providence at work (Deist 1992), though doing so means breaking from the previous technique of revealing only what Saul himself could know. The Philistine threat that lay behind ch. 8 comes to the fore since Saul's stated role is to save the people from the Philistines. This statement sits awkwardly with the statement at the end of ch. 7 about subduing the Philistines for the rest of Samuel's life (Smith 1899: 62 regards it as a direct contradiction), though, as noted, the time reference there probably only intends to cover the period up to the initiation of the monarchy. More importantly, the statement clarifies Saul's role in terms functionally equivalent to those of a judge. The major judges had all 'saved' Israel from an external power, and Saul's role is to follow this pattern. Samson, as the last military judge, had only 'begun' this process (Judg. 13:5), and Saul is to continue it, so that his position is more like a formalized judge than a king as such. Moreover, that Yahweh is responding to the cry of the people indicates that a parallel to the events of the exodus is intended, something that generates irony from the fact that the exodus motif featured most prominently in 4:1 – 7:1, where the theme of the exodus is more of a warning to Israel than one of hope.

17. We revert to the main narrative, so when Samuel sees Saul, Yahweh informs him that this is the one of whom he has spoken. Nevertheless, the verse retains an important ambiguity because of the role assigned to Saul, which is to 'restrain' (not 'rule'; see 'Notes') the people. This implies that Yahweh sees a negating role for Saul, one designed to prevent the people from moving towards chaos. In particular, this links to Judg. 17 – 21, when 'there was no king in Israel, and everyone did what was right in their own eyes' (Judg. 17:6; 21:25; cf. 18:1; 19:1). Saul's role is not one with absolute freedom, something that chimes with the limited perceptions of kingship established by Deut. 17:14–20. However, the element of restraint means a move away from the chaos of Judg. 17 – 21 in order to lead a society reflecting Yahweh's rule. Saul's failure is ultimately because he fails to acknowledge this in chs. 13 and 15. Nevertheless, it is not that Yahweh has set himself against Saul to begin with (against Gunn 1980a: 115–123). The balance retained is that Saul remains personally responsible for his choices, while Yahweh's purposes are also achieved.

18–21. The narrative reverts to Saul's perspective. He approaches someone in the town gate and requests directions to the seer's house, only to discover he is speaking to the seer, Samuel, himself. There is a play on words when Saul asks Samuel to tell him (*haggîdâ*) the way to the seer's house, though Yahweh has said that Saul is to be his *nāgîd*. Both words may come from the same root (the initial nun elides in the verb), but their similarity in sound is what matters. Although Samuel does not immediately anoint Saul, he reveals he is the seer and directs him and his lad to go to the high place where they will eat together; and in the morning Samuel will tell him (*'aggîd*) what is on his heart. Saul hears this in terms of the donkeys, but Samuel has a different point of view and informs him of their safety, indicating he knows the nature of the journey he and his lad have undertaken. This suggests that something other than donkeys is on Saul's heart, though perhaps Saul may not yet recognize it. Samuel then adds a cryptic remark about the desire of the nation and its relationship to Saul. The phrase is enigmatic, suggesting either that Saul and his family are the goal of Israel's desire, or all that is desirable in Israel belongs ultimately to Saul's family (see 'Notes'). The first interpretation suggests Saul fulfils the nation's desire for a king, while the second suggests the nation's wealth will come to Saul and his family, highlighting kingship's wealth and acquisitiveness (see Birch 1998: 1039). Although the latter is more probable, the result is the same for Saul, and the donkeys cease to be the pressing matter. Saul recognizes something of what Samuel is saying, even though the kingdom as such has not been mentioned, and protests his unworthiness. Such protests are characteristic of those called by God in the OT (especially Gideon). There is some validity to Saul's protests, but they must be seen against the background of Yahweh's decision.

22–24. Saul (and his lad) are later taken by Samuel to a banquet in the high place's hall, where Saul is placed in an exalted position. Yet Saul has this position only because Yahweh gave it to him, indicating the limits placed on his role. Saul is also given a special portion of the meal, a portion it now transpires Samuel arranged to set aside. The exact significance of this banquet is unclear. Since Samuel has arranged it in advance and knows there will be a need for a special portion, it is perhaps intended as a pre-coronation meal. There may be some priestly significance, too, but it is never highlighted. More probably, it retains the ambiguity inherent in the process. Saul has been called to a special role, but it has not yet been given content. Samuel knows, but Saul does not. The meal points to special significance, but what that is remains unsaid. What remains clear is that the authority to instigate and negotiate change remains with Yahweh, and he does this through Samuel.

Anointing and signs for Saul: 9:25 – 10:16

9:25–27. After the banquet, Saul stays the night with Samuel, with the roof chosen as the cooler place to sleep during the warmer months. This is necessary for Samuel to tell Saul the things on his heart, but the conversation is delayed until early morning. This conversation is terse, informing Saul that Samuel will send him on, though Saul would have expected this, since he had come only to find the missing donkeys. The narrative brevity is maintained by simply recording that Saul rose, and that then the two of them went out. Once outside, Samuel directs Saul to send his lad ahead, indicating some secrecy in what is to follow. Samuel does so because he is about to announce a word from God. This is why Saul came to see Samuel, though the word he will receive is different from the one he sought. He already knows about the donkeys, so at this point Saul has no idea of what is to transpire.

10:1. The word Saul initially receives is not a message in the traditional sense. Rather, Samuel takes a vial of oil and anoints Saul, announcing through a rhetorical question that Yahweh has anointed him to be the leader over his inheritance, that is, over the people Israel and the land. Anointing was familiar from the Egyptian model, where vassal kings were anointed (EA 51.4–9; Judg. 9:8, 15 suggests it may also have been an old Canaanite practice; see de Vaux 1965: 103–106). So the action declares that Saul is not a ruler with the same authority as other nations; he is Yahweh's vassal. This is clear from Samuel's question in the anointing: although Samuel poured the oil, Yahweh anointed Saul as *nāgîd*. The word 'king' is carefully avoided. The title *nāgîd* is suitably vague – it means a leader, but the details are not defined. By avoiding 'king' or any word associated with the judges, Saul's role is still limited. He will not act with a king's authority, and neither is he another judge; he has a leadership role that will be determined and shaped by Yahweh, one to be exercised under Yahweh, but Saul has not yet been given specific content. Indeed, a striking omission from Samuel's speech is any reference to Saul's role in saving the people from the Philistines.

2–8. As well as anointing him, Samuel also announces a series of three signs that will come to Saul. The first is the meeting of two men at Rachel's tomb (near Bethlehem; see Gen. 35:20) around the otherwise unknown Zelzah, who will confirm that the donkeys have been found and that Saul's father is now concerned for him. This confirms Samuel's initial message to Saul. The second sign is the encounter with three men, going to worship at Bethel and carrying some kids, bread and a skin of wine, who will give Saul two loaves he is to accept. Both point to areas where Saul was previously lacking (regarding the lost donkeys and food). Finally, Saul will meet a prophetic band at Gibeath Elohim (Hill of God) coming down the hill and 'prophesying', most probably in ecstasy associated with music. Such a pattern is known from early Israel (Num. 11:17, 24, though without music), but was not the dominant pattern of prophecy in later times. Most importantly, when this happens, Saul will be changed through an experience of the Spirit of Yahweh that will result in his having a new 'heart'. In declaring the matters that previously concerned Saul, Samuel addresses what is on his 'heart', but now he will receive a changed heart, indicating a complete change covering his rational and emotive self. This will take place when Saul also prophesies. This is the only sign where the fulfilment is described, indicating it is the one the narrator considers to be primary. After announcing the signs, Samuel directs Saul to do that which his hand finds to do, which appears to indicate an attack on the Philistine garrison (Long 1989: 207; see Judg. 9:23), though he is also to be at Gilgal, where he will wait for seven days until Samuel comes to make the necessary sacrifices. Although there may seem to be some tension between the statements of vv. 7–8, they are to be resolved in that the command of v. 7 is tied to the specific moment of the completion of the signs. It is not carte blanche to do anything, but depends upon the presence of the Philistine garrison. The task is an important test, a means of proving his openness to Yahweh's leading and willingness to work under the prophet in matters concerned with the Spirit. Saul will be authorized by his encounter with the Spirit, but remain under prophetic authority and be required to remain faithful to the prophetic message. Although it is unclear at this point, this seven-day wait at Gilgal is preparatory for 13:7b–15, where Saul's loss of the kingdom is first announced.

9–13. From this point, we have the record of the fulfilment of the signs outlined by Samuel. Since the change of Saul's heart is primary, the narrator brings it to the foreground of the fulfilment narrative, and begins with it rather than the signs themselves. Nevertheless, the signs demonstrate the reality of this change. The emphasis is upon the last sign, and we have a full record of the encounter with the prophets, but no detail on the other two. At Gibeah ('the hill', though presumably Gibeath Elohim as in v. 5) Saul met the prophetic band. At this point, the Spirit comes upon him, a phrase reflecting the experience of the judges (Judg. 3:10; 6:34; 11:29; 13:25; 14:6, 19; 15:14), and especially of Samson, who is the only other figure of whom it is previously said that the Spirit 'rushed' (*ṣlḥ*; Judg. 14:16, 19; 15:14) upon him. This may be because of the close association of both with the Philistines, but may also point to the basic instability of character and variable relationship with Yahweh that marks them both (see Judg. 16:20; 1 Sam. 16:14–23; but note David in 16:13). What is important is that Samuel's word comes about and Saul also prophesies, an event paralleled in 1 Sam. 19:18–24 (cf. 18:10), but which there indicates something very different about Saul's status. This experience is said to be the origin of a proverb about Saul's being one of the prophets. The emphasis here is difficult to discern, perhaps because the proverb is ambiguous. But the association of the Spirit of Yahweh with his elective purpose indicates that it is uttered in awe of what has happened. Not all were supportive of Saul, however, and the question 'And who is their father?' in reference to the prophets suggests a negative attitude in that these prophets had no recognizable leader. This perhaps derives from the phrase 'the sons of the prophets', used to describe prophetic bands. From the perspective of Saul's move towards the throne it is positive; it is the point when Saul knows that Samuel's word to him is correct and he will be the nation's leader.

14–16. We suddenly return to Saul's home to conclude the story of the donkeys. That Saul had sought the donkeys is presumed by his uncle's question, but he would be curious to know why they had taken so long (against Eslinger 1985: 334–335, who views the uncle as a literary device). Saul reports that because they could not find the donkeys they went to Samuel, though the role of his lad in making this link is not mentioned. Saul is, after all, the one meant to know what to do, so the lad is marginalized by this report. However, it piqued his uncle's interest, so he asked about Samuel's message, though Saul revealed only the information about the donkeys. Indeed, we are told he kept the matter of the kingdom to himself. Not mentioning the kingdom is remarkable since it is clear throughout that Yahweh is king. Saul's silence raises questions about his future role. As anointed leader, Saul is preparing for a kingdom, but that is not what he has been promised; already there is a point at which Saul appears to be setting himself at cross-purposes with Yahweh, though at this stage he has not acted upon it.

Explanation

The striking thing about so much of this story is that it begins by describing a normal set of events: a farmer loses some livestock and dispatches his son and a servant to find them. There is nothing unusual in this, and coming straight after the events of ch. 8 it seems almost anticlimactic. But these events serve to introduce Saul, and to make the introduction in a manner that initially conceals what the story is about. Saul is the tall, good-looking son of a wealthy Benjaminite, though he is also someone rather lacking in initiative, as his servant repeatedly knows the appropriate thing to do, whereas Saul does not. What the narrator has concealed is that this series of perfectly normal events is not independent of Yahweh's greater purposes. By means of a direct intrusion into the narrative at 9:15–17 we discover that Yahweh has a far more important purpose for Saul than we might have expected, and even the (temporary) loss of the donkeys was not simply an accident but part of Yahweh's providential purpose that involves Saul's appointment as Israel's leader, a leader who will save the people from the Philistines and restrain them from their tendency towards chaos. This tendency was evident in Judg. 17 – 21, but was also latent in their request for a king 'like the nations' in ch. 8. This intrusion is the key to understanding the narrative, as it makes clear the dimensions of Saul's role, something far more important than a possible etymological study of the key term *nāgîd*. Saul will be the leader through whom Yahweh will act for his people since, even with this appointment, Yahweh is still Israel's real king. Saul's election, confirmed through a series of signs that would also appear random if not for their prior announcement through Samuel, thus seems to answer the question raised by ch. 8.

Nevertheless, a number of issues are raised about Saul, issues not immediately significant but that raise questions as the narrative proceeds. As we have noted, it is Saul's servant, not Saul, who is aware of how to approach Yahweh through a prophet. Moreover, Saul's background as a man from Benjamin, and in particular Gibeah, raises a host of questions in the light of Judg. 19 – 21. Saul looks like a king should, tall and handsome, but his lineage is questionable. In part, these questions are resolved by the fact that following the signs, Saul had a special experience of the Spirit and was changed. But the most closely similar experience of the Spirit to that of Saul is Samson, one who 'began' to save Israel from the Philistines (Judg. 13:5), and even if Samson achieved his purpose, he was hardly the sort of model who inspires confidence. Thus there is considerable ambiguity woven through this narrative, even in Saul's characterization. This ambiguity becomes more acute in the way Saul acts after he received the confirmatory signs, in that we are not told that he actually did that which his 'hand found' (10:7). God was present with Saul, but it is not entirely clear what this meant to him. Similarly his silence with his uncle in 10:14–16 is centred on the topic of the kingdom, though a kingdom is never mentioned within the narrative. Even Saul's silence raises questions about what he is doing as leader, enhancing the narrative's ambiguity.

The narrator's skill is seen in how these two elements, Yahweh's overarching providence and the inherent ambiguity seen in Saul (and to a lesser extent Samuel), are held together. Yahweh is acting, and appears to be responding to the matters raised by ch. 8. Saul will be a central figure in this process, but his importance is limited by the extent to which he recognizes he can act only under the greater kingship of Yahweh. It is this kingship that is providentially demonstrated that is to be applied through Saul. What is not yet demonstrated, and indeed remains an open question, is whether or not Saul will appreciate and act within his role's limits.

1 SAMUEL 10:17–27

Translation

[17]Samuel summoned the people to Yahweh at Mizpah. [18]He said to the people of Israel, 'Thus has Yahweh, God of Israel, said, "I brought Israel up from Egypt and I redeemed you from the hand of Egypt and from the hand of all the kingdoms that oppressed you." [19]But today you have rejected your God who saves you from all your calamities and distresses when you said, "No! You shall set a king over us." And now, present yourselves before Yahweh by your tribes and your thousands.' [20]Then Samuel brought near all the tribes of Israel, and the tribe of Benjamin was taken. [21]Then Samuel brought near the tribe of Benjamin by its clans, and the clan of Matri was taken. Then Saul, son of Kish, was taken, and they sought him but did not find him. [22]They asked again of Yahweh, 'Is there yet someone come hither?' And Yahweh said, 'He has hidden himself in the kit.' [23]Then they ran and took him from there. When he stood in the midst of the people, he was taller than all the people from the shoulders up. [24]And Samuel said to all the people, 'Do you see him whom Yahweh has chosen? There is no one like him among all the people.' And all the people shouted, 'Long live the king!'

[25]Then Samuel spoke to the people concerning the justice of the kingship and wrote it in a book and set it before Yahweh. Then Samuel sent all the people home. [26]Saul also returned to his home in Gibeah, and the warriors whose hearts God had touched went with him. [27]But some worthless men said, 'How can he save us?' And they despised him and did not bring him a gift, but he stayed like one who is silent.

Notes on the text

18. McCarter (1980a: 192) reads *mamlākôt* as 'kings' rather than 'kingdoms'. Although possible, and resolving the issue that the qualifying participle is m. rather than f., it is better to retain the normal translation and interpret the gender of the participle as personification, so that kingdoms and the kings become indistinguishable. See Fokkelman 1993: 440.

19. Reading (with some MSS and Tg) *lō'* rather than *lô*. The interchange is common. *'elep* is here equivalent to *mišpaḥâ* in v. 21. This suggests the traditional translation of 'thousand' is less than helpful, as a much smaller number is in view. However, that the word can refer to a military unit may be significant since the king's role was initially conceived militarily.

21. LXX adds a further clause on the bringing forward of the Matrites (an otherwise unknown clan). A longer text regularizing a pattern is suspect, and MT is retained.

22. The people's question is awkward. LXX adds the article to understand Saul as the reference. The translation follows Driver (1913: 84) and presumes the people are looking for someone else.

kēlîm elsewhere refers to military equipment, so the traditional 'baggage' is misleading. 'Kit' allows for baggage, but is more consistent with the military elements.

25. Again, there is a play on *mišpāṭ*. It can mean 'custom' as well as 'justice', but the use here echoes 8:9, 11, where the double meaning was crucial to the dialogue between Samuel and the elders.

26. The warriors who went with Saul are called *ḥayil*, which can also mean 'man of substance' (i.e. wealthy). See the description of Kish in 9:1.

27. A much longer text is found in 4QSam[a], providing possible background to the events of 11:1–13, and is adopted by NRSV. As MT stands, we have a contrast between Samuel's summoning 'cry' in 10:17 and Saul's silence. Such a balance argues for retaining MT. The inclusion of the extra text would not add significantly to our knowledge of the events described, and could conceivably have been generated by MT's awkward phrasing.

Form and structure

Where 9:1 – 10:16 recorded the private encounter between Saul and Samuel, this passage records the beginning of the public recognition of Saul's kingship. This occurred in two stages, as Saul was first recognized as Yahweh's choice by lot and then confirmed as a result of his deliverance of Jabesh Gilead (11:1–15). Saul had done nothing to claim the throne after the confirming signs, even to the extent of keeping the news of his anointing from his uncle. Thus Samuel took the lead to move the process from the private confirmation to Saul through the signs to public recognition of Saul as Yahweh's chosen. Saul's anointed status plays no part in this narrative because it is essential that a public process demonstrates his choice by Yahweh. Yet ambiguity remains, as other literary references in the OT to taking someone by lot (Josh. 7; 1 Sam. 14:36–42) are less than positive. Yet as a result of this, Saul moves from being *nāgîd* to king (*melek*). No longer can Saul hold back. His position is made clear; the ambiguity of being *nāgîd* is removed.

Critical discussion has centred on the sources generally held to be present, as well as noting that this passage may follow on quite naturally from ch. 8 (see Birch 1976: 42–54). The suggestion is often made that we have two sources which suggest that Saul was selected either by lot or by an oracle concerning his height. However, not only does this create sources too fragmentary to be helpful, but it also suggests the editor was particularly clumsy. This narrative works by including tensions, and the technique is included here to heighten the drama of Saul's election and his failure to be found. There is surely irony in someone being so much taller than everyone else but unable to be found in the crowd. There is still a coherent narrative thread that runs through Saul's rise, and it needs to be read as a coherent unit (Long 1989: 211–215), providing a stage in Saul's accession. However, the closing mockery of the worthless men who refuse to bring Saul a gift may contain an intentional irony. They refuse to acknowledge Saul as king, because they wonder if he can save the people. Readers coming back to their comment later may wonder if they had it right.

Comment

Saul selected by lot: 10:17–24

17–19a. After his private anointing, Saul returned to his home in Gibeah. We do not know how long he was there, though some time had passed between his return and these events, since Saul appears to be an adult here. However, given that the dividing line between youth and adulthood is notoriously thin, it would be wiser to set attempts at precision aside. All we know with certainty is that some time had passed before Samuel summoned the people to Mizpah. The selection of Mizpah is significant since it was during the assembly at Mizpah in ch. 7 that Yahweh ensured the Philistines were decisively defeated, indicating that a king was not strictly needed. Also, Mizpah was where Israel had gathered prior to the destruction of the tribe of Benjamin after the events of Gibeah (Judg. 20:1). Saul's status as a Benjaminite has already been noted (9:1, 21), while 10:10 may hint at what is made explicit in 10:26; Saul is also from Gibeah. The negative connotations apparent from Mizpah's choice as the site for this gathering become explicit in Samuel's speech in vv. 18–19a. In v. 18 Samuel speaks with Yahweh's voice, describing the salvation experience of the exodus and the conquest as something he has done. Pointedly, Yahweh claims he delivered the nation from the 'kingdoms' that oppressed them. Their oppressors were peoples with kings, the model Israel was seeking to apply for itself. Hence Samuel concludes that the act of attending the assembly to appoint their own king shows the people are again rejecting Yahweh, since he is always their saviour. The critical remarks directed at the elders in ch. 8 are now directed to the people as a whole as they attend this gathering, though those present are probably still elders.

19b–21. After the fiery start to Samuel's speech, we might have expected a longer judgment statement, but the critique ends there. Samuel has made clear that the decision to move towards a king was flawed, but Yahweh will continue to be a part of the process because he is permitting it. The procedure to find a king requires a selection by lot. This is akin to the taking of Achan in Josh. 7, though the tribal division is here less clearly defined (see 'Notes'). This association with Achan, as well as with

Jonathan's taking in 14:36–42, casts a literary shadow over Saul's selection. If we are to judge by texts like Num. 26:55, Josh. 18:6 or Prov. 16:33, the process of making selections through the casting of lots may be seen as something positive, or at least neutral. But the only times the taking of a person is described apart from this narrative are for someone who is in some way guilty. We must therefore distinguish between Samuel's actions in following this process and the literary interpretation offered by the text. No one present would have regarded it as sinister. But the narrator, by evoking the taking of Achan and preparing for that of Jonathan (which influences subsequent readings), raises questions for us. The process is essentially binomial, with a 'Yes' or 'No' decision, and then once an affirmative choice has been made from one group (initially the tribe) the same process is made from the remaining levels (clan and then father's house, though the narrative is compressed and does not give all the details) until Saul is taken. Saul's selection is not a sham (contra Eslinger 1985: 344) since it is a necessary stage within the process, moving from private to public information before public acceptance, and the control of the lot is evidence of the exercise of Yahweh's sovereignty. The taking of Saul by the lot is remarkable for the fact that Saul himself was apparently not present when the lot was cast in his favour. This is unusual since the assumed process was that each person passed before the community for the lot to be cast, as appears to be the case in v. 21. However, when Saul is taken, we discover he is not present, the lot apparently being cast in his absence. Commentators are troubled by this since it is assumed the person had to be present, but we have insufficient evidence to conclude this. Previously, Saul sought the lost donkeys he could not find, but now it is the people who seek Saul whom they cannot find.

10:22–24. Because of Saul's apparent absence, the people ask Yahweh about his whereabouts, apparently assuming others are still to arrive, and that Saul must be one of them. The process of asking enables the narrator to play with Saul's name in much the same way as in ch. 1, since the name 'Saul' comes from the verb 'to ask'. However, where the play on Saul's name there depended ultimately on his absence, here it depends on his presence. The matter is resolved when Yahweh points out that he is hiding in the kit. Based on this, the people run to find Saul, who is then brought to them, with the first thing everyone noting about him being his great height. There is thus a deliberate echo of 9:2, which in turn points to his apparent suitability to be king, though it makes his attempt at hiding even more bizarre. However, before we hear of any reaction from the people, Samuel affirms that Saul is the one Yahweh has chosen as king, stressing his uniqueness. Thus there is still a tension for Samuel. Although he recognizes the inappropriateness of a king, he has also worked with Yahweh so that the one chosen to be king is still Yahweh's king. Through the combination of the lot as the means by which Yahweh's will is revealed, and the prophetic announcement by Samuel, the people give a great cheer, indicating their recognition of Saul as king.

Samuel and the people: 10:25–27

25. Samuel's role is not restricted to announcing Yahweh's choice of king, because he also proclaims the structure of kingship to the people before inscribing it and placing it in the sanctuary. Strikingly, he uses the same term (*mišpāṭ*) as when he addressed the elders in 8:10. If the term is more than accidental, and it is not necessarily one we expect, then it seems the message he inscribes is negative towards kingship. It may be modelled on Samuel's earlier speech, though it presumably added additional items that regulated the role of the king, much as expected by Deut. 17:18, where the king's task on accession is to make a copy of the book of Deuteronomy. But by using this term, the narrator encourages us to see points of continuity between what Samuel writes and his earlier message, though the extent of their overlap cannot be determined (see Eslinger 1985: 352–355; Youngblood 1992: 631–632). However, we should not see this as a form of covenant (against ben-Barak 1979), because that development is one initiated by David (2 Sam. 5:3). Nevertheless, Samuel resolves the tension between what Yahweh permits and what is desirable for his people, and placing the book before Yahweh, presumably in the sanctuary at that time, means it continues to testify about what is expected of both king and people.

26–27. After this, Samuel sent everyone home, and even Saul returned to Gibeah, though a group, possibly the beginning of a standing army in Israel, accompanied him. However, this is unclear, since the term used can refer to wealth or military prowess (see 'Notes'), so we may have a pointer to the fact that it was the wealthy who supported kingship. Sometimes the term can be used with both senses since normally only the wealthy could indulge in the military training necessary to prepare for army service, and it is likely we should understand the term in that way here. The key, however, is that those who went with Saul did so because Yahweh had touched their heart, so that from the beginning Yahweh was working with Saul. But a stark contrast is provided because another group is mentioned in 10:27. These are the so-called 'sons of Belial', a term for social and religious outcasts (see 2:12), though here is perhaps the term the wealthy use for the socially marginal. Where the wealthy have been touched by Yahweh and journey with Saul, this marginal group voices its doubts openly and does not acclaim Saul as might have been expected. Indeed, their question is worked out in the balance of this passage, as the nation has to discover that it is still Yahweh who saves them. There is a profound irony in that these people do not recognize that Yahweh has indeed chosen Saul, and thus stand in opposition to his purposes, and yet their question raises the issue where Saul will be shown to fail. Saul remains as 'one who is silent', but whether this is from a position of strength or weakness is not yet made clear.

Explanation

There is a profound tension lying at the heart of this passage, a tension that is only partly resolved, between what Yahweh agrees to do and what Yahweh desires to do. The request for kingship has not taken Yahweh by surprise, even though the motivation behind it rejected his final sovereignty over the nation. Although kingship was within his purposes, the model sought by the people was not. Samuel's task was to mediate Yahweh's decision so that the people understood the fault of their request, and yet show that Yahweh had still chosen a king for them, a choice made clear through the process by which Saul was chosen. By reminding the people of their initial failure and then restating, and perhaps expanding, the 'justice of the kingship', Samuel is able to provide a mechanism by which the people's request for a king is reshaped so that it has the potential to conform to Yahweh's will for the nation. But this is not an easy solution, and the conflict kingship brings is apparent in the differing responses to Saul after his public recognition, while the narrator's allusion to the taking of Achan casts a dark shadow over Saul. In a sense it is the partial nature of the resolution that is important here since there are many points at which conflicts like this present themselves. The temptation is invariably to seek a solution that only holds to one side of the tension, but what is offered here is a model in which the tension itself is grasped. In this way it can be acknowledged that God's purposes are being resolved, though the procedures themselves may retain something that is provisional. This does not mean that the identification of such things is easy, but it does mean that awareness of the possibilities needs to remain on the agenda.

1 SAMUEL 11

Translation

[1]Nahash the Ammonite went up and besieged Jabesh Gilead, and all the men of Jabesh said to Nahash, 'Make a treaty with us and we shall serve you.' [2]So Nahash the Ammonite said to them 'On this condition I shall make it with you; that I gouge out everyone's right eye, and thus put disgrace upon all Israel.' [3]The elders of Jabesh said to him, 'Leave us for seven days and we shall send messengers throughout Israel's territory. If there is no one to save us, then we shall go out to you.' [4]When the messengers came to Gibeah of Saul they reported the matter in the ears of the people and all the people raised their voice and wept.

⁵But behold, Saul was coming from the field behind the oxen, and Saul said, 'What is the matter with the people that they are weeping?' So they recounted to him the words of the men of Jabesh. ⁶The Spirit of God rushed upon Saul when he heard these words and his anger was kindled greatly. ⁷He took a yoke of oxen and cut them in pieces and sent them through all Israel's territory by the hand of messengers, saying, 'Whoever does not come out after Saul and after Samuel, so shall it be done to his oxen.' Then the dread of Yahweh fell upon the people and they came out as one. ⁸When he mustered them at Bezek, the men of Israel were three hundred thousand and the men of Judah thirty thousand. ⁹They said to the messengers who came, 'Thus shall you say to the men of Jabesh Gilead, "By the time the sun is hot tomorrow you shall have deliverance." ' When the messengers came and reported to the men of Jabesh Gilead, they rejoiced. ¹⁰The men of Jabesh Gilead said, 'Tomorrow, we shall come out to you and you shall do to us whatever is good in your eyes.' ¹¹On the following day, Saul divided the people into three groups, and they came into the midst of the camp during the morning watch and struck the Ammonites until the heat of the day. Those who were left were scattered, and no two of them were left together.

¹²Then the people said to Samuel, 'Who are the ones who said, "Shall Saul reign over us? Bring them that we may put them to death." ' ¹³But Saul said, 'No one shall be put to death this day, because today Yahweh has wrought salvation in Israel.'

¹⁴Samuel said to the people, 'Come, let us go to Gilgal and renew the kingship there.' ¹⁵So all the people went to Gilgal and made Saul king there before Yahweh at Gilgal. They sacrificed peace offerings there before Yahweh, and there Saul and all the Israelites rejoiced greatly.

Notes on the text

1. 4QSamᵃ (cf. NRSV) continues the longer text (see Josephus, *Ant.* 6.5.1) from 10:27 with a brief chronological note that can also be read on the basis of LXX's (see Mommer 1990: 111) 'about a month later'. The same issues apply as at 10:27, so again the shorter MT is preferred (see Kallai 1996).

2. The expected *bĕrît* is absent from most Masoretic MSS, but present in some of LXX. It is probably to be understood by ellipsis, so those texts that include it make explicit what is implicit.

8. LXX has much higher numbers: six hundred thousand (Josephus has seven hundred thousand) and seventy thousand. Although the number for Judah is supported by 4QSamᵃ, the lower numbers are more likely.

9. LXX has the sg. 'He said', retaining the focus on Saul. MT is retained as the more difficult reading.

12. Polzin (1989: 108–110) insists that this quote can be treated only as a question by emendation. But Fokkelman (1993: 581) points out that second-degree direct speech embedded within a question does not need an interrogative particle, and the question is therefore consistent, albeit framed differently, with 10:27 (see GKC §150a). McCarter (1980a: 201) prefers the direct statement 'Saul shall not reign over us', following LXX (and two MT MSS; see Smith 1899: 81). But the text is explicable.

13. LXX, followed by McCarter (1980a: 202), has Samuel in place of Saul, but this attempts to smooth the narrative flow (see Stoebe 1973: 222).

15. LXX has only Samuel offering sacrifices, and then highlights Samuel's participation in the subsequent rejoicing.

Form and structure

An important technique throughout the account of Saul's accession is the use of 'hinge' passages that close off one stage of the narrative while establishing the context for the next. The technique is evident here. The previous chapter closed with the worthless men's question ('How can he save us?', 10:27), before noting that they failed to bring him any gift. The question sets the scene for this chapter when Saul delivers Israel from the Ammonites through the Spirit. This chapter's close (11:14–15) then closes off the demonstration of Saul as king while preparing for Samuel's speech at Gilgal in ch. 12. However, the move around each hinge is not straightforward. From the events of 10:5–8 we expect the Philistines, not the Ammonites, to be the ones from whom Saul delivers Israel, and it is unusual that the worthless men's question sets the scene for us. Having seen deliverance wrought, one might have expected Samuel to speak positively in ch. 12, whereas he offers a stinging rebuke. The narrator prepares for each new development through the hinges, but undercuts our expectations through the following events.

Critical discussion has long been troubled by the apparently multiple accounts of how Saul became king (see Birch 1976: 54–63; Mayes 1978; Mommer 1991: 110–122), though a number of studies have demonstrated the coherence of the whole of 8 – 12 along the lines developed here, understanding the narrative to describe an incremental approach through which Saul's kingship was gradually established (see Long 1989: 183–190). The victory described here confirms the election recounted in 10:17–27, while also answering the question with which that account ended. Uncertainty has also revolved around Samuel's role in 11:12–15, and it is suggested that vv. 14–15 are a redactional insertion to the tradition. But without these verses, we have no context for ch. 12, and although there is a tension between Samuel's assertion that kingship should be renewed and the people's action of making Saul king, it is arguable that this highlights a meaningful contrast in understanding between them (Fokkelman 1993: 487–491).

It should be noted that the story is a salvation narrative. The principal words related to salvation occur a number of times and, taken as a whole, demonstrate that Yahweh is the nation's saviour. Indeed, that Saul acts like a judge in 11:1–11 in bringing Yahweh's salvation rather than as a king may be preparation for Samuel's address in ch. 12. Thus 11:1–11 may be parallel to ch. 7, affirming that Yahweh's salvation is not dependent upon the presence of a king. Therefore, even a text in many ways positive towards Saul may still suggest that the existing model is sufficient for Israel's crises (Gordon 1986: 122). Yet, even as it offers some positive perspectives on Saul, points of uncertainty remain. Is his return to farming indicating that he is still not taking on his assigned role? In addition, there are clear echoes of the account of the Levite who chopped his concubine into twelve pieces to initiate the Benjaminite war in Judg. 19:29–30 (something that ultimately led to intermarriage between the inhabitants of Gibeah and Jabesh Gilead in Judg. 21), which is hardly an auspicious background. Even as the narrator tells of Saul's successes, are there hints that all is not as positive as it seems, or are Saul's actions a positive counterpoint to that older narrative (Eslinger 1985: 367)? Either conclusion may be drawn, but the hints aligning Saul with negative elements from Judges make it more likely that critical elements are again to the fore. Yet this narrative also recounts the final evidence of Yahweh's appointment of Saul as king. It emphasizes that Yahweh gave the people what they requested, even though their request at heart rejected Yahweh's reign. This in turn highlights the problems caused by having the people's monarchy rather than the one initiated by Yahweh.

Comment

The deliverance of Jabesh Gilead: 11:1–11

1–2. Nahash's assault on Jabesh Gilead represented a serious crisis for the nascent state, especially since Saul is not said to have undertaken actions to ensure the establishment of an Israelite government. Following his election by lot, Saul simply returned to the family farm. By assaulting Jabesh Gilead (about 22 miles south of the Sea of Galilee), Nahash was claiming territory east of the Jordan, an area the Ammonites had claimed during the time of Jephthah (Judg. 10:17–18). Jabesh Gilead also had a specific link to the tribe of Benjamin, most notably by providing four hundred virgins for surviving Benjaminite soldiers after the Benjaminite war (Judg. 21), an association strengthened through Saul's evocation of the Levite who dismembered his concubine when summoning of the Israelite tribes (v. 7). There are again continued allusions to the dreadful events of Judg. 19 – 21 and their motto that 'in those days, there was no king in Israel' (Judg. 19:1; 21:25). These allusions provide negative background to Saul's early achievements that portray him positively. Jabesh Gilead maintained its close link with Saul's house after his death by reclaiming his body for

burial (1 Sam. 31:11–13), so references to the city are boundary markers
for Saul's reign. Jabesh Gilead is where Saul's reign was established, but
also where the kingdom must pass to David. The immediate crisis was how
to deal with Nahash's assault. The city's initial response was to offer a
covenant with Nahash, a relationship involving subordination by Jabesh
Gilead, but that would also bind Nahash. But Nahash's offer of all having
their right eye gouged out does not seem like the terms sought! Nahash was
of the opinion that one-eyed soldiers were less effective than those with
two, and Josephus claims the shield obscured the left eye – so the right eye
was vital for battle (*Ant.* 6.5.1), though the reliability of this is uncertain.
The important point is that Nahash intended to bring disgrace upon all
Israel through his superior power demonstrated on the Jabeshites.

3–4. In response to Nahash's conditions, the city elders requested the
opportunity to send messengers throughout Israel to seek a 'saviour',
which in Judg. 3:9 and 15 refers to a judge and in 10:19 is Yahweh, though
also preparing for the possibility of an answer to the worthless fellows'
question in 10:27. Nahash's response to the request to have seven days to
seek a saviour is odd, but may reflect his immense confidence that he will
either defeat the Israelites easily or that no one will come and victory
will be achieved without an extended siege. However, the wording of the
request from Jabesh is crafty in its formulation. The verb 'come out' (*yṣ'*)
can mean to 'come out in surrender' or 'come out in battle'. The ambiguity
inherent in it represents a crucial irony, as Nahash assumes the former
meaning and is duly taken in, or else he would not have permitted the
messengers to depart. Although the elders had requested the option of
sending messengers throughout Israel, the only ones mentioned are those
who came to Gibeah of Saul. Given that 'Gibeah' simply means 'hill' and
may refer to several sites (note 10:5, 10), the addition of 'of Saul' stresses
that the messengers were specifically looking for Saul, and that Gibeah was
not simply one place on their journey. When they arrived, the messengers
recounted the offer to the people generally. Their response of weeping
parallels Judg. 2:4–5, suggesting that the people saw Nahash's actions as
discipline from Yahweh.

5–8. When the messengers reached Saul, he was working as a farmer,
indicating he had not yet acted to establish the monarchy as an effective
model of government, though in view of Samuel's listing of the 'justice of
the king' (8:10–18) this is not necessarily a criticism. Nevertheless, Saul
has not carried out the directives 10:5–8 led us to expect. His action here is
striking. While the rest of Israel weep, Saul responds by slaughtering his ox
and sending its dismembered pieces around Israel, an action reminiscent of
the events that precipitated the Benjaminite war (Judg. 19:29). There are
significant echoes of that narrative, which lamented the lack of kingship,
but what is decisively different here is that Saul has been elected as king
and this action is related to the work of the Spirit of God (though Bergen
1996: 136 notes a possibly implied criticism in that this is not the 'Spirit of

Yahweh' as with all of the judges, as only Balaam previously received the Spirit of God), something that anticipates success. This is the second account of the Spirit rushing upon Saul (see 10:10), though that the Spirit was only temporarily with him prepares for the Spirit's departure in 16:14. Attached to the pieces of the ox are the words of a curse from Saul, asking that what had happened to the ox happen to the ox of anyone who did not follow Saul and Samuel into battle at Jabesh. The mention of Samuel suggests that Saul did not see himself acting independently as king. Rather, the king acts under the prophet's leadership. Saul's actions are led by the Spirit, so it is no surprise that the 'dread of Yahweh' came upon the nation, with the result that the nation as a whole came out after Saul. They were mustered at Bezek, a couple of miles west of the Jordan, and close enough to Jabesh Gilead to enable the attack without drawing unwanted attention. The army was made up of two distinct groups: three hundred 'thousands' from Israel and thirty 'thousands' from Judah. Probably, we are to understand the 'thousands' as the largest military unit rather than an actual thousand people (see 'Comment' on 4:2 and 10:19), but the division in numbers between Israel and Judah shows that the separation of the Israelite state after Solomon's death had long roots.

9–11. The import of the muster was expressed in a message to the residents of Jabesh Gilead, that on the next day there would be the deliverance for the city, a statement received by them with joy. They repeated their message to Nahash, retaining the fundamental ambiguity about whether they would come out in surrender or battle. Of course, the additional 'You shall do to us whatever is good in your eyes' suggests to Nahash that surrender is what is intended, but if the reference is to battle, the only thing he will see as 'good' will be to fight. The battle is recounted briefly in v. 11. Following a traditional strategy and dividing his forces into three groups, Saul overcomes the Ammonites after launching his assault early in the morning, achieving victory relatively early in the day. The battle can be recounted briefly because it is not the narrative's main concern. Rather, it has answered the question of 10:27, demonstrating that Saul can be the king the people have requested.

Kingship's renewal: 11:12–15

12–13. The victory's importance is established by the question posed to Samuel in v. 12. It recognizes that there are no longer grounds for opposing Saul's elevation to the throne, and asks that those who opposed Saul be put to death. But is this petty vengeance or an attempt to apply the law on blasphemy, since Saul is Yahweh's anointed king whose election is now demonstrated? The narrator leaves this unresolved. Saul rejects this request on the grounds that it is not an appropriate response to Yahweh's salvation, and therefore rules that the law not be applied. More importantly, we now have the first instance of Saul's acting independently of Samuel. The people have approached Samuel, but it is Saul who acts. At the same time, in making this decision at what seems to be the high point of Saul's success, questions about him are raised. If the request for the execution of the doubters applies sacral law, does Saul have the right to overrule it because it may make him more popular? Or is he a wise and just king? The narrative answers neither of these questions, but they lay the foundation for Samuel's speech in the next chapter.

14–15. Samuel responds by summoning the people to Gilgal for kingship's renewal. This perhaps recognizes that monarchy is really present only once Saul begins to act as a king should, and that this needs to be acknowledged. Moreover, there was previously opposition, but with its removal it is now possible to speak of renewal in the sense that the whole nation now supports Saul (Eslinger 1985: 378). But the choice of site is striking since 10:8 indicated that Saul should go to Gilgal and wait there for Samuel, and there is no record of this happening. Hence the people return to Gilgal where, amid great rejoicing and the sacrifice of peace offerings, they make Saul king. This causes some difficulty on the assumption that Saul is king already and because Samuel spoke only of renewing the king. However, at no prior point have the people actually acknowledged Saul as king, and so what is an act of renewal for Samuel is an act of initiation for the people. In spite of this, the answer to the pressing question of 'Can this man save us?' is 'No'. Saul is not the saviour, but if God is prepared to save through a king as he has previously through the judges, then the institution has hope, provided it is recognized that divine authority is always over that of the king. But whether this is what will happen remains to be seen.

Explanation

Mizpah is where Yahweh demonstrates he has chosen Saul as king, but Jabesh Gilead is where Saul demonstrates this, so Gilgal can become the place where the renewal of his kingship is also the point at which the people truly make him king. The question of the doubters in 10:27 appears to have been decisively answered. But has it? While this narrative is a salvation story, it is a reminder that God alone offers salvation for his people, though he may choose to do so through his people and servants. But it suggests that salvation does not reside in the person of his servants; they are instead how his salvation is revealed. While the people wanted a king to lead them in battle, it is in reality still God who provided the lead, this time through the Spirit's presence with Saul. But even though it indicates that salvation is achieved through his servants, the king's role is rendered questionable by Saul's actions, especially through the ambiguous allusions Judg. 19 – 21. The Spirit has provided the deliverance, and even Saul himself realizes this in 11:12–13. But his reaction raises new questions. Has Saul begun to move towards a monarchy structured like that of the nations, whereas in reality the salvation that comes through him occurs when he acts more like a judge? This story offers hope for salvation through God's servants, but implicitly criticizes any model of power that seeks, even through apparently good means, to turn the purposes of God to one's own benefit, because God alone remains his people's saviour.

1 SAMUEL 12:1–25

Translation

[1]Samuel said to all Israel, 'Behold, I have listened to your voice, to all you said to me, and have set a king over you. [2]Now, behold, the king walks before you, but I am old and grey; yet behold, my sons are with you. I have walked before you from my youth until this day. [3]Here I am, testify against me in the presence of Yahweh and his anointed. Whose ox have I taken? Whose donkey have I taken? Whom have I defrauded? Whom have I oppressed? From whose hand have I taken a bribe that I may avert my eyes with it? I shall restore it.' [4]They said, 'You have not defrauded and you have not oppressed us. You have not taken anything from the hand of anyone.' [5]He said to them, 'Yahweh is a witness against you, and his anointed is witness this day, that you have not found anything in my hand.' They said, 'He is witness.'

[6]Samuel said to the people, 'Yahweh, it was, who worked with Moses and Aaron and brought up your ancestors from the land of Egypt. [7]Now, present yourselves, and I shall present you with evidence before Yahweh concerning all the righteous acts Yahweh has wrought for you and your ancestors. [8]When Jacob entered Egypt and the Egyptians oppressed them, your ancestors cried out to Yahweh, and Yahweh sent Moses and Aaron and they brought out your ancestors from Egypt and made them dwell in this place. [9]But they forgot Yahweh their God and he sold them into the hand of Sisera, commander of the host of Hazor, and into the hand of the Philistines, and into the hand of the king of Moab, and they waged war against them. [10]Then they cried out to Yahweh and said, "We have sinned, because we have forsaken Yahweh and served the Baalim and the Ashtaroth. But now, deliver us from the hand of our enemies and we shall serve you." [11]Yahweh sent Jerubaal, Barak, Jephthah and Samuel, and he delivered you from the power of your enemies round about, and you dwelt securely. [12]When you saw that Nahash, king of the Ammonites came against you, you said to me, "No, but a king shall reign over us." But Yahweh your God was your king. [13]Now, behold the king whom you have chosen, for whom you asked. Behold, Yahweh has appointed a king over you. [14]If you fear Yahweh and serve him and listen to his voice and do not rebel against Yahweh's commands, that is, if both you and the king who reigns over you follow Yahweh your God ... [15]but if you do not listen to Yahweh's voice and rebel against Yahweh's command, then Yahweh's hand will be against you and your ancestors.

[16]'Indeed, now, present yourselves and see this great thing Yahweh will do before your eyes. [17]Is it not the wheat harvest today? I shall call to Yahweh that he may bring forth thunder and rain. Then know and see that great is your wickedness which you have done in Yahweh's eyes in asking for a king for yourselves.' [18]So Samuel called to Yahweh and he brought forth thunder and rain that day. And all the people greatly feared Yahweh and Samuel.

[19]All the people said to Samuel, 'Intercede for your servants with Yahweh your God that we may not die, because we have added to all our sins the evil of asking for a king for ourselves.' [20]Samuel said to the people, 'Do not fear. You have done all this evil, yet do not turn aside from Yahweh, but serve Yahweh with all your heart. [21]And do not turn aside, for it is after worthless things that do not profit and do not save, because they are worthless things. [22]For Yahweh will not forsake his people for his great name's sake, because Yahweh was pleased to make you his people. [23]As for me, far be it from me to sin before Yahweh by ceasing to intercede for you, and I shall instruct you in the good and upright way. [24]Only fear Yahweh and serve him in truth with all your heart, for consider what great things he has done for you. [25]But if you still do wickedly, both you and your king will be swept away.'

Notes on the text

3. The textual traditions are diverse here. The variety suggests we have exegetical explanations of the text rather than genuine variants, attempting to make explicit what is implicit in a terse MT.

5. Reading the pl. 'they said' with many MSS, LXX adds 'the people' to make clear the subject of the sg. verb.

6. Most translations interpret '*śh* as 'appoint', but this struggles with the relative pronoun, and is often linked with a repetition of the theme of witness from LXX (e.g. NRSV, ESV), and is contrary to normal usage (Driver 1913: 71). But if *'et* is the preposition 'with' in the first two instances (see Deut. 10:19 and Ruth 2:19 for parallels), then no emendation is needed.

7. The ni. cohortative of *špṭ* is difficult to translate (cf. NIV, NRSV, ESV). The sense is 'plead' or 'enter into judgment', though elsewhere this is usually with God (Jer. 2:35; Ezek. 20:35–36; 38:22). The longer LXX text, supported by NRSV 'and I shall declare to you', is a clarifying expansion.

8. Following LXX, 'and the Egyptians oppressed them'. Many MSS read the sg. of *yšb*, aware that the pl. may attribute the settlement to Moses and Aaron, but the pl. indicates the process began with them.

11. Bedan's identity has puzzled interpreters, while Samuel's presence is odd in a list describing activities of the past, though defence of LXX's 'Samson' (e.g. Smith 1899: 87) on the basis of Samuel's modesty is unpersuasive given 1 Sam. 7:2–14. Jacobson (1992, 1994) defended Abdon (derived from Judg. 12:13–14). This is orthographically plausible, but J. Day's criticisms (1993) remain impressive. LXX reads Barak for Bedan, but may be accidentally correct, as Tsumura (1995) has shown that Bedan may be a phonetic realization of Barak, reflecting the narrator's pronunciation. This remains the best option in spite of Frolov's (2007a) defence of the authenticity of Bedan.

14. Most versions provide a positive apodosis (such as ESV, 'it will be well') presuming this is required by the aposiopesis (GKC §167a). The absence of an apodosis is significant; and it is better to retain the aposiopesis's ambiguity, as its function must be determined in each case (see 2 Sam. 5:8; 23:17). The alternative, that the apodosis begins with *whytm* (e.g. Boecker 1969: 77–79; Youngblood 1992: 648), is unsatisfactory because it is tautologous. However, the initial waw is explicative (GKC §154a [note b]).

15. Stoebe (1973: 234) defends MT (cf. NIV) against the dominant trend of following LXX with 'king' for 'ancestors', though it is not a comparison, as he argues.

21. McCarter (1980a: 212) regards *kî* as incomprehensible, and most EVV omit it, but with Fokkelman (1993: 530) it is the companion to the *min* of v. 20. The unusual use of *tôhû* cannot be limited to idols, but refers to all temptations to deviance from covenant (Fokkelman 1993: 530). With B. T. Arnold (2004), the verse quotes from an ancient source, perhaps as a new application of polemic against Baal worship.

Form and structure

As we have noted, in dealing with monarchy's institution, the text's basic attitude is negative towards monarchy initiated by the people themselves. Such a conclusion stands against one branch of critical orthodoxy that argues that chs. 7 – 12 contain a mixture of texts, some that are for kingship and some against (see Birch 1976: 63–74 and Mommer 1991: 122–133 for evaluations). Rather, whatever the prehistory of the textual units, the finished text represents a critical view of Israel's desire to have a king like the nations. Yet, although this means rejecting Yahweh's reign, kingship is also a gift from him. The people sin in asking for a king, yet Yahweh chooses to give them one. It is this paradox that has often driven critics to presume we have divergent sources that have not been completely homogenized. The presence of such a paradox also leads some to question Yahweh and Samuel's righteousness in this (esp. Eslinger 1985: 383–396 and Polzin 1989: 117–124). If they are critical of the move towards a king, how can they therefore be trusted? That is to say, even if one dissolves the paradox, one is still left with unanswered questions about Yahweh's trustworthiness through it all.

The solution lies in understanding the ambiguity inherent in Israel's initial request, a fundamentally flawed request that set human initiative against what Yahweh was providing. It is because of this that the nation's sin will be exposed. The people asked for a king like the nations, a king whose authority and structure of rule would be absolute. We have begun to see the possibility of such a pattern emerging in Saul's reign following the deliverance of Jabesh Gilead, though throughout the account of his rise the narrator has maintained an ambiguous posture; there is enough in Saul that may be positive if employed properly, and yet hints are also present of a deeply flawed man. We do not yet know if he will rise above his flaws or if they will be the snares that trap him. Crucially, Yahweh is unopposed to kingship as such, and the reality is that where the king keeps the covenant, and thus acknowledges Yahweh's greater reign and is thus a king not like the nations, there is hope. Thus Yahweh's righteousness is shown, for he responds to the people's request, but he has simultaneously shown he does not accept their basic premise. Kingship is God's gift, but this king is one he has permitted, not one he desires. Samuel's position is more complex, and it is essential to the narrator's presentation of him that we see this. But it falls to him in this speech to recapitulate what has happened so far and provide a way forward, because a renewal of kingship (1 Sam. 11:14) is taking place. Kingship has been established, but it needs renewal to conform to Yahweh's will.

All these themes come to their conclusion in this chapter. In form, it represents an address by Samuel, one that is closely akin to those of Moses and Joshua (Deuteronomy as a whole; Josh. 24), which incorporates a number of elements from covenant-making, though without actually forming a covenant as such. These similarities mean it is often interpreted as Samuel's 'farewell address', but this is too limited. It is not that Samuel is going away. Indeed, not only will he play a vital role in a number of subsequent narratives, but this address closes with an assurance of his continued involvement in the nation's life as teacher and intercessor. The importance of the address is not to be found in Samuel himself, but rather in how it brings to a conclusion the move towards kingship and lays out the choices kingship has to make. It is, above all else, a call to covenant faithfulness, faithfulness to be expressed by both king and people.

Comment

Declaration of Samuel's innocence: 12:1–5

1–2. Samuel is about to declare the nature of the nation's sin. Samuel's approach anticipates Jesus' dictum about removing the speck from one's own eye (Matt. 7:4). Before outlining Israel's sin, he asks the people to confirm his innocence in matters where he might have abused his power as prophet, priest and judge. Accordingly, there is an abundance of legal language in the dialogue. Such language is necessary if Samuel is to demonstrate he has the right to raise the issues addressed in vv. 6–15 as a precursor to kingship's renewal. By their testimony about Samuel, the people confirm he has provided an appropriate model of leadership under

Yahweh, where leadership represents tasks done, not the office claimed. This contrasts with the behaviour Samuel earlier described concerning the king (8:10–17). The passage's setting is not specified within this chapter, but since 11:14–15 acts as a hinge between chs. 11 and 12, it is still Gilgal. When Samuel begins, he affirms he has listened to the people's request and appointed a king for them, though this is consistent with Yahweh's directive at 8:22. Samuel has acted appropriately as judge and prophet, one standing between the people and Yahweh. This then prepares for his priestly role as intercessor from v. 19 onwards. More than that, the king is present, apparently as witness to the quasi-legal proceedings initiated, though having mentioned the king, Samuel largely ignores Saul for the balance of the chapter. Samuel points to his age as a factor necessitating change, though it is linked to the fact that he has lived before the community since he was a lad (alluding to his time at Shiloh). In addition, the character of his sons is known, though Samuel does not mention their faults from 8:1–3. Whatever their failings, Samuel is still someone the community knows well since his leadership has been conducted in the public eye, which is how the king is to live. Samuel provides leadership's benchmark, even if the limited reference to his sons tacitly acknowledges they have become like Eli's sons.

3–5. Using legal language, Samuel raises a series of rhetorical questions, a series that is consciously before the anointed and Yahweh. The dominant word here is 'take', the word that was so central to the description of the king's conduct in 8:10–17. Where Samuel saw the king as someone who 'took' from the people, he here asks them to affirm he has not taken from anyone, including the receipt of any bribes, and that he has always acted with justice and integrity. The point is that if one person can challenge him on these grounds, then he has no right to raise the issues central to the subsequent discussion. Even after the people affirm Samuel's innocence, he again turns to legal formulations, affirming that both the anointed and Yahweh are witnesses against the people if they prove false in this matter, and once again the people affirm their position. Being innocent of the potential abuses of kingship, Samuel then addresses the nation's sin in asking for a king.

Evidence of Israel's sin: 12:6–18

6–7. With Samuel's right to speak established, we enter the heart of his address, when he accuses the people of sin in their choice of a king. His emphasis is on Yahweh's provision in working with Moses and Aaron as leaders for their ancestors, and, more importantly, in bringing them up from Egypt. Yahweh has provided for his people and overcome enemies. Against this background, Samuel presents the evidence against the nation. This returns to words based around the root *špt*, also prominent in ch. 8, with the people's request for a king to 'judge' them (see 'Notes'). Samuel insists that their history judges them when seen in the context of Yahweh's actions for them. This is why they are called to present themselves, as those required to make their defence.

8–11. Salvation history, summed up in the exodus and deliverance under the judges, is central to Samuel's point, though like Amos 2:9–12 salvation history is presented to show how Israel has failed in spite of Yahweh's faithfulness. Yahweh has responded to his people's cry and brought deliverance in the face of overwhelming odds, thus undercutting the need for a king. This is emphasized through the exodus, beginning with Jacob's descent into Egypt and the nation's cry, to which Yahweh responded by sending Moses and Aaron to deliver them, deliverance that eventually brought them into the land. But Yahweh's provision had not ended with the exodus. Instead, the nation's sinfulness in forgetting him meant the people had to be disciplined through other nations before Yahweh responded to their cry and confession of sin and raised up a delivering judge. Thus Samuel points to events described in Judges through a list of some judges. The list's structure is confusing since Samuel does not refer to them in the order in which they are recorded, while the names of the judges he mentions are unclear (see 'Notes'), but a common feature among them as we reconstruct the text is that other than Barak they were engaged in conflicts associated with Baal (Judg. 10:6–7; 1 Sam. 7:2–3), a theme highlighted by calling Gideon by his less-well-known name of Jerubbaal (Judg. 6:28–32; 7:1). Barak is required because of the reference to Sisera in Judg. 4. Samuel's speech is not a formal history up to this point; it is an impressionistic account pointing to Yahweh's consistency in responding to his people's cry when they face need.

12. The nature of the people's sin in choosing a king is now driven home. With the events surrounding the invasion by Nahash the Ammonite, the people had chosen a different path, that of appointing a king, an action that rejected Yahweh's kingship. It is difficult to reconcile the presentation of the data here with the events of 10 – 11, though perhaps not as difficult as Klein (1983: 113) suggests. According to these traditions, Saul was privately anointed before this was publicly acknowledged. The people then confirmed the kingship after Nahash's defeat. Here, however, Samuel seems to suggest it was Nahash's invasion that triggered the request for a king. However, 1 Sam. 8 presupposes some sort of threat, and since the Philistines were subdued by Samuel, they cannot be the dominant threat. Nahash was a raider before the events of ch. 11, so he could well be the threat in ch. 8, a possibility strengthened by the fact that Jabesh Gilead is not mentioned here. If this reconstruction is correct, it was the threat of Nahash's raids that triggered the request for a king, and this in turn meant that Saul's defeating him provided the public proof that was sought, though Saul's test was meant to be with the Philistines (10:5–8). From Samuel's point of view the whole approach was fundamentally flawed, because Yahweh had already shown that he was the nation's king.

13–15. With this clarified, Samuel again points to the king, emphasizing that he is the king for whom the people have asked, the king they have chosen, rather than being the one Yahweh will initiate. Yahweh, however, has also given the king to the people, for this could not have happened without his approval, but this kingship was not his choice, even though he chose the king. It is here where we see most clearly that Samuel seeks to renew kingship, because he provides a means by which this kingship can be integrated into Yahweh's purposes. The act of asking for a king was sinful, but Yahweh has graciously provided the king. The question for Israel was whether they would live under Yahweh's greater reign, which is being renewed through the renewal of kingship (see Vannoy 1978: 178). If they did, there was a means by which the king's presence would not be problematic, though by withholding the final affirmation of what could be achieved at the end of v. 14, Samuel adds a degree of ambivalence as to what Yahweh will do. The hint of something positive is there, but there is also the warning in v. 15 of what will happen if the nation does not integrate kingship into a theological system structured around Yahweh's reign. It is this choice that provides the means by which kingship can be renewed. Curiously, the final action that Yahweh could enact against Israel if kingship was not integrated was against them and their ancestors. Such a formula has seemed odd to many (see 'Notes'), but it seems Samuel is deliberately blurring the generational distinctions, showing once again that the people's decision matches a pattern established earlier (see Fokkelman 1993: 523).

16–18. Having introduced the possibility of a future for Israel with a king who reigns under Yahweh, Samuel presents a sign to authenticate his claims. This is important since it demonstrates Yahweh's commitment to his message. The people are not simply called to observation, but also to consideration and reflection. The nature of the sign depends upon the weather conditions of Palestine. The wheat harvest takes place in May–June, during the dry season when rain is virtually unknown (Eybers 1988: 138–143). Thunder and rain are completely unexpected. The sign was terrifying, not only because of the natural fear many had of thunderstorms, but because the rain could damage the harvest, causing some grain to rot. Yahweh responded to Samuel's call by sending the storm, including thunder (not the same word as 2:10), leading to the concluding statement that the people greatly feared Yahweh and Samuel. The nature of this fear is not explored. The fear of God can be understood positively in the OT, but here it may be more than holy awe since it is also fear of Samuel.

Samuel as intercessor: 12:19–25

19. The people's fear after the storm leads also to concern that Yahweh is about to act against them. It is no surprise that the people ask Samuel to intercede on their behalf, recognizing that in addition to their other unstated sins they have compounded their evil in asking for a king. At this point, they still see their situation outside the possibility hinted at by vv. 14–15, because their understanding is based on the model of kingship they have initiated.

20–23. Samuel's reply restates the structure of a renewed kingship, refocusing the people on to the possibility of this model. Even though this chapter is opposed to the nation's model of kingship, describing it as evil they have done, it is not finally negative in what it seeks because its task is one of renewal. With the people's sin acknowledged, the closing emphasis is on national hope, hope found in faithfulness to Yahweh, so that a renewed kingship provides a focus for the nation to express its faithfulness. Thus Samuel counsels them not to be afraid, for, although they have sinned, there remains the possibility of a fresh start with Yahweh, one where the people can live in faithfulness, not turning away, but giving themselves in faithful service. This is the choice laid before them. The alternative is then described, somewhat surprisingly, in terms of idolatry (see 'Notes'). Instead of serving Yahweh, the people may be tempted to pursue idols, though here they are described as 'nothing', for Samuel recognizes that the idols have no separate reality. Although we may expect mention of the king, it seems that kingship initiated outside Yahweh's intent is treated under the broader rubric of idolatry. Against this possible choice by the people, Samuel stresses Yahweh's faithfulness. Idols, and by extension kings, cannot save, but Yahweh will not forsake his people.

23–25. In response to the people's request, Samuel can do nothing else but intercede for them. In fact, failing to do so would be sin on Samuel's part, though intercession is linked with his role as the nation's teacher. However, the responsibility still lies with the people to serve Yahweh faithfully, and so, in language reminiscent of Deut. 10:12, Samuel calls them to faithfulness. This faithfulness is marked by sober reflection on history and present experience, because both become part of the means by which the nation can learn about faithfulness to Yahweh alone. A king cannot supplant Yahweh, but a renewed kingship can be effective provided both king and people understand their limits. But when kingship moves outside this model, there is no future for either king or people.

Explanation

Samuel's task here is complex but centred on the theme of renewal. Kingship was part of Yahweh's plan, but the elders' actions in 1 Sam. 8 had initiated a different approach towards kingship, one where the king's eminence was the point stressed. Saul's rise emphasized that Yahweh was still prepared to offer a king, and Saul was the one Yahweh had chosen. At the same time, there are hints of Saul's potential fallibility, though the significance of these becomes apparent only in the ensuing chapters. Taken as a whole, therefore, chs. 8 – 12 are neither pro- nor anti-monarchic, though Samuel's task in this chapter is to articulate a model by which kingship can genuinely succeed. That is why it is crucial we recognize it as an account of the renewal of kingship, because it describes a process by which a flawed model may be workable, provided king and people understand it is still Yahweh who rules. This represents a seismic shift from before when Yahweh's rule was actualized through figures such as Moses, Joshua and the judges directly called by Yahweh. Now the civil aspects of rule are carried out through a king, while the theological elements are defined by prophets such as Samuel, though the overlap between their roles will itself be a trigger for future conflict between king and prophet. Each side of this structure needs to understand the other's position. The prophet does not control the civil realm, nor the king the sacral. Each has a specific role that has to complement and balance the other. In effect, this speech becomes the point where Samuel cedes his civil authority as a judge, but the king must cede any sacral authority. The choice the people must make is to adopt this as a form of constitutional monarchy where power within certain spheres is separated and thus limited. Although Saul is never named (though there are plays on his name in vv. 17, 19), the possibility for him to succeed and rise above his limitations remains, because there is a broad pattern of obedience within which he may walk (against Gunn 1980a: 65).

Samuel thus speaks powerfully to the needs of the people in his own time, but through Samuel the narrator speaks to later generations. The exiles knew the experience of being swept away along with their king. They knew the sense of pain and loss their sin had brought, and that even though Yahweh had chosen to work with kingship, it was not finally kings who saved. Only Yahweh could do that. But this chapter is not finally condemnation; it is gospel, good news, because it affirms God's commitment to renew those who turn to him, recognizing their sin, and who seek to serve him faithfully. What Samuel affirms is that the God of the Bible is a God of beginnings, a God who saves and delights to summon his people to come once more and join with him. There is thus always hope in repentance and faith.

1 SAMUEL 13

Translation

[1]Saul was [ ] years old when he became king, and he reigned over Israel for two years. [2]Saul chose three thousand men of Israel for himself; two thousand were with Saul at Michmash and in the hill country of Bethel, and a thousand were with Jonathan at Gibeah of Benjamin. The rest of the people he sent back to their tents. [3]Jonathan struck the Philistine garrison that was at Geba, and the Philistines heard. And Saul blew the trumpet throughout the land, saying, 'Let the Hebrews heed.' [4]All Israel heard it said that Saul had struck the Philistine garrison and that Israel

had become odious among the Philistines. So the people were called out after Saul at Gilgal. [5]The Philistines were assembled for battle with Israel – thirty thousand chariots and six thousand horsemen, and an army that was like the sand on the seashore for number. They came up and camped at Michmash, which is east of Beth Aven. [6]When the Israelites saw that their position was difficult and that the people were pressed, they hid themselves in caves and thickets, under rocks and in tombs and cisterns. [7]Some Hebrews crossed the Jordan to the land of Gad and Gilead, but Saul remained at Gilgal, and all the people followed him trembling. [8]He waited seven days, the time that Samuel had set, but Samuel did not come to Gilgal, and the people were scattering from him.

[9]Then Saul said, 'Bring me the burnt offering and the peace offerings.' And he offered up the burnt offering. [10]As soon as he finished offering the burnt offering, behold, Samuel came, and Saul went out to meet and greet him. [11]Samuel said, 'What have you done?' Saul answered, 'When I saw that the people were scattering from me, and you had not come within the appointed days and that the Philistines were assembling in Michmash, [12]I said, "Now the Philistines will come down against me at Gilgal, and I have not sought Yahweh's favour." So I restrained myself and offered up the burnt offering.' [13]Samuel said to Saul, 'You have acted foolishly. You have not kept the command of Yahweh your God that he commanded you, for now Yahweh would have established your kingdom over Israel for ever. [14]Instead, your kingdom shall not be confirmed. Yahweh has sought out for himself a man after his own heart and Yahweh has commanded him to be leader over his people, because you have not kept what Yahweh commanded you.'

[15]Samuel arose and went up from Gilgal to go his own way, but the rest of the people went up after Saul to face the men of war. They came from Gilgal to Gibeah of Benjamin. Saul numbered the men found with him, about six hundred men. [16]Then Saul and his son Jonathan and the people who remained with them stayed in Geba of Benjamin while the Philistines were encamped at Michmash. [17]Raiding parties went out from the Philistine camp in three companies – one group turned toward Ophrah in the land of Shual, [18]another turned toward Beth Horon and another turned toward the border overlooking the Valley of Zeboim towards the wilderness.

[19]A metalworker was not to be found in all Israel because the Philistines had said, 'Otherwise the Hebrews might make swords or a spears.' [20]So all Israel would go down to the Philistines to sharpen their ploughshares, mattocks, axes or sickles. [21]The price was two-thirds of a shekel for ploughshares and mattocks and a third of a shekel for axes and setting goads. [22]So it was on the day of the battle that no sword or spear was found in the hand of all the people with Saul and Jonathan, but they were found with Saul and his son Jonathan. [23]And the Philistine garrison went out to the pass of Michmash.

Notes on the text

1. The verse is lacking in LXX[B], and the MT is a notable crux, though linguistically tenable. However, both numbers are suspect. The first may

read that Saul was 'one year old when he became king'. Though clearly unacceptable, the usual suggestions of thirty or forty are essentially guesswork. We have to assume a number has fallen out, in spite of the endeavours of many (going back to Tg) to retain MT. The 'two year' reign assigned to him seems too brief for describing his total reign (NIV's forty-two years draws on Acts 13:21; cf. Josephus *Ant.* 6.14.9, though in 10.8.4 it is twenty years!). Noth (1960: 176) defends two years, arguing that this agrees with the structure of the Deuteronomistic History. Two years is probably the correct reading, but describes the period of his reign only before his rejection in 15:26, though he was king de facto for a longer period. 'Another' two years (Kreuzer 1996) is improbable.

2. LXX[L] has three thousand.

3. Hebr. *něṣîb* refers to either a Philistine 'prefect' or a 'garrison'. Since a prefect would have a force with him, the emphasis is on the garrison's presence.

6. Hebr. *ḥăwāḥîm* (thickets) is often emended to *ḥôrîm* (holes; see Driver 1913: 99), but this is unnecessary (see McCarter 1980a: 226 and Gordon 1986: 133).

8. Reading *śām* after 'Samuel' with a number of MSS. It appears to have fallen out through homoioarchton. The alternative, *'āmar*, is supported by a few MSS and LXX, but is less easily explained.

10. Although *brk* normally means 'to bless', it sometimes refers to a greeting stronger than *šālôm*. See Gen. 47:7; 2 Kgs 4:29; 10:15.

12. Most versions translate the hith. of *'pq* as 'force'. But the verb does not have this sense in its other six occurrences, so 'restrain' (its normal sense) is preferred (see Long 1989: 89).

13. With many MSS and the versions, reading *'al* for *'el*.

15. MT appears to have suffered a long haplography between the two references to Gilgal. Translation follows LXX.

19. Hebr. *ḥārāš* (metalworker) is traditionally 'blacksmith', but refers to a range of craft skills. The Philistines had an early advantage in iron production, but it seems the reference is broader and includes control of access to bronze. Although Israel was in the Bronze Age, the verse seems to suggest that the Philistines controlled access even to that metal.

20. MT repeats 'ploughshare', but LXX gives 'sickle'.

21. Older versions transliterated *pîm*, but archaeological evidence indicates it is equivalent to two-thirds of a shekel (Báez-Camargo 1980: 318–319).

Form and structure

The events described in ch. 12 established a framework where Saul's kingship might have been successful, a framework where the king understood that he was theologically under Yahweh's rule, and that on such matters Yahweh's authority was mediated through a prophet, in this case Samuel. This was the goal of the renewal at Gilgal since it resolved the ambiguity inherent in the request for a king by making clear that Israel's king was 'like the nations' (see 'Comment' on 8:5) only in that he represented political and military leadership, but Yahweh's greater kingship had to be recognized. Thus the kingdom had been renewed. But an unresolved element from Saul's rise to power remains, which is that in 10:5–8 Samuel told Saul to 'do what his hand found to do' when he went to Gilgal, which in context was to attack a Philistine garrison. The parallel from Judg. 9:33 makes clear that this refers to military action, and although Saul engages with the Ammonites because of Nahash's actions (11:1–11), he has not done so against the Philistines, even though 9:16 indicates that Saul's role was to deal with them (see Miscall 1986: 87). Although the narrative accepts that Saul's rise can be reconciled with Yahweh's reign, Saul has not yet demonstrated acceptance of this. Indeed, it is notable that although the dread of Yahweh came upon the people because of Saul's slaughter of the oxen in 11:7, Saul did not refer to Yahweh, even though his actions were inspired by the Spirit of God. Saul is thus at a point where he needs to demonstrate his commitment to the structure of government developed in Samuel's speech and the unresolved Philistine problem. Hence the narrator moves readers forward to explore the direction Saul's reign will take, knowing that the future of the monarchy cannot be resolved until this question is addressed.

As becomes clear, Saul fails to adhere to the conditions established. We also see the tension between Saul and Samuel hinted at by the earlier narratives in Samuel's response to Saul's sacrifice in preparation for battle. These events prepare for the contrast between Saul and Jonathan that is developed as this story continues in ch. 14, a contrast that begins to take on a tragic note because we know by then that Jonathan, in spite of his manifest qualities, will not succeed his father to the throne. Samuel's rejection of Saul is paralleled in ch. 15, though the tradition of bracketing 13:7–15 (e.g. Mommer 1991: 135) as a later insertion interrupting the narrative misses the importance of the narrator's use of repetitions throughout Samuel, in order to emphasize and develop key themes. Thus it is essential we recognize the importance of the form of the text as we now have it. Taking this seriously means addressing some significant difficulties (see Birch 1976: 75–76), not least the apparent chronological difficulties in relating the events here to those in 10:8. There is also the possibility of confusion between Gibeah and Geba within the narrative, a problem not helped by the fact that the distinction between these places is not uniform within the OT, while vv. 3–4 can also be read as attributing the initial Philistine defeat to both Jonathan and Saul. These last two problems are capable of resolution (esp. if Geba and Gibeah are variant spellings of the one place; so P. M. Arnold 1990: 54–60; but see Shalom Brooks 2005: 120–126 for arguments against this), though the first is undoubtedly problematic, especially for those who assume Saul was a young man in chs. 8 – 12, whereas we have someone mature enough to have an adult son here. There is also a large literary gap, a matter further complicated in that the events of ch. 12 were at Gilgal. Yet, as Long has demonstrated, there are a range of literary patterns at work between chs. 10 and 13 (1989: 43–66), a key element of which is that Saul had not, as directed, attacked the Philistine outpost in 10:7 (see van Zyl 1988: 169). This then points to the need for the renewal process of ch. 12 from which only now does the conflict with the Philistines begin. The irony is that Jonathan, not Saul, initiates it. The seven days of 10:8 thus relate to the time from which Saul attacks the Philistines rather than an absolute date of Saul's initial empowerment through the Spirit. Hence this chapter narrates the point where Saul may enact the charge he has received and prove his worth as king of Israel, a charge he will fail to carry out.

Comment

Conflict with the Philistines: 13:1–8

1. Although certainty concerning the detail of this verse is impossible (see 'Notes'), it has an important narrative function in that it introduces the formal period of Saul's reign. He has hitherto been moving towards kingship, but his accession and reign details (following a regnal introduction form routinely used elsewhere in Samuel and Kings; see 2 Sam. 5:4–5; 1 Kgs 15:1–2, 9–10) mark off this stage. Although there is some variability in the formula (Solomon and Jeroboam do not have one), and an accession age is unusual, these details function to indicate the period the king is officially active. Kingship's renewal at Gilgal has marked this transition, so Saul can now be assessed by the 'justice' of kingship (see Deut. 17:14–20; 1 Sam. 8:10–19; 10:25). Seen in this light, the 'two years' of reign ascribed to Saul may be the period when he is sanctioned by Yahweh as king.

2–4. When Saul received the promise of kingship and its confirmatory signs in 10:1–8, it was clear the Philistine garrison in Gibeah represented a specific challenge he was to face by attacking them. That he had not done so raises questions about his reign, but those questions can be addressed only now he is formally recognized. Saul's choice of three thousand men to join him is the point where he acts on his instructions, in spite of the delay. The men are presumably chosen at Gilgal, which accounts for those sent home. But the army's presence means that what was initially a faith venture for Saul as a sign of kingship is now one where his point of reference is military force. Saul's army was divided into two groups, two thousand with him near Michmash and Bethel (Beth Aven [v. 5] is likely an alternative name for Bethel; see Hos. 4:15; Amos 5:5), and the balance with Jonathan at Gibeah. Jonathan is not introduced at this point as Saul's son, something reported in 13:16 only after Saul's initial rejection, so the first-time reader does not connect Jonathan with Saul's dynasty. If we are correct in identifying Gibeah with Geba, then Jonathan's forces are in the general region, whereas the Philistines are in the town. Saul thus divided his forces either side of the Wadi es-Swenit, a few miles north of Jerusalem, though since Jonathan was on the same side as the Philistines, his position was more dangerous. V. 3 reports Jonathan's successful attack with great brevity, noting that the Philistines became aware of it before mentioning that Saul blew the trumpet to summon the 'Hebrews'. This is not the normal title Israel uses of themselves, though Fokkelman (1986: 30) is probably right that this is a motivating use of a normally derisive term used by enemies. Blowing the horn was ambiguous. It could announce defeat or be a call to arms, but v. 4 declares Saul defeated the Philistines so Israel became offensive to them. Thus the people were called out to join Saul at Gilgal, some 15 miles west. Saul allows the perception to exist that he rather than Jonathan defeated the Philistines. Although the return to Gilgal seems to surrender the initiative, this is the faith element required by 10:8.

5–8. Israel was unprepared for the extent of the Philistine response, as a huge army gathered against them, though chariots would not have been much use in such hilly country. Nevertheless, the Philistines could terrorize opposition, especially a militia not experienced in dealing with them (Long 1989: 84). Having returned to Gilgal, the Philistines could take the territory Saul had previously occupied at Michmash. Hence the Israelites took cover wherever they could, especially the various caves pockmarking the region, with some of the people moving across the Jordan and even into Israel's north. The initial perception is that a king was not a great success in leading the nation in battle (see 8:20). Saul was still at Gilgal, but the evidence pointed more to fear than confidence among those still with him. Of more concern was the fact that after Saul had waited the seven days specified, Samuel had not come to Gilgal and the army was scattering. The opposition was building its forces, and Israel under Saul was doing nothing. Since this was an element of Yahweh's command to Saul it is apparent that this was a part of what it meant for him to demonstrate kingship consistent with its earlier renewal. What is not made clear is whether we have simply reached the seventh day, or whether the seventh day has elapsed.

Samuel and Saul at Gilgal: 13:9–14

9–10. With people leaving, Saul acted, ordering the burnt offering and fellowship offerings to be brought to him, and then he made the burnt offering. Yet at precisely the point that Saul finished making the offering, Samuel arrived. This news was conveyed to Saul, who went out to meet and greet him.

11–12. The narrator passes over formalities, and moves straight to the heart of the dialogue, emphasizing the terse nature of what transpired. Samuel's question is brief, though it need not imply he was aware of what Saul had done. Saul's reply is loquacious, with three separate clauses describing his situation. The reply moves from those who had scattered (the people), to the one who had not come (Samuel) to those who had (the Philistines), before moving to the central point. This includes Saul's reported interior dialogue of his concerns about the Philistines coming against him as far as Gilgal without having sought Yahweh's favour. Saul's words are open to interpretation, especially given that *ḥlh* (pi.) means variously 'to seek favour' (e.g. Zech. 8:21) or 'to mollify' (e.g. 1 Kgs 13:6). The verb's semantic range suggests a view of Yahweh open to manipulation: if Saul acts in the right way, Yahweh is bound to bring blessing. This will be explicit when Saul acts through his curse in ch. 14, so his defence prepares for such a possibility. But the ark's story (4:1b – 7:1) has already demonstrated that such a view of Yahweh is inappropriate. That Saul knew his actions were inappropriate is indicated by his claim to have 'restrained himself' in making the offering, perhaps suggesting he might have gone further. Saul's own words, even though offered in self-defence (remembering Samuel has not accused him) show his problems.

13–14. Where Samuel's initial question was terse, his reply is extensive, matching Saul's length. Nevertheless, he starts with a single-word sentence (in Hebr.), 'You have acted foolishly.' This statement is evocative of a range of texts in Ecclesiastes (where this root is common), especially that the fool is one who is unable to choose right (see 2 Sam. 24:10). The second sentence explains the nature of Saul's folly, which is that he has not kept Yahweh's command. At this point, commentators have frequently sought for the command that Saul has broken, and the common view (e.g. Brueggemann 1990b: 100) is that there is no such command. It is on this basis, in part at least, that Gunn (1980a: 66–67) regards Saul as a tragic victim, caught in a trap generated by the alleged ambiguity of Samuel's earlier message. But it seems clear that Samuel arrived at the end of the seventh day, so in spite of Saul's claims to the contrary, he has breached the command of 10:8 since Samuel was to make the offerings and then direct Saul beyond that point. Saul's sin is not some cultic irregularity but the choice to set aside the command relating to the task he was set. On that basis, Samuel announces Saul's fate, again in two sentences, with an escalation of intensity that moves from potential to actual. Had Saul not breached the command, Yahweh would have confirmed his dynasty for ever; something now deferred until the promise to David in 2 Sam. 7:1–17. Saul's dynasty, like Eli's before him, would not endure, though the theoretical possibility had existed (similarly, Avioz 2005a). Instead, Yahweh has sought out someone who is 'after his own heart' and commanded that this person be ruler (*nāgîd*) over Israel. Saul's actions have triggered this situation, though at this point we do not yet know who that person is. Jonathan's exemplary actions at the start of this chapter may suggest he is the one, though loss of dynasty for Saul dashes that expectation. Only in 16:1–14 will we discover that this person is David, though what 'after Yahweh's heart' means becomes clear only through the subsequent narrative. However, the emphasis is more on the freedom of Yahweh's choice than on David's character (see McCarter 1980a: 229, though note George 2002b).

More conflict with the Philistines: 13:15–18

15–16. The conflict with the Philistines threatened since v. 7 is again central, except that Saul's change of status is now revealed. Where Samuel went is not indicated, but Saul returned to Gibeah with his army, except that it now numbered just six hundred men. Only now is Jonathan called Saul's son, suggesting an element of tragedy since his bravery indicated that he was well qualified to be king, something now impossible because of Saul's sin. The situation of the two sides in the battle is similar to the beginning of the chapter, except that Saul's smaller force is together on one side of the Wadi es-Swenit and the massive Philistine force is on the other.

17–18. With their massive numerical advantage, the Philistines divide their forces, attempting to encircle Saul and his group. The group heading towards Ophrah covers the north, the group heading towards Beth Horon cover the west and the group heading towards Zeboim covers the east. Although one expects a frontal assault on Saul's base, it seems the marauding bands were protecting their own routes back to Philistine territory as well as preventing reinforcements from reaching Saul. What is emphasized is that Saul's position is one where victory appears impossible. His small force is greatly outnumbered and completely surrounded. Philistine victory seems inevitable.

Philistine prices and Israelite weapons: 13:19–23

19–22. Readers unaware of the region's geography tend to find this section somewhat odd, but it is an important aside, developing the impression previously established. Saul's situation seemed militarily impossible, but now we discover there were no metalworkers in Israel because the Philistines controlled metal production and maintenance. The Philistines thus effectively disarmed Israel since all they could access in metal were farming tools for which the Philistines charged outrageous prices for sharpening (possibly also manufacture: *lṭš* covers sharpening or manufacture). The point is that when the battle came, only Saul and Jonathan had the funds to equip themselves properly for battle; all other Israelite soldiers had to manage with inferior weaponry, such as clubs and slings. Although these could be damaging, they were hardly effective against a force equipped with metal weapons.

23. The chapter ends with an additional Philistine force moving out to the fords at Michmash, only a short distance from Saul's force in Gibeah. Saul is surrounded, and defeat seems inevitable. It seems defeat by the Philistines is how Saul's loss of dynasty will be enacted, preparing for the handover to one after God's heart.

Explanation

Although some modern writers see Saul as a tragic figure, with Yahweh and Samuel set against him, this chapter suggests a different approach, provided we realize it is closely linked to 10:5–8. Saul's initial charge involved attacking Philistine forces, a task he did not carry out, in spite of the special enabling of the Spirit. Although there was probably a considerable delay between those events and those of this chapter, Jonathan's attack on the Philistine garrison is the point where that command's requirements are initiated. It is significant that it is Jonathan, and not Saul, launching the attack, though the subsequent report associated it with Saul. Throughout the battle, which runs through to 14:46, it is Jonathan who takes the initiative and expresses faith in Yahweh's provision. Saul does not see Yahweh like this, and although his return to Gilgal to wait for Samuel is consistent with the initial charge, he fails to follow it through and allow Samuel to offer the sacrifices. It is for this, and not some cultic irregularity, that Saul loses his dynastic status, because these actions are associated with his elevation to kingship. Yet he has not lost the kingdom. The renewal ceremony at Gilgal in ch. 12 indicated that kingship's success depended on the king's willingness to remain under Yahweh's greater reign, a reign expressed though his prophet, in this case Samuel. The tragedy of Saul's action is that he offered the sacrifice to mollify Yahweh, when it was his willingness to wait in the face of the Philistine threat that would have demonstrated his commitment to Yahweh's way. It is for this that Samuel condemns him: a king who does not conform to Yahweh's pattern cannot establish a dynasty. Someone else aware that kingship in Israel operates on this pattern is chosen by Yahweh, though we do not yet know who it is.

Following Saul's rejection at Gilgal, the narrative returns to the battle around Gibeah, as a huge Philistine force encircles Saul's forces, a band now shrunk from three thousand to six hundred, and which is not properly equipped. Defeat seems inevitable, a defeat we expect to initiate the selection of Saul's successor. Yet this chapter mentions only Saul's punishment for partial obedience, so the next will make it clear that the whole nation will not be punished for the king's sin. Saul's sin is the only one for which punishment has been announced, though, as the chapter ends, Israel's escape seems impossible.

1 SAMUEL 14

Translation

[1]One day Saul's son Jonathan said to the lad carrying his kit, 'Come, let's cross over to the Philistine garrison on the other side.' But he did not tell his father. [2]Saul was staying on the outskirts of Gibeah, under the pomegranate in Migron. The army that was with him was about six hundred men, [3]along with Ahijah the son of Ahitub, Ichabod's brother, the son of Phineas, the son of Eli, the priest of Yahweh in Shiloh, carrying an ephod. The army did not know Jonathan had gone. [4]Within the passes where Jonathan sought to go across to the Philistine garrison was a rocky crag on one side and a rocky crag on the other. One was called Bozez and the other Senneh. [5]One crag rose in the north before Michmash and the other in the south before Geba.

[6]Jonathan said to the lad carrying his kit, 'Come, let's cross over to the garrison of these uncircumcised. Perhaps Yahweh will work for us, for nothing can hinder Yahweh from saving by many or by few.' [7]His kit-bearer said to him, 'Do all that is in your heart. Reach out. Behold, I am with you as your heart.' [8]Jonathan said, 'Behold, as we cross over to the men we shall show ourselves to them. [9]If they say to us, "Wait for us until we reach you," then we shall stand in our place and not go up to them. [10]But if they say to us, "Come up to us," we shall go up because Yahweh has given them into our hand and this will be the sign for us.' [11]So both showed themselves to the Philistine garrison, and the Philistines said, 'Behold, the Hebrews are coming out from the holes where they hid themselves.' [12]The men of the garrison answered Jonathan and his kit-bearer, 'Come up to us and we shall show you something.' Jonathan said to his kit-bearer, 'Come up after me, because Yahweh has given them into Israel's hand.' [13]Jonathan went up on his hands and feet and his kit-bearer came after him, and they fell before Jonathan, and his kit-bearer killed them after him. [14]In that first strike they made, Jonathan and his kit-bearer killed about twenty men within an area of about half a yoke. [15]There was trembling in the camp, in the field and among all the people. Even garrison raiders trembled, the earth quaked and it was an almighty panic.

[16]Saul's watchmen in Gibeah of Benjamin looked and, behold, the tumult surged back and forth. [17]Saul said to the troops with him, 'Count and see who has gone from us.' They counted and, behold, Jonathan and his kit-bearer were not there. [18]So Saul said to Ahijah, 'Bring near the ark of God,' for the ark of God went with the children of Israel then. [19]While Saul spoke to the priest, the tumult in the Philistine camp increased more and more. So Saul said to the priest, 'Withdraw your hand.' [20]Then Saul and all the troops with him cried out and came to the battle and, behold, each one's sword was against another, and there was very great confusion. [21]Even those Hebrews who had previously been with the Philistines and had gone up with them into the camp turned and joined the Israelites with Saul and Jonathan. [22]When all the Israelites who had hidden themselves in the hills of Ephraim heard the Philistines had fled, they also followed them closely in the battle. [23]So Yahweh delivered Israel that day, and the battle passed over to Beth Aven.

²⁴The Israelite troops were hard pressed that day, and Saul put the people under an oath, saying, 'Cursed is the one who eats food before evening and I am avenged on my enemies.' So none of the troops tasted any food. ²⁵Everyone entered the forest, and there was honey on the ground. ²⁶When the troops came to the forest, behold, the honey was oozing out, but none put their hand to their mouth because they feared the oath. ²⁷But Jonathan did not hear when his father charged the troops, and he put forth the tip of the staff in his hand and dipped it in the honey of the honeycomb and put his hand to his mouth, and his eyes were brightened. ²⁸Then one of the men responded, 'Your father truly placed the troops under an oath, saying, "Cursed be the one who eats food today."' And the troops were faint. ²⁹But Jonathan said, 'My father has troubled everyone. Look, my eyes have brightened because I tasted a little of this honey. ³⁰How much better then if the troops had eaten freely of the spoil of their enemies that they found! For now the strike against the Philistines has not been great.'

³¹That day they struck the Philistines from Michmash to Aijalon, but the troops were exhausted. ³²The troops pounced on the spoil and took sheep, oxen and calves and slaughtered them on the ground, and the troops ate the blood. ³³It was reported to Saul, saying, 'Behold, the people are sinning against Yahweh by eating with the blood.' He said, 'You have acted treacherously. Roll a great stone to me today.' ³⁴Saul said, 'Scatter yourselves among the troops, and say to them, "Each one shall draw near to me with his ox or flock animal, and slaughter them here and eat them and not sin against Yahweh by eating with the blood."' So everyone brought their ox with them that night and they slaughtered them there. ³⁵Saul built an altar to Yahweh; it was the first altar he built to Yahweh.

³⁶Then Saul said, 'Let us go down after the Philistines tonight and plunder them until dawn, and not leave a man among them.' They said, 'Do all that is good in your eyes.' But the priest said, 'Let us draw near to God here.' ³⁷Saul enquired of God, 'Shall I go down after the Philistines? Will you give them over into the hand of Israel?' But he did not answer them that day. ³⁸Saul said, 'Come here, all the chiefs of the people, and know and see how this sin happened today, ³⁹because as Yahweh who saves Israel lives, even if it is in Jonathan my son, he shall surely die.' But there was none from all the troops who answered him. ⁴⁰And he said to all Israel, 'You shall be on one side, and Jonathan and I shall be on the other.' The troops said to Saul, 'Do what is good in your eyes.' ⁴¹Then Saul said, 'Yahweh, God of Israel, why have you not answered your servant today? If the guilt is in me or in Jonathan my son, then give Urim. But if the guilt is in your people, Israel, give Thummim.' Jonathan and Saul were taken and the troops were cleared. ⁴²Saul said, 'Cast the lot between me and my son Jonathan.' And Jonathan was taken. ⁴³Saul said to Jonathan, 'Tell me what you have done.' Jonathan told him, 'I truly tasted a little of the honey on the tip of the staff in my hand. Here I am. I shall die.' ⁴⁴Saul said, 'Thus may God do, and thus may he continue to do, for you shall surely die, Jonathan.' ⁴⁵But the troops said to Saul, 'Shall Jonathan, who has worked this great salvation in Israel, die? Far from it! As Yahweh lives, not one hair from his head should fall to the ground because he has worked with God today.' So the troops ransomed Jonathan, and he did not die. ⁴⁶Then Saul went up from pursuing the Philistines and the Philistines went back to their place.

[47]When Saul had taken the kingship over Israel, he battled with all his enemies round about, with Moab, the Ammonites, Edom, the kings of Zobah and the Philistines, and wherever he went he inflicted punishment on them. [48]So he acted valiantly and struck Amalek and delivered Israel from the power of those who plundered them.

[49]Saul's sons were Jonathan, Ishvi, Malchishua, and the names of his two daughters were Merab, his firstborn, and the younger was Michal. [50]The name of Saul's wife was Ahinoam, the daughter of Ahimaaz. The name of his army commander was Abner, the son of Ner, Saul's uncle. [51]Saul's father was Kish and Abner's father was Ner, the son of Abiel. [52]There was hard battle against the Philistines all Saul's days, so when Saul saw a mighty or valiant man, he brought him to himself.

Notes on the text

2. Although *'am* most commonly means 'people' it can also, as here, refer to an army.

7. MT is awkward, and most EVV follow LXX, though it probably paraphrases a difficult text; Driver's suggested *Vorlage* for the LXX (1913: 107) is not idiomatic. For other attempts at rendering MT, see ESV and NASB.

15. Hebr. *ḥerdat 'ĕlōhîm* may be 'a panic of God' (hence NIV, 'a panic sent by God'; similarly, Klein 1983: 130). It is more likely that *'ĕlōhîm* is used as the superlative, but the ambiguity should be retained, as one may lead to the other.

16. Lit. 'and surged and thither'. Following LXX, the closing phrase is read as *ḥālōm wĕḥālōm*. The textual note to the ESV errs here as the claimed reading of MT is actually that of LXX, as followed in the main text.

18. LXX has 'ephod' rather than 'ark'. In its favour is that oracular decisions are achieved elsewhere through the ephod, not the ark. Conversely, 'ephod of God' does not occur elsewhere, though the 'ark of God' does, and it is easier to explain 'ephod' as a correction of 'ark'. Davies (1977: 15–16) argues that the ark and ephod are equated in 1 Samuel, but depends upon a chain of arguments that are not equally persuasive (Long 1989: 112). MT is retained as the more difficult reading (Stoebe 1973: 260; see van Zyl 1988: 175).

23–24. LXX, followed by NRSV, is much longer. Though supported by McCarter (1980a: 245), it is perhaps an explanatory gloss. However, the folly of Saul's vow is probably present in MT if the anomalous vocalization of the verb *wayyō'el* is a play between the roots *'lh*, 'to place under oath' (hiph.) and *y'l*, 'to be foolish'. LXX may attempt to bring both together (see Long 1989: 117).

25. The beginning of the verse is difficult. Klein (1983: 130), unpersuaded by McCarter (1980a: 245) leaves it blank. However, Gen. 41:57 and 2 Sam. 15:23 (Driver 1913: 113) suggest the problematic *'ereṣ* is hyperbolic, and 'everyone' is a suitable translation, perhaps because of the more limited sense of *'am* in this narrative. Moreover, it prepares for the similar use in 14:29.

27. There is a play on words here between 'curse' (*'rr*) and 'light' (*'wr*).
29. See on 14:25.
41. Following LXX and Vg, there appears to be a clear omission of text through homoioteleuton, though NASU attempts to sustain it by offering 'give a perfect lot' (similarly, NIV). But the context requires the conditional statement provided by LXX. Moreover, *dēloi* elsewhere stands in LXX for Urim (Num. 27:21; 1 Sam. 28:6), meaning that *tāmîm* can reasonably be repointed *tummîm*, 'Thummim', providing the appropriate parallel for Urim earlier in the verse.
43. NIV treats *'āmût* as an indirect question, 'Shall I die?', but is contextually unlikely (Youngblood 1992: 668).
47. The verb *rš'* is difficult, and often emended on the basis of the LXX (e.g. McCarter 1980a: 254). Most commonly, it means 'to act wickedly', but can also mean 'to condemn' in a legal setting (1 Kgs 8:22). In context, where victories are described, the more positive reading (inflicted punishment) is required, though there may be something deliberately ambiguous about the verb missed by the LXX, particularly as 14:48 refers to Amalek, preparing readers for Saul's rejection in ch. 15.

Form and structure

Ch. 14 continues ch. 13, picking up from 13:18 and 23. Nevertheless, it is appropriate to treat these chapters separately. Within this battle with the Philistines, these chapters highlight different flaws in Saul, though the concluding notes in vv. 47–52 indicate he also had his successes. Saul continues to compare unfavourably with Jonathan, who again leads the attack and seems more aware of what it means to lead Yahweh's people in battle. By contrast, Saul's vow (v. 24) is foolish, an attempt to manipulate Yahweh unmitigated by the altar he builds in v. 35. The story must be read against the people's request in 8:20 and Yahweh's declaration of the purpose of Saul's reign in 9:16. The people requested a king to lead them in battle, while Yahweh specifically assigned Saul the task of defeating the Philistines. Critical exegesis has been unusually united in seeing this chapter as a unity, often seeing an old tradition from close to Saul (e.g. Birch 1976: 85–86). Yet how this narrative interacts with earlier material from the Saul narratives is important. In addition to links already noted, how Jonathan is taken is highlighted by its formal similarities to Saul's election in 10:20–21. By collecting these allusions to Saul's election and promotion to kingship, the narrative closes off the main elements of his reign before his rejection by showing how much more effective Jonathan is, though we now know he cannot become king.

This becomes evident through both halves of the main story. The battle is central in vv. 1–23, but it quickly becomes evident that Jonathan, and not Saul, is the one taking the initiative. Whereas Saul reacts, Jonathan creates opportunities and seeks Yahweh's leading in his actions (vv. 6, 10, 12). Conversely, although Saul began to enquire of Yahweh (v. 18), he does not carry through, so the narrator's comment in v. 23 is crucial; in spite of his responsibility, Saul is not leading the nation to victory over the Philistines. Rather, Yahweh achieves it through Jonathan, a victory echoing that against the Philistines in ch. 7. This reinforces the main point. Yahweh gives the victory, though that Yahweh acts apart from Saul already hints at his final rejection. The chapter's second half (excluding vv. 47–52) deals with Saul's vow and its implications, though it pivots on how Saul prevented the troops from eating meat with blood. Although this is a limited success, it was needed because his vow had brought such hunger that the troops acted sinfully. Although Saul is pious, he cannot understand Yahweh's activities, even being willing to put Jonathan to death. There are echoes of the Jephthah story (Judg. 10:6 – 12:7) in this, especially how both Jephthah and Saul seek to manipulate Yahweh. Jonathan is finally saved when the troops make the same declaration as the narrator; they know he has worked with God, so he cannot be put to death (v. 46). Nevertheless, the appendix (vv. 47–52) does show some grudging appreciation for Saul's achievements, though with enough ambiguity to suggest that even these are not to be taken at face value (see Garsiel 1983: 87–93).

Comment

Victory over the Philistines: 14:1–23

1–3. The narrative now returns to Saul and Jonathan as they seek what seems an impossible victory. Israel is outnumbered, under-equipped and outflanked and yet Jonathan seizes the initiative in summoning his kit-bearer to join him in attacking the Philistine garrison, though without informing Saul. Having noted Jonathan's actions, the narrator returns to Saul, who has his camp set up at a pomegranate tree in Migron (location unknown), where he has only six hundred troops. Such a small group has no chance against the vast Philistine force, though Saul also has the priest Ahijah with the ephod (see 'Notes' on 2:28). That the ephod could be used for determining Yahweh's will, probably through the Urim and Thummim, implies something positive for Saul. But Ahijah's presence, from Eli's family, is not so positive when read in the light of 2:36 and 3:14. It seems strange that Samuel's role has been taken by a member of Eli's family (Fokkelman 1986: 49). Even Saul's piety is questionable.

4–5. The ground around Michmash is particularly rugged, and the two crags mentioned cannot definitely be identified (but see Wyatt 1995). The meaning of their names is unclear: the common suggestions that Senneh is 'thorny' and Bozez 'shining' are based on tendentious etymology, and given the conservative nature of toponyms may be pre-Israelite.

6–7. The narrative resumes Jonathan's actions from v. 1, highlighting his appreciation of Yahweh's involvement. Although nothing so far indicates a Yahweh war (*ḥerem*), it seems clear from the fact it reflects events initiated by Yahweh in 10:5–8 that this was seen as one. Saul's test in 13:8–15 is consistent with this. Jonathan does not act on his own, as he involves his kit-bearer in the process. Kit-bearers are mentioned at a number of points and do more than simply carry weapons and other equipment, perhaps acting as a lieutenant to a senior officer. Jonathan's comment invites the kit-bearer to join him in attacking 'the uncircumcised', a derogatory phrase used only of Philistines, though his concern is what Yahweh may do through just the two of them. The second half of v. 6 is a classic confession of faith, a feature of Yahweh war since the battle occurs in the face of overwhelming odds (see Gideon in Judg. 7:1–23). The kit-bearer's response shows his commitment to this understanding of Yahweh's activity.

8–10. Jonathan's means of discerning Yahweh's activity within the battle depended on the Philistines in either directing him and his kit-bearer to stay where they were or to come up to the garrison when they revealed themselves. It was a risky strategy, since making themselves visible meant they were at risk from Philistine spears and had no escape plan. The key for Jonathan was whether or not they would go up to the Philistine garrison, because going up meant they knew Yahweh had given the Philistines over to them.

11–15. The plan in place, Jonathan and his kit-bearer put it into action. Having revealed themselves, the narrator switches to the Philistine perspective, as we hear them speak in derogatory terms of the Hebrews, mentioning their hiding places from 13:6. However, in v. 12a the Philistines express themselves within the terms of Jonathan's test, using terms that confirm Yahweh's actions for Jonathan and his kit-bearer, though the additional 'and we shall show you something' shows their own confidence. Jonathan's comment to his kit-bearer is equally confident, except that he trusts Yahweh rather than superior military force. The conflict's nature as one between Yahweh and the Philistines is thus made clear. The garrison's location was inaccessible from the side used by Jonathan, as he and the kit-bearer went up using their hands and feet, though this may also have been to keep low. This detail is important, as it stresses the advantage of the Philistine position and makes v. 13's conclusion, that the Philistines fell before Jonathan and his kit-bearer, more remarkable. In that strike they killed twenty men in the area of 'half a yoke'. The 'yoke' refers to the area yoked oxen could plough in a day, the basis on which the measurement of the 'acre' was initially based. The battle thus took place in about half an acre. More important is the effect of this assault, which induced panic within the garrison and Philistine raiding parties, a panic emphasized through the verbal and nominal repetitions of *ḥrd* (panic). The Philistines now adopt the Israelite reaction in 13:7. The panic was also associated with an earthquake that created an almighty panic, an expression that might suggest God's activity, while remaining suitably ambiguous.

16–19. The focus turns to Saul at his base in Gibeah as his lookouts report unusual activity in the Philistine camp. Therefore, he finally acts, though it is unclear why he believed from the outset that someone had launched a raid. Jonathan and his kit-bearer's absence is reported, so he only now discovers what Jonathan has kept from him (v. 1). Having discovered Jonathan's absence, Saul sought an oracle from Yahweh, ordering Ahijah to bring the ark forward. We have no evidence elsewhere of the ark being used to receive an oracle, though use of the ephod (14:3) may presume its presence (see Fokkelman 1986: 58). Since 7:2 indicated the ark was at Kiriath Jearim, we must assume that remained its base, but it could still be brought to battle. But, as with 13:8–15, Saul did not wait when he saw the turmoil of the Philistine camp. There may be an implied criticism since, in contrast to Jonathan, Saul did not base his actions on Yahweh's will.

20–23. Saul now enters the fray, resulting in considerable slaughter among the Philistines. This success prompts others to join Saul and Jonathan, as Hebrews who formerly served as mercenaries for the Philistines defect to Israel. The Israelites who have hidden in the hill country of Ephraim (presumably not too far into it) return to the battle too. In spite of Saul's achievement, the narrator is clear – the victory belongs to Yahweh, the one whose will Jonathan has sought, but from whom Saul finally refrains from seeking an oracle. The closing statement of v. 23 quotes Exod. 14:30, associating this victory with the crossing of the Sea of Reeds (Youngblood 1992: 663).

Saul's vow and its outcome: 14:24–46

24. Although the battle's conclusion could have ended the narrative, it gave rise to subsequent events. As was clear from 14:23, the battle continued to Beth Aven (probably Bethel), so, although victory was won, the fighting continued. Probably, it was more skirmishes than outright battle from here, though weariness obviously affected the troops, who were hard pressed. Having had success, Saul placed a curse on anyone who ate before evening or he was avenged on his enemies, with the result that no one ate anything. The curse contrasts markedly with the declaration of the previous verse. The victory belonged to Yahweh, but Saul claimed it for himself (see Hertzberg 1964: 114). Moreover, the oath's enactment sounds suspiciously like an attempt to manipulate Yahweh into following Saul's agenda, echoing Jephthah's fateful vow in Judg. 11:30–31. Although this was a Yahweh war, we should note that there is no indication that the ban (*ḥerem*) was applied, since this had to be initiated by Yahweh (against Edelman 1991: 90). The disastrous outcome of this is worked out in the balance of the narrative.

25–30. Food preparation was time-consuming, so Saul could have banned prepared meals. However, honey in the forest was the ancient equivalent of fast food and could be eaten without loss of fighting efficiency. In spite of their hunger, none of the troops ate any of the honey, because of Saul's curse. Yet just as Jonathan had not informed his father of his activities, Saul had not told Jonathan of the curse. So Jonathan took some honey on his staff as he went, ate and was revitalized. Only then did one of the soldiers inform him of the curse, perhaps because of his own hunger, something the narrator highlights. Jonathan's response is damning, equating Saul's actions with those of Achan (Josh. 7:24–26), whereas eating was obviously beneficial. Fokkelman (1986: 66) highlights the similarities between Jonathan's condemnation of Saul and that of Samuel in 13:13–14. Since Yahweh delivered Israel, Jonathan's final comment suggests Saul's curse went against what Yahweh had achieved for the nation, preventing the Philistine defeat being as great as it might have been (against Polzin 1989: 136). Victory was complete, but v. 52 concludes that there was continual warfare with the Philistines (similarly, Long 1989: 141).

31–35. Jonathan's reference to the possible Philistine spoil leads to the next episode, which increases Saul's culpability as he moves from folly to breach of law. Although the victory could have been greater, considerable spoil was taken as the Philistines were driven east beyond Bethel and towards Aijalon, near the coastal plain. In their hunger, the troops took the captured livestock and slaughtered it where they were. Deut. 12:15–25 allows for localized slaughter of meat, provided the blood was not also consumed, since blood carried life (see Lev. 3:17). However, in their haste, the blood was not drained, and the people ate it with the meat. Saul's complaint of treachery is that the people have not followed his oath, though it may also include the legal breach. However, the narrator is not overly critical of Saul since his decision to set up a battlefield altar where the meat was drained prevented further abuse. This temporary battlefield altar was the first one Saul built. However, the implication is clear. Although Saul prevented further abuse, his oath had created the problem. The foundations for an intriguing irony are laid, since in ch. 15 it is Saul who seizes the booty (Long 1989: 121).

36–39. With Saul's altar, the crisis initiated by his vow seems resolved, but the problem of Jonathan's actions remains unaddressed. With the troops fed, it was possible to strike a final blow against the Philistines, and Saul summoned the troops to join him. But the priest with him, presumably Ahijah, suggested the previously broken-off enquiry of Yahweh be resumed. So Saul enquired of Yahweh, only to find that Yahweh gave no answer that day. The logical conclusion was that Yahweh would not give an oracle because of the people's sin, though Saul's words in v. 39 have an ironic ring, even as they attempt to divert blame. He does not know that Jonathan broke his curse, so his statement is foolish bravado. Also, he swears a further oath by Yahweh as Israel's saviour that the sinner will be put to death. Thus Saul compounds his earlier folly and demonstrates his continuing misunderstanding of Yahweh's ways. Saul seeks Yahweh only when it suits his purposes. The troops' responding silence is ominous since some of them know what Jonathan has done.

40–42. Saul had been taken by lot (10:20–21), and Jonathan is now taken by means of the sacred stones known as the Urim and Thummim. Exactly how they worked is obscure, but it appears questions were asked requiring either 'Yes' or 'No' as the answer, or there was a binary choice. The possibility must exist that there was no answer either. If the text above is correct, an analogy to the Australian game of two-up may be appropriate. This gambling game (legal only on Anzac Day, when the sacrifice of those in war is annually remembered) involves two coins tossed simultaneously, and while the coins are in the air the gambler calls 'heads' or 'tails'. A win occurs if the specified call appears on both coins. The Urim and Thummim might have worked similarly, with the call specifying one pair as 'Yes' and the other as 'No', with the assumption that Yahweh controlled the outcome through the priest. Where a pair did not occur, no answer was given (see Rowley 1956: 28–29). Given the etymology, where Urim means 'accursed' and 'Thummin' 'perfect', 'Thummim' would usually designate the preferred answer, though this is not necessary. The initial choice is made possible here as Saul places himself and Jonathan to one side and the people on the other, with Saul placing himself under 'Urim'. Saul sought the source of the nation's guilt through this process, though it again echoes the Achan story (Josh. 7) where Yahweh identified the source of guilt by means of lots. The irony is that in v. 29 Jonathan identified Saul with Achan. Jonathan and Saul were then taken, so the following process determined in which of them the guilt lay, and the casting of the lot saw Jonathan taken.

43–46. The analogy of Achan continues as Saul's initial question echoes Joshua's to Achan in Josh. 7:19. Jonathan is unrepentant about eating the honey, and speaks boldly of his actions. Saul, in view of his second oath, acts to put Jonathan to death, taking another oath against Jonathan. Normally, this oath formula was self-imprecatory (see 1 Kgs 19:2 for the only other example where self-imprecation is avoided), so the subtle change may suggest he is not taking his responsibility seriously (see Ziegler 2007: 70). This final oath highlights Saul's folly in contrast to the troops who respond with a counter oath by Yahweh that Jonathan will not die. The troops recognize that Yahweh acted through Jonathan, not Saul, because Jonathan genuinely sought to do Yahweh's will. Saul's actions have looked suspiciously self-serving throughout. The allusions to Achan and Jephthah show Saul in a negative light, since he tried to manipulate Yahweh and troubled the nation. Finally, the troops ransomed Jonathan, probably not through a payment but by suggesting that delivering him was costly (see Gordon 1986: 141). The effect is highlighted in v. 46; the remaining Philistines return home as does Saul. Saul could have had the victory in spite of the overwhelming odds, but his failure to act with Yahweh prevented it.

Appendix to Saul's reign: 14:47–52

47–48. The narrator is interested in a narrow range of Saul's activities, specifically this battle with the Philistines and that with Amalek in the next chapter, so a wider range of battles is passed over. There is acknowledgment of other successes, though these are tempered by his failure to deliver the nation from the Philistines completely, a failure preparing for the coming events. The victories described here are east of the Jordan (Moab, Ammon, Edom), north (Zobah) and south (Amalekites), as well those against the Philistines in the west. Saul provided a measure of national security, so his kingship was not necessarily a political failure; but the writer is concerned with the theological failures, not the political successes.

49–51. One of the devices employed in Samuel is bridging sections by listing children and officials (see 2 Sam. 3:2–5; 8:15–18; 20:23–26). The listing of Saul's sons is incomplete, omitting Abinadab (1 Sam. 31:2) and Ish-bosheth (2 Sam. 2:8; unless Ishvi is a variant for both), though mention of his daughters Merab and Michal prepares for the prominent role they play in 18:6–27. Similarly, Jonathan and Malchishua are with Saul at his death (30:2–6). Unlike David, who gradually increased the number of his wives, Saul has only Ahinoam, though this ignores his concubine Rizpah (2 Sam. 21:8) and her children. But like David he has a cousin, Abner, in command of the army.

52. The brief notes in this section could have provided a more positive assessment of Saul: certainly, he did not develop a lavish court and extend taxation. But he did not defeat the Philistines, which 9:16 had indicated was his central task. This failure drives the narrative of his reign, and is highlighted by its placement at the end of this appendix. His military strategy, though wise at one level, was not a success, and the hint that runs throughout this chapter is that this failure was because he had not understood the nature of kingship in Israel. The closing note regarding his recruitment strategy prepares for the handover, since David was the one soldier whose recruitment would be narrated.

Explanation

This chapter represents a surprise reversal of the Yahweh war stories found in Joshua and Judges, though the reversal is hinted at through Saul's association with earlier failures in Israel's story, notably Achan and Jephthah. The reversal is not a failure to defeat an enemy that was militarily overwhelmingly superior. This element, carried over from the conquest accounts and especially the Gideon story (Judg. 7), comes to its expected conclusion. Rather, the reversal is seen in the portrayal of Saul as one who fails to carry out his commission, and whose foolish attempts to manipulate Yahweh through his vows result in Israel's success being limited. The element of reversal explains, in part at least, why the battle account with the Philistines occupies such a minor part of the narrative. Primary focus is placed upon Jonathan's actions because of how he sought to achieve Yahweh's will, actions that show Saul in a harsh contrast. Jonathan and his kit-bearer are not only resourceful soldiers; they discover Yahweh's mode for defeating the Philistines. It does not occur to them that Yahweh will fail to defeat the enemy (14:6–7). It is not that Jonathan is resourceful (though he is); it is that he focuses his resourcefulness on faithful service of Yahweh. Saul, by contrast, is pious, but his piety hinders Yahweh's purposes because it is self-serving (see Brueggemann 1990b: 105). His call was to deliver Israel from the Philistines (9:16), but this he fails to do, while his son begins to achieve this goal. There is great emphasis within the chapter on what Yahweh is doing, and both major panels (vv. 1–23, 24–46) conclude with a statement of Yahweh's activity in giving victory, with the additional emphasis in v. 45 that it was achieved through Jonathan.

It is important to read these narratives in the light of the appendix to Saul's reign in vv. 47–52, for these are not bare annals: they emphasize the real political and military achievements of Saul's reign. But by concluding with continual warfare with the Philistines, the appendix suggests that these successes are seen within the framework of theological failure. Saul's attempts to manipulate and control Yahweh through his oaths are shown to be the seedbed of his failure, a failure that impeded the nation's life. Nothing speaks more eloquently of Saul's loss of status through his actions than Yahweh's silence in 14:37. Silence confirms the earlier rejection of Saul, while hinting at something more. Thus ch. 14 takes the events of the previous chapter one step further, while preparing for Saul's final rejection as king in ch. 15.

1 SAMUEL 15

Translation

[1]Samuel said to Saul, 'It was me that Yahweh sent to anoint you as king over his people Israel. So now, listen to the words of Yahweh. [2]Thus has Yahweh of Hosts said, "I have considered what Amalek did in opposing Israel on the way when they came up out of Egypt. [3]Now go and strike Amalek and devote to destruction all

that is theirs. You shall not spare any but you shall kill man and woman, child and infant, ox and flock animal, camel and donkey." '

⁴So Saul summoned the people and numbered them in Telaim. There were two hundred thousand on foot, and ten thousand men of Judah. ⁵Saul came to the city of Amalek and lay in wait in the valley. ⁶Saul said to the Kenites, 'Go. Flee. Go down from the midst of the Amalekites lest I destroy you with them. For you dealt favourably with all Israel when they came up from Egypt.' So the Kenites turned aside from the midst of Amalek. ⁷Then Saul struck Amalek all the way from Havilah to Shur, which is east of Egypt. ⁸He captured Agag king of Amalek alive, but all the people he devoted to destruction by the edge of the sword. ⁹But Saul and the people spared Agag and the best of the flock and the herd and fatlings, and the lambs and all that was good and would not devote them to destruction. Yet everything despised and worthless they devoted to destruction.

¹⁰Yahweh's word came to Samuel, saying, ¹¹'I regret that I made Saul king, because he has turned from following me, and has not carried out my instructions.' Then Samuel was angry, and he cried out to Yahweh all night. ¹²Samuel rose early to meet Saul in the morning. It was reported to Samuel that 'Saul has gone to Carmel and set up a monument for himself, then turned and passed over and gone down to Gilgal.' ¹³So Samuel came to Saul, and Saul said, 'Blessed are you to Yahweh! I have carried out Yahweh's instruction.' ¹⁴Samuel said to Saul,

> 'Then what is this sound of sheep in my ears,
>   or the sound of the herd that I hear?'

¹⁵Saul said, 'They have brought what the people spared from Amalek from the best of the flock and the herd to sacrifice to Yahweh your God. But the rest they devoted to destruction.'

¹⁶Samuel said to Saul, 'Stop, and I shall tell you what Yahweh said to me last night.' He said to him, 'Speak.' ¹⁷Samuel said, 'Though small in your own eyes, are you not the head of Israel's tribes? Yahweh anointed you as king over Israel! ¹⁸Yahweh sent you on a mission, and said to you, "Go, devote the sinners Amalek to destruction, and wage war against them until they are destroyed." ¹⁹So why have you not obeyed Yahweh's voice and have pounced on the spoil and done evil in Yahweh's eyes?' ²⁰Saul said to Samuel, 'I have obeyed Yahweh's voice, and I went on the mission that Yahweh sent me. I have brought Agag the king of Amalek, but have devoted Amalek to destruction. ²¹The people took from the spoil, flock and herd, the best of that devoted to destruction, to sacrifice to Yahweh your God in Gilgal.' ²²Samuel said,

> 'Has Yahweh as much delight in burnt offerings and sacrifices
>   as in obeying the voice of Yahweh?
> Behold, to obey is better than sacrifice,
>   to heed is better than the fat of rams.
> ²³For rebellion is like the sin of divination
>   and presumption is like iniquity and teraphim.

Since you have rejected Yahweh's word,
  he has rejected you from being king.'

[24]Saul said to Samuel, 'I have sinned because I transgressed Yahweh's command-ment and your directions, because I feared the people and hearkened to their voice. [25]But now, please pardon my sin, and return with me that I may worship Yahweh.' [26]But Samuel said to Saul, 'I shall not return with you. Because you rejected Yahweh's word, Yahweh has rejected you from being king over Israel.' [27]As Samuel turned to go, Saul seized the edge of his robe and it tore. [28]Then Samuel said to him, 'Yahweh has torn the kingdom of Israel from you this day and given it to your neighbour who is better than you. [29]Also, the Enduring One of Israel will not lie nor relent, for he is not a human that he should relent.' [30]He said, 'I have sinned, now please glorify me before the elders of my people and before Israel, and return with me that I may worship Yahweh your God.' [31]Then Samuel turned back after Saul, and Saul worshipped Yahweh.

[32]Samuel said, 'Bring Agag, king of Amalek to me.' Agag came to him trembling, though Agag said, 'Surely, the bitterness of death is past.' [33]Samuel said, 'Just as your sword made women childless, so also shall your mother be childless among women.' Samuel hewed Agag to pieces before Yahweh at Gilgal. [34]Samuel went to Ramah, but Saul went up to his house in Gibeah of Saul. [35]Samuel did not see Saul again to the day of his death, but Samuel grieved over Saul. And Yahweh regretted he had made Saul king over Israel.

Notes on the text

2. Hebr. *pqd* can have a number of senses. A common meaning is 'to visit', either graciously (e.g. Gen. 21:1) or in punishment (e.g. Amos 3:1). It can also mean 'observe carefully' (e.g. 1 Sam. 17:18), or 'appoint' (e.g. Num. 27:16). All these senses are to some extent operative here, creating a sense of play with the same verb in v. 4, where it means 'to number'.

9. Hebr. *hammišnîm* ('the second copy'?) is out of place. Read *hammašmannîm* (fatlings; see BDB on basis of LXX, Tg and Neh. 8:10).

13. A lengthy LXX addition specifies the time of Samuel's arrival as when Saul was finishing his offering.

16. With most MSS, read with Q *wayyōmer* rather than K *wayyōmerw*.

18. Following LXX's *synteleses*. See McKane 1963: 102.

27. 4QSam[a] and LXX include Saul as the subject of the verb *wayyaḥăzēq*. This makes clear what might otherwise be ambiguous in the narrative, though Campbell (2003: 157) suggests that MT might be better read as suggesting that Samuel tore his own robe.

29. Although *nēṣaḥ yiśrā'ēl* is usually translated 'Glory of Israel' (so NIV, NRSV, ESV, NASU), *nēṣaḥ* refers to eminence and enduring nature. Moreover, a distinction in translation with *kābôd* should be maintained. This is the only place where this divine title is used in the Bible.

32. The meaning of *ma'ădannōt* is uncertain. LXX renders as *tremōn*. MT could be 'in bonds', but the phrasing is awkward. LXX understands it to come from *'dn*, 'delicately'. Although possibly a f. allusion (so *DCH*), it may also refer to the trembling way Agag came.

Form and structure

The second stage of Saul's rejection is reached. Ch. 13 saw the loss of dynastic status, but Saul remained as king. Although ch. 14 showed some successes, it was still critical of his leadership, especially compared with Jonathan. Just as Saul moved towards the throne through three key stages (anointing, acclamation, battle victory), his removal takes three stages (loss of dynasty, announcement of loss of rule, and death). His anointing was where the certainty of his rule was confirmed, while Yahweh's announcement of his loss of rule makes certain that he cannot remain king. The only surprise in his fall is that the final stage takes so long, though within that David also passes through two stages (anointing and battle victory) before his final acclamation. Like Saul, David's national acclamation must overcome opposition. Older treatments tended to see chs. 13 and 15 as doublets (e.g. Smith 1899: 129), but this is rejected on source-critical grounds (Birch 1976:105–106), while the literary integrity of 13 – 15 has also been demonstrated (Long 1989: 166–169). This chapter is not anti-monarchic, since monarchy's continuation is assumed, but is highly critical of Saul (Mommer 1991: 147).

This chapter arises from the enduring conflict between Israel and Amalek deriving from Exod. 17:8–16 (see Deut. 25:17–19), where Yahweh promised to 'blot out' Amalek. This is to be carried out through a battle where Amalek is 'devoted to destruction' (*ḥrm*). This represents a process of special consecration whereby something is definitively given over to Yahweh and therefore no longer accessible for common use. The net result is the destruction of the thing or person so consecrated (Lev. 27:28–29; Josh. 6:17–18; see *NIDOTTE* 2:276). Within warfare, the regulations are set out in Deut. 7 and 20 and indicate that only Yahweh may initiate such a battle (Longman and Reid 1995: 33). A range of cultic activities are included (Longman and Reid 1995: 32–47), all of which show that it is Yahweh who wins the battle.

Although it involves a battle report, the battle comprises a relatively small component of the narrative, the greater part of which is dialogue between Samuel and Saul. Dialogue is the central mechanism by which the plot is developed. The dialogue, and to some extent the narration as a whole, is marked by plays on the semantic range of keywords, most importantly those associated with the root *šm'*, which occurs seven times. Depending on context, *šm'* means variously 'hear' or 'obey', and the range between these senses that is explored. It demonstrates that Saul listens to the wrong voice, and his obedience to Yahweh is therefore compromised. This is what leads to his rejection, because ch. 12 has made clear that obedience to Yahweh's will is central to Israelite kingship. Nevertheless, because the demand was so specific, claims that Saul was doomed to fail from the beginning (so Brueggemann 1990b: 108; Gunn 1980a: 71) misread the text. The neighbour who is 'better than Saul' who will replace him (v. 28) must be one who will obey Yahweh's command.

Comment

Samuel's instructions for Saul: 15:1–3

1. A new scene begins here, though no location is specified, as Samuel speaks to Saul. Samuel's speech opens by emphasizing his role in anointing Saul as king at Yahweh's command, stressing that Israel is Yahweh's people. There may be a king, but when a king remains subject to Yahweh the people belong to him, not the king. Samuel uses his role's background as the basis for summoning Saul to hear Yahweh's message. 12:13–15 stressed the importance of both people and king obeying (šmʿ) Yahweh's voice if the experiment with kingship was to succeed, so Samuel stresses this theme here.

2–3. The message proper begins in v. 2, as indicated by the messenger formula, where Samuel claims to be reporting Yahweh's speech. Significantly, the full title 'Yahweh of Hosts' (ṣĕbāʾôt) is employed for the first time since 4:4. The name occurs in clusters in Samuel at points of significant change in the nation's leadership (see 1:3). Yahweh's message is based on consideration of the activities of Amalek (a nomadic group associated with the Negeb and further south, though Edelman 1986, argues for a northerly group) in opposing Israel on the journey from Egypt. Saul is required to strike the people and devote them to destruction (ḥrm). Since Saul's victory over Amalek (1 Sam. 14:48) is regarded as a significant achievement, Amalek must have represented a continuing threat to Israel at this point (against Brueggemann 1990b: 110). The command to Saul switches into the pl. at the point of commanding that Amalek be devoted to destruction, but reverts to the sg. for the rest of Samuel's speech. Although such alternations are common enough, it seems likely that the pl. links king and people since both are under Yahweh's command. The sacral nature of ḥerem must be appreciated; such total destruction is difficult for contemporary readers, but even within Israel it could operate only if its sacral position was appreciated. Although it shows variation in practice, it was ultimately a sacrifice to Yahweh where nothing could be kept for another use. This is highlighted by Samuel's insisting that Saul spare nothing.

The battle with Amalek: 15:4–9

4. Although not apparent in English, the narrator plays with the sense of šmʻ here since the verb is also used of Saul's summoning the people at Telaim. If this is identified with the orthographically similar Telem of Josh. 15:24, it is probably in the southern Negeb and is thus a logical base for an assault on Amalek. The size of Saul's army is problematic since it appears completely out of proportion to that mentioned in ch. 14, where three thousand seemed a significant force. Again, the problem may lie in the meaning of the word ʼelep (traditionally, 'thousand'), which can refer to a military unit or even a clan unit. If the latter is intended, then Saul may have had members of two hundred clans from Israel and ten from Judah, perhaps an army of around one or two thousand. The more important point is the Israel–Judah ratio, since problems in the Negeb affected Judah and not Israel (understood as the northern tribes). The presence of a large northern contingent for a southern problem may suggest Saul was seeking to gain greater support in Judah.

5–7. Having assembled the army, Saul came to the 'city of Amalek'. The site of this city is unclear, not least because the Bible usually presents Amalek as nomadic, as also are the Kenites whom Saul enables to flee before the battle because of their earlier favourable dealings with Israel (Exod. 18:1; Judg. 1:16; 4:11). Although an unusual usage, it is preferable to understand 'city' as referring to a fortified (perhaps semi-permanent) Amalek encampment, notable for their king's presence, rather than as a town (though note Gordon 1986: 143). As such, the valley where Saul lay in wait cannot be identified, though the account is terse, omitting such details as how he informed the Kenites without endangering the attack. If only one encampment was attacked, it would explain why Amalek continued to pose problems later (e.g. 1 Sam. 27:8). The battle account is then given, but is notable for its brevity. It simply notes that Saul struck Amalek from Havilah towards Shur. Given the narrative's geographic difficulties, it is no surprise that we cannot locate these sites with certainty, though perhaps they were difficult to find even at the time of the narrator, since Shur has to be defined as east of Egypt, indicating that the conflict was in the Negeb or the north of the Arabian Peninsula.

8–9. Saul seems so far to have acted appropriately, but the narrator has held back a surprise that is now revealed. The statement that Saul had captured the Amalekite king, Agag (c.f. Num. 24:7, 23), alive raises concerns about Saul's obedience, even though the remaining people are devoted to destruction. No motivation for this is given, and it is only when confronted by Samuel that we hear Saul's dissembling explanation. V. 9 raises the stakes by noting that Saul and the people also refrained (precluded by v. 3) from devoting the best of the livestock to destruction. Only things of lower quality were put under the ban. Although motivation is not provided directly, the narrator suggests a degree of greed since the concept of *ḥerem* meant that everything devoted to destruction was already Yahweh's. As with ch. 14, allusions to Achan in Josh. 7 continue to portray Saul negatively (Berges 1990: 182).

Saul's rejection: 15:10–31

10–12. The narrative shifts its focus to Samuel as Yahweh reveals his own grief (*nḥm*) at having made Saul king because of his failure to keep his directives. In fact, Yahweh does not indicate if there is a specific breach or whether Saul is judged more generally. The accumulation of evidence from 13:1 onwards may suggest a more general statement, though the most recent breach remains the focus within the balance of the chapter. Crucially, Yahweh has come to a point of regret, which he expresses, mirroring the narrator's direct statement in v. 35. (The statement, echoing Gen. 6:7, stands in tension with the statement Samuel makes about Yahweh in 15:29, where the same verb is used to indicate the unchanging nature of Yahweh's decision. As will be seen, the tension is more apparent than real.) There is no indication that Samuel seeks this information, though since Samuel's prophetic role means he makes Yahweh's will known to king and people it is appropriate that the news begins with him. Samuel often appears awkward and prickly, but his anger at what Yahweh has announced is clear from the fact that he spends the night calling out to Yahweh, though the content of his cry is unspecified. Accordingly, he sets off to find Saul early in the morning, apparently journeying to where he expects to find him. Initially he is told that Saul has erected a monument to himself at Carmel (a Calebite city in the Negeb, not the well-known northern site; see Josh. 15:55), before heading to Gilgal. Such a monument, placed strategically for Saul at the southern boundaries of Judah, suggests a process of self-aggrandisement out of keeping with Yahweh's command. The journey to Gilgal meant Saul returned to his power base.

13–15. Samuel's journey to Saul and encounter are telescoped to their meeting at Gilgal. Because Samuel is the subject of the first verb of v. 13, we expect his initial speech to be reported, but the narrator moves straight to Saul. This highlights Saul's claims, especially through his double use of Yahweh's name. The blessing of Samuel is a greeting, foregrounding Samuel and Saul's relationship to Yahweh. Saul's second clause builds on this by claiming to have performed Yahweh's command, meaning the devotion of Amalek and all it owned to Yahweh. Saul's speech contrasts with the points made by the narrator, so we know there will be conflict. Saul's speech has two parallel components, so Samuel's reply consists of two parts that indirectly move towards the conflict, employing a questioning technique similar to Yahweh's in Gen. 3:12. Samuel effectively asks why he can hear livestock if all has been put to death. Having claimed to have performed Yahweh's command, Saul cannot now admit he has not done so. Therefore, his reply focuses on the people's activities, claiming they had set aside the best of the animals to sacrifice (*zbḥ*) to Yahweh, though the rest were devoted to destruction (*ḥrm*). Saul thus permits a change in sacrificial form. The root *ḥrm* refers to sacrifice where something or someone is given over entirely to Yahweh, essentially because it is already his. By contrast, *zbḥ* in sacrificial contexts usually refers to a practice where the participants shared a common meal involving the sacrifice. The change in the sacrificial form implies a change in the livestock's ownership. Under *ḥrm* everything was Yahweh's already and could not be claimed by another, but sacrifices associated with *zbḥ* belonged to the worshipper and were then offered to Yahweh. Although it sounds a noble response, Saul's dissembling is effectively a cover for theft, albeit one attributed to the people.

16–19. Samuel's intervention indicates his frustration with Saul's claims as he indicates he can reveal something extra from Yahweh, something Saul is prepared to hear. The message begins with a brief recitation of the events of chs. 8 – 12, noting that Saul did not consider himself particularly important (9:21), and yet Yahweh anointed him as king over Israel. What is emphasized is that Saul as king remains subject to Yahweh's greater authority. Saul had to carry out Yahweh's command faithfully, in this case devoting Amalek to destruction, with the element of Amalek's sinfulness directly stressed. Samuel's accusation is expressed through a leading question in v. 19. Saul's guilt is assumed, and the element of theft is highlighted by the forceful verb used, which describes Saul's pouncing on the prey and doing evil by not obeying Yahweh. Obedience is crucial for kingship in Israel, and Samuel insists it is lacking. The people cannot be blamed, for responsibility lies with Saul.

20–21. Saul's response seeks to deflect blame, but simply further incriminates him. He repeats his claim of faithfulness to Yahweh's command, though he now introduces Agag, whom Samuel has not mentioned. Unlike v. 9, it is now clear that Saul was personally responsible for Agag's presence, though he continues to blame the people for the livestock. Unlike the people, Saul offers no reason for Agag's presence.

22–23. Samuel's response is justly famous, and like many prophetic oracles is cast in poetry. The importance of obedience is stressed. Where sacrifices are mentioned in the first line of v. 22, each of the three succeeding lines mentions obedience, always in reference to its superiority over sacrifice. Samuel's stress on obedience's priority has echoes in prophetic texts (Amos 5:18–24; Mic. 6:8) and Psalms (Pss 40:6; 51:16). In v. 23 he adds that the choice not to obey is a sin equal to divination, which Deuteronomy unconditionally condemns (18:10; but see 1 Sam. 28:6!). The reference to teraphim is awkward since in some cases their presence as a form of household god is not condemned, but at others they are a means of occult enquiry (Ezek. 21:21), the sense required here by the parallelism (see Klein 1983: 153), so the accusation is more than idolatry (against McCarter 1980a: 268). Essentially, the choice not to obey Yahweh is sin as bad as prohibited behaviour because such practices deny Yahweh's authority. The stunning conclusion comes at the end of v. 23. Saul has rejected Yahweh's command; Yahweh has rejected him as king.

24–26. Only after judgment has been pronounced does Saul confess his sin, admitting he has broken Yahweh's command mediated to him through Samuel. Yet he again seeks to shift the blame on to the people, claiming he feared them and listened (šm') to their voice. Saul claims to have been forced to obey them instead of Yahweh, making his subsequent request that Samuel forgive him awkward because he has not fully accepted his guilt. The only other monarch to express himself in this way is Pharaoh (Exod. 10:16–17; see Frisch 1996: 102), an allusion that hardly strengthens Saul's position. Nevertheless, he recognizes a separation between himself and Yahweh, and understands he needs forgiveness, shown by Samuel's presence, if he is to worship Yahweh again. But virtually quoting his own words in v. 23b, Samuel refuses to return with Saul. Yahweh's rejection of Saul's reign means Samuel cannot accompany Saul.

27–29. As Samuel turns to leave, Saul grabs the edge of his robe and tears it. The wording is significant. David will cut off the same part of Saul's robe in 24:4 and 11, while Samuel's robe will be mentioned the next time Saul sees Samuel when he raises his shade to enquire of it (28:14), echoing Hannah's devotion in annually providing Samuel with a new robe (2:19). A host of associations are established, all more important than the oft-cited parallel of Ahijah (1 Kgs 11:30). Samuel announces that this symbolizes Yahweh taking the kingdom, not just dynastic succession as in 13:13–15, and giving it to Saul's neighbour. David is not mentioned, but we are prepared for his arrival. The neighbour will be better than Saul, though this must refer to obedience to Yahweh's command. The certainty of this is highlighted by Samuel's statement on the unchanging nature of Yahweh's decision. Although v. 29 (see Num. 23:19) may contradict both vv. 11 and 35 (Berges 1990: 190 regards it as an integrated gloss), Samuel is probably referring to this particular decision rather than making a generalized statement about Yahweh. The narrative is clear that Yahweh can regret (raising important questions about Yahweh's immutability), but this decision is one from which he will not turn (see Fretheim 1985: 595–602), a factor emphasized in the unusual title of Yahweh as the 'Enduring (or Eminent) one of Israel'.

30–31. Saul's second confession is the first point where he does not attempt to deflect blame, but it comes too late. Moreover, in seeking honour before Israel's elders, Saul still seeks inappropriate status, even if it is in the context of worship. Although Samuel goes with Saul, forgiveness is not mentioned.

Agag's death and the separation of Samuel and Saul: 15:32–35

32–33. The matter of the surviving livestock is not explored further since the sin to which Saul confessed directly was allowing Agag to survive. Although Samuel appears harsh in putting Agag to death, the narrator sees his actions as faithfulness to Yahweh's command. By stating Agag's crimes (murder), Samuel acts as a judicial executor since Deut. 17:7 required that witnesses to crimes should initiate any execution. Although Samuel is not a direct witness, he acts as Yahweh's intermediary. This action rebukes Saul further (see Long 1989: 165) since Samuel carries out what Saul was commanded to do. That this did not remove all the Amalekites, or even Agag's descendants, is clear from Esther's treatment of Haman, a descendant of Agag (3:1), while hinting Mordecai may be of Saul's family (2:5).

34–35. Samuel and Saul's separation is signified by their return to their homes, to which the narrator adds that because of his grief over Saul (grief ordinarily shown over the dead; Fokkelman 1986: 110) Samuel did not see him again until the day of his death, though Ramah and Gibeah are not far apart. Ordinarily, not to see someone again until the day of death means Samuel never saw Saul again, but this phrase is deliberately used to prepare for 28:3–25. Samuel's pain is mirrored by Yahweh's experience, for Yahweh regrets he has made Saul king. But Yahweh's gift of the kingdom to an unnamed neighbour indicates that kingship has not come to an end, although Saul is rejected.

Explanation

Reflection on this story inevitably focuses on how Saul's sin leads to his rejection. At a most basic level, it is a sin of partial obedience. He carried out some of Yahweh's command, but refrained from fully carrying it out. But the situation is more complex, because Samuel's meeting with Saul enabled Saul to address his shortcoming. Instead, he obfuscated, blaming the people, something that contrasts with David's immediate confession when confronted by Nathan in 2 Sam. 12:13. Only gradually do Saul's failures emerge in this conversation as he lets slip that the survival of the Amalekite king Agag was his decision. Saul could correct his actions but never does. Complicating matters is the interplay between Saul's claim that the livestock were kept for a sacrifice (*zbḥ*) and Yahweh's order that everything be devoted to destruction (*ḥrm*). Both terms refer to sacrificial action. Within Saul's claim, the livestock belong to the people and they can then offer them in a participatory sacrifice akin to a sacred barbecue, where the priestly share is given but the people eat the meat. But *ḥrm* (devoted to destruction) indicates that everything belongs to Yahweh, and is therefore excluded from what can be offered. Saul was partially obedient to Yahweh's command because he was partially obedient to the people, meaning he engaged in a wider range of sin than might be immediately apparent. 1 Sam. 12 established that obedience to Yahweh's command is the defining characteristic of Israel's kings, so Samuel had to announce that Yahweh had given the kingdom to an unnamed other. Yahweh is consistent with his claims, and expects that his servants will be too.

This narrative also highlights Yahweh's repentance/regret (*nḥm*). Such an anthropopathism may surprise, especially if one believes God to be impervious to change. But the text insists Yahweh regretted making Saul king, even as it insists that he will not relent (*nḥm*) of his decision to give the kingdom to another (cf. Gen. 6:7 and Jon. 3:10 for parallels). There is a deeply rooted paradox about God's nature, but his integrity is emphasized: he responds to human actions, but his purposes do not change (Peels 2003: 62–63). God's openness expresses both his freedom and his compassion (B. W. Anderson 1996:21). Though God's sovereignty does not compel obedience, his sovereignty responds to obedience when it comes (Stoebe 1973: 292; Moberley 1998: 114).

Many contemporary readers have difficulty with the concept of anything being devoted to destruction: it begins to sound like the odious 'ethnic cleansing'. No easy answer to the issues raised can be given, but it should be noted that here it is God's judgment on sin. In the NT such judgment becomes eschatological, though Ananias and Sapphira (Acts 5:1–11) are stark reminders that it was not always so. God's judgment on sin remains fixed, even if the form taken is not. This practice of things being devoted to destruction was being phased out by Saul's time, suggesting it had a specific and limited function, tied to the occupation of the land. It was historically and covenantally conditioned and since no modern nation stands in the same relationship to God as Israel in the OT, it is not a right any can claim today (see Wright 2004: 472–480). Nevertheless, we should not lose sight of God's rejection of sin and the biblical claim that sin will be judged, which in this instance saw Saul lose the kingdom through partial obedience.

1 SAMUEL 16:1–13

Translation

[1]Yahweh said to Samuel, 'How long will you grieve over Saul since I have rejected him as king over Israel? Fill your horn with oil, and go; I am sending you to Jesse the Bethlehemite, because I have identified my king among his sons.' [2]Samuel said, 'How can I go? When Saul hears, he will kill me.' But Yahweh said, 'Take a heifer along with you, and say, "I have come to sacrifice to Yahweh." [3]You shall invite Jesse to the sacrifice, and I shall make known to you what you shall do, and you shall anoint for me the one I indicate.'

[4]Samuel did what Yahweh said, and came to Bethlehem. The city elders were terrified when they met him and said, 'Have you come in peace?' [5]And he said, 'In peace. I have come to sacrifice to Yahweh. Consecrate yourselves and come with me to the sacrifice.' And he consecrated Jesse and his sons and invited them to the sacrifice.

[6]When they arrived, he saw Eliab and thought, 'Surely Yahweh's anointed is before him.' [7]But Yahweh said to Samuel, 'Do not consider his appearance, or the height of his stature, because I have rejected him, for God does not see as people see. People consider the appearance, but Yahweh looks to the heart.' [8]So Jesse called Abinadab and presented him before Samuel. But he said, 'Yahweh has not chosen this one either.' [9]Jesse presented Shammah, but he said, 'Yahweh has not chosen this one either.' [10]Jesse presented seven of his sons before Samuel, but Samuel said to Jesse, 'Yahweh has not chosen these.' [11]Then Samuel said to Jesse, 'Is that all your lads?' And he said, 'There is still the littlest, but look, he is keeping the sheep.' Samuel said, 'Send and bring him, for we shall not rest until he comes here.' [12]Then he sent and brought him, and he was ruddy, with fine features and a handsome appearance. And Yahweh said, 'Rise and anoint him, because this is the one.' [13]Samuel took the horn of oil and anointed him in his brothers' presence. And the Spirit of Yahweh rushed upon David from that day onward. Then Samuel arose and went to Ramah.

Notes on the text

1. With many MSS reading '*al* for '*al*.

2. 4QSam[a] and LXX have the imperative 'take' for MT's imperfect. This is probably a clarifying reading since the imperfect here has an imperatival force.

4. The sg. verb is indefinite and functions as a pl. may in English (GKC §141d, though §145u supports emendation instead). The elders' speech is to be read as an unmarked question (GKC §150a).

7. *yr'h h'lhym* has fallen out (also Klein 1983: 158) and is restored from LXX.

11. The sense of the verb *nsb* is awkward. The root *sbb* normally means 'to turn', so the sense here is a derived one in that to rest will be to turn from the task at hand.

Form and structure

Saul has been rejected as king, but Yahweh has not thereby rejected kingship. Since Hannah's Song (2:10) and the man of God's announcement (2:35), it has been evident that Yahweh is moving towards kingship. Samuel's speech at Gilgal (ch. 12) made clear the form such kingship must take, and against that model Saul's leadership had foundered. Saul was not set up to fail, but his choices led to that outcome. Yahweh must now anoint someone new from a different family. Although notoriously difficult to interpret, Gen. 49:10 appears to suggest that kingship is ultimately associated with Judah, so it is natural to expect the next king to come from there, though Saul's reign demonstrated that kings could come from other tribes. But David's anointing demonstrates Yahweh's continued commitment to monarchy, stressing that David is chosen on grounds radically different from those of Saul, though he could also have been chosen on that basis.

It is important to recognize that the text is not interested in providing biographical information on David. We know little about him prior to this time apart from hints provided in ch. 17. Rather, the text is theologically driven by the need to demonstrate Yahweh's choice. That drive may also have resulted in the narrative of chs. 16 – 17 being presented in a dischronologized form (Firth 2005d). This approach is clearly evidenced in 2 Sam. 5:17 – 8:14 and 21:1 – 24:25 (Firth 2001: 209, 214). Although the narrative of Samuel is broadly chronological, there are points where the narrator varies this because of the need to highlight thematic issues. The text leaves evidence to indicate this (incidentally pointing to the respect given to sources, since the awkwardness is allowed to remain), and this evidence hints that a different reading model is required. The beginning and end of chs. 16 – 17 provide these hints. First, in 16:1–3, Samuel is afraid of what Saul will do when he discovers Samuel visited Jesse's family. Such fear is difficult to understand unless Saul is aware of the family's significance, yet 16:4–5 suggests they are a relatively minor family in Bethlehem since Samuel does not include Jesse with the elders. Conversely, in 17:55, Saul does not know David's family, which sits awkwardly with 16:22, where David has been in Saul's service at his request. Possibly, the story's chronology begins with the Goliath story, subsequent to which David was taken into Saul's military service. Saul's jealousy saw David return to his family, a context that explains Samuel's concerns in 16:1–3. David was then anointed, but remained at home. In the light of Saul's blackening moods, David was then brought to the court as someone known for military valour (16:18) as well as musical skill. This makes sense of the clues left in the narrative. It also leads us to ask why this was important.

A partial explanation lies in the structural parallels between the rise of Saul and David (see 'Form and structure' on 9:1 – 10:16; also Grønbaek 1971: 71–74). David follows the same basic path as Saul, though the differences are of considerable importance since they represent key theological emphases. But these are differences within the pattern, not expressions of something different. A second element comes to the fore here – the selection of the new king is based on Yahweh's inscrutable purpose, not human criteria. David's military skill might have been known, but it was not the basis of Yahweh's election, which is still surprising given David's status as the youngest son. Finally, placing the Goliath story at the end of the section gives special prominence to David's words in 17:45–47 as an expression of the ideal of Israel's existence as a witness to the nations (see Gen. 12:1–3), while the enveloping references to Jesse the Bethlehemite in 16:1 and 17:58 mark off this stretch of text (though see 16:18). Thus we already have hints suggesting David has a more profound understanding of Israel's role before the nations than Saul does. The need to highlight these issues, not biography, accounts for the material's shape.

Since McCarter's (1980b) programmatic essay, 1 Sam. 16 – 2 Sam. 5 has usually been considered a defence of David's rise to power, highlighting his refusal to seize power from Saul, and thus his legitimacy. Somewhat unusual twists have been put on this by Halpern (2001) and McKenzie (2000), both of whom charge David with considerably more than the text, though both demonstrate that the account is quite ancient. The detail of their position cannot be examined here, but their position seems too complex for the gains generated, and Ockham's razor suggests that reading the text at more or less face value is more effective (see Provan, Long and Longman 2003: 221–225). By way of contrast, Isser (2003) places the whole account into a folklorist context. Although McCarter's approach can be criticized for being too closely bound up with source criticism rather than the narrative movement of Samuel, the function of these chapters is more or less as he suggests. However, although the text apparently responds to possible criticisms of David, we should not assume (with Halpern 2001) that every point that it offers in David's defence signals David's guilt. The placement of this body of text within the whole of Samuel suggests the narrative wants to demonstrate Yahweh's presence with David, and that this presence led to his success and achievement. This theme runs across David's story in Samuel, highlighting that this text is fundamentally shaped by concerns about Yahweh rather than David's biography and politics, even though such information is shared. The special concern of 16:1–13 is to begin to show how central Yahweh's presence with David really was.

This explanation is achieved with considerable skill and plays on the semantic range of keywords, especially those related to sight. There are significant verbal links with ch. 15, so although this segment commences the account of David's rise (though many, e.g. Klein 1983: 163, and Mommer 1991: 176, prefer 16:14), it is well integrated with the surrounding narratives. There is an element of suspense developed by withholding David's name until 16:13, so a first-time reader is unaware of David's identity until the very end. This fits in with the narrator's insistence that appearance is not what matters since introduction of David's name too soon evokes too many other associations. Yahweh chooses his king, a fact highlighted by the reference to the horn of oil with which the passage begins and ends, and though that king will be David, we must not know it too soon.

Comment

Samuel is sent to Bethlehem: 16:1–5

1. The movement from ch. 15 is abrupt, with no indication of the timescale involved, though v. 1 picks up on the key themes from the chapter's end as Samuel continues to grieve over Saul. There Yahweh relented that he had made him king, and here he acts to resolve the political problems this generates. His speech to Samuel is simple and direct, the question 'How long?' effectively indicating that such grief is no longer required. The reason for this is stated in the reaffirmation of Yahweh's rejection (*m's*) of Saul as king. Samuel had announced this in 15:23 and 26, but now Yahweh reminds Samuel. Yahweh's directives make clear that a new king is to be appointed. For this reason, Samuel was to take a horn filled with oil in order to anoint this king, one Yahweh had chosen from Jesse's family in Bethlehem (also known as Ephrath, Gen. 35:19), a town about 5 miles south of Jerusalem. This is the family's first mention in the Hebrew Bible (Ruth precedes Samuel in English Bibles, but not Hebrew), so we have no knowledge of them. However, there is an immediate contrast with Saul's family since Kish was a man of wealth or power, and no such statement is made here. What is significant is not their prestige, but that Yahweh has identified his new king among them. Saul was the people's choice, but this member of Jesse's family is the one we have expected since Hannah's Song (2:10; cf. 2:35).

2–3. In terms of the information available at this point, Samuel's response is surprising since no reason is given for fearing execution by Saul if he does this. However, the narrative dischronologization (see 'Form and structure') means Yahweh's election is foregrounded in spite of the difficulties it poses. David's military achievements probably mean he had some repute, though as the youngest son it would not change his status within the family, and association with him placed Samuel at risk. In response, Yahweh points out that there were legitimate reasons why Samuel should go to Bethlehem, though the sacrifice could possess a range of meanings. Samuel was to invite Jesse so Yahweh could make clear whom to anoint. Brueggemann's assertion that this process was virtually a lie (1990b: 121) appears to miss the point, assuming that Yahweh's activity excluded prudence. Nevertheless, a sacrifice (*zbḥ*) is ironic. An intention to sacrifice had caused Saul's downfall, but was now how Yahweh would designate his successor.

4–5. Samuel's obedience is emphasized, and the narrative brings us quickly to Bethlehem. The threat of activity by Saul against them was apparently something of which the locals were aware, though when the elders greet Samuel it is also quite likely that they are concerned by what he will do among them. Whatever the anxiety's cause, the town elders tremble when they greet him, wanting to know whether he has come for a peaceable purpose. Only when this is resolved can the narrative move to the town proper. We thus see that the town was aligned with neither Samuel nor Saul. Only when Samuel has been accepted can he initiate the sacrifice, something requiring the consecration of those elders attending. Jesse appears not to be among the elders since they are told to consecrate themselves (make themselves ritually holy), whereas Samuel consecrates Jesse and his sons separately. Although this may simply highlight that the appropriate consecration took place, it suggests this was not a family of sufficient importance for routine involvement with the elders and a prophet.

David's anointing: 16:6–13

6–7. Although others were involved, the narrative is not concerned with anyone apart from Jesse's family. How the events described happened without others knowing is not a matter of concern, though it was presumably possible to have some privacy at the sacrifice. The narrator is much more concerned to describe the events of David's anointing, highlighting that even Samuel did not fully understand Yahweh's ways. Saul's election had, in part, been related to his appearance, and Samuel had not yet learnt that good looks alone do not make a leader of Yahweh's people. Hence the first event described at the sacrifice is when Samuel sees Eliab, and is convinced that he must be Yahweh's anointed. In fact, the narrator does not even indicate that he is Jesse's son, something only made clear retrospectively. To this Yahweh delivers a stunning rebuke in v. 7. Samuel was deceived by the same things as before. Yahweh has different criteria, and appearance is not one of them – otherwise, Samuel may be doing nothing more than appointing another Saul, and in any case Yahweh had already told Samuel that he would indicate whom to anoint (Fokkelman 1986: 120). What matters is the heart, not least because of 13:14, where it was asserted that Yahweh would choose the one after his own heart. That reference more likely concerns Yahweh's freedom in choosing, but is matched here with a concern with the heart of the one chosen, with the heart representing issues such as motivation, thought processes and loyalty. Samuel sees only the outside, but Yahweh looks deeper, a thought possibly reinforced by the use of a different verb for human seeing in comparison with Yahweh's clearer sight.

8–11. That Eliab is Jesse's son is made clear only by the fact that he now presents Abinadab and Shammah, presumably his next-eldest sons, who are likewise rejected. Where Saul's election was presented as a smooth transition from tribe to clan and finally to Saul (10:20–21), this is a process of rejection, as Samuel cannot see the right one. A degree of uncertainty is raised, especially once all seven of Jesse's sons have been presented, making Samuel's frustration also that of the reader. If all Jesse's sons have been presented, where is the next king? Yet Yahweh's opening statement stands, and the next king has been identified from Jesse's family. Samuel's question evokes the imagery of ch. 2, where a 'lad' (*na'ar*) could have been either a servant or a son. Is he leaving scope for Jesse to offer a member of his household rather than a biological son? Jesse's answer leaves hope even as it creates expectation – the least of the sons has not been presented because he is tending the sheep. This creates a sense of hope in that ANE kings routinely styled themselves as 'shepherds', while a recurrent theme in earlier narratives was Yahweh's election of the younger brother (e.g. Isaac, not Ishmael; Jacob, not Esau, Joseph, etc.). The possibility is not lost on Samuel either, and he is anxious for this last son to be presented.

12–13. The youngest son is now brought, but there is a further surprise in store, as the first thing we learn about him is his appearance. Yahweh may not consider the appearance, but apparently it would have worked this time as well, as we discover that the ruddy (reddish) lad is quite good looking. Lit. he had 'beautiful eyes', though this may be a more general comment on his appearance (Leah had 'weak eyes' in Gen. 29:17, the contrast with Rachel suggesting that this is a negative evaluation of her appearance) than anything specific about his eyes. There is inner-narrative logic to this phrase as well in that Yahweh's denial of interest in appearance in v. 7 is literally with reference to the eyes. Had he been presented for popular acclamation, this lad could have been more than acceptable. But the crucial matter is Yahweh's choice, and this is immediately shown when he directs Samuel to anoint the lad. This choice is confirmed when the Spirit rushes upon David, who is only now named. The Spirit's presence had been a sign to Saul of his status (10:6), though the Spirit's coming happened only after his anointing. However, the Spirit came on David from that day onward. David's experience of the Spirit was not only a sign of election on that day; it was an enduring element. The Spirit would leave Saul (16:14), but David was for ever Yahweh's charismatic choice. With that, Samuel returned to Ramah (see 15:34), so we have no other record of an encounter between him and David until 19:18, their only other meeting.

Explanation

Walter Brueggemann observes that 'David is not a human accident but a divine intention' (1990b: 120). This is undoubtedly how to read this narrative, though it also means placing it in the whole of 1 Sam. 1 – 15. We knew from 2:10 and 2:35 that kingship was coming, and that Yahweh would provide his own king. Although Saul had a legitimate opportunity to fulfil this role as the people's choice, his failure means that we now come to Yahweh's choice. It is here we discover that David is that choice. Nevertheless, David's election fits the wider scriptural pattern where Yahweh consistently chooses those who might otherwise have been passed over – notably the younger and the barren. Indeed, David's election brings these elements together in that David is the youngest son of eight (though 1 Chr. 2:13–15 indicates only seven; see Kalimi 2001: 2), and Samuel is the son of a formerly barren woman. The pattern seen in their lives is not restricted to this level, for a great theme of the exodus is that Yahweh did not choose Israel because of their power and prestige but rather for their weakness (see Deut. 7:6–8), and in faithfulness to his covenant with the ancestors – a theme Paul develops in Christian discipleship in 1 Cor. 1:26–31. God's intention has been kingship, but in doing so he has kept to his own pattern of choosing those who otherwise surprise. This reality must not be pressed too far, because the text provides no indication that David was a little boy, in spite of the popularity of that concept. Rather, he is a humanly unlikely candidate because he is the youngest son of an undistinguished family in an otherwise unimportant town. The human propensity is to go for the obvious, as does Samuel in his initial response to Eliab, but Yahweh's ways are not those of humankind. That said, the text does not hide David's physical attractiveness. Good looks, apparently, ran in the family. But God sees things differently, and his thoughts are not our thoughts (Isa. 55:8–9). David may well be attractive, but the text asserts we cannot equate the divine intention with those we would devise ourselves (see Miscall 1986: 117). The divine intention is there, but that does not mean it is always immediately apparent, and how David conforms to Yahweh's heart can be known only as the narrative develops.

The anointing is presented at the beginning of David's story to create a frame of reference for what follows, even if other events may have preceded it. In so shaping the account, the narrator provides us with a means of reading the events that follow, many of which will be less than savoury. David is Yahweh's choice, and the Spirit is powerfully with him. This does justify all he does in his rise or as king, because there are points where Yahweh has to get David out of the trouble he makes for himself (especially in 1 Sam. 27 – 2 Sam. 1). Election to the office of king, and an understanding of what that means in Israel, does not justify everything David does. What it does mean is that he remains within Yahweh's larger purposes, so for all the twists it takes, his move towards the throne from here is inexorable.

1 SAMUEL 16:14–23

Translation

[14]The Spirit of Yahweh left Saul, and a grievous spirit from Yahweh assailed him. [15]Saul's servants said to him, 'Behold, a grievous spirit from God is assailing you. [16]Let our lord now direct your servants who are before you, and they will seek out a man who is skilful at playing the harp. And it will be that whenever the grievous

spirit from God comes upon you, his hand will play and you will be well.' ¹⁷Saul said to his servants, 'Provide for me a man who can play well, and bring him to me.' ¹⁸Then one of the lads answered, 'Behold, I have seen a son of Jesse the Bethlehemite, who knows how to play and is a valiant warrior, a man of battle, discerning of speech, good looking, and Yahweh is with him.' ¹⁹So Saul sent messengers to Jesse and said, 'Send David your son who is with the flock to me.' ²⁰Jesse took a donkey, bread, a skin of wine and the kid of a goat and sent them with David his son to Saul. ²¹David came to Saul and stood before him. And he loved him greatly, and he became his kit-bearer. ²²Saul sent to Jesse saying, 'Let David remain before me because he has found favour in my eyes.' ²³Whenever the spirit from God came upon Saul, David took the harp and played with his hand, and Saul would be refreshed and the grievous spirit would depart from him.

Notes on the text

14. Some MSS read 'from God' instead of 'from Yahweh'.

16. LXX omits 'of God'.

22. The subject of *wayye'ĕhābēhû* is not stated, but is most likely Saul (against Wong 1997).

Form and structure

David's anointing and Saul's rejection create an expectation that we shall quickly move to the point where David replaces Saul as king. In terms of how Kings narrates such changes, it is possible to relate this in only a few verses, and even the story of Jehu (where a new king is anointed while the other is alive) completes the removal of the previous ruling house and Jehu's takeover in only two chapters (2 Kgs 9 – 10), though there Jehu has no hesitation in killing the existing king of Israel, as well as the king of Judah, in the process (2 Kgs 9:14–29). But David's rise to the throne will be strikingly different because the narrative insists on relating the extended process by which this happened, emphasizing that David was never Saul's enemy, though Saul did not always recognize this. Two key themes that emerge through this account are Yahweh's presence with David and how others are drawn to him. These elements are related, and both are emphasized by this account, which stands at the head of his movement towards the throne. One of Saul's servants and Saul himself are drawn to David, while Yahweh's presence with him is itself a key element in the statement of qualities explaining why David should come to court.

David's movement towards the court is balanced by the move of the grievous spirit to Saul, a spirit sent by Yahweh which can be calmed by David's playing. The change in spirit links this narrative to the previous one where the Spirit of Yahweh came upon David (16:13), graphically

COMMENT 187

illustrating Saul and David's relative status before Yahweh. Saul's rejection is worked out by the loss of the Spirit, while David's election is shown by the Spirit's enduring presence. Hence the chapter as a whole has a certain unity, in spite of its seemingly disparate material. A further link appears in v. 22, when Saul writes to Jesse, indicating David has found favour 'in my eyes'. The statement is formulaic, but takes on a special significance due to the unusual use of the word 'eyes' in 16:7, 12. Yahweh rebuked Samuel for seeing the 'eyes', though David has 'beautiful eyes', and it is now in Saul's 'eyes' that David finds favour. In a telling irony, Saul sees only the criteria Yahweh rejected, though what he sees is actually correct. The nature of this problem for Saul is reinforced by the inclusion created by the reference to the grievous spirit with which the passage ends, a spirit that can be calmed only through David. Saul sees what is humanly helpful about David, even experiencing benefit through him, but he does not see what Yahweh is doing. See 'Form and structure' on 16:1–13 for the chronological relationship of the two halves of the chapter.

Comment

14. The Spirit's departure from Saul represents an immediate link between this account and 16:13. There the Spirit came upon David, and now the Spirit departs from Saul. The Spirit's presence signifies election to the role of king, so the contrast highlights the change in status between David and Saul (see Howard 1989: 475–476), even though David will not become king until 2 Sam. 2:4 (Judah) and 5:1–5 (Israel). More troubling is that Saul is afflicted by a grievous spirit from Yahweh. It should be borne in mind that the OT is seldom concerned with secondary causation, and since Yahweh is Lord of all, the spirit is seen as coming from him. But the narrative still holds Saul responsible for his actions while afflicted (18:10–11; 19:10), so though this statement is absolute, the wider narrative indicates that a more nuanced understanding is necessary. A specific psychological assessment of Saul is not really possible, and this first mention being expressed in terms of its absolute cause discourages the attempt. But we should note that the word usually translated 'evil' (here 'grievous') in the OT does not necessarily have a moral force (see Amos 3:6), and that is almost certainly the case here.

15–16. Although this is the first reference to Saul's affliction, it is something with which his servants are familiar. There is no indication of the time that passed between vv. 14 and 15, so these events could have been some time later, which would have given his servants time to develop a strategy for dealing with the problem. Saul's servants are loyal to him and aware that music in some way calms Saul when his condition is at its most severe. Hence they recognize the need for a harpist for those times when the spirit afflicts Saul. All they need is Saul's permission to act for him to seek a man to play the harp when the spirit assails him, so as to calm him.

17–18. Saul agrees with his servant's suggestion, though his speech betrays another important link with 16:1–13. In 16:1 Yahweh could declare that he had provided (*r'h*) himself with a king, whereas Saul can only command that his servants provide (*r'h*) him with a harpist. The harpist's job description is as the servants suggested. At this point we expect a search to find someone with the necessary skills, but it transpires that one servant knows the person needed. This servant (*na'ar*, 'lad') has already seen (*r'h*) a son of Jesse the Bethlehemite (see 16:1), who has skill with the harp, though he lists a wider range of qualifications, a significant portion of which centre on his military prowess. Military skills and musical ability are by no means contradictory, but nothing in the previous discussion suggested it was important to have more than musical ability. In fact, the servant's speech uses twice as many words to describe his military skills as it does his musical ability, and all of it is garnished with the additional observations that he is discerning in speech, good looking and has Yahweh with him. These elements prepare for the central themes that run through David's presentation in the chapters that follow, since each plays some part other than the reference to his good looks. There are some significant ironies in how this is presented as good news for Saul, especially given that Yahweh's presence with this unnamed son is another sign of Yahweh's rejection of him. Yahweh has rejected Saul, and the servant's suggestion hints at what is to come, hints suggesting that this son of Jesse may be Saul's replacement.

19–21. Saul seems to be oblivious to the hints in the servant's speech and issues the command that David be brought. It is only now that David's name is mentioned, so that Saul is the first to speak his name directly in 1 Samuel. In sending the messengers with the demand that Jesse send David back to him, Saul also draws a further link with the preceding passage by noting that David is with the flock. Saul's reference to David locates him in the relatively lowly place where Samuel found him, but the servant's speech has indicated that he is considerably more than that. Saul's description of David pushes him down the social ladder, a mechanism that may in part be a response to the servant's glowing testimony, especially if we are correct in presupposing that these events are chronologically subsequent to the Goliath story (see 'Form and structure' on 16:1–13). Unwittingly, Saul brings his rival to court, preparing for conflicts that will come between David and himself, though his speech may suggest he has his own agenda in having David come. Once the command reached the family, Jesse made the appropriate arrangements to send David to Saul, accompanied by a significant gift, perhaps to indicate the family's loyalty to Saul. The items in the gift represent things Saul encountered when he began his move to the throne (10:1–8), though Jesse's intentions remain ambiguous. When David arrived, he took his place as a courtier and rose to some prominence. This seems to have been initiated by Saul since the most likely interpretation of the ambiguous 'and he loved him' is that Saul loved David. The nature of this prominence becomes clear when David became Saul's kit-bearer, a role that 14:1 suggests was of some importance within Israel's military structures. David came to court as a shepherd and musician, but the broader description of him offered by Saul's servant in 16:17 begins to work itself out, so the context where David would be recognized as the logical alternative to Saul is established. Yahweh has provided a new king for himself, and Saul paradoxically provides the platform for him to come to prominence.

22–23. David's status within Saul's court is confirmed by Saul's decision to ask Jesse for permission for David to remain. This suggests Saul's initial plan was that David should stay only for a specified period, but the status David achieved meant he became indispensable. Saul has not only come to love David; he can even communicate to Jesse that he has found favour in his eyes. This statement is fraught with ambiguities because of this chapter's structure. In 16:7 Samuel was told not to look to the 'eyes', though David had beautiful 'eyes'. Although Saul's speech uses formulaic language, it indicates he has not penetrated the key to David's status: he has not looked on the heart. But Saul is incapable of doing this, for Yahweh is no longer with him but with David. This is graphically illustrated by the closing verse closing off the passage by means of an inclusion where David is shown to be active, doing what he came for and refreshing (a play on the root *rwḥ* from which 'spirit' is derived) Saul by calming him and enabling the grievous spirit to depart. Yahweh is with David, not Saul, and this is reinforced by Saul's condition.

Explanation

Yahweh's presence is central to David's rise. Even when not explicitly stated, it is an element the stories all illustrate. This time the narrator makes the theme explicit because of the story's importance at the beginning of David's rise. However, what it means to say Yahweh is with David is not defined. It is known only by examining how Yahweh brings about his purposes through David. That is to say, Yahweh's presence does not enable David to do whatever he wants. Rather, Yahweh's presence means he is working his purposes through David, and in this instance that purpose is to bring David to the throne. This is not a mechanical outworking of the divine will, because various human characters all play their own part, each taking responsibility for his own actions. Saul may be afflicted by a grievous spirit following the departure of Yahweh's Spirit to David, but he still makes important decisions about David, most importantly that David should remain with him in the court, also appointing him to an important military position. Saul's servants act independently to bring David to the court, even voicing the wider range of David's attributes than were necessary for the musician who calmed Saul. Even Jesse acts positively by contributing a gift to the court. What is remarkable is that at no point is David said to have done anything other than play his harp and calm Saul. He was brought to the court for this one role, but the platform this created meant that he was able to demonstrate his ability before the nation. The wide range of skills voiced by Saul's servant could be seen by all. Thus to say Yahweh was with David is not a generalized statement, a blessing without specific content. It was an affirmation that those things that constituted David's mission were being brought about by Yahweh. Paul makes a similar affirmation about the role of the Spirit in the life of the believer in Rom. 8:18–27, because the NT democratizes the work and role of the Spirit. But this process of democratization does not ignore the fact that God's presence in this way is still tied to the achievement of his purposes.

1 SAMUEL 17

Translation

[1]The Philistines assembled their forces for war and were assembled at Socoh in Judah, and encamped between Socoh and Azekah, in Ephes Damim. [2]Saul and the men of Israel were assembled and were encamped in the Valley of Elah, and they set their battle line to meet the Philistines. [3]The Philistines stood on the hill on one side while Israel stood on the hill on the other, and the valley was between them. [4]A champion came out from the Philistine camp named Goliath of Gath, and his height was four cubits and a span. [5]A bronze helmet was on his head and he wore a coat of scale mail, and the weight of the coat was five thousand shekels of bronze. [6]He wore greaves of bronze on his legs, and a bronze javelin was slung between his shoulders. [7]The shaft of his spear was like a weaver's beam, and the head of his spear weighed six hundred shekels of iron, and his shield-bearer went before him. [8]He stood and called to the Israelite ranks and said to them, 'Why have you come out to form your battle lines? Am I not a Philistine and you are Saul's servants? Choose a man and let him come down to me! [9]If he is able to fight me and kill me, we shall be your servants. But if I prevail against him and kill him, you shall be our servants and shall serve us.' [10]And the Philistine said, 'I defy the ranks of Israel today – give me a man and let us fight together.' [11]Saul and all Israel heard these words of the Philistine, and were dismayed and greatly afraid.

[12]Now David was the son of a man of Ephrath, from Bethlehem of Judah, and his name was Jesse. He had eight sons and in Saul's days he was old and advanced in years. [13]Jesse's three oldest sons followed Saul to the battle. The names of his three sons who had gone into battle were Eliab (the firstborn), Abinadab (the second) and Shammah (the third). [14]David was the youngest, and the three eldest followed Saul, [15]but David went back and forth from Saul to pasture his father's sheep at

Bethlehem. [16]The Philistine drew near morning and evening for forty days and took his stand.

[17]Jesse said to David his son, 'Take this ephah of parched grain for your brothers along with these ten loaves and take them quickly to the camp, to your brothers, [18]and bring these ten cheeses to their unit commander. Visit your brothers to check on their welfare and bring a token from them.' [19]Now Saul and they and all the men of Israel were in the Valley of Elah waging war with the Philistines.

[20]David rose early in the morning, left the sheep with an attendant, took the provisions and went as his father Jesse commanded him, and he entered the secured area as the army was going out to the battle line shouting the war cry. [21]Israel and the Philistines set themselves in their battle lines opposite each other. [22]David left everything in the hands of the keeper of kit, ran to the battle line, and came and sought his brothers' welfare. [23]As he was speaking with them, behold, the champion (Goliath of the Philistines from Gath was his name), came up from the Philistine ranks and spoke as before, and David heard him. [24]When all the men of Israel saw the man, they fled from before him and were very afraid. [25]The men of Israel said, 'Have you seen this man who has come up? Surely he has come up to defy Israel! The king will make whoever kills him very rich and give him his daughter and the house of his father shall be set among the freemen in Israel.' [26]David said to the men standing with him, 'What shall be done for the man who kills this Philistine to remove the reproach from upon Israel, for who is this uncircumcised Philistine that he should defy the armies of the living God?' [27]The people responded in accordance with this message, 'Thus shall it be done for the man who kills him.' [28]But Eliab, his oldest brother, heard him talking with the men, and Eliab's anger was kindled against David and he said to him, 'Why have you come down? With whom have you left those few sheep in the wilderness? I know your presumption and the evil of your heart, because you have come down to see the battle!' [29]But David said, 'What have I done now? Isn't that the issue?' [30]He turned away from him to another and spoke in the same way. And the people answered him as before.

[31]When they heard what David said, they told Saul, so Saul took him. [32]David said to Saul, 'Let no one's heart fall because of him – your servant will go forth and fight with this Philistine.' [33]But Saul said to David, 'You are not able to go against this Philistine to fight him, because you are a lad, and he has been a man of war since he was a lad.' [34]But David said to Saul, 'Your servant has been a shepherd to his father's flock, and when a lion or a bear came and took an animal from the flock, [35]I went after it and struck it and rescued from its mouth. When it rose against me, I seized it by the jaw, struck it and killed it. [36]Your servant has struck down both lion and bear, and this uncircumcised Philistine will be like one of them because he has defied the ranks of the living God.' [37]And David said, 'Yahweh, who delivered me from the paw of both the lion and the bear shall deliver me from the hand of this Philistine.' Then Saul said to David, 'Go, and Yahweh be with you.' [38]Saul dressed David in his gear, and he set a bronze helmet on his head and dressed him in armour. [39]David girded his sword on over his gear, but he was unable to go because he had not tested them. So David said to Saul, 'I am not able to walk in these because I have not tested them.' So David took them off.

⁴⁰Then he took his stick in his hand and chose five smooth stones from the stream and put them in his shepherd's bag, that is his wallet, and his sling was in his hand; and he drew near the Philistine. ⁴¹The Philistine kept moving nearer to David, and his shield-bearer was before him. ⁴²The Philistine looked and considered David and he despised him because he was a lad, ruddy and handsome of appearance. ⁴³The Philistine said to David, 'Am I a dog that you come out to me with sticks?' And the Philistine cursed David by his gods. ⁴⁴The Philistine said to David, 'Come to me, and I shall give your flesh to the birds of the heavens and to the beasts of the field.' ⁴⁵But David said to the Philistine, 'You come to me with sword and spear and javelin, but I come to you in the name of Yahweh of Armies, God of the ranks of Israel, whom you have defied. ⁴⁶This day, Yahweh will deliver you into my hands, and I shall strike you and sever your head, and this day I shall give your corpse and the corpses of the Philistine camp to the birds of the heavens and the creatures of the earth, and the whole earth will know that there is a God in Israel. ⁴⁷This whole assembly shall know that it is not by sword or spear that Yahweh saves, for the battle belongs to Yahweh, and he will give you into our hands.'

⁴⁸When the Philistine rose and drew near to attack David, David hurried and ran toward the battle line to attack the Philistine. ⁴⁹David put his hand in his kit and drew from there a stone. He slung, and he struck the Philistine on his forehead, and the stone sank deep into his forehead, and he fell on his face to the ground.

⁵⁰So David prevailed over the Philistine with sling and stone, and struck the Philistine and killed him. There was no sword in David's hand. ⁵¹David ran and stood over the Philistine and took his sword, drew it from its sheath, killed him and cut off his head with it. When the Philistines saw their warrior was dead, they fled. ⁵²Then the men of Israel and Judah arose, gave a war cry and pursued the Philistines as far as the valley and the gates of Ekron, and the bodies of the Philistines fell on the Shaarim road as far as Gath and the gates of Ekron. ⁵³The Israelites returned from pursuing the Philistines and plundered their camp. ⁵⁴David took the Philistine's head and brought it to Jerusalem, but he put his kit in his tent.

⁵⁵When Saul saw David going out to attack the Philistine, he said to Abner, commander of the army, 'Whose son is this lad, Abner?' And Abner said, 'As your soul lives, O King, I do not know.' ⁵⁶The king said, 'Enquire whose son this stripling is.' ⁵⁷When David returned from killing the Philistine, Abner took him and brought him before Saul, and the Philistine's head was in his hand. ⁵⁸Saul said to him, 'Whose son are you, lad?' David said, 'The son of your servant, Jesse the Bethlehemite.'

Notes on the text

4. Following 4QSamᵃ and most LXX texts as well as Josephus. MT's '6 cubits' is defended by Bergen (1996: 189). Fokkelman (1986: 148) notes that LXX provides the structural progression 4–5–6.

6. *kîdôn* (javelin) may also be a scimitar. Also v. 45.

7. Reading Q *'ēṣ* ('wood', and hence 'shaft') with many MSS and LXX. K *ḥēṣ* (arrow) is improbable.

8. Reading *bḥr* (choose) with LXX.

12–31. These verses are missing from LXX[B]. See below, 'Form and structure'.

12. Following LXX 'advanced in years'. MT 'among men'.

18. Lit. 'commander of their thousand'.

30. See Stoebe (1973: 322) and Fokkelman (1986: 164–165) for the translation. The key is to recognize the polyvalence of *dābār*.

32. LXX has *kardia tou kyriou mou*.

37. LXX omits 'and David said'.

38. LXX omits the reference to armour.

39. LXX omits 'because he had not tested them'.

41. This verse is missing from LXX[B].

46. With McCarter (1980a: 289), LXX's longer reading is preferred, MT having lost text through homoioarchton.

48. LXX omits the second half of this verse.

49. A change in vocalization means David struck Goliath on the knee. LXX recognizes this ambiguity and adds the explanatory note that it was 'through the helmet'.

50. LXX omits this verse.

51. With a few MSS, reading *'al* for *'el*.

55–58. Missing from LXX[B]. The omission continues to 18:5.

Form and structure

1 Sam. 17 is among the best-known OT narratives. Its popular title 'David and Goliath' has proverbial status, so even those hard-pressed to recount the story's details have a theory as to its message. However, this status usually means a focus on the size comparison between the respective national champions, although David is never described as small, and since Saul's armour apparently fitted him, he must have been relatively tall, albeit still smaller than Goliath. David is a lad (*na'ar*) and apparently lacks formal military experience, but the narrative's comparison is not to the champion's size but rather to the means employed to gain victory. The extended discussion of Goliath's appearance demonstrates he is not only larger than anyone else, but that he is equipped with the latest military technology (17:4–7). But to read only from this perspective is to be lulled into a false sense of insecurity, because it follows only terms of the initial Philistine claims. As the narrative proceeds, it gradually moves from description to dialogue, and in particular to David's dialogue, where he shifts the focus from the Philistine's military advantages and on to Yahweh. This process is carefully structured, so we move from Goliath's challenge, where he defines the battle as one between himself and Israel's

army through to David's declaration that the battle belongs to Yahweh and that Goliath's defeat is a testimony to the whole world that there is a God in Israel (17:45–47). David's claims at the point where he meets Goliath are not new. Rather, they represent the end point of a process where each stage of speech involving David gradually sharpened the narrative's theological focus. Thus, where the Israelite army accepts that Goliath defies Israel, David insists that Goliath defies the armies of the living God (17:25–27). Although the dialogue with Eliab at first seems to counter this pattern, it does more than provide David with the opportunity to deny he has come to the battle lines for personal profit; it is the means by which he is taken to Saul (17:28–31). While there, he refocuses Saul's perceptions, because it is not weaponry and military technology that will deliver him from the Philistine; it is Yahweh. Since this central point is driven home so carefully through a number of repetitions in dialogue, the actual battle account can be brief: only vv. 48–49. However, the author's characteristic approach of using repetitions to drive home the point results in the more detailed account provided in vv. 50–53, though this also provides information demonstrating that Goliath's defeat triggered the defeat of the Philistine army as a whole, though not in the terms Goliath had suggested.

Such a reading presumes we are following the tradition found in MT. But 1 Sam. 17 is a point where the text is particularly open to dispute since LXX[B] is considerably shorter. The most obvious omissions are vv. 12–31, 50 and 55–58, though (see 'Notes') there are other points where the LXX is shorter. More importantly, LXX[B] resolves the anomalies apparently present in MT in that David is already with Saul as an established warrior who completes the battle against Goliath; while the story's conclusion at v. 54 means the difficulty of Saul not knowing who David is does not arise. Thus ch. 17 can be seen to follow 16:14–23. For this reason, a number of scholars (e.g. Auld 2004: 81–96; Campbell 2003: 167–193; Tov 1986) have argued that the MT's additional material should be treated as a separate tale (in Auld's case, as an intentional series of supplements) that confuses the otherwise more direct account from LXX. In addition, although LXX[A] includes the material found in MT, it appears to come from a different translation source since it follows MT more closely than does the rest of the narrative in LXX. The material in LXX[A] paralleling the additional text in MT is therefore secondary. There is no need to contest these observations. However, a defence of MT here is still reasonable (Firth 2005d), especially when it is noted that chs. 16 – 17 represent a dischronologized narrative (see 'Form and structure' on 16:1–13; cf. Fokkelman 1986: 144–145). The shorter account only resolves the difficulties posed by 16:14–23 in relation to ch. 17, but not those of the relationship of 16:1–13 to both. Once it is recognized that the account is structured to conclude David's initial move to the court with a battle victory (while leaving clues that this is not the chronological sequence), the need to harmonize ch. 17 with 16:14–23 falls away. The material's presentation has been shaped by the need to begin with David's election by Yahweh, so this is seen separately from his military skills. It then concludes with his killing Goliath, and especially his speech to Goliath, so David's perception of Israel is the highlight of his move towards the court.

These conclusions still presume David actually slew Goliath. But this is not a point of scholarly agreement since 2 Sam. 21:19 seemingly reports that one Elhanan slew Goliath, the argument being that the achievement of a lesser-known warrior was attributed to the better-known one, a process not unknown in folkloric literature (see the summary in Isser 2003: 125). But the retention of Elhanan's story is puzzling because the account of his killing Goliath is brief and could easily be omitted. Although it is common to dismiss the fact that 1 Chr. 20:5 has Elhanan slay Lahmi the brother of Goliath as a late harmonization (e.g. McKenzie 2000: 76), the case for accepting the witness of Chronicles is strong (see 'Form and structure' at 2 Sam. 21:15–21). Although there were certain standard 'type-scene' conventions employed in accounts about the slaying of the Philistine giants, it is reasonable to assume that David did slay Goliath. Although reference to the Goliath incident elsewhere is limited (only 21:9), its significance resounds through other elements in David's story (18:6–9; 25:29; 29:5), and makes a fitting narrative climax in his move towards the court, even if it was probably the earliest story about him.

Comment

Goliath's introduction: 17:1–11

1–3. The nature of events leading to conflict with the Philistines is not explored, though they are probably a continuation of the conflict from chs. 13 – 14. This time the battle's location is in Judah (earlier conflicts were in Benjamin), with Socoh and Azekah a little over 12 miles west of Bethlehem in the Shephelah. This is where the encroaching populations of Philistia and Israel met, with the Valley of Elah running up towards Bethlehem. This was a strategic area to control because it enabled access to the good farming land of the coastal plain and the grazing land of the valley (see Eybers 1978: 43–44). The Israelite highlands were much poorer (note Eliab's dismissive comment in v. 28), so these areas were important to both groups. The exact site of Ephes Dammim is unknown, though the general area can be identified, but requires a small valley in between the two hills where the two sides faced one another.

4–7. The conflict's source is not a matter of interest. More interesting is the activity of the Philistine champion, a giant from Gath, who came out each day to goad Israel into action. Single combat to resolve conflict is not well attested in the region (though known among the Hittites), though since

Goliath's defeat does not result in a Philistine surrender we should not press the concept too far. More likely, the armies cancelled each other out, so the Philistines sent their champion to break the deadlock, hoping to inject sufficient fear into the Israelites by his presence so the Philistines could move to victory. Goliath was an impressive figure, tall, strong and equipped with the most up-to-date military technology – a combination of the Hulk and James Bond! Although probably not as tall as popular tradition imagines (perhaps about 6 ft 9 in.; see 'Notes'), he was probably considerably taller than those present. The writer goes to great lengths to describe Goliath's armour and equipment. The bronze helmet is atypical for Philistines (see Plate 9 in McKenzie 2000), and may relate to his special role, but clearly protects his head. The body armour is described in terms of its weight, roughly 110 pounds, emphasizing his leg coverings. In short, Goliath is an armoured giant, with no apparent weak point, especially given that he has a man carrying a large shield in front of him. His weaponry is particularly threatening. Although the weapon slung across his back cannot be identified with certainty, he carries a large spear with a heavy iron point (roughly 13 lb), though comparison with the weaver's beam is probably to how the shaft had a line wrapped around it. This enabled spin to be imparted so it could be thrown more effectively, though given its weight the range was still limited. The narrator describes Goliath as the Philistines wanted him to be perceived: a threat too great to be overcome.

8–11. The narrator now introduces speech, a technique of crucial importance since the key emphases are made through dialogue. Goliath's opening speech is addressed to the Israelite troops, a strategy that avoids Saul. Goliath ridicules Saul as he contrasts his status as a Philistine with the Israelites' status as Saul's servants. His question teasingly asks why they should come out to battle for an overlord like Saul. Nevertheless, he offers them a way out: choose a soldier to fight him, and their combat can resolve the conflict. The key element is how his speech plays with various senses of 'bd: Israel 'serves' Saul, but victory over Goliath means the Philistines will 'serve' them, though the alternative is that Israel will 'serve' the Philistines if their man is defeated. Goliath's speech subtly suggests discontent with Saul and the opportunity for freedom, with defeat simply meaning a change of master. The tone becomes notably harsher in v. 10 as Goliath's second speech begins by defying (ḥrp: the root implies disdainful contempt, and is used in a range of ways through the chapter; George 1999: 398 prefers 'shame') Israel to engage him in single combat, though there is still no response. Before his size, strength and speech, Saul and Israel are shattered. Mention of Saul is significant, because 13:22 indicated that he was properly armed, while his height was emphasized in 10:23, and a pivotal reason for asking for a king was that he go before the people and fight their battles (8:20). Goliath's speech, by beginning and ending with reference to Saul, demonstrates his failure as king, even as it shows the lack of resolve among the people.

The introduction of David: 17:12–30

12–16. David's introduction parallels the information provided by 16:1–13. If the narrator has deliberately dischronologized chs. 16 – 17, then this apparent doublet can be explained in that David's move to the battle was before his anointing, and required him to be introduced. Now it is a further mechanism for highlighting that the events of this chapter are sequentially earlier, although their significance requires them to conclude the sequence. As with 16:6–10, the sons named are Eliab, Abinadab and Shammah, though Jesse's age is also highlighted. What is more important is Jesse's support of Saul with his three eldest sons at the battle with him. David is again described as the little brother, though in Hebrew as in English this does not necessarily refer to physical size. The account emphasizes that David was not seeking to join the battle, but acted as his father's messenger, moving between his sheep and the battle. In addition, it introduces the motif of David as shepherd that gradually becomes more important as the narrative proceeds (Fokkelman 1986: 153). This movement happened over a period of time, though 'forty days' is probably a shorthand reference to an extended period rather than a specific chronological note. But it points to the cost involved in provisioning the army, explaining David's initial role.

17–18. With David's normal actions outlined, the narrative moves to when he joined the fight, though it begins innocently as his father directs him to take supplies to his brothers and their unit commander and to bring back evidence of their welfare. David is not participating as a soldier; as the youngest brother he acts for their welfare at the direction of his father.

19–23. The focus shifts back to the battle site, where David is to journey, though Saul's place is emphasized again, showing the battle has not moved over its duration. David's arrangements are routine, ensuring the flock is properly kept while he makes the journey and is careful to follow his father's instructions. That he arrived as the army moved out into its daily position means he rose early, since even a brisk walk from Bethlehem would take about four hours. But the timing is important since it means David is present as the army takes up its position. Although this may seem a propitious moment, the last time the army was said to have raised the war cry was in 4:5, and that was followed by the ark's capture, though Israel had won when Yahweh thundered (2:10; 7:10). Nevertheless, David saw the armies lined up and facing each other, and, having left his gear with the keeper, ran to the lines to enquire about his brothers' welfare. David is careful to carry out his father's instructions: he is not looking to engage in the battle. But even as David asks about his brothers, the daily routine repeats itself as Goliath comes out to bring his challenge. Thus David is confronted with the threat that neither Saul nor the army are able to overcome.

24–27. Goliath's impact is graphically demonstrated when the army turn from him in fear, though they flee only as far as the camp and do not leave the battle zone. Nevertheless, they also quote something Saul is reputed to have said, which is that whoever kills Goliath will be greatly enriched and marry the king's daughter, while his family will gain special status in Israel, possibly tax exemption (see Youngblood 1992: 698). We have no record of Saul's saying this, and he does not appear to act upon it, unless that is the point of his question in vv. 55 and 58, but there is no reason to imagine the narrator is offering unreliable information. This is apparent from the record of David's seeking confirmation of the offer from the soldiers. Nevertheless, the shift from indirect dialogue in Saul's case to directly reported speech from David means it is David's speech that begins to reframe Israel's understanding of events. His opening words seek confirmation of the offered reward, though in so doing David sees the conflict differently. Goliath has defied (*ḥrp*) Israel (17:10), but David sees the situation as a reproach (*ḥrp*) that must be removed by killing Goliath. Moreover, David is the first one to introduce a theological interpretation – this uncircumcised Philistine has defied (*ḥrp*) the army of the living God. David's speech exposes the fallacy of accepting things as the Philistine presented them in vv. 4–11. This is not an unbeatable foe. This is someone who has set himself against God. David receives confirmation of the offered reward in this context, though his speech indicates that a reward is not necessary.

28–30. Although David's intent seems positive, not everyone sees it that way, especially his eldest brother, Eliab, who portrays David as abandoning his sheep and coming to the battle to promote his own interests. Bodner's attempt (2003) to see Eliab as a 'double-voiced' character who provides us with a reliable insight into David's heart must be considered unlikely, not least because the narrator's outline of events stands in tension with Eliab's perceptions. This section is unusual in voicing criticism of David, though its function is ironic – because of Eliab's rebuke, David asks other people to confirm what he has heard, and this leads to his being presented to Saul. Eliab's failure to understand what is happening confirms Yahweh's rejection of him in 16:7. What Samuel cannot know of Eliab's heart is revealed through his misunderstanding of David's (see Fokkelman 1986: 163). But David can now see this, as is clear from his question (see 'Notes').

David and Saul: 17:31–40

31–33. The narrative has moved relatively slowly so far but now accelerates, though it is first necessary for David to meet Saul. V. 31 is two terse statements, climaxing with Saul taking David. The king and his replacement are face to face, and though the crown's future is not immediately at stake, it is their comparative understanding of Yahweh's role that is resolving the issue. Saul continues to accept Goliath's portrayal, whereas David sees them in the light of his understanding of Yahweh. David thus instructs Saul about Yahweh, and so demonstrates that he is taking on the leadership role previously imagined for the king (8:20; see Brueggemann 1990b: 130). This is emphasized by our entering the conversation where David continues his process of reframing events, insisting there is no need for despondency, because he, Saul's servant, will battle the Philistine. Although the name Goliath does not occur with great frequency in this chapter, it is notable that no Israelite refers to him by name, a mechanism for dismissing his significance. Saul is astonished by David's declaration, noting that David is only a 'lad', in contrast to the Philistine who has been a warrior since his youth. Saul contrasts David's lack of military experience with that of his opponent, but thus shows he accepts Goliath's perspective.

34–37. David responds with a poetic narrative (Ceresko 1985: 61), showing he can overcome the Philistine with Yahweh's assistance, pointing to his experiences as a shepherd where he overcame lions and bears to recover livestock they had taken. Both lion and bear are more fearsome than Goliath. Interestingly, David describes his encounters with these animals in terms of close combat, though he will not do so when fighting Goliath, suggesting he has not yet formulated a plan involving his sling. However, the central point is not to indicate how he will overcome Goliath; it is to assert that David will kill Goliath just as lions and bears, because Yahweh is with him. Goliath, again dismissed as an 'uncircumcised Philistine', will be defeated because his actions in defying (ḥrp) the armies of the living God show he is Yahweh's enemy. What Saul could not recognize, David makes clear: victory for Israel does not lie in the finest military technology or the greatest physical strength. Victory comes when the nations remember Yahweh's presence. The God who previously delivered David would deliver him this time. Only in response to David's speech does Saul express himself theologically, though his words are purely conventional.

38–40. That Saul has not grasped the import of David's speech is apparent from his attempt to clothe him in his own armour. There is no indication that it does not fit David, so he too must have been tall, and there is nothing in the narrative to suggest Saul would be so militarily foolish as to put David into something particularly ill-fitting. Nevertheless, Saul was responding within Goliath's frame of reference: if one wants to fight a heavily armed giant, one should go out heavily armed. Saul intends that David fight on Goliath's terms – even down to such similarities in armour as a bronze helmet, a mail coat and a significant sword. The problem is that David cannot use them because he has not tested them. Instead, he takes what is familiar, the gear a shepherd would use: a stout stick, a sling and a selection of five stones, probably about the size of tennis balls, taken from the brook. David goes forth depending upon what he knows (military equipment in the form of a sling) but also certain that this is Yahweh's battle.

The encounter with Goliath: 17:41–54

41–44. As we move towards the narrative's climax, the focus shifts momentarily back to Goliath's perspective, though he is dismissively referred to as 'the Philistine' in each sentence in this section. Finally, Israel has a champion, but there is a sense of disappointment for Goliath. He approaches the battle with all his equipment and the cover of his shield, prepared for battle, but when he looks more closely, all he sees is a good-looking youth (see 16:12). This is hardly a challenge to one so powerful, and in a comparatively rare psychological comment we are told he despised David. This becomes prominent in his speech where he wonders if he is a dog that someone should come and fight him with sticks, though as Birch (1998: 1112) points out, we already have a record of David's killing a lion and a bear. Goliath's hubris emerges, though in a form heavy with irony, as he curses David by his gods. As a battle technique, this is unsurprising, but it foregrounds the question of Yahweh's authority that is central to David's speech through the chapter. Do the Philistine gods (perhaps Dagon among others; see 5:1–5) have any authority? Goliath believes so as he invites David to come to battle so that his corpse can become carrion. The battle is not merely between David and Goliath; it is between competing systems of religious belief, only one of which can be vindicated, even if Goliath believes the deck is stacked to his advantage.

45–47. The narrative's focus returns to David as he responds to the Philistine's speech with a superbly crafted piece of rhetoric that reframes Goliath's perspective, just as he previously attempted with Saul. Thus he highlights the problem inherent in Goliath's curse: Goliath does not depend upon his gods but upon the military technology he employs. David, by contrast, comes in the name of Yahweh of Hosts. Although the title probably refers to the armies of heaven and insists that these belong to Yahweh, its presence in Samuel marks points where Yahweh acts to change Israel's power structures (see on 1:11). David introduces this name, highlighting that Yahweh is bringing change through him, for Goliath has defied (*ḥrp*) Yahweh. Therefore, Yahweh will give Goliath into David's power, so Goliath and the Philistine army will become carrion. This is not simply a matter of each side claiming the authority of their God, for David goes on to insist that his victory will be a testimony to the reality of the God of Israel to the whole world. David has grasped the special nature of Israel's role before the nations in a way that Saul never does – Israel exists as a witness to the nations of the reality of Yahweh. It is this truth that needs to be emphasized. There is also a point of understanding immediately accessible, that Yahweh does not depend upon military might and technology to achieve victory. This theme is also evidenced in chs. 5 – 7, but takes on a special poignancy here because of Goliath's might. Yahweh will defeat Goliath, and in so doing the rest of the Philistine army will be given into Israel's control.

48–51. Given this chapter's length, the battle account is remarkably matter of fact. The Philistine's initial charge is apparently an attempt to claim the advantage and terrify his opponent, but David draws on his mobility advantage and calmly slings a stone that strikes Goliath on the forehead, a spot apparently vulnerable in spite of his armour. Goliath's weakness was his lack of manoeuvrability, brilliantly exploited by David, though it also took an extraordinarily good shot to hit the giant, since moving targets are harder to hit. Kellermann (1990) has sought to demonstrate on the basis of endocrinology that Goliath was weakened by aspects of gigantism, though this remains speculative. But the writer does not dwell on David's ability with the sling (unlike Halpern 2001: 1–13, who virtually accuses David of cheating by not competing on Goliath's terms), because all that was needed was to show that David's claims were vindicated. Goliath had not defied Saul and Israel; he had defied Yahweh, and Yahweh had overcome him. Goliath, face down in the ground like Dagon (5:3–4; see George 1999: 407), was an eloquent testimony to this fact. To highlight this, the narrator pauses in v. 50 to summarize David's victory: he killed Goliath with only his sling, not with a sword. Thus the central theological themes from David's speeches are highlighted, though it is necessary to resume the main narrative in v. 51 by reporting that David did in fact finish the job by taking Goliath's sword and severing his head, just as he had said would happen in v. 46. Goliath's defeat precipitated panic among the Philistines, who fled from the battle, indicating that Goliath's initial offer was not to be taken seriously.

52–54. David's speech had indicated that his victory would testify to his own troops about Yahweh's power, and the Philistines would accordingly be given into their power. The narrator is careful to indicate the precise ways in which David's declarations resolve themselves as the Israelite army rise and pursue the Philistines with another battle cry, this time from a people who know that Yahweh is fighting for them. Thus they are able to pursue the Philistines along the valley as far as Ekron, possibly the nearest Philistine city, before returning to plunder their camp. Nevertheless, a crack begins to appear almost immediately, as they are described as the men of Judah and Israel, not Israel alone. David came from Judah, and there may here be the first hint of the division that affects so much of the nation's life. But the emphasis at this stage is one of victory, specifically victory won by Yahweh in accordance with David's speech. Israel and Saul have discovered they must understand events from the perspective of covenantal faith in Yahweh, all of which is a testimony to the whole world of this reality. To this is appended a note that David takes Goliath's head to Jerusalem. Since the city is not captured until David is king (2 Sam. 5:6–10), the note must refer to later actions. Bergen (1996: 198) rejects this, unpersuasively arguing David took Goliath's head to Jerusalem as a possible sign to its inhabitants. Goliath's sword ends up at Nob (21:8–9), though David placed all of his kit in 'his tent'. This reference is ambiguous since it could refer to either David's or Goliath's tent. If the reference is to an immediate action, then Goliath's is meant, since as a visitor to the battle David would not have a tent, but if this is a telescoped note (as seems more likely), then it is more probable that David took it with him. The process by which the sword reached Nob remains unknown.

Saul and Abner: 17:55–58

55–56. Saul has been a bystander, but as king the narrative returns to him. He has seen David demonstrate what he claimed, that victory comes from Yahweh, not from power. Yet, as one who has been gathering capable warriors (14:52), David was someone Saul would want. But the focus of his question to Abner, his army commander, is on a more particular issue – to what family does David (again, a *na'ar*) belong? The question is important because of the offer in v. 25, and was clearly not discussed in his interview with David (see Dietrich 1996: 183–184). If Eliab had brought David to Saul, this might not have arisen, but since other soldiers had done so, an answer was needed. Abner was ignorant, so Saul required him to enquire further as to the lad's family.

57–58. With the Philistine dead, Abner brought David to Saul, with Goliath's head ominously in his hand. Their exchange is full of tension. Saul does not ask David for his name, but for that of his family. We cannot presume Saul was ignorant of David's own name since the report in v. 31 would have included it, but the question of family is important. Polzin (1989: 175) exceeds the evidence base (see Birch 1998: 111) in insisting Saul is asking David to change his loyalty from that of his biological father. Nevertheless, he has highlighted how this one wary answer creates the possibility for additional conflicts – David remains opaque to Saul, and Saul knows a threat when he sees one.

Explanation

The story of David and Goliath remains one of the best-known and most potent stories from the OT. It has shaped the presentation of innumerable scenes in fiction where the hero overcomes a powerful foe through quick thinking and skill, such as Mark Twain's *A Connecticut Yankee in King Arthur's Court* (see Halpern 2001: 11–12) or the market scene in Steven Spielberg's *Raiders of the Lost Ark*, when Indiana Jones overcomes a seemingly unbeatable swordsman by drawing his pistol and shooting him. Consistently, the emphasis is placed upon the hero's ability to overcome the seemingly overwhelming foe, a contrast stressing the comparative size of the combatants. Yet this is a relatively minor theme, a feature that becomes evident when one notes that David's slaying Goliath takes one verse, whereas his final speech to Goliath, which lays out his theological understanding of the events (and that of the narrator), takes three times as long. Indeed, the narrator has played with readers when presenting Goliath with his mass of weaponry and armour without dwelling on his lack of mobility, because it was these elements that terrorized his opponents. By way of analogy, the Australian bushranger Ned Kelly (whose armour was similar in weight to Goliath's) used the same tactic in his final shootout at Glenrowan and was also brought down by a well-aimed shot. Goliath's presentation is how the Philistines want us to see him in order to demonstrate the impossibility of defeating him. As the narrative progresses, we see that the Israelite army, and Saul in particular, accept this perspective. The narrative world apart from David is notable for being a world without reference to Yahweh, a world where the Philistine perspective dominates.

The narrator does not overthrow this perspective too quickly, for otherwise the narrative's tension would be undone. Rather, it is through David's speeches that we gradually develop a different appreciation of the situation. David is the first to bring a theological perspective in his dialogue with the men of the army, where he shifts the perspective from Goliath's defying Israel to his defying God (v. 26). This element is continued in his meeting with Saul, where Saul continues to accept the Philistine construal, whereas David reframes it in terms of his experience of Yahweh. If bears and lions can be overcome, then so can Philistine giants, and one does not need Saul's armour to achieve this. So far one might have thought the point was indeed that God can overcome the seemingly insurmountable, but David's final speech refines our understanding (vv. 45–47). This conflict is not simply about Yahweh's ability to overcome any foe; it is meant instead as a testimony to the whole world of the reality of the God of Israel. What is at stake is not a question of power, but the underlying reality of who Yahweh is. This truth is demonstrated by David's victory over the giant, a victory that occurs just as David has announced. Thus the narrative's climax transcends the issue of overcoming the powerful foe (though without removing it altogether) and develops the missiological impulse that runs through Israel's story since Abram's call (Gen. 12:1–3). This is what marks David out from Saul, and provides the final reason why this story, though chronologically prior to the events of ch. 16, has been placed at the end of this initial sequence of stories about David. David demonstrates an understanding of the central purpose of Israel's election, and this understanding has shaped his actions. Saul, by contrast, allowed the Philistine discourse to shape his perceptions, so even after David's victory he is ineffectually seeking more information about David's identity instead of celebrating Yahweh as the God at work in Israel, and whose purposes for the nation were directed towards his commitment to creation (Gen. 9:8–17). David's knowledge of Yahweh transforms his actions, whereas for Saul it has no visible effect. Now their differing understandings of

Israel's role have been demonstrated, we can trace David's and Saul's paths in a more or less chronological process.

1 SAMUEL 18

Translation

[1]When he had finished speaking to Saul, Jonathan's soul was knit to David's soul, and Jonathan loved him as his own soul. [2]Saul took him that day and did not permit him to return to his father's house. [3]Then Jonathan made a covenant with David because he loved him as his own soul. [4]Jonathan stripped himself of the robe that he was wearing and gave it to David, along with his armour, including his sword, bow and belt. [5]David went and was successful wherever Saul sent him, so Saul set him over the men of war. This pleased all the people, even Saul's servants.

[6]When they were coming home, as David returned from killing the Philistine, the women came out from all the cities of Israel singing and dancing, to greet King Saul with tambourines, joy and musical instruments. [7]The women sang as they played and said,

> 'Saul has killed his thousands
>   And David his tens of thousands.'

[8]Saul became very angry, and this matter grieved him. He said, 'They have given tens of thousands to David, but they have given me thousands! So, surely the kingship is his!' [9]Saul watched David closely from that day on.

[10]The following day a grievous spirit from God rushed upon Saul, and he prophesied in the midst of the house while David, as usual, played the lyre. Saul's spear was in his hand. [11]Saul hurled the spear, for he thought, 'I shall strike David against the wall.' But David evaded him twice.

[12]Saul was afraid of David, for Yahweh was with him, but had departed from Saul. [13]Then Saul removed him from his presence and appointed him as commander over a thousand. Then he went out and came in before the people. [14]David was successful in all his ways, because Yahweh was with him. [15]When Saul saw how greatly he succeeded, he dreaded him. [16]But all Israel and Judah loved David because he went out and came in before them.

[17]Then Saul said to David, 'Here is my elder daughter, Merab. I shall give her to you as a wife. Only, be a valiant man for me and fight Yahweh's battles.' (Saul thought, 'My hand shall not be against him, but the hand of the Philistines will.') [18]But David said to Saul, 'Who am I, my kin, my father's clan in Israel, that I should be the king's son-in-law?' [19]So when Merab should have been given to David, she was given to Adriel the Meholathite for a wife.

[20]But Saul's daughter Michal loved David. They told Saul and he was pleased. [21]Saul thought, 'I shall give her to him and she will be a snare to him, so the

Philistines' hand will be against him.' So Saul said to David a second time, 'You shall now be my son-in-law.' [22]Saul commanded his servants, 'Speak to David secretly, saying "The king delights in you, and all his servants love you, so now, become the king's son-in-law."' [23]Saul's servants spoke these words in David's ears. David said, 'Is it trifling to you to become the king's son-in-law since I am a poor man and lightly esteemed?' [24]Saul's servants reported to him, 'This is how David spoke.' [25]Saul said, 'Thus you shall speak to David: "The king desires no bride-compensation except one hundred Philistine foreskins, to take vengeance on the king's enemies."' Saul planned to bring down David by the hand of the Philistines. [26]When his servants reported these words to David, it pleased David to become the king's son-in-law. Before the days had expired, [27]David arose and went with his men and struck two hundred Philistines, and brought their foreskins in full number to the king to be the king's son-in-law. So Saul gave him his daughter Michal as a wife. [28]When Saul saw and knew that Yahweh was with David, and that Saul's daughter Michal loved him, [29]Saul was even more afraid of David. So Saul was a continual enemy of David.

[30]The Philistine leaders went out to battle, and whenever they went out David was more successful than all Saul's servants, so his name was highly esteemed.

Notes on the text

1–5. These verses are absent from LXX, continuing a lacuna from 17:55. See 'Form and structure' on 1 Sam. 17 for a defence of MT at this point.

1. With Q, reading *wayye'ĕhābēhû*.

4. NIV renders *maddāyw* as 'his tunic' (cf. 17:38). Although plausible (the word normally refers to something made of cloth), the context requires something military and armour could be made of heavy cloth or leather rather than metal.

6. The opening clause is absent from LXX. The sense of *šālišîm* is uncertain. It is seemingly a musical instrument, though perhaps less generic than our translation implies. The word may derive from a root meaning 'three', perhaps indicating a triangle or something with three strings.

7. Reading, with Q, *'ălāpāyw*.

8. Reading, with Q, *'ôyēn*.

10–11. Absent from LXX.

12. The second half of this verse is absent from LXX.

17–19. Absent from LXX.

18. Revocalize *ḥayyay* as *ḥayyî*.

23. 'Is it trifling' and 'lightly esteemed' represent a play on the similar roots *qll* and *qlh*.

26b. Absent from LXX.

27. LXX conforms to 2 Sam. 3:14 and has one hundred foreskins. However, the reference there is to Saul's nominated price, not the amount paid. MT is more likely original.

28. LXX has 'all Israel loved David'. Although this leads easily into the statement of Saul's fear, it seems like a scribal correction to a perceived error.

29b–30. Absent from LXX.

Form and structure

The battle against the Philistines has been won. With David's anointing and battle victory recounted, it is possible to return to chronologically linear narration. Indeed, although each chapter does not necessarily immediately follow its predecessor, the whole of chs. 18 – 26 (apart from components of 21:10 – 22:5) are a set of episodic narratives, where each depends upon the completion of its predecessors, though still complete in itself. This technique is dropped from 1 Sam. 27 – 2 Sam. 1, where the narrative is serial, and each narrative is directly dependent upon its antecedent, though in this case two separate narrative strands are followed. The return to linear narrative causes some harshness, but the benefits of the dischronologized structure of 16 – 17 (See 'Form and structure' at 1 Sam. 16) are greater than the cost. Hence we have the difficulty that David appears to have been brought to court in 16:14–23, where he was already a warrior, and yet this narrative recounts his arrival there. Yet v. 10 presumes the earlier account, suggesting it is written in full awareness of the difficulties. Once we recognize that this is where the seams are rejoined, the difficulties become more apparent than real. 16:14–23 summarizes the process by which David came to court as a musician also known as a warrior. The reasons why David was known as a warrior have now been disclosed, though an exact chronology is difficult to determine. V. 2 must be a shorthand summary of a larger cycle of events, so the timescale is more general than it initially seems. As part of the shift in form, the narrator begins to provide extensive insight into the inner life of every character other than David (see Polzin 1989: 177).

This section's larger goal is to show the nature of David's life at court and how Saul begins to seek David's death. We begin with Jonathan's love for David, something standing in opposition to Saul's dread. However, a second contrast is Yahweh's presence, since Yahweh is now with David but not Saul. Instead, Saul endures a grievous spirit from God. All this pivots on the women's song as David and Saul return to base. The song may honour David by belittling Saul, which is how Saul understands it. Lying behind his response in vv. 8–9 are Samuel's words in 15:28. Saul knows Yahweh is taking the kingdom from him; he does not know who the neighbour who is better than him is. He may not expect to bring his replacement in with him, but there may be a hint in v. 8 that he is beginning to realize who this is. In contrast to Saul's dread, Jonathan's love for David is echoed by the people when they see his activities for them. The narrator does not leave us guessing why this is; as 16:18 has suggested, it is Yahweh's presence that is determinative, enabling David to escape when Saul first tries to kill him. The second half of the chapter explores Saul's further attempts to kill David through the apparently positive gesture of offering him the chance to marry one of his daughters. The offer of Merab does not proceed when David declines, but Saul sees his chance when he is informed that his younger daughter, Michal, also loved David. His expectation is that this provides a mechanism for the Philistines to kill David. The reasoning behind this becomes clear in the Michal story, where he nominates a bride price of one hundred Philistine foreskins. Given that Philistine warriors would hardly have yielded these willingly, it seemed a perfect way to kill David without appearing to do so. But the narrator informs us that Saul's plan failed because of Yahweh's presence with David (18:28), something that even Saul could recognize. Saul's plan is a dark foreshadowing of how David will kill Uriah (2 Sam. 11:14–17). This chapter not only records David at court, but is an important theological statement about why he achieves the recognition and success he does.

This reading presumes that we are following MT. As is evident from the 'Notes', the LXX represents a considerably shorter text, without vv. 1–5, 6a, 10–11, 12b, 17–19, 26b and 29b–30. LXX generally represents a tradition more positive to Saul than the MT, since apart from v. 21, it omits information about Saul's attempts to kill David, as well as his statement in 9b about David's claiming the kingdom. Defenders of the LXX (e.g. Klein 1983: 187) regard the MT as expanding the earlier LXX narrative, claiming there would be no need for David to express surprise at being offered the chance to marry Michal if he had already been offered the chance to marry Merab. But a psychological assessment of David cannot resolve the issue, especially if the offer of Merab was regarded as fulfilling 17:25 since David would by then have declined the reward for his earlier combat. Saul may intend it differently, but having declined the reward it is unnecessary to imagine that another offer would be made. A similar conclusion leads Grønbaek (1971: 100–109) to posit several redactional levels within the story. It is better to regard the variations in LXX as continuing the changes made in ch. 17, which we have already seen as less likely, and retain the narrative found in MT.

Comment

Friendship between David and Jonathan: 18:1–5

1. The chapter's opening is set after the events just narrated. However, it is clear a new narrative is beginning as we focus on those who love David, and whose love stands in contrast to Saul's growing fear. Jonathan's commitment to David is immediate and strong, though again we are not

told of reciprocation by David. The reason for this probably lies in the fact that the verb 'love' in these accounts is not so much an emotion or expression of friendship as a commitment to David's political position. There was a real and deep friendship between them, but the political dimension is essential (Thompson 1974). Yet it means we must reject approaches that see a homoerotic relationship between David and Jonathan (see Zehnder 1998 for linguistic and narrative substantiation; Nissinen 1998: 58 suggests that modern readers are more likely to see homosexuality as a possibility than ancients). More probably, Jonathan sees David as the one likely to succeed to the throne and commits himself accordingly.

2. Jonathan's commitment to David is initially mirrored by Saul, though without love (though see 16:21). That it was 'on that day' does not necessarily mean it was immediately after the defeat of Goliath, since the phrase can have a more general sense, which is required as the narrative returns to a linear structure. Saul's decision to draft David is consistent with his policy from 14:52. Although logical, it may hint at resistance to the announcement of 15:28, though this theme will be developed more fully in subsequent chapters. Where Jonathan sees a possible successor to the throne, Saul sees someone who may strengthen his reign.

3–4. The contrast between Saul and Jonathan is illustrated by the covenant Jonathan makes with David. Again, emphasis falls upon Jonathan's actions. We are never told how David sees things. We are not told of the content of this covenant either, though if it was directed towards securing Jonathan's position after David became king, we may have a hint of it in 2 Sam. 9:1. That the covenant was essentially political seems apparent from Jonathan's actions in removing his robe, armour, sword, bow and belt. The text gives prominence to the gift of the robe, perhaps because, as we have seen, the robe is a prominent motif in the book. Samuel was marked out by the robe his mother brought him (2:19), and it was Samuel's robe that Saul tore (15:27). In 24:4 (cf. 24:11) David cut the corner of Saul's robe, while in 28:14 the robe enables Saul to recognize Samuel's shade. Tamar's robe (2 Sam. 13:18) marks out her status. Clothing is of considerable importance, especially as it is frequently a marker of special status. By giving his robe to David, Jonathan effectively passes over his badge of rank, acknowledging tacitly that David will succeed to the throne. This is highlighted by the provision of his military equipment, which 13:22 indicates is a gift of considerable value. David had no need of such equipment to fight Goliath (17:38–39), but the symbolism here is different. It is not a denial of Yahweh's work in his life, but a means of accepting the support of one who acknowledges the validity of his rise.

5. This section closes by returning to David's role with Saul, highlighting his success in all of the military positions to which Saul sends him. This theme develops through the chapter (cf. 18:14, 30), and is paralleled by Saul's growing fear of him. At this point, fear is not the issue for Saul,

which is why he appoints David to a position of command. When fear becomes an issue, Saul will exploit this appointment as the means of having David killed. In the meantime, everyone, even Saul's servants, is happy with the situation.

Love and fear of David: 18:6–16

6–9. The turning point in relations between Saul and David comes from a seemingly innocuous event. David and Saul are returning from battle with the Philistines. Although the MT reads 'the Philistine', it is unlikely that the reference is directly to Goliath (though the sg. may emphasize Goliath as the classic example); so the gentilic refers to the Philistines in general (against Fokkelman 1986: 211). David has established himself as the most successful of Saul's commanders, and has, with Saul, been engaged in further battle against them. This allows for David to have sufficient fame along with Saul for women from the whole country to meet them on their return. Their music and dancing are reminiscent of Miriam (Exod. 15:20–21), suggesting that the victory belongs to Yahweh, even as they sing (cf. 21:11; 29:5) of the nation's heroes. Although they sing of both champions, they are only said to go out to meet Saul. This may provide a clue to their song's meaning, though the narrator may intend it to remain ambiguous (similarly, Gunn 1980a: 149). The parallelism may suggest David and Saul are treated as equals in battle, a possibility strengthened by the fact that the word translated 'ten thousands' may simply mean 'myriads'. Moreover, 'thousands' and 'ten thousands' are a stock pair (e.g. Ps. 91:7). Read this way, the two lines are synonymous, so David and Saul are placed on a par, effectively saying David and Saul have both killed many Philistines. On the other hand, this may be intensifying parallelism (Alter 1985: 19; 1999: 113), in which the second line heightens the meaning of the first, but this time with a change of subject, so David is exalted over Saul. Whatever the women's intent, Saul interprets their song as a slight, and this interpretation shapes subsequent events. Even if David is interpreted as Saul's equal, Saul sees the threat posed, as his authority is no longer unique. Rather than the king leading the nation in battle (8:20), both Saul and David do so. Saul wonders if the women's song marks out David as the next king. Saul has a clue as to the identity of his 'neighbour' (15:28), creating a context of suspicion where a careful watch on his potential adversary is kept.

10–11. See also 19:9–10. Again Saul is afflicted by a grievous spirit from God (cf. 16:14). That it occurred 'the next day' indicates this was something that happened intermittently to Saul, understood as evidence of divine punishment. When the spirit came upon Saul, we are told he 'prophesied'. Most English versions have 'raved' here, but this loses the force of the parallelism with 10:10 and 19:23. The experience at 10:10 was a largely positive sign of Saul's election, while 19:23 effectively points to his rejection because it occurs in the context of an attempt on David's life. This experience stands between those two, so we may know Saul is still among the prophets, but are prepared for the negative evaluation of that in 19:24. At this point, David is still with him to play the harp, but there is no indication that music is effective. This indicates how Saul is subject to this spirit, though even as he prophesies he grasps the spear at his side and makes a determined effort to kill David. Saul is not completely under the spirit's control; he still makes decisions and expresses his thoughts, even if they are murderous. But David eludes him twice.

12–16. The narrator provides a means of interpreting these events through the prism of what Saul sees. Saul fears David. He knows Yahweh is with David and not him. Saul sees what everyone else seems to know, but for him it is destructive. The first part of this is what his servants affirmed in 16:18, but it takes on special meaning for Saul now. Yahweh's presence with David makes him a threat, the one likely to claim his throne, but for the same reason a difficult rival to remove. Saul could not risk having David so close, so he removed him from a position that was effectively a leader within his own bodyguard to make him commander of a 'thousand', the largest of the Israelite military divisions. This was probably a demotion (Gordon 1986: 160), though it put him in closer contact with the general population. David's job was to go out to battle against the Philistines, the people from whom Saul was supposed to deliver Israel (9:16). There is heavy irony here. In removing David from his immediate household, Saul gave him the job he was supposed to do. It is no surprise that David is successful, but again we are reminded of Yahweh's presence. David's success may be put down to skill (and the verb used for 'succeed' often has overtones of wise actions; see AV), but they are not to be interpreted in that way. Yahweh's presence makes the difference. Saul's perspective is employed again in v. 15. He sees David's success, and dreads him. For Saul this represents a heightening of tension, as the verb employed (*gûr*) is stronger than that for fear. But Saul's dread is balanced by the love of all Israel and Judah for David. Their love is generated by the same thing that causes Saul's dread, David who leads the nation in successful battle; so loyalty to David seems appropriate. But Saul sees what this portends.

Saul's attempts to kill David through marriage: 18:17–30

17–19. A central narrative technique employed in Samuel is repetition, where similar narratives are told, but with some variation to develop the point. As such, the two marriage offers made to David by Saul must be interpreted in relation to one another. The offer of Merab is probably in fulfilment of the promise of 17:25, though it has taken some time to come to fruition. This time Saul's approach is made directly to David, a hearty-sounding invitation to become his son-in-law. Attached to it is the statement that David should be a warrior and fight Yahweh's battles, which suggests that Saul intends the gift of his daughter to depend upon what David does in the future. Merab's perspectives are never explored, but we are provided with a key indicator of Saul's motivation. If David takes on the role associated with marriage into the royal family, he will be engaged in so many battles that the Philistines will kill him. Ironically, David's hand will not be against Saul. Rather, Saul will die in battle against the Philistines at his own hand (31:3–6; similarly, Arnold 2003: 275). Saul believes he need do nothing but wait. As such, he has not grasped what Yahweh's presence with David means, and of course is unaware that David is Yahweh's anointed. David declines the offer, suggesting he comes from too minor a family to take on this position, though phrasing this as a question leaves some ambiguity. David's response may be largely formal, but Saul sees the attempt's failure, and gives Merab to Adriel the Meholathite instead. The children of that marriage come to a tragic end because of Saul's sin (2 Sam. 21:8). Thus the narrator prepares us for the compounding effect of sin.

20–21a. Merab's feelings remain unclear, but the same is not true for her sister, Michal. The first thing we are told about her is that she loved David, something reported to Saul (who was apparently unaware) and saw in it an opportunity to further his plans against David. This is the only time in OT narrative that we are told of a woman's love for a man (but note Song 1:7; 3:1–4), and it is easy to interpret this in romantic terms. Although it cannot be excluded, political loyalty dominates the other expressions of love for David, and it is most likely that Michal's attitude functions in the same way. Saul is not playing primarily with Michal's emotions so much as her loyalties, and sees her as a baited trap for David, waiting to be sprung (cf. Amos 3:5). Saul's plan is that David be placed in a situation where the Philistines will kill him.

21b–25. Initially, Saul appears to make a direct approach to David, but the narrative breaks off before David's reply. That Saul engages in subterfuge, instructing his servants to provide David with off-the-record briefings of his high regard for him, as well as the servants' love, suggests David declined the offer. The servants were faithful to Saul's command, suggesting they at least did not love David, and engaged in a process of private ('in his ears'; cf. 8:21) briefings to urge him to become the king's son-in-law, apparently more important than being Michal's husband. Again, David claims to come from too low a station, though his comparative poverty is an element not present when he declines to marry Merab. When this is reported to Saul, Saul sees his opportunity, instructing his servants to indicate he does not need cash as bride compensation (the exact social function of the *mōhar* is disputed; see Wright 1990: 191–194). All he needs is one hundred Philistine foreskins to be avenged on his enemies since the Philistines, like the Egyptians, did not practise circumcision. But Saul's words and thoughts are not the same, because his goal was to enable the Philistines to kill David.

26–27. Since this needed to be reported to David indirectly, the servants are again involved as intermediaries, and only now is David pleased to become the king's son-in-law. But Saul has a cruel surprise coming, because even before the specified time, David returns with his men from killing two hundred Philistines. He duly presents their foreskins to become the king's son-in-law. Saul is stuck; he has made the offer and now needs to follow the process through, though in doing so he grants additional authority to David, since he can now claim status within the royal family (see Grønbaek 1971: 108).

28–30. Again the narrator shows events through Saul's eyes. Saul sees and knows that Yahweh is with David. If Michal's love for David is essentially a political statement, then it provides Saul with additional evidence, because others in his family can see this. This is why Saul's fear of David increases, and why he sets himself as David's permanent enemy. The first one to love David is the first to become his enemy. Saul's fears are confirmed by David's continuing success against the Philistines. Where David saw himself as only lightly esteemed (18:23), it now transpires his name is highly esteemed.

Explanation

Three themes interweave themselves through this chapter: Saul's fear of David manifesting itself in three attempts on his life, the people's love for David (including members of Saul's family) and Yahweh's presence with David. It is impossible to separate these because each depends upon the others for its development. However, it is probably appropriate to see Yahweh's presence with David as central since without it there would be no basis for the love and fear he inspires. But Yahweh's presence with David is never an abstract truth, something without impact on the reality of his life. Yahweh's presence with David is something that Saul (18:12, 28) and the people (18:14) see working itself out in David's activities. David evades Saul's attempts on his life and is the most successful of Saul's commanders because Yahweh is with him. It is this that leads to Saul's murderous plans, yet also the extraordinary expression of loyalty seen in Jonathan, and possibly Michal as well. In all this, Saul remains responsible for his actions. He is not fated to fall before David because the decisions he takes are real decisions, real choices. Already he can see how Samuel's statement of 15:28 is working out, but his choice is to oppose the one he begins to recognize as the 'neighbour' who is better than him. Saul represents one way where one can respond to Yahweh's presence, but Jonathan represents the alternative, choosing to follow Yahweh's leading, even if it is not one he would otherwise have chosen. Throughout, David remains opaque, because his motivation is not central, and his actions are a foil to Saul's. In modelling these responses to Yahweh's presence, the narrator poses questions to the reader. In particular, we are asked about our own response. Jesus indicated that we recognize false prophets, and presumably those who are faithful, by their fruit (Matt. 7:15–20). If we take this chapter seriously, then fruit of those with whom God is present ought to be evident in real experience. The question that remains is whether we are able to respond to this presence by surrendering our own goals rather than resisting it because our own ambitions take priority. Although David's story has further to travel, it suggests that only one approach is appropriate, and the evidence for this is plain from the destructive way Saul's resistance to Yahweh's clear purpose works itself out in both his life and that of his family.

1 SAMUEL 19

Translation

[1]Saul spoke to Jonathan his son and all his servants that they should kill David. But Jonathan, Saul's son, delighted greatly in David. [2]Jonathan reported to David, 'My father Saul seeks to kill you. So now, be on guard in the morning. Stay in a secret place and hide yourself. [3]I shall go and stand at my father's side in the field where you are and will speak to my father about you and see what I can report to you.' [4]Jonathan spoke well of David to Saul his father, 'Let not the king sin against his servant David because he has not sinned against you, and because his deeds have greatly benefited you. [5]For he took his life in his hand when he struck the Philistine and Yahweh wrought great deliverance for all Israel. You saw it and rejoiced. Why should you sin against innocent blood and gratuitously kill David?' [6]Saul listened to Jonathan's voice. Saul swore, 'As Yahweh lives, he shall not be put to death.' [7]Then Jonathan called David and reported all this to him. Jonathan brought David to Saul, and he was in his presence as before.

[8]There was again war. David went out and fought against the Philistines and struck them heavily, so they fled before him. [9]But a grievous spirit from Yahweh came upon Saul as he sat in his house with his spear in his hand, and David was playing the lyre. [10]Saul sought to strike David against the wall with his spear, but David evaded Saul. The spear struck the wall, but David fled and escaped that night.

[11]Saul sent messengers to David's house to watch him and kill him in the morning. But David's wife, Michal, told him, 'Unless you save your life tonight, you will be killed tomorrow.' [12]Michal let down David through a window, and he fled and escaped. [13]Michal took the household idol and placed it on the bed and put a quilt of goats' hair at its head and covered it with clothes. [14]When Saul sent messengers to take David she said, 'He is sick.' [15]Saul sent messengers to see David, saying, 'Bring him up to me on his bed that I may kill him.' [16]The messengers came and, behold, it was the household idol on the bed, with the quilt of goats' hair at its head. [17]Saul said to Michal, 'Why have you misled me and sent my enemy away

that he escaped?' But Michal said to Saul, 'He said to me, "Send me away. Why should I kill you?" '

[18]David fled and escaped and came to Samuel at Ramah, and reported everything Saul had done to him. Then he and Samuel went and stayed in the huts. [19]It was reported to Saul, 'Behold, David is at the huts in Ramah.' [20]Saul sent messengers to take David. When they saw an assembly of prophets prophesying with Samuel standing as their head, the Spirit of God came upon Saul's messengers, and they also prophesied. [21]They told Saul, and he sent other messengers, but they also prophesied. Saul sent a third group of messengers and they also prophesied. [22]Then he also went to Ramah and came as far as the great well at Secu. He asked, 'Where are Samuel and David?' Someone said, 'Behold, they are at the huts in Ramah.' [23]He went there, to the huts in Ramah. The Spirit of God also came upon him and as he went he prophesied until he came to the huts in Ramah. [24]He also stripped off his garments and he too prophesied before Samuel, and lay naked all that day and all that night. Therefore they say, 'Is Saul also among the prophets?'

Notes on text

9. LXX renders 'spirit from God' (*pneuma theou*) in conformity with 18:10. With a few MSS, read *běyādô*.

13, 16. The sense of *kābîr* is uncertain, and is variously rendered as 'quilt', 'net' or 'pillow'. The word occurs only here, both times in construct with 'goats' hair'. The context requires that it be something braided, appropriate for a bed, so some sort of quilt is preferable. *těrāpîm* is pl., but is treated as a sg. noun.

14. The messengers in LXX report that David is sick. The f. verb has probably been conformed to the m., so preference is given to MT.

18. *nāyôt* is often treated as a proper noun 'Naioth' (e.g. NIV, NRSV, ESV), but is more likely a common noun since it is in the town of Ramah. McCarter (1980a: 328) links it to where shepherds stay, hence 'camps', but something more permanent is required; hence 'huts'. Prophetic bands might have stayed in such places.

20. The required pl. verb is indicated by LXX. The meaning of *lahăqâ* ('elderly', Prov. 30:17, though textually uncertain) is unclear. LXX suggests reading *qěhillâ*, the change brought about by metathesis. Similarly, Tg.

22. LXX provides the expected pl. verb in response to Saul's question. But LXX is considerably longer and may reflect a different *Vorlage*. MT is intelligible (cf. ESV) and is retained.

Form and structure

Ch. 19 develops the main themes of ch. 18, recording three more attempts by Saul on David's life, the last of which (19:11–24) runs through several stages. There is a pattern of repetition running through these accounts, especially the highly similar 18:10–11 and 19:9–10, which are often treated as doublets, as also are 10:1–13 and 19:18–24. However, a key element of repetition within Samuel is how the second narrative develops the first one's themes, thus providing new insight into how Yahweh engages with David and Saul. The pattern of repetitions means we are not dealing with doublets but a carefully structured narrative where key themes are woven together in contrasting ways. The ways this chapter develops ch. 18 can be seen in the following table:

David and Jonathan	18:1–5	19:1–7
Philistine war	18:6–9	19:8
The grievous spirit	18:10–11	19:9–10
David and Saul's daughters	18:17–30	19:11–16

Such an analysis hides as much as it reveals, but the presence of so many similarities suggests chs. 18 and 19 are matching panels of a diptych. David and Jonathan's friendship is shown to have real substance, while Michal's love for David also resolves itself in concrete action, though her subsequent speech is ambiguous. However, there are also key differences. First, where Saul prophesied in 18:10, his prophesying is delayed until 19:17–24, so this account becomes the theological climax of his attempts on David's life, while also concluding the account of David and Michal. This is part of a number of subtle changes that suggest Yahweh's activity for David has reached a new level. Previously, Saul could throw his spear at David while prophesying, but now Yahweh prevents Saul from acting. Ch. 18 was replete with observations on Yahweh's presence with David (18:12, 14, 28), something absent here. The theme is still present, but demonstrated rather than announced. Tensions have reached a new level, but through the commitment of those who love him, and Yahweh's involvement, Saul cannot kill David, though Saul's plots have become overt. Ch. 19 still has an internal unity generated by the repetition of key roots (e.g. *mwt*, *mlṭ*, *šlḥ*; see van Zyl 1989: 57). That chs. 18 and 19 are closely linked is also apparent from the presence of an inclusion between 18:1 and 19:24, with both referring to the removal of royal clothing, though for Saul (19:24) this has now become satire.

Comment

Jonathan saves David's life: 19:1–7

1. Where Saul previously attempted to kill David secretly, he now moves publicly. But Saul made a bad choice with the people he directed to kill David, since we know that Jonathan (18:1) loves David. This time, we are not told of his love, but that he 'delighted' (*ḥpṣ*) in David, the term Saul had used when he misrepresented himself to David in 18:22. Saul's approach from the outset is flawed in both conception and practice.

2–3. Rather than killing David, Jonathan warned him. That David needed to be on guard in the morning highlights the threat's imminence, meaning he needed to remain hidden. While David hid, Jonathan would speak to his father, apparently bringing him into the field where David was, so David could overhear some of the conversation. Against Hertzberg (1964: 163; cf. Stoebe 1973: 359), this does not mean we have a composite narrative, because there were still elements Jonathan might have needed to explain for his argument to be accepted (Gordon 1986: 165). If it was rejected, it should have been evident to David, so he could flee in safety.

4–5. Jonathan's speech about David is a masterpiece of compressed rhetoric, with his own points emphasized by the narrator's initial summary statement. His speech begins with a jussive (expressing a mild command or strong wish), emphasizing that Saul must choose not to act against David. Jonathan's choice of words is important, stressing that the decision to kill David would be to sin against him. It cannot be a judicial execution of someone who has committed treason. David is Saul's servant, who has not sinned against Saul. David has acted for Saul's welfare, risking his own life against 'the Philistine', so Yahweh wrought national deliverance, something Saul has seen and over which he rejoiced. Jonathan touches on Saul's most sensitive areas but also demonstrates the lack of grounds for his killing David. Thus, just as his speech began with reference to the potential killing of David as sin, so it closes with a rhetorical question that echoes throughout the chapter. Why should Saul gratuitously kill an innocent man (cf. 25:31). Jonathan never accuses Saul, though the fact of his order suggests he is already guilty. Instead, Jonathan encourages Saul to revoke his decision.

6–7. Convinced by Jonathan's argument, Saul invokes Yahweh in an oath that he will not kill David. Saul's last oath was his folly in 14:24, making this oath suspect; but Jonathan is convinced. Having reported Saul's decision to David, he restores him to the court. David is again active in Saul's court, helped by Jonathan's friendship. Saul's oath, though sworn by Yahweh, is all that protects David, and is a very thin shield.

David eludes Saul again: 19:8–10

8. 19:8–10 closely follows 18:10–11, but the developments indicate we are to understand them separately. The note that David evaded Saul twice in 18:11 is possibly a displaced summary of the two accounts, though certainty is impossible. This verse functions to refocus on the Philistine war, and David's importance and success. It therefore reprises 18:6–7 and 13–16, though is extended by noting that the Philistines now fled before David.

Previously, his success meant that Israel was in awe of him. That awe now extends to the Philistines, a theme that will be developed in 21:11.

9–10. Saul is again afflicted by a grievous spirit. As with 16:14, the spirit is from Yahweh, whereas in 18:10 the more generic 'God' is used. For the ethical issues this raises, see on 16:14. Unlike before, Saul does not 'prophesy', so there is no sense he is acting outside his normal volition, though 18:11 indicates that even while 'prophesying', Saul retained responsibility for his actions. This time, Saul was calmly seated in his house, but his spear's presence meant he had the weaponry to kill David, though his reasons are unsaid. David was present to play his lyre, though it is not said that this was his custom. These small differences suggest that in spite of the similarity between here and 18:10–11, we are dealing with events the narrator regards as discrete, where David is in a different relationship to Saul, and his presence with Saul can no longer be taken for granted. David now has a different way of spending his time, leading the army against the Philistines, so Saul's action is more opportunist than before. Nevertheless, the result is similar. David evades Saul, though this time he does so only once. Finally, David flees from Saul on that night: a decisive breach has been reached in their relationship.

Michal saves David's life: 19:11–17

11–12. Saul's failure to kill David is compounded as his daughter Michal expresses her love for David by enabling him to escape. The chronological note in 19:10 shows it is the same night as Saul's attempt, but unlike 18:10–11, he here continued his assault. Messengers were sent with the brief of guarding the house so that David could be killed in the morning, though who would carry out the execution is unclear. Responsibility, however, lay with Saul. But Michal saw the danger and informed David, advising him to flee that night, letting him down through a window to escape. David's house must have been on the town wall (cf. Josh. 2:15; 2 Cor. 11:33) since otherwise Saul's guards would have seen him. It is important that Michal takes the initiative, so her actions mirror Jonathan's. David remains on the run until Saul's death.

13. Once David escaped, Michal initiated a ruse to buy him some time. Taking the teraphim (household idol), she placed it in the bed and covered it with clothing and bedding, so if someone glanced into the room they would see a figure they could mistake for David. The description of the teraphim (see 15:22) suggests it was close to life-sized, contrasting with Gen. 31:34, where the teraphim were small enough to be placed in Rachel's saddle. Teraphim are generally rejected because of their association with divination (see 2 Kgs 23:24; Zech. 10:2), but Michal is not condemned here. There is no embarrassment in the presence of a teraphim in David's house, though as with Michal's subsequent lie, the narrator may be playing with ambiguity. The narrative links Michal with Rachel in Gen. 31, since both use teraphim and deceive their father with a lie to further their husband's interests (cf. Youngblood 1992: 716). Laban was powerless because he could not find the teraphim; Saul is powerless when he does (cf. Fokkelman 1986: 275–276).

14–15. With Michal's ruse in place, the narrator returns to Saul. V. 14 is terse, simply stating that Saul sent messengers to seize David, but they were diverted by Michal's claim that he was ill. Still, this opens new questions. Did they see the teraphim in the bed? Has Saul begun a new initiative that will not wait for morning, for he seeks to kill David immediately? These questions are never answered; Saul moves to this more forceful approach only after David has fled. A recurring theme in the ensuing chase is that Saul is always too late. This theme is emphasized almost immediately, as Saul returns his messengers, instructing them to bring David back immediately, even if he is still in his bed. There is no more ambiguity: Saul will kill David himself, because Saul sees David as his enemy.

16–17. The focus is now on the messengers' experience as they enter the room, and we share their surprise at how they have been duped. Immediately, the narrative returns to Saul, who now knows he has been outwitted, as we hear his conversation with Michal. Saul's tone is accusatory, and his charge that Michal has misled him has overtones of treachery (cf. Prov. 26:19). Strikingly, the woman at Endor speaks to Saul in almost identical terms (28:12). Michal's response is a surprise. Jonathan's speech was resourceful and positive, and although Michal took the initiative in sending David away, she seeks to deflect blame from herself, claiming David threatened her. The narrator does not accuse Michal of sin, in spite of her manifest untruth, leaving readers to decide whether the means justified the end of David's freedom and her continuing ability to work for him.

David safe with Samuel at Ramah: 19:18–24

18. David's movement is surprising in that going to Samuel means journeying about 8 miles north and west, away from his power base in Judah. Yet Judah, and especially Bethlehem, may be where Saul expects him to go, so going to Ramah may be tactically astute. Samuel had established himself as Yahweh's authentic prophet. He had anointed David, so it made sense to go there. Moreover, Samuel had previously criticized Saul, so providing Samuel with full information would ensure his continued support for David. However, as always, David's motives remain opaque. With Samuel informed, they went and stayed in what were probably local shepherd's huts (cf. 'Notes'), suggesting that they were unconcerned about David's presence becoming too well known.

19–21. Whatever David and Samuel's intention, reports reached Saul of David's presence in Ramah. As before, he sent messengers to arrest David.

But when they encountered a group of prophets prophesying with Samuel at their head, they too prophesied when the Spirit of God came upon them. In a narrative style similar to 2 Kgs 1:9–16, where Ahaziah sent three groups of messengers to Elijah, so Saul sent two further groups who had the same experience. David is the anointed one, and the Spirit of God will not allow Saul to arrest him.

22–24. In a narrative parodying the account of the confirmation of his anointing (10:1–13), Saul set out to apprehend David. On the way, Saul stopped at the great well at Secu. This location is unknown; it is presumably on the road between Gibeon and Ramah (Khirbet Shuwei-keh is suggested but is unlikely because it is about 2 miles further north). While there, he requested and received confirmation that David and Samuel were in the huts at Ramah, and so continued his journey. By including this information, the resolution is delayed, enabling us to journey with Saul on to Ramah. But his journey does not continue as expected, because on the way the Spirit comes upon him again, as in 10:10. There the Spirit's presence had proved he was Yahweh's chosen king. This time, as he prophesied on his way to Ramah, it decisively proved that he was opposing God, because the Spirit prevented him from carrying out murder. Mention of Samuel's presence creates some tension with 15:35, but it is possible that the earlier reference referred only to a formal meeting. In a telling irony, Saul now removes his garments, echoing Jonathan's actions in 18:1. Jonathan had displayed his love for David because he recognized his position in the nation; in resisting David, Saul is shamed in his nakedness (cf. Gen. 2:24). Jonathan's removal of his garments was voluntary, passing his rights to David. Saul's are involuntary, yet symbolize the same thing. Saul's actions against David have become more overt; so have God's against Saul. The proverb that once proved Saul's status as elect king is now a mocking adage.

Explanation

Saul initially sought to kill David discreetly. The Philistines could do the job for him, but this would not work; so he moves in this chapter to attacking David overtly. Ch. 18 showed that Saul could recognize Yahweh's presence with David, but was unable to appreciate what that meant. Without saying so directly, the narrator continues to show what this means, so the harder Saul works to destroy David, the more his sin comes back on himself. Saul is in a spiral of sin. Initially, he was open to persuasion as Jonathan presented a reasoned case for protecting David. But this became problematic when, afflicted by the grievous spirit from Yahweh, he made further attempts on David's life. This was compounded by his attempt to seize David from his own home, an attempt prevented by the resourcefulness of his daughter Michal. Thus his family work against his goals. But it is ultimately God who has set himself against Saul, and this is nowhere more evident than the concluding account of Saul's attempt to arrest David at Ramah. Events that had previously shown God's presence with him, proof that he was the chosen king, work the other way. No longer is the proverb 'Is Saul also among the prophets?' a sign of God's grace. Now, as was becoming evident in 18:10, Saul's prophesying is a sign of God's rejection. This is clear as he lies prostrate and naked before Samuel, prophesying day and night. His garments have been removed, but not by his choice. He no longer has the badges of rank and honour that mark him out as king. Jonathan had voluntarily removed his and given them to David. Saul, where he seeks to destroy David, discovers that God has done the same to him. David does not usurp Saul, but Yahweh will; so the next time Saul has his garments removed (31:8) it will be by the Philistines, the point where he finally discovers that the wages of sin is death (Rom. 6:23). A response to these events, perhaps dedicated to David rather than written by him, is found in Ps. 59, the title of which is specifically linked to 19:11–17.

1 SAMUEL 20:1 – 21:1 [ET 20:1–42]

Translation

¹Then David fled from the huts in Ramah and came and said before Jonathan, 'What have I done? What is my iniquity and what is my sin before your father that he seeks my life?' ²But he said to him, 'Far from it! You shall not die. Behold, my father does nothing great or small without revealing it to me. So why should my father hide this matter from me? It is not so.' ³But David vowed again, 'Your father surely knows that I have found favour in your eyes. So he has thought, "Do not let Jonathan know this lest he be grieved." But as surely as Yahweh lives and you live, there is only a step between me and death.' ⁴Jonathan said to David, 'Whatever you say, I shall do for you.' ⁵David said to Jonathan, 'Behold, tomorrow is the new moon, and I should surely be seated with the king to dine. But send me away, and I shall hide in the field until the third evening. ⁶If your father attends to me, say, "David asked me earnestly to run to his city Bethlehem because there is an annual sacrifice there for all the clan." ⁷If he says "Good," then it will be well for your servant. But if he is enraged, then know that he has determined harm. ⁸And may you show steadfast love to your servant, because you have brought your servant into a covenant of Yahweh with you. But if there is iniquity in me, then kill me yourself! Why bring me to your father?' ⁹Jonathan said, 'Far be it from you! For if I knew my father had determined harm against you, would I not tell you?' ¹⁰David said to Jonathan, 'Who will tell me if your father answers you harshly?' ¹¹Jonathan said to David, 'Come, let us go out into the field.' So they both went out into the field.

¹²Jonathan said to David, 'By Yahweh, the God of Israel, when I have sounded out my father, about this time tomorrow or the third day, if he is well disposed to David, shall I not send to you and disclose it to you? ¹³Thus may Yahweh do to Jonathan,

and more also, if your harm pleases my father and I do not make it known to you and send you away that you may go in safety. May Yahweh be with you as he has been with my father! [14]And if still I live, shall you not show me the steadfast love of Yahweh that I may not die, [15]that you may never cut off your steadfast love from my house, not even when Yahweh cuts off David's enemies from the face of the earth?' [16]Jonathan made a covenant with the house of David, saying 'Let Yahweh exact it from the hand of David's enemies.' [17]Again Jonathan caused David to swear on account of his love for him, because he loved him as himself.

[18]Then Jonathan said to him, 'Tomorrow is the new moon, and you shall be missed when your seat is empty. [19]On the third day go down quickly and enter the place where you hid yourself on the eventful day, and stay by the stone Ezel. [20]I shall shoot three arrows to the side, as though to a target. [21]Then, behold, I shall send the lad, saying "Go, find the arrows." If I say to the lad, "Look, the arrows are across from you, bring them here," then you shall come and, as Yahweh lives, it will be well for you. There is nothing in it. [22]But if I say to the young man, "Look, the arrows are across from you and beyond," go, because Yahweh has sent you away. [23]As for the matter of which we spoke, Yahweh is between me and you for ever.'

[24]So David hid in the field. Now, it was the new moon, and the king sat at the feast to eat. [25]As was his custom, the king sat on his seat, the seat by the wall, while Jonathan was opposite and Abner sat at Saul's side. But David's place was empty. [26]Saul said nothing about it that day because he thought, 'It is an accident. He is not clean; surely he is not clean.' [27]But the next day, the second day of the new moon, David's place was empty. Saul said to Jonathan his son, 'Why has the son of Jesse not come, both yesterday and today, to the feast?' [28]Jonathan answered Saul, 'David implored me that he might go to Bethlehem. [29]And he said, "Please send me, because there is a clan sacrifice in our city, and my brother has commanded me; so now, if I have found favour in your eyes, let me please slip away that I may see my brother." Therefore, he has not come to the king's table.' [30]Saul's anger was kindled against Jonathan, and he said to him, 'You son of a perverted, rebellious woman! Don't I know that you are choosing the son of Jesse to your own shame and to the shame of your mother's nakedness? [31]For as long as the son of Jesse is alive on the earth, you and your kingdom shall not be established. Now, send and bring him to me, because he is a dead man.' [32]Jonathan responded to Saul his father, 'Why should he die? What has he done?' [33]Then Saul hurled a spear at him to strike him, so Jonathan knew his father had determined to kill David. [34]Jonathan rose from the table in a rage and did not eat the meal on the second day of the new moon because he was grieved over David, because his father had humiliated him.

[35]In the morning Jonathan went into the field for the appointment with David, and a small lad was with him. [36]He said to his lad, 'Run. Please find the arrows that I shoot.' The lad ran and he shot the arrows beyond him. [37]The lad came to where the arrows Jonathan had shot were, but Jonathan called after the lad and said, 'Is not the arrow beyond you?' [38]Jonathan called after the lad, 'Hurry! Quick! Do not stay.' So the lad picked up Jonathan's arrows and came to his master. [39]But the lad did not know anything. Only Jonathan and David knew about the matter. [40]Jonathan gave his kit to his lad and said to him, 'Go, take this to the city.'

⁴¹The lad went and David rose from the south side and fell with his face to the ground and did obeisance three times. They kissed each other and wept, David the most. ⁴²Jonathan said to David 'Go in peace, because both of us have sworn in the name of Yahweh, saying "May Yahweh be between you and me, between my seed and your seed, for ever."'

²¹꞉¹Then he arose and went, but Jonathan entered the city.

Notes on translation

20:2. Reading *lō' ya'ăśeh* with Q and many MSS. Cf. LXX.

3. *peśa'* is a hapax legomenon, but the meaning 'step' seems secure. There may be a play with *peśa'*, normally 'transgression'. Understood reflexively, a non-theological sense of 'slip-up' is possible.

10. Reading *'im* with LXX in place of MT *'ô mah*.

12. The text is often emended to follow Syr, 'Yahweh is Witness' (see ESV; McCarter 1980a: 336). But two medieval MSS read, 'as Yahweh lives'. This suggests the text's terse form was seen as an oath lacking certain expected features. The presence of different solutions suggests these are emendations rather than distinctive text types. With Stoebe (1973: 374), MT is retained as *lectio brevior* and *lectio difficilior*.

13. The expected negation in Jonathan's protasis is not directly expressed, but is included in the asseveration. See GKC §149d. The introduction of direct speech is understood from context.

14. Three occurrences of *wĕlō'* make this verse very difficult. LXX omits the second. The first is read as an asseveration, though we normally expect *wĕ'im lō'* rather than *wĕlō' 'im*. The second introduces a question through emphasis (GKC §150a; see 1 Sam. 11:12) and the third an apodosis.

16. *bĕrît* is understood, the object omitted by ellipsis within a common formula (GKC §117g).

23. LXX adds *martys*, so Yahweh is a witness between David and Jonathan. This is probably an explanatory addition.

25. For MT *wayyāq'm* read *wayyĕqaddēm*. Rebera (1989) defends MT on the basis of semantic vacancy, but there are insufficient markers for this.

33. *kālâ hî'* is unintelligible. Emendation to *kālĕtâ hî'* is justifiable since it conforms to 20:7, and the loss of one letter is explicable. McCarter (1980a: 339) objects that the emendation lacks MSS support, but is easier to explain than his preferred reading, LXX.

21:1. EVV treat this as the end of 20:42.

Form and structure

Ch. 19 showed Saul's attempts on David's life cannot succeed because of Yahweh's involvement, although this usually occurred through intervention from Saul's children. This theme is now demonstrated through an extended narrative rather than the vignettes previously employed, though close linguistic (cf. van Zyl 1989: 58) and thematic links remain. In particular, the field was not exploited in ch. 19, something causing readers to wonder about its inclusion. The reason now becomes clear as the field is again used, this time for an extended process where David remains hidden while Jonathan determines his father's attitude to him. Similarly, Michal misled her father about David in 19:17, but now Jonathan does so. The themes come together, so 20:1 – 21:1 acts as a capstone to chs. 18 – 19. David remains for ever out of Saul's reach.

The narrative development presumes either Jonathan is largely unaware of the events of 19:8–24, or contact with his father is not reported when the decision to kill David is revoked. The other possibility, that the narrative is out of chronological sequence (Klein 1983: 205), is less likely in this instance. The issue is that Jonathan, not David, needs to be convinced of Saul's intentions, though it is possible that it belongs chronologically after 19:7. However, this requires us to downplay 20:1. What is clear is that kerygmatic matters were prioritized (Arnold 2003: 296), as is apparent from how this narrative closes a sequence of shorter accounts with a long narrative, just as the Goliath story closed the accounts of David's move to court. Just as chs. 16 – 17 were enveloped by references to Jesse the Bethlehemite, so also chs. 18 – 20 are bounded by references to David and Jonathan's friendship and covenants (18:1–5; 20:42 – 21:1 [ET 20:42]). Although this chapter is often suggested to be a self-standing tradition (Grøenbaek 1971: 120), it is still possible to read it as a development of what previously transpired (Polzin 1989: 188). The narrator does not fill this gap for us, because the key point is Jonathan's loyalty to David in the face of the obligations owed to his father (Exod. 20:12). Jonathan has to assume his father's oath to him is still binding (19:6), and his attitude is shaped by that concern. Jonathan's discovery of his father's duplicity is central, a theme paralleled by the formal content given to the covenant relationship between himself and David.

Saul's portrayal also adds new dimensions to his characterization, especially his response to Jonathan when he tries to excuse David's absence. As well as abusing Jonathan (20:30), Saul indicates for the first time that he knows David is his chosen replacement (20:31). Jonathan cannot have a secure kingdom as long as he is alive. Though Saul follows the ritual elements of Yahwism, he effectively declares himself against Yahweh. It is no surprise when Yahweh later will not answer Saul (28:6). Saul's speech highlights the central theme explored: Who can choose to do Yahweh's will in spite of its cost? This will is more than just David's escape; it is that David, not Jonathan, should succeed Saul. Saul knows his kingdom cannot endure, though he does not know David will not claim it by force. Saul is driven by the need to retain what Yahweh has begun to remove. By contrast, Jonathan reinforces 18:1–5, acting for David's good because he knows David is Yahweh's chosen. Jonathan follows Yahweh's costly will where Saul does not. But this establishes an irresolvable paradox for Saul since his actions are ostensibly to ensure Jonathan's succession, although Jonathan has shown he will not accept it. The pain this generates is demonstrated through the extensive use of familial language. Thus the narrator explores the cost of faithfulness while grounding it in real choices.

Critical discussion has focused on the place of 20:12–17 and 40–42 in terms of Deuteronomistic redactional layers (e.g. McCarter 1980a: 342–343, though McCarter also includes 20:11). The reason is that it provides a link to 2 Sam. 9, and so joins the History of David's Rise to the Succession Narrative (see 'Introduction', 'Sources'), which are presumed to be separate sources. The key issue centres on 20:12–17, since 20:40–42 is only redactional if the earlier verses are. Such an approach creates a circular argument: the source is posited, and verses that counter the theory are redactional additions. A certain literary roughness in the shift from v. 10 is insufficient to justify such a change, because v. 23 already presumes a covenant with more content than 18:3. Indeed, Fokkelman (1986: 309) believes vv. 11–24 follow smoothly from v. 10. The narrative presumes the development of the covenant relationship explored in 20:12–17. In fact, there are several internal narrative difficulties (see Campbell 2002: 212–217), but these are capable of resolution within the plot.

Comment

Jonathan agrees to test Saul's intentions: 20:1–23

1–4. David moves from his hiding place at Ramah to contact Jonathan again. That he flees suggests he knows the dangers of staying where he is known, notwithstanding Yahweh's protection. Accordingly, he returned to Jonathan, presumably at Gibeah, though the city is unnamed. The meeting's details are of no interest. Instead, we plunge into David's searching questions of Jonathan. Although asking Jonathan for information, they functionally declare his innocence, as also in some psalms (e.g. 7, 17, 26). By phrasing his declaration of innocence as questions, David enables Jonathan to engage with him since questions are open to exploration. David asserts only what he considers to be generally known: that Saul seeks his life. But Jonathan is operating on the basis of his father's oath from 19:6, and expresses both shock and outrage at the suggestion, because he considers himself to be in Saul's inner cabinet, and no such decision will be made apart from him. The language is similar to Amos 3:7, but Jonathan is unaware that his father acts independently. The narrator shows Jonathan's commitment to his father, but also that he has been duped. That is why David must swear an oath to justify his view, which is that Saul already distrusts Jonathan because of his commitment to David.

David insists he is only one slip from death. The oath convinced Jonathan, who committed himself to David before he knew what David would ask.

5–8. With Jonathan's promise received, David showed how he could demonstrate that Saul had determined to kill him, possibly intending to provoke a reaction from Saul (Polzin 1989: 189). The process involved a deception not dissimilar to Samuel's in 16:2, employing claimed worship as cover for an alternative action. The plan hinged on the expectation that David would eat with Saul at new moon, traditionally the month's beginning, when celebration and sacrifices were required (Num. 10:10; 28:11–15). Celebrating a feast might suggest that Sabbath and new moon coincided, a combination that could provide a setting for a family sacrifice since it occurred only a couple of times a year. That the feast ran for two days might indicate that Israel was not entirely confident of its astronomy. That is why David's plan required him to hide in the field until the third day. Jonathan was to attend the feast and provide the agreed excuse if Saul noted David's absence. The forceful language suggests David was also providing cover for Jonathan. If Saul was unconcerned, it would demonstrate that David's understanding was wrong, but if Saul was enraged, then Jonathan would know that Saul intended to kill David. It is clear from the outset that David is right, but what matters is that Jonathan accepts this. David then summons Jonathan to show steadfast love (ḥesed) to him on the basis of their covenant (18:3). David describes himself as Jonathan's servant because he is dependent upon Jonathan. The language is strong because of the bond between them. Because covenant requires absolute fidelity, David concludes by insisting that if he is guilty of any crime against Saul, then Jonathan should fulfil his familial and covenant obligations and kill David himself. It is not expected that he will do this, because this again functions as a denial of guilt, forming an inclusion with his words in v. 1.

9–11. Jonathan had forcefully denied that his father would kill David. Now he is equally forceful in denying that he will hide information about this from him. He will not act against David. Instead, he will ensure that if David is correct he will keep him informed. Only now does David see a weakness in the plan: How will Jonathan tell him if Saul has determined to kill him? Once he has given David's excuse, Saul's anger will not permit Jonathan to meet David. But the narrator introduces a delay; rather than answering David's question, Jonathan invites him to go into the field.

12–17. Leaving David's question aside, we are provided with a development of their covenant. This relationship provides the basis for their future engagements, although they meet only once more (23:15–18), where they again form a covenant. Indeed, whenever David and Jonathan meet, they form a covenant. However, when Jonathan speaks here, we do not expect a covenant, though it is clear he is using oath language when he insists he will report back to David irrespective of his father's response. David's question of v. 10 begins to be answered, though that he may have to 'send' to David implies the possibility of intermediaries. The force of

Jonathan's commitment is demonstrated by the oath language in v. 13, where Yahweh's punishment is directed upon himself should he fail to keep his word (cf. Ruth 1:17; also building on *ḥesed*). That Jonathan concludes this oath with the blessing that Yahweh should be with David as he had been with Saul indicates he already believes what becomes explicit in 23:17, which is that David is the next king. The language of vv. 14–16 is difficult and condensed (see 'Notes'), but is capable of being understood. The narrator has employed the technique of confused language as evidence of a character's stress in 4:17, 9:12–13 and 17:38, and the same is probably done here (see Rendsburg 1999). The extended question of vv. 14–15 (see 'Notes') is designed to elicit a specific response, where David demonstrates the same commitment (*ḥesed*) to Jonathan as Jonathan demonstrates towards David. The implication is that although David and Jonathan will work with and for each other, it is ultimately Yahweh who destroys all David's enemies, perhaps an oblique reference to Saul (Evans 2000: 94). From here Jonathan made a covenant with the house of David, and not David alone. It recognized that their commitment had to be worked out beyond the two of them, reaching to their descendants, and is an element on which Jonathan comments in 20:42. A striking aspect of the whole paragraph is how Jonathan takes the initiative, even making David swear in response. It is unclear whether David swears by his own love for Jonathan, or by Jonathan's love for him, since either is possible. Since oaths are normally sworn on the basis of one's own commitment, and this interpretation is marginally preferable syntactically, it is likely to be an expression of David's own love. If so, this is noteworthy because elsewhere we hear of others who love David, not of David's love for them. But whichever way we read this clause, the personal commitment between them is profoundly political, but both the personal and the political are subjugated to Yahweh's will.

18–23. Jonathan's speech picks up elements introduced by David in 20:5, but provides specifics as to how matters will be resolved. Again, Jonathan takes the initiative. The new moon near, indicating a degree of urgency, though Saul's celebration over two days means David cannot know the outcome until the third day, when he is to return to the place where he hid on the 'eventful day', presumably alluding to 19:2. While there, he was to hide near a prominent stone known as Ezel (departure). This agreed rendezvous probably also provided David with a good view. A procedure was agreed so Jonathan could indicate whether or not David was safe by firing three arrows and by the coded advice he gave his lad. If Jonathan told the lad the arrows were close, David was safe, but if he said that the arrows were beyond him, David had to flee. The intention was that David and Jonathan need not meet, though they did not follow through on this exactly. What mattered most was their covenant relationship, and Yahweh's abiding commitment to them both. Although committed to one another, it was to Yahweh that they both needed to look.

Saul's intentions confirmed: 20:24–34

24–26. The test is now carried out. Saul has previously been discussed, and is now the major actor. Saul does not know the events are a test where his attitudes to David are demonstrated to Jonathan since Jonathan must be convinced that Saul wished to kill David. Hence David hid in the field while Jonathan went to the new moon celebration. The narrator describes the table arrangements carefully since the scene is quite intimate, with places for Jonathan, Saul's general, Abner and David. It is a meal where anyone's absence would be noted. Indeed, Saul misses David, but is not initially troubled. This is revealed by recording his thoughts on the matter, concluding David must be ritually unclean, and so unable to attend since sacrificial meat cannot be eaten by the unclean. There were many ways to become unclean, such as touching an unclean thing (Lev. 11:39–40) or touching a corpse (Num. 19:11), though often, after washing, one returned to normal life quite soon. One night's absence need occasion no concern. Touching a corpse (a common problem for soldiers) resulted in being unclean for seven days, so a longer period could be explained, though for the test the second day mattered. Nevertheless, after the first day of the test, Jonathan has no reason to doubt his father.

27–29. On the second day, David's absence is once again noted, but this time Saul asks why, directing his question to Jonathan. Saul knows that Jonathan, not Abner, who is notionally David's commander, will know about David's position. The narrative emphasizes Jonathan's conflict between David and Saul by specifically calling him Saul's son, a conflict developed through Saul's question. David is not named; he is simply 'the son of Jesse', a phrase indicating that David lacks Jonathan's status and that Saul will not name him directly. Saul's question is deceptively simple – it seemingly seeks information, but actually suggests a hierarchy of relations where David is below Jonathan. In response, Jonathan repeats the agreed answer: David has gone to Bethlehem to attend an annual family sacrifice, adding a reference to his brother's command. Yet Jonathan thus picks up a keyword from the previous chapter (*mlṭ*; 19:10, 12, 17–18). This time it must mean David has slipped away rather than fled, though in every other occurrence it meant 'to escape' (see 1 Kgs 18:40; Job 1:15; Amos 9:1). It leaves an open ambiguity. Jonathan seeks to provide the agreed cover, suggesting David simply follows orders. He is, therefore, unlikely to seek power for himself. Yet it could be understood as saying David knows the risks at court and has fled somewhere safer where he can threaten the king. Jonathan's confused speech under pressure in vv. 14–16 has its narrative pay-off here. Under pressure, his speech leaves open more possibilities than it closes, meaning that Saul interprets it as the opposite of what he intends. Jonathan's language is careful to follow court form, addressing Saul in the third person as 'the king', but though his additions were meant to clarify, they work against his goals.

30–31. Jonathan's statement completes the test, as Saul's anger is directed against him because Saul realizes Jonathan is working with David. No doubt Saul is angry with David, but Jonathan is the focus of his anger. Although Saul addresses Jonathan as the son of a perverted and rebellious woman, it is unlikely this suggests a negative evaluation of Ahinoam, since the parallel clause indicates Jonathan has shamed her. Rather, it insults Jonathan while distancing him from Saul since he does not describe him as his own son (English has similar dysphemisms). Saul complains that in siding with David, Jonathan brings shame on both himself and his mother's nakedness. This normally refers to someone's genitals (e.g. Gen. 9:22; Lev. 18:6; 20:17; Ezek. 16:8), though not through the process of giving birth. All this strongly suggests that Saul is using coarse language throughout to attack Jonathan. Saul insists Jonathan's failure is that he has not understood that siding with David means his own kingdom can never be established. Yet this is a fundamental difference between Saul and Jonathan. Saul has set himself against Yahweh's purposes, opposing both the loss of dynasty in 13:14 and the loss of kingdom in 15:28. Saul also reveals he knows David will be king. Saul's supposed clinching argument really proves Jonathan's choice. Saul is oblivious to this, and concludes by demanding Jonathan arrest David and bring him to Saul, because David is a 'son of death'. This idiom is striking, unique to Samuel, but reverberates through David's stories, recurring in 26:16 and 2 Sam. 12:5 (the similar 'man of death' occurs in 2 Sam. 19:29 and 1 Kgs 2:26). In both subsequent cases it is David who speaks these words, once condemning Abner and once unintentionally condemning himself. The phrase is probably more forceful than 'he deserves death'. 'Son' can be used in Hebrew to indicate essential characteristics. For example, age can be expressed as being 'a son of x years' (Gen. 7:6; 11:10). If this is the intent here, then it suggests that David has already reached the state of death in that judgment is passed on him. From Saul's perspective, David is already dead.

32–34. Saul accepted Jonathan's argument for David before (19:4–7), so Jonathan follows the same strategy here. The narrator emphasizes that Saul is his father, the element of their relationship Saul's earlier comments sought to downplay. Rather than arguing the case, Jonathan poses a pair of questions with both emphasizing David's innocence. There is no basis for David's execution. This only triggers Saul's wrath more directly against him, so Saul hurls his spear for the third time (18:11; 19:10), this time at Jonathan. Saul seems not to have been blessed with a particularly good aim, but this was enough to convince Jonathan. The test's goal had been realized, and now Jonathan knew that David was right about Saul. Thus Saul's anger is matched by Jonathan's as he rises from the table and leaves the feast. Jonathan's grief confirms David's view that Saul did not always tell him of his plans (20:3). Instead of being shamed by his support for David, Jonathan has been humiliated by his father. Jonathan will not abandon Saul, but neither can he allow an attempt on David's life.

Jonathan and David part: 20:35 – 21:1

35–40. With Jonathan convinced of his father's intentions, the narrative works through the remaining elements quite swiftly. Jonathan initially follows through with the plan, bringing a young lad with him at the agreed time and place, but there are minor modifications. That the lad is specifically described as 'young' indicates he was less likely to notice anything unusual taking place. A minor variation is that Jonathan seems to send the lad off before he shoots, though this is because he intentionally aims in the direction required for David to know he is in danger. By shooting beyond the lad, Jonathan does not have to confuse the lad since he will have seen the arrows land. This means he is unlikely to suspect something else is happening. Jonathan's directions to him conform to the agreed advice to inform David of his danger. However, the intensity of Jonathan's concern is shown by his speech, as he urges the lad three times to move quickly in gathering the arrows, though these words may also be directed to David as the one who overhears. We might have expected Jonathan to leave the site once the arrows were gathered, so David could escape unseen. Instead, after the narrator emphasizes the lad's ignorance of what was happening, Jonathan passed over his kit and told him to take them back to town.

20:41 – 21:1 [ET 20:41–42]. With Jonathan alone in the field, David moves quickly from his hiding place to greet his friend. In doing so, he shows respect for what Jonathan has done and reveals his commitment to their relationship. Indeed, providing some insight into David's experience is quite unusual since David normally remains opaque. In bowing down to Jonathan, David recognizes his current political status, but that they kiss (a normal form of male greeting) indicates that the political dimension is only one aspect of their relationship. Politics are highlighted by David's bowing down three times, something unique in the OT. In spite of the political dimension, it is an intensely personal moment, as both weep, but especially David. For David, it is the point at which he knows he must flee and cannot remain with his friend. For Jonathan, it is the point where he acts on what he now knows about his father, though he will not abandon Saul. Grief operates at a number of levels, even as both agree that David's perceptions about Saul are correct. Although the main plot was initiated by David, Jonathan initiated most subsequent action, and that continues here as he reiterates the content of their covenant relationship. In doing so, there is important development, so it is not just a covenant between the 'house' of David and Jonathan (20:15), but also through their descendants. This commitment will begin to work itself out through Mephibosheth (2 Sam. 9), a commitment that involves Yahweh's activity in watching over them both. This conclusion is important, stressing that their parting expresses their respective faithfulness to Yahweh and also their future dependence upon him. For now, there is only the wish of peace as each goes his separate way.

Explanation

This long story takes themes narrated in brief accounts in the previous chapters and explores them through an extended piece. At its heart is the question of faithfulness to Yahweh. What does this mean, and what does it cost? Although David is an important character, this is really Jonathan's chapter. David is a foil who allows this exploration to take place. Jonathan's faithfulness is seen in the contrast with Saul. Jonathan knows, and acts upon, the assumption that David will succeed his father to the throne; but this is costly faithfulness. This means rejecting his father's intentions for him, a rejection that provides an astonishing insight into how the fifth commandment (Exod. 20:12) had to be worked out. Commitment to parents could not claim priority over commitment to Yahweh, but neither can one abandon one's parents. Jonathan returns to town at the narrative's end because he cannot abandon his father. He continues to sustain his father, even dying with him in battle (31:2), but he does not allow this commitment to supplant his prior commitment to Yahweh. Just as Ruth shows her commitment to Naomi by refusing to obey her demand that she return to her mother's house (Ruth 1:16–18), so Jonathan shows commitment to his father by refusing to claim the throne. Jonathan's practice anticipates Jesus' call of discipleship in Matt. 10:37–39. Saul cannot accept this. He is not prepared to lose kingship and dynasty, so his rage is directed at Jonathan because Jonathan is prepared to lose these things. Jonathan discovers the extent of this cost in his own life only by exploring the question David initiated about Saul's intentions. For readers, his intentions are already perfectly clear, but Jonathan does not initially know this. Moreover, it is because of his commitment to his father that we appreciate the personal cost involved for him. From now on Jonathan fades from the narrative apart from brief cameos in 23:16–18, the mention of his death and David's song for him and Saul (2 Sam. 1:19–27). In narrative terms, this achieves what Jonathan has determined for himself. Personal greatness, at least becoming king, was not his path. Paradoxically, it is perhaps because he chose the path of decreasing that David might increase (cf. John 3:30) that we see Jonathan's greatness, a greatness that knows that one's commitment to God must have priority. For David, this means leaving his friend under a cloud of suspicion, suspicion readers know to be misplaced.

1 SAMUEL 21:2 – 22:5 [ET 21:1 – 22:5]

Translation

²David came to Nob, to Ahimelech the priest. Ahimelech came to meet David trembling, and said to him, 'Why are you alone and have no one with you?' ³David said to Ahimelech the priest, 'The king charged me with a matter and said to

me, "Let no one know anything about the matter concerning which I am sending you, and with which I have charged you." But I have directed the lads to a certain place. [4]Now, what do you have to hand? Give me five loaves of bread, or whatever can be found.' [5]The priest answered David, 'There is no ordinary bread to hand. But there is the holy bread – if the lads have kept themselves from women.' [6]David answered the priest, 'Indeed, women are kept from us whenever I go on a mission. The lads' bodies are holy when it is an ordinary journey. How much more will their bodies be holy today?' [7]So the priest gave him the holy bread, because there was none there except the holy bread, the bread of the presence, which is removed from before Yahweh to set hot bread in its place when it is taken away.

[8]But there was a man from Saul's servants restrained before Yahweh that day named Doeg the Edomite, the chief of Saul's shepherds. [9]David said to Ahimelech, 'Is there not perhaps a spear or a sword on hand here, for I have brought neither sword nor kit with me because the king's command was urgent?' [10]The priest said, 'The sword of Goliath the Philistine whom you struck down in the Valley of Elah – look, here it is, wrapped in a cloth behind the ephod. If you want it for yourself, take it, because there is no other here.' David said, 'There is no other like it. Give it to me.'

[11]David arose and fled on that day from Saul and came to Achish, king of Gath. [12]Achish's servants said to him, 'Is this not David, the king of the land? And was it not to this one they sang as they danced,

'Saul has killed his thousands,
    and David his tens of thousands'?

[13]David took these words to heart, and was greatly afraid of Achish, king of Gath. [14]So he changed his behaviour before them and acted like a madman in their hands and scribbled on the doors of the gate and let his saliva run down into his beard. [15]Achish said to his servants, 'Behold, you can see he is acting like a madman. Why have you brought him to me? [16]Am I lacking in madmen that you have brought this one to act the madman in my presence? Shall this one come to my house?'

[22:1]David went from there and escaped to the cave of Adullam, and his brothers and all his father's house heard and came down to him there. [2]Everyone who was in distress or in debt or bitter in soul gathered to him. So he was their commander, and there were about four hundred men with him. [3]David went from there to Mizpeh of Moab. He said to the king of Moab, 'Let my father and mother come to you until I know what God will do for me.' [4]He left them with the king of Moab, and they stayed with him all the time David was in the stronghold. [5]The prophet Gad said to David, 'Do not stay in the stronghold. Leave, and go into the land of Judah.' So David departed and went to the forest of Hereth.

Notes on the text

21:3. The po. *yôda'tî* is a hapax legomenon. A causative sense, a feature of the po. (and other intensive forms) is required, though the existence of the

hiph. for the root *yd'* makes this an unusual choice. A range of emendations suggested either that it might be the hiph. (GKC §55b, though
opting for MT) or derived by metathesis from the root *y'd* ('appoint',
'designate'; see BDB). None of these changes the text's meaning, and MT's
awkwardness may be a sign of originality.

3. *pĕlōnî 'almōnî* is an idiom employed when something specific is
intended but there is reticence against a formal identification. See the closer
kinsman in Ruth 4:1.

4. LXX smooths a rough MT by omitting *mah yēš*.

5. MT *'el* appears corrupt, and is omitted in 4QSam^b. LXX and 4QSam^b
add a note permitting the men to eat the bread, though this is understood
in MT.

6. Not all MSS read *'im*. 'Bodies' renders *kĕlê*, commonly 'vessels'. Here it
is a metaphor for their body, though with a euphemistic element. Paul
plays with the same metaphor/euphemism in 1 Thess. 4:4, also discussing
holiness.

7. 4QSam^b's sg. *mûsār* is more regular than MT's pl., but is probably a
correction. R. W. Klein (1983: 212) rightly suggests that the MT pl. is by
attraction.

8. For a defence of the MT's title for Doeg, see Aster (2003: 354–356).

9. McCarter (1980a: 348) regards *'în* as 'unintelligible'. It is retained
here, but read as an irregular pointing of *'ên*, showing possible Aramaic
influence. The odd combination of the particles of non-existence and
existence may be intended to indicate David knows the sword is there, but
still needs to make a request. LXX paraphrases. See Fokkelman 1986: 731.

22:1. *wĕkōl* is omitted by LXX.

3. MT *yēṣē'* is awkward, but is difficult to explain MT from the LXX or
other versions. We might have expected *yšb* to be used, as in Syr and Vg,
but it is probably better to retain MT, understanding the verb to mean
'come out from where they are' with 'to this place' understood. The
versions would then be paraphrases.

4. *wayyanĕḥēm* is here vocalized as *wayyanaḥēm* (i.e. hiph. of *nwḥ*, not
nḥḥ as currently in MT).

Form and structure

David's fugitive status has been confirmed. He is now on the run from Saul.
Typically, the narrative of this period begins with a set of related shorter
vignettes that prepare for the longer narrative in 22:6–23. This pattern
was also evident in the short narratives of ch. 16 before the extended
Goliath narrative, and the matching panels of chs. 18 – 19 before the
extended narrative of ch. 20. That these three narratives should be read
together is evident from how the brief note about Doeg in the first (21:8
[7]) prepares for the narrative of the slaughter of the priests at Nob. In fact,

each unit introduces themes and elements that become significant later in David's story. The meeting with Ahimelech sets the scene for Saul's murder of the priests, but also prepares for the priestly support David will receive (22:20–23). Achish is duped by David's feigning madness, but will be significant in chs. 27 – 31, where he will be duped in other ways. David's gathering of a band of supporting warriors and prophetic support through Gad initiates a series of accounts referring to them (23:13, 25:13, 27:2, 30:9–10 all refer to David's band, while Gad reappears in 2 Sam. 24). Each vignette has its own integrity but prepares for other elements in David's story.

These narratives are also joined by presenting David as a resourceful figure, determined to survive, though none is entirely complimentary. David lies to Ahimelech, feigns madness before the Philistines and associates with Moabites, none of which would ordinarily be considered positive. But we end with David in the forest of Hereth, around 12 miles from Nob, a point that is important because it shows that David is not near the town when Saul orders the slaughter of the priests (22:6–23). More importantly, David's final speech to the king of Moab (22:3) shows he is now waiting on God to lead him; his resourcefulness has not been completely effective, even if others have joined him and begun to recognize his authority. Until this point, God has not been mentioned apart from passing reference to priestly practice in 21:7 [6]. But this statement establishes a new pattern for David, though the horror unleashed by his approach is still worked out in the following account. David is innocent of the priests' murder (McCarter 1980b: 500), but not entirely innocent.

The literary function of these observations means we need to be careful in dealing with attempts to reorder these events, such as the proposal that 21:2–10 originally followed 19:17 (e.g. Hertzberg 1964: 178). Chronological concerns are not always primary in the material's arrangement concerned with David, so Campbell (2003: 222) is correct in suggesting that the dominant question was how to present it. The impact of this becomes more apparent in 22:6–23, but we can make the preliminary observation that although it covers a range of traditional materials, chs. 21 – 22 are a carefully structured literary panel where vital information is both presented in advance and withheld until later for effect (22:9–10; 22:22). The point where narrative information is revealed is itself important in assisting readers to assess the reliability of things that will be claimed.

Comment

David at Nob: 21:2–10 [ET 21:1–9]

2–3. If David was in Gibeah, then flight to Nob was logical. Although still in Benjamin, it brought David closer to Judah. About a mile east of

Jerusalem, it was about 8 miles from Gibeah, and close enough for David to reach the day he left Jonathan and before news of his outlaw status arrived. David's intent was to reach Ahimelech the priest, a descendant of Eli (see 22:9). David's presence obviously signified some danger, because Elimelech was trembling when he met David (echoing the Bethlehem elders when they met Samuel in 16:4), a sign he was not altogether comfortable about the meeting. His discomfort may be expressed by his question about the absence of David's men, though it may be simple surprise that David is alone. David's response is immediate, but false. He unhesitatingly claims Saul's support even though he is fleeing him. Admittedly, David is somewhat oblique, and 'the king' may conceivably refer to Yahweh (Fokkelman 1986: 396). But even if there is a double entendre, David means Ahimelech to hear that he has Saul's support. That David is on a secret mission means he cannot provide Ahimelech with any details, which conveniently closes off unwanted questions about his journey. Claiming he has his troops nearby, directed to some undesignated point, may hint at desperation on his part given his subsequent request for weaponry. Nevertheless, it is a calculated approach that seeks vital resources from Ahimelech.

4–7. David's need of resources is made specific as he asks for five loaves of bread, an amount insufficient for his men but more than David himself needed. But why ask the priest? Though not a large place, there would have been other places in Nob to obtain food. Nevertheless, the narrator refrains from answering this question. David's question plays with the word 'hand' (*yād*): he wants what is under Ahimelech's hand to be placed into his, and if Ahimelech doesn't have the five loaves, he wants whatever is available. Ahimlech's response introduces an important subtheme running through the balance of their discussion. There is no common (*ḥōd*) bread, only the holy (*qōdeš*). The answer deals in opposites, as the common and the holy cannot be mixed. The bread is that laid out by the priests each Sabbath, which only they can eat (Lev. 24:5–9). Ahimelech indicates his willingness to allow a broader interpretation of this and permit David and his men to eat, provided they have kept themselves from sexual relations with women. Although no Pentateuchal law specifically requires this for military service, Lev. 15:18 indicates that sexual intercourse made one unclean. Sexual abstinence was an element of ritual preparation for warfare, an indication of holiness, and is probably included even at points where it is not specifically mentioned (e.g. Josh. 3:5; cf. Uriah in 2 Sam. 11). David's answer presumes this, claiming sexual abstinence is a mark of his men's holiness whenever they are on duty, and their holiness in this regard was even more important when undertaking such a crucial mission for the king. Close analysis highlights problems with David's dissembling – if he is on an urgent and unplanned mission, how can he be sure his men have retained ritual purity unless none was married? Ahimelech does not notice this and gives David the holy bread of the presence. The importance of this bread is underlined by the extended way it is described, with a cluster of references pointing to its holiness. This was not bread that would ordinarily go to a soldier, but the principle of the priority of human need seems to have guided Ahimelech, a point Jesus affirms (Mark 2:25–26). David's need was genuine, even if the need he represented was not.

8. The narrator now introduces an aside, mentioning that Doeg the Edomite, one of Saul's servants and a senior shepherd (possibly a military title; see Aster 2003: 357–361), was detained (see Saul's role in 9:17) before Yahweh. We are not told why he was there, but the terms used to describe him point to the possibility of problems for David. He is Saul's servant and an Edomite, a nation with whom Israel had a deep-rooted antipathy, seen most clearly in the refusal of its king to permit them to pass through on their way to the land (Num. 20:14–21). Although Deut. 23:7–8 limits the antipathy between the nations, it still restricted Edomites from entering the sanctuary before the third generation. How this might have brought trouble is not made clear until 22:9. But there are enough hints in Doeg's characterization to know he means trouble.

9–10. David's other need was for weaponry, and so his second request is for a sword. The manner of his request suggests he knew that Goliath's sword was there, but needed to ask in a way that allowed Ahimelech to offer it. As such, David continued to ask about what might be under Ahimelech's hand, allowing for the possibility of either sword or spear. Again the request requires some dissembling, a mixture of truth and falsehood, where David's obvious lack of weapons was explained by something just plausible, that the king's command was so urgent that he could not obtain his equipment before departing. As before, Ahimelech either does not notice or chooses not to notice the implications of David's question, and offers him Goliath's sword (against Reis 1994, who suggests that Ahimelech colluded with David). The sword was probably David's primary objective, and the bread, though necessary, secondary. It is Ahimelech's apparent *naïveté* that allows him to be interpreted as an innocent caught in the wrong place or as someone who supported David while masking his actual role. Though the former is perhaps more likely, there is enough there for someone as suspicious as Saul to see conspiracy and act against it. The narrator subtly prepares for the coming slaughter of the priests. At the moment, the interest is in David's gaining the equipment he needs, and he is glad to retrieve the sword from behind the ephod (presumably, here the priestly garment) because there is none like it. Although 17:54 indicated David had kept Goliath's equipment, it is intrinsically likely that the equipment of a vanquished enemy would end up in a sanctuary, just as the ark had in 5:1–5. The reference to the ephod here carefully introduces a theme word of growing interest over the next few stories, because ultimately it will be the presence of a priest with the ephod that enables David to flee from Saul, even when it seems impossible for him to do so (23:6). Although complete in itself as an account of how David was provisioned, this also sets the scene for what follows.

David at Gath: 21:11–16 [ET 21:10–15]

11–12. David's flight takes an unexpected turn to the east as he heads across to the Philistine city of Gath, probably Tell es-Safi, a large site on the border of the Shephelah and the Philistine plain, though the exact site is disputed. No reason is given for his choosing this as a place of sanctuary, though David's urgency is conveyed by noting he arose and fled on that day. His stop at Nob was enough only to gain provisions before heading to Gath. More important than the place itself is its king, because David specifically came to Achish, to whom he will return (27:2). The designation 'king' is unusual since earlier references were to the Philistine rulers (e.g. 5:8), but the term is probably applying only the standard title for a local ruler. Although David fled to Achish, the narrator delays any account of his response, preferring instead to recount his servants' advice, quoting the song from 18:7. The implication is clear: if David slew so many Philistines, then he is a dangerous figure. More strikingly, they call David 'the king of the land'. Saul may be the de facto king of Israel, but these Philistines recognize David as king. Is this a slip on their part? Although possible, it is unlikely that the narrator would have been the first to acknowledge David's kingship as an accident. More likely, this comment is retained because it shows that whereas Saul's servants oppose David because they see he will claim the throne, the servants of a Philistine king see the deeper reality. Their quote of the old song thus brings with it a new nuance. For Saul it signified that there was nothing more for David than to claim the throne. For the Philistines it shows David is indeed king.

13–16. David's position was complicated by Achish's servants. They knew he was more than just a refugee from Saul, so staying with Achish was as dangerous as remaining with Saul. David's fear was well placed. Just as he misled Ahimelech at Nob, so David sought to mislead Achish. This time, he feigned madness, scribbling on the city's doors and gates and letting saliva run through his beard. It was a desperate attempt to remain free. David must have been an effective actor, because Achish complained he did not need another madman in his presence. The title of Ps. 34 (and probably Ps. 56) links it to this time in David's life. Curiously, Achish's question receives a positive answer in 27:3 when David returns, though then there will be no need for him to feign madness. For now he intends it only as evidence indicating why David cannot gain admission to his house, though it is possible he intends it as a mildly sarcastic jibe at his courtiers as well (Fokkelman 1986: 370).

David at Adullam and Moab: 22:1–5

1–2. How David left Achish is unclear, but he escaped from there back into the south of Judah to the cave of Adullam. The most likely site for Adullam (Khirbet esh-Sheik Madkur) is not far back into Judah, perhaps close to the scene of the battle with Goliath. If so, it may have been contested territory, where neither Saul nor the Philistines held clear control, and thus the sort of place where someone like David could operate. Bethlehem was within a day's walk, so news of his presence could reach his family so they could visit him there. But David also began gathering a group of men around him, drawing on those suffering economically or politically under Saul. That this represented a body of four hundred men suggests there was considerable unease with Saul, especially within Judah. Nevertheless, it is worth noting that the text does not indicate that all those who joined David were Israelite, so it is possible that he drew on disaffected Philistines as well. Indeed, he later has a Philistine bodyguard (2 Sam. 15:18) made up of six hundred, who followed him from Gath. At this point, David has four hundred with him, though it will rise to six hundred by 23:13. Again a key element of this narrative is the introduction of elements important for the following accounts. The group's size also suggests Adullam was a complex of caves rather than a single cavern.

3–4. The future role of the four hundred is left aside as David journeyed to Moab, a journey across Judah's south, though the site of Mizpeh in Moab is not known. No reason for this choice is provided, though Ruth 4:13–17 indicates David had a Moabite background, and the association of family with David throughout 22:1–5 may indicate he came to family here too. The pivotal change in David is made clear in his speech to the unnamed Moabite king: he wants his parents to remain until he sees what God will do for him. Where dissembling and deceit marked his opening encounters after leaving Saul, this third one indicates a different approach, one that demonstrates itself by his two refusals to kill Saul (chs. 24, 26). David is now concerned for others as well as himself, and this is expressed in terms of his own faith in God. Accordingly, David left his parents with the Moabites while he was in the 'stronghold'. Against McCarter (1980a: 357), it is unlikely that the 'stronghold' is Adullam, because Gad tells David to leave it to return to Judah, suggesting it is somewhere in Moab. If so, David's parents might not have stayed there too long.

5. The emphasis on God's input into David's life from here is emphasized by including a comment from the prophet Gad. He has not been mentioned previously, and remains unmentioned until 2 Sam. 24:11 (but see 1 Chr. 29:29). However, he initiates a new element in David's story, which is that he is subject to prophetic leading, a key element that ch. 12 indicated was vital for the effective rule of an Israelite king. David's relationships with prophets never takes on the acrimonious tone we see between Saul and Samuel, but this brief statement from Gad, and David's prompt acceptance of it, immediately sets him apart from Saul. The prophetic word, whether guidance (2 Sam. 24:18), redirection (2 Sam. 7:5–16) or rebuke and judgment (2 Sam. 12:1–14; 24:12–14) is something David accepts. By concluding this panel of stories that introduce David's period as an outlaw in this way, the narrator lays the ground for the more significant contrasts with Saul that will be developed. Faithful to Gad's word, David returned to Judah, staying in the forest of Hereth, a site that cannot be precisely located, though it was clearly in Judah's south.

Explanation

Having fled Saul, David faces life as an outlaw. The difficulties of such a life are immediately apparent as he moves across Judah's south through Nob to Gath, then back again to Moab via Adullam, and then finally to the forest of Hereth. These are the journeys of a man in danger, who has no safe haven in his homeland, but who cannot settle outside Judah either. The narrator does not simply recount these movements, but uses them to introduce themes that recur in the balance of David's rise. The move from Saul closed off many possibilities, so the narrator introduces components that become fully significant only later.

The narrative's artistry is that it is more than an introduction of motifs or elements to come; it is also an account showing David growing and developing in his response to Saul. Whereas the first two stories within the panel show him dissembling and deceitful (even if with a sense of humour while with Achish), the final segment (22:1–5) shows him taking more seriously his role as Yahweh's anointed. He is now the one around whom the disaffected rally, suggesting his leadership may be the opposite of what Samuel has warned about (8:10–18). Moreover, he demonstrates the beginning of a theology that sees his future in God's hands, as seen in his comments to the Moabite king and acceptance of Gad's prophetic direction. More than anything else, this sets David apart from Saul. David is an outlaw, but not a brigand. He knows and accepts God's authority. But this was not something reflected in his earlier actions, and his sin there will still bear its bitter fruit. In addition, these narratives show a developing appreciation of David's role by others: Ahimelech had to be duped, the Philistines recognized David even if he had to feign madness, the oppressed gathered to him as a leader and the Moabites deal with him as a person of standing. David is increasingly recognized as the coming king with whom God is present, even when he has left the court. There is nothing astonishing here like Saul being forced to prophesy (19:24), but there is still assurance that Yahweh is with David, and David is beginning to recognize this.

1 SAMUEL 22:6–23

Translation

[6]Saul heard that David and the men with him were discovered. Saul was sitting in Gibeah under the tamarisk tree on the height, his spear was in his hand, and all his attendants were standing around him. [7]Saul said to his attendants who were standing around him, 'Hear now, sons of Benjamin! Shall the son of Jesse give each of you fields and vineyards? Shall he appoint each of you as commanders of thousands and commanders of hundreds? [8]For all of you have conspired against me. No one informs me when my son makes a covenant with the son of Jesse. None of you feels regret for me or informs me that my son has stirred up my servant against me, to lie in wait as it is this day.' [9]Doeg the Edomite, who stood by Saul's servants, answered, 'I saw the son of Jesse come to Nob, to Ahimelech ben Ahitub, [10]and he enquired of Yahweh for him, gave him provisions, along with the sword of Goliath the Philistine.'

[11]Saul sent to call Ahimelech, the son of Ahitub the priest, and all his father's household – the priests who were in Nob – and they all came to the king. [12]Saul said, 'Hear now, son of Ahitub.' He said, 'Here I am, my Lord.' [13]Saul said to him, 'Why have you conspired against me, you and the son of Jesse, in that you gave him food, a sword and enquired of God for him, so that he has risen up against me to lie in wait as it is this day?' [14]Ahimelech answered the king, 'But who among all your servants is as faithful as David – the king's son-in-law, captain of your bodyguard and honoured in your house? [15]Have I just begun to enquire of God for him today? Of course not! Let the king not impute anything against your servant, against all my father's house, for your servant knew nothing of all this, trivial or important.' [16]But the king said, 'You shall surely die, Ahimelech, you and all your father's house.' [17]The king said to the runners attending him, 'Turn and kill the priests of Yahweh because their hand is also with David; because they knew he was fleeing, but did not disclose it to me.' But the king's attendants were unwilling to put forth a hand to execute the priests of Yahweh. [18]Then the king said to Doeg, 'You turn and execute the priests.' So Doeg the Edomite turned and executed the priests. On that day he killed eighty-five men who bore the linen ephod. [19]He also struck Nob, the priests' city, with the edge of the sword, men and women, children and infants, ox, donkey and flock animal with the edge of the sword.

[20]But one of Ahimelech ben Ahitub's sons named Abiathar slipped away and fled after David. [21]Abiathar told David that Saul had slain Yahweh's priests. [22]David said to Abiathar, 'I knew that day when Doeg the Edomite was there he would surely tell Saul. I am responsible for the life of all your father's house. [23]Stay with me. Do not be afraid, because the one who seeks my life seeks your life. Your security is with me.'

Notes on the text

8. 'Covenant' is absent from MT, understood from the idiom. LXX's *diathēkē* is interpretative rather than evidence of the underlying text.

ḥôleh, elsewhere 'to be sick', is difficult, but suggested emendations (e.g. Driver 1913: 142) miss the play with *gôleh*. For 'feel regret', see Jer. 5:3.

13. With many MSS reading *'alâ* for *'ēlâ*.

14. With LXX reading *śār* for MT's *sar*.

15. The translation of the first half of the verse is a conundrum because its sense is dependent upon its ambiguity. It may introduce a real condition (as above) phrased to agree that an enquiry has taken place. But it can equally be an unreal condition, and rendered 'Did I this day for the first time enquire for him of God?' (Alter 1999: 138), so a denial is meant: he has not previously enquired, so why should he start now? The grammatical ambiguity is essential to the narrative's development because of what it leaves open.

17. With Q reading *'znî*. Hubbard (1984) has demonstrated that *pg'* is a legal term referring to judicial slaying, and is thus 'to execute'.

18. LXX has 305 men killed, while Josephus has 385. On the 'bearing' of the ephod, see 'Notes' on 2:28.

22. MT *sabbôtî* is difficult, and often emended with LXX to *ḥabtî* (e.g. McCarter 1980a: 363). But *sbb* is a *Leitwort* in the chapter, and David's use of it transforms Saul's (vv. 17–18), so the verb should be retained and read causatively (see Gordon 1986: 175).

Form and structure

After the diversions of David's time at Gath and Adullam, the narrative resumes the account broken off at 21:10 [ET 21:11]. The elements established in the diversions are not simply scraps of tradition about David; they establish important elements for what ensues, while allowing a narrative break that builds tension as we await Saul's response to David's journey to Nob. The careful mention of Doeg in 21:8 [ET 21:7] prepared for the fact that David's visit there would not go unnoticed, though we cannot expect the carnage that follows. Indeed, elements in the preceding narrative that seem to be merely scenery, such as reference to the ephod, turn out to be important components of the whole account.

Although this narrative is anti-Saul, it does not exonerate David, as is clear when David accepts responsibility for what happened to Abiathar's family. No comment is made on his earlier dissembling since David's own words convict him. The narrative works out the tensions inevitably felt when rivals make a claim for power, even though David sought to avoid conflict. But greater blame is laid at Saul's feet, as the combination of madness and violence developing since his rejection in 15:28 expresses itself in a sacrilege that insists his right to power is more important than his submission to Yahweh.

The narrative is carefully structured, built around several key repetitions. It includes two accusations of conspiracy lodged by Saul, first against his attendants (22:7–8) and then against Ahimelech (22:13), both starting with 'Hear now' and addressing those hearing as 'son of...' After each accusation, an action by Doeg advances the narrative; first, when he offers an alternative to Saul's claim of a conspiracy against him by his attendants (22:9–10), and then when he kills the priests after the attendants have failed to do so (22:18–19). Both references to Doeg follow a reference to the attendants. Finally, there are two movements of the priests; first, when Ahimelech and his family come to Saul (22:11), and then when Abiathar flees to David (22:20). The narrative is also held together through the use of the roots *šmʿ* (hear) and *sbb* (round) as *Leitworte*, while the root *šʾl* is variously employed to refer to the act of seeking guidance from Yahweh or for Saul's name, though Saul is never said to have enquired of Yahweh. The interweaving of these elements makes the whole more complex than Youngblood's (1992: 734) otherwise appealing chiasm suggests.

Comment

Saul accuses his attendants: 22:6–10

6. How Saul knew David and his men had been discovered is not indicated, though Doeg's presence at Nob shows David's visit there would not go unreported. There is no indication of the delay between David's arrival at Nob and this account since we do not know how long Doeg was detained before Yahweh (21:8 [ET 21:7]). Nob is only a few miles from Gibeah, so it is possible that Doeg reported to Saul on the same day, though some time may have passed. But Saul knows where David has gone. Saul has also heard of men with him. This may mean he has a report of David's claimed support when he spoke to Ahimelech, or he has heard of the band that have begun to join him. While the former is more likely, that it was false would not change Saul's response since he believed it to be true. Saul was based at Gibeah, and is said to be under a tamarisk tree 'on the height'. Since tamarisks were rare in this area, it might have been considered a place of some importance (see Judg. 4:4–5), and was apparently used by Saul to hold court. This is clear from the presence of his attendants around him. There is also a hint of coming violence since we are told Saul had his spear in his hand, a statement that consistently prefaced unnecessary violence from him (18:10–11; 19:9–10; 20:33).

7–8. Saul addresses his attendants, accusing them of conspiracy against him. He calls them 'sons of Benjamin', suggesting he had a narrow power base. Rather than making his accusation directly, Saul begins with a pair of questions about the rewards David could give those faithful to him. The questions are laced with irony since he believes David can give neither property nor promotion. But more irony is generated when Saul effectively claims he can give these, though they are the things against which Samuel has warned the nation (8:12–14). In claiming to be the just king, Saul reveals how little he understands the role. Saul intends the questions to undermine his attendants' supposed support for 'the son of Jesse', and to show why they should not conspire against him. But the narrator thus suggests there was no reason to support Saul. Saul specifies two areas of the purported conspiracy where his attendants are implicated because of their failure to inform him. First, his son (Jonathan, like David and Ahimelech, is never named by Saul in this chapter) has conspired with David and made a covenant with him. This covenant is mentioned in 18:3 and 20:8, while a further covenant will be made in 23:18. Secondly, Jonathan has stirred up David to lie in ambush for him, an accusation he will also make against Ahimelech (22:14). The first accusation is true, though whether or not Saul's attendants were aware of it is unclear. We have only Saul's accusation. But the second is false (against Green 2003b: 86) as David twice has the chance to kill Saul but refrains each time (chs. 24 and 26).

9–10. None of Saul's attendants, save Doeg, responds, so we do not know if they supported David. Doeg was present when Saul made his accusations, though he seems to be separate from the other attendants, either as one 'beside' or 'over' them. He is separated from the main body, and may speak from a perspective of personal self-interest. When he speaks, he carefully picks up Saul's language and refers to David by Saul's dismissive 'son of Jesse'. One may think he offers nothing more than a simple recount of events when David came to Nob, but there is considerable development because of his reference to the ephod. Ahimelech had taken Goliath's sword from there, but Doeg appears to make this the basis for his claim that Ahimelech had enquired of Yahweh for David since the priests used the ephod for enquiries. The combination of enquiring of Yahweh, providing provisions and a sword, makes it appear Ahimelech also conspired against Saul. Doeg omits as much as he tells, failing to mention David's lies, so the truth is carefully manipulated to agree with Saul's inferences (see Fokkelman 1986: 389).

Saul accuses Ahimelech: 22:11–19

11–13. Although Doeg mentioned only Ahimelech, Saul summoned all the priests at Nob. A seemingly innocent detail, its significance becomes clear only later. When confronted with the priests, Saul addresses himself only to Ahimelech, dismissively calling him 'son of Ahitub', putting him on the same level of contempt as David. His accusation is cast in the plural, providing a further link to the accusation against his attendants. Although this could be an accusation against all the priests, Saul qualifies the remark so it is made clear that his accusation is against Ahimelech and David. Saul's charge is that Ahimelech has encouraged David in his rebellion by providing food, a sword and enquiring of God. The conspiracy charge presumes Ahimelech wittingly engaged in these actions, knowing David was rebelling against Saul and therefore chose to join it so David could lay in wait for Saul. The subsequent narratives, especially chs. 24 and 26, indicate David does not do this, but Saul's accusation is based on perception alone.

14–15. Ahimelech's response is a masterpiece of compressed rhetoric, building an argument through two main steps, both rhetorical questions. This avoids the problem of accusing the king of making a wrong accusation, though each question generates a coherent position. His two questions mirror those posed by Saul in v. 7. Consistent with court style, he avoids addressing Saul directly, speaking only in the third person of 'the king'. First, he points out that David is a highly important person in the court. Evidence for this is found in David's status. David is trustworthy, the king's son-in-law, commander of his bodyguard and honoured in the king's house. Nevertheless, Ahimelech does not admit directly to having enquired for David (see 'Notes'), and probably intends his last question to deny the charge to which he could claim innocence irrespective of David's status. The argument's climax is developed in v. 15b, where Ahimelech moves from questions to a conclusion, though the use of the court style enables him to avoid making a directive statement, and functions instead as a request. The king should not impute any blame to him or his family, because he had no basis for knowing there was any dispute between David and Saul. The argument is that he acted in ignorance, and could not have been involved in any conspiracy.

16–17. Ahimelech's question about enquiring of Yahweh is grammatically ambiguous, and although he probably intends it as a denial, Saul interprets it as an admission. The grammatical ambiguity is crucial to the narrative's development, a masterpiece of narrative art. Saul's judgment is immediate: Ahimelech and his family will die. It is a judicial statement, presumably drawing on the ANE tradition that all divination oracles had to be reported to the king (Roberts 1999). As such, Saul interprets Ahimelech's statement as additional evidence of his complicity. Israel's laws do not record any such requirement of disclosure, and their emphasis upon the priesthood's independence would probably argue against its validity. The studied use of court style by Ahimelech has thus condemned him for something he probably did not do and for which he should not be convicted in Israel. The narrative's emphasis is not that Saul is 'demented' (e.g. McCarter 1980a: 365), but that he applies a different legal structure to that which operated in Israel. Saul is becoming a classical Near Eastern king, falling into the pattern against which Samuel warned (8:10–17). Saul directed his runners, troops who travelled with him as an elite guard (2 Sam. 15:1; 1 Kgs 1:5; 14:27), to kill Yahweh's priests because of their conspiracy with David. Saul's words unwittingly allude to the events at Nob, where David consistently asked what was under Ahimelech's hand (21:3, 8), and Saul now characterizes their action as having put their hand with David. Innocent terminology is now freighted with accusation. Saul's judgment assumes the priests knew David was on the run, even though this was specifically denied. Since seeking an oracle required the one making the request disclose key information, Saul assumes David had to reveal his actual status, though this is far from necessary. But Saul's runners are unconvinced, and refuse to carry out the command. The narrator continues to play with the senses of 'hand' here, as their refusal is characterized as not putting their hand against the priests.

18–19. Saul's speech to Doeg repeats what he previously said to his runners, except for two careful changes. First, the second imperative moves from 'kill' to 'execute' (see 'Notes'). He thus makes explicit the legal framework in which he believes he operates. Secondly, he omits 'of Yahweh' when describing the priests, though this is probably by ellipsis. Doeg's actions then follow Saul's commands precisely, though the narrator, using language that savagely parodies holy war terminology, only now reveals the extent of the group present, as we are told that Doeg killed eighty-five priests. What Saul would not do to Amalek, he does to Yahweh's priests. The description goes further, and states that the priests 'bore the linen ephod', a phrase evocative of 2:28, where the man of God announced Yahweh's judgment on Eli's family. Even where Saul acts most like an oriental despot, he still achieves Yahweh's announced purpose. This tragic connection points to Saul's own struggle: if his attempt to destroy his enemy actually achieves Yahweh's purpose, there is no way he can thwart David's move to the throne. Moreover, he cannot be the anointed one before whom the survivor comes to beg (2:35–36). That Saul carries out Yahweh's judgment on the Elides does not exonerate him, because it is clear that he moved out of the realm of acceptable kingship. One of the key insights of the OT is the tension it retains between divine sovereignty and human responsibility, insisting that humans are free and responsible for their choices, but Yahweh's purposes will be fulfilled. Doeg is likewise responsible, though his responsibility is linked to Saul's, as he struck everyone in the town of Nob, killing human and livestock alike. The narrator shifts the verb again, so this is no longer execution – it is vengeance wreaked by a jealous sovereign. Saul's revenge is mindless bloodshed.

Abiathar flees to David: 22:20–23

20–21. Despite Saul's violence through Doeg, the narrator has held back a surprise – Abiathar, one of Ahimelech's sons survived and came to David. The language of Abiathar's escape picks up the terminology of David's flight from his house (19:12, 18), though he specifically flees to David. Saul can never find David, but one young priest can. Abiathar's report again changes the language of the priests' death, introducing the verb *hārag*. Although it can refer to judicial executions (e.g. Exod. 32:27; Lev. 20:15), this is comparatively rare, and also refers to indiscriminate or revenge killing (Gen. 34:25; 2 Sam. 3:30). Abiathar reports from his own perspective, so the broader term is more natural, but he does not use the more legally tinged *pg'* that was previously employed. No one reports an event like this neutrally.

22–23. Only now does David acknowledge the effect of Doeg's presence when he came to Ahimelech. Yet the narrator retains a veil of ambiguity. Was David intentionally vague with Ahimelech because he knew Doeg was there, or did he not want to draw Ahimelech into his plans? Either way, David took a calculated risk that brought terrible consequences for the priests and the town of Nob, and admits his responsibility for this. Yet David still invites Abiathar to join him, because he is safer with him. David's argument may seem awkward in that his reason is that the one who seeks Abiathar's life also seeks his. But when seen in the light of his status as Yahweh's anointed, it should be understood as a profound expression of confidence. Yahweh is bringing David to the throne, and provided Abiathar stays with David, he must be safe. David gains benefits from Abiathar's presence (23:6), but the narrator withholds that information for the moment, so David's confession of responsibility and hope is this narrative's climax. The title of Ps. 52 links it to David's reflections on these events.

Explanation

The nature of divine sovereignty and human responsibility runs through this account. Two central elements are present: Yahweh's purposes inevitably come about and humans are fully responsible for their actions, even when their sin results in Yahweh's greater purpose being fulfilled. Yahweh's purpose is both announced and mysterious. It is announced in that the man of God previously declared the Elides' fall and destruction, while Samuel anointed David. But it is mysterious in that the Elides' fall comes through morally flawed actions by both David and Saul, though only David admits any responsibility. Yet, through all this, David is still moving to the throne.

Saul's sin is tied in with his own sense of paranoia, something he voices when he accuses his attendants of conspiring with David. In doing so, he sounds like the king against whom Samuel warned. This accusation is never removed, but Saul is diverted by Doeg's recollection of events he saw at Nob. Once the priests are summoned, Saul begins acting like a classical ANE monarch, assuming he should be told of all oracles. Saul claims the right to unique access to God's intentions so he can serve his own purposes, compounding the picture of him as a king no longer acting in a manner consistent with the terms of ch. 12. The final evidence for this is demonstrated through his execution of the priests on the charge of sedition. Saul's actions can never be defended. Yet this is also how Yahweh's purposes are worked out, and Saul's sin completes the judgment of the Elides. Saul is never compelled to act against his will, and it is notable that there are no references to the baleful spirit from Yahweh here. Yet David accepts his guilt, even if the extent of this acceptance is never made entirely clear. David's confession also points to his own move to the throne. Saul's sin thus serves Yahweh's purposes in two ways: it completes the judgment of the Elides, and points to Yahweh's judgment of him. Saul no longer has access to priestly support, but because of his actions, David does (Hertzberg 1964: 188). Yahweh's mysterious purposes do come about, and humans are fully responsible for their actions. The temptation is always to emphasize one of these at the expense of the other, but the narrative will not allow us to do that. The tension between them must always be held.

1 SAMUEL 23:1 – 24:1 [ET 23:1–29]

Translation

[1]They told David, 'Behold, the Philistines are fighting against Keilah, and plundering the threshing floors.' [2]So David enquired of Yahweh, 'Shall I go up and strike these Philistines?' Yahweh said to David, 'Go, and strike the Philistines and save Keilah.' [3]David's men said to him, 'Behold, we are afraid here in Judah. How much more if we go to Keilah against the ranks of the Philistines?' [4]So David again enquired of Yahweh, and Yahweh answered him. He said, 'Arise, go down to Keilah, for I shall give the Philistines into your hand.' [5]David and his men went to Keilah and fought the Philistines. He led away their livestock and struck them with a great blow. So David saved the inhabitants of Keilah.

[6]When Abiathar ben Ahimelech fled to David at Keilah, the ephod came down in his hand. [7]It was reported to Saul that David had come to Keilah, and Saul said, 'God has sold him into my hand because he has been shut up by going into a city with gates and bars.' [8]Saul summoned all the people for battle, to go down to Keilah and besiege David and his men. [9]But David knew Saul was devising evil against him, so he said to Abiathar the priest, 'Bring the ephod here.' [10]David said, 'Yahweh, God of Israel, your servant has surely heard that Saul seeks to come to Keilah to destroy the city on my account. [11]Will the lords of Keilah surrender me into his hand? Will Saul come down as your servant has heard? Yahweh, God of Israel, please tell your servant.' Yahweh said, 'He will come down.' [12]David said, 'Will the lords of Keilah surrender me and my men into Saul's hand?' Yahweh said, 'They will surrender you.' [13]So David arose along with his men, about six hundred of them, and they went out from Keilah and went to and fro where they could. When Saul was told David had slipped away, he stopped the pursuit. [14]David remained in the strongholds in the wilderness, and stayed in the hill country in the wilderness of Ziph. Saul pursued him constantly, but God did not deliver him into his hand.

[15]David was afraid because Saul came out to seek his life while David was in the wilderness of Ziph at Horesh. [16]Saul's son Jonathan arose and came to David at

Horesh and strengthened his hand in God. [17]He said to him, 'Do not be afraid, because the hand of my father Saul will not find you. You shall become king over Israel and I shall be second to you. Even my father Saul knows this.' [18]The two of them made a covenant before Yahweh. David remained at Horesh and Jonathan went home.

[19]The Ziphites went up to Saul at Gibeah, saying, 'Is not David hiding with us in the strongholds at Horesh, on the hill of Hachilah which is south of Jeshimon? [20]And now, O King, according to all your deepest desire to come down, come down. Our part will be to surrender him into your hand.' [21]Saul said, 'May you be blessed by Yahweh because you had compassion on me. [22]Go, make yet more sure. Find out and discern his place, where his foot is, and who has seen him there, for it is reported to me that he is very cunning. [23]Locate and seek out every hiding place where he hides, then return to me with sure information, and I shall go with you. If he is in the land, I shall search him out from all the thousands of Judah.' [24]They arose and went to Ziph ahead of Saul, but David and his men were in the wilderness of Maon, in the Arabah south of Jeshimon. [25]Saul and his men went seeking him, but they told David and he went down to the rock and stayed in the wilderness of Maon. When Saul heard, he pursued David in the wilderness of Maon. [26]Saul went to one side of the hill while David and his men went on the other. David was hurrying to escape from Saul, while Saul and his men were trying to surround David and his men to arrest them. [27]But a messenger came to Saul, saying, 'Hurry and come, because the Philistines have raided the land.' [28]So Saul turned from pursuing David and went to engage the Philistines. Therefore, they named that place Sela Hammahlekoth.

[24:1]David went up from there and stayed in the strongholds of Engedi.

Notes on the text

23:6. The verse poses several difficulties (see Veijola 1984: 68–70). LXX is considerably longer and may be defended on the basis of haplography (so McCarter 1980a: 369). However, it may also be an attempt to resolve the difficulty of when the ephod arrived, allowing David to have it for the initial enquiries. NIV retains MT by rendering *yārad* as a pluperfect. MT is retained as a synchronization with 22:20–23 (similarly, Fokkelman 1986: 422), while explaining why David's men were unconvinced by the answer. The peculiar phraseology effectively personifies the ephod (Fokkelman 1986: 423).

7. *nikkar*, often considered corrupt, is emended to *sgr* or *mkr*. While the verb is rare, MT is defensible since the root *nkr* occurs in Ugaritic with the meaning 'acquire, sell', the sense required here. LXX's *pepraken* is perhaps a fortunate guess. So Barr (1968: 267, 331).

11. The use of *ba'alîm* for the town leaders is paralleled in Josh. 24:11; Judg. 9:22. See Driver 1913: 146. NRSV follows 4QSam[b], but MT is retained because it introduces the keyword *sgr*.

15. Reading *wayyirā'* with Youngblood (1992: 744) and Birch (1998: 1153).

23. Many MSS reverse the opening verbs, but LXX supports *BHS*. LXX omits everything from the opening verbs to 'sure information'.

25. A waw has dropped off from *lĕbaqqēš*, but is restored on the basis of LXX.

24:1. ET 23:29.

Form and structure

The technique of setting similar accounts together is again employed. Both stories in this chapter describe how David is delivered from Saul when it seems he cannot escape. The two stories interpret one another, though the second story enriches the first's detail, so the themes are not straight repetition, something highlighted by the chapter beginning and ending with a Philistine attack. The elements of thematic repetition are significant:

1. Both are set in Judah's south.
2. Both have locals prepared to betray David.
3. Both have David seemingly trapped, with escape impossible.
4. Both have David escape and continue to live in Judah's south.

Repetition's importance is such that these elements are narrated in the same order so as to highlight the parallels. But woven into these repetitions are crucial differences highlighted through the juxtaposition of otherwise similar elements. When David escapes from Keilah, we discover that Abiathar had brought the ephod with him (23:6), so David could enquire of Yahweh. Whether or not Ahimelech had done so for him before, David now has access to this crucial tool, something Saul apparently assumed belonged only to the king. That David is the next king is confirmed when Jonathan finds him and affirms that both he and Saul know this (23:16–17). Saul has hinted at this before (20:31), but Jonathan makes it explicit. That their meeting occurs between the two escape stories emphasizes its importance. A final development is David's means of escape. He can leave Keilah because of Abiathar's use of the ephod (23:12), so Yahweh's involvement is specific (23:14). His escape from the Ziphites comes when Saul is summoned at the last moment to engage the Philistines (23:27). This pattern, of explicit deliverance by Yahweh and events that seemingly conspire to protect David, has been encountered before (see 19:11–17 and 18–24), but both are means of stressing Yahweh's protection of David. Jonathan's affirmation of David's status, and his covenant with him, forms the chapter's heart, but the elements it stresses are the themes the rest of the panel demonstrates.

David's status as the coming king is also demonstrated through his actions, especially at Keilah (23:1–14). What is most notable is that the self-interest demonstrated in 21:2–16 [ET 21:1–15] has receded, and the concern for others at which 22:1–5 hinted has now become apparent. As an outlaw, David has no responsibility for Keilah, but still chooses to deliver it from the Philistines, which is what the king should do. By contrast, Saul's obsession with David allows the Philistines to attack in the Ziph narrative (23:15 – 24:1 [ET 23:15–29]). Again narrative components combine to emphasize elements made directly through dialogue or direct narrative comment. The sequence of covenant narratives involving David and Jonathan (18:1–5; 20:12–17) contributes to the goal of highlighting David's status in that they moved from a situation where Jonathan was sovereign to one where David now is (Wozniak 1983: 218). This development, and the integration of each covenant to its narrative, argues against Veijola's suggestion that 23:16–18 is a Deuteronomistic addition (1975: 88–90). Similarly, the chapter's tight integration argues that it should be read as a complete work and not through a putative redactional history (Veijola 1984: 73–80).

Comment

David at Keilah: 23:1–14

1–5. Like Saul, David appears to have had access to sources of information, so David responded when a Philistine raid on the town of Keilah was reported. Keilah was in Judah, a couple of miles south of Adullam, in the area disputed with the Philistines, and thus prone to raids. This raid occurred in summer when the harvest had been brought in, since the raid's target was the threshing floor. In this setting, David begins to act as the king should by applying the theologically sensitive approach suggested by 22:3. Specifically, David enquires of Yahweh (the action that led to Saul's executing the priests), though the means of his enquiry is not yet stated. The enquiry shows David in a positive light, since his concern is with the town of Keilah. Although within Judah, and more likely to be loyal to him (unless it was still an independent Canaanite city; see Edelman 1991: 182–183), David had nothing to gain by delivering the city, but his enquiry is directed to that end. In spite of Yahweh's positive response, David's men were unconvinced. The Philistines were a threat within Judah – how much more if David's men attacked them? Accordingly, David enquired further, and was promised that Yahweh was giving the Philistines into his hand (note the frequency of 'hand', *yād*, throughout chs. 22 – 24; see Miscall 1986: 139). The language of Yahweh's two responses is crucial, because they echo the initial statements about Saul (9:16). Saul was to save (*yšʿ*) Israel from the Philistines, yet David will now do so. Moreover, the promise of giving the Philistines over to David draws on the Yahweh war tradition (Longman and Reid 1995: 33–34), the tradition Saul subverted by ordering the priests' deaths. David is again marked out as the coming king by fulfilling royal responsibility, and he receives the promises associated with it. The battle report can therefore be brief since David does what Yahweh said, and saves (*yš'*) the town's inhabitants, while also plundering the Philistines of their livestock, perhaps the beasts used to carry their equipment (Baldwin 1988: 142). David has fulfilled a king's role in a way that Saul has not, because the one time Saul brought back beasts it was an act of sin (15:9).

6–8. Only now are we told that when Abiathar fled to David he brought an ephod with him, and the ephod was a means of enquiring of Yahweh. Since Abiathar arrived when David was at Keilah, he could not have used the ephod in the previous enquiry, perhaps explaining the fear of David's men in spite of the initial answer. David has acted as the king should, and so the narrator now reveals that he has royal access to Yahweh through a priest. Saul destroyed his access to Yahweh through the ephod, but David now has this access. The narrative's focus then switches to Saul. Unlike David, Saul is solely dependent upon human information. He may speak of God, but has no knowledge from God. He is told that David has gone to Keilah, and sees an opportunity. The folly of his position is not stated. Instead, the narrator uses his own words to show how little Saul understands, claiming God has sold David into his hand because David can be trapped in a city with barred gates. Abiathar's presence with David with the ephod shows how flawed Saul's view is, since this signifies Yahweh's presence with David. David's presence in the town as Yahweh's appointed deliverer also stands against this. What Saul does not say is equally important. He does not delight that the Philistines were defeated. He sees only the possibility that he might vanquish his foe, a possibility he seeks by summoning all his forces to besiege David and his men at Keilah, even though this abdication of royal responsibility left the nation open to Philistine attack.

9–12. The awareness David and Saul show of each other continues, though this time we are told David knew of Saul's plan, not that he was told of it. This points to David's acute military awareness, though it is only when he enquires of Yahweh that he substantiates the report. This time, we are told David employed Abiathar with the ephod to enquire of Yahweh. As in 23:2–4, David enquires of Yahweh twice. The first enquiry asks whether the lords of Keilah will betray him and whether Saul will come down against him. Only the second question is answered, so David again asks whether the town's lords will betray him, to which he receives a positive answer. No reason is given for the perfidy of the lords of Keilah, in spite of David's actions for them. Of more interest is that David repeatedly enquires of Yahweh and receives answers, whereas Saul presumes to know what God is doing but shows only his misunderstanding. We are thus prepared for Yahweh's silence when Saul enquires of him in 28:6.

13–14. Armed with information from Yahweh, David and his men escape. Six hundred men (an increase of two hundred since 22:2) may have been no match for Saul, but could still leave the town, although they seemingly had no particular destination. Once Saul was told David had again slipped away (*mlṭ*; see 19:10, 12), he called off his expedition. David remained in the region, making use of natural defences and moving to the region of Ziph, to the south of Hebron. The narrator then comments directly on this period, which is that in spite of Saul's continued efforts, God did not give David over to Saul. David was not too difficult to find, as is clear from those who joined him and from Jonathan's subsequent visit. But Saul could not find him because of God's actions, of which the events at Keilah were a specific example.

David at Ziph: 23:15 – 24:1 [ET 23:15–29]

23:15–18. V. 15 acts as a hinge, joining David's escape from Keilah with what follows, repeating the geographical note that he was in the wilderness of Ziph, but adding that this was at Horesh, an unknown location meaning 'wooded height'. This is tied to the previous account by noting that Saul sought David's life. While David was afraid because of this, Jonathan did what Saul could not and found him. Jonathan is specifically named as Saul's son, stressing his status within the royal family. Jonathan came to encourage David, doing so in theological terms since he 'strengthened his hand in God' (see 30:6). The encouragement's content is developed through Jonathan's speech when he counsels David not to be afraid. There are two main reasons for this. First, Saul will be unable to find David; and secondly, because David will be king. The first expresses a faith that understands the narrator's point from v. 14, but that has been clear since ch. 19. Try as he may, Saul cannot catch David, even though others can. That David will be the next king develops themes latent in the previous accounts, though also providing a context where Jonathan's choice not to seek the throne is made explicit. This has been evident since he passed across his robe and armour (18:1–5), and was confirmed when he enabled David to escape. Jonathan adds two clarifying remarks, each of which develops the theological heart of this chapter. First, he expects to be second to David, an expansion on their previous covenant (20:12–17), but consistent with it. The second remark is more important – even Saul knows David will be the next king. This was implied in Saul's outburst in 20:31, but is made explicit here. The fundamental conflict is made clear. David is Yahweh's elect king, and cannot be harmed. But Saul has set himself against Yahweh, even though he deludes himself that God still works for him (23:7). Jonathan sides with David because this is working with God. As is typical, we have no record of David's response (Alter 1999: 143). Jonathan thus voices themes the rest of the chapter develops in a more understated way. All of this is confirmed in the final covenant made between David and Jonathan, a covenant explicitly made before Yahweh before they separated (see Sheriffs 1979: 61). This is their last recorded meeting, and Jonathan remains unmentioned until his death (31:2).

19–20. Where David's betrayal by the lords of Keilah was never carried out, the second betrayal by the men of Ziph is initiated. The narrative thus demonstrates the increasing danger with which David lived, even if Jonathan's speech has indicated the outcome of this threat. The chapter is marked by a gradual increase in the specificity of David's location, so it is now the hill of Hachilah south of Jeshimon in Horesh. None of these places can be identified, but the point is that Saul now has an exact location where he can find David. No reason is given for the Ziphites' actions (though Saul describes them as compassion), but it is striking that two communities in Judah were prepared to betray David. Whatever their reasons, the Ziphites were keen that Saul should satisfy his own desire and come so that they might surrender David (using the same term, *sgr*, as the lords of Keilah and the Ziphites) to Saul.

21–24. As previously, Saul responds in theological terms, blessing the Ziphites by Yahweh. But his speech serves only to condemn him, since Jonathan has already made clear that Saul knows he is acting against God by seeking David. Despite this, Saul was acutely aware that finding David was a difficult challenge, which is why he sent the Ziphites back to confirm their initial information. The importance of this for Saul is evident in the piling up of imperatives directing the Ziphites to establish their information, and to expand on it by noting who else goes to David. Jonathan's visit was obviously just in time since a subsequent visit would be reported by Saul's spies. Saul also wanted to know about the hiding places available to David. The extensive information sought is evidence of a detailed military plan, one from which David could not possibly escape. Once Saul had certain information, he would join the Ziphites, and wherever David was hiding, he would find him. There is no attempt to recount the Ziphites' confirmation. Instead, the account moves directly to Saul's departure, at which time David had moved on slightly in the same area to the wilderness of Maon, about 8 miles south of Hebron.

23:25 – 24:1 [ET 23:23–29]. David remained as well informed as Saul, so when Saul sought him David was informed and went to a rock, presumably a secure place, in the wilderness of Maon. But Saul heard and pursued him in Maon, meaning they were now at their closest since David's flight. Indeed, they were so close that as Saul passed along one side of a hill, David and his men passed alongside the other, with David hurrying to escape even as Saul and his men were surrounding him in a pincer movement. In spite of Jonathan's claims, and those of the narrator in v. 14, it seems David could not escape. But at that point, a messenger urgently summoned Saul to confront the Philistines who were again raiding the land. Saul had no choice, and had leave to deal with the Philistines. The place thus became known as Sela Hammahlekoth, meaning something like 'Rock of Escape' or 'Rock of Parting'. David then moved to the region of the Dead Sea and stayed at Engedi. Where it seemed impossible, the claim of v. 14 was shown to be true: in spite of Saul's effort, God did not give David into Saul's hand (though see Bergen 1996: 236).

Explanation

The two narratives that make up this chapter are closely related. Both are accounts of treachery, and both recount David's escape from seemingly impossible situations. Both times it is evident that Yahweh enables him to do this. One theme running through David's story is the statement that Yahweh was with him. This is not stated here, but is demonstrated in how the stories are told. Yahweh's promise to David was sure, and even when circumstances seemed to point in another direction, David's position was secure, although there remained a mystery in Yahweh's ways: once he delivered David through direct communication, and once through circumstances that would be considered coincidental were it not for the strong emphasis on providence stated in v. 14.

But this is not the only element developed, because the theme of kingship is closely bound to God's presence with David. Chs. 21 – 22 showed David in a not altogether positive light: his dissembling with Ahimelech led to the slaughter of the priests, and he continued to be less than honest in his dealings with Achish. Even his acceptance of responsibility when Abiathar fled to him was less than convincing. This chapter presents a positive image of David as someone living as the anointed king should to underline his fitness for the role. Therefore, this chapter shows David's acting as the king should. He delivered Keilah from the Philistines, an act that did not serve his own interests, but in doing so he does what an Israelite king is supposed to do. By contrast, Saul continues to misunderstand God, claiming divine support where it cannot be. The contrast between David and Saul strengthens the claim that David is the nation's just king, since he models the ideal of kingship, whereas Saul is tied up in his own ambitions. Most importantly, the king's task is to submit himself to God's greater rule. David does this through a series of points where he enquires of Yawheh. The title of Ps. 54 associates it with this period in David's life, providing a further reflection on these events in terms of trusting Yahweh. As Jonathan makes clear, Saul has set himself against God because he knows David will be king. Jonathan's visit is how David is encouraged, but also how we see the certainty of the promise to David. Thus the chapter assures readers of the certainty of God's promises, and yet ties these into the need to do God's will. David and Jonathan, not Saul, do this, and continue to receive the promises.

1 SAMUEL 24:2–23 [ET 24:1–22]

Translation

[2]When Saul returned from following the Philistines, they told him, 'Behold, David is in the wilderness of Engedi.' [3]Saul took three thousand chosen men from all Israel and went to pursue David and his men before the Rocks of the Ibexes. [4]He came to the sheepfolds by the road. There was a cave there and Saul went in to relieve himself. But David and his men were staying in the inner recesses of the cave. [5]David's men said to him, 'Look, today Yahweh says to you, "Behold, I am giving your enemy into your hand." And you shall do to him as is right in your eyes.' So David arose and secretly cut off the corner of Saul's robe. [6]But after he had done so, David's heart struck him because he had cut off the corner of Saul's robe. [7]He said to his men, 'Yahweh forbid that I should do this thing to my lord, to Yahweh's anointed, to put forth my hand against him, because he is Yahweh's anointed.' [8]David divided his men with words, but he did not permit them to rise against Saul. Saul rose up from the cave and went on his way.

[9]David arose afterward and came out from the cave and called after Saul, 'My lord, the king.' When Saul looked behind him David did obeisance with his face to the ground. [10]David said to Saul, 'Why do you listen to human words saying, "Behold, David seeks to harm you"? [11]For this day your eyes have seen that Yahweh gave you into my hand today in the cave, and it was said that I should kill you, but my eye pitied you. I said, "I shall not put forth my hand against my lord, because he is Yahweh's anointed." [12]But, my father, see! Yes, see also the corner of your robe is in my hand. Since I cut off the corner of your robe but did not kill you, know and see that there is neither harm nor transgression in my hand. I have not sinned against you, though you lie in wait to take my life. [13]May Yahweh judge between me and you and may Yahweh avenge me from you. But my hand shall not be against you. [14]As the proverb of the ancients says, "From the wicked comes forth wickedness." So my hand shall not be against you. [15]After whom has the king of Israel come out? Who are you pursuing? A dead dog? A single flea? [16]May Yahweh be judge and give judgment between me and you. May he see and argue my case, and may he vindicate me from you.'

[17]When David finished speaking these words to him, Saul said, 'Is this your voice, my son David?' Then Saul lifted his voice and wept. [18]He said to David, 'You are more righteous than me, because you dealt fairly with me, but I have dealt unfairly with you. [19]You have declared today how you have treated me fairly when Yahweh sold me into your hand but you did not kill me. [20]For if a man finds his enemy, will he let him go safely away? So may Yahweh recompense you with good for what you have done to me this day. [21]Now, behold, I know that you surely will be king, and the kingdom of Israel shall be established in your hand. [22]So now, swear to me by Yahweh that you will not cut off my seed after me, and that you will not destroy my name from my father's house.' [23]David swore to Saul. Saul went to his house, but David and his men went to the stronghold.

Notes on the text

3. For 'ibexes', see Danin 1979.

4. To 'relieve himself' is lit. to 'cover his feet'. The euphemism refers to exposure of male genitals (see Judg. 3:24), referring particularly to defecation. This is clear from the similar idiom for urination in Isa. 36:12. A similar expression occurs in Isa. 6:2, but the verb is different.

5–8. NEB follows a common suggestion, reordering these verses as 5a, 7–8a, 5b–6, so David's remorse concludes the section. The arrangement's value is dubious, and creates more problems than it solves (with Gordon 1990: 143–144).

5. Following Q. K reads 'enemies'. Most EVV treat the men's claim as a previous promise from Yahweh (e.g. ESV, NRSV, NIV), but Driver's (1913: 149–150) treatment of *'ăšer* shows it cannot refer to a previous event, and thus an interpretation of what is happening.

6. With a number of MSS and LXX, restoring *hammĕ'îl*.

8. MT *wayĕšassa'* is difficult, and usually emended along the lines of LXX (i.e. 'I was not willing'), though McCarter (1980a: 381) thinks this is a contextual guess. Stoebe (1973: 435) thinks there may be a local idiom. MT can be retained, with the pi. understood iteratively, meaning David's decision created ongoing conflict. The pressures this generates may explain events in ch. 26, where David initiates a similar situation. Wordplay is also prominent: David has cut off the corner of Saul's robe, and now he cuts up his men (Gordon 1990: 144).

11. Fokkelman (1986: 734) rightly defends *wĕ'āmar* as impersonal. *'ênî* is understood after *wattāḥās*.

23. Reading *'el* with many MSS.

Form and structure

Ch. 23 has emphasized Yahweh's protection of David from Saul. In spite of his military might, Saul cannot find David. But is Saul safe from David? Since David is anointed by Yahweh to succeed Saul, can he use Yahweh's protection to destroy Saul? More broadly, will David use force to gain his own ends? This issue runs through the whole of chs. 24 – 26, and it is vital that this chapter be seen within that complex, though as Gordon points out, its roots reach back to 23:14 (1980: 40). In spite of Klein's (1983: 236–237) extensive list of parallels (not all equally persuasive), this chapter is not simply a doublet of ch. 26 (see Gordon 1980; Edenburg 1998). This has been the dominant critical approach, with scholars divided over which is the earlier account. Rather, the two accounts of David's sparing Saul are important because of the developments between them and how they balance the Nabal story in ch. 25. The accounts' similarities are important only in that they generate differences interpreted through the Nabal story. Here David could use violence against Saul, but though he regards Yahweh as the opportunity's source (v. 11), he declines to do so. In the Nabal story David is prepared to use violence, but discovers through Abigail's intervention that Yahweh has prevented him (25:32–34). Ch. 26 therefore is where David demonstrates this understanding both to Saul and also his men when he initiates the opportunity to kill Saul. The need for a second demonstration may be implied by v. 8 (see 'Notes'). Here David can only express the wish that Yahweh would reward his actions, but in 26:23 he treats this as a certain outcome. David here takes a risk based on what has previously happened. David in ch. 26 demonstrates what he knows.

This chapter is less concerned with the actual events than with the dialogue between David and Saul. Although the overarching issue of David's preparedness to use force to grasp the throne is present, the chapter's focus is on how David and Saul express their understanding of what it means to be Yahweh's anointed. This can be seen in that the narrative of David's not killing Saul is completed by 24:8 [ET 24:7], whereas vv. 24:9–23 [ET 24:8–22] constitutes a pair of lengthy speeches. David's speech (24:9–16 [ET 24:8–15]) carefully insists he poses no threat to Saul, though Yahweh has provided him with the opportunity to kill Saul, before expressing the wish that Yahweh act as the final judge between them. Saul accepts David's claims before making his own confession. He knows David will be king (24:21 [ET 24:20]). Jonathan previously indicated this, but this is the first time we hear it from Saul. But the confession will not prevent Saul from continuing to pursue David.

This reading assumes the chapter's literary integrity, but critics are not agreed on this. An older generation tended to see 24:5–8 [ET 24:4–7] as dislocated, requiring David's refusal to attack Saul before he cut off the corner of the robe (e.g. Smith 1899: 217–218; see NEB, 'Notes'). But this is unnecessary. As McKane (1963: 147–148; cf. Gordon 1990: 142–144) has shown, this creates more serious difficulties than it resolves since David would then be filled with guilt for having cut off the corner of the robe, the very act he would have proposed as an alternative to killing Saul. Veijola (1975: 91–93) has argued that most of 24:18–23 [ET 24:17–22] consti-tutes a Deuteronomistic addition to the narrative since Saul's oath meant there would be no need for ch. 26. The argument that these verses are Deuteronomistic may itself be doubtful, but the greater problem is that this fails to attend to the dynamics of the larger narrative. In any case, Saul has previously shown willingness to oppose Yahweh's purposes for him, so the continuation of his pursuit of David is not altogether unlikely. Saul's subsequent opposition to Yahweh's purposes contrasts with the theme developed through chs. 24 – 26, which is that Yahweh's purposes will be fulfilled.

Comment

David spares Saul in the cave: 24:2–8 [ET 24:1–7]

2–4a. David had fled to Engedi, on the western coast of the Dead Sea after Saul was called off to fight the Philistines (24:1 [ET 23:29]). Saul's battle against the Philistines is of no interest beyond proving Yahweh's providential protection of David, so the account simply resumes his pursuit of David. Once Saul had returned from fighting the Philistines his information network kicked in again, reporting David's general whereabouts. Saul's pursuit is serious, for he selects three thousand of his best men, a force that makes David's six hundred seem insignificant. Saul's intelligence was more specific than just the region of Engedi, since he brought his troops directly to the Rocks of the Ibexes, apparently a prominent local formation. Ibexes are still prominent in the area, but the particular rocks cannot be identified. His intelligence may have been more specific since the expression 'before' (*'al pĕnê*) can mean 'east', which leaves only a narrow area between the rocks and the Dead Sea. Yet Saul could never find David, though in an account spiced with scatological humour, David finds Saul. Sheepfolds were often constructed around caves as the natural formation provided some protection for the animals, as well as shelter for the shepherd. A sheepfold indicated a sufficiently large cave for Saul to relieve himself in private.

4b–5a. But Saul did not know that David and his men were stretched out along both sides of the cave. Had Saul looked, he could have found David. Instead, David finds him. David's men see the possibility this offers. They interpret it as evidence of Yahweh's providence (see 'Notes'), that he has delivered Saul into David's hand (*yād*, a key term from chs. 21 – 23). Saul is characterized as David's enemy, so the men present David with a simple temptation to do what he thinks right, a euphemism for killing Saul.

5b–8. But interpreting providence is complex. Presented with the temptation, David instead sneaked forward. Somehow, he cut off the corner of Saul's robe (*mĕ'îl*). In spite of Gunn's sexual interpretation (1980a: 92–95), the narrator more likely alludes to 15:27–28. There Saul tore the corner of Samuel's robe (*mĕ'îl*), which Samuel interpreted as signifying Yahweh's tearing the kingdom from him. David cuts off the corner of Saul's robe as a symbolic claim to the kingdom – note that in Mesopotamia a robe's fringe could be used a symbol of authority, though the sense of this is varied (see Long 1989: 158–162). David has not followed his men's suggestion, but claims the kingdom. It is this, as much as David's protestation of innocence of a direct assault on him, that convinces Saul of David's position as the next king. Yet David's move is premature. If David is dependent upon Yahweh's timing, then this symbolic claim goes too far, and so David's heart is said to strike him (see 2 Sam. 24:10). David knows he has moved too close to the violence that Saul is prepared to enact. That is why

David expresses himself in a forceful oath before Yahweh. He knows he has nearly succumbed to the temptation of violence, and he cannot employ violence against Yahweh's anointed, even though he too is anointed. If Yahweh can anoint two men, then Yahweh must resolve the resulting conflict. Saul is still king, so David's description of him as 'my lord' is not mere convention. It also indicates why he cannot act against Saul, because David's status as Yahweh's anointed is activated fully only when Yahweh has removed Saul. But Saul is still Yahweh's anointed. This view divides David's men, some of whom interpret providence, as they initially suggested, while others accept his case. But David's authority remains and he will not permit them to rise against Saul. Instead, Saul can rise and go, oblivious to events that take place around him.

David's speech to Saul: 24:9–16 [ET 24:8–15]

9. David arose after Saul, taking a great risk in calling after Saul since the king's men would be outside the cave, though if Saul was acting outside the camp (Deut. 23:12–13), he would perhaps not have been immediately present (see Bergen 1996: 240). David's address is polite, reflecting the position of honour he has previously used when addressing his men, calling Saul 'My lord, the king.' The titles are more than honorific. They represent the status David knows Saul retains. Hearing this, Saul turns and sees David with his face to the ground in a position of obeisance. Saul has been in David's power; now David is in Saul's. Saul has been prepared to use violence, but David is struck with guilt even by violence's symbolic application. The narrator thus creates intense conflict, though it will be resolved through dialogue.

10–12. David's position is precarious, but his speech is a fine example of rhetoric in demonstrating that he does not threaten Saul. Initially, this is done by his asking Saul to consider the reasons for Saul's pursuit. David sets up a conflict between human information and Yahweh's purposes, and the two disagree. Saul has listened to human speech that suggested David sought his harm. Instead, David picks up his men's argument about Yahweh's providence, and presents it in a new light. He accepts their claim that Yahweh has put Saul into his hand in the cave, but uses it in demonstrating he does not seek Saul's harm. David does not simply present evidence for this. Instead, he twice asks Saul to consider. Yahweh has given Saul into David's hand in the cave when some told David to kill Saul. David's speech here uses impersonal forms to refer to his men obliquely in case Saul does not accept the argument; but the reference is clear enough. Given that opportunity, David has shown Saul pity. He did not take the opportunity to kill Saul because he still accepted Saul's status as Yahweh's anointed. As evidence for this, David again invites Saul to examine the evidence, the corner of his robe he cut off, which is now in his hand.

David's speech moves into familial language here, for he calls Saul 'my father'. As his father-in-law, this is appropriate, but the intention is to indicate a close relationship between them. It moves from the formality of 'my lord the king' into language that acknowledges Saul's position while suggesting that David is not removed from him. Saul is thus presented with the chance to examine the corner of the robe David holds while listening to David's testimony and his affirmation of innocence of both action and intent against Saul. David insists Saul's life is safe. He intends him no harm, a point he reinforces through a series of synonyms to emphasize this, all the while insisting that Saul can now know this. David has not acted against Saul, and neither will he. The conclusion that David draws is simple. Saul is hunting him even though he poses no threat to him.

13–16. Vv. 13–16 are bound together as the second component of David's speech by the opening and closing references to Yahweh's acting as the judge between him and Saul. What is demonstrated is that their conflict's resolution cannot be something David will resolve. Yahweh must judge between their competing claims. Vengeance belongs to Yahweh, not to David or any other human, and David claims that he will not therefore act against Saul. The cumulative case is that David did not act against Saul when Yahweh gave him the opportunity. Final resolution can come only through Yahweh's direct action separate from David. David also points to an old proverb, and effectively claims that if he were as wicked as Saul's informants claimed, then Saul would already be dead. But David insists that he is not like this, employing a series of rhetorical questions to show how little a threat he poses. Saul is really pursuing a dead dog or a flea (see 26:20, and Mephibosheth before David in 2 Sam. 9:8). David insists that he poses no threat, though by putting this through questions he invites Saul to reach this conclusion rather than stating it directly. David can thus conclude by wishing again that Yahweh judge between them, making it clear that David will not act against Saul, even though he is confident of the outcome.

Saul's speech to David: 24:17–23 [ET 24:16–22]

17. Having recorded David's speech without interruption, the narrator now records Saul's. Saul must first recognize David, and he does this through a rhetorical question where he too employs familial language, as he calls David 'my son' (see 26:17). Saul appreciates the immensity of what David has done, which is no doubt why the king weeps, while the familial language brings David symbolically closer to Saul.

18–20. Saul addresses David directly, asserting that David is more righteous than him because he has not killed Saul (see Gen. 38:26). David has not sought to repay Saul for what he has done, although Saul has sought David's harm. David's testimony shows this, though just as in Gen. 38

neither Judah nor Tamar was wholly innocent, Saul perhaps implies that there is still some guilt in David, in spite of his asseveration of innocence. Saul accepts that Yahweh has sold him into David's hand (which Keilah's lords would have done to David), and that David has not killed him. This is indisputable, and Saul ties this into a proverb himself in v. 20. Thus Saul expresses the hope that Yahweh repays David for the good he has done this day. In spite of its seemingly positive nature, the speech remains narrow in focus. Is this day representative of what David does, for which he should receive divine recompense or a unique event that cannot, in the long run, overcome the harm Saul still believes he will do? Saul accepts David's evidence for this day without commenting on David's wider claims. Yahweh's judgment for this day is that David is more righteous than Saul, but Saul's comments do not necessarily go beyond that.

21–22. We now come to Saul's first confession that David will be king, the point to which Jonathan earlier referred, but that we have not heard directly from Saul. The confession makes clear what readers have known for some time: the kingdom is passing from Saul to David. But that Saul requires David to swear an oath that he will not kill his descendants suggests he is not entirely committed to David's view on Yahweh's vindication. If vindication belongs to Yahweh, then Saul's descendants are safe. Although Saul does not know it, David previously swore as much to Jonathan (20:42), though 2 Sam. 21:1–14 indicates that David can be selective in this. Saul's concern for his descendants is explicable since usurpers often killed all members of the royal family to stop any further call on the throne (Judg. 9:5; 2 Kgs 10:1–11; 11:1), so an oath can be explained. But an oath still suggests that Saul is less confident of how Yahweh's judgment will be resolved. Saul may not be as adept with words as David, but like many modern politicians he can still shroud his words with enough possibilities that they may not mean what they at first seem. Nevertheless, though Saul continues to resist Yahweh's will, the kingdom's transfer is certain. The only question is how it will happen.

23. The narrative closes with a brief note suggesting that both David and Saul appreciate a remaining degree of ambiguity. David swears the oath Saul requested, though it does not later prevent him from killing a significant number of Saul's family. Only Jonathan's line is really safe. But David knows all is not yet settled, which is why he returns to his stronghold, possibly Adullam, while Saul returns home. Saul cannot now strike David, but though they are probably given sincerely, Saul's assurances are not as clear as they might seem.

Explanation

How is providence to be understood? That question lies at this chapter's heart more forcefully than the parallel account of David's sparing Saul in ch. 26. The narrator never speaks of God in this chapter. Rather, we hear about God only as the characters express their understanding of what he is doing. In so doing, we see providence interpreted differently along with the rights of those who have received God's promises in respect of it.

The one thing on which all speakers are agreed is that Yahweh put Saul in David's power when Saul entered the cave to relieve himself. Saul can never find or catch David because Yahweh is with David, but Saul can be placed in David's power. But that Yahweh enabled the situation does not provide any guidance on how David should act. His men, however, are sure. They believe that Saul's presence in the cave shows Yahweh is enabling David to act against Saul, and even if their suggestion of 'you shall do to him as is right in your eyes' is expressed euphemistically, their meaning is clear: Yahweh has provided the opportunity for David to kill Saul. Though he will be grieved by his action, David reaches out against Saul, cutting off part of his robe. This is symbolic of a larger action against Saul, and though David has not attacked Saul's person, he has denied him his proper status. This is the source of David's guilt, and perhaps why he excoriates his men for their view. David's guilt makes clear to him that even a symbolic attack on Saul is not acceptable, and whatever the opportunity, violence is not open to him.

David's guilt enables him to understand this providential event differently, daringly announcing it to Saul. Though their words were veiled, it was clear his men wanted him to kill Saul, but David took the piece of cloth and showed it as evidence that he would not act maliciously against Saul. Yahweh's providence meant David could show he would not attack Saul, even when the opportunity presented itself, and therefore Saul had no need to continue pursuing him. More than that, David concludes his speech by insisting that Yahweh will finally judge between Saul and himself, precisely because he knows that Yahweh's providence can be trusted. Accordingly, David knows he must trust God and not take matters into his own hands. Yahweh's purposes will be worked out, but David has to wait for Yahweh to do them. Yahweh's will is achieved in Yahweh's way and Yahweh's time: David cannot shape Yahweh's will to his own ends. The canonical tradition associates Pss 57 and 142, which express a similar perspective, with this time in David's life.

Saul too accepts that Yahweh has placed him in David's power, though Saul may be less positively disposed towards Yahweh. He regards Yahweh as having given him over to David's power in the same way as he intended the Ziphites to give David over to him in 23:20 (note the repetition of the verb *sgr*). Saul accepts that Yahweh should repay David for what he has done this day, and even sees in these events evidence that David will become king. This is actually more than David sought, though given the events before and after this, Saul is still not prepared to surrender to Yahweh's will.

Through this, a theme begins to develop where David avoids bloodshed, either because of his own insights into Yahweh's ways, or because of the intervention of others (Abigail in ch. 25). Providence's exact function is not always discernible by all, but what becomes clear is that it cannot be used to justify practices otherwise contrary to Yahweh's will.

1 SAMUEL 25

Translation

[1]Now Samuel died. All Israel assembled and mourned for him and buried him at his house in Ramah.

David rose and went down to the wilderness of Paran. [2]Now there was a man in Maon whose business was in Carmel. The man was very rich, and had three thousand sheep and a thousand goats. He was shearing his sheep in Carmel. [3]The man's name was Nabal, and his wife's name was Abigail. The woman was discerning and beautiful, but the man was harsh and badly behaved; he was a Calebite. [4]When David heard in the wilderness that Nabal was shearing his sheep, [5]he sent ten lads. David said to the lads, 'Go up to Carmel and go to Nabal and greet him in my name. [6]You shall say to my kinsman, "Peace to you, peace to your household and peace to all that is yours. [7]I heard that you have shearers. Now your shepherds were with us and we have not harmed them, and the whole time they were at Carmel nothing of theirs was missing. [8]Ask your lads, and they will tell you. Let my lads find favour in your eyes, because we have come on a festive day. Please give whatever you have to hand to your servants and your son David."'

[9]So David's lads came and spoke all these words in David's name to Nabal, and waited. [10]But Nabal answered David's servants, 'Who is David? Who is the son of Jesse? Today there are many servants who are breaking away from their masters. [11]Shall I take my bread, my water and the meat I have butchered for my shearers and give it to men who come from I know not where?' [12]David's lads turned to their way, returned and came and reported to him all this. [13]David said to his men, 'Every man strap on his sword!' Each man strapped on his sword, and David also strapped on his sword. About four hundred went up behind David, while about two hundred stayed with the kit.

[14]One of the lads reported to Nabal's wife, Abigail, 'David sent messengers from the wilderness to greet our master, but he shouted insults at them. [15]But the men were very good to us. They did not harm us, and we did not miss anything while we were out with them in the fields, as long as we were with them. [16]They were a wall to us both day and night, the whole time we were with them keeping the sheep. [17]Now know and see what you should do, because harm is determined against our master and his entire house, and he is a son of Belial, so no one can speak to him.' [18]Then Abigail hurried and took two hundred loaves of bread, two pitchers of wine, five prepared sheep, five seahs of parched grain, one hundred bunches of raisins and two hundred fig cakes and loaded them on donkeys. [19]She said to her lads, 'Pass over before me; I am coming after you.' But she did not tell her husband, Nabal. [20]And it happened as she was riding on the donkey, coming down

under the cover of the hill, that David and his men came down toward her. So she met them. [21]David had said, 'Surely it was in vain that I kept all that belongs to this man in the wilderness so that nothing of his was missed. So he has repaid me evil for good! [22]Thus may God do to David and thus may he continue to do if by morning I spare as much as one who pisses against the wall.'

[23]When Abigail saw David, she hurried and got down from her donkey and fell before David's anger upon her face and bowed to the ground. [24]She fell at his feet and said, 'May the iniquity be on me alone, my lord. May your maidservant speak in your ears; hear your maidservant's message. [25]Let not my lord lay to his heart this man of Belial, Nabal, because he is like his name. Nabal is his name, and folly is with him. As for me, I did not see your lads you sent. [26]But now, my lord, as Yahweh lives and as your soul lives, since Yahweh has restrained you from entering into bloodshed and saving with your own hand, may your enemies seeking to do evil to my lord be like Nabal. [27]Let this blessing that your servant has brought be given to the lads who accompany my lord. [28]Please forgive the transgression of your maidservant, for Yahweh will surely make a sure house for my lord because my lord fights Yahweh's battles, and evil shall not be found in you throughout your life. [29]When men arise to pursue you, to seek your life, then your life shall be bound in the bundle of the living with Yahweh your God, but the lives of your enemies he shall sling out as from the hollow of a sling. [30]When Yahweh has done for my lord all the good he has said concerning you, and appoints you as leader over Israel, [31]then there will be no cause of grief or stumbling of heart for my lord on account of gratuitous bloodshed or my lord taking vengeance for himself. And when Yahweh has dealt well with my lord, then remember your maidservant.'

[32]David said to Abigail, 'Blessed be Yahweh, God of Israel, who has sent you to meet me today! [33]Blessed be your discernment, and blessed be you, who has kept me today from bloodshed and delivering myself by my own hand. [34]Indeed, as Yahweh who has kept me from harming you lives, unless you had hurried to come and meet me, truly there would not have been left so much as one who pissed against the wall from all belonging to Nabal.' [35]David took what she had brought to him from her hand, and said to her 'Go up in peace to your house. See, I have heard what you say and have granted your request.'

[36]So Abigail went to Nabal, and he was holding a feast in his house like a royal feast. And Nabal's heart was merry within him since he was very drunk. So she did not tell him anything at all until the morning light. [37]In the morning, when the wine had gone out of Nabal, his wife told him these things. Then his heart died within him and he was like a stone. [38]And about ten days later Yahweh struck Nabal so he died.

[39]When David heard Nabal had died, he said, 'Blessed be Yahweh, who has pleaded my cause for my reproach from Nabal's hand and restrained his servant from wrongdoing, but has brought back Nabal's wrongdoing on his own head.' David sent and spoke to Abigail to take her as his wife. [40]David's attendants came to Abigail the Carmelite and said to her, 'David has sent us to you to take you to him as a wife.' [41]She arose and bowed down to the ground and said, 'Behold, your

maidservant is a servant to wash the feet of my lord's attendants.' [42]Abigail quickly arose and mounted a donkey with her five maids attending her. She followed David's messengers and became his wife. [43]David had also taken Ahinoam the Jezreelite, and both of them became his wives. [44]But Saul had given his daughter Michal, David's wife, to Paltiel ben Laish from Gallim.

Notes on the text

1. LXX has Maon for MT Paran. This harmonizes with the previous chapter, though if Paran is used more generally it could still describe the area. Typically, Paran is the wilderness in the Sinai Peninsula (Gen. 14:6; 21:21; Num. 10:12; 12:16; 13:3, 26), whereas Maon is west of the Dead Sea, in the hill country of Judah (Josh. 15:55). But if Paran is used to mean 'southern wilderness', then it could include Maon.

3. Reading *klby* with Q. K has *klbw*, which would offer 'according to his heart'. LXX has *kynikos*, 'doglike', but this is simply a different pointing. It may point to a pejorative pun on Calebites (Grønbaek 1971: 171). The name 'Nabal' is often thought to be a nickname since parents are unlikely to call a child 'fool'. But other derivations are possible, and it is more probable that the name is one that is easily distorted rather than intentionally insulting.

6. Many EVV (e.g. NRSV, ESV) simply omit the difficult *leḥāy*. NIV (cf. NEB) takes it as a greeting, 'Long life' (see Fokkelman 1986: 484), though the Masoretic punctuation would be odd. The Vg understands it as 'to my brother'. Youngblood tentatively supports this, assuming elision of the aleph (1992: 765). This is possible, but 18:18 has already shown that *ḥay* can mean 'my kin', in which case the Vg's reading can be supported without emendation.

11. LXX has 'my wine' for my 'water'. In such a dry area, water is valuable.

18. Five seahs is a little over six quarts.

22. With LXX, omit *'ôybê*, as the curse must be uttered against the speaker (see Sanders 2004: 95–96). Bergen (1996: 250) defends MT.

23. Abigail lit. falls 'to David's nose'. The verse is frequently emended with LXX (cf. NRSV), though it offers the sort of emendation we might expect. The key is that *'ap* not only means 'nose, nostril' (e.g. Gen. 2:7; Job 27:3; Amos 4:10), but also 'anger' (e.g. Gen. 27:45; Exod. 32:12). Abigail not only interposes herself before David; she does so specifically before his anger.

25. The name 'Nabal' and 'folly' come from the same root (*nbl*), though so also does the 'pitcher' used for the wine in v. 18.

27. 'Blessing' here is a gift, but the more literal sense is retained because of the root's use (*brk*) in David's subsequent speeches (similarly, Alter 1999: 157). Many MSS read *hby'h* for *hby'*.

29. *hā'ādām* is a generalizing sg., best translated as a pl., though the sg. may create an allusion to Saul (Fokkelman 1986: 506–507).

35. 'Granted your request' is lit. 'lifted up your face' (Heb. *wā'eśśā pānāyim*). The idiom can be used in a number of ways. For this sense, see Gen. 19:21; Job 42:8–9.

36. For the idiom of *lēb ṭôb* referring to drunkenness, see Esth. 1:10; 5:9.

Form and structure

This account is the pivot between the narratives where David spares Saul's life. As there, this one is primarily developed through dialogue. Although Nabal is a character in his own right (albeit, never developed beyond the plays on his name), he clearly stands in place of Saul (Biddle 2002: 626), though care should be taken not to equate the two directly (Nicol 1998: 135). The chapter's contribution is to provide David with evidence of the rightness of the decision he made in the previous chapter not to kill Saul. An important contrast between chs. 24 and 26 is how the chance to kill Saul is generated. In ch. 24 it is considered providential, whereas in ch. 26 it is initiated by David, though under Yahweh's protection (26:12). This chapter shows why David can confidently act as he does, because here he is prepared to use violence to kill a foe, but is prevented by Yahweh. That this happens through Abigail does not change the story's thrust, because David clearly sees her as sent by Yahweh for this purpose (25:32). David is prepared to use violence in both chs. 24 and 25, though in both he is prevented from doing so. By ch. 26 David knows that violence is not how he achieves Yahweh's purpose, however providential the situation may seem to others (26:9–11). Thus the narrative also prepares for situations where David responds to those who admit having used violence against kings (2 Sam. 1:1–16; 4:5–12), a feature aided by the concentration of legal language here (Adam 2007: 114).

Before this, a new complication is introduced through the notice of Samuel's death (25:1a). Since the end of ch. 3, Samuel has been Yahweh's principal mouthpiece, also anointing David and protecting him when he fled from Saul (19:18). Although Gad was involved (22:5), Samuel has dominated. His death makes David's position more problematic since Samuel was clearly opposed to Saul. As well as resolving the question of whether or not David can use violence to achieve his ends, this account also demonstrates that David continues to experience Yahweh's favour without Samuel.

Finally, the narrative highlights David's marital situation, explaining how he married Abigail, as well as noting his marriage to Ahinoam of Jezreel and Saul's action in giving his wife Michal to Paltiel. Each is important for the subsequent narration, so the links this chapter generates cannot be limited to chs. 24 and 26. Marriage to Abigail, legitimized by Nabal's death at the hand of Yahweh, provided David with access into the Calebite clan, the group centred on Hebron where David first becomes king over Judah (2 Sam. 2:1–4). Although Stoebe (1973: 454) overemphasizes this point, making David's marriage to Abigail the narrative's purpose, it is not to be ignored. Ahinoam (not Saul's wife mentioned in 14:50; see Gordon 1980: 44) provided David with important links to the rest of Judah. Michal's removal, however, separates David from the northern tribes. By the chapter's end, David knows he cannot claim the kingdom by violence, though he might do so through politically astute marriages, even if Saul undercut this by giving Michal to another. David remains under Yahweh's favour even without Samuel's presence, although how he will come to the throne is not yet demonstrated.

Comment

Samuel's death: 25:1a

1a. Samuel has been unmentioned since 19:22, so mention of his death here is a deliberate action of the narrator. Samuel's death, along with the national mourning and his burial at Ramah (see 1:1), needed to be recounted in the midst of David and Saul's conflict, and is not just a preparation for ch. 28. As Birch observes (1998: 1166), Samuel's death is noted only after Saul confesses that David will be king (24:21 [ET 24:20]). Hence his death closes off one stage of David's move towards the throne. Saul's loss of the throne was announced in 15:28, while David was anointed in 16:13. Samuel was involved in both events, helping to set in motion the conflict the narrative is currently resolving. But Saul's confession shows he accepts that David will be king, though this might mean only his loss of dynasty, not that he has lost the throne itself. Samuel also offered David a point of security (19:18), security no longer available. Yet the authority of Samuel's word as Yahweh's word (3:19 – 4:1a), a word that announced both Saul's loss of the throne and David's status as Yahweh's anointed, continues to shelter David. By keeping David from his own latent violence, this narrative demonstrates that Yahweh's word continues to resolve itself, even when the one who announced it has died.

David prepares to kill Nabal: 25:1b–13

1b–3. Some time after Samuel's death, David journeyed to the wilderness area of Judah's south (see 'Notes'). Within this area was a man of great wealth. His introduction is reminiscent of that of Job (Job 1:3), with a listing of his substantial livestock holdings and the notice that his business was in Carmel, which must refer (as in 15:12) to the town in the hill country of Judah, not the better-known northern site. The narrator is careful to characterize the man as wealthy and to enumerate his wealth before revealing that his name is Nabal, and that his wife is Abigail. Since Nabal can mean 'fool' in Hebrew (though the word can also mean 'wineskin'), the presence of such wealth may already signal problems, since fools and wealth were considered a dangerous combination (Prov. 30:22). By contrast, Abigail was both prudent and beautiful. Her looks were a match for David's (16:12), while her prudence would also generate favour (Prov. 13:15). Nabal's introduction starts with his wealth, whereas Abigail's focuses on her character. Finally, the narrator returns to Nabal, pointing out that his behaviour is as one expects from a fool. But there is an additional note. Nabal is a Calebite, and thus a member of a prominent regional clan. The clan was centred on Hebron, the city initially given to Caleb (Josh. 15:13), and it would be in Hebron that David established his initial kingdom (2 Sam. 2:1–4). But Nabal is rich, surly and a man with powerful connections.

4–8. Sheep-shearing was a special time (Matthews and Benjamin 1993: 56), so given the size of Nabal's flocks, David would naturally have heard about it. David's actions towards Nabal are not described. Instead, we hear them through the speech David directs ten of his lads to give to Nabal at Carmel. Although some take this as suggesting David was running a protection racket (Halpern 2001: 284), Nabal's servants later agree with David's construal (25:14–16), indicating David did not threaten Nabal. This is borne out by David's greeting of peace to Nabal and his household. David also addresses Nabal as a kinsman (see 'Notes'), so he anticipates some mutual respect towards each another (Hertzberg 1964: 202). Thus, although the narrative shows David's latent potential for violence, violence is not present from the outset. In the speech David points out that he and his men have been with Nabal's shepherds, who suffered neither harm nor loss in that time. Since this is verifiable, David requests that he and his men join Nabal for the feast at the conclusion of shearing. The speech is carefully constructed to emphasize the kinship relationship between David and Nabal, even if its exact nature is never explained. David's claim is that the service he rendered is worthy of payment, perhaps as something for which Nabal should have prepared. Yet, although the favour David seeks is really something earned, there is a hint of violence simply because David asks as the leader of a band of six hundred men, greatly increasing his request's force.

9–11. The narrative quickly recounts David's men's following of his directions before waiting for Nabal's answer, the only point emphasized being that they asked in David's name. Nabal's initial characterization (vv. 2–3) indicated he could be harsh, so his response is in character, even if it surprises David. Nabal's response is harsh, but focused on David's name. The question 'Who is David?' is not concerned with information; instead, it stresses that David is of no importance. Nabal emphasizes this when he asks about David as 'son of Jesse', repeating Saul's dismissive way of referring to David (20:30–31; 22:7–9, 13). David's name is his reputation, the basis on which his appeal is made, but Nabal denies that it has any significance. His reasons are demonstrated in the balance of v. 10. Here he claims many slaves have rebelled against their master, indicating that David is one of them. David may have expected support from a kinsman, and depended upon the laws requiring care of the sojourner (e.g. Deut. 10:19; see O'Rourke Boyle 2001: 417), but has instead discovered a supporter of Saul. Nabal's dismissive rhetoric returns to questions in v. 11. Here he effectively denies the validity of David's claim of having protected him. In claiming he does not know David and his men, Nabal cannot be claiming a lack of information since he knows who David's father is. Instead, he refuses to recognize David. Neither David's reputation nor deeds justify Nabal's providing for him and his men during his feast.

12–13. With Nabal's words ringing in their ears, David's lads returned, providing a full account. The violence latent within David thus came to the fore as he directed his men to arm themselves to go against Nabal. In preparation for the anticipated battle, David left two hundred men with the kit while he took four hundred with him, a policy he repeats (for different reasons) in 30:10. Thus it seems Nabal's surliness and failure to recognize his mutual obligations have paved the way for battle. David's anger means he stands on the brink of violence.

Abigail's intervention: 25:14–35

14–17. David is prepared to fight, but before that the narrative switches to Abigail as she acts for Yahweh in preventing David from exacting retribution. This happens through the intervention of one of Nabal's lads, who reports David's embassy and Nabal's hostile response. The irony is that Nabal accused David of being a servant rebelling against his master, but that is what Nabal's servant does here. Any report contains biases, and this lad's report to Abigail is no different. It omits any reference to David's request that he and his men share in the shearing feast. Only David's greeting is noted. The lad clearly supports David's position, because his account of David and his men in v. 15 closely matches David's claim in v. 7. The lad provides the testimony David had suggested Nabal seek to confirm his claims. The lad adds the additional point that David and his men had both refrained from doing any harm and had also provided protection from outsiders, being a wall around them day and night. The lad draws no conclusion, because that was not his role. But by asking Abigail to understand and decide what to do in the light of David's anger and determination to avenge himself he clearly suggests that David and his men should partake of the feast. How the lad knows David's intentions is unclear since David was not with Nabal, but the lad can point to Nabal's obstinacy, in particular that he is a 'son of Belial' (see 2:12), as showing he is not competent to respond appropriately to David.

18–19. The lad's hints were not lost on Abigail, who immediately gathered significant resources of food and drink to send to David. The amounts involved were so large that we have to presume she was drawing on resources already prepared for the feast (explicitly so for the sheep), because otherwise the preparation would have been impossible. Even so, it is noted that Abigail hurried (*mhr*) to prepare everything, an expression David picks up in his response to her (25:34). Her actions show urgency because of the threat David brings. That threat also requires tact about how she approaches David, as seen when she sends her attendants ahead of her, much as Jacob did before confronting Esau (Gen. 32:13–23). But picking up on the lad's theme that there was no talking to Nabal, she does not tell him what she is doing.

20–22. David's encounter with Abigail is similar to when Saul almost captured him (23:26). Abigail apparently came down a hill pass where she was invisible to David so he was unaware of her, though they were on the same road. The narrative focuses on their dialogue, leaving aside the part played by her attendants. David's dialogue with Nabal was cool and distant, but this is immediate and passionate. Before the dialogue can be reported, the narrator provides a flashback in vv. 21–22 to David's earlier comments because of his anger against Nabal. David's speech there reflects his earlier statement to Nabal that Nabal's lad had verified to Abigail, providing a third reference to the good David has done for Nabal, good repaid by evil. But David now believes his previous actions were in vain (*šeqer*), though this view is revealed only after David has met Abigail with her provisions. Nevertheless, the threat David posed is made clear by the oath formula in v. 22. Here David expresses the wish that God will kill him if he fails to kill so much as one who pissed against the wall (the males) within Nabal's household. David's language is intentionally crude, and its force should not be muted in translation (though cf. NIV, NRSV, ESV). The idiom is always used in the context of group extermination (25:34; 1 Kgs 14:10; 16:11; 21:21; 2 Kgs 9:8), the vulgarity demeaning those to be killed. For all this, there is an irony inherent within the oath, because we know God will not kill David as his anointed replacement for Saul. Having encountered Abigail, we know David will not kill Nabal and his men, but we also know Yahweh will not punish David for an otherwise foolish oath. Yahweh has other plans for David, as Abigail will make clear.

23–25. Having been delayed by the flashback to David's earlier oath, the main narrative thread resumes in Abigail's speech. It is carefully constructed, emphasizing her humility before David, but also stressing that Yahweh will bring about his purposes for David without David's resorting to violence. Her care in dealing with David is emphasized by her hurry (*mhr*) to dismount and fall down before David, recognizing the risk she takes in interposing herself between David and his anger (see 'Notes' on v. 23). She must negotiate from this place of danger with care and humility. This is emphasized by repeating 'and she fell', the second time at his feet, thus presenting herself as a supplicant before a king. Her posture is also evident from her language, addressing David as 'my lord', and characterizing herself as David's 'maidservant' (*'āmâ*) and 'servant' (*šipḥâ*). Although largely interchangeable, she uses *'āmâ* (×6; vv. 24, 25, 28, 31, 41) to reflect her subordinate position, but hinting that David has an obligation towards her. By contrast, *šipḥâ* is used twice (vv. 27, 41) to refer to a gift and willingness to serve, possibly suggesting a more servile position (Chisholm 1998: 42). But she consistently places herself physically and socially below David. From here she achieves rhetorical force, claiming she should bear Nabal's guilt while requesting an audience with David. As she does, she points out Nabal's weaknesses. His character is like his name: he is a man of Belial (repeating her servant's position, 25:17) and his actions are consistent with his name. Nabal means 'fool' (in the sense of moral obtuseness), so the obvious link is that he is characterized by folly (*nĕbālâ*) (for the wordplay, see Isa. 32:5–6). But *nebel* can mean a 'wineskin' (see 25:18), and though a cognate form *nĕbālâ* is not attested, it may refer to one marked by wine (see 25:36). Finally, the root *nbl* can refer to something dropped, and its cognate noun *nĕbēlâ* means 'corpse', which is what Nabal finally becomes. There is a host of wordplays, and each is evident in the ensuing narrative. 'Folly' is the most immediate connection with Nabal's name, and explains why David should not be concerned with him. In contrast, Abigail suggests she would have taken a more gracious approach had she seen David's lads when they came, thus preventing the problem from developing.

26–31. The second half of Abigail's speech seeks to explain why David should not employ violence. In spite of obvious difficulties, Abigail recognizes Yahweh's hand in leading her, a point reinforced with an oath taken by Yahweh and David. Yahweh has previously prevented David from incurring bloodguilt, so she wishes that all his enemies might be like Nabal. Nabal has not yet died, so some relocate this verse, but it is better to see this as an example of the so-called precative perfect, where Abigail expresses an imprecation against David's enemies. By contrast, Abigail's gift should be shared with David's men. She also points to the certainty of the house Yahweh will build for David as explaining why she should be forgiven for her delay. Abigail's language echoes the man of God in 2:35 while anticipating Nathan's oracle in 2 Sam. 7:16. Because David fights Yahweh's battles, she suggests he cannot fall prey to violence's lure since it is contrary to his calling. The implications are then worked out in two colourful metaphors in v. 29. If someone arises to pursue David, then David will be protected as one 'bound in the bundle of the living'. The image is protective, something important to God, like the bundle of myrrh to the woman in Song 1:13. By contrast, David's enemies will be slung out like a stone from a sling.

The allusion is to David's victory over Goliath, hinting at how Nabal will be defeated. In fact, 'stone' imagery will be used somewhat differently (25:37), but the point remains. David must not exact vengeance: that is for Yahweh alone (see Prov. 25:21–22; Rom. 12:14–21). Thus when Yahweh's promises to David are complete and he is leader of the people, he need not be troubled by memories of violence. Abigail's speech aims carefully to ensure that David does not move into violence, but rather wait for Yahweh's resolutions. Abigail's own certainty of David's future is made clear by her request that David remember her, a request not simply about facts, but that he act positively towards her. In the light of subsequent events, this could be a veiled offer of marriage (see Edelman 1991: 214–218).

32–35. Abigail understood herself to be acting for Yahweh in confronting David, and David accepts this, praising Yahweh for sending Abigail. Abigail is thus sent by Yahweh, but David balances this by praising Abigail's discernment and actions preventing him making the move into bloodshed and evil. Understanding providence was a key theme in ch. 24, and that continues here, showing Yahweh acts to prevent violence, sometimes through human intervention. Praise speech is picked up again in v. 39, when it is again seen that retribution belongs to Yahweh alone. David thus refers back to his vulgar language when left to kill Nabal and his men (v. 22), acknowledging that he would have been guilty of pointless violence without Abigail's intervention. This insight is reinforced by the oath David employs in v. 34, so his speech becomes a testimony to Yahweh's ways. So David accepted her gift and sent her back to her house in peace because he had granted her favour.

Nabal's death and David's marriages: 25:36–44

36–38. Following David's directions, Abigail returned home as Nabal was holding a feast that the narrator compares to a royal feast. The irony is that Nabal refused to serve an anointed king while showing royal pretensions. As in Esther, the feast (*mišteh*) was as much the consumption of drink as food (Esth. 1:3, 5; 5:5–6; 7:1–2), so Nabal's drunkenness is unsurprising. Accordingly, Abigail told him nothing until morning. When morning came and he was no longer drunk (though the unusual phrase here may also be a vulgar play on his name; see Leithart 2001), Abigail reported what had happened. Nabal did not die immediately, but his 'heart died' within him (not a technical medical diagnosis [see O'Rourke Boyle 2001], though still indicating a serious illness). This prepares for his death, the stone reference alluding to Abigail's statement in v. 29 about David's enemies. The narrator then summarizes, noting that ten days later Yahweh struck Nabal and he died. Thus the narrative bears out Abigail's claims. Retribution belongs to Yahweh alone. Even as Yahweh's anointed, David cannot claim the right of retribution. David's throne cannot be claimed by violence.

39–42. This theme is reinforced by David's praising Yahweh when he hears of Nabal's death. David's praise accepts that he was prepared to use force, but Yahweh overcame his foe and avenged Nabal's slight. Yahweh, not David, must resolve such issues. David cannot wrongly bring about a just cause. With Nabal removed, David was free to marry Abigail. Such a marriage was political more than anything else, as David knew he needed support from the Calebites, which marrying into the clan could ensure. For Abigail the marriage promised security, linking her clan to the nation's future king. Nabal's death also changed the power dynamics between David and Abigail, so rather than being a powerful chieftain's wife she was a widow dependent upon others. This perhaps explains her otherwise obsequious response when David's men come and invite her to marry him. Yet her actions throughout are highly astute, so her language may simply be conventional. Hence she comes to David as a person of importance, as is evident from her retinue.

43–44. That marriage with Abigail was primarily political is apparent from the fact that we are told immediately of another marriage of David's, not previously narrated, to Ahinoam of Jezreel. Most probably, the Jezreel referred to is a few miles north-west of Carmel in the hill country of Judah (Josh. 15:55), not the well-known northern town. Marriage to Abigail meant David could establish influential links in the region, and marriage to Ahinoam achieved this with another important town. In spite of this, Saul continued to oppose David, even taking Michal from him and giving her to another. The legality of this is doubtful given that David had paid twice the fee of one hundred Philistine foreskins to marry her (18:27; cf. 2 Sam. 3:14), but Saul knew the importance of retaining political support. In spite of this, the chapter suggests such actions cannot succeed.

Explanation

Sandwiched between the accounts of David's not killing Saul, this narrative demonstrates that violence, even for a just cause, is not something David can initiate. Refusing to kill Saul when the opportunity arose in the previous chapter opened up inevitable questions. Since he also was Yahweh's anointed, could he claim the throne by force? Samuel's death makes the problem more immediate since Samuel acted as a mediator of Yahweh's will, though David had little contact with him after fleeing Saul. This narrative avoids until the final verse Saul's actions against David, though it is more than a coda here: it insists that although David had not killed Saul, Saul still opposed David. Here David is confronted by a less powerful foe, and the problem he faces is a serious slight rather than something putting his life at risk. Yet this reduction in risk leads David to respond with violence to Nabal's insults. Indeed, his vow of violence far exceeds the slight received. David knows he should not use violence to claim the throne, but is prepared to employ it when others cross his path.

Yet David is stopped through Abigail's intervention and both she and David ultimately recognize it as Yahweh's intervention. Abigail's involvement goes beyond simply stopping David from killing her husband. She sees a deeper issue where violence can never be justified in achieving Yahweh's purposes. To do so means using evil, and good cannot be achieved this way. David has received Yahweh's promise that he will be king, but he cannot obliterate minor enemies any more than can Saul. He must wait on Yahweh's intervention. This was what he sought in his earlier encounter with Saul (24:16 [ET 24:15]), but Abigail extends this to cover a range of possible actions. Nabal's death is finally attributed to Yahweh, happening ten days after his encounter with David. Through this, David is shown that retribution belongs to Yahweh alone. He cannot initiate violence. Yahweh's purposes for David are achieved when David accepts that Yahweh will achieve them for him, though it does not prevent David from taking suitable marriage opportunities when they appear. Providential opportunities may arise, but they are not grasped through violence. The principal established through Nabal's death confirms David's decision in ch. 24, but also extends it. Yahweh will act for David in a similar way with all his enemies, something that puts his dealing with Saul into a clearer perspective. David was right to show restraint in ch. 24, even as he had to be restrained here. The narrator is careful to emphasize that this is Yahweh's way for his people. Tragically, the account of Uriah (2 Sam. 11) demonstrates that David was not always prepared to learn this, so numerous tragic echoes of this story recur in 2 Sam. 11 – 12 (Youngblood 1992: 765).

1 SAMUEL 26

Translation

[1]The Ziphites came to Saul at Gibeah, saying, 'Is not David hiding at the hill of Hachilah, which overlooks Jeshimon?' [2]Saul arose and went down to the wilderness of Ziph along with three thousand choice men of Israel to seek David in the wilderness of Ziph. [3]Saul camped at the hill of Hachilah which overlooks Jeshimon, by the road, but David stayed in the wilderness. When he saw Saul had come out to the wilderness after him, [4]he sent scouts and confirmed that Saul had come. [5]Then David arose and came to where Saul had camped. David saw where Saul lay along with Abner ben Ner, his army commander. Saul was lying within the entrenchment, and the troops were camped around him.

[6]David then asked Ahimelech the Hittite and Abishai ben Zeruiah, Joab's brother, 'Who will go down with me into the camp to Saul?' Abishai said, 'I shall go down with you.' [7]David and Abishai went to the troops by night and, behold, Saul lay asleep in the entrenchment with his spear pushed into the ground at his

head, while Abner and his troops lay around him. [8]Abishai said to David, 'Today God has delivered your enemy into your hand. So now, let me strike him with the spear to the ground one time, and I shall not do it to him again.' [9]David said to Abishai, 'Do not destroy him, for who can put forth a hand against Yahweh's anointed and be innocent?' [10]David said, 'As Yahweh lives, surely Yahweh will strike him, or his day will come and he will die, or he will go down into battle and perish. [11]Yahweh forbid that I should put my hand against Yahweh's anointed! But now, take the spear that is by his head and the jug of water, and let us go.' [12]David took the spear and jug of water from beside Saul's head, and then they left. No one saw or knew or awoke, for they were all asleep since a deep sleep from Yahweh had fallen upon them.

[13]David crossed to the other side and stood on top of the hill at a distance, with a great space between them. [14]David called to the troops and to Abner ben Ner, 'Will you not answer, Abner?' Abner answered, 'Who are you that calls to the king?' [15]David said to Abner, 'Are you not a man? And who is like you in Israel? Why have you not guarded your lord the king, when one of the people came to destroy your lord the king? [16]This thing that you have done is not good. As Yahweh lives, you are a dead man, because you have not guarded your lord, Yahweh's anointed. So now, see where the king's spear is with the jug of water from beside his head.'

[17]Saul recognized David's voice and said, 'Is this your voice, David my son?' David said, 'It is my voice, my lord the king.' [18]He said, 'Why is my lord pursuing his servant? What have I done? What evil is in my hand? [19]Now may my lord the king hear his servant's words. If Yahweh has incited you against me, let him accept an offering; but if it is people, let them be accursed before Yahweh because they have driven me out today so I am not joined to the heritage of Yahweh, saying, "Go, serve other gods." ' [20]But now, let my blood not fall to the ground away from Yahweh's presence, for the king of Israel has come out to pursue a single flea, just as one pursues a partridge in the mountains.'

[21]Saul said, 'I have sinned. Turn back, David my son, for I shall no more do you harm since my life was precious in your sight today. Behold, I have acted foolishly and erred greatly.' [22]David answered, 'Here is the king's spear. Let one of your lads come across and take it. [23]Yahweh rewards a man for his righteousness and faithfulness; when Yahweh delivered you into my hand today I was unwilling to put forth my hand against Yahweh's anointed. [24]But behold, just as your life was precious in my sight today, so may my life be in Yahweh's eyes and may he deliver me from all tribulation.' [25]Saul said to David, 'Blessed are you, my son David. You will do many things and will surely succeed in them.' So David went on his way, and Saul returned to his place.

Notes on the text

4. '*el nākôn* is awkward; one expects a place name after *bā*' (Driver 1913: 159). Accordingly, *nākôn* could be a corruption of a place name, though LXX's Keilah is not plausible. However, *wayyēda'* is read here as seeking confirmation, in which case MT can be defended. McCarter (1980a: 405) opts for Hachilah, which is plausible, but the process by which such a corruption originated seems too complex.

22. Reading Q. K would read 'the spear, O King'.

23. Reading the possessive with many MSS. *BHS* reads *yād*.

Form and structure

This chapter closes off Saul's pursuit of David in the wilderness while simultaneously reinforcing key themes about David's refusal to claim the throne from Saul by force. Within the smaller cluster of chs. 24 – 26, it also enables David to show that the lesson learnt in ch. 25 can be applied. Yahweh removed Nabal, so Yahweh must resolve the problem of Saul (see Gordon 1980: 42–43).

Many themes developed here have already arisen in ch. 24. As argued, it is important not simply to see these chapters as doublets. The decisive difference here is that it is David who takes the initiative. Although Abishai urges David to kill Saul while he is asleep before him (v. 8), the possibility arises only because David sneaked into Saul's camp. In ch. 24 David and his men respond to circumstances; this time they generate them. A further difference lies in Yahweh's role. Although David, his men and Saul spoke frequently about Yahweh in ch. 24, it is never said that Yahweh acted. All the characters seek to explain Yahweh's activity, but the narrator never comments directly on what Yahweh does. But this time we are told of Yahweh's activity in v. 12b, which is the chapter's pivot. Yahweh's activity is consistent with 25:38, where he struck down Nabal, enabling the narrator to affirm the reality of Yahweh's providence in this account. Although the characters still speak about Yahweh and seek to understand his activity, this one statement confirms that Yahweh works for David, showing that David's refusal to kill Saul is correct.

These elements indicate that although there are repetitions between chs. 24 and 26, development runs through them, and their similarities are therefore to be read in a new light. There is reason to interpret 24:8 (see 'Notes' there) as suggesting that David's actions against his men initiated ongoing conflict that generated pressure for direct action against Saul. If so, it is probable that there were two times when David refused to kill Saul, with the underlying patterns meaning the accounts were similarly related (see Grønbaek 1971: 169). But the important point is that David now acts because he knows what Yahweh is doing. Moreover, Saul also shows new insights. Previously, he acknowledged that David was more righteous (24:18), but this time he confesses his own sin (26:21). In 24:12 David claimed he had not sinned against Saul, but now Saul acknowledges he has sinned against David. Further, although he first acknowledged in 24:21 that David would be king, he now goes further and blesses David (26:25).

Their enmity remains, but the similarities have enabled the developments in both to be seen.

Comment

Saul comes to the wilderness: 26:1–5

1–3a. This account begins with another Ziphite report (see 23:19 – 24:1 [ET 23:19–29]) to Saul about David's location. The location is much the same as 23:19: Hachilah, which overlooks Jeshimon. The site cannot be identified, but David has remained in the same area as before. Their report is phrased as a question, implying that if they can find David, there is no reason Saul cannot do better. This Ziphite encounter is more compressed, so the narrative immediately recounts Saul's taking three thousand of his best men down to the wilderness of Ziph to pursue David. David had obviously moved slightly by the time Saul arrived since Saul set up his camp on the hill of Hachilah, but David was further out in the wilderness.

3b–5. The narrative switches from Saul to David. The Ziphites were Saul's information source, but David had his sources, and learned that Saul was back looking for him. David also sent spies to the reported location to confirm Saul's presence, and perhaps to determine the size of his force. The spies' report is not recounted, as the narrator moves swiftly to tell of David's coming to Saul's camp. Having moved the narrative forward quite quickly, v. 5 slows the pace, explaining that David could see where Saul lay along with Abner, his military commander. The narrator emphasizes that he could see Saul lying down within a central defensive area in the camp (*ma'gāl*, most probably an entrenched area, or one that contained snares). The narrative thus emphasizes David's boldness in entering the camp and reaching Saul since he had to pass three thousand troops, and enter the central defensive zone.

David in Saul's camp: 26:6–12

6–7. Immediately, focus switches from what David sees to what David does. It is not a question of whether or not David will enter Saul's camp, but of who will accompany him. Two companions are mentioned: Ahimelech, the Hittite, and Joab's brother, Abishai. Ahimelech the Hittite is not mentioned elsewhere, his title distinguishing him from the priest of the same name. Uriah will be another Hittite working for David. Abishai is introduced as Joab's brother, though Joab himself is not introduced until 2 Sam. 2:13. These three along with their brother Asahel are the 'sons of Zeruiah'. Samuel does not explicitly connect David and the sons of Zeruiah apart from their work for him, but 1 Chr. 2:16 has Zeruiah as

David's sister. More important in Samuel are their acts of violence and military prestige. Abishai was a senior officer among David's mighty men (2 Sam. 23:18), and thus an important warrior (2 Sam. 10:10–14), though his involvement in Joab's murder of Abner (2 Sam. 3:30) points to the family's propensity for violence. Although this information is revealed later, his decision to accompany David into Saul's camp is consistent with this. David's entry was bold, but not foolhardy, as he waited for the cover of darkness. Entry of the outer camp is of no interest, so we are brought immediately to the entrenchment where Saul slept. Saul's spear was a frequent threat in his pursuit of David, even if he could never hit his intended target (18:10; 19:10; 20:33). But here it is stuck in the ground alongside Saul's head, with Abner also asleep there.

8–11. The temptation to violence is a constant theme in these chapters. In 24:5 [ET 24:4] David's men urged him to kill Saul in the cave. Confronted by Nabal's obstinacy, David was prepared to kill him himself (25:21–22). The temptation this time comes from Abishai, who claims Yahweh has delivered (*sgr*) Saul into David's power, echoing Saul's interpretation of events at Keilah (23:7). Abishai knows David previously refused to kill Saul because he could not touch Yahweh's anointed (24:7 [ET 24:6]), so he offers a simple solution: he will kill Saul. David would thus remain technically guiltless since another would actually kill Saul. Abishai displays an element of bravado, claiming he will do so with a single stroke of Saul's spear, so the weapon that had twice missed David would finish Saul. But David will have none of this casuistry, and dismisses it with the same argument as before. David would not be free of guilt if he ordered another to kill Saul. David has developed a new insight out of ch. 25: that Yahweh must remove Saul. Previously, this was a wish (24:13–16 [ET 24:12–15]), but now it is declared, even asserted with an oath that names Yahweh. David does not know how Yahweh will do this – the options of direct action of Yahweh (as with Nabal), old age or battle covers most possibilities – but knows Yahweh will act. David refuses to accept an argument that associates providence with the right to initiate violence. But David does take Saul's spear and water jar before leaving, since these will prove he was in the camp.

12. These events occurred even though Saul has a significant force, and normal military procedures mean that some soldiers were on watch. Yet David entered the camp and left, carrying Saul's equipment with him. Knowing this needs explanation, the narrator intrudes directly to provide explicit theological comment, affirming that no one in Saul's camp was aware of David's presence because Yahweh caused a deep sleep to fall on all there. The 'deep sleep' (*tardēmâ*) is more than just the slumber of the weary, since its other occurrences in narrative contexts (Gen. 2:21; 15:12) are initiated by Yahweh for significant purposes, while in Job 4:13 and 33:15 it is the type of deep sleep where Yahweh is claimed to reveal himself. Conversely, in Isa. 29:10 Yahweh pours it out on those who do not know him. David was here able to achieve his purposes in Saul's camp because Yahweh sent this sleep, sleep so deep no one would stir.

Dialogue between Saul and David: 26:13–25

13–14. The narrative speeds up as we follow David across the valley to the neighbouring hill, creating a great space between Saul and himself, space that is symbolic of the gap in outlook and destiny between them (Gordon 1980: 60). But the dialogue is of the most interest, as is evident from how it dominates the balance of the chapter, the bulk of the narrative simply indicating who speaks at each point. David's address is not initially to Saul, but to the troops and then to Abner. Since we have no reported speech to the troops, the assumption is that David used them to attract attention before focusing on Abner. The dialogue proper begins with Abner. David's speech commences with a question loaded with implied accusation, drawing Abner into the position where he must answer, even if he wants to ignore David. Yet Abner can play the same game, recognizing that David is using him to approach the king, so his answer is a question that implies more than it asks. By linking the identity of the one he addresses with right of access to the king, Abner suggests David has no right to address the king.

15–16. Where David and Abner initially traded a single question, David replies with three, each developing the accusation, before closing with an oath that insists Abner has failed in his responsibilities. He never answers Abner's initial question, treating it as an attempted diversion. David thus sidesteps the suggestion that he has no right to call to the king. The questions build their effect cumulatively. The first two, 'Are you not a man?' and 'Who is like you in Israel?', both offer a perspective on Abner that would not be contested since Abner occupied an important position as Saul's kinsman and army commander (14:50). Both questions may be positive, but David presents them in terms of the responsibility they require through his third question when he asks why Abner has not protected Saul when someone came to destroy him. The identity of that one is unstated, though Abishai may be meant. But David is not concerned to identify anyone. Rather, his question accuses Abner of failing to protect Saul, whom David consistently calls Abner's 'lord the king'. The double title points to Saul's importance and Abner's responsibility. Accordingly, David moves in v. 16 to make direct statements, declaring that what Abner has done is not good, asserting with an oath ('As Yahweh lives') that Abner is effectively under a death sentence (see 20:31). David's inference is wider than Abner alone, since he here addresses Abner in the plural, so all the troops stand under this judgment. The importance of this is emphasized when David introduces a new title for Saul into the conversation, calling him Yahweh's anointed. Abner may well deny this since he has been under the deep sleep, but David now introduces his key evidence: Saul's spear and water jug. They are incontrovertible proof that David was close enough to Saul to kill him, and this possibility indicates the danger of Abner's position. By again phrasing this as a question, David leaves Abner with the need to ponder his position.

17. David has not directly addressed Saul, but now Saul intrudes into the dialogue, so we never hear Abner's response. Saul, too, commences with a question, repeating his question after the incident in the cave in 24:17 [ET 24:16]. Saul's address is intimate, seeking confirmation that it is David and calling him 'my son'. Since Saul recognized David's voice, the point is not to determine the identity of the one speaking to him but to ask David to identify himself formally. This is subtler than Abner's question, which acted more as an accusation. David identifies himself, though he does not respond to Saul's use of familial language, continuing to address him as 'my lord the king'.

18–20. David's dialogue with Saul is also shaped by questions that imply more than they ask. In asking why Saul pursues him, David calls himself Saul's servant (*'ebed*), a title that both moves away from family language and asserts that David is not Saul's opponent, making Saul's quest inappropriate. The first question develops into two more that depend upon the first, both of them implying David has done nothing to justify Saul's actions against him. With the questions as his claim of innocence, David moves to more direct speech, though he is still careful to use court language, a form of speech appropriate to his stated role as Saul's servant. David offers two reasons why Saul pursues him: either Yahweh has incited him, or people have. David rejects the first proposition but suggests if it was Yahweh, then an offering would resolve the matter. His language concerning people is far stronger, for he curses them before Yahweh for driving him out of Yahweh's heritage, effectively directing him to worship other gods. Since the land of Israel was Yahweh's heritage for his people, driving him from the heritage was driving him to other lands where other gods were worshipped. This was foreshadowed in 21:11–16 [ET 21:10–15], and becomes a key concern in 1 Sam. 27 – 2 Sam. 1 when David lives in Philistine territory. David does not want to leave the land because he does not want to die outside Israel. That Saul need not pursue David is reinforced by the assertion that Saul is seeking a single flea (see 24:15 [ET 24:14]). David then compares Saul's activities to how partridges (*qôrē'*, a pun on Abner's question in v. 13) were hunted in the hills, being continually chased until they collapsed since when pursued they tend to run along the ground rather than fly. Saul's is a position of power, but he applies his power to one who offers no threat.

21. Saul's response is brief, but contains two confessions. The first is that he has sinned against David in pursuing him, even though David regarded his life as precious. The second is that he acted foolishly and committed a great error in doing this. The folly is not directly linked to the previous chapter since Saul employs the root *skl* rather than *nbl*, but since they are in the same semantic domain some overlap is probably intended. However, in the midst of his confessions, Saul directs David to 'turn back'. What he means is unclear. He may be asking David to return to his household, or perhaps simply to stop seeing Saul as an adversary. Whatever Saul's intent, it will not lead to a rapprochement between them.

22–24. Hearing Saul's confession, David declares he has the spear, which answers his question to Abner in v. 16, so reference to the spear creates an inclusion around the dialogue with Saul. David was prepared to have one man come and collect it, though there is no further reference to the water jug. Attempts to see David holding the jug as a continued threat against Saul's life (see Green 2003b: 388) are beside the point – with a group the size Saul has brought, access for one man to water is hardly an issue. Saul's spear has been a key motif, and its return presages its next reference in 2 Sam. 1:6. David's central point is developed in vv. 23–24. First, he draws on a general principle, that Yahweh rewards people for their righteous behaviour, before reaffirming that he acted righteously towards Saul in not killing him when he had the chance, although he could claim Yahweh provided the opportunity. David's argument is that as Saul was Yahweh's anointed, it was illegitimate for him to use violence to destroy him. Therefore, he draws his conclusion in v. 24, though expresses it as a wish. David believes that just as he has protected Saul's life, so Yahweh will protect his. Indeed, this sums up the lesson that David has learned over the whole of chs. 24 – 26. David cannot claim the throne by violence, but Saul cannot successfully attack him. Yahweh's purposes for both mean that David must live with this tension, though his experience has demonstrated that Yahweh will do what David suggests here.

25. Faced with this, Saul blesses David, again, calling him 'my son'. Saul thus regards David as blessed by Yahweh, and therefore able to succeed in whatever he attempts. In one sense, this is anti-climactic, since in 24:21 [ET 24:20] he declared that David will be king. But this statement builds on the earlier one, so he not only asserts David will be king, but also implies David will have success in the role that has eluded him. The blessing may not be as glowing as Brueggemann (1990b: 188) suggests, nor as indecisive as Jobling infers (1998: 92), but it is still a crucial record of Saul's last words to David. Curiously, in spite of the blessing, Saul never mentions God in this chapter (Fokkelman 1986: 551), a literary absence that mirrors an experiential absence. But with his blessing on David declared, they part, never to meet again.

Explanation

The relationship between providence and the right to enact violence continues to be explored through this second account of David's sparing

Saul's life (see ch. 24). Although chs. 24 and 26 have much in common, Miscall (1986: 158) is right to indicate that the key difference is that here we have a 'demonstration of David's ability to kill Saul'. In ch. 24 the opportunity presented itself, but this time David sought out the opportunity to confront Saul. Moreover, Yahweh's work for David is shown in a way never made explicit in ch. 24 by the narrator pointing out that David and Abishai's raid on Saul's camp succeeded because of the deep sleep Yahweh had put on the whole camp (v. 12). This element is held back initially, but its revelation at the chapter's heart makes clear that David prospers because of Yahweh's presence. Yahweh is committed to David, so David succeeds. Even Saul has to acknowledge this (v. 25).

But providence is awkward to interpret, and the text never makes clear how conscious David is of its work. What is clear is that David will not allow some casuistry to justify something otherwise unacceptable on the basis of providence. A policy of not killing Yahweh's anointed subsequently works to David's advantage, but his concern here is presented only in terms of doing Yahweh's will. Abishai's offer to kill the sleeping Saul provides a real temptation, but the implication would be the same if he killed Saul himself and is thus rejected. David in the preceding chapter has learnt something about providence through Nabal's death: the one under Yahweh's blessing can wait for Yahweh to resolve the difficulty of his enemies without taking the law into his own hands. David thus understands the implications of providence, even if he cannot explain its process.

David's understanding is what sets him apart from both Abner and Saul when the text moves to dialogue from v. 13 onwards. His questions to Abner elicit a response from him, though in reality they are a vehicle to address Saul. But in addressing Abner, David still expresses himself in terms of responsibility before Yahweh. When Saul enters the conversation, David again keeps Yahweh at the heart of his discussion. But neither Abner nor Saul responds in theological terms, although David's statement in v. 23 makes explicit the link between faithfulness and providence. The divide between David and Saul is thus made explicit, preparing for Saul's act of desperation in 28:3–25. David is under Yahweh's blessing, but also appreciates the practical implications of Yahweh's presence. Saul no longer speaks theologically, and this absence points to the larger gap in his life. Providence affects both, but only David appreciates its significance.

1 SAMUEL 27:1 – 28:2

Translation

[1]David said in his heart, 'Now, one day I shall perish by Saul's hand. There is nothing better for me than that I escape to the land of the Philistines so Saul will despair of seeking me any more in all the borders of Israel. Thus I shall escape from

his hand.' ²So David arose and crossed over, he and the six hundred men with him, to Achish ben Maoch, king of Gath. ³David settled with Achish in Gath, he and his men each with his household, and David with his two wives, Ahinoam the Jezreelite and Abigail, the widow of Nabal the Carmelite. ⁴When it was reported to Saul that David had fled to Gath, he did not seek him any longer.

⁵David said to Achish, 'If I have found favour in your eyes, let them give me a place in one of the country towns that I may dwell there. Why should your servant dwell in the royal city with you?' ⁶So that day Achish gave him Ziklag. Therefore, Ziklag has belonged to the kings of Judah to this day. ⁷The number of days David lived in Philistine territory was one year and four months.

⁸David arose with his men and they raided the Geshurites, the Girzites and the Amalakites, for they had been the land's inhabitants from of old, as you come into Shur, even as far as the land of Egypt. ⁹David would strike the land and not permit a man or woman to live; he took sheep, cattle, donkeys, camels and clothing and then returned to Achish. ¹⁰Achish would say, 'Where have you raided today?' David would reply, 'Against the Negeb of Judah' or 'Against the Negeb of the Jerahmeelites' or 'Against the Negeb of the Kenites.' ¹¹But David left neither man nor woman alive to bring news to Gath, thinking, 'Lest they report against us, saying, "Thus has David done."' This was his custom all the days that he dwelt in Philistine territory. ¹²Achish trusted David, thinking, 'He has surely made himself odious to his people Israel, so he shall always be my servant.'

²⁸:¹In those days the Philistines gathered their armed camps for war against Israel, and Achish said to David, 'You must understand that you shall go out with me in the camp, you and your men.' ²David said to Achish, 'Thus you shall see what your servant can do.' And Achish said to David, 'Thus I appoint you as my bodyguard for life.'

Notes on the text

27:7. *yāmîm* here has the sense of 'year'. See Driver 1913: 163 for analogies. It is absent from LXX, which has only 'four months' (defended by Smith 1899: 236), but its omission is more easily explained.

8. Retaining K. Q offers 'Gezirites', a known group but too far north, so is probably attempting to replace an unknown group with a known one. Twelve LXX MSS read 'from Telam' rather than 'from of old', but the reason is unclear (see NRSV and McCarter 1980a: 413 for the evidence). McCarter favours 'from Telam' (see Smith 1899: 237), but accepts it is conjectural (thus rejected by Youngblood 1992: 775). MT is awkward, but 'from Telam' may be exegetical rather than a different base text. Stoebe (1973: 475) wonders whether something has dropped out. It may be a northern boundary to balance Shur.

10. MT is impossible, so read *'ān* for *'al*, supported by a couple of MSS, plus Syr and Tg. LXX's *epi tina* presumes Hebr. *'al mî*, which is more difficult to explain. With many MSS, read *'al* for final *'el*.

Form and structure

Ch. 27 initiates a new section running through to 2 Sam. 1, which can be called 'The Accession Narrative' (Firth 2007) since it describes events by which David finally became king. This section is set off from what precedes it by a shift in narrative form. Chs. 16 – 26 employ episodic form narration where each account is more or less complete in itself and where chronological sequence is not necessarily reflected in the presentation order. By contrast, 1 Sam. 27 – 2 Sam. 1 employs serial narration where each episode requires and builds on those that preceded it, climaxing in David's lament over Saul and Jonathan. This is a sophisticated example of a bifurcated narrative that simultaneously follows both David and Saul, constantly cross-referencing them through 'tiling' (see Ska 1990: 10–11). This is where one narrative's end sequence overlays the beginning of the parallel account's next stage (see Josh. 10:16–27 for another example). Here the technique allows for the parallel narration of Saul and David's experiences, while also enabling construction of a series of 'cliffhangers', so each segment concludes with an unresolved issue that remains unaddressed until we return to the particular narrative stream. Hence, in 28:2, David seems bound by his promise to serve the Philistines, even though this means engaging in battle against Israel. But resolution of this problem is delayed until after Saul's visit to Endor. This in turn sees Samuel's shade announce Saul's death in the coming battle, but this is delayed by two further accounts where David is rejected by the Philistines and then travels to the Negeb, well away from the battle, so he could not have been involved in Saul's death. Only then is Saul's death recounted. Episodic narration then dominates until 2 Sam. 9 – 20, where serial narration returns.

Despite its specific features, the Accession Narrative is not disconnected from chs. 16 – 26 since these chapters provide the assumed background. Moreover, the strategy of repetition employed throughout Samuel remains important, as we have the second account of David's going to the Philistines (see 21:11–16 [ET 21:10–15]), while 29:6 provides the third occurrence of the song first mentioned at 18:7. Moreover, Saul's death vindicates David's statement in 26:10. The Accession Narrative is not a separate source but an element within David's move to the throne given special prominence by its narrative form.

In the light of the narrative form, 27:1 – 28:2 should be seen as the first element of a double introduction to the Accession Narrative, the second being Saul's visit to Endor in 28:3–25. This chapter's function is to create the problem for David that he is aligned with the Philistines when they are about to go to war against Israel. David is forced into a delicate situation, as is evident from the careful ambiguity of his response to Achish in 28:2. David twice indicated he would not kill Saul, but engaging in battle against Israel makes that a real possibility and he would genuinely become as odious to Israel as Achish believes him to be after his disingenuous reports of his activities in 27:10–12. David's attempt to flee from Saul places him in an extremely difficult position. This problem is not resolved immediately because it helps maintain interest over the whole Accession Narrative.

Comment

David flees to the Philistines: 27:1–7

1. A key feature of this chapter is the use of interior monologue where we access the characters' thoughts and thus understand their motives. The interest is heightened by the fact that David's interior monologue in 27:1 accurately interprets, whereas Achish's in 27:12 displays a flawed understanding of David. The narrator thus shows how effectively David has duped Achish. David's speech demonstrates that, in spite of the apparent rapprochement in ch. 26, Saul continues to threaten him. David does not flee because he wants to but because of necessity, though his attitude stands in tension with his confidence in 26:9–11. Nevertheless, Edelman's judgment of David as losing sight of his special relationship with Yahweh (1991: 232) is too harsh. As in 21:11–16 [ET 21:10–15], David flees to the Philistines, even though his previous attempt was less than successful. David's hope lay in his previous success in duping Achish, though his victories over the Philistines were too recent a memory for him to remain. Finding security with the Philistines was a bold but risky move for Israel's would-be king, but David concluded that the doubtful security of the Philistines was better than being on the run from Saul.

2–4. David's interior monologue is matched by action, except that whereas he initially spoke only of going over to the Philistines, his move to Achish is made explicit. Gath's location is unknown, but is possibly Tell es-Safi, on the border of the Judean Shephelah and the Philistine plain. Achish's father is mentioned, but otherwise unknown, while the title 'king' is unusual, but paralleled in 1 Kgs 2:39. More importantly, David is able to retain support in spite of the risks inherent in his decision as his six hundred men and their families continued with him, as also did the two wives he gained in ch. 25. The appropriateness of his decision is made explicit by the comment in v. 4 – Saul ceased to pursue David only when it was clear Saul could no longer reach him. When David flees from Absalom, he is again followed by six hundred soldiers, except this time they are Philistines (see Fokkelman 1986: 560).

5–7. The narrative passes over David's arrival. On his first visit he had to feign madness, but there is nothing similar here. Instead, the text moves immediately to where David is acceptable to Achish. These details' absence indicates how compressed this account is, perhaps because such details constitute a story in their own right, whereas the concern here is how David's actions (where he again dupes Achish) will seemingly place him in an impossible position from which only Yahweh can deliver him. However, at this point such an outcome appears improbable. This is clear from the fact that the biblical usage of the polite question 'If I have found favour in your eyes' when put to a foreign king normally presumes that the questioner has indeed won the favour of the one spoken to (Gen. 50:4; Esth. 5:8; 7:3; 8:5). How David found favour with Achish is not recounted. What matters is that he uses this position to his advantage. David's goal is to find a base where he is protected by Achish but sufficiently remote that he can run his own affairs, which is why he requests allocation of a country town. His argument to Achish is that he should not be a burden on royal resources in Gath, an argument that carries some weight given the size of his retinue. Achish therefore gave David Ziklag. The town is in the northern Negeb, initially listed as belonging to Simeon (Josh. 15:31; 19:3). The exact location is disputed (see Seger 1984), but the general region is clear enough. Crucially, the town is remote enough that Achish would not know everything that happened there. This suggests it was a town where the Philistines were not heavily involved, perhaps because of its location on the Israelite border, though it would therefore be advantageous to Achish to strengthen his control by placing troops there. David's offer appears to suit Achish, though in reality it suits David. The narrator then appends a note that the town has remained under the control of Judah's kings, a note that cannot originate before the ninth century since it presumes the division of the kingdom. Such a note already hints at David's coming triumph. That David was not there for long is shown by v. 8, which indicates a period of sixteen months (see 'Notes'). That, however, was long enough for him to improve his own position while appearing to aid Achish.

David's raids: 27:8–12

8–9. With his base established at Ziklag, David could raid various regions. Ziklag was well placed for raiding Judah, but that would have been politically dangerous for David, so instead he raided to the south, in the wilderness towards Egypt. The Geshurites were inhabitants of the Negeb, in the south of Judah (Josh. 13:1–2), but had never been completely removed. The Girzites are otherwise unknown (see 'Notes'), while the Amalekites had been Israel's enemy since the exodus (Exod. 17:8–16), and were meant to have been destroyed by Saul (1 Sam. 15). David's policy was to raid the peoples Israel was meant to have devoted to destruction when they entered the land. Although the language of Yahweh war (ḥerem) does not formally appear, David's decision to leave no one alive conforms to this (Bergen 1996: 262), though his regular collection of booty suggests it was a policy born of political necessity as much as religious concern. The absence of Yahweh war terminology may be intentional since it was, at least in part, Saul's decision to allow the best livestock to live in ch. 15 that led to his condemnation. That David returned to Achish after his raids suggests Achish received a share of the spoils (but see 30:27–31), as would be expected after deeding over Ziklag.

10–12. David had to report to Achish after his raids, no doubt so Achish could claim his share. In doing so, David needed to explain the source of the livestock he brought. Raids in the wilderness towards Egypt would not necessarily have troubled Achish, but by placing David in Ziklag the expectation was that he would raid Judah. David previously had no trouble in dissembling (see ch. 21), so continuation of that policy here is no surprise. David's reports claim he was raiding Judah's territory or those groups related to them, such as the Jerahmeelites (1 Chr. 2:25), or who supported them, like the Kenites (1 Sam. 15:6). Achish hears what he wants, without the risk of someone else telling him the truth. Indeed, the report of David's thoughts shows he could not risk someone else telling the truth since it would remove his façade of service to Achish when he was really acting as a faithful Israelite, which is why he maintained this custom throughout his time among the Philistines. Achish was completely taken in and trusted David, believing David could never gain the support of Israel, and so would serve him henceforth.

Preparations for battle: 28:1–2

1. David's control of his position could not avert the risk of war between the Philistines and Israel, but this happened at the end of his sixteen months among the Philistines. Moreover, Achish's complete trust of David now causes David his greatest difficulty. As the Philistine war camps assemble, Achish is clear that David can have no other expectation than that he and his men join the camp with him. David is seemingly caught in his own cleverness. All his efforts in duping Achish were so that Achish would trust him while David furthered Israel's interests. That trust now means he must join Achish in war against Israel, something that will completely undercut David's goals.

2. Faced with this, David's response is intentionally ambiguous. His language carefully employs court style, which is why he styles himself as Achish's servant. But the promise that Achish will see what he can do works in two ways. What Achish hears is that he can see first hand what has previously been reported to him, but David's statement can equally mean that Achish will see David's true colours. Achish does not recognize the ambiguity and expresses his trust by making David his lifetime bodyguard. It is an important position, though one where it would be extremely difficult for David to act against him and survive. Because of his trust in David, it is unlikely that Achish places David here to watch him (against Alter 1999: 170). It therefore seems that David's careful manipulation of events has led him into an insoluble problem. He cannot fight for the Philistines against Israel because that will generate implacable opposition to his claim to the throne. Yet Achish's trust has placed him at the point where his own survival suggests he has no choice. We now expect the battle to begin, but the narrative is deliberately broken off so the account of Saul's movement towards the same battle can begin.

Explanation

Like a soap opera, this account leaves readers with an unresolved narrative. David has fled from Saul to the only safety he can see, which means placing himself in the embarrassing position of living among the Philistines. For a future king of Israel, nothing worse could be imagined. In spite of this, and that Samuel is generally pro-David, David is not presented as a spotless hero, and the chapter's art lies as much in what it does not say as what it does. It leaves readers waiting to find out what happened next, something they will not discover until ch. 29.

The most obvious, and perhaps crucial, omission here is any reference to God. David never speaks of Yahweh, and neither does the narrator reveal Yahweh's response to events. Instead, we have David duping Achish and gaining an advantage for himself. Yet the advantage he gains, security from Saul, subsequently leads Achish to place David in a position where it seems he can only lose. Once the Philistines join battle with Israel, David's position as future king becomes impossible. All his care in raiding and destroying Israel's traditional enemies seems lost. The narrative sets up this reality for us and leaves us hanging at the end without resolution, only ambiguity.

How are we to read these events? Do they celebrate David's skill and guile, or express a loss of faith? Such a dichotomy is probably too harsh, because both elements are present. David is not lacking in guile and persuasion, but in doing so he moves to excessive levels of violence. No doubt many in Israel enjoyed hearing accounts of his success, but that he was not strictly carrying out the ban (*ḥerem*) cautions against reading these accounts as something entirely positive. For all the skill he displays, David still ends up in a situation where he has no resolution, and no amount of dissembling covers this. Indeed, his own cunning put him into this position. In this we may have a hint of the narrator's attitude. David's skill is admired, but the absence of references to God also suggests that David has created a position for himself from which only God can extricate him. But since we end on a cliffhanger, we must wait for another narrative to resolve itself into its own cliffhanger before we return to this one.

1 SAMUEL 28:3-25

Translation

³Samuel had died and all Israel mourned for him and buried him in his city Ramah. And Saul had removed the mediums and necromancers from the land. ⁴The Philistines gathered and came and camped at Shunem, and Saul gathered all Israel and they camped at Gilboa. ⁵When Saul saw the Philistine camp, he was afraid and his heart trembled greatly. ⁶When Saul enquired of Yahweh, Yahweh did not answer him, whether by dreams, Urim or prophets. ⁷So Saul said to his servants, 'Seek for me a woman, a spirit mistress, so I may go to her and enquire of her.' And his servants said to him, 'Behold, there is a woman who is a spirit mistress at Endor.'

⁸Saul disguised himself and put on other clothes and went, he and two men with him, and they came to the woman at night. He said, 'Divine for me by a spirit and bring up for me whomever I tell you.' ⁹The woman said to him, 'Behold, you surely know what Saul has done, how he cut off the mediums and the necromancers from the land. Why are you striking at my life so as to kill me?' ¹⁰Saul swore to her by Yahweh, saying, 'As Yahweh lives, no punishment shall come upon you in this matter.' ¹¹So the woman said, 'Whom shall I bring up for you?' And he said, 'Bring up Samuel for me.' ¹²When the woman saw Samuel, she cried out with a great voice. And the woman said to Saul, 'Why have you deceived me? For you are Saul!' ¹³The king said to her, 'Do not be afraid. What do you see?' The woman said to Saul, 'I see gods coming up from the ground.' ¹⁴He said to her, 'What is his form?' She said, 'An old man is coming up and he is wrapped in a robe.' Then Saul knew that it was Samuel, so he bowed with his face to the ground and did obeisance.

¹⁵Samuel said to Saul, 'Why have you disquieted me by bringing me up?' Saul said, 'I am greatly distressed, the Philistines are waging war against me and God has turned aside from me and no longer answers me, whether by prophets or dreams. So I summoned you to make known to me what to do.' ¹⁶Samuel said, 'Why are you asking me when Yahweh has turned aside from you and become your adversary? ¹⁷Yahweh has done what he said by my hand. Yahweh has torn the kingdom from your hand and has given it to your neighbour, to David. ¹⁸As you did not obey Yahweh and carry out his burning anger against Amalek, Yahweh has done this to you today.

¹⁹'Yahweh shall also give Israel with you into the hand of the Philistines, so tomorrow you and your sons will be with me. Indeed, Yahweh will give Israel's camp into the hand of the Philistines.'

²⁰Saul fell at once full-length on the ground and was greatly afraid because of Samuel's message. There was no strength in him for he had not eaten anything all day and night. ²¹The woman came to Saul and saw he was terrified, so she said to him, 'Behold, your maidservant obeyed you. I took my life in my hands and listened to the words you spoke to me. ²²Now, you also obey your maidservant. Let me set a morsel of bread before you; so eat and have strength as you go on your way.' ²³He refused and said, 'I shall not eat.' But his servants urged him, along with the

woman, and he listened to their words. Then he arose from the ground and sat on the bed. [24]The woman had a fattened calf at the house, so she went quickly and slaughtered it. She took flour and kneaded it and baked unleavened bread [25]and presented it before Saul and his servants, and they ate. Then they arose and went off that night.

Notes on the text

4. 'Mediums and necromancers' renders *hā'ōbôt wĕ'et hayyiddĕ'ōnîm*. The derivation of *'ōb* is uncertain, but the combination may be an idiomatic reference to male and female mediums rather than describing different classes of those consulting the dead. The often-proposed derivation for *'ōb* suggesting these are ancestral spirits or their images is unpersuasive (see Johnston 2002: 161–166; Blenkinsopp 2002: 53). The woman is a medium, not a witch (S. Fischer 2001: 29).

12. With LXX and Syr, omit *lē'mōr*.

16. A few MSS agree with LXX and omit waw before the interrogative. *'āreka* is difficult, but may be an Aramaizing variant of *ṣar* (see Ps. 139:20; Fokkelman 1986: 737). Klein (1983: 268) rejects the etymology, but his proposed metathesis (see McCarter 1980a: 419) presumes another word has fallen from the text.

17. Understanding *lô* as a reflexive ethical dative. See GKC §§119s, 135i. A few MSS support LXX and read *lāk*, but this is conforming the text to a simpler form.

19. McCarter (1980a: 419) considers this verse corrupt in all witnesses, arguing for a reduced text. But a supposed conflation does not constitute text-critical evidence, so a redactional argument is more likely. Given the importance of parallelism in Samuel (Firth 2003), there is probably an intentional emphasis here that includes development. Similarly, Youngblood 1992: 785.

23. MT *wyprṣw*, 'and they broke out' is impossible. We read by metathesis *wypṣrw*. This verb occurs only seven times (cf. 1 Sam. 15:23), which accounts for the error.

Form and structure

Having recounted David's move to the Philistines and its associated problems, the narrative returns to Saul. It is therefore necessary to recount Saul's experiences so they can be thematically paralleled by David's in preparation for battle. Where 28:2 had the Philistines prepared for battle and David caught up in their midst, we now turn to Saul and the events surrounding him before the battle at Gilboa (28:4), though the bulk of this chapter is at Endor. A key element of the Accession Narrative is how it defers the battle account, an effect achieved here with Saul's journey from Gilboa to Endor to enquire of Samuel through a spirit mistress. The outcome of this encounter is that Saul too heads towards the battle from a seemingly impossible position.

The narrative works on a thematic paralleling of Saul and David, not a chronological one. This is not immediately apparent from chs. 27 – 28, but becomes clear in chs. 29 – 30. The geographical notes in 28:4, 29:1 and 29:11 show these chapters are presented out of chronological order since the journey from Philistia to Shunem in the north (28:4) could have happened only after passing through Aphek (29:1). Aphek is well south of Shunem, but lies on the logical route from Philistine territory (see 'Comment', below). However, the assumption that the narrative should be presented in a strict chronological sequence has often resulted in the suggestion that 28:3–25 has been displaced from after ch. 30 (see McCarter 1980a: 422; Kleiner 1995: 7). Once the geographical and chronological elements are noted, a range of other issues are sometimes introduced to suggest this is a late intrusion, assigned to a redactional layer within the Deuteronomistic History (Foresti 1984: 133–136 provides a useful summary). Of most importance here is how this narrative displays awareness of other texts within 1 Samuel and builds upon them. Yet this should not pose a problem unless one is dependent upon certain source theories. A passage occurring late within a text but part of an extended narrative would naturally be aware of other elements within the larger text of which it is a part. Moreover, since both thematic and textual repetitions and dischronologized narratives are frequently occurring features in Samuel (see Firth 2001, 2003, 2005a and 'Form and structure' on 1 Sam. 16 – 17), its presence here should not surprise us (also Edelman 1991: 238). Assigning the narrative to the Deuteronomist is rendered problematic by the absence of distinctively deuteronomistic language. Rather, the narrative is presented in this order so both the introductory narratives of 27:1 – 28:2 and 28:3–25 end on an unresolved tension. Both section endings require us to read through to the climactic battle between Israel and the Philistines at Gilboa, though the battle account will again be deferred by narratives about David, though these resolve at least part of the tension before Gilboa.

Comment

Saul arranges to visit a medium: 28:3–7

3. The Accession Narrative has a double introduction, and this account has two introductory elements. Although they may seem distinct from one another, this verse's two halves deal with the same issue. Saul can no longer access the numinous, whether by authentic enquiry through Samuel or by means Israel's law deemed illegitimate. Samuel's death was noted in 25:1, but its repetition provides a crucial parallel with David. In ch. 25 David had to resolve the effects of Samuel's death by discovering how Yahweh would continue to lead him. There, when it seemed David would resort to illegitimate violence, he discovered that faithfulness to Yahweh was still the only way (25:32). This parallel now provides Saul with the same dilemma, but shows him seeking what Yahweh opposes. Samuel's death has removed Saul's key means for seeking Yahweh's will. An alternative option, necromancy, also seems removed by Saul's actions since he previously removed mediums and necromancers from the land. This was a positive action since all such occult activities were prohibited (Lev. 19:31; 20:6, 27; Deut. 18:11; Isa. 8:19–20), though for Saul it functions only to generate a problem he seeks to overcome by contradicting his earlier actions.

4. The introduction's second element is the Philistine location as they prepare for battle. The Philistines have pressed well into Israel's north, with Shunem lying in the Jezreel valley, about 15 miles south-west of the Sea of Galilee. They must, therefore, have travelled along the coastal plain through Aphek before entering the Jezreel valley. Saul's forces were gathered on Mount Gilboa, roughly 6 miles further south. It is from this context of military threat, and the seeming impossibility of divine guidance, that the narrative traces out Saul's response.

5–7. The relative size of the armies is not stated, but seeing the Philistine force struck fear into Saul's heart. A characteristic of Saul in ch. 14 was a constant desire to receive specific instructions about the campaign, and that resurfaces here as he enquires (*š'l*) of Yahweh. But Yahweh does not answer, though Saul was open to guidance from a range of means such as dreams, Urim (shorthand for Urim and Thummim) or prophets. Each was a legitimate means of receiving divine guidance, though the range of guidance offered differed. Examples of each form occur earlier in Samuel: Urim and Thummim in 14:41, prophets in 22:5, and a case could be made for Samuel's initial experience of Yahweh being a dream (3:3–14). The unstated irony is that Saul's actions against the priests at Nob (22:18–19) robbed him of access to the ephod, a means of guidance now with David (23:6), which David employs in 30:7–8. Faced with this, Saul issues a desperate order for his servants to find a spirit mistress so that he can enquire through her. The intent is to employ necromancy to access the divine will, something against Israel's law (see on v. 3). The narrative here may be compressed since we receive an immediate response from Saul's attendants, but this woman may be well known so no research is required to pass on local information. In any case, they inform him of a spirit mistress in Endor. As a town Manasseh could not effectively remove (Josh. 17:11–12), Endor might have remained a Canaanite enclave, but the important point for Saul was that it lay approximately 12 miles north. The Philistine camp at Shunem and Endor were respectively south and north of the Hill of Moreh (Gen. 12:6), so Saul might have passed through Philistine lines to reach there, though this is not as certain as Birch (1998: 1184) suggests. That Saul contemplated this enquiry at such a difficult location is clear evidence of his desperation.

Saul's enquiry: 28:8–14

8–10. Since Saul had driven out other necromancers from the land, he had to go in disguise to see the woman at Endor. Also the possibility of passing through Philistine controlled territory could have provided additional motivation, though it is clear his main concern was disguising his identity from the woman. Curiously, whenever kings disguise themselves in Samuel–Kings, the result is their condemnation (Coggins 1991), so this note prepares readers familiar with the genre for Saul's fate. The dangerous journey with two attendants is passed over because the main concern is Saul's encounter with the woman, whom he meets at night. The meeting's formalities are passed over to focus on Saul's imperious demand that the woman employ a spirit, possibly a familiar spirit, and bring up whomever he names. The demand is deliberately vague, not specifying who is to be summoned. The woman carefully protects herself, pointing out that Saul has cut off (possibly executed) all the necromancers in the land (see v. 3). The fact is well known, and leads to a question that is also an accusation: Saul's request is an attack on her that will lead to her death. Saul's response is a stunning irony, swearing by Yahweh that the woman will not be held guilty for her actions, though Saul's desired means of enquiry is counter to what Yahweh desires. Indeed, in 15:23 Samuel told Saul that rebellion was 'like the sin of divination (*qsm*)', but Saul now directs the woman to 'divine' (*qsm*) for him. Saul's experience, as well as the law, indicate that his actions are unacceptable, making this oath absurd.

11–12. Despite its limitations, Saul's oath convinces the woman, who returns to Saul's demand and asks whom she is to bring up. Saul's response is still a demand, but is formed to highlight Samuel's name. We have not previously been told Saul's goal, though the narrator's repetition of Samuel's death notice in v. 3 has prepared for it. The narrative's compression is evident in that we go straight to when Samuel's shade has been raised with no description of the processes of necromancy or the spirit employed by the woman. Instead, we have her response to Samuel's appearance when she sees him. The woman's ability to raise Samuel surprises modern readers, but the OT only condemns necromancy; it never questions its possible effectiveness (see Johnston 2002: 150–166). It later becomes apparent that Saul cannot see Samuel, but the concern here is with the woman's cry when she sees him, and her subsequent question, which is again an accusation. This question accuses Saul of deceiving her since Samuel's presence somehow enables her to realize Saul's identity.

How seeing Samuel leads to this is unclear, though perhaps the combination of Samuel and Saul enable her to recognize one from the other's
presence.

13–14. Saul responds by telling the woman not to be afraid. The reason
for this soon becomes evident. Saul is concerned to discover the necromancy's outcome, and asks her to describe what she sees, which indicates
he cannot see the shade. Most modern EVV (e.g. NIV, NRSV, ESV, NASB) treat
her response as describing a single divine being (*'ĕlōhîm*) coming from the
ground. But the participle pl. is normally a reference to pagan gods, so AV
renders it as a pl. Linguistically, this is preferable, though since *'ĕlōhîm* can
refer to judges (Exod. 22:8; Ps. 82:1–2), there may be deliberate ambiguity
in her phraseology. A plurality of gods fits with a pagan world view, but
may also be a hint of coming judgment. Isa. 8:19 might suggest that
necromancy's objects were called *'ĕlōhîm*, so the phrasing may be a
conventional means of describing the preternatural (see Arnold 2003:
374; Stoebe 1973: 485). The vagueness in her response leads to a clarifying
question from Saul that is cast in the sg. Even if she sees a plurality of
beings, Saul is interested only in Samuel. Taking this cue, the woman's
response employs the sg. She describes an old man dressed in a robe (*mĕ'îl*).
This response might considered equally vague, except for the keyword
mĕ'îl. This term was regularly associated with Samuel (2:19; 15:27), as
well as moments where royal power's transfer is signified (15:27; 18:4;
24:5, 12 [ET 24:4, 11]). As with 15:27, both elements are present, though
here it is enough for Saul to identify Samuel. Knowing Samuel's authority,
Saul falls face down on the ground to offer reverence to Samuel.

Samuel's message: 28:15–19

15. The woman is deftly placed in the background, enabling Saul and
Samuel's conversation to be directly recounted, a technique also employed
in Esth. 4 where the eunuch who acted as the messenger between Esther
and Mordecai is gradually removed to report direct speech between them.
It is unclear whether Saul now sees Samuel or if he depends on the woman,
but this technique brings a degree of immediacy to the dialogue as Samuel
shows himself less than pleased with Saul. As with the woman, Samuel's
accusation to Saul is expressed as a question, since the act of disturbing the
dead was unacceptable (see 13:11–12; Fokkelman 1986: 610). Saul's
response shows him in a similar light to ch. 14, where his actions were
for ever hamstrung by a desire for specific guidance. Saul's answer is
lengthy, but is made up of a collection of brief statements that tumble out
one after the other. The paradox, seemingly lost on Saul, is that the more
he expresses himself like this to Samuel, the more likely he is to be
condemned. The climax of Saul's distress is his inability to receive divine
guidance (with a listing largely repeating the narrator's from v. 6), which is

why he has summoned Samuel to provide that guidance. Saul does not consider that he may be responsible for his own difficulties.

16–19. Samuel's response is predictable to all but Saul. The announcement of judgment is initially framed as a question that plays on Saul's name and the verb 'to ask' (*š'l*). Saul can gain nothing by making this enquiry because Yahweh has turned from him, so Samuel cannot offer Saul something Yahweh will not, especially when Yahweh has become Saul's adversary. Accordingly, Yahweh has done what he announced in tearing the kingdom from Saul (15:27) and giving it to David, confirming Saul's own insight at 24:21 (Miscall 1986: 170). Saul may still be king, but the kingdom is no longer his. The reason for this is tied to Saul's failure to destroy Amalek in ch. 15, where his rebellion was compared to divination (15:22), the sin he has committed here. Saul can therefore no longer receive divine guidance. He has rejected earlier guidance and so cannot expect to receive more here. But Samuel does announce something new in v. 19, though in a sense it applies the law of Lev. 20:6. That law specifies that Yahweh will cut off anyone who resorts to necromancy. Samuel's judgment speech declares this fate not only of Saul, but also of his sons, all of whom will be dead by the following evening, while Israel will be defeated by the Philistines. Saul's desperation to receive guidance for the battle is what finally defeats him. He was called to deliver Israel from the Philistines (9:16), but instead delivers the nation over to them.

Saul's meal and departure: 28:20–25

20–22. Saul's response to Samuel's message, in falling full length on the ground, is immediate. This is not a collapse on his part, but a demonstration of the fear Samuel's message generates. Klein (1983: 272) points to the irony of a king who is head and shoulders taller than the rest (9:2) now face down on the ground. But we are now also told of Saul's weakness due to a fast. Although there is no evidence of a vow, it is eerily reminiscent of 14:24 when the whole army was too weak to fight because of the fast ordered by Saul. However we judge the woman, she still shows compassion towards Saul when she sees his terror. She argues that she obeyed Saul and put herself in his power by carrying out his instructions; now he should obey her. Accordingly, she offers to prepare a snack so he will have the strength to leave. The form of argument suggests her motives are not particularly altruistic: she must, in some way, keep Saul under her power so he does not cut her off after he has gone.

23–25. Saul initially refused the woman's offer, perhaps because of the implication of accepting her authority. However, his attendants persuaded him to accept the offer so he agreed to have the meal. Accordingly, he rose from the ground and sat on the bed while the woman prepared the meal. In fact, she did considerably more than her initial offer, for instead of a portion of bread, she slaughtered a fattened calf and made unleavened bread for Saul. Both activities take several hours, so Saul remained with the woman for a considerable period. This is so even if one accepts Reis's suggestion (1997: 19) that the meat was eaten raw, though it is more likely that cooking the meat is elided within the narrative. As the amount of meat eaten in Israel was low compared to modern Western consumption, slaughtering a fattened calf was a gesture of considerable generosity, since only the wealthy would normally eat such animals (see Amos 6:4; Luke 15:23). The value of the gift was itself probably intended to place an obligation on Saul. But the delay meant Saul left at night to return to his troops at Gilboa. The darkness provided him with cover so he could escape Philistine notice, but is also symbolic of his own condition as he returned to his forces with Samuel's word of condemnation ringing in his ears.

Explanation

This is a story deliberately told outside its chronological sequence. Leaving David in his self-generated moment of crisis with the Philistines, this narrative recounts how Saul generates his own crisis in the face of the Philistines. The geographical clues throughout chs. 27 – 29 make it clear that David's crisis was resolved long before Saul's journey to Endor, but the narrative form requires an introduction to the problems each has generated. It is only from the perspective of understanding the actions of the two that we appreciate how Yahweh continues to work for David, even as Saul's rejection is ultimately confirmed. Thus chs. 27 – 28 constitute a double introduction to the Accession Narrative, enabling the narrator to explore key differences between David and Saul as Yahweh's two anointed.

It is also possible to read this story as a discrete unit, though it finds its fulfilment in ch. 31. Saul is confronted by his inability to receive guidance from Yahweh while also confronting a Philistine assault deep in Israelite territory. His responses to crisis are similar to those previously encountered, except this time he explicitly transgresses the legitimate means by which one may seek information from Yahweh by engaging a medium to employ necromancy for him. Saul believes he can discover the needed divine guidance only from Samuel, even though divination is the sin Samuel previously said is equivalent to his earlier rebellion (15:23). For the Chronicler, this was Saul's decisive sin for which Yahweh put him to death (1 Chr. 10:13–14), though within 1 Samuel it is the climax of a history of sin that reaches back to at least his earlier moments of rebellion in chs. 13 and 15. Although this narrative can stand as a discrete unit, it is filled with allusions to earlier parts of Saul's story, which is why this is the climax of his sin.

The story's nature requires that it be read with its own narrative dynamics, and yet with sensitivity to the whole of Saul's reign. We have known ever since the rejection of Saul's dynasty in 13:14 and Saul himself in 15:28 that the kingdom is moving to Saul's neighbour. Saul recognized David as this neighbour who would receive the kingdom in 24:21 [ET 24:20], though this information is never revealed to him directly. Now it is revealed with one other point: Saul will die within twenty-four hours. Saul sought to force Yahweh's hand, but this only makes his failings clearer because Yahweh's hand may not be forced. Saul is finally a weakened man, the symbolic removal of his royal robes pointing to the reality fast approaching. The spirit mistress finally serves him a meal fit for a king when his reign is about to end. Saul's story confirms necromancy's futility, but even more so demonstrates the tragedy of the king called to deliver his people from the Philistines (9:16), whose fear of the Philistines leads to this sin, so he will meet his own end before theirs.

1 SAMUEL 29

Translation

[1]The Philistines gathered all of their camps to Aphek, while Israel was camping at the spring which is in Jezreel. [2]While the Philistine lords were passing by in hundreds and thousands, David and his men were passing by in the rear with Achish. [3]The Philistine commanders said, 'What about these Hebrews?' Achish said to the Philistine commanders, 'Is this not David, the servant of Saul, king of Israel, who has been with me these days and years? I have found no fault in him from the day he defected to me until today.' [4]But the Philistine commanders were angry with him. The Philistine commanders said to him, 'Send the man back that he might return to his place which you allocated to him. Do not permit him to come down with us into the battle, so he does not become an adversary for us in the battle. For with what could this fellow be reconciled to his lord except the heads of these men? [5]Is not this David, to whom they sang in the dances,

> 'Saul has slain his thousands,
>   But David his tens of thousands'?

[6]Achish summoned David and said to him, 'As Yahweh lives, you are upright, and it pleases me that you go out and come in with the camp, because I have not found anything wrong in you from the day you came to me through to today. But you do not please the lords. [7]So now, turn back, go in peace, that you might not displease the Philistine lords. [8]David said to Achish, 'What have I done? What have you found in your servant from the day I came before you until today that I should not go out and fight against my lord the king's enemies?' [9]Achish answered David, 'I know you are as pleasing in my eyes as an angel of God. However, the Philistine commanders said, "He shall not come up with us in battle." [10]So now, rise early in the morning, along with the servants of your lord who came with you, and go as

soon as you have risen and have the light.' [11]So David and his men rose early to depart in the morning, to return to the land of the Philistines, while the Philistines went up to Jezreel.

Notes on the text

3. With LXX, reading *'ēlî* after *nîplô*.

4. LXX omits the second 'Philistine commanders', but this is probably a natural shortening of clumsy phrasing rather than evidence of a different text.

6. McCarter (1980a: 426) omits the second *lō'* (with LXX[B]) as introducing unnecessary confusion, but his argument presumes that only the Philistine commanders were suspicious of David, suggesting David's questions in v. 8 are otherwise superfluous. But David's questions there focus specifically on Achish's response to him as a deliberate rhetorical strategy, so the text-critical link is unnecessary. Similarly, Deboys 1989.

10. NRSV follows LXX (cf. NEB, REB), including the longer text, which inserts 'and go to the place that I appointed for you. As for the evil report, do not take it to heart, for you have done well before me' after 'the servants of your lord who came with you'. Although smoother, Youngblood (1992: 789; cf. Edelman 1991: 261–262) rightly observes that MT fully addresses David's concerns, and the longer text adds no new information and is thus more likely an expansion.

Form and structure

After the Accession Narrative's double introduction in chs. 27 – 28, chs. 29 – 30 return to David, picking up from 28:2 where he became a member of Achish's bodyguard. Thus we explore how Yahweh delivers David from the seemingly impossible position in which he has placed himself, though given that ch. 23 recounts two other points where David is delivered from seemingly impossible situations such deliverances are not altogether surprising. But we must answer the question generated by 27:1 – 28:2: How will David avoid involvement with Saul's death in the coming battle? More broadly, as one who successfully duped Achish but became a trusted bodyguard, how can David avoid battle against Israel, battle that will for ever damage his position and limit his effectiveness as king? How can he fight for Israel without the Philistines killing him immediately since his position stops him acting as a double agent?

Just as the Accession Narrative begins with a double introduction, so there is a double answer to these questions, an answer pointing to Yahweh's providential involvement, a providence that is only comprehensible from the perspective of David's final accession, and not at various points along the way. Thus the first element is David's dismissal from the Philistine forces. This is paralleled by the journey into the Negeb in ch. 30 to retrieve the families of David and his men. The two narratives combine to show that David was as far as possible from Mount Gilboa when Saul died and was working for Israel's good at the time. What seemed an impossible situation was resolved, though unlike 27:1 – 28:2, there was no dissembling from David.

The suspense generated by the double introduction is partly a feature of how the whole narrative is presented. As noted previously (see 'Form and structure' on 28:3–25), the events of chs. 29 – 30 chronologically precede those of 28:3–25. But chronology is not the central concern, although geographical notes are kept – so a chronological harmony is possible. Suspense, and its resolution, is a priority for the Accession Narrative, and here we have the beginning of one such resolution.

This chapter's contribution to the account must still be noted. Brueggemann (1989) has noted how this chapter triangulates David, Achish and the Philistine leaders in the form of a trial, though one where the Philistine accusers never directly contact David. Against Achish's thrice-stated affirmation of David's innocence, the Philistine leaders continually assert his guilt, a pattern that Brueggemann (1989: 30–33) notes recurs in three accounts of Jesus' trial in Luke 23:2–15 and John 18:38 and 19:4–6. That David is said to be innocent more times than guilty contains a deep irony, because from the Philistine perspective he really is guilty. But for Israel, he is innocent of the one charge that will prevent his rise to the throne. Not only did he refuse to kill Saul, the hidden providence that proved so hard to read in chs. 24 and 26 also prevented him from incurring guilt unintentionally. David is not just lucky. Achish may be the only one here to name Yahweh, but the longer narrative makes clear that Yahweh is indeed present with David.

Comment

The complaint against David: 29:1–5

1. The geographical note places the events about to be described chronologically before 28:3–25. Aphek is on the Sharon plain about 40 miles south-west of Shunem (29:4), on the coastal route most naturally taken up into the Jezreel valley. The Israelite forces were at Jezreel, only a few miles north of Mount Gilboa, and used a spring there. This note also shows that the following events were not generated by the imminence of conflict, but from widespread distrust of David among the Philistine commanders.

2–3. The scene envisaged has the Philistine forces parading by. 'Hundreds and thousands' are the typical military units, although they were probably considerably smaller than their names suggest. David and his men are in the parade, bringing up the rear with Achish. David's position there generates conflict from the Philistine commanders, whose concern is evident in their dismissive question, a question not directed to anyone in particular. The question also plays on the root 'br, from which both 'passing by' and 'Hebrews' are derived; but this only accentuates their negative judgment of the group. Yet Achish is as innocent as ever, and provides an introduction for David and his men that emphasizes David's trustworthiness. He knows David was formerly Saul's servant, but has now defected to him, and has found nothing unworthy in him throughout the time he has been with him. As an affirmation, it is strongly positive. Yet the narrator has shown that Achish's perspective is flawed since 27:5–12 demonstrates that David duped Achish. It is a positive commendation that contains its own limitations. Achish points only to what he has not found, though the earlier narrative indicates he would have found a great deal had he looked. Moreover, that David has defected perhaps suggests he is more an opportunist than a loyalist, so the features Achish so greatly values might also be what makes David a threat to the Philistines.

4–5. David's potential threat was not lost on the Philistine commanders. Where their first question was open, this time it is stated that they gathered against Achish and insisted that David be directed to return to Ziklag, the place Achish had allocated to him. The reason for this is that he could not then enter the battle with the Philistines because that might enable him to act as an adversary (śāṭān) against them. This would actually be extremely difficult since David would have been particularly vulnerable, but as someone in the rear he could well assassinate Achish. Their view of David's loyalties is clear from their closing questions, both of which function as assertions about the threat he poses. First, they ponder how David could most effectively ingratiate himself with his lord, by which they mean Saul, not Achish. The answer is with a collection of Philistine heads. What they do not realize is that it was a collection of Philistine foreskins that convinced Saul of the threat David posed (18:27–29), but theirs was a logical deduction. Moreover, there is a nice irony included, because in appointing David to his bodyguard, Achish had literally appointed him as keeper of his head (28:2). Given that David previously kept Goliath's head (17:54), there was perhaps good reason for the Philistines to wonder about David and their heads, though David had not given even Goliath's head to Saul. The second question is posed by quoting the song first recorded in 18:7 (see 21:12 [ET 21:11]). For the Philistines, the song's interpretation is clear. Saul poses a threat, but David is a greater threat, an interpretation consistent with Saul's own (18:8). Their argument is forceful, insisting David be placed where he can do no harm. The commanders are not prepared to countenance Achish's position, which is that the enemy of their enemy might be their friend. Proper preparation for battle requires a more cautious approach.

David's dismissal: 29:6–11

6–7. Faced with implacable opposition from the Philistine commanders, Achish summoned David to announce he had to leave the Philistine forces. Achish's approach is pastoral, reaffirming the positive assessment he gave earlier to David, both in terms of his upright character and as someone whose dealings with Achish are satisfactory. From Achish's perspective it is only right that David continue with the Philistine forces because Achish has found no fault in him. Remarkably, this affirmation of David's character is prefaced with an oath sworn by Yahweh. Even more notable, the only reference to God during David's time among the Philistines comes from Achish, not David. Of course, all of this underscores how far Achish has been taken in, because the one thing readers of 27:1 – 28:2 know is that David has not dealt honestly with Achish. They are normally called 'lords', but in v. 3 it is the commanders of the Philistines who are distinguished from the lords of v. 2 who made the complaint against David. Achish appears therefore to upgrade the source of the complaint from the commanders (the military leaders) to the lords, thus claiming greater support for his position. What he reports is that the Philistine lords distrust David. From Achish's point of view, he reports a misunderstanding. In reality, the Philistine lords have understood more fully than he. The impact of this is the point to which Achish builds: David must leave the camp since his continued presence displeases the Philistine lords.

8. David's response is a series of questions directed to Achish, not to the position of the wider Philistine leadership. This lets him protest the decision without actually contesting its grounds. First, David asks if there is something particular he has done that has led to this decision, a question echoing his earlier affirmations of innocence through a question in 17:29, 20:1 and 26:18 (see Miscall 1986: 175). This is crucial; it may point to something recent that the other leaders have against him but that Achish does not. Of course, this time David's affirmation of innocence is not true (see Gordon 1986: 199), but Achish must understand it in the same way as the earlier statements. Then David asks if Achish has found any fault in him. Achish has already made clear that he has found no fault at all, but the context of the initial question allows this to be clarified. By retaining a focus on Achish's response to him, David can avoid the wider grounds of complaint utilized by the Philistine lords and commanders. There is also a careful ambiguity here. When David protests that he should have the opportunity to fight against the enemies of his 'lord the king', he does not indicate who that lord is. Although Achish does not realize it, the possibility exists that David did plan to act as the Philistine leaders had suspected.

9–11. David's questions allowed him to offer a seemingly valid protest, yet without addressing the concerns expressed by the Philistine leadership. Moreover, by phrasing them as questions that Achish alone could answer,

David could keep the conversation within manageable bounds. Achish recognizes none of this and reasserts his previous statement, going so far as to say that David is as blameless as an angel of God. The only problem, he insists, is a Philistine leadership that will not allow David to go to battle with them. Accordingly, he directs David and his men to prepare to leave early the next morning. This indeed David does, while the Philistines go north to Jezreel, the place v. 1 indicated was the site of the Israelite camp.

Explanation

The narrative in 27:1 – 28:2 had been left deliberately unresolved. David faced a seemingly impossible situation where he would be forced to fight for the Philistines against Israel, facing the risk that he would kill Saul himself, and the almost certain loss of Israelite support. But the signs of Yahweh's providence that proved so difficult to read in chs. 24 – 26 become clearer here as David is removed long before the battle begins. There is no direct theological statement of this, though the absence of direct theological observation is a feature of the Accession Narrative. However, within the larger flow of David's story it is clear that this is what has happened. Just as occurred twice in ch. 23, so here David is delivered from an impossible situation. What seemed like simple distrust from Philistine commanders is actually evidence of providence ensuring the divine promise to David would be fulfilled. David must still be an effective actor in dealing with Achish, but the God who called him ensures he does nothing contrary to what is expected. This does not mean David is without fault, for he is clearly less than truthful with Achish. Rather, it points to God's faithfulness to his promise, even if the processes involved are less than neat and tidy. Whether by design or accident, David will not incur the bloodguilt that would have accrued had he killed Saul, and this is a greater sign of Yahweh's presence with David than the simple fact of David's removal from the battle scene.

1 SAMUEL 30

Translation

[1]When David and his men entered Ziklag on the third day, the Amalekites had raided the Negeb and Ziklag. They struck Ziklag, burned it with fire [2]and captured the women and all in the town, both small and great. They did not kill anyone but took them off and went on their way. [3]When David and his men came to the city, then, behold, it was burned with fire and their wives, sons and daughters had been taken captive. [4]David and the people with him lifted up their voices and wept until they had no more strength to weep. [5]David's two wives were taken captive,

Ahinoam of Jezreel and Abigail the widow of Nabal of Carmel. ⁶David was greatly distressed because the people spoke about stoning him, because all the people were bitter, each one concerning his sons and daughters. But David strengthened himself in Yahweh his God.

⁷David said to Abiathar the priest, the son of Ahimelech, 'Bring me the ephod.' So Abiathar brought the ephod to David. ⁸David enquired of Yahweh, 'Shall I pursue this band? Shall I overtake them?' He said to him, 'Pursue, for you shall surely overtake and you shall surely rescue.' ⁹So David went, he and the six hundred men who were with him, and they came as far as the Wadi Besor, where those left behind remained. ¹⁰David and four hundred men gave chase, but two hundred who were too exhausted to cross the Wadi Besor remained.

¹¹They found an Egyptian man in the field, and took him to David. They gave him food that he ate and water that he drank. ¹²They gave him a piece of fig cake and two bunches of raisins. When he had eaten, his spirit revived, for he had not eaten food or drunk water for three days and three nights. ¹³Then David said to him, 'To whom do you belong? And where are you from?' And he said, 'I am an Egyptian lad, a servant of an Amalekite, but my master forsook me because I was ill three days ago. ¹⁴We had raided the Negeb of the Cherethites and against what belongs to Judah, and against the Negeb of Caleb, and we burned Ziklag with fire.' ¹⁵David said to him, 'Will you take me down to this band?' He said, 'Swear to me by God that you will not kill me or deliver me over to the power of my master. Then I shall take you down to this band.'

¹⁶Then he took him down, and behold they were spread out across the face of the land, eating and drinking and revelling because of the great amount of spoil they had taken from the land of the Philistines and from the land of Judah. ¹⁷David struck them from first light until the evening of the following day, and not a man of them escaped except four hundred lads who mounted camels and fled. ¹⁸David recovered all Amalek had taken, and David recovered his two wives. ¹⁹Nothing was lacking, whether small or great, their sons and their daughters, the spoil or anything they had taken. David brought back everything. ²⁰David also took all the flocks and the herds. They drove that livestock before them and said, 'This is David's booty.'

²¹David came to the two hundred men, those too exhausted to follow David and left at the Wadi Besor. They came out to greet both David and the people with him. When David drew near the people, he greeted them. ²²Then the wicked and worthless fellows from the men who had gone with David answered, 'Since they did not go with us, we shall not give them anything from the spoil we recovered except that a man may lead away his wife and his sons and depart.' ²³David said, 'You shall not do so, my brothers, with what Yahweh has given to us. He protected us and gave over this band which came against us into our hand. ²⁴Who will listen to you in this matter? The portion of the one who went down into battle will be the same as the portion of the one who remained with the kit. They shall share alike.' ²⁵He made it a statute and an ordinance for Israel from that day and onward unto this day.

²⁶When David came to Ziklag, he sent some of the spoil to Judah's elders, his friends, saying, 'Behold, a gift for you from the spoil of Yahweh's enemies.' ²⁷It was

for those in Bethel, in Ramoth of the Negeb, in Jattir, [28]in Aroer, in Siphmoth, in Eshtemoa, [29]in Racal, in the cities of the Jerahmeelites, in the cities of the Kenites, [30]in Hormah, in Bor Ashan, in Athach, [31]in Hebron, and to all the places where David and his men had wandered.

Notes on the text

2. Reading 'and all' with LXX.

3. Reading 'his sons' with Q.

7. LXX omits Abiathar's bringing of the ephod, but redundancies are more likely to be omitted than added, so MT is retained.

8. Reading 'shall I pursue' with LXX. MT has 'I shall pursue', though Driver (1913: 172) notes that the initial interrogative is not strictly necessary.

9–10. In these verses logic is often treated text-critically (see Smith 1899: 248; McCarter 1980a: 431), but the difficulty of the order of the numbers is a more awkward expression. Fokkelman (1986: 583) sees a narrative device of numbers reducing in units of two hundred.

16. The verb *ḥgg* is often rendered 'danced' (see ESV, NRSV), but this is over specific. It principally refers to the pilgrim feasts. This may include dancing, but is not restricted to it.

17. *nešep* is normally 'twilight'. But this means moving from twilight one night to the following evening, twenty-four hours of close combat. However, Job 7:4 and Ps. 119:147 have the sense offered here (see *DCH*, LXX offers 'dawn'). Taken this way, David initiated his attack at first light, pressing it until evening when the light failed. That it happens on 'the following day' means the battle occurred the day after he arrived, since he needed the first day's light to assess the raiders' position and prepare his attack (Collins 1991).

20. Reading *lipnêhem* for *lipnê*. See Alter 1999: 187.

21. Rather than David's greeting the people (lit. asking about their welfare), LXX has the people approach David. With Gordon (1986: 200), MT is retained.

22. Reading *'imānû* with several MSS, LXX, Syr and Vg.

23. *'ēt 'ăšer nātan yhwh lānû* is awkward. It is read here (with Hertzberg 1964: 225) as an object to the previous verb.

Form and structure

David, dismissed from the Philistine forces at Aphek, returned to his base in Ziklag, a three-day journey to the south. The timing of this journey makes it impossible for him to be at Gilboa when Saul was slain, an important apologetic point. Although David was associated with the

Philistines when Saul died, he had no part in it. We should not read the narrative in a reductionist manner, as if providing David with an alibi for Saul's murder (Halpern 2001: 78–81; cf. Robinson 1993: 146) was its only purpose, because the apologetic concern is woven into a larger frame where this is only one concern. This is particularly clear from Fokkelman's (1986: 594) chart of synchronisms, which demonstrates that David was engaging with the Amalekites while Saul consulted the spirit mistress at Endor. Fokkelman's view may not persuade on every detail, but his general position is sound. The synchronization does provide David with an alibi, but it also leads to a comparison between David's and Saul's actions at that time. A contrast between the claimants for Israel's throne is drawn by showing the actions of each during a crisis.

This chapter is also the second account concerning David in the current sequence. As noted ('Form and structure', 1 Sam. 27), the Accession Narrative makes significant use of doubled accounts. There was a double introduction and will be a double narrative of Saul's death. Here we have a second account concerning David during the Philistine muster against Israel. These narratives mutually inform one another. In 1 Sam. 29 the narrative focuses on Yahweh's removal of David from the Philistine army, and thus his avoiding having to face Saul in battle. A feature there, and of 1 Sam. 27:1 – 28:2 when David first went to Achish, is the comparative absence of reference to Yahweh. Indeed, Yahweh is never mentioned in 1 Sam. 27:1 – 28:2, with the only direct reference being from Achish in 29:6. By contrast, Yahweh is mentioned frequently in this chapter. In 30:6 we are told that David 'strengthened himself in Yahweh', while 30:7–8 shows David enquiring of Yahweh through the ephod. When confronted by the troops who did not wish to share the Amalekite plunder, David affirms that it has come from Yahweh (30:23), and when he distributes gifts to friendly towns, he specifies that it is plunder from Yahweh's enemies (30:26). This represents a fundamental shift in David's approach since he arrived in Philistine territory, and presents him in a theologically positive manner. The one about to be made king shows patterns of behaviour expected of an Israelite king because he submits to Yahweh's greater rule.

This assessment of David is informed by the implicit contrast with Saul in 28:3–25. As Birch notes (1998: 1191–1192), both are accounts of leaders under stress. Saul has tried to enquire of Yahweh (28:6), but has received no response, something to be understood in the light of his murder of the priests and the ephod's subsequent deliverance to David (23:6). Faced with this, Saul resorted to the spirit mistress, engaging in practices prohibited in Israel and acting against his own decisions (28:3). The dialogue between Saul and the woman makes use of theological language, but is flawed. Only Samuel's shade uses Yahweh's name appropriately. By contrast, when under pressure because of his men's desire to stone him when they returned to Ziklag, David strengthened himself in Yahweh, something demonstrated by his subsequent actions. Saul is portrayed as thinking only of himself, but David acts as the just king who ensures a fair distribution of plunder for all. The moment of stress is when Saul fails to act as Yahweh's servant whereas David does. In fact, there is a double comparison running through this chapter, because Saul's failure to deal with the Amalekites as directed by Yahweh in 1 Sam. 15 is contrasted to David's actions when confronted by them at Ziklag. Saul's failure to destroy the Amalekites made clear he would lose the throne (15:26), whereas David acts with absolute faithfulness (see Garsiel 1983: 135). David's suitability for the throne is thus emphasized through these comparisons in advance of the accounts of Saul's demise.

Comment

David's return to Ziklag: 30:1–10

1–3. After their dismissal from the Philistine forces, David and his men journeyed over 50 miles from Aphek to Ziklag, arriving on the third day. Instead of a secure home, they found the town and the wilderness to its south raided by the Amalekites. Saul failed to destroy them in spite of the directions given to him in 15:1–3 (see there on Amalek). David had been raiding among them (27:8), so a retaliatory raid while he was away is unsurprising (similarly, Edelman 1991: 263). The raid was devastating, burning the city, looting it and taking all there captive. The one hopeful note is that, unlike David's raids against the Amalekites (27:9), no one was killed, presumably because the Amalekites hoped to sell their captives as slaves. This hopeful note drives the narrative. Thus David and his men returned to a burned city, with their wives, sons and daughters taken captive. David and his men cannot have initially known of their families' survival, but the narrator foregrounds what can be known only retrospectively to prepare for the coming chase.

4–6. The response of David and his men was natural but powerful, mourning the loss of their families, weeping until they had no more strength. The narrator then discusses David's loss more specifically, emphasizing that both his wives, Ahinoam and Abigail, had been taken. David was not exempt from the loss affecting his men. But as leader David could be blamed for leaving insufficient protection for the town while they were away, though as someone under Achish's authority he might have had no choice. Moreover, it was because David had led them into Philistine territory that they faced this trauma. The blame was acute and David clearly felt pressured as the people's bitterness came to the fore when some spoke of stoning him. But here the narrative takes an important turn, declaring that David strengthened himself in Yahweh (cf. 23:16). Overtly theological language has been lacking during David's Philistine period, and perhaps such an attitude could be expressed only because the Philistine forces were well to the north. But David's attitude represents a key development in the narrative, introducing expressly theological themes that run through his remaining actions in Philistine territory. The narrative thus makes a subtle key change. David remains the astute politician, but he is again the politician who knows how much depends upon his relationship to Yahweh.

7–10. David's theological motivation was demonstrated when he sought Yahweh's guidance about what to do (see Stoebe 1973: 512), requesting Abiathar to bring the ephod. While Saul sought divine guidance through the spirit mistress, David sought guidance through Yahweh's priest (Bergen 1996: 276). As in 23:11, where David also enquired of Yahweh by this means, the request is presented as a pair of related questions. David wanted to know if he should pursue and if he would overtake the Amalekites, important issues given their head start. Of course, any group loaded with captives and plunder moves more slowly than an unencumbered body of armed men, even after a tiring journey. But this was Amalekite territory, a difficult area they knew well. David's urgency was matched by Yahweh's double response, which went beyond David's request. The first part directs David to pursue the raiding band because he will overtake them. But an added assurance is given, that David will indeed rescue those taken. Both of Yahweh's statements are emphatic, stressing the certainty of this outcome. Suitably reassured, David set out with his six hundred men, heading either west or south-west for between 15 and 25 miles towards the Wadi Besor (probably the Wadi Ghazzeh). After so much travel it is unsurprising that two hundred of David's men were too tired to journey further and were left behind, leaving a reduced group of four hundred to confront the Amalekites. On the problematic order of vv. 9–10, see 'Notes'. The reduction of David's force is a motif consistent with Yahweh war, as for example when Gideon's massive army was greatly reduced (Judg. 7:2–8), a theme more important than Stoebe's (1973: 513) supposed aetiological foundation for David's decree in v. 24. Along with the reassurance from Yahweh through the ephod, this reinforces the point that the victory will be Yahweh's alone.

David defeats the Amalekites: 30:11–20

11–12. Yahweh's work for David is shown by the seemingly chance discovery of an Egyptian in a field. The man was hungry and thirsty, having been abandoned three days earlier by his Amalekite masters. Brought before David, he was fed not only bread and water, but also figs and raisins. Bergen (1996: 277) suggests that the meal's details show David as faithful to the legal requirements concerning aliens (see Exod. 22:21; 23:9; Lev. 19:34; Deut. 23:7). This might have been so, though the sugars in figs and raisins also helped to speed the man's recovery. There might also be a contrast with Saul's meal in 28:24–25. Both meals take considerable space in otherwise terse narratives, and both involve someone famished from an extended period without food. But the contrast is crucial. David shows compassion in faithfulness to Yahweh, whereas Saul accepts the hospitality of one whose actions are the antithesis of such faithfulness. Where Saul was terrified and lost all strength because of his rebellion against Yahweh and the punishment announced by Samuel, this man receives David's provisions and his spirit is restored. But David's motives here are not altruistic. He wants the man to recover for the information he can provide.

13–14. David's focus on information is clear from his questioning. Just as with the ephod, David again asks a double question, both of which are terse and direct. David needed to know whether the man was a slave, and where he came from. The man's answers are somewhat longer, but provide a context for his answers as well as developing the narrative's timescale. His answers reverse the order of David's questions, identifying himself as an Egyptian before indicating he is a slave to an Amalekite. David's double question through the ephod elicited a three-part answer, and this man also provided additional information to explain why he was found there. Three days previously he had been ill and abandoned by his owner, presumably because he was delaying a group that was already rather slow. Beyond the personal information David initially requested, the man described a series of Amalekite raids on the Negeb, culminating in the burning of Ziklag, as well as a raiding of the wilderness areas to the south of Judah in territory allotted to Caleb (Josh. 14:6–15). Although within Judah's boundaries, Caleb's association with Hebron and its surrounds was regarded as distinct. David and his men had protected Nabal, who was specifically identified as a Calebite (1 Sam. 25:2–8), against such raids. The Negeb of the Cherethites is probably in the south of Philistine territory. The Amalekite band would have begun its raid there before moving east into Judah, then south towards Hebron and its surrounds before heading west to Ziklag and further west again into the traditional Amalekite territory.

15. David's goal in dealing with the man is made clearer as he asks whether the man will lead him to the raiding band. The assumption is that they have a regular base from which raids were carried out. But the man needed reassurance that David would not simply hand him over to his owners, a statement that suggests he had not so much been left behind as taken the opportunity to escape: a master would hardly punish a slave he had left behind but would certainly act against an escapee. That is no doubt why he wanted David to swear an oath that he would neither kill him as a captive of war nor hand him back to his owner. The importance of the oath is made clear by his desire that David swear by God that he will not act in these ways. But if David agrees, he will lead them to the raiders' camp. There is no record of David's swearing this oath, though since the man led them to the raiders' camp, we must assume he did. This approach is consistent with Deut. 23:16 [ET 23:15], which stipulates that slaves are not to be returned to their masters, and uses language very similar to here.

16–17. True to his word, the man led David's band to the raiders' camp. The military discipline David practised was not evident here as the raiders were spread out and celebrating their plunder. The sense of Yahweh's providence, initially indicated by the Egyptian's discovery, is heightened in that this is the ideal moment for a small group to attack. David launched his attack at first light (see 'Notes'), taking advantage of the raiders' condition, pressing home his attack until light failed that evening, so only four hundred men who mounted up were able to flee. David overcame a numerically superior force, as Gideon had done (Judg. 7:19–23), because of Yahweh's presence. Saul failed to destroy Amalek in spite of Yahweh's command (1 Sam. 15). With Yahweh's presence, David succeeded where Saul had failed.

18–20. That this was Yahweh's work for David is made clearer when David rescued everything the Amalekites had taken, including his two wives, just as Yahweh had promised (30:8). The extent of his success is emphasized by the addition of vv. 19–20, which are not strictly necessary since v. 18 has already stated that David was completely successful. They emphasize David's success by stressing that everything taken was recaptured. Both goods and family members were recaptured, nothing was lost, and even the livestock was brought back. The assertion that the spoil was David's marks a reversal from the earlier adversity towards him, so he is now the people's hero. Gunn (1980a: 111; see Fokkelman 1986: 589) argues that because David took Amalekite spoil whereas Saul was condemned for it, Saul was therefore one of God's victims. However, there are clear differences, the most important of which is that Saul contradicted a specific command related to a particular point in time. In addition, this is recapturing Philistine and Israelite material. The general principle remains – Saul failed in respect of Amalek whereas David succeeded – but the particulars of each account are not to be pushed to create unintended parallels.

David's policies: 30:21–31

21–25. The narrative quickly returns to the Wadi Besor, where the two hundred previously exhausted men remained with the kit. On seeing David, this group greeted him and exchanged the normal pleasantries. This seemingly trivial detail is included to show there was no general animosity between David and this group, while preparing for the contrast with the 'wicked and worthless fellows' (*bĕlîyaʿal*; cf. 2:12) who sought to prevent them from receiving back anything more than their family. Given that the four hundred who went with David had engaged in the battle, this could have been a persuasive position, which implied that only those who participated in combat shared the spoil. But this loses sight of Yahweh's involvement in the process, for the success is what Yahweh promised when David enquired of him. David's view is to let everyone see that the spoil was given to them by Yahweh, and that gift belongs to the whole band. All who had set out were responding to Yahweh's guidance, so the spoil could not be divided. All who remained faithful to Yahweh could share the plunder, and that applied equally to those who remained with the kit. The importance of this decision becomes clear when it is said to have become a statute in Israel from that day. Although he has not yet ascended to the throne, David acts as 1 Sam. 12 indicated a king should act: with justice that is also submission to Yahweh. This is what 28:3–25 shows that Saul would not do, while the link to 15:10–23 highlights the further contrast that Saul sinned because he listened to the people, but David's leadership was shown when he did not (Fokkelman 1986: 590). A similar policy is described in Num. 31:27 and Josh. 22:8, but the theological foundation for the division is not as explicit as here (Ackroyd 1971: 224).

26–31. The plunder taken included Philistine material as well as spoil from Judah. Hence David could ensure his positive relationship with the neighbouring towns in Judah by sending gifts to them from what had been captured, though it is unclear if these towns received as much as was originally taken. The gifts were characterized as coming from Yahweh's enemies, which stressed the common faith that bound David and Judah, even though his political base in Ziklag was then among the Philistines. The narrative has also stressed Yahweh's activity for David, so the gifts can truly be seen in this light. David's characterization of the gift is both historically accurate and politically astute, as it provided him with the means to improve his support base in Judah. However, the exact interpretation of David's gifts remains tentative because many of these towns cannot be identified. Hebron along with Jattir and Eshtemoa were priestly centres in Judah (Josh. 15:48; 21:11, 14), while Hormah was in Simeon (Josh. 15:30). Aroer was in Judah, about 12 miles south-east of Beersheba. The other towns were presumably also in Judah and Simeon and thus close to where David was. This is certainly the case with Ramoth Negeb since its name required it to be in the wilderness to Judah's south. The Bethel mentioned here cannot be the larger town in southern Ephraim since it was remote from the others and needed to be in the area where David and his men roamed. The general principle, however, is clear. David ensured that, as well as sharing the plunder with all his men, he also shared it with towns whose support he needed to become king. The importance of this goal is stressed by the list ending with Hebron, which is where he became king. This time, there was no share for Achish, suggesting that David was both preparing Judah for his arrival and cutting his Philistine ties.

Explanation

The double narrative of David's actions during Saul's conflict with the Philistines comes to its close here. Although this account provided David with an alibi explaining why he was not associated with Saul's death even though he was a Philistine vassal, the narrative offers considerably more than that. By creating a series of parallels where David is contrasted with Saul in 1 Sam. 15 and 28, the narrative offers an apology that shows why David became king. At the two pivotal points where Saul failed because he was unfaithful to Yahweh, David succeeded because he remained faithful. The argument for this is centred on the fact that in the time of crisis David not only found his strength in Yahweh (30:6), but also demonstrated the effects of this when dealing with Yahweh's people and enemies.

On his return from Aphek, David and his men were confronted with the devastating sight of the burnt remains of Ziklag and the loss of their families. It was a time of tremendous pressure for David, with his men prepared to stone him. But whereas Saul in his distress sought the guidance of a spirit mistress (28:3–25), David strengthened himself in Yahweh, demonstrating this by enquiring of Yahweh through the ephod. It is not that the answer strengthened David: rather, he received the answer because he had found his strength in Yahweh. David's commitment to Yahweh's ways was worked out through his decision to pursue the Amalekite raiders, in which he is completely successful, retrieving all that had been taken and providing equally for all. Saul failed when Yahweh had directed him against Amalek (15:1–22) but David succeeded because he was faithful to Yahweh's directions. David's success was marked by a policy of giving, first to some of his men who were too tired to complete the journey, and then to towns in Judah's south. It was a spirit of giving that Brueggemann (1990b: 205) appropriately links to the parable of the workers in the vineyard (Matt. 20:1–16), because this was giving equal shares to all and not simply rewarding work done. David modelled actions appropriate for Yahweh's king because he modelled the principles of the kingdom of God. This did not prevent David from being politically astute in his giving – he was both as wise as a serpent and as innocent as a dove (Matt. 10:16). But the principle of recognizing what comes from Yahweh first was central.

Running in parallel is a strong emphasis on providence, which emphasizes Yahweh's involvement in all that happens. It is because of Yahweh's directions that David pursued the Amalekites (30:8). Although it is not stated directly, the discovery of the Egyptian slave after receiving this direction is also evidence of Yahweh's providential involvement, as is the timing of David's arrival at the Amalekite camp and their lack of readiness for battle. This is why David recovered all that had been captured. Indeed, David recognized as much when he insisted that the spoil had been given to him by Yahweh (30:23), while the spoil sent to the Judean towns had come from 'Yahweh's enemies' (30:26). All of this points to Yahweh's providence, providence David recognized. Such providence is another part of the presentation of David as the next king because it shows that Yahweh was indeed with him. David acted as the king should, by finding his strength in Yahweh, while Yahweh demonstrated his commitment to his chosen king by providing for him. David was eligible to be the next king because he showed his commitment to Yahweh, while Yahweh showed his commitment to him. All that remained was Saul's final removal, completing the process announced in 15:28.

1 SAMUEL 31

Translation

[1]Meanwhile, the Philistines battled Israel, and the men of Israel fled from the Philistines and fell slain on Mount Gilboa. [2]The Philistines overtook Saul and his sons, and the Philistines struck Jonathan, Abinidab and Malchi-shua, Saul's sons. [3]The battle was heavy against Saul, and the archers found him and he greatly feared the archers. [4]Saul said to his kit-bearer, 'Draw your sword and run me through with it lest these uncircumcised come and run me through and deal ruthlessly with me.' But his kit-bearer was unwilling because he was greatly afraid, so Saul took the sword and fell on it. [5]When his kit-bearer saw Saul was dead, he also fell upon his sword and died with him. [6]So Saul and his three sons, his kit-bearer and all his men died together on that day. [7]When the men of Israel who were across the valley and those across the Jordan saw that the men of Israel had fled and that Saul and his sons were dead, they abandoned the cities and fled. Then the Philistines came and dwelt in them.

[8]When the Philistines came the following day to strip the corpses, they found Saul and his three sons fallen on Mount Gilboa. [9]They cut off his head and stripped his kit and sent messengers through the land of the Philistines to bear the good news to the house of their idols and their people. [10]They put his kit in the temple of Ashtaroth and fastened his body to the wall at Beth Shan. [11]When all the inhabitants of Jabesh Gilead heard what the Philistines had done to Saul, [12]all the men of valour rose up and went through the night and took the corpses of Saul and his sons from the wall of Beth Shan and came to Jabesh and burned them there. [13]Then they took their bones and buried them under the tamarisk at Jabesh and fasted seven days.

Notes on the text

2. Reading *wayyadběqû* as a hiph. See GKC §53n.

3. With several MSS, reading *'al* rather than *'el*. See 1 Chr. 10:3. LXX is broadly followed by many modern EVV in the final clause (e.g. NIV, NASB, NRSV, ESV), suggesting Saul was seriously injured. The emendation to *wayyāḥel* for this is slight and widely supported (see Youngblood 1992: 801). But this requires that *min* after a passive mean 'by', something difficult to substantiate (Fokkelman 1986: 739). LXX may be confused by the root *ḥll* (corpse) in v. 2 and carries this over in its translation where MT's vocalization understands it to be *ḥyl* (*ḥwl* in BDB). Fearful writhing is contextually better in the light of Saul's fear in 28:5.

6. LXX omits Saul's men, apparently harmonizing with v. 7. But these men would be Saul's bodyguard, so there is no contradiction.

11. LXX[B] omits *'ēlāw*, smoothing over difficulties since the word is redundant. But 1 Chr. 10:11 adds *k'l*, and that is read here.

Form and structure

After the double accounts of David being removed from the battle (chs. 29 – 30), we now have two accounts of Saul's death (31:1–13; 2 Sam. 1:1–16). Because of the Accession Narrative's structure, these accounts are separated from 28:3–25, although those events immediately preceded these. This was required because David had to be shown to be in the south at this time (chs. 29 – 30). Although often treated as contradictory doublets (Smith 1899: 251; Robinson 1993: 155–156), the two accounts fulfil different narrative functions. As with the accounts of David's sparing Saul (chs. 24, 26), these do not simply replicate one another. Instead, they develop our understanding of events, though both are woven closely into the Accession Narrative through the repetition of keywords. The presence of these terms means they are not random pieces of tradition that the narrator could not resolve but integrated components within the narrative. In 1 Sam. 31:1–13 this is evident through repetition of the root *pšṭ* in vv. 8–9. This was a key term in 27:8, 10, 30:1 and 14, where it meant 'raid' rather than 'strip for plunder' as here. The root also means 'raid' in 23:27, while in 18:4 and 19:24 it refers to removing clothing, though not as plunder. This creates echoes within Saul's story, while the closing references to the actions of the men of Jabesh Gilead (31:11–13) means they bookend his story (cf. 11:1–11). The Amalekite's report of Saul's death to David in 2 Sam. 1:1–16 provides alternative links within these chapters.

This chapter offers a third person account of Saul's death, whereas the Amalekite's report is first person. That the Amalekite speaks with personal interest means that his report is probably less reliable, and this explains the key differences between the accounts (see 'Form and structure' on 2 Sam. 1:1–16 and B. T. Arnold 1989, who demonstrates that the differences are not as great as sometimes suggested). This chapter recounts how Saul and his sons died and what happened to their bodies to remove the possibility of conflict between David and Jonathan for the throne. Saul has died, along with his sons, and David can now advance towards the throne. Moreover,

Saul died exactly as 28:19 indicated he would, he and his sons together. By contrast, 2 Sam. 1:1–16 explains how David received Saul's badges of rank. Since David was not at Gilboa, they must have been removed by someone before the Philistines arrived the next day and brought to him. Each account has its own integrity, but they must be read together to see how they develop one another.

Comment

The death of Saul and his sons: 31:1–7

1–3. The narrative thread from 28:25 is renewed here. After his night with the spirit mistress, Saul returned to his troops on Mount Gilboa to face the Philistines. It was a battle where he had little hope, and in these verses any remaining hope is gradually stripped away as Saul's forces become ever smaller. First, as battle raged, the Israelites fled from the Philistines, though in the process many died, their bodies falling on the mountain. Then the narrative comes closer to Saul as the Philistines overtook him and his sons as they fled. Three of Saul's sons, Jonathan, Abinidab and Malchi-shua, were killed by the Philistines. Jonathan and Malchi-shua are mentioned in 14:49, along with another son named Ishvi. If Ishvi is Ish-bosheth (Eshbaal in Chronicles), then his absence from this list prepares for the conflict between David and Ish-bosheth in 2 Sam. 2 – 4. That the three sons died at the one time links back to 28:19, and prepares for Saul's death. This echoes the death of Eli and his sons, which also happened on one day during war with the Philistines (4:11, 18). It will not, however, come quite as one might expect, because although the Philistines had caught up with Saul they did not kill him. Instead, v. 3 focuses on Saul himself, delaying his death by emphasizing his difficulties and the fear it generated in him (see 'Notes'). With his troops having fled or been killed and his sons dead, the narrative focuses on Saul alone. He has good reason to fear, perhaps more than in 28:5, because he can see the announcement of 28:19 resolving itself in the reverse order of that announcement. Only Saul's death remains, and it cannot be delayed because he must die on the same day as his sons.

4–5. Although we expect Saul to be killed by the Philistines, the narrative takes an unexpected turn. Although he dies because of their pressure, he dies at his own hand. Although 28:19 might create an expectation that the Philistines would kill Saul, it refrains from saying this, an ambiguity explored through this account. Faced with what he judged as overwhelming odds, we discover that Saul had his kit-bearer with him (see 14:6–15). Although they carried equipment for senior officers, kit-bearers were themselves active soldiers and assisted those in command. David had entered Saul's service in this role (16:21). Saul commands this man to run him through with his sword and kill him because of his fear of what the Philistines will do. Saul still speaks dismissively of the Philistines as 'uncircumcised' as had Jonathan (14:6) and David (17:36), but even this casts a tragic shadow across him. Jonathan and David had faced seemingly overwhelming Philistine opposition and yet won, but for Saul this is the language of defeat. Saul's fear of how the Philistines will treat him is well founded (see the same verb in Judg. 19:25), but he does not want this to happen in life. Yet the kit-bearer is unwilling, his fear perhaps related to David's refusal to touch Yahweh's anointed (24:7 [ET 24:6]; see Stoebe 1973: 526–527). Saul chooses instead to commit suicide by falling on his sword, an act followed by his kit-bearer. This was a possibility for Saul's end David had not contemplated in 26:10. Suicide is comparatively rare in the Bible, and apart from Saul and his kit-bearer only five others are recorded: Abimelech (Judg. 9:52–54), Samson (Judg. 16:25–30), Ahithophel (2 Sam. 17:23), Zimri (1 Kgs 16:15–20) and Judas (Matt. 27:3–5 / Acts 1:18–19). None of these is considered a noble death: each is the outworking of tragic circumstances and sin. Razias' suicide in 2 Maccabees 14.42 differs as it is seen as a noble death, but this opposes the dominant view of suicide in biblical and Jewish sources.

6–7. With the deaths recounted, the narrator summarizes, tying together the elements of 28:19. Saul, his sons, his kit-bearer and his men die on the one day. Samuel's post-mortem prophecy has resolved itself. Saul's death led to chaos among the Israelites as those closest to him across the valley from Mount Gilboa (Jezreel), and eventually those across the Jordan, abandoned the cities and fled when they saw Saul was dead. Although this would have taken a few days, it points to the difficulties of Israel's situation, since the Philistines then controlled large areas of Israel's north, especially the valuable trade routes through Jezreel. Mention of the territory across the Jordan cannot mean they occupied too much there, since the men of Jabesh Gilead were unaffected and Ish-bosheth's rump kingdom began in the Transjordan. But it suggests they occupied enough to control the trade route from the north of Israel through to the cities on the coastal plain. With Saul's death, Israel lost both its government and one of its principal areas of revenue.

The treatment of the corpses: 31:8–13

8–10. That Saul's fear of Philistine ruthlessness in their treatment of him was well founded is clear, as they came the following day to strip (*pšṭ*) the corpses on Mount Gilboa. The delay between Saul's death and the Philistines' arrival left space for the Amalekite to take his badges of rank and escape before bringing them to David (2 Sam. 1:10). The description suggests the Philistines were not particularly seeking Saul so much as stripping the corpses to gain whatever spoil might be available. Thus they found Saul and his sons on Mount Gilboa. The narrative focus is on their treatment of Saul, highlighting the severing of his head by mentioning it first, though he would have been stripped of at least some equipment first. David had also cut off Goliath's head (17:51). Just as with the ark's capture (5:1–4), the Philistines followed the normal practice of taking Saul's relics as spoils of war to a temple (Dagon's temple in 1 Chronicles). It is likely that the pi. of *šlḥ* here emphasizes that they not only sent messengers with the good news (see the messenger to Eli in 4:12–17) of Saul's demise, but also sent his relics. Saul's armour ended up in the temple of Ashtaroth (see 7:3), which is probably a generic way of referring to Philistine goddesses rather than a specific identification of the deity concerned (similarly, Youngblood 1992: 800; see *NIDOTTE* 3:562–563). His body, however, was impaled on the wall at Beth Shan, a town about 5 miles east of Gilboa.

11–13. Although the Israelite troops had scattered, some areas remained loyal to Saul. In particular, Jabesh Gilead was where he demonstrated his election to the throne (11:1–11), so it is unsurprising that its valorous men journeyed through the night to take the bodies of Saul and his sons down from the wall at Beth Shan. The town was about 12 miles south-east of Beth Shan, in range for a nocturnal recovery mission. The absence of reference to battle might suggest that although these towns were under Philistine control, the level of occupation was small since they brought the bodies back to Jabesh Gilead. Once there, they burned the bodies before burying them under a tamarisk tree by the town and fasting seven days. Fasting to signify mourning is normal (Judg. 20:26; 1 Kgs 21:27; Zech. 7:5), though seven days is severe. But burning the bodies is unusual because Israelites did not normally practise cremation, and Amos is particularly stern in condemning some Moabites who burned the bones of an Edomite king to lime (Amos 2:1–3). The Chronicler apparently felt some discomfort with it, omitting the burning (1 Chr. 10:12). It is unlikely that burning the bodies was from concern with contagion (so Baldwin 1988: 171) because that assumes a modern understanding of the spread of disease, and Baldwin's only supporting reference (Amos 6:10) is textually doubtful. Nor can we assume this was only burning spices (see NEB) since the syntactical support is too slight (similarly, Edelman 1991: 294). The Tg also offers this interpretation and notes it was a local practice (Gordon 1986: 204). Perhaps a better option is to assume a local practice, which, though non-orthodox, was intended to honour Saul and his sons at Jabesh Gilead. A seven-day period of uncleanness typically followed contact with a corpse (Num. 19:11), and this may also explain the fast's length, suggesting the burning and fast were local responses to contact with a corpse, though with some memorial content. When commending the town's loyalty to Saul, David does not mention the burning (2 Sam. 2:5–7). If burning is non-orthodox, then even the final attempt to honour Saul might offer less than intended. It could be a final and somewhat ironic observation on his reign. The intentions were right, but the practice never quite worked out as it should have.

Explanation

Saul's death has long been expected. It has been coming since his rejection in 15:28 and David's anointing in 16:1–13. More precisely, Samuel's post-mortem prophecy in 28:19 made clear that it would happen here. While David was in the south defeating a traditional enemy (Amalek), Saul faced the Philistines, the people from whom he was meant to deliver Israel (9:16). The paralleling of chs. 30 and 31 provides additional pathos, even though the outcome for Saul was partially known in advance. It was only partially known because it was not expected that he would commit suicide, begging for the help of his kit-bearer to avoid dishonour as Israel's first royal pretender, Abimelech, had done in Judg. 9:52–54. The narrative never directly comments on Saul's death, but by joining allusions to Abimelech and Eli, whose deaths were more tragic than noble, there is an implied observation on Saul. Unlike 1 Chr. 10:13–14, there is no theological statement. Yahweh is never directly mentioned in this chapter, and yet his word hangs heavy throughout.

The tragedy is not restricted to one man's death. Saul's sons and men died with him, and Israel's north came under Philistine subjugation. The evidence of Philistine victory is clear, for Saul's relics are paraded in their temples, and the bodies of Saul and his sons are nailed to the wall in Beth Shan. Only the people of Jabesh Gilead act for Saul, coming through the night to retrieve their bodies and give them what they apparently judge to be an honourable burial. But this one note stands against everything else. Defeat is all around for Israel. The nation whose pressure seemingly triggered Israel's request for a king to lead them in battle (8:20) seems to have won as they now control the coastal plain in the south and the rich Jezreel valley in the north. Israel is reduced to small groups in the Transjordan.

Against this background we should note the double references to the coming of Yahweh's king in both Hannah's Song (2:10) and the man of God's announcement (2:34). Kingship may seem to have failed, but both of these references point to the king Yahweh will bring. Pointedly, in 12:1 Samuel described Saul as the king for whom the people asked. Saul was Yahweh's anointed, but in renewing kingship in ch. 12, Samuel had to outline a model of kingship that was submitted to Yahweh's greater reign. Yet Saul in chs. 13 – 15 showed he did not understand this. David, by contrast, is Yahweh's chosen and anointed, and without a public request. The conflict between David and Saul that dominated chs. 18 – 31 derives from this and it is memory of this that continues to provide hope even in the midst of tragedy here. Saul's death opened the way for David to accede to the throne. It created the possibility for a king who would reign under Yahweh's greater reign. By showing David's acting as a king ought to in ch. 30, the way forward has been shown before Saul's death is recounted, though the events of these chapters are parallel to one another. Saul's death was tragic in itself, and it was a tragedy for Israel because of the Philistine occupation, but it opened the door for fulfilment of Hannah's Song. That Yahweh has another anointed one means there is still hope, even when all seems bleak. That hope may be evident from the parallels with the defeat at Ebenezer in 4:1b–11. Afterwards the ark was taken as a trophy to Dagon's temple, but the Philistines quickly discovered that this was not the victory they wanted, and arranged to return their trophy. Saul's relics were paraded in the same way. Yet defeat at Ebenezer was how Yahweh brought about new and effective leadership through Samuel, and hope remains for something similar here. The Philistines also discovered that Yahweh was not defeated as easily as Israel. The Philistines may claim victory, but the earlier story's echoes suggest this is not how it must remain.

2 SAMUEL 1

Translation

[1]After Saul's death, when he returned from striking Amalek, David stayed two days in Ziklag. [2]On the third day, behold, a man came from Saul's camp, with his garments torn and dirt on his head. When he came to David, he fell to the ground and did obeisance. [3]David said to him, 'Where have you come from?' He said, 'I escaped from Israel's camp.' [4]David said to him, 'How did things go? Tell me.' He said, 'The army fled from the battle. Many of the army fell and died; also Saul and his son Jonathan are dead.' [5]David said to the lad reporting to him, 'How do you know Saul and his son Jonathan died?' [6]The lad reporting said to him, 'By chance I happened to be on Mount Gilboa and, behold, Saul was leaning upon his spear, and behold, the chariots and cavalry officers were closing in on him. [7]When he turned around, he saw me and called to me and I said, "Here I am." [8]He said to me, "Who are you?" and I answered, "I am an Amalekite." [9]He said to me, "Please stand over me and kill me because the death throes have seized me, yet life is still in me." [10]So I stood over him and killed him because I knew he could not live after he had fallen. Then I took the crown on his head and the armlet on his arm and I brought them here to my lord.'

[11]Then David seized his clothes and tore them, as also did all the men with him. [12]They mourned, wept and fasted until evening for Saul and Jonathan his son, for the people of Yahweh and for the house of Israel because they had fallen by the sword. [13]David said to the lad who reported to him, 'Where are you from?' He said, 'I am the son of a sojourner, an Amalekite.' [14]David said to him, 'Why were you not afraid to put forth your hand to destroy Yahweh's anointed?' [15]David summoned one of the lads and said, 'Go. Execute him.' So he struck him and he died. [16]David said, 'May your blood be upon your own head because your mouth testified against you, saying, "I killed Yahweh's anointed."'

[17]Then David chanted this lament concerning Saul and Jonathan his son, [18]and

ordered the sons of Judah to be taught the harsh realities. Behold, it is written in the Book of Jashar:

> [19]'The honour, O Israel, is slain upon your high places.
>   How the mighty warriors have fallen!
> [20]Tell it not in Gath,
>   Nor announce the good news in the streets of Ashkelon,
> Lest the daughters of the Philistines rejoice,
>   Lest the daughters of the uncircumcised exult.
> [21]Mountains of Gilboa
>   Let neither dew or rain be upon you,
>   nor upland fields;
> For there the shield of the mighty warriors was defiled.
>   The shield of Saul was not anointed with oil.
> [22]From the blood of the slain, from the fat of the mighty warriors,
>   The bow of Jonathan did not turn back
>   and the sword of Saul did not return empty.
> [23]Saul and Jonathan, beloved and pleasant in their life,
>   and in death they were not separated;
> They were swifter than eagles,
>   they were mightier than lions.
> [24]Daughters of Israel weep for Saul,
>   who clothed you luxuriously with scarlet,
>   who put ornaments of gold on your apparel.
> [25]How the mighty warriors have fallen
>   in the midst of battle.
> Jonathan lies slain on your high places,
> [26]I am distressed for you, Jonathan my brother;
>   you were very pleasant to me.
> Wonderful was your love for me,
>   exceeding the love of women.
> [27]How the mighty warriors have fallen,
>   and the implements of war have perished.'

Notes on the text

4. *'ašer* introducing direct speech is unusual but not unparalleled (GKC §157c).

6. *na'ar* is ambiguous, but would not refer to the man's youth. As an Amalekite sojourner it may suggest he was a servant (so Fokkelman 1986: 639). The clause *niqrō' niqrêtî* appears to confuse the roots *qr'* and *qrh* and is corrected in several MSS so that the inf. abs. conforms to the finite verb. But the correction is intrinsically suspect. Both roots can mean 'befall' in ni. (e.g. Deut. 22:6 and Num. 23:4), so correction is unnecessary as they can be treated as byforms. *ba'alê happārāšîm* is unparalleled, but cannot just be 'horsemen' (as in NIV, NRSV, ESV, NASB), which requires only *happārāšîm*. The meaning 'masters' for *baʿalê* is well attested in construct relationships (see Gen. 14:13; 37:19; 49:23; Exod. 24:14; Deut. 15:2; Neh. 6:18), so the reference is probably to the officers (so McCarter 1984: 57).

7. 'Here I am' is technically correct for *hinnēnî*, but masks the structural development through the use of *hinnê* in vv. 6–7, and as the last word in the man's speech in v. 10, where it remains untranslated for reasons of English style. See Edelman 1991: 301.

9. *šābāṣ* is a hapax legomenon. The most obvious root, *šbṣ*, means 'to weave' (Exod. 28:20, 39), but it occurs only twice in the OT, and this noun's relationship to it is unclear (see BDB). LXX's 'terrible darkness' is probably a contextual guess. Perhaps the mixture that seizes Saul is being at the point between life and death, which then makes sense of the following clause. Hence 'throes of death' as the point where death and life seem to be mixed, but death has not yet triumphed. For the last clause's syntax, see Anderson 1989: 4.

15. For *pgʿ* as 'execute', see 1 Sam. 22:18; 1 Kgs 2:25, 34, 46 (also Hubbard 1984).

18. *qešet* (bow) is difficult and is tempting to omit (see McCarter 1984: 67–68, pointing to some LXX evidence), but it is difficult then to see how it arose. It is often retained as the lament's title, hence 'Song of the Bow', though evidence is not strong (see Gordon 1986: 210–211). AV (see Spero 1991) takes 'bow' as the direct object, but needs the article. Fokkelman's solution (1986: 651) is elegant, treating *qešet* as the defective pl. noun *qāšōt*.

19. LXX reflects a doublet of the end of *bāmôt*. McCarter (1984: 74–75; cf. Barrick 1997) treats *bāmôt* anatomically. Although possible, the link to high ground throughout the poem renders this unlikely.

21. *śĕdê tĕrûmâ* is difficult, but not impossible. Although *tĕrûmâ* is elsewhere an offering (Deut. 12:6, 11; Ezek. 20:40; Num. 15:19–21), it comes from a root meaning 'high'. We assume that *tĕrûmâ* can be used in a secular sense, as also can *bāmôt*, so it refers to an upland area (Youngblood 1992: 815–816).

24. A number of MSS have *ʿal* for MT *ʾel*, but the two can be interchangeable. Some correct *hammalbiškem* to *hammalbišken*, conforming to the f. subject, but such confusion is common with pl. suffixes, not all of which are fully represented in HB. See GKC §135o and examples there.

26. *niplĕʾatâ* is odd, but is perhaps a lamed-alpeh verb adopting lamed-he vowels. See GKC §75oo.

Form and structure

Saul's death was narrated in 1 Sam. 31. Because David was in the far south fighting Amalekites while Saul was in the far north fighting the Philistines,

David could not have known Saul was dead. Having been sent from the battle (1 Sam. 29), he knew conflict with Saul was coming, but could not know the outcome. Thus it is appropriate that 2 Samuel opens with his hearing of Saul's death (vv. 1–10). Within the structure of the Accession Narrative (1 Sam. 27 – 2 Sam. 1), in which all accounts are part of doubled structures, we expect a full account to be given to him even though it would be possible simply to note Saul and Jonathan's deaths were reported to David. But the doubling strategy always offers more through the second account, this time explaining how Saul's badges of rank reached David. That does not require this report to be entirely reliable (see 'Form and structure' on 1 Sam. 31; Fokkelman 1986: 641–542; B. T. Arnold 1989; but note Bergen 1996: 288, whose harmonization follows Josephus, *Ant.* 6.370–372), since it is only through recording inconsistencies that we see how the Amalekite is driven by his own goals. Mauchline's observation (1971: 197) that the Amalekite's story 'rings true' is rendered improbable by the narrative's poetics.

As with Saul's death in 1 Sam. 31:1–13, this account is linked to the surrounding material through key terms. The most obvious is that the man reporting to David is an Amalekite, a member of the nation Saul failed to destroy in 1 Sam. 15. David was raiding them in 1 Sam. 27:8, and they raided Ziklag in 1 Sam. 30, leading to David's pursuing them. But there is a further verbal link in that the man came to David on the third day (v. 2), which was also the time David took from Aphek to Ziklag (1 Sam. 30:1) and the period another Amalekite was abandoned in the wilderness (1 Sam. 30:13). These verbal associations indicate that this Amalekite account is an integrated component in the narrative, not an addition from another source. However, Polzin's (1993: 5–6) tortuous attempt to see the Amalekite as a stand-in for David himself is not required. The Amalekite's literary associations are so strongly with Saul's failures that he stands only as a counterpoint to David in terms of reacting to Saul's death and the possibilities opened up.

Most commentators treat vv. 17–27 separately from 1–16. As a poem it is clearly substantially different. Nevertheless, it is appropriate to treat it here because it follows naturally from vv. 1–16. In one sense it breaks the doubling structure that has run since 1 Sam. 27, since this is the only poem. Yet the content continues the repetition strategy since both David's decision to execute the Amalekite and his lament over Saul and Jonathan represent two responses to the news of their deaths. 2 Sam. 1:1–16 is thus a hinge that provides the parallel to Saul's death in 1 Sam. 31 and David's response to it, with David's second response in 2 Sam. 1:17–27. This structural device prepares for the end of the Accession Narrative as a component in Samuel, while also highlighting the lament's importance as the climax of the whole. That we move into a different section of the book is apparent from the return to episodic narration in 2 Sam. 2.

The lament is carefully structured (see A. H. van Zyl 1998: 667), gradually moving its focus from Saul to Jonathan. It is built around its refrain (vv. 19b, 25a, 27a), though there are also repeated references to 'high places' (vv. 19a, 25c), while Saul and Jonathan together are beloved and pleasant (23a), themes repeated for Jonathan individually (26b, c). Both the 'daughters of the Philistines' (23c) and the 'daughters of Israel' (24a) are mentioned, the two forming a contrast between those who should not exult and those who should mourn. These repetitions bind the poem together, while reference to the Philistine women as daughters of the uncircumcised links it to Saul's reference to the Philistines in 1 Sam. 31:4.

The poem's placement here provides both the Accession Narrative's climax and also a theological reflection that closes off the whole of Samuel so far. Structurally, Samuel is built around three major poetic blocks: Hannah's Song (1 Sam. 2:1–10), David's lament (2 Sam. 1:17–27) and David's two reflective pieces (2 Sam. 22:1 – 23:7). Kingship is central in each poem. Hannah's Song anticipates kingship. In David's lament, Saul's failure to provide the kingship required is considered, while the reflective pieces consider how kingship can make a positive contribution. Hannah's Song and the reflective pieces are at the book's boundaries, and the lament is its turning point as we move from Saul to David. The lament refuses to condemn Saul and Jonathan. Their memory is to be honoured. At the same time, it prepares for David's arrival as king, even if that is incomplete until 5:5.

Comment

The Amalekite's report: 1:1–10

1–2. The synchronizations that have aligned David and Saul since 1 Sam. 28:3 continue, noting that David returned from defeating the Amalekites (1 Sam. 30) and remained two days in Ziklag. This shows that David was not involved in Saul's death, though it also prepares for a repetition of the 'third day' motif when a messenger arrived with news of Saul. The allusions to the death of Eli (1 Sam. 4:11–18) in 1 Sam. 31 continue as this messenger is described in words almost identical to those used for the Benjaminite who reported in 1 Sam. 4:11, reinforcing the changeover in power taking place here. It is unclear if this messenger was in Saul's forces, or that he merely came from Saul's camp, but his torn garments and the dirt upon his head were traditional signs of grief. The narrative initially refrains from identifying the messenger, reporting only that he approached David with proper respect, prostrating himself as one would do before a king.

3–4. Although the man comes as a messenger, David commences the discussion, asking where the man comes from. His reply is terse, indicating that he has escaped from the camp of Israel's army. The use of *mlṭ* (escape, slip away) evokes David's escapes from Saul (1 Sam. 19:10, 12, 17–18), but retains the ambiguity present in Jonathan's use of the verb in 20:29.

Has he escaped as one who fled from the battle, or as one who decided to save his life and go somewhere safer? David does not necessarily see the ambiguity but knowing that a battle had been about to take place asks for information about it. His question is short and direct but coupled with a command demanding clarity, 'Tell me.' The man's appearance indicates the battle went badly, but David indicates he is not to be spared any details. Responding to David's two-part question, the man answers with three elements that gradually move closer to Saul and Jonathan's situation: the army has fled from the battle, many have fallen and died, and, finally, Saul and Jonathan are dead.

5–10. Only now does David know of Saul's fate, though he lacks information on how they died, or how the messenger knows these things. Hence he questions the messenger more closely, beginning by asking how the man knew Saul and Jonathan had died. The man's response provides an account of how they died as well. It is not an account that squares with the previous chapter, though not as different as sometimes suggested. Indeed, there are enough similarities to suggest that the man has introduced changes only where he believes it will present him more favourably to David. The man's words are carefully chosen, indicating only that he was on Mount Gilboa by chance and Saul was leaning on his spear. It is unclear what condition Saul was in. He might have been badly wounded or he might simply have been tired. The man also reported that Saul faced the imminent arrival of the Philistine cavalry and chariots, though the presence of the latter on Gilboa is odd since chariots would be better suited to the Jezreel valley below rather than the mountain's slopes. But he could have meant the mountain's lower slopes, so this is not necessarily evidence of unreliability. The man claims that Saul saw and summoned him, and that he had acknowledged this summons. Saul had asked for more information, so the man had told him he was an Amalekite. In the context of the man's report, there is nothing exceptional about this, but within the larger narrative this triggers a range of important associations (see above, 'Form and structure'). Amalekites within this narrative are intrinsically untrustworthy, enemies of God's people. The man's speech now operates at two levels: it recounts what he claimed took place, while allowing the narrator to hint that these may be the actions of an unreliable character who stands within a pattern of actions opposed to Yahweh's will. The man does not know this, and continues with his account, claiming that Saul asked him to stand over him and kill him since he knew he would die anyway and wanted only a comparatively merciful ending. This the man had done. In response to David's question of how he knew Saul and Jonathan were dead, he claims not only that he was an eyewitness, but that he was the one who had finally killed Saul at his own request. But he is silent about Jonathan's death. The man's evidence of how he knew of their death was Saul's crown and armlet, his badges of rank, which he presented to David. From the man's point of view, this proved Saul and Jonathan had died as he claimed, though it also demonstrates that David had not taken the crown and armlet by force. The kingdom and its signs were coming to him; he was not seeking them.

David executes the Amalekite: 1:11–16

11–12. David's response, along with that of his men, is traditional, showing the normal signs of public mourning with torn clothes, weeping and fasting until evening. Yet, though traditional, his response is surprising since an enemy's death would not normally be marked like this. Certainly, it would surprise the Amalekite, who imagined he was bringing David good news from which the Amalekite might profit. David not only mourns for Saul and Jonathan, though the lament places them at the centre of his actions; he mourns for the whole of the army and the nation. He knows this was a devastating defeat, and the whole of the north now comes under Philistine domination. Saul's death was significant for the whole of Israel, and David mourns for the whole of the nation.

13–16. After the period of mourning, David again spoke to the Amalekite, though this time it was more an interrogation. The Amalekite apparently believed David would approve of his actions. David's first question was a surprise, asking where the man had come from. The man has already indicated he is an Amalekite (v. 8), so David is not asking for his ethnicity. Rather, he needs to know if the man is subject to Israelite justice. Bloodguilt would probably apply anyway, but indicating that he is a resident foreigner means he is subject to Israelite law (see Epsztein 1986: 115–118). The man is ethnically Amalekite, but places himself within Israel's social context. This adds poignancy to David's second question about why the man was not afraid to destroy Yahweh's anointed, not least because David is also Yahweh's anointed (Alter 1999: 198). In 1 Sam. 24:7 [ET 24:6] and 26:9–11 David used similar language to indicate why neither he nor Abishai should kill Saul, in spite of the benefits David would receive from Saul's death. In 1 Sam. 24 he refused to kill Saul himself. In 1 Sam. 26 he declined Abishai's offer even though it meant he did not personally bear the guilt for Saul's death, although he would have authorized it. Here he can accept the benefits of Saul's death without having authorized his killing. David's question, however, shows he still will not approve of Saul's killing, a point emphasized by not recording the Amalekite's response. Instead, David orders the man's execution, stating that his own words show his guilt since they are a virtual confession. David's language is forensic, describing the man's speech as testimony, though the crime is not only murder (Exod. 20:13), but more specifically the killing of Yahweh's anointed. David's view in 26:10 was that only Yahweh could end Saul's life, so any human action against him was rebellion against Yahweh.

David's lament over Saul and Jonathan: 1:17–27

17–18. David's first reaction to Saul and Jonathan's deaths is to execute the man who has confessed to killing Saul. His second is to lament, the authenticity of which is widely accepted (see Birch 1998: 1205, though note Robinson 1993: 158). The lament (*qînâ*) is a traditional funeral song (Ezek. 28:11–19; Amos 5:1–2), and so entirely appropriate. Typically, these laments look back on the life of the dead, sometimes addressing them directly, though the form was borrowed for a range of contexts. Hence, although there are none in Psalms, the book of Lamentations employs the *qînâ* in its reflections on the fall of Jerusalem. Although the *qînâ* is sometimes said to follow a particular metre, that is not evident here as the metre is irregular (see Fokkelman 1986: 677). Of more importance is how the dirge allows David to express his own sorrow over the deaths of his king and his friend, though this sorrow was not restricted to him alone. Rather, Saul and Jonathan's deaths pointed to the harsh realities of life in the face of the Philistine threat (see 'Notes'), and the song should be taught to Judah so all would understand. That David's instructions were concerned only with Judah might point to the division between the northern and southern kingdoms he would work to overcome, though the concern was probably that his own supporters understood the situation. However, the song's wider role in instruction is clear from its recording in the Book of Jashar (the Book of the Upright), a collection of ancient songs mentioned in Josh. 10:13.

19–20. The song proper begins here. In it David addresses Israel, insisting its honour is slain on its high place. Yahweh is neither addressed nor mentioned in the song. Apart from v. 21's addressing of the battle site, it is always addressed to Israel. The opening word 'honour' (*ṣĕbî*) can also mean 'gazelle' and there may be an intentional play on these homonyms given the later references to Saul and Jonathan's speed (v. 23). The pl. of the word also occurs in Song of Songs as a play on the name Yahweh of Hosts (2:7, 9, 17; 3:5), though the hosts here are Israel's army. But it is the nation's honour that lies slain on its high places (*bāmôt*). Although high places are subsequently rejected as places of pagan worship (1 Kgs 12:31–32), the religious connotation is absent here, and the word simply points to Israel's mountains as where they were killed. The place where Saul sought to gain his tactical advantage was where he was defeated and died. This death was a tragedy as is evident from the exclamation at the end of v. 19, 'How the mighty warriors have fallen' (cf. 1 Maccabees 9.21). This works as a refrain in the song, recurring in 25a and 27a. David does not refer to the whole of Israel's army. The warriors whose deaths he mourns are Saul and Jonathan alone. If Israel's honour lies fallen, then Israel must remain silent, so this news cannot be announced in the representative Philistine cities of Gath (see Mic. 1:10) or Ashkelon. For them, these deaths would be good news (*bśr*) to be announced, but for Israel silence is required. Moreover, should this news be announced by Israel to their enemies it would be the Philistine women who rejoiced. This links to the Israelite women's rejoicing when David and Saul returned after Goliath's death (1 Sam. 18:6–7). Then they sang and rejoiced after David had slain the 'uncircumcised' Philistine (1 Sam. 17:36). Now the risk is that the daughters of the uncircumcised exult. In reality the Philistines would make this known, but Israel should not give them extra reasons for celebration.

21. The song's focus shifts to the battle site, effectively wishing that it be cursed by the lack of dew or rain. A place without water becomes uninhabitable, and David wishes that for where Saul and Jonathan died, so it no longer has rich fields on its lower slopes (similarly, Gilgamesh's lament for Enkidu, *Gilg.* 8.1, 4–22; see Yee 1988b: 570–571 for parallels). The link between this curse and their deaths is made explicit in the second half of the verse. Gilboa was where the shield of these warriors was defiled by death, so Saul's shield would no longer be oiled in preparation for battle. David's use of 'anointed' in describing Saul's shield is striking, since *māšîaḥ* elsewhere in Samuel refers to the anointed king. The rubbing of shields with oil to keep them in good condition is well attested, but there is special poignancy generated through the associations triggered by this word. Reference to the shields also initiates a series of references to Saul and Jonathan's equipment in the next verse, a theme closed off by the song's last line.

22–23. David now celebrates Jonathan and Saul's military achievements, their names presented in an ABBA chiasm, which emphasizes their closeness in life and death. The references to military equipment from the previous verse continue, showing that both Jonathan and Saul were effective warriors. Although lamenting their fall, David stresses their achievements as warriors before whom many had fallen. The song celebrates Jonathan's effectiveness with the bow and Saul's with the sword, though these are representative of their weapons. Where v. 22 looks back, v. 23 reflects on their death. Jonathan and Saul together are described as beloved and lovely, terms David uses again to describe his relationship with Jonathan in v. 26. Saul's inclusion again indicates David's commitment to him. Saul had pursued him, but David could still see that he was beloved in the nation. Jonathan and Saul's beauty is seen in their unity: just as they were together in life, so also in death. David's eulogy even sees them swifter than eagles and stronger than lions, phrases pointing to them as surpassing warriors. Such expressions might seem strange within David's story – Saul and Jonathan quarrelled over David (esp. in 1 Sam. 20), and Saul could never actually catch David. But a lament is not the place to point to someone's failings, and David's is gracious towards Saul. Their life and death was to be remembered, and their achievements were elevated in memory.

24–25a. David now addresses the Israelite women, summoning them to weep for Saul. Jonathan is not included here, so v. 24 speaks only of Saul, whereas vv. 25b–26 speak only of Jonathan, with the refrain closing off each section and covering both. The address to these women balances the earlier reaction of the Philistine women when they heard of Jonathan and Saul's death. The Philistine women should not rejoice, but the Israelite women should weep. The reason given is that Saul had enabled them to be clothed lavishly in scarlet cloth and gold jewellery. These lines of the lament are linked by a play on the similar sound of 'ădānîm (luxuries) and 'ădî (ornaments) that come between the two references to garments and create a minor chiasm within the song. Again the song goes beyond the experience of most Israelite women, for whom Saul would hardly have provided any significant wealth, but may suggest times when Saul shared the bounty he had won for the nation. Perhaps the crucial point is that David will not declare Saul's rule a failure, and so closes this section on Saul with the refrain from v. 19b.

25b–27. The song's closing section focuses on Jonathan alone before closing with the refrain. The language describing Jonathan as fallen on the high places picks up the terminology of v. 19a. It is unlikely that David suggests that Israel's honour there refers only to Jonathan (against Fokkelman 1986: 670; Baldwin 1988: 181) since the song celebrates both Jonathan and Saul, but by returning to this language the song still offers Jonathan special honour. Where David summoned others to weep for Saul, his comments about Jonathan are much more personal. The hyperbole prominent in vv. 22–24 is absent. This is David's grief following Jonathan's death in all its raw agony, though without precluding poetic skill. David speaks of his distress at Jonathan's death, a distress made worse by the friendship they had shared. His distress is shaped by the strength of the relationship he had shared with Jonathan, a relationship that was very pleasant, so much so that Jonathan's love for David exceeded that of women. The choice of this terminology is partly shaped by the fact that David deliberately echoes his description of Saul and Jonathan in v. 23, though the roots n'm (pleasant) and 'hb (lovely, beloved) are reversed, creating another minor chiasm within the lament. In spite of the reference to the love of women, Jonathan's love for David was not homoerotic (see on 18:1 and literature cited there; also A. H. van Zyl 1998: 672), but Jonathan had absolute political commitment to him, demonstrated through his enabling David to escape in 1 Sam. 20, and the constant covenant-making between them (1 Sam. 18:3; 20:8; 23:20). Jonathan's love for David was deep and abiding, of a different type to that of women. This love was prepared to sacrifice personal gain for a friend, surrendering a claim to the throne for the one recognized as more fitted to the role. It is the loss of this love that is distressing to David. On this note, the lament returns to the refrain from vv. 19b and 25a, adding that along with the loss of Saul and Jonathan, the implements of war have also been destroyed. Israel stands on the brink, without their king or his son, and without weaponry to proceed. It is powerlessness marked by a power vacuum in the centre. Such are the hard times for which David required this song to be recorded and taught.

Explanation

The climactic account of David's move towards the throne comes to its conclusion. David's rise continues as the subsequent chapters follow him from Judah's throne to that of Israel and Judah, but the section begun at 27:1 is concluded. It retains the central narrative elements present through this section with their constant references to Philistines and Amalekites and the final set of doubled accounts. This time we have the second account of Saul's death in vv. 1–16, which acts as a hinge by also recording the first of David's two responses to the news of the father and son's death with the execution of the Amalekite who claims to have killed Saul. David's second response is presented in the elegy he required the people of Judah to know so that they would understand hard times.

As is typical of Samuel, each account adds something new, extending what we knew before. In terms of Saul's death, David learns some of the truth from an unreliable narrator, an Amalekite who claimed to have finished off Saul himself. The claim is false but part of the man's strategy to ingratiate himself with David and justify his bringing of Saul's badges of rank. It is thus shown that David did not seize the throne, and that he retained his policy of respecting the life of Yahweh's anointed. David had twice previously refused to claim the throne by violence (1 Sam. 24, 26). Instead, he waited for Yahweh to bring it to him. Because of this policy, we are introduced to the first element of David's response, which is to execute the man. He was probably a scavenger who found Saul's remains before the Philistines did and saw his opportunity to take them to David for reward. Yet he did not realize that, in accordance with the synchronized chronology of the whole of 1 Sam. 27 – 2 Sam. 1, while the Philistines were defeating Israel, David was overcoming an Amalekite band. We are twice told this man was an Amalekite, once as information volunteered (v. 8) and once under questioning from David (v. 13). The label is enough to generate suspicion, but he is executed by David for claiming to have killed Saul. David does not have the account from 1 Sam. 31, and so acts on the information given to him, but the central point remains that David would not seize the throne. It could come only as Yahweh brought it. Violence, though ever present, could not bring the kingdom.

David's second response is the beautiful lament in vv. 19–27. The song is a moving tribute to Saul and Jonathan, and underscores the main point from his response to the Amalekite – David would not deliberately destroy them. The song is infused with David's sense of loss, though showing more grace towards Saul than Saul showed David, while highlighting his profound sense of loss with Jonathan's death. But as something intended to be taught, we already see David acting as king. He ensures that Judah understands that having a king is no guarantee of safety. The mighty fall in battle and the nation still face difficulties more profound than it imagines.

The lament offers concluding reflections on Israel's first attempt at monarchy. Hannah's Song (1 Sam. 2:1–10) anticipated monarchy (1 Sam. 2:10), while the two songs in 22:1 – 23:7 look back over David's reign. Samuel is structured around these poetic reflections. Hannah's Song looks forward, David's closing songs look back, while this song provides a hinge into the next section, the beginning of David's reign. As such, it looks back over Saul and Jonathan with fondness, but fondness shaped by the knowledge that Saul has failed. The nation asked for a king to lead them in battle (1 Sam. 8:19–20), while Yahweh's goal for Saul was to deliver Israel from Philistine control and to restrain the nation (1 Sam. 9:16–17). The threefold lament 'How the mighty warriors have fallen' tacitly highlights these points, because Saul achieved neither. These things the nation must learn. Saul's death also resolves the issue which has endured since David's anointing in 1 Sam. 16:13. Now there is only one who is Yahweh's anointed, and David knows that Saul has not done what was set before him. His failures in 1 Sam. 13 and 15 made clear that he did not understand the constitutional monarchy set forth in 1 Sam. 12. The future lies with David. But it is a future that has hope only if the people and the incoming king learn the lessons of the past.

2 SAMUEL 2:1–11

Translation

[1]After this, David enquired of Yahweh, 'Shall I go up into one of the cities of Judah?' Yahweh said to him, 'Go up.' David said, 'Where shall I go up?' So he said, 'To Hebron.' [2]David went up there with his two wives, Ahinoam the Jezreelite and Abigail the widow of Nabal of Carmel. [3]David also brought his men who were with him, each with his household, and they stayed in the cities of Hebron. [4]Then the men of Judah came and anointed David as king over the house of Judah there.

When they told David, 'It was the men of Jabesh Gilead who buried Saul,' [5]he sent messengers to the men of Jabesh Gilead and said to them, 'May you be blessed by Yahweh because you have shown this loyalty to your lord Saul, and buried him. [6]Now may Yahweh show you loyalty and faithfulness, and, for myself, I will also establish this friendship with you since you have done this thing. [7]Now strengthen your hands and be valiant, because your lord Saul has died, but the house of Judah has anointed me as king over them.'

[8]But Abner ben Ner, commander of Saul's army, took Saul's son Ish-bosheth, brought him to Mahanaim, [9]and made him king for Gilead, the Ashurites and Jezreel and over Ephraim, Benjamin and all Israel. [10]Ish-bosheth ben Saul was forty

years old when he became king over Israel, and he reigned for two years, though the house of Judah went after David. [11]The time David was king in Hebron over the house of Judah was seven years and six months.

Notes on the text

4. Retaining *'ăšer* in the final clause creates a wordy sentence. It is omitted by LXX, Syr and Vg. But awkward composition is an insufficient basis for omission. 4QSam[a] has lost text at this point through homoioteleuton (see Fincke 2001: 118).

5. LXX could suggest *ba'alîm* (leaders) and is supported by McCarter (1984: 81). But Anderson (1989: 27) is probably correct to suggest this is a deliberate alteration because of context.

6. The demonstrative *zō't* is awkward unless one recognizes *ṭôbâ* as a treaty term meaning 'friendship' (NRSV, 'reward' is inappropriate). Previously bound by a form of treaty to Saul, David offered the same relationship to the town (see McCarter 1984: 85).

8. It is generally agreed that Ish-bosheth is a deliberately corrupted form of Eshbaal (or perhaps Ishbaal), as in 1 Chr. 8:33. In the tenth century BC, *ba'al* probably did not refer to Canaanite worship and may have been a title for Yahweh meaning 'lord' or 'husband' (see Hos. 2:18 [ET 2:16]). The word *bōšet* means 'shame' and is regularly used in Samuel for names that compound with *ba'al*. Hence, instead of Eshbaal, ''Baal (the lord) exists', we have Ish-bosheth, 'man of shame'. Similarly, Meribaal becomes Mephibosheth in 2 Sam. 4:4. Curiously, in 1 Sam. 12:11 the form Jerubbaal is retained for Gideon, but in 2 Sam. 11:21 the form Jerubbesheth is used. This indicates the substitution comes from sources associated with David's court.

9. Ashurites are mentioned in Num. 24:22, 24; Ps. 83:8. Syr and Vg suggest Geshurites, but the difficulty is that they were known to have their own king then (2 Sam. 3:3; see Fokkelman 1990: 368). Tg has 'Asher', which is plausible if understood as part of a claimed realm (standing for the whole of Galilee), not an actual one (see Gordon 1986: 213–214). Ashurites is retained as the more difficult reading.

9. The prepositions *'el* and *'al* are frequently interchangeable, but some distinction is recognized, since the first three referents for Ish-bosheth's reign are governed by *'el* and the second three by *'al*.

Form and structure

After many twists since David's anointing in 1 Sam. 16:13, we finally reach the point where he begins to reign (see 'Form and structure' on 1 Sam. 9:1 – 10:16 on Saul and David's accessions). Saul is dead, and the people can freely acknowledge David as king. However, nothing runs smoothly, because as Judah anointed David as their king, Abner appointed Saul's son Ish-bosheth king over a section of the northern tribes. David's long rise to the throne is not over yet, something passed over in 1 Chr. 11:1–4. By describing only the end of the process, it could give the impression of a smooth transition. Instead, we move into a new section of Samuel with rival claimants to the throne, though only one is anointed. Hence there is conflict between these claimants until Ish-bosheth's murder in 2 Sam. 4. The major issue of how David dealt with Saul is resolved, but it leads to the parallel problem of Ish-bosheth and Abner, Saul's military commander who was the power behind Ish-bosheth. The themes of the longer conflict narrative between David and Saul are repeated through the following account. The use of such a narrative patterning recurs in 2 Sam. 20. There the short account of Sheba's rebellion follows the longer account of Absalom's. This patterning highlights the continual struggles David faced in establishing his realm.

The narrative consists of three brief reports dealing with David's move to Hebron at Yahweh's direction, his attempt to develop sound relations with Jabesh Gilead and Abner's decision to appoint Ish-bosheth as king over the north. Although originating separately, they contrast these kings and their kingdoms, and are joined by their concluding references to David as king of Judah (see Fokkelman 1990: 25). David's actions are marked by devotion to Yahweh. He goes to Hebron only at Yahweh's direction, and when he arrives he is anointed by the townspeople. David's dealings with Jabesh Gilead are similarly marked by concern for Yahweh, specifically asking that Yahweh show them the same loyalty (*ḥesed*) they showed Saul, even as he asks them to recognize the legitimacy of his reign. By contrast, Yahweh is unmentioned in Abner's appointment of Ish-bosheth as king at Mahanaim. A reference to Ish-bosheth's anointing is conspicuous only by its absence. The narrative thus points to David's legitimacy, while denying any such claim for Ish-bosheth. In the light of Saul's experience and these statements about Ish-bosheth, there can be only one winner in this conflict. Nevertheless, the narrative insists that David was not involved in the murders that finally led to his accession over the whole nation. Although David now enters combat as Judah's king, he still will not seize power for himself. It must be Yahweh who brings power to him.

Comment

David becomes king in Hebron: 2:1–4a

1. No attempt is made to indicate how long David remained at Ziklag after hearing of Saul and Jonathan's deaths (1:3–10), or how long he mourned. Instead, there is a generalizing statement indicating that at some point he began the process by which he would formally become king. There is also no reference to Philistine attitudes, though when Saul died he was (notionally) a Philistine vassal (see Anderson 1989: 25, but contrast Cartledge 2001: 365). These issues do not concern the narrator. Rather, the focus is on how Yahweh determined David's actions. The form of David's enquiry suggests use of the ephod Abiathar had brought (1 Sam. 23:6), and that he used in determining to pursue the Amalekites following their raid on Ziklag (1 Sam. 30:7–8). But this is not made specific. Rather, two questions are recorded (see 1 Sam. 23:1–4, 9–13; 30:8), where David is first told he should go up to one of the towns in Judah, and then to Hebron. Some 20 miles south-west of Jerusalem and at an elevation of about 3,000 feet, Hebron is the highest town in Israel, so the verb 'go up' ('ālâ) is particularly appropriate. After defeating the Amalekites, David had distributed booty in Judah's south and especially in Hebron (1 Sam. 30:31). It was thus a city likely to support him.

2–4a. Faithful to Yahweh's instruction, David went up to Hebron, taking his two wives with him. Since David also took his men and their households, mention of his wives might be considered redundant. But both women retained links to the region of Hebron. Ahinoam came from the Calebite town of Jezreel, while Abigail is again identified as Nabal's widow from Carmel (see 1 Sam. 30:5). Both towns are close to Hebron, and suggest possible support for David from local clans (see 'Comment' on 1 Sam. 25:39–44), a good reason for mentioning them here. Along with his wives, David took his men, presumably the six hundred who served him (1 Sam. 27:2) and their households. Such a large group could not be housed in Hebron alone, which is no doubt why they settled in the 'cities' of Hebron, its surrounding settlements. So many soldiers and their households could be seen as a regional takeover. Instead, the men of Judah as a whole came to David and anointed him there. This anointing says nothing of David's legitimacy as king since that depended on Samuel's earlier anointing. Just as Saul was secretly anointed and subsequently recognized, so also Judah now publicly recognizes David's status as king.

David negotiates with Jabesh Gilead: 2:4b–7

4b. Following his accession in Judah, David was told of the actions of the inhabitants of Jabesh Gilead in retrieving Saul's relics and burying them (1 Sam. 31:11–13). It is unclear if we are to understand this as something the men of Judah told him when he was anointed, or if v. 4b commences a new section, in which case the verb is impersonal. What matters here is not that Saul was buried, but that the men of Jabesh Gilead did it. Jabesh Gilead is a considerable distance from Hebron and there is no particular reason why the Judahites would have passed on this news, so an impersonal verb is more probable. The important point is that Jabesh Gilead represented northern Israel, so this news provided David with an important test. An abiding issue was the apparent division between north and south. David was confronted with an important challenge: Should he confirm his power at home before interacting with the northern tribes?

5–7. David's response was engagement, interacting with the north in a way that recognized their contribution while also enhancing his position. His message is notable for its carefully phrased language, which is built around references to the loyalty (*ḥesed*) of the Jabesh Gileadites and reference to Saul as their lord (*'ādôn*). In the midst of this he introduces reference to Yahweh to emphasize the bonds that united all the tribes. Hence he expresses two wishes: that they would be blessed by Yahweh because of their loyalty to their lord, and that Yahweh would show similar loyalty to them. It is astute political language, though no less meaningful for that. But to these wishes David adds two further comments that deal with his relationship with them. First, because of their loyalty to Saul, he desires to establish a similar friendship with them (see 'Notes'). He has evidence of their loyalty, and wishes to experience something similar. Secondly, he encourages them to strengthen themselves in the light of Saul's death, since Judah has anointed him as king. They are effectively invited to align themselves with David and Judah. But David does not compel their loyalty. Faced with Saul's most loyal supporters, he chooses to invite them to join him, making no threats if they do not. David will still not compel loyalty, but invites a group who are not his natural supporters to join him in a treaty relationship that recognizes him as king. The possibilities of such an invitation need time to be worked out in the light of the Philistine threat, but it is an important attempt to cultivate northern support and work towards national unity.

Ish-bosheth becomes king at Mahanaim: 2:8–11

8–9. The unity David sought faced an immediate challenge. While he was king in Judah, Saul's kinsman and general Abner (1 Sam. 14:50) took Saul's son Ish-bosheth and made him king in Mahanaim. The key contrast is that everything occurs at Abner's initiative. There is no anointing, public recognition or evidence of Yahweh's involvement. This is a political act that sought to retain the power of Saul's family, though suggesting that the real power remained with Abner since the verbs all refer to his actions. Ish-bosheth appears passive before him. Mahanaim, the site of this coronation, is in the Transjordan, on the south of the Jabbok (see Gen. 32:3 [ET 32:2]), and later becomes an important site for David during Absalom's rebellion (17:27). The key point for Abner is that it was away from both David and the Philistines, representing a base where he could build his power.

Ish-bosheth apparently survived the battle at Gilboa (1 Sam. 31:2). Mahanaim was a logical place to claim authority over Gilead, but the influence that could be wielded over Jezreel, Ephraim and Benjamin, all of which were west of the Jordan, would be limited. This is especially so when we recognize that these areas were under Philistine control, if not occupation, after Saul's defeat. The location of the otherwise unknown Ashurites cannot be determined, but taken with the other elements they probably represent a claim that Ish-bosheth governed an extensive territory summed up as 'all Israel', here meaning the northern tribes. It is doubtful that he actually governed these areas, and what we have here is empty propaganda claiming these areas for him. At best he had limited support in Gilead and Benjamin.

10–11. A chronological note is inserted to explain the time of Ish-bosheth's rule and David's time in Hebron, with Ish-bosheth said to be forty when he became king, subsequent to which he reigned for two years. David, by contrast, was in Hebron as king of Judah for seven years and six months. Although these numbers are sometimes thought to be problematic (Haelewyck 1995a: 184, suggests they indicate David had claimed Judah while Saul was still king), they are difficult only if we assume David and Jonathan were about the same age, since then Ish-bosheth would appear older than Jonathan given that David was thirty when he became king (2 Sam. 5:4–5). But if Jonathan was about ten years older than David, which is possible since in 1 Sam. 13:2 he was a military commander, while David is still a 'lad' (*na'ar*) when he encounters Goliath (1 Sam. 17:33), the difficulty is less acute. Ish-bosheth's age might be approximate, but would be near enough, and he would then be Saul's second son, otherwise known as Ishvi (1 Sam. 14:49; see Provan, Long and Longman 2003: 199–201). The more awkward question revolves around Ish-bosheth's rival reign of only two years, yet David reigned in Hebron for seven years and six months, moving to Jerusalem where he was king over Israel and Judah for thirty-three years. Since the narrator sees no difficulty, we have to assume that the differences in regnal periods are explicable. The most likely possibility is that Abner made Ish-bosheth king some time after David's recognition in the south, so some of the time is explained that way. Since David's capture of Jerusalem occurred after his accession to the throne of Israel and Judah (5:1–9), we should assume that the periods in 5:4–5 are rounded off and that David was king over Israel as well as Judah for a short period before he captured Jerusalem and made it his capital (see 1 Chr. 11:4). Perhaps more important than the specific chronology is the distinction between 'Ish-bosheth reigned...' whereas 'Judah followed David'. Ish-bosheth's statement refers to claimed status, whereas David had real support. Their conflict's outcome is thus subtly announced in advance, though it will be resolved through a complex series of political double-dealing, murders and Yahweh's inscrutable involvement.

Explanation

Following Saul's death, David finally moves to the throne. However, the narrative carefully shows that David does not seize it, even though he remains as Yahweh's anointed. Instead, David seeks Yahweh's will, even to the extent of deciding on his return to Judah and the city where he goes. Although Yahweh's chosen king, David cannot grasp power for his own purposes. He must still submit to Yahweh's purposes for him, and the validity of this submission is demonstrated when the men of Judah anoint him as king at Hebron. This anointing does not have the sacral authority of Samuel's earlier anointing of David (1 Sam. 16:13) but represents the point when David's right to rule as king is formally recognized for the first time.

As Judah's king, David faced two challenges, the effects of which are narrated to the end of 2 Sam. 4. First, he needed to win over the north, especially those loyal to Saul. To this end, he sent an embassy to Jabesh Gilead after he heard of their loyalty towards Saul in rescuing his remains and burying them. Although impressed by their actions, his larger concern was clearly that they now support him as the nation's legitimate king. Politics and faith are not separate as David offered a treaty relationship to Jabesh Gilead, even as he pointed out that Judah had anointed him as king. Thus they were invited to join him in the new direction Yahweh was leading the nation. This is tied into the second challenge, which is that Abner had taken Saul's surviving son, Ish-bosheth, and made him king over the north, although in reality his power base may never have been more than the region around Mahanaim. The seeds for conflict are generated as David must win over the north and deal with Ish-bosheth, and especially Abner as the power behind the throne.

In all this, the narrative hints at David's ultimate victory. Only he is Yahweh's anointed to whom Judah has voluntarily given allegiance. By contrast, Ish-bosheth was made king in the north by Abner. Saul's story showed that power did not have to be grasped, and even though David continued to face the challenge of the Saulides through Ish-bosheth, that principal remains. David sought Yahweh and now begins to become king of Israel. Even as he faces an unexpected challenge, that process remains. Power comes as Yahweh delivers it – it cannot be grasped as an end in itself.

2 SAMUEL 2:12 – 3:5

Translation

[12]Abner ben Ner went out with Ish-bosheth ben Saul's servants from Mahanaim to Gibeon. [13]But Joab ben Zeruiah and David's servants went out and met them by the pool of Gibeon. One group sat on one side of the pool, and one on the other. [14]Abner said to Joab, 'Let the lads get up and compete before us.' So Joab said, 'Let

them get up.' [15]So the lads got up and passed over by number, twelve for Benjamin and Ish-bosheth ben Saul and twelve from David's servants. [16]Each seized his fellow by the head and stabbed him in the side, so they fell together. So that place was called Helkath-Hazzurim, which is at Gibeon. [17]The battle was very severe that day, but Abner and the men of Israel were defeated before David's servants.

[18]Now the three sons of Zeruiah were there, Joab, Abishai and Asahel, and Asahel was light on his feet, like a gazelle of the field. [19]Asahel pursued Abner and did not turn aside to the right or the left from after Abner. [20]Abner looked behind him and said, 'Is that you Asahel?' He said, 'It is me.' [21]Abner said to him, 'Turn aside to your right or left and grab one of the lads and take his plunder for yourself.' But Asahel was unwilling to turn aside from following him. [22]Abner continued to say to Asahel, 'Turn aside from following me. Why should I strike you to the ground? How could I lift up my face before Joab your brother?' [23]But he refused to turn aside, so Abner struck him in the belly with a back thrust of his spear, so the spear came through his back. So he fell there and died on the spot. All who came to where Asahel had fallen and died stood still.

[24]Joab and Abishai also pursued Abner. The sun was setting when they came to the hill of Ammah which lies before Giah on the way to the wilderness of Gibeon. [25]The Benjaminites assembled behind Abner and became one band and stood on top of a hill. [26]Abner called to Joab, 'Shall the sword devour in perpetuity? Do you not know the end will be bitter? How long shall you not tell the people to turn from following their brothers?' [27]Joab said, 'As God lives, if you had not spoken, the people would not have given up the pursuit of their kin before morning.' [28]Joab sounded the trumpet and all the people stood and no longer pursued Israel, nor did they continue the battle.

[29]Abner and his men went through the Arabah all that night, walked the whole Bithron, and entered Mahanaim. [30]Joab returned from pursuing Abner and gathered all the people; nineteen men and Asahel were missing from David's servants. [31]But David's servants had struck down three hundred and sixty Benjaminites with Abner. [32]They carried Asahel and buried him in his father's tomb in Bethlehem, then Joab and his men walked all night and day and broke on them at Hebron. [3:1]The war between the house of Saul and the house of David was prolonged, but David continued to become stronger, while the house of Saul was weakening.

[2]Sons were born to David in Hebron. They were his firstborn, Amnon, to Ahinoam the Jezreelite, [3]and his second, Chileab, to Abigail the widow of Nabal the Carmelite, and the third, Absalom the son of Maacah, the daughter of Talmai the king of Geshur, [4]and the fourth, Adonijah, the son of Haggith, and the fifth, Shephatiah the son of Abital, [5]and the sixth, Ithream, to David's wife Eglah. These were born to David in Hebron.

Notes on text

2:16. Reading *wĕḥarbô* as a verb is required. Because the verb is rare, the infinitive plus pronominal suffix could be mistaken for the noun. BDB proposes emending *haṣṣurîm* to *haṣōdîm*, which is attractive as it links the field's name to the use of the word 'side' (*ṣad*), though the resulting 'Field of plotters' is less persuasive within the narrative context.

18. Some MSS omit *šām*, but attestation in the versions suggests its antiquity.

23. Most EVV have Abner using his spear's butt. But this is impossible as one could not penetrate the abdomen without something sharp. This translation takes *'aḥărê* adverbially. Elsewhere *'aḥar* occurs adverbially in nominal clauses in Gen. 22:13 and Ps. 68:26, admittedly as an adverb of space, but the pl. (as here) can describe motion (1 Sam. 12:20; 2 Kgs 19:21 = Isa. 37:22). Similarly, REB.

27. LXX supports 'Yahweh' for 'God', but 4QSam[a] supports MT. Reference to Yahweh in oaths is more common, which would explain LXX.

3:3. The name of the second son varies. Josephus (*Ant.* 7:21) follows 1 Chr. 3:1 with 'Daniel', while LXX reads 'Dalouia', possibly supported by 4QSam[a]. Other versions follow MT.

Form and structure

Abner's appointment of Ish-bosheth over some of the north while David ruled in the south meant inevitable conflict between David and the house of Saul. But rather than following this directly through David and Ish-bosheth as the group leaders, the conflict is actually worked out between their generals, Abner and Joab. The importance of this lies in that Abner eventually tries to defect to David, but the conflict between Abner and Joab makes this impossible, resulting in Joab's murdering Abner (2 Sam. 3:26–30). David is distanced from the conflict to show his innocence in respect of Abner's murder. By focusing on the conflict between David and Ish-bosheth through their generals, the way is prepared for 3:6–39 while also showing David becoming more powerful than Ish-bosheth.

This section contains two separate but linked battle reports (2:12–17; 2:18–28), to which a summary statement on casualties (2:29–32) and a concluding remark on the relative strength of both sides (3:1) is appended. Evidence for David's strength is provided by the list of his children born in Hebron (3:2–5). Such lists are an important element in the account of David's reign. A further list of sons born in Jerusalem is provided in 5:13–16, while lists of officials are given at 8:15–18 and 20:23–25. The son lists are combined in 1 Chr. 3:1–9. The first list of officials also includes David's sons (2 Sam. 8:18), thus linking the lists. The function of these lists has been variously interpreted, but it seems clear that they help to structure the account of David's reign. At the same time, there are formal differences between them. For example, the son list in 5:13–16 does not mention the mother of each son, though this is important here. Youngblood (1992: 859) suggests that 3:2–5 concludes the account of David's rise over

Hebron, and 5:13–16 concludes his rise in Jerusalem, while the two lists of dynastic officials close off the initial account of his reign and then the conflict within his family (Youngblood 1992: 909). This interpretation of the second son list and the lists of dynastic officials is workable, but the interpretation of the first is forced since we already know of David's position in Hebron (2:1–7). It seems better to assume that these lists have multiple purposes, and may not so much close off sections of 2 Samuel as provide bridges between them, giving information relevant at later points. Hence this son list indicates David's security, but also provides seed information for events from later in David's story. Something similar can be said for 5:13–16 and both lists of dynastic officials. This suggests that although 3:2–5 is inserted between 3:1 and its logical continuation at 3:6, the insertion is not random. Rather, it provides a complex tool for showing David's position while foregrounding elements that become important later.

Comment

Conflict at Gibeon: 2:12–17

12–13. How the conflict developed between the houses of Saul and David does not interest the narrator. All that matters is that the conflict exists and has its roots in Saul's earlier pursuit of David. Accordingly, we plunge straight into military hostilities, with Ish-bosheth represented by Saul's general, Abner, and David by Joab. We have been told that Abner established Ish-bosheth in Mahanaim (2:8) and that Ish-bosheth's claimed territory was in the north while David's was in the south. Accordingly, Abner's decision to bring his forces from Mahanaim across the Jordan to Gibeon was an important territorial claim since Gibeon lies more or less on the country's north–south divide, perhaps near the border between them. About 6 miles north-west of Jerusalem, Gibeon (modern el-Jib) was traditionally Benjaminite territory and close to Saul's capital at Gibeah. But it was also traditionally non-Israelite, its status reaching back to events in Josh. 9. We cannot assume the city was favourably disposed towards the house of Saul since 21:1–14 indicates considerable animosity. Abner may have wanted to take a strategic site that strengthened his southern border, or at least claim authority within the area. David could not permit such a claim, and was represented by Joab, who along with his two brothers is known as a 'son of Zeruiah' (see 'Comment' on 1 Sam. 26:6–7). One of his brothers, Abishai, was introduced in 1 Sam. 26:6–12, while a third brother named Asahel features in 2:18–23. But Joab is a central figure in the story of David as king. He is David's hard man, but one who has his own agenda. Quite what the Philistines made of this as the dominant power after Saul's death is unclear since David threw off their yoke only after moving to Jerusalem (5:17–25), though they may have fondly imagined David was working for them. In any case, both sides met at a pool in Gibeon, a component in the city's extensive water system (see Jer. 41:12), with each side taking a position opposite the other.

14–16. The details of the resulting conflict are unclear (which is partly why Polzin 1993: 33, regards the account as stylized), but it seems to be representative combat, such as the single combat proposed by Goliath in 1 Sam. 17:1–11. Rather than single combat, Abner and Joab each agreed to count off twelve men to fight each other, with the fighting described euphemistically as 'competing'. Abner's men are called Benjaminites, suggesting that Ish-bosheth's support was localized. Since Abner suggested this, he might have felt it would be to his advantage, though it did not work out that way. Again, the terminology shows that the conflict was between David and the house of Saul, even though neither David nor Ish-bosheth was present. Unfortunately, no clear result was achieved, as the representatives seem to have stabbed each other with knives carried during wrestling, so that all fell. Everyone might not have died, as some might have fallen wounded, but no clear winner emerged. A number of ancient reliefs depict scenes similar to this, including one from Syria more or less contemporary with these events (Alter 1999: 205). Because of the conflict, the place became known as Helkath-Hazzurim. The name's meaning is unclear (see 'Notes'), and the consonants can mean either 'field of adversaries' or 'field of flint knives' (i.e. the knives the men used). Either would be appropriate in the light of the events described.

17. Single combat between David and Goliath did not resolve conflict (1 Sam. 17:52–53), and representative combat was similarly unsuccessful here. Instead, full battle was now joined, a battle noted for its fierceness. If Abner hoped to gain an advantage through representative combat, such a possibility was not only lost to him but his forces were beaten back by David's. Saul could never overcome David, and neither could his house after him.

Conflict between Abner and the sons of Zeruiah: 2:18–28

18–19. Although a wider conflict is described as the battle moves away from Gibeon, the narrator's focus is narrower. Of Zeruiah's three sons, only Joab's presence was previously noted, but we are now told that her three sons were present, including the previously unmentioned Asahel. Asahel's importance is highlighted by the fact that whereas Joab and Abishai's presence at the battle is noted, we immediately focus on one characteristic of Asahel, his speed as a runner, which is compared to a wild gazelle (cf. 1:23; in 2 Sam. 23:24 Asahel is listed among David's elite troops). This element is highlighted because his speed separates him from his brothers, enabling him to pursue Abner once the battle turns in favour of David's forces. His speed was not, however, matched with the tactical awareness to realize he should not be separated from his own forces. Asahel's pursuit of Abner is single minded and committed, and 'did not turn aside to the right or the left', introducing a key phrase in Abner's attempted negotiations with him.

20–21. As Abner left the scene, he was aware of pursuit, though he needed to question his pursuer to confirm his suspicion that it was Asahel. Presumably, Asahel was well known, though Abner might have known him from before. Certainly, he was conscious of the need to avoid creating an additional feud with Joab. With Asahel's identity confirmed, Abner asks him to turn aside to the right or left, precisely what he has not previously done, though he suggests Asahel attack one of his soldiers and claim whatever spoil he might. Asahel's single mindedness in the pursuit is made clear as we are again told he is unwilling to turn aside.

22–23. Again, Abner asks Asahel to turn aside, this time effectively threatening him, even though it is phrased as a question. Each stage of the dialogue has raised the stakes in the pursuit, so the danger to Asahel is now made clear. Nevertheless, Abner's concern about how he will lift his face in Joab's presence (be able to dialogue with him) should he kill Asahel indicates that his greater concern is with the blood feud that might be generated even if Asahel is legitimately killed in battle. Joab was clearly known as someone not to be crossed, something that becomes clear in later narratives. Again Asahel refuses to turn aside, so Abner defends himself with a back-stab of his spear into Asahel's stomach. Asahel must have been lightly armoured to have run so fast, but it is still a sign of considerable force that Abner can force the spear right through him. Asahel must also have run ahead of most of his forces, and they stop when they reach the spot where he lies (see 20:12). Abner averts pursuit but initiates the blood feud he dreads.

24–25. The focus switches to Joab and Abishai as they arrived with the rest of the troops after Abner. That sunset came while they were still in the vicinity of Gibeon suggests the initial conflict occurred late in the day (unless we emend the text to refer to Gibeah or Geba; so Baldwin 1988: 186), though the exact site of the hill of Ammah or Giah is unknown, but must be sufficiently far to allow for Asahel to have gone far enough ahead of his brothers that they could not offer support. Unlike their brother, and perhaps because of their troops stopping to see Asahel's body, Joab and Abishai could not catch Abner, as the Benjaminite troops rallied and united with Abner on top of another hill.

26–28. With a clear gap between them, Abner employed the same technique as David in 1 Sam. 26:13–16, standing on a hill and calling to his adversaries. But where David had taunted Abner, he tries to break off hostilities. Rather than making direct statements, Abner poses three rhetorical questions to Joab, each asking him to consider the point in continuing the conflict. The first, asking whether the sword should consume for ever, asks Joab to decide whether the casualties that will be suffered makes battle worthwhile since Abner now holds the high ground. Yet there is an ironic element here, because David's message to Joab following Uriah's murder uses the same phrase (11:25). Along with David's son list in 3:2–5, it is one of the 'future echoes' set up here for the longer narrative of 2 Sam. 9 – 20. The point of the first question is reinforced in the second, since the end to which Abner refers is the death of many of Joab's soldiers. Thus the third question constitutes Abner's actual goal, though without directing Joab as to how to act. Rather, by posing a question to him about how long it will be before he tells his men to turn back, Abner leaves the final decision to Joab, creating the possibility of both men living to fight another day but with face saved. Joab sees this possibility, and so with a blast on his horn stops the pursuit to halt the battle.

Summary of outcomes: 2:29 – 3:1

2:29. The narrative summarizes the subsequent activities of both groups while demonstrating that the advantage had gone to David, even if nothing was decisive. Abner and his men needed to march east through the night, crossing the Jordan valley, passing through Bithron to return to Mahanaim. Bithron's location is unknown, though it must be a district rather than a town, unless it is a time reference. Given Mahanaim's location near the Jabbok, it may be somewhere along the valley. The larger point is that this was a long and tiring march.

30–32. The record of Joab's return is deferred until the end of this section so as to highlight the comparative casualty figures, which show David's advantage. Only nineteen of David's men were killed apart from Asahel, a marked contrast to the three hundred and sixty from Abner's troops. But the greater concern is with Asahel's loss and burial in his family tomb in Bethlehem before the troops returned to Hebron, arriving as day broke. Like Abner's forces, this was a long march of approximately 25 miles, but one made all the more sorrowful by Asahel's death. His death triggers a blood feud, even though Abner killed him in battle.

3:1. One battle had ended, but the larger conflict between David and the house of Saul was incomplete. Ish-bosheth is completely marginalized by this statement, because it makes clear that, though dead, Saul was in a real sense still David's principal enemy. The long conflict could only benefit David, who became progressively stronger while the house of Saul continued to weaken. The casualty figures from Gibeon represent the longer pattern that develops through the war. Yahweh's choice of David is evident even when it is not directly mentioned (see Hertzberg 1964: 253)

David's sons from Hebron: 3:2–5

2a. David's strength was not only demonstrated in his victories over Abner. His security was seen in his ability to have children while in Hebron, something that had apparently not happened while he was an outlaw. Indeed, his power and prestige are such that he has developed a significant harem. Mentioning sons here is important, because they create the possibility of a dynasty. As it happens, none of the sons born in Hebron will succeed him, but the possibility is generated. However, the son list is important because three of them feature prominently in the internecine rivalry that threatens to destroy David's family after his murder of Uriah.

2b–5. The list of each son follows a fixed pattern, in which their rank is given followed by their name and then their mother's name, with one son listed for each mother. The first, Amnon, will rape his sister Tamar (13:11–14) and be killed by Absalom (13:28–29). His mother, Ahinoam, was introduced in 1 Sam. 25:43. The second, Chileab (see 'Notes'), is not mentioned again, and presumably died young unless he was counted as a levirate descendant of Nabal (Bergen 1996: 306), though the case is not strong. His mother was Abigail, whom David married after Nabal's death (1 Sam. 25:39–42). The birth of the first sons provides a link with David's past, while pointing to his future. The third son is Absalom, who both kills his eldest brother and leads a revolt against David (2 Sam. 15 – 19). His mother, Maacah, was from the royal family in Geshur, immediately to the north of Ish-bosheth in Mahanaim. David's marriages to Ahinoam and Abigail had a strong political edge, and this one undoubtedly did too as it enabled him to pressure Ish-bosheth from the north. The fourth son was Adonijah, the first of David's sons to have a name including a reference to Yahweh. Adonijah became Solomon's rival claimant to the throne when David was dying (1 Kgs 1:5–10). Adonijah's mother, Haggith, like the other wives, is not mentioned in other narratives, so nothing is known about her (though curiously only Eglah is called David's wife). The same is true of his fifth and sixth sons, Shephatiah and Igleam respectively. They complete the list, but the narrative's interest is in three of their elder brothers.

Explanation

Two claimants for the one throne could lead only to conflict. One could claim to be Yahweh's anointed ruler; the other, the son of Yahweh's anointed ruler. It was a context ripe for claim, counterclaim and violence. Although the account of their accessions allows for a protracted war between David and Ish-bosheth, a period to which 3:1 points, the narrative of military conflict is limited to this passage. Although Yahweh is barely mentioned, the clear thrust is to show that the kingdom was passing to

David, and being removed from the house of Saul. That this was a conflict with Saul's house rather than Ish-bosheth in particular is clear from the fact that Ish-bosheth is always mentioned as a member of Saul's family, while the summary statement in 3:1 ignores him to focus on Saul's house. Since Abner was a member of Saul's family, he is presumably included, though the key emphasis is that the earlier conflict between David and Saul is continuing. Characterizing events in this way is important, because it reminds us to read them in the light of David's earlier encounters with Saul. Saul repeatedly tried to catch David, but never succeeded because of Yahweh's presence with David. Evoking that background creates the context for reading this narrative.

The military context is best understood by noting that Gibeon was a marginal, yet strategic, town. Its location made it of interest to both groups in order to strengthen their boundaries. Abner's choice of it as a point to encounter David's forces may suggest that he was the aggressor, though this is not explicit. The initial confrontation seems to have been inconclusive, representative combat, ultimately leading to a full-scale battle. Yet the narrative refrains from describing the whole battle, giving only a summary in 2:17 that points to the success of David's forces. Instead, it focuses on the encounter between the sons of David's sister Zeruiah and Saul's general, Abner. Initially, this conflict is concerned with the pursuit of Abner by the youngest of Zeruiah's sons, the fleet-footed but dim-witted Asahel; but it is a conflict that was destined to escalate because Abner knew that killing Asahel would initiate a blood feud with his eldest brother, and David's military commander, Joab. Abner may have been the initial aggressor, but he was keen to avoid an escalation of tension; yet Asahel made this unavoidable. His back-thrust with a spear killed Asahel, but also set in train a series of events that resulted in his own murder (3:27). Although Abner subsequently convinced Joab to refrain from further military activity at that time, the seeds of his own end were sown. Moreover, there was already good evidence from this conflict that only David could win, especially given that Abner's casualties were nearly twenty times those of Joab.

Stage by stage, Yahweh was bringing all the kingdom to David, and this was made evident through David's growing strength and the weakening of Saul's house. The narrative says nothing more about the weakening of Saul's house at this point, suggesting that the casualty figures were enough. But listing David's wives and the sons born to him while at Hebron is further evidence of this. It is a secure king who can build a harem (even if most of the marriages were apparently political, and multiple wives may hint at criticism; see Deut. 17:17) and have a line of succession with six sons. As David became more secure, so the evidence of Yahweh's presence with him grew. Nevertheless, there is another element in this list of names that not only links to David's past, but also prepares for his future. Within this list are the seeds of the conflict that will nearly tear David's kingdom apart when David turns from what Yahweh requires. The kingdom thus remains something not to be grasped, but to be accepted from Yahweh, even if the timing of its arrival is complex. The house of Saul cannot grasp that which no longer belongs to it, and in this list which points to David's own strength is a reminder that even he, as the chosen and anointed one, cannot do so either.

2 SAMUEL 3:6–39

Translation

[6]While there was war between the house of Saul and the house of David, Abner strengthened himself in the house of Saul. [7]Saul had a concubine named Rizpah bath Aiah, and Ish-bosheth said to Abner, 'Why have you gone in to my father's concubine?' [8]Abner was very angry about Ish-bosheth's words and said, 'Am I a dog's head belonging to Judah? Today I deal loyally with the house of Saul your father, to his brothers and to his friends and have not delivered you into David's hand. But today you accuse me of iniquity concerning a woman! [9]Thus may God do to Abner, and thus may he continue to do to him, for I shall do for David as Yahweh swore to him, [10]to transfer the kingdom from the house of Saul and establish David's throne over Israel and over Judah, from Dan to Beersheba.' [11]He could not answer Abner another word because he feared him.

[12]Abner sent messengers to David on his behalf, saying, 'To whom does the land belong? Make your covenant with me and behold, my hand shall be with you to bring all Israel around to you.' [13]He said, 'Good. I will make a covenant with you. I ask only one thing of you. You shall not see me unless you bring me Saul's daughter Michal when you come to see me.' [14]David sent messengers to Saul's son Ish-bosheth, saying, 'Give me my wife Michal, whom I betrothed to myself for the price of one hundred Philistine foreskins.' [15]Ish-bosheth sent and took her from her husband, Paltiel ben Laish. [16]Her husband came with her, weeping after her all the way to Bahurim. Abner said to him, 'Go, return.' So he returned.

[17]Abner's message came to Israel's elders, saying, 'For some time you have sought David as king over you. [18]Now, do it, because Yahweh has said to David, "By the hand of my servant David shall I save my people Israel from the hand of the Philistines and the hand of all their enemies." ' [19]Abner also spoke to Benjamin, and then went to speak with David in Hebron concerning all that was pleasing in the eyes of Israel and in the eyes of the whole house of Benjamin. [20]Abner came to David at Hebron with twenty men, and David gave a banquet for Abner and the men with him. [21]Abner said to David, 'I will arise, go and gather to my lord the king all Israel, that they may make a covenant with you and that you shall be king over all you desire.' David sent Abner and he went away in peace.

[22]But behold, David's servants and Joab were returning from a raid and brought much spoil with them. Abner was not with David at Hebron because he had sent him and he had gone in peace. [23]When Joab and all the army with him came, they

told Joab, 'Abner ben Ner came to the king, and he sent him away and he went in peace.' [24]Joab went to the king and said, 'What have you done? Behold, Abner came to you. Why then have you sent him away, and he has gone? [25]You know Abner ben Ner, that he came to deceive you, to know your going out and your coming in, and to know all you are doing.'

[26]When Joab came out from David, he sent messengers after Abner and they returned with him from the cistern of Sirah. But David did not know. [27]When Abner returned to Hebron, Joab took him aside to the middle of the gate to speak with him privately, and he struck him there in the belly. So he died on account of the blood of Asahel his brother.

[28]When David heard about this later, he said, 'I and my kingdom are innocent for ever before Yahweh from Abner ben Ner's blood. [29]May it whirl about upon Joab's head and all his father's house, and may the house of Joab never lack one who has a discharge or who is leprous or who holds the spindle or who falls by the sword or who lacks bread.' [30]For Joab and his brother Abishai murdered Abner because he killed their brother Asahel in the battle at Gibeon.

[31]David said to Joab and to all the people with him, 'Tear your garments and dress yourself in sackcloth and mourn before Abner.' King David followed the bier. [32]They buried Abner in Hebron, and the king lifted his voice and wept before Abner's tomb, and all the people wept. [33]The king lamented over Abner and said,

> 'Shall Abner die as dies a fool?
> [34]   Your hands were not bound;
>   your feet were not fettered.
> As one who falls before sons of injustice have you fallen.'

All the people wept over him again. [35]Then all the people came to persuade David to eat something while it was still day. But David swore, saying, 'Thus may God do to me, and thus may he continue to do, if I taste bread or any morsel before sunset.' [36]All the people recognized it and it was pleasing in their eyes, just as all the king did was pleasing in the eyes of all the people. [37]So all the people knew, and all Israel on that day, that it was not the king's will to put Abner ben Ner to death. [38]The king said to his servants, 'Do you not know that a prince and a great man has fallen this day in Israel? [39]And I am powerless today though anointed king. But these men, the sons of Zeruiah, are harder than me. May Yahweh repay the evildoer according to his evil.'

Notes on the text

7. Reading 'Ish-bosheth' with a few MSS, though it is contextually required. LXX, and probably 4QSamª, has 'Mephibosheth', Aquila, Theodotion, Symmachus and Vg all support MT. The same issue arises in 3:11; 4:1, 2.

   12. *taḥtāw* means either 'where he was' or 'on his behalf'. Although the former is more common (cf. 2:23), the latter is preferable, though mildly

tautologous. The second *lē'mōr* is awkward but secure in the MS tradition, and is understood here epexegetically (see Fokkelman 1990: 371).

15. Paltiel is called Palti in 1 Sam. 25:44, but there is textual confusion at 2 Sam. 21:8, where Adriel is probably Merab's husband.

18. Reading *'ôšî'a* with many MSS and all versions.

29. Most EVV render *ḥûl* as 'fall', though this is the only place where it is so trans. Normally, the verb means 'to dance', 'writhe' or 'whirl about'. Since the emphasis in David's curse is upon the enduring nature of the punishment, 'fall' is to be rejected. 4QSam^a reads the verb here as sg. in agreement with the antecedent *dām*, but the pl. indicates bloodguilt arising from Abner's murder.

29. *pelek* is rendered variously as 'staff' (and by extension, 'crutch'), 'chain gang' (Holloway 1987) or 'spindle'. Prov. 31:19 suggests 'spindle' as the most likely sense here (see Layton 1993).

34. With many MSS, read the pl. 'hands'.

39. The last half-verse may be absent from 4QSam^a (e.g. McCarter 1984: 112, who calls it a 'pious addition'). But Fincke (2001: 24) shows it may be original.

Form and structure

The conflict between Joab and Abner that Asahel's death initiated resolves itself here as Joab exacts his revenge. But this account of a personal blood feud is set in the larger context of rivalry between Israel's claimant kings. Ironically, Ish-bosheth inaugurated events here when he accused Abner of having sex with one of Saul's concubines. The claim's validity is never confirmed (unless, with Smith 1899: 275, one follows LXX^L, which asserts his guilt). But this accusation drives Abner to offer his services to David, claiming he can bring the whole nation to support David instead. David received him as a potential ally, though as a power broker he could also be dangerous. Thus it initially seems that this is how the northern tribes will switch their loyalty to David, but it quickly becomes clear that the blood feud is the controlling issue.

The blood feud's centrality becomes apparent when Joab returns to Hebron shortly after Abner's departure in v. 22. Discovering Abner's visit, Joab berates David for allowing Abner to spy on them (3:24–25) before sending messengers to bring Abner back and then murdering him in the city gate. The key to understanding the horror with which the narrative views these events lies in the prominence of the word *šālôm* (peace) in vv. 21, 22 and 23. All affirm that Abner left David in peace, twice through the voice of the narrator and once through the unnamed residents of the town who tell Joab. But after Asahel's death (even though it was in battle), Joab will not allow Abner peace. That Joab acts against *šālôm* provides the narrative with its sense of horror, something reinforced when David describes the sons of Zeruiah as harder (*qāšeh*) than him, and hopes that Yahweh will repay (again the root *šlm*) them as evildoers (3:39).

David's innocence is thus emphasized, though this has not stopped many from believing that this covers his involvement (most recently, McKenzie 2000: 117–122; Halpern 2001: 82–84). David does not punish Joab directly for this murder, unlike those who claimed to have killed Saul (2 Sam. 1:14–15), and Ish-bosheth (2 Sam. 4:10–12), but this does not indicate David's complicity. Indeed, were David guilty, then it is odd that he is presented as too weak to deal with Joab, something he finally leaves to Solomon's 'wisdom' (1 Kgs 2:5–6). A king who cannot deal with someone of strength is open to challenge, so this narrative actually prepares for the rebellions of Absalom (2 Sam. 15 – 19) and Sheba (2 Sam. 20). In both of these rebellions we also find Joab ignoring David's instructions to achieve his own goals (2 Sam. 18:9–15; 20:9–10). Joab is intensely loyal to David's reign, but his loyalty always has its own agenda. David can exploit this (2 Sam. 11:14–21), but can never be free of Joab's influence. Although this narrative is well disposed towards David, its portrayal of his weakness suggests the narrative is not a propagandistic whitewash. In his innocence we see how he is bound to Joab through weakness, weakness from which he can never escape. Only through Solomon, and after his own death, can David deal with Joab.

In spite of this, the situation can still be positive for David, even if he has not controlled circumstances to his favour. Abner clearly felt he should have control, with Ish-bosheth as a figurehead king. For David, having both Joab and Abner seeking to control events might have been too much. Yet Abner could bring a legitimate link to Saul's house, which was the one element David constantly needed, as is clear from his demand for Michal's return (vv. 14–15). There is thus an ambiguity about David's situation by the end of this narrative that can be resolved only when others take matters further than Abner and deliver Ish-bosheth's head to David.

Comment

Abner accused by Ish-bosheth: 3:6–11

6–7. After the list of David's sons born in Hebron, the narrative returns to the conflict between the houses of David and Saul. However, the focus has shifted because this account is not just one of conflict, but a narrative of the processes by which David became king over all Israel. The son list divides the conflict into periods of consolidation and extension for David. As before, Ish-bosheth is marginalized, so the conflict is not between David and Ish-bosheth but David and Saul, though worked out through the representatives of their houses (similarly, Adam 2007: 53). Abner was the strength behind Ish-bosheth's throne, and it is clear that the period of conflict meant his position within Ish-bosheth's court continued to strengthen. Concentrating power within a court in someone other than a king is invariably destabilizing, and at some point Ish-bosheth accused Abner of having a sexual relationship with one of Saul's concubines, a woman named Rizpah bath Aiah, who reappears as one particularly loyal to Saul in 21:10–14. A concubine was typically an auxiliary wife where no financial transfer took place to enable the marriage, but sexual congress with one was apparently tantamount to claiming the throne (cf. 16:21; although it is doubtful that Abishag was a concubine, this is probably the basis for Solomon's judgment of Adonijah in 1 Kgs 2:17, 21–25). Abner's guilt in this is not confirmed (against Brueggemann 1990b: 226, who assumes his guilt; Anderson 1989:56 suspects his innocence), though Rizpah's later loyalty towards Saul suggests she would not have been a willing party (Scholz 2004 interprets it as rape). However, Abner's guilt is left unresolved because what matters is not his guilt but his response to Ish-bosheth's accusation and need to restrain Abner's power.

8. Abner responded with fury. If it was true, his anger was presumably that someone as weak as Ish-bosheth would challenge him. If false, there would be the natural anger of those wrongly accused, especially of what could be a capital crime. Although his anger is clear, he offers a well-structured response. Although he never denies the accusation, his claim of loyalty to Saul should probably be assigned this function. Abner's language is forceful, and though the expression 'dog's head' is unique, it is clearly a dysphemism. He argues that he is not so low that he would do something that favours Judah. Instead, he has shown loyalty to the whole of Saul's house, including his brothers and friends, perhaps suggesting there was some internal conflict that might initially have prevented Ish-bosheth's accession apart from the challenge from David. The charge is completely counter to all Abner has done for the family, though the final clause might suggest that such a charge would be trifling rather than a matter of substance even if it were true.

9–11. Ish-bosheth's accusation initiates a series of events by which Abner vows to deliver the whole kingdom to David. The force of his position is emphasized by an oath where he places himself under a self-curse before God should he fail to do so (for a similar self-curse, see 1 Sam. 25:22). But there is a striking note here, because Abner vows to carry out what Yahweh has sworn to do for David. Abner acknowledges to Ish-bosheth what readers have known for some time: Yahweh is giving David the kingdom. How Abner knows this is not made clear. He could have concluded this from political and military outcomes, though the oracular language here and in v. 18 suggests he has received a prophetic word not otherwise recorded. Abner believes he can do this for David, and that he can deliver the whole of the country, which he defines by the traditional description from north to south as 'from Dan to Beersheba'. Although this narrative does not charge Abner, he does claim too much, because he is unable to do as he vows and will die as one unable to bring David the kingdom. In any case, his language oversteps what he can claim, since Beersheba lies in the south and is already well within David's territory. But in the face of such forceful claims, Ish-bosheth's weakness is made clear, as he is unable to respond.

Abner negotiates with David: 3:12-21

12-13. True to his word, Abner contacted David, initially doing so through intermediaries whom Ish-bosheth was unable to stop. Abner's approach to David is careful, framed as a rhetorical question emphasizing that the land belongs to David, though unlike his statement to Ish-bosheth there is no theological observation. However, the question marginalizes Ish-bosheth, so there are only two power brokers to consider, Abner and David. With this acknowledged, Abner makes his offer: if David enters a covenant with him he will both work with David and bring the whole nation over to him. The nature of the covenant is unclear, though it is intended to be one of equals. It is a dangerous game for both players, because it means David's accepting Abner on terms similar to those faced by Ish-bosheth, for how else can he accept one who brings across so many supporters whose first loyalty may well be to Abner? Yet Abner, having begun to cut his links with Ish-bosheth, needs a figurehead and cannot alienate David. This is partly why David insists he will see Abner only if Abner brings Michal with him, because with Michal David has a member of Saul's house in his own household. Abner's offer is acceptable, but only if someone represents Saul within David's household so Saulide loyalty will not be with Abner. We should not imagine there is anything romantic in David's request; it is *Realpolitik* working itself out in the quest for advantage.

14-16. Abner contacted David through messengers, so David initiated contact with Ish-bosheth the same way. The assumption is that his demand to Abner for Michal's return allows this to happen. David's message to Ish-bosheth is brusque and direct, and pays no heed to Michal or her second husband, Paltiel. However, from David's perspective he still had a valid marriage because he had met Saul's terms for the wedding (1 Sam. 18:20-27). Saul's decision to give Michal to Paltiel (1 Sam. 25:44) was invalid, and questions about remarriage after divorce (Deut. 24:1-4) do not arise. Ish-bosheth was faced with a powerful foe demanding his legal right, the denial of which could trigger more open warfare, but the acceptance of which could see more of his support ebb away. Lacking strength to resist, Ish-bosheth arranged to bring Michal from her home in Gallim. Her new husband followed weeping as far as Bahurim. Both villages were probably a few miles north-east of Jerusalem, so he might not have come too far before being sent back by Abner. Abner, too, knew that this was a key political manoeuvre, and whatever Paltiel's feelings, nothing was going to hinder it. But of Michal we know nothing. She is simply claimed and sent, and the narrator refrains from providing any insights into her experience or reception by David.

17–19. The negotiations needed to include Israel's elders, who also had to agree to someone being king. Therefore, Abner invited them to make David king. That Ish-bosheth had a very narrow power base is evident when Abner acknowledges that they previously wanted David to be king. Accordingly, he directs them to make David king, though emphasizing that he remains the kingmaker. Yet, in so doing, he confirms to them publicly what he has already admitted to Ish-bosheth, that David is the one chosen by Yahweh. Evidence for this is an otherwise unattested oracle that Yahweh will deliver Israel from the Philistines (who remained the dominant presence through this period) and all their enemies through David. Saul was supposed to deliver the nation from the Philistines (1 Sam. 9:16), but this role is transferred to David. The power of Saul's house is further undermined by this admission, so even as kingmaker Abner shows his position's weakness. As well as his general embassy to Israel's elders, Abner also speaks to the tribe of Benjamin, perhaps indicating the special sensitivities they might feel, before reporting the willingness of all involved to David at Hebron.

20–21. Meals are important in the OT for cementing relationships and rites of passage (Blomberg 2005: 40–49), so it was important that David welcome Abner and his delegation with the proper formalities. Abner is portrayed as being conscious of the demands of the situation, but is still trying to be kingmaker. It is notable that his speech three times states what he will do for David. To Ish-bosheth and Israel's elders Abner emphasizes that David is Yahweh's choice, which is why they must support him. But to David, as part of his own claim for power, Abner emphasizes that he will bring over all Israel so that they may enter into a covenant. David, in return, will reign as king over all he desires. It is a delicate balance that both retain, but behind it all remains the hint implied in David's son list, that the kingdom cannot be grasped. David sends Abner away in peace, because David desires what he offers, but the narrator may question the validity of this by focusing on the political trading involved. That David deals in peace with Abner indicates he was not involved in the following events, so no matter how many compromises were involved, David dealt honourably with Abner.

Joab murders Abner: 3:22–30

22–25. David may have dealt honourably with Abner, but his whole court did not support opening negotiations through him. Abner left in peace, but left enemies behind. Among them were members of the court who told

Joab, when he returned from a successful raid, of the contact with Abner.
Abner could not have left long before Joab's return, perhaps trying to avoid
contact with Joab given 2:18–23. However, on Joab's return he was
told of Abner's visit and peaceful departure, the report replicating the
narrator's comment, emphasizing that Abner had come to David. Rather
than acting against him, David had sent him off in peace. This was too
much for Joab, who saw the king to ask about his actions and insist that
whatever claims Abner made, he had really come to spy on David to know
what he was doing. If this charge was lodged against anyone else, it would
have been tantamount to treason. In fact, the narrator carefully shows
that Joab's accusation is false. We know Abner intervened in Michal's
return and spoke with Israel's elders. Joab could scarcely be unaware of
this, so there is a sense that his arguments are what he wanted to believe
about Abner, not what is necessarily true. However, there is enough in
Joab's accusation that could be true, though not in the sense of acting
against David. Abner, like Joab, is more concerned with obtaining his own
goals than anything else. No response from David is recorded, perhaps
paralleling him to Ish-bosheth, who was likewise unable to control his
general.

26–27. Abner must have left shortly before Joab's return since Joab
could send messengers to bring him back. Sending messengers is an
important theme in this chapter with each new sending linked to claims
of political power, so Joab's sending messengers is significant. These
messengers were to bring Abner back, though this is apparently not by
compulsion. Abner had not gone far, reaching only a cistern at Sirah
(probably modern Ain Sarah), a little over a mile north of Hebron. But
David's ignorance of all this is emphasized. Joab acted of his own volition.
When the messengers brought Abner back, Joab took him aside within
the town gate as if to speak privately. As a developed area a town's gate
was the logical place to conclude a discussion (see Malul 2003: 2.1).
Instead, Joab struck Abner in the belly and killed him to avenge his
brother Asahel's death. No blood feud should have existed over Asahel
because he was killed in war, but Joab worked to his own rules. Joab did
not recognize David's peace under these circumstances, as is evident from
this very public execution. It is an approach Joab later employs with
Amasa (20:9–10).

28–30. Just as Joab heard about Abner's visit to David, so David heard of
Joab's actions. Like Ish-bosheth with Abner, David was placed in a dilemma
because of Joab's power within his household. David needed to achieve two
things here: to assert his own innocence, and introduce appropriate punishment for Joab. The narrator has made clear David's ignorance of Joab's
plans towards Abner (v. 26), but now records David's declaration of
innocence, a declaration that functions legally and is probably expressed in
a public statement (Bodner 2005: 58). For reasons the narrative does not
explore, David could not act directly against Joab. Instead, he curses Joab's

whole family. The curse is extensive, asking that the effects of his actions continually swirl around him, a perennial burden for him and his family. The curse covers his father's house (though Joab's father is never named; he is described only as the son of his mother, Zeruiah), a mechanism for including his brother Abishai since David considers him to be involved as well. The curse's content is not as extensive as some (cf. Ps. 109:6–19), though similar to several psalms (e.g. Ps. 69:29–37 [ET 69:28–36]). David wishes that Joab and his family never lack those who are weak or in some way effeminate. The flow to which David initially refers is typically a woman's flow of blood (Lev. 15:19, 25), while use of the spindle (see 'Notes') was typically associated with women. The first element could refer to disease (and thus uncleanness in general), but the combination is forceful. The element of disease and exclusion is reinforced by the inclusion of 'leprosy' (not Hansen's disease), an illness leading to social exclusion (Lev. 13:1 – 14:32). In combination these elements point to weakness and death, points that naturally lead into the final elements of violent death or constant hunger. In short, the opposite of what Joab and Abishai seek for themselves through violence is what David asks that they receive because they murdered Abner in an illegitimate blood feud.

David mourns Abner: 3:31–39

31–34. Having cursed Joab and Abishai, David needed to demonstrate his innocence by organizing a proper funeral for Abner. Hence he accorded Abner the honours given to someone of importance, actions perhaps directed towards the northern tribes so they would see his commitment to Abner. The rending of clothes, wearing of sackcloth (a rough cloth) and weeping are all typical signs of mourning. Both David (called king for the first time by the narrator here) and the people participated in this way to show their respect. In addition, David composed a lament for Abner, much as he had done for Jonathan and Saul (1:17–27). The lament's first line is addressed directly to those who hear, while the balance is addressed directly to Abner, though rhetorically to those who heard. The opening question is rhetorical, suggesting Abner has died a death that is beneath him. He was no fool, but an astute politician, and this should not have happened. In addressing Abner, David still addresses the crowd, but helps them empathize with Abner. That he was unbound makes clear he was not a prisoner. However Joab might present things, this was murder, not execution. Abner died like a convicted murderer, but his killers are those who practise injustice. Thus David testifies to all who hear that what was done to Abner was unacceptable, tacitly pointing out to Joab and Abishai the reality of their guilt (see Fokkelman 1990: 110).

35–37. If David's goal was to ensure that his innocence was recognized, then it is clear he was successful. After David's lament, a delegation of the people tried to persuade him to eat since he had apparently begun to fast (see 1:12). Instead, David placed himself under a self-curse (see 1 Sam. 25:22) so God would punish him if he ate anything that day. The people still needed convincing of David's innocence, and it was this self-curse that finally convinced them he was not involved in Abner's murder. But their support is also clear from the fact that this was not only the sort of action that pleased them.

38–39. Whereas the previous utterances were public, these verses record private comments from David. In effect, they contrast David's public position against what he privately knows he can achieve. The question to his servants is rhetorical. They know an important and powerful leader has died. What they may not appreciate, though, is that David, the anointed king, is too weak to act against the sons of Zeruiah. David knows that although kings rule, they do so only with their generals' support and he can thus not attack Joab and Abishai outright. Instead, he can only wish that Yahweh repay them for what they have done. David's curse seeks justice, but here he concedes he himself can do no more. Only when Solomon is taking over will David initiate Joab's punishment (1 Kgs 2:5–6). David knew the power that lay with the army commander. He was prepared to work with Abner, and now knows he must continue to work with Joab.

Explanation

After the extended wait while Saul was on the throne, the beginning of this narrative seems to offer the desired resolution. Ish-bosheth's accusation against Abner meant Abner was prepared to bring the kingdom to David. Instead of a divided kingdom, Judah and Israel could be united under a single throne. Moreover, Abner twice insisted that he and the northern tribes knew this was Yahweh's sworn purpose (vv. 9, 18). All seems to be falling into place. Nevertheless, it could not be achieved yet. Partly this was because of the blood feud Joab and Abishai maintained against Abner for killing their brother Asahel, ignoring its place in battle (2:18–23). Yet there are hints of a deeper problem, hints suggesting that just as David could not seize the kingdom while Saul was alive, neither can it be seized for him now.

The reasons for this become clear when we explore the relationship between the two kings and their generals, and how religious faith is twisted to suit political purposes. Above all else, this is politics at work, and it makes for unpleasant reading. Neither Ish-bosheth nor David can control their generals, with both seeing themselves as in some sense independent of their king's authority. They served the king only when their own purposes were secured. Abner clearly acted like this, as is evident from the fact that (to justify taking the kingdom to David) only after he was accused did he cite the prior promise of Yahweh. Thus he claimed to know of a promise from Yahweh to David that he previously acted against. Although the narrative shows Abner acting faithfully with David once negotiations began, it is faithfulness already shown to be suspect. David treated him with peace, even making a covenant with him (vv. 12–13), and is an invariably canny negotiator in their encounters (note his technique to ensure Michal's return), but questions about Abner's goals are subtly raised throughout. Yet if Abner's characterization is double-voiced, Joab's is clearly critical. His encounter with David where he accused Abner (vv. 24–25) has enough truth to convince those who want to believe him, but is shown to be flawed by earlier elements in the narrative. In any case, he directly countermanded David's peaceful arrangements with Abner by arranging to return Abner to Hebron, where he murdered him in the gate complex. With Abner's death the opportunity for immediate unification of the kingdoms evaporated. While this weakened Ish-bosheth, it also weakened David because it made him less trustworthy to the northern tribes. In addition, David's internal position was shown to be weak since he could not punish Joab and Abishai as their crime deserved.

Although we hear nothing more about Ish-bosheth in this chapter after the handing over of his sister Michal, the last element of the narrative provided David with the opportunity to state his innocence. The narrator makes his innocence clear (v. 26), but David also voices it before arranging a state funeral for Abner. Here, David must not only state his innocence, but must demonstrate it publicly so that lingering suspicions can be offset. In the end, the one who has seemed likely to gain the whole kingdom is shown to be weak before his general. The whole kingdom was coming to David, but he could not seize it or have it seized for him. Abner rightly stated Yahweh's purposes for David and Israel, but these purposes are not worked out through power politics that only weaken all those involved. Yahweh's processes are more complex than that.

2 SAMUEL 4

Translation

[1]When Ish-bosheth, Saul's son, heard Abner had died in Hebron, he lost courage and all Israel was dismayed. [2]Saul's son had two men who commanded his raiding bands, one named Baanah and the second named Rechab, the sons of Rimmon the Beerothite from Benjamin – for Beeroth is reckoned to belong to Benjamin [3]since the Beerothites had fled to Gittaim and have been there as sojourners until this day.

[4]Saul's son Jonathan had a son crippled in his feet. He was five years old when the news about Saul and Jonathan came from Jezreel. His nurse took him up and fled, but in her haste to flee he fell and became lame. His name was Mephibosheth.

[5]Now the sons of Rimmon the Beerothite, Rechab and Baanah departed and came to Ish-bosheth's house during the heat of the day while he was taking his noonday rest. [6]So they came into the middle of the house while collecting wheat but struck him in the belly. Then Rechab and his brother Baanah fled. [7]When they entered the house as he was lying on his couch in his bedroom and struck him and killed him, they removed his head and went by way of the Arabah all night [8]and brought Ish-bosheth's head to David at Hebron. They said to the king, 'Behold, the head of Ish-bosheth ben Saul, your enemy who sought your life. Yahweh has today granted my lord the king vengeance from Saul and his seed.' [9]David answered Rechab and Baanah his brother, the sons of Rimmon the Beerothite, 'As Yahweh lives, who has delivered my life from every distress, [10]when one reported to me saying, "Behold, Saul is dead," and thought he bore good news, I seized and killed him in Ziklag – this was the reward I gave him for his news! [11]How much more when wicked men kill an innocent man in his house, upon his couch! Now, shall I not require his blood from your hand and destroy you from the earth?' [12]David commanded the lads and they killed them and cut off their hands and feet and hung them beside the pool at Hebron. But they took Ish-bosheth's head and buried it in Abner's tomb in Hebron.

Notes on the text

1. Ish-bosheth's name is absent from the MT here and v. 2 (cf. 3:7, 11). See note on 3:7. 'Lost courage' is lit. 'his hands dropped'; see Isa. 13:7; Jer. 6:24; Ezek. 7:17; Zeph. 3:16 for the idiom. Reference to 'hands' (vv. 1, 11, 12) and 'feet' (vv. 4, 12) mark out the chapter. Thus Baanah and Rechab's execution aligns itself with the weaknesses of the Saulides.

4. As with Ish-bosheth (see 'Notes' on 2:8), Mephibosheth's correct name is masked in 2 Samuel because of a Baal compound. The original Meribaal is maintained in 1 Chr. 8:34 and 9:40, though with spelling variations. Another member of Saul's family with this name is mentioned in 21:8.

6–7. The translation follows MT, understanding *hēnâ* as an adverb rather than a f. pronoun. LXX has a very different text, which is widely supported (see RSV but not NRSV), but retroverting this to a text from which the alternative readings can be explained is problematic, requiring an otherwise unattested meaning for *mlṭ*. 4QSam[a] seems to omit the verse altogether. The difficulties might have been generated by v. 7's apparent replication of the killing after the brothers' escape in v. 6. But a similar repetition occurs in 1 Sam. 17:50–52, where the severing of a head is narrated after the killing. V. 7 can be read as a clarifying repetition, and understood as pluperfect. Although some textual damage is possible, MT can be understood, and is retained as *lectio difficilior*. It is doubtful that the participle *lōqêḥî* can mean 'intending to take' since the participle here should recount a single act (GKC §§116–117).

12. 4QSam[a] and some LXX MSS have only David taking and burying Ish-bosheth's head. This is less likely as it removes MT's unexpected pl. forms.

Form and structure

There are important parallels between this chapter and 1:1–16. In both, a messenger comes to David with evidence of the death of a member of Saul's family expecting reward. Instead of reward, David executed those claiming to have killed, whether as mercy killing (1:6–10) or murder (see Carlson 1964: 51). Both deaths benefited David in that he moved closer to the throne. But there are wider elements of patterning involved that prevent us from examining the parallels too narrowly. As noted above (see 'Form and structure' on 2:1–11), there is extensive patterning across the whole of Samuel, so the account of the long rivalry between David and Saul (1 Sam. 16 – 2 Sam. 1) is followed by a short rivalry between David and the house of Saul (2 Sam. 2 – 4). This creates the context for the long rebellion narrative climaxing in Absalom (2 Sam. 13 – 19) and the short rebellion narrative focused on Sheba ben Bichri (2 Sam. 20). Both the short rivalry account and the short rebellion include murders by Joab where he stabs a rival in the belly (*ḥōmeš*; 3:27; 20:10). Moreover, 2:1 – 5:16 begins with David's accession to Judah's throne and ends with his accession to the throne of Judah and Israel. The components are variously linked by David's son lists (3:2–5; 5:13–16) and officials (8:15–18; 20:23–26, the first also referring to David's sons). Finally, we note that the bloodshed that occurs in each instance also involves killing, where someone is struck in the belly (*nkh* + *ḥōmeš*; 2:22; 3:27; 4:6), phraseology exclusive to 2 Samuel (similarly, Polzin 1993: 50, who links it to fraternal terminology). This web of associations suggests that the narrative is not solely interested in defending David from claims of involvement in Ish-bosheth's death (see Haelewyck 1997: 152–153). It does insist he was innocent of any wrongdoing and that he acted justly in executing Ish-bosheth's killers, but the narrative is more complex than that. It sets David's final accession in a context of continual violence where David must overcome those who use violence to achieve their own ends. Ultimately, David will be seduced by the possibilities of violence (2 Sam. 11), but the narrative shows first what he could achieve when he placed worship at the heart of his kingdom (5:17 – 8:18), a theme that recurs in chs. 21 – 24. This reading assumes the chapter's basic unity, but is a contested point (see Haelewyck 1997: 146–149). Although v. 4 breaks the main narrative (see 'Notes' on 4:1), it is an important intrusion, and once v. 7 is understood as a repetition that qualifies the initial information (see 'Notes'), then the text's artistic unity becomes evident (see Youngblood 1990: 843).

Comment

Sons of Saul: 4:1–4

1. The point at which Ish-bosheth knew of Abner's death is unclear. Given Abner's vow to deliver the kingdom to David he might not have expected him to return, so a considerable gap between this statement and the previous chapter is possible. However, the important point is the effect of this news, which is that Ish-bosheth's courage failed (see 'Notes'), while the whole nation was dismayed. This may have been because Abner was seen as holding the kingdom together, but was more probably fear of David. Reports to Ish-bosheth would not necessarily emphasize David's innocence (note Shimei's comments in 16:8), so he might have been afraid of what David would do to him. If so, the irony is that David ultimately had nothing to do with his death. Instead, like many ancient monarchs, Ish-bosheth was assassinated by those closest to him.

2–3. David had supported himself in Ziklag with marauding raids, a practice seemingly followed in Hebron (3:22), though these would not have been against northern sites given his hope of ruling them. Ish-bosheth followed a similar principle, with raiding bands commanded by Baanah and Rechab, who are identified throughout as sons of Rimmon from Beeroth. Since Baanah is introduced first it is likely he was older, though Rechab is subsequently mentioned first (vv. 5–6, 9), suggesting he was the leader. They came from Beeroth, a village a few miles south-west of Bethel. A note explaining this is necessary since according to Josh. 9:17 it was a Gibeonite city, so any involvement with Benjamin would have been notional. However, the original Beerothites are said to have fled to Gittaim, possibly to the west of Beeroth. It is possible that this is the event behind 21:1–14, where David avenged the Gibeonites for Saul's violent actions against them.

4. The narrative suddenly breaks off to include a note about Jonathan's son Mephibosheth (see 'Notes'). We are told he was five years old when Jonathan died, but had been injured and left lame as a result of an accident when dropped by his nurse. This is intrusive to the account of Ish-bosheth's murder, but not completely out of place, delaying the main story, which would otherwise proceed quite swiftly. Previously, we knew of only one surviving male in Saul's family. But before his death is recounted, another is introduced, a descendant of Saul through Jonathan. Mention of Mephibosheth is thus important because of the covenant between David and Jonathan and their commitment to each other's descendants (1 Sam. 20:15, 42). David has an obligation to Jonathan's descendants that he does not have to other Saulides. Nevertheless, because of Jonathan's statement in 1 Sam. 23:17, Jonathan's son should not pose a threat to David, though popular sentiment can be different, as is apparent in the accounts of Ziba and Shimei (16:1–8). His lameness makes him an unlikely claimant for the throne. Mephibosheth's introduction is carefully timed to coincide with what seems like the end of Saul's family, in order to stress David's continuing responsibility to them and that they have not been completely destroyed. It builds on the promises made earlier by David to Jonathan and prepares for Mephibosheth's introduction as a major character in ch. 9.

Ish-bosheth's murder: 4:5–12

5–6. After the digression about Mephibosheth, the narrative returns to Rechab and Baanah as they arrive at Ish-bosheth's house in the heat of the day. Although they are Ish-bosheth's raiders, nothing indicates that they come back from a raid, though being soldiers they can enter the king's house armed. Since the heat makes work debilitating, it is common in warm climates to have an afternoon sleep, which is what Ish-bosheth is doing when they arrive. It is unclear whether they come with a deliberate plan, or act opportunistically to kill Ish-bosheth. Rather than suggesting that they pretended to collect wheat (so ESV, NASB, NRSV, NIV), they more probably saw their opportunity while collecting some (see 'Notes'). Ish-bosheth was clearly not well protected, though since these men were probably part of his bodyguard it may not have been relaxed as sometimes suggested (Baldwin 1988: 193). As with the deaths of Asahel (2:23) and Abner (3:37), Ish-bosheth was killed when struck in the belly. With their murder carried out, the brothers fled.

7–8. Although the account of Ish-bosheth's death could have been complete in v. 6, the narrative pauses to provide additional details, with v. 7 functioning as a flashback. V. 6 provides a simple statement of murder, but v. 7 provides its details. Rechab and Baanah entered Ish-bosheth's house while he slept and killed him, cutting off his head, which they took with them as they travelled that night across the Arabah (the lower Jordan valley, see 2:29) and came to David at Hebron. The distance between Mahanaim and Hebron (possibly in excess of 60 miles, depending upon Mahanaim's location) shows their urgency. The reason for urgency is clear, for they travelled with Ish-bosheth's head and would know that capture by Ish-bosheth's supporters would grant them the same fate. David's position as Ish-bosheth's rival meant he appeared to offer both a safe haven and the possibility of reward. The desire for reward becomes clear in their speech. Just as the Amalekite who reported Saul and Jonathan's death brought evidence of their fate, so the brothers proffer Ish-bosheth's head as proof of their claims. Importantly, they are said to speak to 'the king', affirming David's status, while stressing that Ish-bosheth was Saul's son. The link with Saul emphasizes that the brothers are on David's side, while seeking to make Ish-bosheth guilty by association with his father. It was Saul, not Ish-bosheth, who had sought David's life, though their language is carefully ambiguous, leaving open the option of understanding them as claiming that Ish-bosheth sought David's life. But that Saul was the main problem is clear in their second claim, that Yahweh had granted David vengeance on Saul and his descendants. Saul, they assert, was David's enemy and he could only be overcome through his son's death, a murder for which they claim Yahweh's sanction, though no such sanction is recorded. Apart from Yahweh's directing David to Hebron (2:1), it is notable that throughout the account of David and Ish-bosheth Yahweh is spoken about as justifying actions (3:9–10, 18), but not acting directly again until 5:10. While claiming divine sanction for violence is not unusual, the narrator subtly flags that this is an unsustainable claim.

9–11. David's response is marked by a full introduction to the brothers, perhaps emphasizing their separation from him. The brothers claimed Yahweh's involvement, so David's answer is framed as an oath shaped by Yahweh's existence and that Yahweh has delivered him from adversity so that he needs no human intervention (see Anderson 1989: 71). In context, adversity would primarily refer to Saul's inability to catch David, though as a broad term 'adversity' (ṣārâ) also includes the types of situations described in 1 Sam. 17:34–37. This allows David to bring in as the pattern to follow here his response to the Amalekite who reported Saul's death (1:1–16). There the Amalekite presumed he brought good news (bāśār) and expected reward. His reward was execution, and David follows this pattern for their murder of an innocent man (though unlike Saul, Ish-bosheth is not described as Yahweh's anointed). Yahweh's actions have kept David from irresponsible bloodshed, and those who claim Yahweh's justification for violence have thus misunderstood his ways. David thus ordered their execution (for legal traditions, see Exod. 21:12; Lev. 17:4; Num. 35:31). Although execution remains a necessary judicial tool, David insists that Yahweh's kingdom cannot be construed on the basis of violence, reaffirming the principles established throughout 1 Sam. 24 – 26.

12. The account of the execution is brief. At David's command the brothers are killed and have their hands and feet removed (see Judg. 1:6–7) before their bodies are dishonoured through exposure (see Josh. 10:22–27) by the pool at Hebron. By contrast, Ish-bosheth's head received a proper burial in Abner's tomb. David shows proper respect for one who was murdered and enacts justice against his killers.

Explanation

David has been continually offered mechanisms for seizing the kingdom, and the offers normally come with some theological garnish. Sometimes his own men suggested that Yahweh had provided him with the opportunity to kill Saul (1 Sam. 24:5 [ET 24:4]), or at least with the chance to have one of them kill him on David's behalf (1 Sam. 26:8). Neither of these options was taken, though each raised the issue of providence. The Amalekite messenger who arrived in 1:1–16 claimed to have resolved the problem for David by finishing off a dying Saul, though not being Israelite he made no claim about Yahweh. But this time David was offered the chance to accept that Yahweh had provided him with the kingdom because Rechab and Baanah had killed Ish-bosheth at home. It is a seductive reading of providence. After all, David was clearly prevailing in the battle with Saul's house, and Abner's death meant the north was becoming alarmed (v. 1). Apart from Ish-bosheth, the only Saulide of note was Jonathan's son Mephibosheth, a cripple who could be no more than twelve years old at this point. David neither killed Ish-bosheth himself nor gave the order for his killing. Thus he could claim the kingdom, and assert that Yahweh had enabled these events.

Providence can be difficult to discern, but David here sees through the temptation. Earlier experiences had made clear that he could not claim the throne by violence, and violence against the innocent claimed to be from Yahweh was wrong because this was inconsistent with the values of the kingdom. Subtle variations in theology so that means are justified by a desired outcome are unacceptable. The throne had to come to David; he could not seize it. The paradox is that this was the final element that enabled him to accept the throne when it was offered. The paradox is not unlike that of Judas, who was fully responsible for his betrayal of Jesus, yet at the same time the means by which God's purposes were resolved (Matt. 26:17–56). David's tragedy is that he is ultimately seduced by the importance of holding power rather than seeing it as something God alone can give, but here at least the possibilities of accepting the gift rather than seizing power by means that justify the unjustifiable are held out.

2 SAMUEL 5:1–16

Translation

[1]Then all the tribes of Israel came to David at Hebron and said, 'Behold, we are your bone and your flesh. [2]Previously, when Saul was king over us, you were the one who led Israel out and in. And Yahweh said to you, "You shall shepherd my people Israel and shall be leader over Israel." ' [3]Then all Israel's elders came to the king at Hebron, and King David made a covenant with them at Hebron before Yahweh and they anointed David as king over Israel. [4]David was thirty years old when he began to reign, and he reigned for forty years. [5]He reigned over Judah in Hebron for seven years and six months and over all Israel and Judah in Jerusalem for thirty-three years.

[6]The king and his men went to Jerusalem, against the Jebusites who lived in the land, who said to David, 'You shall not enter here, for the blind and the lame shall turn you away' (thinking 'David cannot enter here'). [7]But David captured the

stronghold of Zion, which is the City of David. ⁸David said on that day, 'Whoever would strike down the Jebusites, let him approach via the conduit "the blind and the lame" whom David's soul hates.' Therefore it is said, 'The blind and the lame shall not enter the house.' ⁹So David dwelt in the stronghold and called it the city of David. David built all around from the Millo and inward. ¹⁰David continued becoming greater, for Yahweh of hosts was with him.

¹¹Hiram king of Tyre sent messengers to David with cedar timbers, carpenters and masons and they built David a house. ¹²So David knew Yahweh had established him as king over Israel and had exalted his kingdom for the sake of his people Israel.

¹³David took more concubines and wives from Jerusalem after he came from Hebron, and more sons and daughters were born to David. ¹⁴These are the names of the sons born to him in Jerusalem: Shammua, Shobab, Nathan, Solomon, ¹⁵Ibhar, Elishua, Nepheg, Japhia, ¹⁶Elishama, Eliada and Eliphelet.

Notes on the text

2. Read *hammôṣî' wĕhammēbî'* with Q.

4–5. Seemingly absent from 4QSamᵃ.

6. *wayyōmer* is sg. because it treats the Jebusites collectively (see Tg), but needs a pl. for English style.

8. An extremely difficult verse. Driver's observation (1913: 199) that it is easier to say 'what it does not mean than what it does mean' still holds true (see Frolov and Orel 1999: 609; Oeming 1994: 408–409). A key problem is the meaning of *ṣinnôr*, occurring elsewhere in the OT only in Ps. 42:8 [ET 42:7]. There it means 'cataracts' or 'waterfalls'. McCarter (1984: 139–140) argues that although rabbinic Hebrew used the word to mean 'water pipe', its meaning in the tenth century BC included the throat or gullet, and translates as 'windpipe', though there is no definite usage with this meaning. Other suggestions, such as 'grappling hook' (see NIV mg.) derive from cognate roots, though their link is difficult to prove. Frolov and Orel (1999: 614) suggest 'door post', but ignore the parallel in Ps. 42. That *ṣinnôr* is a water shaft has been defended by Kleven (1994b), using the sound principle that one should primarily work with established meanings. The translation interprets *wĕyigga'* as jussive in meaning, something made explicit in 4QSamᵃ, obviating the need for an object to have fallen from the text (see AV; Anderson 1989: 80), and *ṣinnôr* as a conduit, though not necessarily Warren's Shaft. Although *ng'* can mean 'to strike', a more limited sense of 'touch' or 'draw near' is possible (for 'touch', see Gen. 3:3; Exod. 19:12; Judg. 6:21; for 'reach', Judg. 20:34, 41; Jon. 3:6), the preposition on *ṣinnôr* thus describing the means by which David's men can approach the 'blind and the lame'. With 4QSamᵃ, read *śānē'â*, so 'the blind and the lame' are the object of David's hatred.

9. For *bāyĕtâ* as 'inward', see Exod. 28:61.

13. That David took his wives *min* Jerusalem may indicate they were Jebusite (see Hill 2006: 130). The parallel in 1 Chr. 14:3 uses the preposition *bĕ*, and these possibly overlap to suggest that the reference is to the timing of David's marriages. That some were Jebusite and part of David's political integration remains probable.

14–16. The names of David's sons recur in 1 Chr. 3:5–8 and 14:4–7 with minor spelling variants. However, Eliada appears as Beeliada in 1 Chr. 14:7, a Baal compound rather than one using El (God). The vocalization in Chronicles has been conformed to here, so the name was probably Baaliada, but later changed when Baal compounds were understood to refer to a Canaanite fertility deity rather than Israel's God.

Form and structure

Where Chronicles has an orderly handover of the throne from Saul to David (1 Chr. 11 – 12), Samuel's account is more complex because of the continuing conflict between the house of Saul and David until Ish-bosheth's death (see Knoppers 2006: 193–200). Now the kingdom David could neither seize nor have seized comes to him. The coming of the kingdom is not simply the moment he is crowned: it also includes those elements where he establishes himself as king over the whole nation. Although it contains several discrete elements, it is important to see this section as a unity where David moves from accepting the offer of the kingdom of Israel to the point where he is securely established as ruler over it in a new capital city that belongs to neither side of the Judah–Israel divide. Yahweh's activity is highlighted in each component, unlike the period of Ish-bosheth. As with 3:2–5, the son list in 5:13–16 divides one section of text from what follows.

We are probably to understand this section as describing several events from across David's reign and not events that closely followed one another. It offers an introductory summary of David's career (similarly, Klement 2000b: 13–14). This is clear from how the account moves from his formal accession to the total period of his reign, and ends with an extensive son list born while David was in Jerusalem. Also, Hiram could be described as king in Tyre for only about the last ten years of David's reign (Bright 1980: 84 has their overlap as 969–961 BC). It is thus a summary that climaxes with the certainty that Yahweh had established David's reign (v. 12), with the son list providing additional evidence of this. This builds on the statement of Yahweh's involvement with David in v. 10. The declaration of Yahweh's involvement is the climax of the whole, because it demonstrates what was illustrated through the preceding chapters: the kingdom must be Yahweh's gift.

Jerusalem's capture (vv. 6–9) poses several difficulties (see 'Notes'). We are not told why David captured the city, while the account itself is difficult to interpret. The chronology is also difficult. A cursory reading might suggest Jerusalem was captured soon after David's accession, and both here and 1 Chr. 11:1–9 recount the city's capture immediately after David's accession. Given the summary nature of this section, this cannot be taken for granted. Yet the rest of 2 Samuel assumes Jerusalem is the capital, so the city was probably taken relatively early in David's reign, though it remains possible that part of the difficulty in reconciling the periods mentioned in 5:5 with 2:10–11 may be that Jerusalem's capture needs to be fitted in there. David's reasons for capturing the city can only be guessed, but national unity is highly probable. Jerusalem was an old and well-established city close to the Benjamin–Judah border, but was never fully captured (Judg. 1:8, 21; see Youngblood 1992: 854) and had remained Jebusite (Judg. 19:10–12). As such, Jerusalem offered neutral territory, belonging to no tribe but joining the north and the south. It was also established as a royal city, emphasizing its continued independence even when integrated into Israel as a whole. The throne needed to be a national rallying point, and a neutral capital was an important tool in achieving this.

Comment

David's accession to the throne of Israel: 5:1–5

1–2. The moment of full accession that has been anticipated since 1 Sam. 16:13 has finally come. David is still in Hebron, but all the tribes gathered to him to declare their links with him and to assert that he was not only their choice of king, but Yahweh's. They provide several reasons why David should be king. First, they link themselves to him as family, noting that they are his 'bone and flesh', a phrase indicating a blood relationship (Gen. 29:14; Judg. 9:2; in 2 Sam. 19:12–13 David uses the same phrase when reclaiming the throne) that also provides the basis for covenant. As family, they are joined to him. Secondly, even during Saul's reign (Ish-bosheth and Abner are tactfully ignored) David had provided the military leadership that according to 1 Sam. 8:20 was why Israel needed a king. David had acted as a king should, and the tribes therefore sought to formalize this. Finally, they point to an oracle where Yahweh had said David would shepherd Israel and was thus the nation's leader (*nāgîd*; see 'Form and structure' on 1 Sam. 9:1 – 10:16). As with Abner's speech in 3:18, we cannot point to any oracle given in Samuel, but the statement is consistent with previous events. That David will 'shepherd' the nation is novel to this verse in Samuel (but see Ps. 78:71) but draws on a common ANE kingship motif. Previous use of the shepherd motif pointed to the actual keeping of flocks (e.g. 1 Sam. 16:11; 17:15), but it now describes royal rule (7:7). Familial, practical and theological reasons unite to indicate why David must be king, though they carefully avoid the word itself at this point.

3. Where v. 1 spoke of all Israel, the language now concerns all the elders, though the elders practically represented the people. Where kingship language had been avoided, the text is now explicit that they came to the king (*melek*), and that he made a covenant with them. Rather than representing an alternative account to vv. 1–2 (e.g. Robinson 1993: 170), the repetition foregrounds David's status. Although Samuel had announced the rights and duties of kingship (1 Sam. 10:25), it is only with David that a formal covenant is instituted (see 3:21). That David made the covenant with them suggests it was at his initiative, and that the covenant was solemnized before Yahweh. The covenant's content is not reported, though it could explain why David captured Jerusalem for his capital. It would, in any case, regulate both David and the people of Israel in their relationship and responsibilities toward one another (Brueggemann 1990b: 239). Kingship is about mutual responsibilities, not just the exercise of power. In response to this, the elders anointed (see 2:4) David as king (*melek*). David's preparatory state as leader (*nāgîd*) is past. Finally, he is king.

4–5. The chronological note (given in round numbers) initially replicates the statement on David's period in Hebron (see 'Comment' on 2:11), but extends it by noting that his age at accession in Judah was thirty and that he also reigned for thirty-three years over Israel and Judah in Jerusalem. The kingdoms are listed separately, so David reigns over a united kingdom, not a single nation. The union was divided again under Rehoboam and Jeroboam (1 Kgs 12). Given the length of David's reign, it is striking that the narratives concerning him tell us so little of it. Mention of Jerusalem here also introduces the next segment of this account.

Jerusalem's capture: 5:6–10

6–7. Without introduction, the account moves straight to Jerusalem's capture, though the repetition of the title 'the king' for David ties this to the accession. We are not told why David went to Jerusalem with his men (presumably his personal militia, though in 1 Chr. 11:4 they represent 'all Israel'), and the account's focus is only on how he captured it and its subsequent importance to him. Jerusalem was well known in the third and second millennia BC (Ebla tablets, Amarna letters), and is known in Gen. 14:18 as Salem when Abram meets Melchizedek. The point for David is probably its political and military importance (see 'Form and structure'). Moreover, it was to David's advantage to remove a Canaanite enclave within the land, though little is known about the Jebusites. According to Gen. 10:15–19, they were ethnically associated with Sidon, while Gen. 15:21 includes them among those occupying the land before Israel. Little is heard of them after this, and they may have been gradually assimilated into Israel. Since Jerusalem sits on top of Mount Zion it is a highly defensible location, and this seems to be the force of the Jebusite taunt that David could not enter the city – and even the blind and the lame could prevent him. Reference to the blind and the lame is important because they are mentioned twice more in v. 8. Here the sense seems to be literal, though a more symbolic sense develops in v. 8. Yet in spite of the Jebusites' confidence, v. 7 is remarkably laconic in asserting that David captured the stronghold. This is the first reference in the Bible to Zion and probably refers to the south-east corner of Jerusalem overlooking the Kidron valley rather than the modern Mount Zion on the south-west of the city. Zion is also called Ophel (2 Chr. 27:3; 33:14, Mic. 4:8). David not only captured the city, but asserted its independence by calling it 'The city of David'. Jerusalem, or at least part of it, was David's city.

8. Having announced David's capture of the city, the narrative returns to note how he did so. Unfortunately, because of textual difficulties (see 'Notes'), nothing certain can be said about this, and archaeology has not offered significant clarification. It seems David recognized the impossibility of direct assault, thus agreeing with the Jebusite claim in v. 6. Instead, he directed a secret attack through a water conduit. This may be Warren's Shaft, a water tunnel known since 1867 that predates David (so Kleven 1994a, yet note Oeming 1994: 411), but this is not accepted by all (Shanks 1999a), and access through the Gihon cave is possible (Kleven 1994b: 203). It may be that the attack was on the water supply itself rather than on the city through the water tunnel. In giving his instruction, David speaks dismissively of all the city's inhabitants as 'the blind and the lame', a phrase describing them as in some way unclean (rather than being an oblique reference to Mephibosheth and Zedekiah; see Carlson 1964: 87; Ceresko 2001: 24), though the law excludes such people only from the priesthood (Lev. 21:18) rather than seeing them as unclean. This statement offers an aetiology of a popular aphorism (the phrase is not to be attributed to David) explaining why such people could not enter the temple, since 'house' most likely means 'temple' (as in 7:5) rather than David's palace (similarly, Olyan 1998: 219–220, against NIV). Birch (1998: 1237) objects that this is contrived since the temple did not yet exist, but this ignores reference to a temple in Shiloh in 1 Sam. 1 – 3, which suggests that wherever the ark was kept could be described in those terms.

9–10. With Jerusalem captured, a compressed summary of David's time there is offered. Once the city was captured, David established it as his place of residence, occupying a site not traditionally associated with an Israelite tribe (see 'Form and structure'). The city's status as a royal centre is emphasized by David's naming it 'The City of David', making explicit what was hinted at in v. 7. Royal cities need both grandeur and defensive capability, and David recognized this by establishing a building programme from the Millo and inwards. Unfortunately, it is impossible to identify the Millo (see 1 Kgs 9:15, 24; 11:27; 2 Chr. 32:5), but the presence of the same term at Shechem (Judg. 9:6, 20) suggests it is a generic element in fortified cities. NIV's 'supporting terraces' may be correct, and points to the construction of improved outer defences. However, the construction work covered more than this and included other elements of the city that are not defined. The conclusion the narrative draws from this is made explicit in v. 10. Throughout his reign, David continued to become greater because Yahweh was with him. Yahweh's presence with David is an important theme (1 Sam. 16:13, 18; 17:37; 18:12, 14, 28; 20:13), though this is the first time that the full title 'Yahweh of Hosts' is used in the formula. The title's importance in Samuel is that it occurs in clusters in the context of significant changes in social structure (see 'Comment' on 1 Sam. 1:3, 11), probably emphasizing Yahweh's authority to make such a change. David's successes and the change in Israel's royal family are tied together by Yahweh's presence with David.

David established in Jerusalem: 5:11–16

11–12. Given that Hiram's accession in Tyre came late in David's reign (see 'Form and structure'), the events described here come from later than Jerusalem's capture. Hiram is noted in the Bible as someone who provided building resources, something that fits well with his role as king of Tyre (in the south of modern Lebanon), where he also engaged in major building works, especially temples, while greatly expanding Tyre's role as a trading city-state. He is elsewhere associated with Solomon and the construction of both the temple and Solomon's palace (1 Kgs 5:2, 7–12) along with Solomon's trade programme (1 Kgs 9:27; 10:11, 22), though this is linked to his relationship with David (1 Kgs 5:1). The relationship with Solomon eventually soured through a dispute over the quality of towns offered by Solomon in a land exchange (1 Kgs 9:11–14), which Solomon presumably offered to pay off debts. An alliance between Israel and Tyre was advantageous to both in terms of trade access and resource sharing, as seen here in the craftsmen Hiram sent to David for the construction of his palace. But the narrator refrains from interpreting this in political or commercial terms. The focus is on how this affected David (see Frisch 2004). For him this involvement with Hiram and its benefits for Jerusalem demonstrated the point made explicitly in v. 10. Not only could it be said that Yahweh was with David; David could see the evidence around him and know Yahweh had established him as king and had exalted his kingdom because of his people Israel.

13–16. Another list of David's sons is given (cf. 3:2–5), this time those born during his time in Jerusalem. Again this list summarizes an extended period in his reign. There may be a hint of criticism because David continued to take both concubines (see 2 Sam. 3:7) and wives, something contrary to Deut. 17:17. However, it seems that the main concern there, the faith issue of foreign wives, is is not a problem here. Such 'taking' echoes Samuel's warnings in 1 Sam. 8:11–18, again hinting at some criticism. But the main concern is to show that Yahweh continued to bless and strengthen David by providing him with numerous sons and daughters, though only sons are listed. From these sons (see 'Notes'), only Solomon reappears in a narrative context, though within Samuel his name is a dark foreboding of David's relationship with Bathsheba. In summarizing David's reign, such issues are not highlighted because the emphasis falls on the evidence of Yahweh's continued presence with him.

Explanation

Ever since Samuel anointed David in 1 Sam. 16:13, readers have waited for him to be established as king. After many twists and turns, and a partial beginning in 2:1–4, that point is reached when the northern tribes come and make him king. The long and involved account of David's conflicts with Saul and Ish-bosheth are put into perspective, though from a rather surprising source since it is the northern tribes who confess Yahweh's election of David as king. Those who resisted Yahweh's purposes for David the longest now recognize and confess those purposes. David must be king, though he cannot be like Saul, something emphasized by the covenant he made with the Israelite elders. Kingship is established by Yahweh's will and is acknowledged by all in his presence.

The narrative does not dwell on this point. Rather, it immediately moves on in vv. 6–16 to reflect on the whole of David's reign, a reign marked by Yahweh's presence. This is a highly compressed collection of materials, recounting David's capture of Jerusalem, the development of his construction programme there and listing David's sons born in Jerusalem. Although followed by a longer reflection on the whole of his reign (see 'Form and structure' on 5:17–25), this collection emphasizes Yahweh's presence with David throughout his reign. Previously, Yahweh was seen to be with David in his rise to power, but the point emphasized here is that this never ceased during his reign in spite of the events narrated in chs. 11 – 20. Yahweh was present with David, and David realized this and so had a perspective from which to view his reign. This does not mean we have a sanitized David presented in these verses. There may be a hint of the acquisitive David who took and destroyed in his multiplication of concubines and wives, and Solomon's mention (5:14) points to events that happen later, but this does not detract from the larger purpose of emphasizing Yahweh's presence with David throughout his reign.

We cannot ignore the fact that Jerusalem's capture did more than provide David with a secure capital city. It certainly did that while cutting across tribal loyalties (and functions as a model for Washington, DC, in the

USA and Canberra as the heart of the Australian Capital Territory in establishing capitals separate from existing power blocs), but its significance is greater than that. It is from this that we have the birth of the Zion traditions (e.g. Isa. 2:2–4; Mic. 4:1–5; Ps. 47), which provide so much of the OT's hope and ultimately transcend all David was or would be while still celebrating Yahweh's presence. And it is ultimately in the temple, hinted at in v. 8, that the blind and the lame came to Jesus and were healed (Matt. 21:14). These texts go beyond the horizons of this one, but could not exist without it.

2 SAMUEL 5:17–25

Translation

[17]When the Philistines heard they had anointed David as king over Israel, all the Philistines went up to seek David; but David heard and went down to the stronghold.
   [18]The Philistines came and spread out in the Valley of Rephaim. [19]So David enquired of Yahweh, 'Shall I go up against the Philistines? Will you give them into my hand?' Yahweh said to David, 'Go up, for I will surely give the Philistines into your hand.' [20]So David entered Baal Perazim, and there David struck them. David said, 'Yahweh has burst through my enemies before me like waters burst through.' Therefore, that place is called Baal Perazim. [21]They left their idols there, and David and his men carried them away.
   [22]Again the Philistines came up and spread out in the Valley of Rephaim. [23]When David enquired of Yahweh, he said to him, 'You shall not go up. Circle around to their rear and come against them from before the balsam trees. [24]When you hear the sound of marching on the tops of the balsam trees then be alert because Yahweh has gone before you to strike the Philistine camp. [25]David did as Yahweh had commanded him and struck the Philistines from Geba as far as Gezer.

Notes on the text

17. *māšḥû* is a generalizing pl. Against McCarter (1984: 151), emendation to a ni. on the basis of LXX and 1 Chr. 14:8 is unnecessary since these have simply opted for a more elegant expression.
   18. LXX, attempting to translate 'Rephaim', renders it as 'giants'. It can mean 'giants' (Gen. 14:5; Deut. 2:11; 3:11) or underworld inhabitants (Ps. 88:11; Job 26:5; Isa. 26:14). In 21:15–22 David confronts the descendants of Rapha, who are Philistine giants. LXX (see 1 Chr. 14:9) suggests *pšṭ* (to raid; also v. 22) for MT's *nṭš*. The similar letters explains the confusion, but the linguistic evidence favours MT (see McCarter 1984: 151).

20. *qārā'* is understood impersonally.

23. The botanical identification of *běkā'îm* is uncertain, and may be a shorthand reference to a grove in the Baca valley. 'Balsam trees' is retained as the most popular suggestion, though with no particular confidence.

25. LXX and 1 Chr. 14:16 have Gibeon rather than Geba, but these are probably textual corruptions due to the similarity in the spelling of the two place names.

Form and structure

With David established as king, the narrative focuses on his work in nation-building, establishing Israel's security and structure. This process begins here and is continued through to 8:14 with a series of narratives drawn from the whole of David's reign. This narrative block is arranged as a chiasm (Firth 2001: 212; cf. Flanagan 1983):

> A.   Military victories with Yahweh's help, 5:17–25
> B.   Worship of Yahweh: bringing the ark, 6:1–23
> B^1. Worship of Yahweh: Nathan's oracle, 7:1–29
> A^1. Military victories with Yahweh's help, 8:1–14

This structure, remarkably similar to that of 2 Sam. 21 – 24 (Firth 2001: 215; see 'Form and structure' at 21:1–14), provides an overview of David's entire reign where Yahweh's activity is emphasized and David's commitment, expressed in public worship, is also highlighted. It provides a grid through which readers approach the darker tales in 2 Sam. 9 – 20. There David's failures are manifest, but the overall assessment of his reign is positive because of his commitment to Yahweh's worship. This provides the marker by which Kings assesses all subsequent kings of Israel and Judah.

This narrative thus prepares for the following events. But it also addresses a pressing issue for David, the question of Philistine influence. David had been a Philistine vassal before gaining Judah's throne (1 Sam. 27 – 2 Sam. 1), and reference to the Philistines in the period of his conflict with Ish-bosheth was notably lacking. Securing Israel's future first required freedom from the Philistine control established following Saul's death (1 Sam. 31:7), and reaching back to events at Aphek (1 Sam. 4:1b–11). This is narrated through a panel of two closely parallel battle accounts where David's actions are limited to those chosen by Yahweh. The accounts are parallel, but not identical in that David's second enquiry (v. 23) is elided, and how Yahweh gains the victory changes. Apart from these elements, they are almost identical, even down to parallel wordplays in each report (Fokkelman 1990: 169–176). However, this structure is also linked to earlier narratives. The doubled account closely mirrors the technique employed in 1 Sam. 27 – 2 Sam. 1, while David's enquiry is similar to 1 Sam. 23:6–13 and 30:7. Reference to the Philistines spreading out (*nṭš*) echoes the ark's capture in 1 Sam. 4:2 (cf. 1 Sam. 30:16). This echo becomes more important in the following account when David brings the ark to Jerusalem, the capture of which was probably later than these battles. Finally, 1 Sam. 9:16 required Israel's king to deliver them from Philistine control, something alluded to by Abner in 3:18, and that is achieved here. The elements from the past, all of which have shown David in a positive light, combined with the fact that Israelite kingship now begins to achieve its goal, suggests this passage is a carefully chosen hinge that draws on past elements while providing a platform to look forward.

Comment

The first battle: 5:17–21

17–18. The context for conflict with the Philistines is established once they hear that Israel anointed David as king. His anointing was tantamount to rebellion, especially given their control of much of the country after Saul's death (1 Sam. 31:7). Accordingly, they mustered for war and came up looking for David. As the anointed king, it was in their interests to defeat or kill him as soon as possible to quell Israel. While the Philistines went up, David went down to the stronghold. The stronghold is unnamed, but is unlikely to be Jerusalem (against Bergen 1996: 325), not least because one normally goes up to Jerusalem, but also because 2 Sam. 5 is presented thematically, not chronologically (see 'Form and structure' on 5:1–16). Indeed, defeating the Philistines here may almost be a requirement for capturing Jerusalem. Earlier references to David's stronghold (1 Sam. 23:14, 19; 24:1 [ET 23:29]) were to the region of Engedi, though Adullam (22:1) cannot be ruled out here since the two appear to be identified in 23:13–14. Both are south of Jerusalem, but close enough that David could bring his forces to the Valley of Rephaim (see 'Notes'), which runs southwest from Jerusalem to the Valley of Elah. That the Philistines spread their forces out suggests they arrived first and thus chose the battle site.

19. As before (1 Sam. 23:11; 30:7), David enquired of Yahweh by two questions, both of which can be answered either 'Yes' or 'No', and with the second dependent upon the first. David presumably employs the ephod, and Abiathar, though omitting mention of this, emphasizes the fact of the enquiry rather than the means (for a possible mechanism, see 'Comment' on 1 Sam. 14:40–42). David needs a directive from Yahweh to enter battle and an assurance of victory, so the victory belongs to Yahweh. Yahweh's response addressed David's questions, though the second answer is emphatic, stressing victory's certainty.

20–21. Fully reassured, David entered the battle at Baal-Perazim (possibly Mount Perazim in Isa. 28:21), which was presumably south-west of Jerusalem, though the exact location is unknown. The name was given only after the Philistines' defeat, the naming taking attention away from the statement that David struck them and focusing instead on Yahweh. It is clear from personal names that the epithet Baal (meaning 'lord' or 'master') was used then for Yahweh and not the Phoenician deity later venerated by some in Israel. The aetiology suggests the experience of Yahweh's involvement was similar to flood waters breaking through and overwhelming all around. David celebrated that victory comes from Yahweh, a point remembered through the location's name. So complete was the victory that the Philistines left their idols when they fled, and David and his men claimed them as tokens of victory. This victory thus reverses the earlier loss of the ark (1 Sam. 4:11). 1 Chr. 14:12 adds that David burned these idols, but the narrator here is more concerned to show the parallels with the account of the ark.

The second battle: 5:22–25

22–24. The second battle account is closely patterned on the first, so the differences introduced are significant (see Murray 1998: 95–103). Initially, it seemed there would be an exact repeat as the Philistines again entered the Valley of Rephaim. Again David enquired of Yahweh, but here the accounts diverge. The content of David's enquiry is not given (though some LXX MSS do fill the presumed gap) but proceeds straight to Yahweh's reply. This is probably because the answer to David's first question (presumably the same as 5:19) is negative, thus voiding the second question. More importantly, it foregrounds Yahweh as the one who both gives victory and also sets the tactics for it. It is possible (though complex) to reconstruct a series of questions with 'Yes'/'No' answers that lead to the ensuing directive, but they are elided for brevity and to maintain the focus on Yahweh's leadership. Rather than attacking directly, David was to circle around and attack from the rear, taking cover from a grove of trees (see 'Notes'). Permission to launch his attack is given in v. 24, which specifies that he is to do so only on hearing the sound of marching in the tree-tops, presumably the sound of wind passing through them. However, the permission still limits David's role. He is simply to be alert because this sound means Yahweh has gone before him (cf. Judg. 4:14) to strike the Philistine camp (cf. 1 Sam. 7:10).

25. David's obedience is emphasized, highlighting his success when he does Yahweh's will, an emphasis complementing 5:10. David has become greater because Yahweh is with him, but that means David's leadership is shaped by obedience to Yahweh's command. Yahweh took the lead, but David was still involved in the battle and pursued the Philistines from Geba to Gezer, about 20 miles west of Jerusalem. As McCarter notes (1984: 157), David drove the Philistines from the Israelite territory they had occupied since 1 Sam. 4. Moreover, the promise from Yahweh cited by Abner in 3:18 is being fulfilled. Yahweh is delivering the nation from the Philistines through David, though according to that oracle this is only the beginning of Yahweh's deliverance. This victory thus indicates the greater things Yahweh will achieve through David.

Explanation

As a former vassal, the Philistines would worry about David being able to unite all Israel. Thus we have two parallel accounts of their attempt to kill David and destroy the nascent Israelite unity. But what the Philistines failed to consider was that David was the one through whom Yahweh would fulfil his purposes for Israelite kingship (see 1 Sam. 9:16; 2 Sam. 3:18). Israel was meant to point to Yahweh as the living God at work in Israel (1 Sam. 17:45–47), something that was a witness to all the earth. In these battle accounts we begin to see those elements come together in a way that has not been evident since David defeated Goliath in 1 Sam. 17. The Philistines could not overcome David because Yahweh was working out his purposes for the nation through him. David is the key instrument for Yahweh's purposes, though these purposes go far beyond David. However, there is an important balance here because Yahweh's sovereignty is joined with human faithfulness. David is the king who understands the claim made in 1 Sam. 17:47 (Yahweh is the one who wins), so he submits himself to Yahweh's purposes to lead his people to the success that can be theirs. The victories still belong to Yahweh, but the text acknowledges the importance of David's leadership in this. By way of analogy, the NT looks to the certain triumph of the gospel of Jesus Christ, but understands this happening through the faithful witness of God's servants. Thus Paul describes the gospel as something of which he is a steward, and yet at the same time something greater than all forces that oppose it (Eph. 3:1–14). That tension between the certainty of God's purposes and the importance of human faithfulness is equally evident here.

2 SAMUEL 6

Translation

[1]David again gathered all the chosen men in Israel, thirty units. [2]Then David rose and went, and all the people with him, from Baale Judah to bring up from there the ark of God, which is called by the name of Yahweh of Hosts who sits enthroned on the cherubim. [3]They placed the ark of God on a new cart and carried it from

Abinadab's house on the hill. Uzzah and Ahio, the sons of Abinadab, were driving the new cart [4]with the ark of God, and Ahio went before the ark.

[5]David and the whole house of Israel were celebrating before Yahweh with all kinds of musical instruments of cypress wood, with lyres, harps, timbrels, rattles and cymbals. [6]When they came to the threshing floor of Nacon, Uzzah reached out to the ark of God and held it because the oxen unsteadied it. [7]But Yahweh's wrath was kindled against Uzzah, and God struck him there because of the negligence, so he died there with the ark of God. [8]David was angry because Yahweh had burst forth against Uzzah, so that place is called Perez Uzzah to this day. [9]David feared Yahweh that day, and said, 'How can the ark of Yahweh come to me?' [10]David was unwilling to bring the ark of Yahweh with him to the city of David, but removed it to the house of Obed Edom the Gittite. [11]The ark of Yahweh stayed in the house of Obed Edom the Gittite for three months, and Yahweh blessed Obed Edom and his entire house.

[12]It was reported to King David that 'Yahweh has blessed the house of Obed Edom and all that is his because of the ark of God.' So David went and brought up the ark of God from the house of Obed Edom to the city of David with rejoicing. [13]When those bearing the ark had taken six paces, he sacrificed an ox and a fatling. [14]David danced before Yahweh with all his strength and wore a linen ephod. [15]David and the whole house of Israel brought up the ark of Yahweh with shouting and the sound of the horn.

[16]As the ark of Yahweh came to the city of David, Saul's daughter Michal looked through the window and saw King David leaping and dancing before Yahweh and despised him in her heart. [17]They brought the ark of Yahweh in and set it in its place inside the tent David had pitched for it. David offered up burnt offerings and peace offerings before Yahweh [18]When David finished offering his burnt offerings and peace offerings, he blessed the people in the name of Yahweh of Hosts [19]and distributed food portions to all the people, to the whole multitude of Israel, to both men and women, to each a cake of bread, a portion of meat and a raisin cake. Then all the people departed, each one home.

[20]David returned to bless his house, but Saul's daughter Michal came out to meet David and said, 'How the king of Israel has glorified himself this day when he uncovered himself today in the sight of the handmaids of his servants when he uncovers himself like one of the vulgar fellows uncovers himself!' [21]David said to Michal, 'It was before Yahweh, who chose me above your father and his entire house to appoint me as ruler over Yahweh's people, over Israel; so I will rejoice before Yahweh. [22]I will be more lightly esteemed than this and will humble myself in your eyes, but with the handmaids of whom you spoke, with them I will be honoured. [23]And Saul's daughter Michal had no child to the day of her death.

Notes on the text

1. The initial aleph of *'sp* is elided (GKC §68h). LXX's 'seventy thousand' exaggerates. As elsewhere, 'thousand' (*'elep*) probably refers to a military unit, not a specific number (see 'Comment' on 1 Sam. 4:2).

2. 1 Chr. 13:6 clarifies that Baale Judah is also Kiriath Jearim (see Youngblood 1992: 879). This ensures it is read as a place name (see Kleven 1992: 303) and not 'citizens of Judah' (as Campbell 1975:171), but is probably explanatory rather than original (against Driver 1913: 203), though note Josh. 15:9. LXX (cf. NRSV, ESV) correctly omits the second *šēm* as dittography, as also may 4QSam[a].

3. Although rendering 'Ahio' as a proper name has a venerable tradition in EVV, LXX regards it as 'his brothers', while Campbell (1975: 129) takes it as the sg. 'his brother'. Certainty is impossible.

4. MT includes *wayyiśśā'uhû mibêt 'ăbînādāb 'ăšer baggib'â* by homoioteleuton from v. 3, and is to be omitted (cf. LXX).

5. *běrôš* can be either cypress or fir. 'Musical instruments' is implied and supported by LXX's *organos*.

6. The name (if it is one) of the threshing floor's owner varies considerably in the textual tradition, and is variously 'Nodar' (LXX), 'Nodan' (4QSam[a]) and Kidon (1 Chr. 13:8). The verb *šmṭ* is unlikely to be intransitive, so the ark is the implied object.

7. *haššal* has long vexed interpreters. BDB's proposal, presuming only a fragment of a longer text, is altogether too neat. Fokkelman (1990: 378) argues for 'negligence' on the basis of a parallel Aramaic root, though the word's presence at the time is uncertain. But the same result can be obtained if we read this as an otherwise unattested noun from the root *nšl*, 'to slip or drop'. The nun's elision is explicable, and the word's rareness meant its meaning was lost early.

13. Against McCarter (1984: 166), the text requires a single sacrifice six paces after the ark was safely moved, not a sequence of sacrifices.

16. One expects *wayyěhî* (so 4QSam[a]) rather than MT *wěhāyâ*, but retain MT as more difficult reading (Campbell 1975:131).

19. *'ešpār* is uncertain, occurring nowhere else other than the parallel 1 Chr. 16:3. 'Portion of meat' is traditional, but *DCH* suggests 'date-cakes'.

20. Michal's combination of inf. const. + inf. abs. (*higgālôt niglôt*) is unique in biblical Hebr., perhaps an emphatic way of stressing David's exposure.

22. 'your eyes' follows LXX. MT 'my eyes' lacks the contrast implicit in David's statement.

Form and structure

The ark's delivery to Jerusalem represents a highlight in David's reign, though the narrative still points out flaws in David's approach. But it emphasizes his intention to worship Yahweh, an intention expressed through his celebration before Yahweh as the ark arrives and also his conflict with Michal. This conflict then distinguishes David's reign from Saul's in that David recognizes Yahweh's authority over him as king, conforming his reign to 1 Sam. 12. Michal represents the house of Saul as one that did not lead the nation in worship. The ark's delivery also prepares for the momentous events in 2 Sam. 7 when Yahweh enters into covenant (Firth 2005b) when David expresses his desire to build a temple as a resting place for the ark (2 Sam. 7:2). Including material about Michal is thus a crucial component in highlighting how David appreciates the role of Israel's king in contrast to the view of the house of Saul.

This account not only prepares for the next chapter, but also joins with elements that precede it. The most frequently noted point is that this chapter appears to resume the ark's story otherwise left off in 1 Sam. 7:1, picking up the story initiated in 1 Sam. 4:1b (see 'Form and structure' there). There are important points of contact, notably the use of a new cart to carry the ark (1 Sam. 6:7; 2 Sam. 6:3) and rhetorical questions to express awe at how Yahweh's presence is manifested (1 Sam. 4:8; 6:20; 2 Sam. 6:9; see van der Toorn and Houtman 1994: 222). Similarly, just as there is a gradual movement towards using Yahweh as the preferred divine name rather than Elohim, as in the previous narrative, so Elohim is dropped here after v. 7 (see Fokkelman 1990: 180). Although the ark was left at Kiriath Jearim in 1 Sam. 7:1 and is here brought from Baale Judah, these are probably variant names for the one site (see 'Notes' on 6:2). Yet it is unlikely that the continuous source postulated by Rost (1982) would make such a change (Miller and Roberts 1977: 23). Moreover, if the ark was mentioned in 1 Sam. 14:18 (see 'Notes' there), then the twenty years specified in 1 Sam. 7:2 during which the ark was largely ignored ended then, even if it was kept at the same place. Therefore, 2 Sam. 6 was probably written with awareness of the earlier account, but not direct dependence upon it. This is consistent with the fact that 2 Sam. 6 assumes knowledge of David's relationship with Michal from 1 Sam. 18:17–30, 19:11–16, 25:43 and 2 Sam. 3:14–16.

Links also exist with 5:17–25 at 5:18, 21 and 22, suggesting that the whole of 5:17 – 8:14 develops themes concerning the ark. But the verbal links with this chapter are also important, especially the use of the root *prṣ* in wordplays explaining place names in 5:20 and 6:8. These observations, combined with 7:2, render improbable Campbell's (1975: 126) claim that neither 2 Sam. 5 nor 7 is concerned with the ark. Rather, 2 Sam. 6's emphasis on the ark is woven into its context while developing the overall narrative. At the heart of 2 Sam. 5:17 – 8:14, therefore, is the point that David allows the ark to create a context for public worship, something Saul's family did not. David's victories in 5:17–25 and 8:1–14 are understood in that context. Worship's priority is also recognized by Ps. 132, which reflects back on this chapter.

Comment

The first attempt to bring the ark: 6:1–11

1–2. That David again gathers his troops, especially thirty elite units, leads us to expect combat with the Philistines. But warfare is set aside until 8:1, and instead he travelled with them (the troops are the people mentioned in v. 2) to Baale Judah (see 'Notes') to bring the ark to Jerusalem. Such a large group suggests the ark's removal is intended as both public worship and a national proclamation of David's faithfulness, though given the ark's proximity to Philistine territory a significant force may also have conveyed a message to the Philistines (Bergen 1996: 328). More importantly, the ark had earlier defeated the Philistines (1 Sam. 5:1 – 7:1), and David has just done the same, the link stressing Yahweh's involvement throughout (see Carlson 1964: 60). David engaged in nation-building by creating a centre of government that united civic and sacral authority, but in so doing he also promoted his own position. The importance of this becomes particularly clear when he encounters Michal at the end of the chapter and a contrast is drawn between David and the house of Saul. The ark's importance is also emphasized by the use of the extended title 'the ark of God, which is called by the name of Yahweh of Hosts who sits enthroned on the cherubim'. The ark has not been called by this full title since 4:3, though there it emphasized Yahweh's power in an ironic way since the subsequent narrative showed that Yahweh was not manipulable. That David had a double purpose here and so placed himself under threat from the ark is suggested by this name. David will also discover that honouring Yahweh while extending one's own position creates dangerous ambiguity.

3–4. David's approach to bringing the ark to Jerusalem is patterned on that of the Philistines in 1 Sam. 6:7, with the ark placed on a new cart pulled by oxen. That it was a new cart follows the Philistines in acknowledging that something used for a holy purpose could not otherwise be used for common work. Thus the ark was loaded on to the cart at Abinadab's house on the hill at Baale Judah, and driven along by Abinadab's sons Uzzah and Ahio (see 'Notes'), with Ahio in the lead and Uzzah bringing up the rear. The consistency with the Philistine approach, and Abinadab's sons' familiarity with the ark (though Eleazar was responsible for it: 1 Sam. 7:1) doubtless made this seem reasonable. But Num. 4:1–16 sets out a different approach, stipulating that the ark was to be covered and carried on poles inserted into it by the Kohathite clan of Levites (see Exod. 25:15; Num. 7:9), and it is unclear that Abinadab's sons were Kohathites (against Bergen 1996: 329). David's careful preparations are noted, but their flaws are suggested by what he has not done.

5–7. David's parade was both a public statement and a genuine act of worship where Yahweh's presence in the ark was celebrated. But this celebration's language evokes the women who greeted Saul in 1 Sam. 18:6

after Goliath's death. Their rejoicing and singing was, unknown to Saul, a precursor of his own failure, and it will also prove to be for David. Nevertheless, this allusion serves the larger purpose of showing David in a more positive light than Saul since David learns from his mistake in ways Saul did not. Moreover, David also joins with those who rejoice with music before Yahweh. But this rejoicing would not continue, for, when they reached the threshing floor of Nacon (site unknown), Uzzah reached out to steady the ark after the oxen had upset it. Like David, Uzzah's action was well intentioned, but the result was devastating because God struck him for his negligence (see 'Notes'). Those responsible for the ark knew it was not to be touched since this breached its holiness, and his family had a long enough association with it to be aware of this. Although final responsibility for Uzzah's death lay with David because he transported the ark in this way, Uzzah was still struck by Yahweh because his own actions breached the ark's holiness. David's position mirrored that of the men of Beth Shemesh in 1 Sam. 6:19. Ps. 99, which also refers to the ark, suggests Yahweh transcends his holiness by reaching out to bring justice and righteousness to a sinful world, but this narrative stresses instead the dangers his holiness poses to those who do not take it seriously. That was Uzzah's problem, however well intentioned his actions were.

8–11. David's anger in response parallels Yahweh's, but is phrased to suggest that David has become Yahweh's enemy. In 5:20 Yahweh had burst (*prṣ*) against the Philistines, and now he has burst (*prṣ*) against Uzzah. David had followed the Philistines in dealing with the ark, and now stood in the same place as them. Just as Baal Perazim commemorated Yahweh's victory in 5:20, Perez Uzzah does the same against David, explaining David's fear of Yahweh. This is not reverence but the fear of an adversary. That David was transporting the ark with mixed motives is demonstrated when he asked how he could bring the ark to himself. The ark would become central to Israel's worship, but David needed to learn that it was not his to control. Here it seems as if David was defeated by Yahweh, and was accordingly unwilling to have such a dangerous object as the ark in his city. Instead, he sent it to the house of a Gittite called Obed Edom. 1 Chr. 15:17–19 indicates he was a Levite, so 'Gittite' cannot mean he was from the Philistine city of Gath but that he was from an Israelite town (such as Gath Rimmon or Gath Padalla, mentioned in the Amarna letters 250.11–14; see Anderson 1989: 105) that used 'Gath' (which means 'wine-press') within the toponym. Here Yahweh blessed Obed Edom and his house, suggesting that the ark was a source of hope where Yahweh's holiness was properly regarded.

The second attempt to bring the ark: 6:12–19

12–13. David's mixed motives in bringing the ark are clarified here. News that Obed Edom's house was blessed by Yahweh because of the ark's presence became the trigger for David's bringing it from there to Jerusalem. The rejoicing associated with this is less defined than the first attempt, though the use of such a positive motif suggests his fear of the ark has been overcome. A key royal motif is also introduced. David is referred to as 'King David' for the first time in the chapter, highlighting the element that becomes the source of conflict with Michal when the ark arrives (vv. 16, 20). A key theme of the chapter is the proper understanding of kingship in Israel and this subtle change in terminology for David prepares for it. The ark's initial movement was celebrated with a sacrifice when the bearers had moved it six paces (see 'Notes'), signifying the legitimacy of its removal. This time, the ark was carried on its poles. David thus shifted from a Philistine model of moving the ark to one consistent with Torah, though this is stressed more in 1 Chr. 15:1–15.

14–15. David's rejoicing is not simply expressed in his sacrifice. Rather, it is expressed through dance, though this is free expressive movement rather than formal liturgy or a fertility rite anticipating his encounter with Michal (against Carlson 1964: 87). Nevertheless, that David wore a linen ephod, a garment typically associated with priests (e.g. 1 Sam. 2:18, 28), is curious (1 Chr. 15:27 speaks of a fine linen robe, though Smith [1899: 295] thinks it is a strip of cloth). Bergen (1996: 329–330) suggests that David acquired a priestly role with Jerusalem's capture, a theme hinted at in Ps. 110:4. If so, his removal of the ark joins with the psalm in linking priestly and royal roles, and may also explain the fact that Jerusalem is never directly named in this chapter but is always 'the city of David' (vv. 9, 12, 16), something consistent with Ps. 132:1–10. Given Michal's later comments, we should not think of the ephod as anything too grand. David's rejoicing was not unique, and though there is undoubted hyperbole in v. 15, it emphasizes that David was one among many who celebrated the ark's movement to the city.

16. Amid the general celebration a discordant note is introduced. When the ark entered the city, Michal looked out of the window (see Judg. 5:28 and Bietenhard 1999: 7–8 for biblical parallels), saw David dancing and despised him in her heart. That this is not simply a matter of marital relations is clear from Michal's description as 'Saul's daughter'. That is also why it is noted that David danced before Yahweh, something not previously made explicit. The contrast between David and Saul was ultimately seen in their understanding of the king's position before Yahweh. This is foregrounded here by linking Michal with Saul and noting that David danced before Yahweh. No reason is given for Michal's response, leaving the narrator's statement that David danced before Yahweh as the only interpretation of his actions. Michal's reasons are voiced when she meets David, but are left aside here to insist on the validity of David's dance.

17–19. The validity of David's worship is emphasized by the record of the preparations he made for the ark's arrival, including pitching a tent for

it. This is consistent with its treatment in the wilderness period when it was
kept within the tabernacle (Exod. 25:10–22; 26:33–34; 30:6, 26; 40:1–5,
20–21). The ark was placed in this tent and David offered sacrifices to
Yahweh, so that sacrifice began and ended the ark's journey to the city.
The sacrifices were both burnt offerings, where the whole offering was
immolated and associated with atonement (Lev. 1:3–9), and peace
offerings, where portions of the animal were distributed for food (Lev.
7:11–18). David also blessed the people (another priestly overtone) in the
name of Yahweh of Hosts (see 'Comment' on 1 Sam. 1:3 on the narrative
significance of this epithet) and distributed additional portions of food to
all. Such actions are typical of an enthronement, so what is celebrated is
Yahweh's enthronement over Israel. David is the ark's guardian, and
clearly desires to have it in his city, but he reigns under Yahweh's greater
authority. David has authority only because of Yahweh's primacy.

David and Michal clash: 6:20–23

20. After sharing gifts with the people, David returned to his house to bless
it. The use of the word 'house' is striking (cf. v. 21), preparing for its key
use in ch. 7. The narrative does not indicate whether he began to bless it or
not, concentrating instead on the encounter with Michal hinted at in v. 16.
The clash of royal houses is stressed by again calling Michal 'Saul's
daughter'. Returning after such an event, David might have expected a
degree of honour but is immediately undercut by Michal's sarcasm. In her
speech, her first recorded word to David, 'honour' is something David has
not received as a result of his dance. Unlike the narrator, who noted that
David danced before Yahweh, Michal does not speak of his dancing, but
claims he has exposed himself before the lowest of the low: the handmaids
of his servants. This, she claims, is something only the most vulgar Israelite
would do. The emphasis upon exposure is so marked that *glh* (uncover) is
used three times (see 'Notes'). Although she refers to David as Israel's king,
she clearly does not consider him worthy of that position. To what extent
David exposed himself physically cannot be determined purely on the basis
of this verb. It could refer to his exposing his naked body, or at least
genitals while dancing, but reference to the ephod suggests he remained
clothed. The exposure that troubles Michal is more probably that David
has revealed himself as one who does not behave in a manner she believes
befits a king (see Gunn 1978: 74).

21–22. David's response denies Michal's fundamental assertion. He did
not dance before the serving girls but before Yahweh who had chosen him
in place of Saul and his house and appointed him as leader, something
stressed by the form of the sentence. This brings Yahweh and his election of
David to the beginning and closes by insisting again that David's actions
were before Yahweh. Hence David insists there is no problem in appearing

like this before serving girls since they will honour him, even though it will produce more approbation from Michal. David takes Michal's sarcastic jab about honour and turns it around. An Israelite king is honoured because he worships enthusiastically with the people, not by behaving like traditional kings. An Israelite king must function before Yahweh, and this cannot be for personal grandeur. The narrator is aware that David's motives in bringing the ark were not altogether pure, but this does not undercut his claim's validity.

24. Nothing more is said of the day's events. Instead, the narrator closes by observing that Michal remained childless. No reason for this is given. Unlike Hannah (1 Sam. 1:5), we are not told that Yahweh closed her womb. It could be Yahweh's judgment, but it could equally be that David no longer associated with her. But the reason is unimportant. What matters is that the rift between the house of Saul and David is now complete. No heir will unite the families. Israel's unity will instead be found in its worship of Yahweh.

Explanation

David's role in 5:17 – 8:14 is nation-building, constructing a context where Israel can define itself. The key elements were establishing a military setting where the nation could operate with freedom and centring the nation's life in the worship of Yahweh. This worship is central to the next chapter, but the close links between this account and that of 5:17–25 shows that the two elements could not be separated. Nevertheless, this narrative also sounds a note of warning against the accumulation of royal power. Yahweh's authority must predominate, and the king must understand his place.

The warning note is crucial. David clearly had mixed motives at several points, not least in his anger that he could not bring the ark to himself (v. 9). In his first attempt to bring the ark, he followed the Philistine pattern from 1 Sam. 6:1–9, which was successful in a context where Yahweh accepted the intent of their actions. But that narrative ended with Israel's struggling to know how to cope with Yahweh's holiness manifested in the ark when they did not respect the ark properly (1 Sam. 6:19–20). David's first attempt to move the ark, in spite of its benefits for the nation, did not accord with the law, and ended in disaster with Uzzah's death as he reached out to steady the ark, a death matched for its suddenness only by that of Nadab and Abihu (Lev. 10:1–2) and Ananias and Sapphira (Acts 5:1–11). David's anger is directed towards Yahweh, but also at himself. Yet the ark offered real possibilities, as is clear from the blessing it brought to Obed Edom, prompting David to make his second attempt to bring the ark to the city. This time the proper procedures were followed, and the removal succeeded. But the issue of the king's power relative to Yahweh continued in David's encounter with Michal. She embodied Saul's family and despised David when he danced in an apparently scanty ephod. Her speech drips sarcasm as she insists that David has dishonoured himself before the nation. By contrast, both the narrator and David insist he was celebrating before Yahweh, so Yahweh has more authority than the king. David understood the principles of kingship established in 1 Sam. 12 in a way that Saul's family never did, and his encounter with Yahweh's radical holiness in the first attempt to bring the ark has made this clear to him. Kings are for building the nation, but only as they point to Yahweh, something not dissimilar to John the Baptist's attitude in relation to Jesus (John 3:30). David is a far from perfect king, but understanding this is what distinguished him from Saul. He was to lead the nation to worship Yahweh, not to agglomerate power in his person. The temptation to do this remains (see 2 Sam. 11), but the principle is clear.

2 SAMUEL 7:1–17

Translation

[1]Now when the king sat in his house and Yahweh had given him rest from all his surrounding enemies, [2]the king said to Nathan the prophet, 'Look, I dwell in a house of cedar, but the ark of God remains within curtains.' [3]Nathan said to the king, 'All that is in your heart go and do, because Yahweh is with you.'

[4]But that night Yahweh's word came to Nathan, [5]'Go, and say to my servant, to David, "Thus has Yahweh said, Shall you build me a house in which to dwell? [6]I have not dwelt in a house from the day I brought up the children of Israel from Egypt until this day, but have wandered in a tent, that is, in the tabernacle. [7]In all my wanderings among all the children of Israel, have I ever spoken a word to one of the tribal leaders I commanded to shepherd my people Israel, saying, 'Why have you not built me a house of cedar?' [8]Now, thus shall you say to my servant, to David, 'Thus has Yahweh of Hosts said, I took you from the pasture, from behind the flock, to be leader over my people, over Israel. [9]I was with you wherever you went and cut off all your enemies before you. I will make a great name for you like the name of the great ones of the earth. [10]I will appoint a place for my people, for Israel, and will plant them so they shall dwell securely and not be disturbed again. Those who practise violence shall no longer afflict them as from the beginning, [11]since the time I appointed judges for my people Israel; and I will give you rest from all your enemies. Yahweh declares to you that Yahweh shall build you a house. [12]When your days are fulfilled and you lie with your forefathers, I shall raise up your offspring after you who will come forth from your body and will establish his kingdom. [13]He will build a house for my name and I will establish the throne of his kingdom for ever. [14]I will be a father to him and he will be a son to me. When he commits iniquity, I will reprove him with the rod of men, with human blows. [15]But my steadfast love shall not depart from him as I removed it from Saul whom I

removed from before you. [16]Your house and your kingdom will be confirmed before me for ever, your throne will be established for ever.'"' [17]Nathan spoke to David according to all these words and all this vision.

Notes on the text

4. Several MSS specify that Nathan is a prophet, though this is probably explanatory.

5. Many MSS and most versions omit *'el* (also vv. 7–8, 10). But omission is easier to explain than inclusion, so we assume the doubling of prepositions is intentional specification.

6. Reading the waw before the tabernacle as explicative.

7. *šibṭê* is usually 'tribes' or 'rods'. Since no tribe was commanded to rule Israel, we assume 'tribe' is incorrect. Unless *šibṭê* means 'those bearing rods' (i.e. rulers; McCarter 1984: 192), then 'rods' is also improbable. *šôpĕṭê* ('judges', 1 Chr. 17:6; see ESV) is attractive, but seems like a correction. However, in 2 Sam. 5:1 *šibṭê* means representative rulers from tribes, an appropriate sense here, perhaps conflating the word's two senses (similarly, Fokkelman 1990: 381). This avoids awkward emendations (e.g. Murray 1987; cf. Begg 1988).

10. *māqôm* refers neither to temple nor to land, but the quality of life to be experienced (Murray 1990), yet linked to the promises to Abraham (Firth 2005b: 90).

12. With many MSS read *'im* for *'et*.

16. Omit the kaph of *lĕpāneykā*.

Form and structure

2 Sam. 7 is often said to represent the high point of the whole of the so-called Deuteronomistic History (Birch 1998: 1254), principally because here the Davidic dynasty is established. Such an assertion is defensible because of the role David's house plays in the balance of Samuel and Kings, though it can be overstressed. An important result of this is that the passage has spawned a massive body of secondary literature looking at its prehistory and evidence of redaction, as well as its significance for biblical theology (for a helpful summary, see Anderson 1989: 112–116; Ulshöfer 1977: 78–98 critiques claimed literary-critical divisions into redactional layers). Yet many of these studies tend to extract the text from its current setting, whereas the attempt here is to read it as a whole within its setting in Samuel (see Avioz 2005b: 43–68; Fokkelman 1990: 207; and the structural analysis of Botha 1986: 68).

It is also commonly noted that the Davidic covenant is initiated here, though *bĕrît* (covenant) is notably, and somewhat surprisingly, absent. Later poetic reflections (e.g. 2 Sam. 23:1–7; Pss 89, 132) speak of this passage as a covenant, a position that can be defended on the basis of the language used and the clear links to the promises to Abraham (Firth 2005b: 84–94). In spite of this, several scholars have claimed either that there was no understanding of a Davidic covenant before the exile (Mettinger 1976: 282) or that there never was a Davidic covenant among those taken in by Yahweh's rhetoric (Eslinger 1994: 90). Mettinger's view requires the allocation of 2 Sam. 23:5 to the exilic period, though the grounds for doing so are not strong, and it is likely that 23:1–7 represents an old tradition (see 'Form and structure' there). Eslinger's more radical view is weakened by his failure to consider the rhetorical goals of the final narrator who controls our reading through later references that treat it as a covenant (Firth 2005b: 94–98; see the parallels in Calderone 1966: 42–57; Laato 1997: 248–257). Like Gen. 15 (with which there are extensive links: Hagelia 1994: 190–191), this is an essentially promissory covenant that does not require any specific action on David's part. Although this is often described as unconditional, it is truer to say that the conditions are implied rather than explicit (see Waltke 1988).

The text must be seen within its literary context and not as an independent artefact. That it is placed relatively early in the account of David's reign does not mean that it is an early event, as 2 Sam. 5:6 – 8:13 is dischronologized through to its chiastic structure. The heart of the chiasm is in chs. 6 and 7, both of which focus on worship, and thus balance the equivalent items in the chiasm of chs. 21 – 24. Both structures emphasize the importance of worship in David's reign, with the first item (2 Sam. 6 and 22) concerned with public aspects of Yahweh's presence with David, while the second item (2 Sam. 7; 23:1–7) is concerned more with formal elements of David's relationship with Yahweh. Moreover, the two sections are linked in that both 7:1 and 22:1 speak of Yahweh's delivering David from all his enemies. Also in 2 Sam. 23:1–7 David offers a formal assessment on his reign, an assessment based upon Yahweh's promises in this chapter. Thus there are clear and deliberate links requiring these passages to be read in the light of each other. Such a structure requires us to recognize 2 Sam. 7:1–17 as the foundational text of the Davidic covenant.

The chapter's central structuring device is the diverse ways the word *bayit* is used in the dialogue. Although the meaning 'house' is well established, it here refers variously to a personal dwelling, a temple or a dynasty (see George 2002a: 24). It is the interplay between these senses that drives the narrative as the focus shifts from David's desire to build Yahweh a house through to Yahweh's promise that he will build David a house, a lasting dynasty. David cannot build a house for Yahweh, though this was accepted royal practice (see Carlson 1964: 98–99), because David remains under Yahweh's authority.

Comment

David's desire to build a temple: 7:1–3

1. There is a clear break between the events described here and what precedes. The time frame is vague, and of no particular interest to the narrator. Of more importance is the link to 2 Sam. 22:1, which is also said to derive from when Yahweh had delivered David from all his enemies, emphasizing the links between these passages. The narrative suggests that David has reached a point where temple construction is possible (see Deut. 12:10–11). Kings constantly engaged in warfare, as did David from 2 Sam. 5:6–8, 17–25 and again in 2 Sam. 8, and lacked the time for major building projects since these signified a settled state. But David has not achieved this condition through his own efforts. Rather, as both chs. 5 and 8 indicate and 22 and 23:1–7 celebrate, the rest enabling this came from Yahweh. David is acting in gratitude, not grasping for power and recognition from God. Deut. 12:1–14 expects that when Israel receives rest in the land, they will destroy Canaanite shrines and worship only at the central place, providing the context in which to understand David's plan. The stability indicated must have existed for some time since David now dwells in his own substantial house, one made of (or perhaps panelled with) cedar (5:11), a sign of a significant building. The rest David received is what Yahweh promised, so what was sought since Joshua has been attained.

2–3. In this context David expressed to Nathan a desire to build a house for Yahweh. This is the first time Nathan is mentioned, and his importance is underlined by the narrator calling him a prophet (see Jones 1990: 19–30). David's address to him contrasts the grandeur of his cedar house when the ark is kept in 'curtains'. Most commonly, 'curtains' refers to elements making up a tent rather than the tent itself, and especially the tabernacle (Exod. 26:1–14), though in poetic parallelism (Jer. 4:20) 'curtains' can be synonymous with 'tent'. It seems clear that the word is chosen to highlight the contrast between David's house and the place of the ark. This contrast is made starker by 2 Sam. 6:17's reference to a tent David erected for the ark. David knows the security from his enemies that enables him to build his house comes from Yahweh, so contrasts his home with where the ark is kept. Nathan's response is positive, insisting that David should build a temple. Although this may sound like an obsequious attempt to ingratiate oneself with the king, it is consistent with the narrator's opening observation: David is secure because of what Yahweh has done, thus demonstrating his status before Yahweh (Youngblood 1992: 885). Later passages show that Nathan is no yes-man, but Yahweh is clearly with David (5:10). Surely, therefore, it was appropriate to encourage David to build the temple.

Yahweh to make a house for David: 7:4–11a

4–7. Nathan's response appears to conclude the matter, but though Yahweh is the source of David's security, Yahweh's presence does not automatically make it necessary for David to build a temple. Thus that night Yahweh's word came to Nathan, in the longest message from Yahweh since he spoke to Moses (Bergen 1996: 336), directing Nathan to report to David. David's status is maintained from the outset because he is called Yahweh's servant (elsewhere used to describe Moses, Josh. 1:2, 7), indicating that although his plan will be rejected, David's own status is not under threat. In addition, such language is classically that of the suzerain in covenant texts, so the language shows that David is addressed in covenantal terms. The message's opening in v. 5b is a rhetorical question, indicating that David will not build Yahweh's temple. The reason for this is established in the following verses as Yahweh explains that he has never dwelt in a temple but has been mobile, living among the people when he brought them from Egypt, always free to move among them. This poses a problem given earlier references to Shiloh as a temple (1 Sam. 1:9; 3:3), though, as noted ('Comment' 1 Sam. 1:9), this may relate to Eli's quasi-royal presentation, and that building might not have been intended as a permanent structure. A temple might threaten Yahweh's authority and freedom in that it limited his location. V. 7 expresses this concern in another rhetorical question, though the implication is essentially the same. The question expects the answer 'No' because Yahweh has never asked any of the nation's leaders to build him a house of cedar. It is Yahweh, not David, who introduces the theme of cedar for the temple, though David's comment at v. 2 probably indicates an intention to build in cedar. Moreover, Yahweh refers to his dwelling as a 'tent', suggesting something a little more than 'curtains' is involved, and implying that this has been sufficient. Was Yahweh permanently opposed to a temple? The movement into Kings would suggest not since in 1 Kgs 5 Solomon is the temple's authorized builder (see v. 13), but the point is that temple-building cannot be humanly initiated (similarly, Avioz 2005b: 16–23), even by someone like David, any more than kingship can be initiated by Israel's elders (1 Sam. 8:4–9). Yahweh's authority and freedom mean that a temple can be constructed only by his nominee (similarly, P. R. Williamson 2007: 125–127).

8–11a. A new stage in Nathan's oracle begins here, a stage again marked by reference to David as Yahweh's servant and a report of what it is that Nathan is to say. Where vv. 5–7 focused on the reasons why David should not build a temple, these verses focus on what Yahweh has done for David, reinforcing the point made by the narrator in v. 1. A new title is introduced for Yahweh within the narrative, naming him as 'Yahweh of Hosts', an epithet used in Samuel only at points of significant social change (see 'Comment' on 1 Sam. 1:1–3). Although possessing warlike overtones, the title is never explained in these terms and within Samuel points to Yahweh's authority to institute change. This change looks back to 1 Sam. 15 – 17 with David's election as anointed leader over Yahweh's people. The reference to 'my people' is rich in covenantal allusions that reach back to Exodus 19:4–6 since it reflects Israel's special status, and therefore David's status within that covenant. Yahweh's language also refers to what he has previously done for David, journeying with him and cutting off his enemies, precisely the claims we expect a suzerain to make, and that Samuel has been careful to demonstrate. The second half of v. 9 moves from a historical statement, essentially the historical prologue, on to the suzerain's promise to his servant, which is that he will make his name great (on the linguistic issues, see Fokkelman 1990: 223–225). This promise is rich in allusions to Abraham (Gen. 12:2), as well as contrasting with the builders at Babel (Gen. 11:1–9). The earlier Abrahamic and Sinai covenants are evoked to demonstrate that the promise to David is understood in similar terms. But the promise is not for David alone, since it is characteristic of covenantal texts to look to Yahweh's greater purposes. Therefore, the promise moves from David to the nation's future status in v. 10. However, since this promise is based on a place for the nation, it too evokes the Abrahamic covenant in that a secure dwelling place is tied to the land promise (Gen. 15:7–21). What is different is that the nation is no longer to be disturbed, although this has been their experience. Thus David's rest is the paradigm for the nation's rest, rest that previous methods of government have not enabled, but rest that Yahweh will give through David (see Evans 2000: 168).

Dynasty: 7:11b–17

11b–13. V. 11b is set off from what precedes and what follows by its use of the third person, whereas elsewhere Yahweh's speech is reported in the first person. By v. 12 we are back into direct address to David, but cannot ignore the rhetorical importance of 11b. By deliberately changing the structure of what is said, it highlights it as a crucial matter since it is reported from Yahweh (similarly, Murray 1998: 185). Thus it introduces those elements of the promise of post-mortem interest to David, as Yahweh promised that David's family would constitute an enduring dynasty, creating a new meaning for the word 'house' within the chapter. The promise is rich in Abrahamic allusions, especially in language concerning the 'seed' to come from David's own body. Since David has not had difficulty in fathering children such a comment is technically redundant, but is included because of the contact it makes with Gen. 17 in pointing to an unborn son. As Yahweh establishes a house for David, it will not be through the sons he has, rejecting primogeniture, but through a son who is to come. Yahweh will establish the son's kingdom, a promise not previously made concerning David. The promise's future reference obliquely refers to Solomon's kingdom, though the NT (and indeed later use of Pss 2 and 132) takes this in a messianic sense.

The son will build a house for Yahweh's name, which is the temple, just as Yahweh has given David a great name. Again, there is a play on the word 'house' because Yahweh will establish David's throne for ever. Yahweh does not object to a temple, but rejects human endeavours to determine when it should be built (similarly, Avioz 2005b: 35). On the other hand, Yahweh retains the right to establish a royal dynasty. David may have come perilously close to repeating the problem generated by the people's request in 1 Sam. 8 of seeking to determine and limit Yahweh's role, but where Saul was ultimately rejected, David remains acceptable to Yahweh because of his special role.

14–15. Covenantal language occurs again in v. 14, where the terminology echoes Exod. 19:4–6, though it is limited to the promise concerning the son. This time, we are to understand the singular distributively, since the promise of an enduring dynasty goes beyond the initial son, even if he would build the temple. The father–son language, like the reference to David as Yahweh's servant, is typical of covenant texts. The suzerain always retains the right to discipline his subjects, and Yahweh does so with David's line, but what is crucial is the promise that Yahweh will never remove his covenant commitment (*ḥesed*) from the son. Saul forfeited it, but this is not to be the experience of David's line.

16. Here we return to direct address to David, with specific focus on the establishment of a sure dynasty and kingdom for him, though describing this as confirmed (*ne'man*) evokes the promise of the faithful priest of 1 Sam. 2:35, while the multiple references to the word 'house' also set David against Eli's family. It is David's family who know Yahweh's promises, who have the assurance that Yahweh will establish their throne for ever, a messianic theme slightly more explicit in 1 Chr. 17:14 through a change in pronoun.

17. Nathan reported to David as directed, the importance of this note being to stress that this is Yahweh's word rather than something mediated through Nathan.

Explanation

As this chapter begins, it appears to prepare for a standard ANE narrative where a king sought and received permission from the deity to build a temple. This honoured the deity, but also enabled the king to gain power since the temple would support the claim of divine support for his rule. David's status as one to whom Yahweh has given rest provides the opportunity to make such an offer, and initially it seems this will happen, as Nathan, seeing Yahweh's presence with David, agrees he should construct a temple. David is not presented as grasping the power this will bring, because his motivation comes from the contrast between his own grand house and the poor condition of the tent where the ark is housed. But there is a surprise, because Yahweh takes the initiative from David by sending a message through Nathan that indicates through a series of questions that he will not build a temple. The reason for the prohibition is that Yahweh has never previously requested such a building, preferring freedom of mobility, though v. 13 shows that this is not a permanent prohibition. Rather, just as Saul had to learn that in sacral matters he must submit to Yahweh's word through the prophet Samuel, so also David must submit to Yahweh's word through Nathan. Kings do not determine what Yahweh does, and although Yahweh will accept a temple, it must be on his terms. David cannot initiate this process; only Yahweh can do so, and he will permit it only through a son to be born to David. In doing this, Yahweh not only explains what David may not do for him; he also outlines what he will do for David. Above all else, this involved the establishment of a dynasty for him, the very thing that was removed from Saul. It was through this dynasty, a dynasty that would endure where others had not, that Yahweh would achieve his purposes for the nation.

Although the word *běrît* (covenant) does not occur here, it is so full of covenantal language that one must conclude that it establishes a covenant with David. If so, this is a vitally important covenant, and not only because it is the central point from which the messianic hope sprang. Its importance within the books of Samuel must be noted, because here we have the point where Yahweh's promises find their focus through deliberate reference to older covenant texts, as well as the whole complex of Joshua–Kings (McCarthy 1965: 137). It is in David that these covenants find their meaning, and it is through David that the covenant relationship continues to develop. Its importance within the OT is immense, and is referred to in a wide range of subsequent texts, including Pss 2, 72, 89, 132; Isa. 7:10–17; 9:2–7; 11:1–5; Jer. 33:14–26; Ezek. 34:23–24; 37:24–28 (Clements 1989: 12; for a more comprehensive treatment, see Schniedewind 1999: 51–139). In sum, reflection on this text from within the OT alone justifies the claim that it is the seedbed of the messianic hope (see Kaiser 1988: 77–83).

It is unsurprising that the NT makes considerable use of this passage. Although it cites it directly only twice (2 Cor. 6:18; Heb. 1:5), there is an extensive body of allusions to it. In doing so it does not lose sight of the fact that the promises had to be meaningful in the time of David and Solomon, as well as for later generations of Israelites who heard this text, but it insists that the text's ultimate fulfilment is seen in Jesus of Nazareth. Repeatedly, he is called Son of David (Matt. 1:1; Mark 10:47), is seen as the one who builds the true temple (John 2:19–22; Heb. 3:3), and the one who ultimately inherits David's throne, which is an eternal kingdom (Heb. 1:8). The connections the NT establishes are more than simply the direct references, because it also builds upon the extensive allusions already present within the OT, especially the Psalms. Taking the example of Ps. 2 alone, it points to Jesus not only as the king who came in fulfilment of the promise to David (Heb. 1:5), but also the one who now reigns (Acts

4:23–30) and is to come (Rev. 19:11–16). Thus the NT (and also Qumran; see 4QFlor) enters a world of exegesis and theology established within the OT. What is distinctive of the NT's witness is that the promise of the Davidic covenant finds and is finding its fulfilment in Jesus. God's reign through David is now expressed in Jesus.

2 SAMUEL 7:18–29

Translation

[18]Then King David came and sat before Yahweh and said, 'Who am I, Lord Yahweh, and who is my house that you should bring me thus far? [19]And yet this was a small thing in your eyes, Lord Yahweh. You have also spoken concerning the distant future of your servant's house, and this is instruction for humans, Lord Yahweh. [20]What more can David say to you since you know your servant, Lord Yahweh? [21]Because of your word, and according to your heart, you have done all this greatness to reveal it to your servant. [22]Therefore, you are great, Lord Yahweh. There is none like you and there is no god besides you according to all we have heard with our ears. [23]And who is like your people Israel whom God led along to redeem to be his people and make himself a name, doing great and awesome things for them, driving out before your people, whom you redeemed for yourself from Egypt, a nation and its gods? [24]You have established for yourself your own people, Israel, for ever, and you O Yahweh became their God.

[25]'Now, Lord Yahweh, confirm the word you have spoken concerning your servant and his house for ever, and do as you have spoken. [26]So your name will be magnified for ever, saying, "Yahweh of Hosts is God over Israel," and the house of your servant David will be established before you. [27]Because you, O Yahweh of Hosts, the God of Israel, have uncovered your servant's ear, saying, "I will build a house for you." Therefore, your servant has found courage to pray this prayer to you. [28]Now, Lord Yahweh, you are God and your words are true, and you have promised this good thing to your servant. [29]And now, be pleased and bless the house of your servant that it may continue for ever before you, because you have spoken, O Lord Yahweh, and with your blessing shall your servant's house be blessed for ever.'

Notes on the text

19. *lĕmērāḥôq* is unusual in having two prepositions, but the same form occurs in Job 36:3. The word is more commonly spatial, but the temporal sense here also occurs in 2 Kgs 19:25 = Isa. 37:26. The last clause is often emended (see McCarter 1984: 233), but the need to do so by blending with 1 Chr. 17:17 cautions against rejecting MT (see Anderson 1989: 124). NIV's conversion to a question is to be rejected.

21. Hiph. *yd'*, with God as the subject, always refers to revelation, not simply passing on information (see *NIDOTTE* 2:411–412).

22. Many MSS (see LXX, Tg, Syr) have 'Yahweh God' (see vv. 28, 29). But this comes from conforming the text to 1 Chr. 17:16–27, which does not use *'ădônāy yhwh* in David's prayer.

23. Revocalize *hālakû* to the infinitive *hōlikô* (McCarter 1984: 234). *lākem* is absent in 4QSam[a] and LXX, while some MSS have *lāhem*. 4QSam[a] and LXX probably correct an awkward text, but *lāhem* could refer back to the people, understood collectively (similarly, Fokkelman 1990: 382–383). In place of *lĕ'arṣekā* one could follow 1 Chr. 17:21 and read *lĕgārēš* (so Youngblood 1992: 900), but Fokkelman's (1990: 383) suggested byform of the hiph. of *rwṣ* (with confusion between aleph and he) achieves this without disturbing the consonantal text, so Chronicles offers a slight paraphrase for clarity.

25. With a number of MSS, read *'ădônāy yhwh*. See 7:22.

28–29. See 'Notes' on 7:22.

Form and structure

David's prayer is closely tied to the dynastic promise Yahweh gave him in 7:3–16. The prayer cannot be interpreted apart from that context and is separated purely for analysis since its own form throws up issues distinct from the first part of the chapter. McCarter (1984: 239–240) has argued that absence of reference to the temple suggests this prayer was originally associated with the ark's arrival in 6:1–19, though he acknowledges the impact of the canonical arrangement. However, since David was precluded from building a temple, there is no reason for him to mention it. Conversely, the frequent use of the words 'house' (*bayit*; ×8 in 7:1–17; ×7 in 7:18–29), 'for ever' (*'ôlām*; ×2 in 7:1–17; ×4 in 7:18–29) and 'servant' (*'ebed*; ×2 in 7:1–17; ×10 in 7:18–29) suggests a close link with the preceding section, so the prayer is here interpreted in the light of Nathan's oracle (similarly, Avioz 2005b: 38–42). Despite attempts to trace the prayer's redactional levels (see McCarter 1984: 240), Carlson's case for its unity (1964: 127) remains sound.

The frequency of servant language points to the prayer's formal setting where David uses elevated forms of address for God, eight times (see 'Notes' on 7:22) addressing the deity as 'Lord Yahweh' (*'ădônāy yhwh*, a title not otherwise used in Samuel) and twice using 'Yahweh of Hosts' (see 'Comment' on 1 Sam. 1:1–3), this epithet's last occurrence in Samuel. This demonstrates that David is highly deferential before Yahweh, though appropriately because Yahweh has declined his offered temple (albeit temporarily), thus demonstrating his authority over David. Yet deference is mixed with a determination that Yahweh should both establish the promise (7:25) and also bless David's house (7:29).

The prayer is more tightly structured than some recognize (e.g. Anderson 1989: 125) beyond the fact that vv. 18–24 are basically thanksgiving and 25–29, petition. The thanksgiving is built around three rhetorical questions (vv. 18, 20, 23), while the petition employs three segments introduced by 'and now' (wĕ'attâ). There are two petitions within this section (v. 25, 29), each using paired imperatives. The prayer thus builds to the request for perpetual blessing as that which confirms the promise, tying the Davidic covenant more closely to the Abrahamic (Gen. 12:2–3; similarly, Wright 2006: 228. See Clements 1967: 53–59, who reverses the literary relationship).

Comment

Thanksgiving for the promise: 7:18–24

18–19. Since 7:17 indicates that Nathan brought Yahweh's message to David, it was necessary for David to enter Yahweh's presence, presumably in the tent mentioned in 7:2. This suggests this is a public prayer rather than a simple response, which explains the care with which it is formulated. This movement underscores David and Yahweh's relative power in that David wanted the ark moved to a temple because of the splendour of his house, but now must enter Yahweh's presence in the tent to speak with Yahweh (see Murray 1998: 201; cf. the repetition of *yāšab* from 7:1). The prayer's opening is a paired rhetorical question. The questions are effectively synonymous because they indicate that neither David nor his house has sufficient status before Yahweh to have received such promises. But linking the questions allows us to see David and his house as indivisible, something important for the rest of the prayer as well as 23:1–7. Yet David confesses that the fact that he and his house have received an elevated status before Yahweh is a small matter for Yahweh because Yahweh's promise extends well into the future. David does not yet speak of for ever, because this will be the petition in 7:29. The last clause of v. 19 is difficult to interpret, but probably means that the evidence of grace in such actions by Yahweh acts as instruction (*tôrâ*) for all people, linking David's prayer to his earlier declaration in 1 Sam. 17:46 on the universal importance of Yahweh's actions in Israel.

20–22. The second rhetorical question acknowledges that David can say nothing more, not only because of the promise given but also because Yahweh knows David. David cannot hide from Yahweh (Ps. 139:1–16; Amos 9:3–4) because Yahweh knows him completely, something he will regret after the events of 2 Sam. 11. Yahweh's actions for David do not therefore respond to David's merit. Rather, Yahweh acted in accord with his own purposes (lit. 'his heart'; see 1 Sam. 13:14), and David can only be thankful and deferential that his part within them has been revealed. This leads David to doxology, praising God for his greatness and uniqueness, drawing in themes expressed more widely in the OT (Deut. 4:35; Ps. 86:8; see Anderson 1989: 127). However, the key text for interpreting this is found in Hannah's Song (1 Sam. 2:2)

23–24. The third rhetorical question focuses on Israel's status, so the position of David and his house is seen within the larger question of the nation and its relationship to Yahweh. The text of v. 23 is difficult (see 'Notes'), but the general thrust is clear enough. Israel, like David, could not claim anything from Yahweh but had experienced the blessing of being brought by Yahweh from Egypt into the land promised to Abraham (Gen. 15:18–21). Israel's entry into the land had settled them, but Yahweh had also expelled the previous occupants and thus gained renown for himself while granting Israel a status given to no other nation. The importance of this is emphasized in v. 24, which draws on the covenant tradition, where the mutual relationship between Yahweh and his people is stressed (cf. Exod. 6:7; Hos. 2:23). The thanksgiving thus praises Yahweh in specifically covenantal terms, but also links Israel's position to David's through the rhetorical questions, all of which pivot on the assertion of Yahweh's incomparability in v. 22. As well as expressing thanks, this section lays the foundation for the coming petitions.

Petition for blessing: 7:25–29

25–27. The rhetorical questions of the thanksgiving are paralleled by three uses of 'and now', which introduce each section of the petitions. As with the questions, the three are related to one another in developing the petitions, though there are only two actual petitions in vv. 25 and 29. Having established the context where Yahweh was expected to act and a basis on which he would, David asks that Yahweh confirm his promise for ever, linking his house's status with that of Israel in v. 24. At first blush, such a request seems unnecessary because Yahweh has already promised a perpetual relationship in 7:16, though it may refer only to the throne and not David's house. Yet David's requested confirmation is directed outwards, so Yahweh's greatness would be demonstrated and acknowledged by others, though this is still tied to the establishment of David's house. But this is not simply an attempt to make Yahweh the state patron (against Brueggemann 1985: 80), because the request is rooted in what Yahweh has already initiated, and in initiating it Yahweh rejected David's own temple initiative. David is aware that his position, and that of his dynasty, is bound up with what Yahweh does, so his future is the continuation of what Yahweh has already done and is bound to what Yahweh has revealed. The promise revealed is what enabled David to pray, so Yahweh's name will continue to be magnified.

28–29. Although both vv. 28 and 29 commence with 'and now' (*wĕʿattâ*), they should be treated together as both link to the second petition in v. 29. V. 28 returns to doxology, paralleling v. 23 in the thanksgiving, though the emphasis is upon the certainty of Yahweh's acting in accordance with his word (Isa. 55:11). This certainty provides the context for David to ask that Yahweh bless his house for ever, with the blessing defined as remaining in Yahweh's presence (cf. Ps. 27:4). The understanding of Yahweh's blessing is that once it is spoken it endures for ever, and this knowledge is sufficient for David. Although David wants glory for his own house, he seeks it in a way consistent with the honour due to Yahweh, honour that needs to look outwards from Israel.

Explanation

Having heard Yahweh's rejection of his planned temple but also his promise of an enduring dynasty for his family, David moved from his palace to the tent where the ark was kept. Originally, he believed this tent was not grand enough for Yahweh's presence through the ark (7:1–2), but now it is where he sits in Yahweh's presence rather than the glory of his palace. It is here that he prays in response to the promise made to him, though through his prayer the narrator provides readers with guidance on how to understand the promise. Even before noting that, the fact that David goes from Nathan to Yahweh's presence after the rejection of his proposal for a temple marks out the distinction between David and Saul. In 1 Sam. 13 and 15 Saul responded to Yahweh's message of judgment by attempting to negotiate a better outcome for himself. David's prayer accepts Yahweh's right to overrule the monarch. This contrast is surely intentional, as it reinforces the point made in 1 Sam. 12, that the king's rule is limited by Yahweh's greater authority.

David is not only presented as praying: we are also given his prayer's content. This may be because it was a public prayer, but it is also because the prayer's content is important for what it says about the covenant with David. An enduring question in understanding OT theology hinges on the relationship between the various covenants (Noah in Gen. 9:1–7, Abraham in Gen. 15, 17 and the Sinai covenant from Exod. 19, 24; see B. W. Anderson 1999: 74–78). Although David's prayer does not answer all the associated questions, it provides a starting point by linking itself directly with both the promise to Abraham and the exodus and conquest traditions. Thus it sees itself as continuing the themes of the earlier covenants without replacing them. It is a supplement, a further step in the *Missio Dei*, rather than replacing what has gone before. Moreover, by making the promises the prayer's centre, it emphasizes the importance of praying the promise, something that provides the pattern for Ps. 89:39–52's [ET 89:38–51] insistence that Yahweh should honour his promises to David, with these promises creating a set of intertwined relationships between Yahweh, David and Israel.

Nevertheless, David's prayer does not simply ask that Yahweh fulfil his promises, though this is crucial to both the thanksgiving and the petition. At crucial points, possibly v. 19 but certainly 26, it looks beyond his own household's experience and perhaps even beyond the borders of Israel. These promises can function like the law in Deut. 4:6–8 and provide the basis for others magnifying Yahweh. This confirms David's attitude in 1 Sam. 17:46, so that both the beginning of David's rise and this moment of his greatest splendour look beyond his immediate experience to its significance for all.

2 SAMUEL 8

Translation

¹After this, David struck the Philistines and subdued them, and David took Metheg Ammah from the hand of the Philistines.

²He struck Moab and measured them with a cord and made them lie down on the ground. He measured two lengths of cord to put to death and one full length to keep alive. So Moab became David's servants, bringing tribute.

³David struck Hadadezer ben Rehob, king of Zobah as he went to restore his rule at the River. ⁴David captured from him one thousand seven hundred horsemen and twenty thousand foot soldiers. David hamstrung all the chariot horses, but left enough for one hundred chariots. ⁵When the Arameans of Damascus came to help Hadedezer king of Zobah, David struck twenty-two thousand men of Aram. ⁶David put garrisons in Aram of Damascus, and Aram became David's servants, bringing tribute. So Yahweh gave David victory wherever he went. ⁷David took the gold shields Hadadezer's servants had and brought them to Jerusalem. ⁸So from Tebah and Berothai, Hadaezer's cities, King David took very much bronze.

⁹Toi, king of Hamath, heard that David had struck Hadadezer's whole army. ¹⁰Toi sent his son Joram to King David to ask about his welfare and to bless him because he had fought with Hadadezer and defeated him, for Hadadezer was often at war with Toi. He brought items of silver, gold and bronze with him. ¹¹These also King David dedicated to Yahweh along with the silver and gold he had dedicated from all the nations he had subdued, ¹²from Edom, Moab, the Ammonites, the Philistines, Amalek and the spoil of Hadadezer ben Rehob, king of Zobah.

¹³David made a name for himself when he returned from striking eighteen thousand Edomites in the Valley of Salt. ¹⁴He put garrisons in Edom – through all Edom he set garrisons – and all Edom became David's servants. So Yahweh gave David victory wherever he went.

¹⁵David reigned over all Israel, and David exercised justice and righteousness for his people. ¹⁶Joab ben Zeruiah was over the army, Jehoshaphat ben Ahilud was the recorder, ¹⁷Zadok ben Ahitub and Ahimelech ben Abiathar were priests, Seraiah was secretary, ¹⁸Benaiah ben Jehoiada was over the Cherethites and Pelethites, and David's sons were priests.

Notes on the text

1. 'Metheg Ammah' becomes 'Gath and its environs' in 1 Chr. 18:1. This is probably an exegetical conclusion rather than a textual one (thus overcoming Smith's 1899: 306 objection) since the place name is otherwise unknown and may be translated 'control of the mother city' (see 20:19; Driver 1913: 215; though more lit. 'bridle of the forearm'), which is identified as Gath.

3. Q, many MSS and LXX (see 1 Chr. 18:3) gloss the River as 'Euphrates'. But 'the River' often has this sense (Jer. 2:8), so this simply makes the point explicit.

4. With MT, but LXX, 4QSam^a and 1 Chr. 18:4 have one thousand chariots and seven hundred horsemen.

6. *něṣîb* is either a prefect or a garrison, but as in 1 Sam. 10:5, 13:3, the garrison includes the prefect and is rendered accordingly.

8. For 'Tebah', MT has 'Betah', but 1 Chr. 18:8, Syr and some LXX MSS suggest Tebah is correct.

12. Some MSS read Edom for Aram. The two are easily confused in Hebr., but Edom could be thought to go with Moab and thus be a scribal correction (see Fokkelman 1990: 385).

13. With a few MSS, Syr and LXX, read Edom for Aram. See Ps. 60's superscription.

18. Insert *'al* to explain Benaiah's relationship to the Cherethites and Pelethites (with 1 Chr. 18:17). David's sons as priests is problematic, especially given Zadok and Ahimelech's designation in v. 17. Chronicles says the sons were 'chief officials in service of the king' (ESV). G. J. Wenham (1975: 79–80) rightly argues that the Chronicles text does not arise from theological concerns with the idea of priestly activity by the royal family. However, his case for reading *sknym* (administrators) is less persuasive, since one corruption (the absence of *'al*) does not require another. Chronicles may be paraphrasing this text to avoid confusing a later generation unfamiliar with such practices, in which case the inclusion of Seraiah and Benaiah before David's sons distinguishes the different classes of priest. 20:26 also mentions a separate priestly class.

Form and structure

Although this may seem like a collection of disparate pieces concerning David, with an annalistic collection of battle reports (vv. 1–14) and an appended list of state officials (vv. 15–18), it is actually of considerable importance. There is an obvious distinction between these sections, and similar lists of officials occur in 20:23–26 and 1 Kgs 4:2–6. The lists of officials appear to come from ancient records. They are used as hinges in Samuel, enabling the move in and out of the Court Narrative of chs. 9–20 (see 'Form and structure' on 2 Sam. 9). In 1 Kgs 4 the list's function is similar but not identical as it is followed by a more detailed exposition of Solomon's administration. The official lists are used like David's earlier genealogical lists (3:2–5; 5:13–16), to some extent presuming them, since David's sons are mentioned. The lists are thus separate from the battle reports. Nevertheless, the text joins them because the battle reports refer to administrative processes initiated by David (vv. 6, 14), while one result of David's victories was an increased level of tribute (vv. 2, 6–8, 10–12), requiring more administration in Jerusalem. The current list thus looks back on David's earlier activities while also looking forward by introducing previously unknown characters and groups who feature in the Court Narrative (see 'Comment' on v. 18). Hence the list is a hinge (see also 'Comment' of 3:2–5), tying together what has gone before and preparing for what follows.

The battle accounts are annalistic, lacking plot or characterization, and probably representative (and mostly proleptic) summaries of David's actions (similarly, Fokkelman 1990: 256). The parallels between 8:3–8 and 10:6–18 are not problematic if one remembers that 5:17 – 8:18 is a summary of all David's reign and that 10:6–18 probably comes from before the period described here (see 'Form and structure' on 5:17–25). Conversely, the defeat of the Philistines is probably resuming the thread from 5:25, with two accounts of David in worship (2 Sam. 6 – 7) inserted to summarize David's reign. However, the accounts in 5:17–25 do contain some plot, suggesting that they are not from the same source but are linked by the narrator's repeated interpretative comment: Yahweh gave David victory wherever he went (vv. 6, 14). Placing these statements in a text otherwise lacking in detail causes them to stand out, and creates an immediate parallel with the two accounts of Yahweh's giving David victory in 5:17–25.

Halpern (2001: 133–141) has argued that 8:1–14 derives from an ancient source, perhaps a display inscription, which explains its annalistic and thematic (rather than chronological) form, though one does not have to accept his minimalist conclusions of David's achievements. However, the key point is how they are employed within this stretch of text as a summary demonstrating that the victories described earlier fitted into a wider pattern. David is victorious because of Yahweh's presence (vv. 1–14), while effectively administering the kingdom as Yahweh required (vv. 15–18).

Comment

David's victories: 8:1–14

1. The time reference in 'after this' is uncertain. If a link with 5:17–25 is intended, then the victory over the Philistines described here is subsequent to those previously narrated. Indeed, since those battles were about securing Israelite territory whereas this account refers to capturing of Philistine land, then it must be a later battle. However, the events of ch. 7 must be later still because 7:1 refers to the point where Yahweh gave David rest from all his enemies. So a precise chronology seems impossible. As well as defeating the Philistines, David also subdued them, enabling him to control some of their land, possibly around Gath if Metheg Ammah is so identified (See 'Notes'). The Philistine control of Israel established after Saul's death (1 Sam. 31:7) was thus overthrown, so Israel had freedom on its south-western flank. However, there is no claim that the Philistines became subservient to David, though the Pelethites (8:18) were probably Philistine mercenaries who served him.

2. As well as the Philistines, David also defeated Moab, a people east of Israel. It is unnecessary that this success came after that over the Philistines since there are no chronological markers describing these victories in relation to one another. It is unclear why David engaged in battle with Moab since they had sheltered him and his family while fleeing from Saul (1 Sam. 22:3–4), and Ruth indicates that David had Moabite ancestry (Ruth 4:18–22). However, the battle accounts do not indicate the initiator of any conflict, and 10:1–5 shows that relationships could quickly change. The savagery of David's treatment of the Moabite captives, using a measuring cord to determine the two-thirds of their troops to execute, could suggest Moab began the fight; though, in a world where all captured troops could be put to death, David's actions might be viewed as lenient (Bergen 1996: 347). The important point is that Moab became subservient to David and accordingly began to pay tribute.

3–4. The next campaign is well to the north and associated with a specific king, Hadadezer of Zobah. Zobah is north of Damascus (roughly 60 miles north of the Sea of Galilee), and might be thought to be outside David's active range, though Saul's battle list in 1 Sam. 14:47–48 includes 'kings of Zobah'. This suggests extended campaigns in the region, while Zobah's inclusion in 10:6–8 also points to a continuing regional problem for David. The name Hadadezer recurs in 1 Kgs 11:23 from late in Solomon's reign, though this is presumably a different king with the same name. V. 3 is ambiguous in that it does not make clear whether David or Hadadezer sought to restore control at the river. Although the last clause of the verse may mean to set up a stele, the effect is the same since only a king who claimed control could do so. If 10:6–8 is earlier than this, then David defeated Hadadezer when he sought to reclaim his territory by the Euphrates (see 'Notes'). In defeating Hadadezer, David also captured a significant body of his armed forces (though on these numbers see 'Comment' on 1 Sam. 4:2), although Israel was not then noted for its chariotry. As with Moab, David needed to render the enemy inoperable against himself, which is why he hamstrung most of the horses (cf. Josh. 11:6–9), retaining only enough for Israel's limited chariotry (though McCarter 1984: 249 notes that this punishment is recorded only against mercenaries and may have been particular to them). Such actions may also fit with Deut. 17:16, which prohibits kings from accumulating horses (also Gordon 1986: 244). Halpern (2001: 139) notes that hamstringing would not prevent their use in agriculture.

5–6. Since Zobah is north of Damascus, David had to pass through Aramean (modern Syrian) territory to reach it, so it is unsurprising that the Arameans assisted Zobah. The two were also hired against David by the Ammonites in 10:6–8. Again David overcame a large and powerful force, and subsequently placed his own garrisons in Aram, so Aram joined Moab as subservient and paying tribute. A display inscription was intended to glorify the king's achievements, but here the narrator includes the statement that Yahweh gave victory to David wherever he went. This note has two important functions. First, it shows that the glory from these battles belongs to Yahweh, not David. Secondly, it explains how David defeated such significant forces. No record of Israelite casualties is provided because such information would not be released on public documents and was probably not available to the narrator. But however much this might have provided David with prestige, the prestige is no longer his but Yahweh's, so these battle reports contribute to the statements in 7:1 and 22:1. A cynical reader might suggest that David's success was linked to the lack of interest in the Levant from the great powers, but for the narrator that is simply more evidence of Yahweh's involvement. We have thus an effective demonstration of the earlier statements that Yahweh was with David (1 Sam. 16:18; 18:12, 14, 28; 2 Sam. 3:1; 5:10; see Arnold 2003: 493).

7–8. The northern victory gave control of key cities and considerable wealth. Hadadezer had apparently made golden shields (possibly quivers) as a sign of his own prestige, but David transported this to Jerusalem, along with a large amount of bronze from some of his cities. According to 1 Chr. 18:8, Solomon used this bronze to make the bronze sea and some of the temple vessels. That David could transport all this material safely back to Jerusalem indicates his control of the trade routes north of Israel, creating a context where Israel's wealth could be increased.

9–12. Presumably on the basis that the enemy of my enemy is my friend, David was approached by Toi (also known as Tou), the king of Hamath, after Hadadezer's defeat. Hamath was a neo-Hittite city north of Zobah and there had apparently been considerable conflict between Toi and Hadadezer. However, Toi needed to be careful not to offend an obviously powerful new figure in the region, which is perhaps why he sent his son Joram as his ambassador to David. According to 1 Chr. 18:10, his name was Hadoram, which would mean 'Hadad is exalted', whereas Joram is a good Israelite name meaning 'Yahweh is exalted'. As with Ish-bosheth (2:8) and Mephibosheth (9:6), it is probable that Chronicles has recorded the actual name, the authors of Samuel apparently not wishing to see David honoured by someone with a name honouring another deity (Hadad is often identified with Baal in Ugaritic texts), though names compounded with Hadad are quite common. Joram's role was to ensure that Hamath remained on good terms with David, and perhaps to formalize this with gifts made from bronze, silver and gold. That Yahweh had given David victory was recognized by David when he dedicated this material, plus his gains from other campaigns, including some not mentioned against the Ammonites and Amalek. These campaigns fill in the geographic ring around Israel since Edom is to the south-east, Ammon to the north-east and Amalek to the south. When linked with the victories over Moab, the Philistines and Hadadezer, it becomes clear that David secured all Israel's borders. Also this list indicates that for the first time Israel occupied the territory promised in Gen. 15:18–21 (see Carlson 1964: 115). That David did not keep the wealth or the horses for himself shows he was acting consistently with Deut. 17:14–20, and could be considered a just king.

13–14. Although David's victory over Edom was intimated in v. 12, it is now described (see 'Notes'). This time he strikes down eighteen thousand in the Valley of Salt, which probably runs south of Beersheba towards the Dead Sea, securing Israel's southern border. Edom also joined the list of nations subservient to David and offering tribute. The point is not so much the victory over another significant force, but the renown David gained through it. On its own, this statement might suggest David achieved this through his own skill, but the narrator again intrudes to observe that David gained victory only because Yahweh gave it to him. The natural tendency is to attribute empire to human achievements, but the narrator insists that the glory belongs to Yahweh.

David's administration: 8:15–18

15. Hints of David's administration were made in terms of his northern garrisons, but we now receive the first direct insight into his administration. Unlike Saul, there is evidence of the establishment of the machinery of state. Such machinery is open to abuse, and will be abused by David, which is why the overall summary of his reign needs to stress his positive achievements. As Campbell (2005: 84) observes, 'No empire survives long without justice at home.' David can be described as the model of the just king, and he worked for all Israel rather than the Israel–Judah divide apparent at his coronation (5:1–5), which recurred after Absalom's revolt (19:41–43). The description of David's reign uses forensic language, indicating that he acted as a final court of appeal for contentious issues, providing the basis for the supposed cases presented to him in 12:1–6 and 14:4–7. Absalom exploited this same structure to begin his rebellion (15:1–6). In spite of his failings, this verse is unequivocal in insisting that the ultimate assessment of David is positive.

16–18. As well as David, we are given a list of David's officials, which is made up of various pairs. The exact roles of Jehoshaphat and Seraiah (the only member of the list without a patronym) cannot be determined precisely, though both were senior administrators within David's civil service. As well as two administrators, the list refers to two military commanders: Joab (see 2:13), who was over the regular army, and Benaiah, who commanded David's mercenary bodyguards, the Cherethites and Pelethites. The names of the latter respectively suggest people from Crete and Philistia, though reference to the 'Negeb of the Cherethites' (1 Sam. 30:14) suggests they had settled there for some time. Both groups may have originated in the six hundred men David built around himself in Ziklag. Joab is a significant figure in the rest of David's story, but Benaiah is a marginal figure in David's story (see 23:20–22), coming to prominence in establishing Solomon's reign (1 Kgs 1 – 2). There are also two priests, Zadok and Ahimelech, the latter the son of Abiathar, the priest who joined David after Saul's slaughter of the priests at Nob (1 Sam. 22:20–23) and thus the last priest in Eli's line. Polzin (1993: 94) insists that this means David was taking over the divine prerogative to appoint the high priest, but there is nothing here to support such a claim. The parallel list in 20:23–26 has Zadok and Abiathar as the priests, but this is probably a case of a grandson bearing his grandfather's name. Of those named here, Joab, Benaiah, Jehoshaphat and Zadok are active in the second list. The final administrative role is that David's sons were priests, though not in the Levitical sense. Zadok and Abiathar's previous mention suggests they took the lead in worship, though 6:12–19 showed that David sometimes acted in a priestly manner. This suggests that certain actions were acceptable for the royal family, though perhaps not in public, which accounts for the terminology in Chronicles (see 'Notes'). In 20:26 Ira the Jairite is also described as David's priest, perhaps indicating a role akin to a court chaplain (similarly, Birch 1998: 1268). David's sons may have had a similar role, but certainty is impossible.

Explanation

Ch. 7 saw David promised not only a dynasty, but also national rest and security (7:10). The events compiled for this chapter show this happening. However, they did not occur simply because David was an effective military leader nor because of a lull in regional interest from the major powers. Both are plausible explanations that modern historians might prefer. But the narrative insists that Yahweh's promises are completed because Yahweh ensures their fulfilment. The importance of this is seen in that the relentless listing of victories is twice broken by the pivotal assertion that Yahweh gave David victory wherever he went (vv. 6, 14). The promises fulfilled are not, however, simply those received by David, for the land controlled by the chapter's end matches that promised to Abraham in Gen. 15:18–21. The chapter explores both how the promises to David were being fulfilled and the further question of how the Davidic covenant is related to the Abrahamic, so the two mutually interpret one another.

Yet David's actions are emphasized, because Yahweh's actions and those of his servants are not absolutely discrete. There is much here that modern readers find difficult, especially the treatment of the Moabites and the Aramean horses. Knowing that David's actions were lenient by ancient standards does not necessarily resolve this, but it does indicate we should not assess David by contemporary standards. In terms of the fulfilment of the promises, David must still engage in battle, because it is only there that he experiences Yahweh's deliverance. David recognized this when he dedicated his captured wealth in vv. 11–12. If Yahweh grants the victory, then the spoils belong to him too. The refusal to increase his own wealth, including the accumulation of horses, resonates with Deut. 17:14–20's declaration of how Israelite kings should reign.

But David's actions were rooted in a just home administration, without which his expansionary campaigns were impossible. The list of David's officials in the context of the statement that David exercised justice and righteousness for the people is also consistent with Deuteronomy's vision for Israelite kings. But Yahweh's promises to David are not fulfilled because David acts like this. Rather, because he has received the promises he must act with justice and provide a state where justice can be done.

By the chapter's end we see David at his greatest, and are enabled to assess the whole of his reign positively. David is under Yahweh's blessing. But the narrative carefully shows that not everything David does is acceptable. David could not, for example, build the temple, while some of his actions (such as killing the Moabites) are left without comment. The narrator does not want readers to praise David without limit. The reasons for this become clearer in the following chapters, where David's failings are more than apparent. But, for the moment, it is enough to know what can be achieved with Yahweh.

2 SAMUEL 9

Translation

[1]David said, 'Is there anyone remaining from the house of Saul that I might deal kindly with him for Jonathan's sake?' [2]Now Saul's house had a servant named Ziba, so they summoned him to David. The king said to him, 'Are you Ziba?' He said, 'Your servant.' [3]The king said to him, 'Is there no longer anyone in Saul's house that I might show him the kindness of God?' Ziba said to the king, 'There is yet a son of Jonathan's who is crippled in both feet.' [4]The king said to him, 'Where is he?' Ziba said to the king, 'Behold, he is in the house of Machir ben Ammiel in Lo Debar.' [5]King David sent and brought him from the house of Machir ben Ammiel

in Lo Debar. [6]Mephibosheth ben Jonathan ben Saul came to David and fell upon his face and did obeisance. David said, 'Mephibosheth.' He said, 'Here is your servant.' [7]David said to him 'Do not be afraid, for I will surely deal kindly with you for the sake of your father Jonathan. I shall return to you all your grandfather Saul's fields and you shall eat at my table regularly.' [8]Then he did obeisance and said, 'What is your servant that you should regard a dead dog like me?'

[9]The king called Ziba, Saul's lad, and said to him, 'I have given your master's grandson all that belonged to Saul and his house. [10]You shall tend the land for him, you and your sons and your servants, and you shall bring in the produce that your master's grandson may have food to eat. But your master's grandson Mephibosheth shall regularly eat at my table.' Now Ziba had fifteen sons and twenty servants. [11]Ziba said to the king, 'All that my Lord the king has commanded his servant thus shall your servant do.' So Mephibosheth ate at David's table like one of the king's sons. [12]Mephibosheth had a young son named Mica, but everyone living in Ziba's house was Mephibosheth's servants. [13]Mephibosheth stayed in Jerusalem, for he regularly ate at the king's table, and he was lame in both his feet.

Notes on the text

3. NEB takes *ḥesed 'ĕlôhîm* as a superlative, 'outstanding kindness'. This seems unlikely, but see Anderson 1989: 140.

7. On the semantic range of *'āb*, see Seiler 1998: 277–279.

11. With LXX, read 'David's table'. MT's 'my table' requires this to continue Ziba's speech. Fokkelman (1981: 449) regards the clause as a gloss. However, it is simplest to assume that MT was influenced by the form of vv. 7–10 (similarly, Smith 1899: 312). We then revocalize *'ōkēl* as the expected *'ākal*.

Form and structure

Since Rost (1982), this chapter has generally been regarded as the beginning of the 'Succession Narrative', a source he claimed runs (more or less, since the beginning was unclear, though Rost 1982: 85–87 included 6:16, 20b–23) from 2 Sam. 9 – 20, plus 1 Kgs 1 – 2. According to Rost, it was written to glorify Solomon as David's successor. Rost's work has generated a mass of literature, and continues to underpin numerous studies (e.g. Seiler 1998: 319–321, who upholds a Solomonic composition date). Both its beginning (Gunn 1978: 8; Kaiser 1988: 6; Seiler 1998: 283–294) and its end are disputed. Rost maintained that the narrative concluded in 1 Kgs 1 – 2, and worked back from there to conclude that David's succession was the central theme (see Whybray 1968: 10–55). But this suffers from research which sees 1 Kgs 1 – 2 as a separate document, albeit one aware of 2 Sam. 9 – 20 (McCarter 1981:

361–362 and esp. Keys 1996: 54–70). If 1 Kgs 1 – 2 was not part of the narrative, then succession is not the dominant motif. Even those who believe the narrative originally continued through to 1 Kgs 1 – 2 disagree over whether or not one can speak of a 'Succession Narrative' (Ackroyd 1981). Recognizing this, it seems best to adopt the more neutral title of 'Court Narrative' for these chapters. This permits one to trace a number of themes, though sin and punishment emerge as central (Keys 1996: 123–141). This enables us to move from Rost's source-critical focus where the source could be studied in its own right to consider its function within Samuel. In particular, it enables us to read chs. 9 – 20 in full awareness of 21 – 24 rather than seeing them as an appendix to be skipped before resuming the supposed main narrative thread (Firth 2001).

This chapter forms the beginning of an extended narrative that runs to ch. 20, describing events in David's reign that counter the positive overall assessments provided in 5:17 – 8:18 and 21:1 – 24:25. The chronological relationship of 9 – 20 in relation to these blocks is uncertain because Samuel's structure is thematic and theological, not chronological. Thus, although a good case can be made for seeing 21:1–14 as chronologically prior to that narrated here (McCarter 1984: 260, but see Campbell's criticisms 2005: 89), it is more important to understand the reasons for the present arrangement. We understand how a Saulide came to hold a prominent place in David's household because of his significant role in 16:1–4 and 19:25–31. The issues raised in these passages depend on those found here (Fokkelman 1981: 28). The chapter itself, although it has its own theme, especially the *ḥesed* ('loyalty' or 'kindness') of David, forms part of the introduction to the longer story. As an introduction, it portrays David positively, and shows him acting in faithfulness to God and others. A similar theme is developed in 10:1–19, which also shows David's practising *ḥesed*, though there it is rebuffed. As with the Accession Narrative (1 Sam. 27 – 2 Sam. 1), the Court Narrative begins with a paired narrative. Care must be taken to ensure that the Court Narrative is not divorced from the text around it. As well as the possibility of 21:1–14, Gunn (1978: 68) has shown strong links with chs. 2 – 4. Most strikingly, Mephibosheth was first introduced in 4:4, while the covenantal basis for David's showing *ḥesed* towards him stems from 1 Sam. 20:14–17, 42.

Apart from the introduction and conclusion, the chapter is built around three dialogue units, respectively between David and Ziba, David and Mephibosheth and David and Ziba again. Through each the focus remains upon David's faithfulness towards Jonathan's family since it is David who consistently takes the initiative. An important marker of the dialogue's shifts is seen in the designation of David. In general speech or conversation with Mephibosheth he is always 'David', whereas in his dialogue with Ziba he is always 'the king'. The labels enable the narrator to build a picture of the power relations between them. This is also seen in how David subtly alters his language in his discussions with them both. David's actions are rooted in *ḥesed*, but this does not remove the power relations running through the chapter. In addition, by building so much around reported speech rather than editorial comment, the narrator leaves open a number of questions. For example, is David genuinely caring, or is he controlling a possible adversary? Do Ziba and Mephibosheth accept David's offer as grace or to improve their own power base? None of these issues is explicitly explored because they need to be left open for when David encounters Ziba and Mephibosheth on his escape from Jerusalem and ultimate return. Issues are established, but narrative reticence ensures not everything is resolved.

Comment

1. The chapter's opening is abrupt, especially given that it follows a list of David's officials. We hear David asking if there is a survivor from Saul's house to whom he can show kindness (*ḥesed*) on account of Jonathan. David's faithfulness to 1 Sam. 20:15 could happen only once Yahweh had established him; and the events narrated in ch. 8 allow for that, though, as noted, it is unnecessary to assume that ch. 8's events were all earlier than ch. 9. David's question indicates some doubt as to the probability of such a survivor. His desire to show kindness (*ḥesed*) to Saul's house comes from his relationship with Jonathan rather than with Saul. However, he broadens the basis for this by including Saul's whole family, perhaps because he wishes to address the injured aspirations of the whole family. Thus, although there is a clear relationship of *ḥesed* between David and Jonathan (1 Sam. 20:14–17, 42), which is the primary motivation behind David's actions, the narrative hints at wider political concerns (Gordon 1986: 248).

2–4. In response to David's request, we are informed that a servant of Saul's house is still available, a man named Ziba. Once he arrives we see his political skill. Although described as Saul's servant, on meeting David he designates himself as David's servant. In reality, he still serves Saul's house, and to some extent the exchange in v. 2 is purely formal. The change of title for Ziba, however, already indicates something of his shrewdness. Again David expresses the desire to show *ḥesed* to the house of Saul, though without mentioning Jonathan and the *ḥesed* is associated with God. Since Yahweh's direct involvement in affairs in chs. 9 – 20 is less marked than before, this may be an important comment to include, because it stresses that God continues to work through his servants. David is addressing a loyal Saulide and words his question carefully to ensure he receives the appropriate information. Ziba's reply introduces an unnamed son of Jonathan. We simply know he is lame, a curious point to emphasize in view of 5:8. Since 2 Sam. 4:4 has already named him as Mephibosheth (see 'Comment' there), we know his identity. Further enquiries reveal he is staying with Machir (see 17:27) in Lo Debar. Although the town's exact location cannot be established, it is generally believed to be in the

Transjordan, and is perhaps to be identified with Debir (Josh. 13:26). This would be consistent with where Ish-bosheth had established his court at Mahanaim.

5–8. With Mephibosheth's identity and location (though not his name) established, David arranged for him to be brought to the royal court. The structure of vv. 5–6 allows a neat irony since although David brings him, Mephibosheth (who is only now named) comes to David. Like Ziba, Mephibosheth was aware of appropriate court behaviour. This is indicated both by his falling before David to give obeisance (a challenge for someone crippled), and his self-designation in response to David as 'your servant'. Indeed, he commences and closes his interview with David by paying homage. Describing himself as David's servant shows the same reserve as Ziba, indicating that both treat David as a typical eastern potentate. In response, David tells Mephibosheth not to be afraid, classically the beginning of a salvation oracle (e.g. Gen. 15:1; 21:17; Josh. 10:25), though it can also be (as here) a more general expression of encouragement (e.g. Gen. 35:17; 50:19, 21; Exod. 20:20). His agenda is not what Mephibosheth imagines. David gives a strong assurance of this by indicating that he will deal with Mephibosheth on the basis of *ḥesed*, specifically in terms of his relationship with Jonathan. The evidence of this is the return of Saul's farmlands to Mephibosheth (possibly the whole of Saul's estate, which was presumably held by the state until an heir was located rather than being confiscated by David; ben-Barak 1981: 81–84) and that he will regularly eat at David's table (cf. 2 Kgs. 25:27–29). This latter expression may be a polite form of house arrest (Hertzberg 1964: 300), where David keeps a close eye on Mephibosheth to prevent any attempt to restore the throne to the Saulides. However, in view of the return of lands it is probable that Mephibosheth is given a prince's status, though the move enables David to head off any pro-Saulide movement. Mephibosheth's response, although self-deprecatory, is formal. Ironically, David described himself as a dead dog before Saul (1 Sam. 24:15). But the phrase neatly describes Mephibosheth's actual position before David without the polyphony Schipper suggests (2003: 348) since he is now dependent upon him. He has accepted David's terms.

9–11. Again the plot is driven through a dialogue initiated by David. This dialogue ties up the loose ends generated by the scene with David and Mephibosheth. As a handicapped court resident, Mephibosheth could not directly manage the estate returned to him. David resolved this by appointing Ziba as estate manager, with specific responsibility for farming the land and bringing in its produce. Although Mephibosheth ate with the king, he may have been expected to contribute to the royal table. The estate's size is apparent from the fact that Zibah had fifteen sons and twenty servants. The dialogue follows formal court procedures since Zibah accepts a lower position relative to David, still designating himself as David's servant. This dialogue also demonstrates that David carried out his promise to Mephibosheth, who was not only given an elevated social position at the king's table, but was also given considerable wealth. The narrator's statement at the end of v. 11 also fulfils this function.

12–13. These verses return to the narrator's voice, indicating that what could be developed by dialogue is complete. Curiously, before Mephibosheth's restoration, we are told of his son Mica. The narrative makes no further mention of him, though he is obviously considered important. Possibly, the narrator wants to show that Mephibosheth's family benefited from David's generosity, although David would also have benefited from knowing where the next generation of Saulides were. However we interpret this note, Mephibosheth was cared for fully with both servants and a place at David's table. The conclusion, that he was lame in both feet, is a reminder of the extent of David's generosity, though highlighting that Mephibosheth did not threaten David. Perhaps Mica was the threat since Saul's line continued through him, so David both honoured his commitment to Jonathan and also allowed Saul's line to endure.

Explanation

Told with great restraint, this chapter draws together existing themes and prepares for new ones, even as it presents its own story. It draws together existing themes by recounting how David enacted covenant obligations he had entered into with Jonathan (1 Sam. 20:14–17, 42), while providing a context to interpret the otherwise unexpected reference to Mephibosheth in 4:4. The keyword throughout is *ḥesed*, an expression of loyalty and kindness that flows from covenant. David's desire to show *ḥesed* to Saul's house is not attempting to curry favour with Saul's house. By locating and bringing Mephibosheth to his house and table and providing him with sustenance through both land and an estate manager, David demonstrates the nature of covenanted kindness. This does not mean this did not benefit David since it might have limited any action against him by Saul's supporters, and we know from 21:1–14 that David could deal ruthlessly with Saul's family. But the story suggests David's actions were expressing genuine loyalty, since the crippled Mephibosheth was treated like one of David's own sons. That Mephibosheth's son Mica also survived meant that Saul's line was not to be brought to an end, as beneficial as that might have been for David, because his covenant commitments to Jonathan prohibited it.

The chapter also prepares for coming events, especially the conflicts caused by the claims of both Ziba (16:1–4) and Mephibosheth (19:25–31). The issues that their claim and counterclaim generate can be understood only through the background of this chapter as it begins the long narrative run to the end of ch. 20. By foregrounding the theme of *ḥesed* it also prepares for the events of ch. 10, where David's expression of *ḥesed* is received rather differently. Thus chs. 9 – 10 serve as the doubled introduction to the Court Narrative, though at this stage few of its details are before us.

But we cannot read the chapter solely for what it does with earlier texts or as a preparation for later ones. Above all else, it needs to be read as an example of loyalty through covenant, even when that involves committing oneself to a potential adversary. David had to take this risk, and it is this that Ziba exploits in 16:1–4. It is the sort of action Jesus indicates in Luke 10:25–37 he expects even outside covenant. Here David demonstrates fidelity to his word that goes beyond finding the minimum point of satisfaction. The irony is that this also begins the larger narrative that will show how far short of this David can fall.

2 SAMUEL 10

Translation

¹After this the Ammonite king died, and his son Hanun became king in his place. ²So David said, 'I will deal kindly with Hanun ben Nahash as his father dealt kindly with me.' So David sent his servants to comfort him concerning his father, and David's servants came to the Ammonites' land. ³But the Ammonite princes said to Hanun their lord, 'Do you think David honours your father because he sent you comforters? Isn't it to search the city, to spy on it and overthrow it, that David sent his servants?' ⁴So Hanun took David's servants and shaved off half their beards and cut their garments in half as far as their buttocks and sent them away. ⁵When they told David, he sent to greet them because the men were deeply humiliated. The king said, 'Stay in Jericho until your beards have grown, and then return.'

⁶When the Ammonites saw they had become odious to David, the Ammonites sent and hired Aram of Beth-Rehob and Aram of Zobah, twenty thousand foot soldiers, and the king of Maacah with a thousand men, and the men of Tob, twelve thousand men. ⁷When David heard, he sent Joab and all the host of the mighty men. ⁸The Ammonites went out and formed their battle lines at the entrance of the gate, while Aram Zobah, Rehob and the men of Tob and Maacah were by themselves in the open country.

⁹When Joab saw he was confronted by battle both to the front and the rear, he chose some of Israel's elite troops and arrayed them to confront Aram. ¹⁰He placed the rest of the people under the command of his brother Abishai and arrayed them to confront the Ammonites. ¹¹He said, 'If Aram is stronger than me, you shall deliver me; but if the Ammonites are stronger than you, I shall come to deliver you. ¹²Be strong, and let us be courageous for the sake of our people and the cities of our God, and may Yahweh do what is right in his eyes.' ¹³Joab and the people with him drew near to battle against Aram, and they fled before him. ¹⁴When the Ammonites saw that Aram fled, they fled from Abishai and entered the city. Then Joab returned from conflict with the Ammonites and entered Jerusalem.

¹⁵When Aram saw they had been defeated by Israel, they gathered themselves together. ¹⁶Then Hadadezer sent and brought out the Arameans who were across the River. They came to Helam, and Shobach, commander of Hadadezer's army,

was their head. [17]When it was reported to David, he gathered together all Israel, crossed the Jordan, and came to Helam. But Aram arrayed themselves against David and fought him. [18]Aram fled from Israel and David killed seven hundred Aramean charioteers and forty thousand horsemen. He struck Shobach, their host's commander, and he died there. [19]When all Hadadezer's vassal kings saw they were defeated before Israel, they made peace with Israel and served them. So Aram was afraid of again delivering the Ammonites.

Notes on the text

2–3. Pi. *nḥm* occurs nowhere else in Samuel (cf. 1 Chr. 19:2, 3) except 12:24. The term's careful placement highlights the links across the whole of chs. 10 – 12.

4. LXX (cf. 1 Chr. 19:4), supported by McCarter (1984: 267); Anderson (1989: 145) omits 'half' for the men's beards. Although MT may conflate the shaving with the cutting off of their garments, it is also possible that the peculiarity of half a beard (which half?) may have led to the shorter text, so MT is retained.

6. 4QSam[a] appears to omit Maacah's thousand men (cf. 1 Chr. 19:7) but both MT and LXX retain it.

8. Although *'îš ṭôb* is sg., and may therefore refer to a local ruler since Tob was a very small state, it is more likely a collective expression (cf. ESV, NASU).

9. 1 Chr. 19:9 and some LXX MSS have 'the city' for the gate, but this probably conforms the text to a more common idiom.

16. The spelling of Hadadezer varies, with many MSS reading Hadarezer. These are easily confused, but since the name is probably based on the god Hadad, Hadadezer is retained. As with 8:3, 'the River' is unnamed, but is probably the Euphrates since Aram was well established there. Although the Jordan or even Yarmuk are possible, this would involve bringing reinforcements from areas David controlled, whereas it is more probable they would come from other areas. Hebr. *ḥêlām* could be 'their army', but is more likely a toponym.

18. The traditions vary as to the numbers David killed and whether they were charioteers, horsemen or foot soldiers (see McCarter 1984: 269). 1 Chr. 19:18 has seven thousand horsemen and forty thousand foot soldiers. For a possible reconciliation, see Youngblood (1992: 925–926), though the conflict with Chronicles may be from textual corruption there.

Form and structure

Although displaying its own narrative form, this chapter's main function is to provide the context for 11:1 – 12:25, which then provides the trigger for the rebellions in chs. 13 – 20. Although this chapter shows that Aram is defeated, it leaves the conflict with Ammon unresolved, remaining so through a framing technique until 12:26–31. This chapter records the war's beginning and establishes a precedent for David's not going out to battle. Instead, Joab leads the army, and David comes in only at certain points, particularly when victory is near, providing information to interpret David's actions in the next chapter. Without this information, some of his actions could be misunderstood. The account's chronistic nature is commonly noted, leading some to suggest it might have come from the royal archives (Hertzberg 1964: 303), though this has not gone unchallenged (Bailey 1990: 61–71; though see Seiler 1998: 223–228). If this chapter comes from an archive, that would explain why this is the only chapter in the Court Narrative other than ch. 9 portraying David favourably.

Although it establishes the context for subsequent events, this chapter also links with 8:3–8 and 9:1–13. It is clear from 2 Sam. 8:3–8 that the Arameans were subject to David, so the events of this chapter are probably prior to the situation described there, but still a part of how Yahweh gave him victory wherever he went (8:6, 14). V. 2 also refers back to ch. 9, so David's desire to show *ḥesed* to Hanun is paralleled with his actions towards Mephibosheth. This time, however, there is no positive response to his initiative, so whatever political ambitions lay behind the move were not achieved.

This chapter is a fairly straightforward account of the origins of the Ammonite war and subsequent Aramean conflict. Although 2 Sam. 8:3–8 summarizes the whole Aramean war, the narrator here provides a more expansive backdrop because of the desire to develop the storyline more fully. The narrative is careful to show that Ammon is defeated in battle, but by omitting an account of their suing for peace (unlike the Arameans) the chapter can conclude on a point of both resolution (Aram) and non-resolution (Ammon). McCarter (1984: 273–275) has argued that these accounts are displaced, and should follow Absalom's revolt, but his argument depends upon the subsequent reference to another of Nahash's sons (Shobi, 17:27) working for David. But the narrative makes sense as it stands since it would be an obvious attempt to restore the relationship between the families and their nations.

Comment

The war's origins: 10:1–5

1. The opening words suggest a link between chs. 9 – 10, though chronological markers in Samuel are often vague and perhaps more to do with redactional seams than chronology (Bailey 1990: 54–57). The time marker places these events some time after Mephibosheth's arrival. How much later is not stated, but it is possibly early in David's time in Jerusalem. A number of echoes between the two chapters indicate a close link between them (Youngblood 1992: 921). The opening event here is the death of the Ammonite king, Nahash. He is presumably the person mentioned in 1 Sam. 11 as Saul's enemy, though we are not told when the good relationship with David developed. Nevertheless, as Saul's enemy he would be a natural supporter of David, and another of his sons supports David in 17:27. Ammon was a kingdom east of the Jordan, north of the Arnon River but south of the Jabbok, with Moab to its south.

2–5. David's expressed wish is to show *hesed* (a phrase with covenantal overtones) to the new Ammonite king, Hanun, as he has done with Mephibosheth. This time, however, he will not receive a positive response as Hanun's advisers tell him David is spying out the city, presumably Rabbah (11:1; 12:26). Given David's expansionist policy towards the Philistines this is understandable advice, but tragically wrong. Their response to David may have been a coarse joke, a provocative insult, and indicates a serious error in assessing his strength. Normally, envoys were granted something akin to diplomatic immunity, and to insult them was a breach of all diplomatic courtesies. Shaving off half their beards attacked their dignity as adults since Israelite males had a full beard apart from expressions of mourning (Jer. 41:5), while exposing their buttocks and genitals was something normally done only to prisoners of war (see Isa. 20:3–5). This was a serious insult to David and Israel. David must have had an efficient intelligence service since the men were told to stay in Jericho (perhaps the region rather than the city, which may not have been occupied at the time), which was where they would re-enter Israel, until their beards had grown. As with David's attitude towards Mephibosheth, this shows his concern for his servants' welfare, though this makes the events of ch. 11 only that much more shocking. More remarkable still is that the narrative refrains from recording any response by David toward the Ammonites (see Fokkelman 1981: 45). In spite of the insult, we see the initial mobilization only from the Ammonite perspective. Throughout, David is not the aggressor.

The Ammonite campaign: 10:6–14

6–8. No war declaration is made, but the Ammonites realized the effect of their actions (they lit. 'stank' before David) and brought in a large Aramean contingent. Again (see 'Comment' on 1 Sam. 4:1–3) exact numbers are difficult to determine, but the army must have been quite large. The troops came from the region of modern Syria, including a collection of petty kingdoms. Tob was north of the Jabbok, with Maacah further north again and just east of the Sea of Galilee, but south of Rehob and Zobah, which are in the anti-Lebanon. These troops were somewhere between vassals and mercenaries. According to 1 Chr. 19:7, they camped 'before Medeba', which is odd given that it is over 20 miles south, unless they were first blocking moves to the south. With the war's background outlined, the narrative moves to the conflict proper. Given the account's nature it is unsurprising that little attention is paid to character development, although there is a reference to Joab's piety. V. 7 again indicates the effectiveness of David's intelligence service since, rather than direct aggression, he responds to a report of what the Ammonites are doing. Although the Ammonite forces were large, David sent only Joab with the standing army, without additional forces that might be raised from the land (von Rad 1991: 76). A primary concern is to show David's legitimately remaining behind during war, preparing for ch. 11. Against Joab were the Ammonite forces and their Aramean troops. The Ammonites are portrayed as standing before the 'gate', presumably of Rabbah (modern Amman), although the city's name is not mentioned until 11:1. Their additional troops are in open country, creating a pincer movement against the Israelite forces as they come up from Jericho.

9–12. Joab apparently saw the Aramean forces as the greater danger, perhaps reasoning that professional soldiers might be more dangerous than the Ammonites themselves. This was borne out when Joab selected the elite soldiers to be under his command against the Arameans, while the others were placed under Abishai's command to take on the Ammonites. The brothers agreed to help each other, though if both were under pressure nothing could be done. The only remarkable element was Joab's piety when referring to the 'cities of our God' (perhaps Transjordanian cities threatened by Ammonite expansion) and the hope that Yahweh would do what was good in his eyes. Such expressions are more typical of David than Joab. This is part of a process of character reversals running through chs. 10 – 12, where David becomes a murderer, Joab expresses piety and a Hittite is the most faithful Yahwist of all, though Joab reverts to type when conspiring with David to murder Uriah. In addition, the use of *ḥzq* twice in v. 12 consciously echoes the holy war tradition, though it is not a holy war per se (Youngblood 1992: 925). Thus the narrative makes clear that the victory belongs to Yahweh, even taking into account Joab's preparations.

13–14. With the context established, the narrative recounts the Israelite success. Both the Arameans and the Ammonites fled in spite of their superior numbers. But Joab did not press home the advantage and take the city. No reason is given for this, though 11:1 may suggest it was the wrong time of year to besiege a city. At this point, Ammon and Aram are defeated but not subjugated.

The Aramean campaign: 10:15–19

15–16. Where the first campaign was directed against the Ammonites and their Aramean support, the second campaign responds to the Arameans alone. Under Hadadezer (see 8:3–4) the Arameans regrouped to continue the war with reinforcements from the region of the Euphrates (see 'Notes'). These troops were commanded by Shobach, while the battle was at Helam. This unknown site, probably in the Transjordan, represents a move back into Israelite territory, thus distinguishing these events from the first campaign outside Israel's borders.

17–19. Again there is evidence of David's intelligence network's activity since he responded to the threat of action, not a direct attack. The army this time is 'all Israel', showing this was a greater danger, as may also be indicated by David's presence. David is present when the threat is greater, as he is also for the moment of decisive victory (12:26–31). The Aramean coalition is no more effective than the combined Ammonite and Aramean forces of the first campaign, and they too flee before the Israelites. This time the advantage is pressed home, with the Arameans suffering heavy losses. Unfortunately, textual difficulties (see 'Notes' on v. 18) make it difficult to be certain of the figures, though they are extensive, and include their commander, Shobach. The result is that David, and hence Israel, now controlled the region into Aram. Ammon was isolated, with her allies defeated and thus ripe for an assault by David's forces (Campbell 2005: 93). Like 2 Sam. 8 the narrative shows the territorial promise of Gen. 15 being fulfilled through Israel's expansion.

Explanation

Reading this chapter requires attention in three directions, each of which contributes to its artistry and meaning, even though the text lacks obvious artifice. First, it requires attention to what has gone before. David previously acted faithfully in terms of his covenants with Jonathan and showed kindness to Jonathan's son Mephibosheth. Before that, ch. 8 pointed to David's military successes across the whole of his reign, though without providing many details. Both of these texts impact the reading of this chapter, where David again sought to exercise loyalty, this time to the new Ammonite king Hanun following his father's death. Where Mephibosheth accepted David's kindness, Hanun accepted his attendants' advice and rebuffed it, insulting David's envoys and triggering a conflict that drew in the Aramean states to the north. This story thus interacts with its predecessors to show that David's offers of kindness could be rejected, but when that happened he would respond with force because kindness (ḥesed) is not softness. In doing so it also sheds light on the events of ch. 8. There we encounter a series of conquest narratives as David gradually expanded Israel's territory to cover that promised in Gen. 15:18–21. This could point to an expansionary policy on David's part, but the reality here is that it was just as much a matter of defending Israel's interests. God's promise was being fulfilled, but perhaps not as one might expect.

Secondly, the chapter must be read on its own terms. It carefully presents David as positively as possible. He is a loyal diplomat who cares for his men when they are humiliated and sent back to Jericho. Through this cameo we can see why David generated such commitment from so many people. We also see David as an astute administrator, staying behind in the Ammonite war where he is not needed, but coming to the forefront when a greater threat comes from the Aramean coalition. A key reason for wanting kingship is to lead the nation in battle (1 Sam. 8:20), but David knows that not every battle requires the king's presence. Yet, when needed, he is there. Remarkably, even Joab is presented positively, trusting Yahweh to achieve the victory against Ammon, even when he has led the army into a trap. Joab's words echo those of 8:6, 14, emphasizing that victory comes from Yahweh alone, a theme that reaches back to 1 Sam. 2:10 and David's victory over Goliath (1 Sam. 17).

Finally, this chapter prepares us for what follows, so as we come to the events in chs. 11 – 12 we have to reread and reassess what is here. We know from this chapter that the king can remain home during battle, so there is nothing intrinsically wrong when David does so in 11:1, but this opens up the possibility of royal abuses of power because the warriors are away. David may have been loyal to Mephibosheth, Hanun and his envoys, but all of this contrasts with his treatment of Uriah. Ch. 9 acts as a foil for this chapter because we now know how *ḥesed* can be rebuffed. But both these chapters then stand as a foil to the events about to unfold as David demonstrates the worst he can be.

2 SAMUEL 11

Translation

[1]At the turn of the year, the time when messengers go forth, David sent Joab, and his servants with him, and all Israel, and they destroyed the Ammonites and besieged Rabbah. But David stayed in Jerusalem.

[2]When evening came, David rose from his couch and walked about on the roof of the king's house, and saw from the roof a woman bathing; and the woman was very beautiful. [3]David sent and enquired about the woman, and one said, 'Is this not Bathsheba, the daughter of Eliam, the wife of Uriah the Hittite?' [4]David sent messengers and took her and she came to him and he lay with her. (She had been purifying herself from her uncleanness.) Then she returned to her house. [5]The woman conceived and sent and informed David and said, 'I am pregnant.'

[6]David sent to Joab, 'Send to me Uriah the Hittite.' Joab sent Uriah to David. [7]Uriah came to him, and David asked about the well-being of Joab, the army and the battle. [8]David said to Uriah, 'Go down to your house and bathe your feet.' So Uriah went out from the king's house, and a gift from the king was sent after

him. [9]But Uriah lay down at the entrance to the king's house, with all his lord's servants, and did not go down to his house. [10]They told David, 'Uriah has not gone down to his house.' David said to Uriah, 'Have you not come from a journey? Why have you not gone down to your house?' [11]Uriah said to David, 'The ark and Israel and Judah are staying in booths, and my lord Joab and my lord's servants are camping in the open country, so should I go to my house to eat, drink and lie with my wife? As you live, and as your soul lives, I will not do this thing.' [12]David said to Uriah, 'Stay here today as well, and tomorrow I will send you on.' Uriah stayed in Jerusalem that day. The following day [13]David summoned him and ate before him and gave him drink and made him drunk. Then he went out in the evening to lie down on his couch with his lord's servants, but he did not go down to his house.

[14]In the morning David wrote Joab a letter and sent it by the hand of Uriah. [15]He wrote in the letter, 'Set Uriah in the front line of the fiercest battle, then pull back from him that he may be struck down and die.' [16]As Joab kept watch on the city he placed Uriah at the point he knew the valiant men were. [17]The city's men came out to fight Joab, and some of David's servants among the people fell, and Uriah the Hittite also died. [18]Joab sent and reported to David all the battle's events. [19]Joab commanded the messenger, 'When you finish telling the king the battle's events, [20]if the king's anger rises and he says to you, "Why did you approach the city to fight? Didn't you know they would shoot from the wall? [21]Who struck Abimelech ben Jerubesheth? Wasn't it a woman who threw an upper millstone from the wall so he died at Thebez? Why did you draw near to the wall?", then you shall say, "Your servant Uriah the Hittite has also died."'

[22]The messenger went and came and reported to David all Joab had sent him to say. [23]The messenger said to David, 'The men prevailed against us and came out against us in the open country, but we drove them back to the entrance of the gate. [24]The archers shot at your servants from the wall and killed the king's servants. Also your servant Uriah the Hittite has died.' [25]David said to the messenger, 'Thus you shall say to Joab, "Let not this matter be evil in your eyes because the sword consumes one as the other. Strengthen your fight against the city and overthrow it." So strengthen him.'

[26]Uriah's wife heard Uriah her husband had died, and she mourned for her husband. [27]When her mourning was over David sent and brought her to his house and she became his wife and bore him a son. But the thing David had done was evil in Yahweh's eyes.

Notes on the text

1. Most commentators and translations accept many MSS, the LXX (and some Syr MSS), offering *malkîm* (kings) for MT, best vocalized *malā'kîm* (messengers, as per some MSS). This reading is so well established that many EVV do not note the change. But Fokkelman (1981: 50–51, followed by Baldwin 1988: 231, also GKC §23g) is right that the change to 'kings' creates unnecessary redundancy. Moreover, *mal'āk* functions as a *Leitwort* through the chapter and this introduces it. On possible intentional ambiguity, see Polzin (1993: 109–112), Bodner (2005: 80–84).

3. Birch (1998: 1284; cf. Bailey 1990: 85) regards the statement identifying Bathsheba as David's, but since he enquired it is more likely that *wayyōmer* is impersonal. 4QSam[a] has Uriah as Joab's kit-bearer but this is probably a scribal comment (cf. Josephus, *Ant.* 7.131).

4. NIV mg. suggests that Bathsheba was purifying herself after sex with David. However, this requires a consecutive verb, not a circumstantial participle.

11. The absence of the interrogative particle is common. See GKC §150a.

12. Following Fokkelman (1981: 450), *ûmimmāḥărāt* is construed as the start of the following verse.

15. LXX appears to read a hiph. imperative of *bw'* for MT's *hābû*. The corruption is easily explained, but the sense is similar. LXX may be paraphrasing a relatively uncommon verb.

21. Gideon is known as Jerubbesheth only here, though the name is an obvious corruption of his alternative name, Jerubbaal (Judg. 8:32), following the pattern of Eshbaal–Ish-bosheth and Meribaal–Mephibosheth.

22. LXX includes a long addition where David says what Joab has said, but this is unnecessary because both Joab and the messenger are creative interpreters of the situation. McCarter (1984: 282–284) relocates this to v. 24, but this misses the narrative dynamics of the astute messenger.

24. The spelling of archers is anomalous and appears to have generated paraphrases in LXX. Some LXX (see OL) MSS specify the Israelite casualties as eighteen.

Form and structure

Arguably the most famous chapter in Samuel after David and Goliath in 1 Sam. 17, this is normally called 'David and Bathsheba'. Although there are reasons for this, such a title in some senses distorts the form of the narrative. Bathsheba is mentioned only in vv. 2–5 and 26–27. Both the first and last times she is mentioned before her marriage to David refer to her as Uriah's wife (vv. 3, 26; cf. Matt. 1:6). Moreover, Bathsheba is a largely passive figure (similarly, van den Bergh 2008). She is seen and summoned by David. David lies with her. She is acted upon, so other than coming and going from her house under escort (v. 4), the only active verbs describing her are when she purifies herself (v. 4), reports her pregnancy (v. 5) and mourns for her husband (v. 26). Apart from her beauty (v. 2), we receive no insight into her character. Indeed, apart from v. 3 she is never called Bathsheba, but always spoken of in terms of others. Her role is within the narrative introduction to the central plot of David's attempts to kill Uriah. These attempts are related throughout vv. 6–25, and are arguably present in vv. 2–5. Indeed, as heinous as David's adultery with Bathsheba is, it can be argued that David uses sex not as an end in itself (satisfying lust), but rather as part of an assault on Uriah that ultimately requires his murder (see Firth 2008).

Bathsheba is not the only character for whom no motivation is provided. David and Joab commit despicable acts, but their reasons are never given. This reticence suggests the narrator had no intention of providing such information, preferring to leave the ambiguity created as something to be negotiated by readers (see Sternberg 1985: 190–193).

The subject matter's horror contrasts with the skill with which it is narrated. It picks up themes from ch. 10 while preparing for 12:1–25 and beyond, yet leaves gaps for readers to explore. Indeed, although ch. 10 possesses an apparent lack of artifice, it has laid the foundation for a number of key references here, so its artistry is best appreciated only with hindsight. The most obvious link is that, unlike the Arameans, the Ammonite conflict was unresolved. Ammon was defeated but not subjugated. This provides the setting for Joab's going to battle in the spring and besieging Rabbah. But smaller links through shared vocabulary provide continued reminders of the previous events. Notable examples include reference to the open country (*śādeh*), where the Arameans had been (10:8) and Israel now camps (11:11), and the place of battle with Ammon (11:23). The same term described Saul's estate in 9:7 when it was returned to Mephibosheth. Linked to this is the unusual phrase 'the entrance of the gate' (otherwise Josh. 8:29; 20:4; Judg. 9:35, 40, 44; 1 Kgs 22:10; 2 Kgs 7:3; 10:8; but only combat-oriented in Judges; Uriah also lies down at the palace entrance, v. 9), which occurs in 10:8 as the place where the Ammonites prepared for battle and the point to which they were driven back in 11:23. The phrase creates strong links with Abimelech's story (Judg. 9:35, 40, 44), links made explicit in the speech Joab imagines David will make in response to the news of the soldiers' death (v. 21). The links to Abimelech, an account of royal power's abuse (however limited in Abimelech's case) creates the context for understanding David's abuses.

The most striking link with ch. 10 is the repeated use of the root *šlḥ* (send). It seems unobtrusive in ch. 10 (×8); after all, commanders send armies. But there is a high concentration here (×12), so it becomes a *Leitwort* for the whole narrative, preparing for the irony of Yahweh's sending Nathan in 12:1. Ch. 11 also has other recurring key terms, most notably 'messenger' (*mal'āk*; ×6; see 'Notes' on v. 1) and the root *dbr* (×5) which never has its most common sense of 'word' but always refers to some action. In addition, various uses of the root *škb* occur throughout, variously referring to a couch (vv. 2, 13), the act of lying down (vv. 9, 13) or as a euphemism for sex (vv. 4, 11), a pattern repeated in ch. 13. The narrative thus creates a web of allusion that contrasts with the narrative's content. Moreover, the final phrase stresses that David has done evil in Yahweh's eyes (v. 27), the very phrase David used to encourage Joab not to be concerned about his losses (v. 25). This irony, with its delayed revelation, is surely intentional. Through it all, David is completely enmeshed in sin: he has become the monarch about whom Samuel warned.

The key to the chapter's interpretation lies in its closing statement, 'the thing David had done was evil in Yahweh's eyes'. Yet what is this thing? A traditional reading considers it to follow a process where David commits adultery and then attempts to cover his mistake given the complication of Bathsheba's pregnancy (e.g. Birch 1998: 1283). This reading depends in part on emending v. 1, so David was wrong to remain in Jerusalem. But we have rejected this (see 'Notes'). It also emphasizes Bathsheba, though, as noted, her narrative role is quite small, and fails to attend to the emphasis placed on her as Uriah's wife. The cover-up reading also fails to note that David's initial sexual contact with Bathsheba was not altogether private – he had sent an escort to bring her, but only after she was identified as Uriah's wife (v. 3). Moreover, some time would have passed between Bathsheba's being aware of her pregnancy and Uriah's return, and even if the gestation period was not known precisely, any birth would have been suspiciously early. Finally, this reading does not address the function in chs. 9 – 20 of sexual congress with another man's wife. When Nathan denounces David in 12:8, he insists Yahweh has not only given David Saul's house, but Saul's wives too. After Absalom took control of Jerusalem, he accepted Ahithophel's counsel to have sex with David's concubines when David fled (16:20–23). Both texts refer to sexual activity that was in some sense public, and that attempted to claim authority from the other. The cover-up approach promotes the subplot above the main plot. Rather than uncontrolled lust, David's actions with Bathsheba attempt to claim authority from Uriah. The pregnancy may have been an unexpected by-product that David needed to address, but all that follows is an attempt to kill Uriah. This is explicit once David sends his letter to Joab (v. 14), but it is arguable that encouraging Uriah to have sex with his wife attempts to convict Uriah of a breach of Israel's Yahweh war traditions, a breach liable to the death penalty. David's sin is deep, but more than covers a mistake: as an attempt to kill a rival it breaches Israel's expectations of kingship. Why David regarded Uriah like that is never explicated. Bailey speculates on why David acted like this (1990: 89–90), but his suggestions depend upon unacceptable textual reorganization. One can observe only that Uriah was one of David's elite troops (23:39) and may have seemed to David to be the sort of threat he had been to Saul, though this can be only supposition. But this is the grasping David (Gunn 1978) whose personal life conflicts with his public persona. He must resolve this conflict in chs. 21 – 24.

Comment

David's adultery with Bathsheba: 11:1–5

1. The narrative opens with a contextual note: that it is the turn of the year when messengers go forth. The statement is abrupt but complete, requiring no reference to warfare. It prepares both for David's sending Joab and the army, and the messengers each sends. Probably, the 'turn of the year' refers to spring since after the wet season the roads could be passed, some grain was available for the army, and men were not yet required for harvest, though it could refer to the anniversary of the events initiated in 10:1. David's normal policy might have been to go with the army, but the precedent for remaining at home was set in the Ammonite conflict, when David went out only when the conflict was sufficiently demanding (10:15–18). If so, the commonly voiced criticism of David's remaining home has no basis. Even 1 Sam. 8:20 does not require the king to lead every fight.

2–4a. David and Bathsheba's adultery is described in a matter-of-fact way. We are given no psychological insights into either character. We do not know their motivation, and seeking to discover it can make us miss the narrative's point. We are simply told that David had risen from an afternoon sleep (something of a necessity in Israel in spring) and was walking on the palace roof. No particular purpose is suggested, but it is understandable as a normal action of the time. From the roof he could see a beautiful woman bathing on her roof, which was a normal place for this to happen, especially in the heat of late spring, and might not have involved anything more than her using a bowl; so she was not necessarily naked (against Berlin 1982: 72; see also the examples from art in Cartledge 2001: 498–499, Bezuidenhout 1997). Bathsheba is entirely passive, and attempts to make her an equal partner or even temptress (Hertzberg 1964: 309; Nicol 1988) miss the point. She is seen, described, named, summoned and lain with. What she thought of the affair is left unsaid. Equally, the narrative simply describes David's actions. He initiates the process because he desires to know Bathsheba's identity, and where passive terms are used of Bathsheba, active ones are used for David. He sees, asks about, sends for, takes and lies with Bathsheba, though claims that he rapes her probably state too much (see Nicol 1997). Most strikingly, it is only *after* he is told that Bathsheba is Eliam's daughter (often linked with 23:34, and thus Ahithophel's granddaughter, but this is supposition) and Uriah's wife that he summons her. Although Uriah is a Hittite, he is apparently a thorough Yahwist, so the label 'Hittite' probably refers simply to his ancestry. David does not send for a woman because he sees her beauty. He sends for her because he knows who she is, and that identity is important to David (see 'Form and structure') in his assault on Uriah through Bathsheba. To whatever extent Bathsheba is also guilty, the narrative's primary focus is on David's guilt. His sin is primary, and the narrator shows it relentlessly. David has become the king who takes (*lqḥ*), the king of whom Samuel warned (1 Sam. 8:10–18). Why David assaults Uriah through his wife is not stated, perhaps because such knowledge might lead to attempts at mitigation. What matters is that this is a massive abuse of power.

4b–5. The affair took place just after Bathsheba had purified herself after her ritual impurity (Lev. 15:19–24). This is seven days from the beginning of menstruation, and indicates a high probability of pregnancy (Krause 1983). More importantly, Uriah cannot be the father. Bathsheba's only speech is to report her pregnancy to David (and no more than that), setting in train the ensuing events.

Attempted grounds for execution: 11:6–13

6–7. David acts in response to Bathsheba's report, summoning Uriah to join him. This is commonly interpreted as an attempted cover-up by David, but since his sexual liaison with Bathsheba is hardly a secret (he asked about her identity and brought her by escort) a cover-up is futile. The pregnancy complicates his position because female fertility is something he cannot control, so rather than attacking Uriah through his wife he now needs to eliminate him to claim the child. He is not trying to cover his tracks but rather trying to create a legal pretence for Uriah's execution. Uriah is one of David's 'servants' (v. 1) besieging Rabbah in the Ammonite war. David's actions parallel those with Bathsheba, sending for someone who comes to him. Uriah cannot know why he is summoned and must presume he is reporting from Joab. David asks about the welfare (*šālôm*) of Joab, the army and the battle. The irony is that *šālôm* is the one thing with which he is not concerned.

8–9. With the formalities complete, David encourages Uriah to go home and 'wash his feet'. Although this could refer to the normal procedure for welcoming a traveller to a house (Gen. 18:4), the use of 'feet' as a euphemism for the male genitalia (Judg. 3:24) could hint that David was suggesting he have sex with his wife. It is possibly intentionally ambiguous (Yee 1988a: 248), though Uriah's comments in v. 11 suggest he understands it sexually. By not making David's position explicit, the narrative suggests his subtlety. Since Deut. 23:10 [ET 23:11] (see David's comments to Ahimelech in 1 Sam. 21:5–6 [ET 21:4–5]; also Exod. 19:15) requires sexual abstinence from active soldiers, David appears to have tried to have Uriah commit a potentially capital offence, thus 'legally' removing the problem (Anderson 1989: 154). But David cannot make the suggestion directly. David is not trying to cover his paternity. He is exploiting his power as king, using the law to his advantage. Through this, Uriah models covenant faithfulness, and sleeps at the palace entrance with other attendants. Indeed, the narrator insists he did not go down to his house, even though it was near.

10–11. Armed with reports that indicate Uriah has not gone home, David needs a new strategy to create a pretext for Uriah's execution. Thus with Uriah present, David questions him about why he has not gone home, the unstated implication being that he should have gone to his wife. Uriah responds in his only speech with a series of questions, each of which compels David's agreement. The questions are effectively a series of assertions, but phrasing them as questions means he can employ court style and not imply royal ignorance of such matters. The first two questions are essentially parallel, indicating that the ark is in a temporary shelter and that Joab and the army are camped in the open. Only now is the ark mentioned within the Ammonite war, but this suggests that troops must be consecrated, precluding sexual contact with one's wife. Uriah aligns himself with Israel's covenant military traditions. In parallel with this he identifies with the troops camping in the open, the implication being that one identifies with one's comrades while on active service, even when in the rear with the king. These questions lead to the third, which is the sequence's logical conclusion. A soldier serving under such circumstances could not go home to pleasant meals, wine and sex. The importance of this is indicated by the oath he swears through an unusual double reference to David, asserting that he can do no such thing. The double reference to David in the oath affirms Uriah's absolute commitment to his king, unaware that his king has set out to destroy him (against Sternberg 1985: 201–213). His loyalty to the king is what leads to his own death.

12–13. Confronted by this loyalty, David sent Uriah back the following day. Uriah waited to be summoned, and was met by David with substantial food and drink, two of the three things he had previously declined. Crucially, David managed to get him drunk, intending that in this state he should go home (cf. Song 5:1). But even this attempt to get him to sleep with Bathsheba failed. There is some ambiguity intended as Uriah goes out to lie down on his couch since the language could be euphemistic, but it is expressly stated as the place where the king's other servants were, with the narrator repeating the conclusion from v. 9 that Uriah did not go home. As Ackroyd (1977: 102) observes, 'Uriah drunk is more pious than David sober.' The 'legal' problems remain, and David cannot execute Uriah.

Murder by proxy: 11:14–25

14–17. Lacking a legal pretext for Uriah's execution, David moved to murder by stealth. The importance of the conspiracy involved is seen in that the murder itself is described briefly, whereas considerable space is given to the reports about it (see Fokkelman 1981: 61). To achieve this, David sent Joab a letter the following day, using Uriah as his messenger. Uriah arrived thinking he was Joab's messenger, so taking a letter back was appropriate. Unaware he was duped and cuckolded, Uriah carried his death sentence to Joab. Had Uriah read the letter he would have broken its seal, thus committing a capital offence (Garsiel 1993: 259); he was trapped by his role. David's instructions left Joab with a difficultly, and he did not follow them exactly since they were much too obvious, though he was not queasy about murder. To kill Uriah through an obvious withdrawal, as David had asked, would place blame upon Joab and could damage morale. His method, placing Uriah where the strongest opposition was and inciting a counter-attack, cost the lives of others (LXX suggests eighteen men), but covered the murder. For Joab this looked like a moment where possible victory overcame caution, and, though distressing, unlike David's plan his competence would not be questioned. Joab was more competent than David expected because he understood his king's intent without creating additional problems. But Uriah still died as a brave and loyal soldier, fighting for a king who betrayed him at the most basic of levels. He was innocent, and other innocent men died with him that the guilty might go free.

18–21. In reporting to David, Joab carefully provided enough information without indicating his complicity to the messenger. Thus he carefully primed his messenger, anticipating David's responses, expecting a risky attack close to the city wall would raise objections from David. But Joab's allusions to Judg. 9 do more than provide a piece of military history. By referring to Abimelech's bloody attempted kingship in Shechem and death at Thebez (Judg. 9:52–53) they point to an earlier story in Israel's history where monarchy abused those it was meant to serve, thus linking this narrative's abuses with the earlier one. Such objections are easily anticipated, and even if David did not mention them, represent the sort of complaint he would make because of the futile loss of troops. But now Joab provided his trump card, telling the messenger to inform David of Uriah's death. Even this was carefully masked, with Uriah described as David's servant, terminology that keeps the messenger from knowing the truth but that rings hollow from conspirators who together murdered Uriah and an unknown group of others.

22–24. The messenger, like Joab, is true to the intent, but also finds creative ways to fulfil them without risking himself. He goes one step further than Joab, seeking to prevent David from having reason to be angry. Accordingly, he sets his battle report within a context of ebb and flow near the city so that there is no sense of negligence in a group ending up near the city gate where the archers can attack them, killing a number of the troops. Further, he informs David of Uriah's death before David can respond, indicating he was astute enough to know that this was the crucial information Joab had wished to communicate.

25. David's response is a veiled attempt to thank Joab. David tells Joab not to let 'this matter be evil' in his eyes, with the identical expression used of Yahweh in response to David in v. 27. David effectively congratulates Joab for doing his job well, not least because he made it seem like Uriah's

death was an accident of war, denying any moral issues in what had transpired. Nevertheless, by introducing a platitude about the devouring power of the sword (though Uriah may have been killed by archers), David's speech prepares for Nathan's use of the same term in his judgment speech against David (12:9–10). David's guilt is manifest. He could not manipulate the law to execute Uriah, but he could commit murder without it appearing to be so. Joab is also involved, but the narrative resolutely focuses on demonstrating David's guilt.

David marries Bathsheba: 11:26–27

26–27a. With the 'problem' of Uriah resolved, this part of the story closes with David's marrying Bathsheba after the period of mourning, perhaps seven days (Gen. 50:10; Sirach 10.12). We are not told how Bathsheba heard of her husband's death, only that she did and had observed proper protocols. Then David again sent for her, brought her and married her to claim the child as his own and as legitimate. We are then told a son was born, though the child is never named. From David's perspective everything now seems resolved (Lawlor 1982: 200).

27b. The narrator has refrained from comment but now observes that the matter was 'evil in Yahweh's eyes'. This directly parallels David's words to Joab over Uriah's murder (also A. Fischer 1989: 55–56), showing that the stress is on the murder, though adultery is included. As the narrative has steadfastly sought to prove, the whole of David's behaviour was sinful because from the outset it abused royal power. Since the commandments against murder, adultery, theft (Exod. 20:13–15) and coveting (Exod. 20:17) were breached, while an attempt was made to distort the commandment against false testimony (Exod. 20:16), Yahweh's perspective is hardly surprising, but foregrounds the theological dimension. An Israelite king's actions cannot be understood apart from Israel's covenant traditions, so there is more to come from Yahweh.

Explanation

Everything we have seen about David to this point encourages us to see him positively. He was the man after Yahweh's heart (1 Sam. 13:14), the neighbour better than Saul (1 Sam. 15:28). We might imagine David possessed some moral superiority, and his persistent refusal to kill either Saul (1 Sam. 24, 26) or Ish-bosheth (2 Sam. 2–4) and seize the kingdom might lead to this conclusion. David had Yahweh's anointing, was marked out by the presence of Yahweh's Spirit (1 Sam. 16:13) and waited for Yahweh to give him the kingdom (1 Sam. 26:10–11). Even David's most doubtful moments, when he served the Philistine king, Achish (1 Sam. 27:1 – 28:2; 29:1–11), were still times when he honoured Yahweh and worked for Israel's good. Saul tried to hunt down David (1 Sam. 23–24, 26), but David was always loyal to Yahweh's promise that he would be king. David could not be like the king of whom Samuel warned (1 Sam. 8:10–18), one who took for himself. Rather, he had to act in the terms of 1 Sam. 12, and structure his reign as one under Yahweh's greater authority. The result of this is finally seen in Yahweh's promise to David in 2 Sam. 7:1–17. Where Saul could never establish a dynasty, Yahweh promised David his dynasty would endure (7:11b–16). The possibility was raised that David's descendants might sin and require Yahweh's discipline, but the prospect of David's sin was not considered.

Against this, 2 Sam. 11 emerges as a shock, a shock that must be understood against its immediate background in chs. 9 – 10 as well as the wider context of the book, though much of its significance is only established in the light of material we read later and are thus forced to reread this chapter (Firth 2008). Here we see David's ruthlessly dealing with someone he believes to be a rival. No reason is given for this belief and though the narrative employs considerable restraint throughout in describing anyone's motivation, this absence may be significant. Although 1 Samuel showed that Saul was fundamentally wrong to pursue David since David would not seize the throne, there was some basis for his actions. After all, David had been anointed by Samuel and even if Saul did not know this he was certainly aware of the adulation David received after slaying Goliath (1 Sam. 18:7), and progressively aware of the covenant bond between David and Jonathan (1 Sam. 20:30–34). Moreover, even Saul eventually accepted that David would be the next king (1 Sam. 24:21 [ET 24:20]). Saul may have attributed false motives to David, but the text is clear that David rivalled him for the people's affection, and also had Yahweh's support. But the absence of any such statements about Uriah may be significant, especially as he is otherwise portrayed as loyal to David and Yahweh. David's actions against Uriah are more irrational than those of Saul. Indeed, David becomes like Saul, a monarch determined to protect his own prestige rather than govern for his people's well-being.

How David does this is seen in the three stages of his assault on Uriah, an assault that occurs against the backdrop of chs. 9 – 10, where the theme of *hesed* (loyalty, kindness) was prominent, because that is what David does not show. First, by taking Uriah's wife, Bathsheba, as a sexual partner he engaged in a process that subsequent chapters indicate was not simply an act of lust but a claim of power over a rival. But David could not control everything, and 'Uriah's wife' conceived. David's assault became more direct as he needed to claim the child as his own. In the second stage he sought a legal pretext to execute Uriah since for him to have sex with his wife while on duty breached the law. But, in spite of David's blandishments and attempt to make him so drunk he did not know what he was doing, Uriah did not comply with David's wishes. David could not control either human fertility or human faithfulness. Finally, he brought Joab into his conspiracy to murder Uriah by proxy, though dressed up as an accident of war. David's destruction of his adversary is complete when he marries his wife and their child is born.

David's position seems secure. Yet, the chapter's closing note raises important questions. David's actions are known to Yahweh, and are evil. Even Yahweh's favourites cannot abuse their position and escape without censure. The nature of that censure awaits ch. 12, but already questions are raised. Saul was rejected for failing to keep Yahweh's word (1 Sam. 13, 15). Can Yahweh continue to work with David? By becoming like Saul, does David forfeit the dynastic promise? Already we know David's sin will be addressed by Yahweh. What we cannot know yet is how it will play itself out.

2 SAMUEL 12

Translation

¹Then Yahweh sent Nathan to David. He came and said to him, 'There were two men in a certain city, one rich and one poor. ²The rich man had very many flocks and herds, ³but the poor man had nothing save one little ewe lamb he had bought. He reared her and she grew together with him and his children. She ate from his morsel, drank from his cup and lay at his breast. She was like a daughter to him. ⁴Now a traveller came to the rich man but he was unwilling to take from his flock or herd to prepare for the wayfarer who had come to him, so he took the poor man's ewe lamb and prepared her for the man who had come to him.' ⁵David's anger was kindled greatly against the man, and he said to Nathan, 'As Yahweh lives the one who has done this is a son of death! ⁶He shall make restitution for the lamb fourfold because he did this thing and had no pity.'

⁷But Nathan said to David, 'You are the man! Thus has Yahweh, the God of Israel, said, "I anointed you king over Israel and delivered you from Saul's hand. ⁸I gave you your lord's house and your lord's wives at your breast and gave you the house of Israel and Judah, and if that had been too little I would have added much beside. ⁹Why have you despised Yahweh's word to do evil in his eyes? You struck Uriah the Hittite with the sword and took his wife as your wife. Yes, you killed him with the sword of the Ammonites. ¹⁰So now, the sword shall never depart from your house because you despised me and took Uriah the Hittite's wife to be your wife." ¹¹Thus has Yahweh said, "Behold, I am raising evil against you from your own house, and I will take your wives before your eyes and give them to your neighbour, and he will lie with your wives in the sight of this sun. ¹²You acted in secret, but I will do this before all Israel and before the sun."' ¹³David said to Nathan, 'I have sinned against Yahweh.' Nathan said to David, 'Yahweh has also put away your sin. You shall not die. ¹⁴Nevertheless, because you caused Yahweh's enemies to blaspheme in this matter, the son born to you shall surely die.' ¹⁵Then Nathan went to his house and Yahweh struck the child Uriah's wife bore to David, and he was sick.

[16]David sought God for the lad, and David fasted and went in and lay all night on the ground. [17]Then the elders of his house rose up beside him to raise him from the ground, but he was unwilling and did not eat food with them. [18]On the seventh day the lad died, but David's servants were afraid to tell him the lad had died, for they said, 'Behold, while the child was yet alive we spoke to him and he did not heed our voice. How can we say to him, "The child has died"? He may then harm himself.' [19]When David saw his servants whispering to each other, David perceived that the child was dead. David said to his servants, 'Is the child dead?' They said, 'He is dead.' [20]Then David rose from the ground, washed and anointed himself and changed his clothes, then entered the house of Yahweh and worshipped. Then he came into his house. When he asked, they set food before him and he ate. [21]His servants said to him, 'What is this thing that you have done, for while the child lived you fasted and wept, but once the child died you rose and ate a meal?' [22]And he said, 'While the child lived I fasted and wept because I thought, "Who knows, Yahweh may yet be gracious to me that the child may live?" [23]But now he has died, why should I fast? Can I bring him back again? I will go to him, but he will not return to me.'

[24]Then David consoled his wife Bathsheba; he went in to her and lay with her and she bore a son and he named him Solomon. And Yahweh loved him. [25]Yahweh sent by the hand of Nathan the prophet, and he named him Jedidiah because of Yahweh.

[26]Joab fought Rabbah of the Ammonites and captured the royal city. [27]Joab sent messengers to David and said, 'I have fought Rabbah and even captured the city of waters. [28]But now, gather the rest of the people and encamp against it and capture it lest I capture the city and it is called by my name.' [29]David gathered all the people and went to Rabbah and fought it and captured it. [30]He took their king's crown from his head (its weight was a talent of gold and a precious stone was in it), and it was placed on David's head. He brought out a very great amount of spoil from the city. [31]But he brought out the people who were in it and he set them to work with saws, iron picks, iron axes and made and set them to labour in the brickworks. He did this to all the Ammonite cities. Then David and all the people returned to Jerusalem.

Notes on the text

1. A few MSS agree with LXX, Syr, adding 'the prophet' after Nathan. This merely conforms the text to 7:2. The Lucianic tradition of LXX (also McCarter 1984: 294) includes an expansion directing Nathan to pass judgment on David. Although he does this, a direct statement runs counter to the text's narrative reticence.

6. LXX has 'sevenfold'. Although proverbial, there is no reason David could not have made an immediate connection to Exod. 21:37.

9. For this use of waw, see GKC §154aNb.

14. 'Enemies of Yahweh' is often deleted as euphemistic (so McCarter 1984: 296) and from the unusual sense of n'$\d{s}$ required. The argument for a euphemism partly depends on David's sin being secret (so McCarter), but I have rejected this. Although *n's* elsewhere means 'to spurn', the pi. can be causative (Fokkelman 1981: 451). This verb links David with Eli's sons (1 Sam. 2:17).

17. With many MSS read *brh* for *br'*.

20. With Q, read the pl. 'clothes'.

21. Following LXX, read *bĕʻōd* for *baʻbûr*. McCarter (1984: 298) follows LXX and OL with David's keeping a vigil, but this is probably explanatory (similarly, Anderson 1989: 159).

23. *zeh* is omitted by a few MSS and, though a simpler construction, loses the emphasis it provides. See Driver 1913: 225.

24. Q (read by several MSS, Syr and Tg) has Bathsheba name the baby.

30. Most witnesses have 'their king', but some LXX MSS read, 'Milcom their king', though this may be dittography (but see NRSV). Include *ûbāh* on basis of 1 Chr. 20:2 and Tg. Although reference to the crown on the idol Milcom is possible (the consonants being the same as 'their king'), David more probably took the king's crown to claim the rule of the city. Although the crown's tremendous weight is difficult, the text says only that it was placed on David's head, not that he wore it. See Youngblood 1992: 953.

31. Reading *heʻĕbîd* for MT *heʻĕbîr* since the context is one of servitude, not execution. With Q read *malbên*, which is perhaps 'brickworks'.

Form and structure

Ch. 11 ended by noting that David's actions displeased Yahweh. That statement's outcome is resolved here as Yahweh sends Nathan to confront David and announce his punishment. Similarly, ch. 10 ended with the Ammonite war left incomplete. As noted, this forms a narrative frame, so the war's completion is reported once the events of David and Uriah are fully settled. The closure of one is linked to closure of the other.

It has long been noted that one could read straight from 11:27 to 12:15b without sensing any loss. Seiler (1998: 258–266) also argues for a complex redactional history within this section. Although the main observation is correct, it does not follow that Nathan's encounter with David is necessarily secondary. Rather, this encounter provides the mechanism for interpreting what follows. David's attitude, especially when explaining himself to his servants in 12:21–23, needs the dialogue with Nathan to make sense (see Jones 1990: 109). It is thus preferable to see 12:1–15 as a second narrative stream, with plot elements from both streams combining to interpret what follows. Veijola (2000) goes further, arguing we should read from 11:27a straight to 12:24b, making Solomon the firstborn of David and Bathsheba. But apart from the textual surgery required, his argument depends upon a chronological structure for the whole of 2 Sam. 10 – 12, an argument weakened by the extent to which large sections of

Samuel are dischronologized for narrative purposes (see 'Form and structure' on 1 Sam. 16:1–13), while failing to name the first child is part of an intentionally shocking literary strategy.

Although chs. 11 – 12 contain the main action of their own plot, they also introduce the theme of family conflict that runs to the end of ch. 20, again indicating that succession is only one theme in these chapters (e.g. Hagan 1979 highlights deception), although it is central in 1 Kgs 1 – 2. But if 1 Kgs 1 – 2 is of separate origin (see 'Form and structure' on ch. 9), then making succession the key theme through 2 Sam. 9 – 20 is misguided. The announcement of David's punishment sets in place the major theme of chs. 13 – 20, which shows how the sword was active in David's family. Equally, it indicates that David's punishment can be complete, so the throne cannot be removed from his family (see Waltke 1988: 140). Yet, although Yahweh accepted David's repentance, punishment was still necessary to address the problem of his sin.

Comment

Nathan sent to David: 12:1–15

1a. Ch. 11 ends by noting that David's actions displeased Yahweh. Now we see what he will do about it. Initially, this involves sending (*šlḥ*, a *Leitwort* of chs. 10 – 11) Nathan (see 7:1–3) to David to announce his word. Nathan may have been attached to the court as the 'house prophet', but he was still Yahweh's prophet, not a state employee.

1b–4. Nathan's message is presented to David through what is best thought of as a parable, provided one does not match this to the specifics of Jesus' parables. It fits within the *māšāl* as an OT genre including riddles, extended metaphors and the like, the basic idea being of comparison (*NIDOTTE* 4:1134–1136). Although some are troubled by the lack of agreement between what Nathan presents and David's crime and are therefore uncomfortable with calling it a parable (e.g. Coats 1981: 368–377 unconvincingly suggests 'fable'), this misses the point even though some details are picked up later, especially the verb *ḥml* ('unwilling' in the parable, but later with the sense of 'pity'). Likewise, there are key linguistic links to the previous chapter (Coxon 1981: 249). David's actions are like those of the rich man, irrespective of their case details (though Schipper 2007: 386–389 believes David tries to depict Joab as the rich man). As Gordon (1986: 257) notes, the 'genius of Nathan's parable is that it so aptly depicts David's behaviour without the latter's realizing it'. Given that David has already murdered Uriah, it is important that Nathan employ care in bringing David to this point. The parable's structure is deceptively simple, alternating between the rich man and the poor man and their comparative wealth (see Altpeter 1982: 47–50). Their contrast is initially emphasized by the narrator providing more detail about the poor man. It is enough to know that the rich man has plenty of sheep and cattle. For the poor man we discover not only that he had just the one ewe lamb he had bought, but also how important she was to him, a close pet rather than livestock. The unmotivated action of the rich man in thus providing for the traveller is shocking. Nathan thus draws David into a state of righteous indignation over the rich man's actions. The rich man's 'taking' parallels David's 'taking' in the previous chapter, as both abuse the less powerful.

5–7a. Suitably drawn in by the story, David expresses his righteous anger. David's declaration over the rich man is that he is a 'son of death' (on this idiom see 'Comment' on 1 Sam. 20:31). Although commonly taken to announce the death penalty, it more likely expresses the idea that his behaviour has sunk to the lowest level. That the death penalty is not intended is indicated by the expected payment of four sheep in reparation (Exod. 21:37 [ET 22:1]). David acts as the upholder of justice, which is precisely what Nathan sought. David's final observation that the man lacked pity (*ḥml*) not only provides an important emotional response to the parable, but also the bridge needed to return to Nathan. Hence Nathan can conclude, 'You are the man!' He thus reveals his use of fiction to expose the truth about David and his actions, an exposure that makes David cognitively aware of his sin, but also makes him feel its emotional force. David identifies with the poor man, but Nathan thus reshapes his perceptions to identify with the rich (Altpeter 1982: 51). The judge is being judged.

7b–10. Nathan then outlined the parable's implications for David in a classic judgment speech broken into two oracles. The first stresses the interaction between David's callousness in taking from Uriah and his role as king. This is shown to be especially heinous in the light of Yahweh's giving to him. Yahweh had given much to David so that he possessed everything he needed. This includes his anointing, saving his life from Saul and the gift of all that had been Saul's, including his wives. Although Saul is known only to have had one wife and one concubine, this does not preclude a larger group, all of whom were apparently taken by David. Giving Saul's wives to David symbolized the gift of the kingdom, but Yahweh claims he would have given David more had he asked. This is contrasted with David's taking Uriah's wife. The oracle's climax is reached in v. 9 where Nathan turns from describing the past to interrogate David, asking why he despised Yahweh's word, rejecting what Yahweh had done for him. In context, Yahweh's word is not a specific promise but a reference to Yahweh's absolutely faithful character. Before David can answer, Nathan announces the specifics of David's sin, which is Uriah's murder and the taking of his wife, which is explained through David's ultimate action in killing Uriah through the Ammonites. It is not that murder is worse than adultery or the other way round. Everything David had done attacked Uriah (see 'Form and structure' for ch. 11) and rejected Yahweh's grace. The outcome of this was continued violence in David's household. David had made the sword central (11:25), and so would experience the sword for the rest of his life, hinting at Absalom's revolt as well as that of Sheba. David took and became the monarch of whom Samuel had warned (1 Sam. 8:10–19). Now he will discover the bitter fruit of such a choice.

11–12. The second oracle expands the punishment already announced, focusing on what will come from within David's 'house', language negatively evoking the promise of 7:4–16. The conflict will come from David's family, but Yahweh is the initiator. Because David took Uriah's wife in secret, Yahweh will give David's wives to a neighbour who will publicly do what David has done with her. The language of the 'neighbour' evokes 1 Sam. 15:28, highlighting how close David has come to emulating Saul and losing the kingdom. The punishment reverses what Yahweh has previously done for David. The two references to the sun in this judgment statement probably show that the public nature of David's punishment is both just and judicial. In many cultures the sun was associated with justice (through the god Shamash), but in Israel this was subsumed through the king. David's sin meant he had to be returned to the realm of justice, and Yahweh would achieve this by ensuring his punishment was seen by the sun and carried out before it (van Wolde 2003: 267). This judgment statement prepares for chs. 13 – 20, where Absalom does this with David's concubines who remained in Jerusalem (16:20–23).

13–15. Confronted with his sin, David confesses to Nathan, specifically noting that it is against Yahweh. This does not deny sinning against Uriah (and Bathsheba), but that all David's sin is against Yahweh's election of him (cf. Ps. 51:6 [ET 51:4], space for the reading of which is left in some medieval MSS). His assault on Uriah rejected the principles on which he had come to the throne where he waited for Yahweh's gift. Nathan's response stresses that his sin is dealt with immediately, and David will not receive the death penalty his actions merited (Lev. 20:10). However, his actions created a context where Yahweh's enemies would revile him (see 'Notes') because his actions were contrary to those expected of an Israelite king. There is therefore one further penalty: the child to be born will die. David cannot avoid his sin's consequences, and neither can he enjoy the blessing of life within it. We are not told why the child should die, though it is possible that David could claim Uriah's estate through him, deriving benefit from his attack on Uriah. Evans (2000: 190) rightly notes that we must distinguish between consequences and punishment, but the child's death is still difficult. The announcement's effect is seen immediately in narrative terms: Nathan returned to his house and Yahweh struck the unnamed child with illness. The tragedy of this is emphasized by the refusal to name Bathsheba as anything other than Uriah's wife, since that was her identity when the child was conceived.

One son's death, another's birth: 12:16–25

16–17. No details of the illness are provided other than its seven-day duration. We do not know if this was the child's age at death or just the period of the illness. If the former, it explains why no name is given, since children were named on the eighth day. What is remarkable is how David acts. He is a mourner from the outset, fasting, prostrating himself on the ground, and refusing food and assistance from senior staff.

18–20. Seven days was the normal period of mourning following a death (Gen. 50:10), so when the child died David had completed the full period. Nevertheless, his activities were so striking that palace staff, fearing self-harm, tried to withhold the news of the death. But, from their whispered comments, David recognized what had happened, and so not only returned to his normal routine but symbolized this by washing and anointing himself, wearing clean clothes and entering the house of Yahweh (see 7:1–3) and worshipping. Such behaviour was highly unusual, but we must note that with the child's death David's specific penalties were completed. Although the child was not a sacrifice (against Hertzberg 1964: 316), it is still clear that this aspect of the punishment was complete. But normal life, symbolized in a meal, happens after worship, the point where David again recognized that he lived under Yahweh's greater authority.

21–23. A more complete explanation of David's behaviour is provided by his response to his servants' puzzled question since David's actions were the reverse of what would be expected. Fasting and weeping were signs of mourning, not celebrating a child's birth (see Job 1:20–21; Esth. 4:1–3). Yet, as long as the child lived, David suggested that he hoped Yahweh would relent and offer a full pardon (Exod. 34:6–8). David mourned in the hope that the child would not die. But with the child's death, David knew he could do no more. He could not restore the child, but he too would die. Although some (e.g. Baldwin 1988: 241) see a nascent hope of life after death here, David more probably affirmed that Sheol was his fate too.

24–25. There is, however, an element of grace in the story. For the first time since 11:3 Bathsheba is named, and now called David's wife. Only once the punishment is complete can this occur. After comforting her, there is close repetition between the verbs of v. 24 and 11:4–5 (via 11:27), though the verb 'take' (*lqḥ*) is notably absent. Bathsheba gave birth to a son they named Solomon. The name may mean 'peace' (see 1 Chr. 22:18) or 'replacement' (Veijola 2000: 347 thinks the child replaces Uriah, though McCarter 1984: 303 argues it is the unnamed first child), though more importantly it echoes events of ch. 11, especially David's threefold use of the root *šlm* in his initial conversation with Uriah (11:7). More importantly, Yahweh loved him, and sent (again *šlḥ*) a message through Nathan naming him Jedidiah, 'beloved of Yahweh'. This latter name appears nowhere else, and may have been a family nickname, although it is also possible that Solomon was a throne name. It also puns David's name since both are built on the root *dwd*. In any case, it signifies Yahweh's grace.

The conclusion of the Ammonite war: 12:26–31

26–28. Since the war framed these events, it is now necessary to report its conclusion. The events of 11:1 – 12:25 must have taken about two years, so it is possible that war was already over. But narrative function prioritizes the frame over the order of events. As with most of ch. 10, we return to a fairly annalistic account, indicating that 10:1 – 11:1 and 12:26–31 were originally part of a continuous narrative. These verses describe Joab's initial success in completing the siege with the royal citadel's capture, which is presumably the city of waters. This probably means the outer fortress protecting the city's water supply was captured. Once this was controlled, a siege would end quickly, so David was summoned since Joab recognized that David should lead the final assault since the glory had to go to the king, irrespective of the work of his general.

29–31. The assault was successful, and David captured the city, also taking the king's crown and plundering the city. The crown's weight (see 'Notes') indicates it was not normally worn since a talent was roughly 75 pounds in weight, and must have been purely ceremonial. The spoil was also extensive, with 'a great amount' punning Rabbah. David's treatment of the city's inhabitants is uncertain (see 'Notes'). The slight emendations offered here understand David to employ corvée to support his building programme. Irrespective of this, by recording Rabbah's capture *after* the resolution of David's sin, the narrator shows that the blessing on David's reign depended upon his relationship with Yahweh. Although problems would continue, he could still reign effectively because of his repentance.

Explanation

The events of ch. 11 raised an important question. The promise to David in 7:12–16 envisaged the possibility of David's descendants needing Yahweh's discipline for sin, but this was not considered for David himself. Yet, through his sustained assault on Uriah, and seeming success following his marriage to Bathsheba and the birth of their son, David had raised the stakes. Yahweh had rejected Saul (1 Sam. 13, 15); might he reject David too? The problem is significant because Saul's sin was ultimately claiming autonomy from Yahweh's greater authority, and David has done the same. Yet David's house did endure and needs explaining. The key is that David, unlike Saul, ultimately recognized Yahweh's greater authority.

How this transpires is important because it happens at Yahweh's initiative yet requires the right response from David. Having reported that Yahweh regarded David's actions against Uriah as wrong, we are told he sent Nathan to David. We are not told if Nathan's parable was a stroke of genius or part of Yahweh's message since he quotes Yahweh only from v. 7, but it certainly was effective. Nathan had to negotiate an extraordinarily difficult set of circumstances in confronting a king who had effectively claimed absolute authority. David had murdered Uriah, so confronting the king with his sin required extraordinary faithfulness and courage. The parable succeeded in eliciting the required response when David was outraged by the rich man's actions, enabling Nathan to announce Yahweh's judgment on the king who thought he was the judge. David sought to deceive throughout the previous chapter, but Nathan's deceptive parable exposed the truth.

The truth for David was incredibly painful. He was king because of Yahweh's gift. David had not reached his position by taking but by receiving. Yet now he has taken. Adultery with Bathsheba and Uriah's murder are part of a complex whole where David rejected the central tenets of what it meant to be Yahweh's king. David is therefore judged by Yahweh. He will be attacked as he attacked Uriah, and just as the sword brought death to Uriah, so the sword will be active in David's family. Yet David's response is stunning, for he confesses simply, 'I have sinned against Yahweh.' Ps. 51, which reflects on these events, makes a similar claim. Unlike Saul, David makes no attempt to justify his actions, and neither does he seek any amelioration. He accepts Yahweh's authority, and for this receives forgiveness, though his sin's consequences remain. We might think it unfair, especially from the perspective of Uriah's family or the soldiers killed at Rabbah, that forgiveness is given so easily. Yet forgiveness is always unfair: that is what makes it grace. But sin's consequences cannot be avoided, as David discovers in the death of his unnamed son. The child's death is only the beginning of the consequences, and these are narrated over the next eight chapters. But in the midst of this there is grace in Solomon's birth and his acceptance by Yahweh. Moreover, as a forgiven king, the account of the battle of Rabbah can be completed. David, a forgiven king, can continue to reign. And this is how the narrator knows David's house endures where Saul's failed: David confessed his sin and received forgiveness. Forgiveness enables his house to endure, although the wages of sin (Rom. 6:23) still worked themselves out. As a forgiven king, we know the promise of 2 Sam. 7, and the messianic hope included with it, continues, and of course is picked up again in Matt. 1:6, where Jesus' descent through Solomon is through 'Uriah's wife'.

2 SAMUEL 13:1–38

Translation

¹Afterwards, Absalom, David's son, had a beautiful sister named Tamar, and Amnon, David's son, loved her. ²Amnon was frustrated to the point of making himself ill because of his sister Tamar because she was a virgin and it seemed impossible to Amnon to do anything to her. ³But Amnon had a friend named Jonadab ben Shimeah, David's brother, and Jonadab was a very wise man. ⁴He said to him, 'Son of the king, why are you like this, weak every morning? Won't you tell me?' Amnon said to him, 'I love Tamar, my brother Absalom's sister.' ⁵Jonadab said to him, 'Lie on your couch and feign illness. When your father comes to see you, then say to him, "May my sister Tamar please come and feed me, and let her prepare the food before me so I may see it and eat from her hand."' ⁶So Amnon lay down and feigned illness. When the king came to see him, Amnon said to the king, 'May my sister Tamar please come and make a couple of cakes before me that I may eat from her hand.'

⁷David sent home to Tamar saying, 'Please go to your brother Amnon's house and prepare food for him.' ⁸Tamar went to her brother Amnon's house where he lay and took the dough, kneaded it, prepared the cakes in his sight and cooked the cakes. ⁹She took the pan and dished them out before him, but he refused to eat. Amnon said, 'Send everyone out from me.' So they went out from him. ¹⁰Amnon said to Tamar, 'Bring the food to the chamber that I might eat from your hand.' So Tamar took the cakes she had made and brought them to her brother Amnon in the chamber. ¹¹She brought them to him to eat, but he seized her and said to her, 'Come, lie with me, my sister.' ¹²She said to him, 'No, my brother. Do not humiliate me, because such a thing is not done in Israel. Do not do this disgraceful thing. ¹³As for me, how could I remove my shame? And you would be like one of the disgraceful fools in Israel. But now, please speak to the king because he will not withhold me from you.' ¹⁴But he was unwilling to heed her and being stronger than her, he humiliated her and laid her.

¹⁵Then Amnon hated her intensely, for the hatred with which he hated her was greater than the love with which he had loved her. Amnon said to her, 'Get up. Go.' ¹⁶She said to him, 'No, my brother, for this wrong in sending me away is greater than what you have already done to me.' But he would not heed her. ¹⁷He called his attending lad and said, 'Please send this one outside away from me, and lock the door after her.' ¹⁸Now she was wearing a special garment, for thus were the king's virgin daughters robed. So his attendant brought her outside and locked the door after her. ¹⁹Tamar put ashes on her head and tore the special robe she was wearing. She laid her hand on her head and went away, crying out as she went.

²⁰Absalom her brother said to her, 'Has your brother Amnon been with you? Now my sister, keep quiet, because he is your brother. Do not take this matter to heart.' So Tamar stayed desolate at her brother Absalom's house. ²¹When King David heard all these things, he was very angry. ²²But Absalom did not speak with Amnon, whether bad or good, because Absalom hated Amnon because he had humiliated his sister Tamar.

²³After two full years, Absalom had shearers at Baal Hazor near Ephraim, and Absalom invited all the king's sons. ²⁴Absalom came to the king and said, 'Behold, your servant has shearers. Would the king and his servants please come with your servant?' ²⁵The king said to Absalom, 'No, my son. Let us not all go so we are not a burden upon you.' Although he urged him, he was unwilling to go, but he blessed him. ²⁶Absalom said, 'If not, then let my brother Amnon come with us.' The king said to him, 'Why should he go with you?' ²⁷But Absalom urged him, so he sent Amnon and all the king's sons with him. ²⁸But Absalom had commanded his lads, 'Look for when Amnon is glad of heart from wine, and when I say to you, "Strike Amnon," then kill him. Do not be afraid. Am I not commanding you? Be strong, men of valour.' ²⁹Absalom's lads did to Amnon what Absalom commanded, then all the king's sons arose; each one mounted his mule and fled.

³⁰While they were still on the road, a report reached David saying, 'Absalom has struck all the king's sons. Not one of them is left.' ³¹The king got up, tore his garments and lay upon the ground, and all his servants stood by with torn garments. ³²But Jonadab ben Shimeah, David's brother, spoke up and said, 'Let not my lord think they have killed all the lads, the king's sons, for Amnon alone has died. For by Absalom's intent this has been determined since the day he humiliated his sister Tamar. ³³So now let not my lord the king set this matter to heart, thinking, "All the king's sons have died," for Amnon alone has died, ³⁴but Absalom has fled.'

The lad who was watching lifted his eyes and saw, and behold, many people were coming from the road behind him beside the mountain. ³⁵Jonadab said to the king, 'Behold, the king's sons are coming; it has happened as your servant said.' ³⁶As he finished speaking, behold, the king's sons came, lifted their voice and wept. The king also, along with his servants, wept very bitterly.

³⁷But Absalom fled and went to Talmai ben Ammihud, king of Geshur, and David mourned for his son every day. ³⁸Absalom fled and went to Geshur and was there for three years.

Notes on the text

6. The meaning of *lbb* ('cakes'; NIV 'special bread') is unclear. Seemingly from the same root as 'heart', this may suggest the food's shape, or perhaps that it was (in an English idiom) 'hearty'. Some form of invalid food is required.

9. *mašrēt* is a hapax legomenon, but the context (and Aram. cognate) indicates the meaning.

14. When the verb *škb* is used as a euphemism for sexual intercourse, it normally includes the preposition *'im* (with). Its absence here is striking and represented through the equivalent dysphemism 'he laid her'.

16. *'al 'ôdōt* is difficult (though see NASB) because elsewhere it is used with *'al*. From the LXX^L one could reconstruct *'al 'āḥî gĕdōlâ hārā'â hazzōt mē'aḥeret*, which fits the context (similarly, Fokkelman 1981: 452).

17. The pl. *šilḥû* is unexpected, and usually emended. But Absalom may be trying to suggest more attendants than he had.

18–19. *kĕtōnet passîm* (identical to Joseph's robe, Gen. 37:3, 23, 32) cannot be translated confidently. 'Many coloured' is linguistically improbable, and it could be a long garment reaching either wrists (for sleeves) or feet. 'Special garment' recognizes its importance without being prescriptive. *mĕʿîlîm* (robes) is frequently emended to 'from of old' or 'from puberty', but, though awkward, should stand because *mĕʿîl* is a *Leitwort* through Samuel, always appearing at crucial narrative points.

20. The waw before *šōmēmâ* is explicative (GKC §154aN1b).

21. Most commentators follow LXX (and 4QSam^a as reconstructed), including the comment that because Amnon was his firstborn David did not curb Amnon's excesses (see NRSV). Although plausible, it could be a marginal scribal comment that has entered some traditions. As with 2 Sam. 11, this chapter is marked by narrative reticence, and the balance of probability is marginally towards MT's shorter reading (similarly, Smith 1990: 40).

25. Reading *pṣr* for MT *prṣ* with 4QSam^a and LXX.

27. See note for 13:25 except that 4QSam^a is unavailable. LXX expands on Absalom's feast, but may be a gloss (Campbell 2005: 126 is similarly reserved).

32. LXX suggests, 'My lord the king', but may conform the text to a common formula.

34. Anderson (1989: 179) rightly regards *wayyibraḥ ʾabšālôm* as concluding Jonadab's speech, and thus not misplaced information to be omitted. LXX is longer in the verse's second half, but MT is not necessarily corrupt.

37. With Q and many MSS read Ammihud for Ammihur. With many LXX MSS supply 'David' as subject of final verb.

Form and structure

Nathan's announcement of David's punishment specified continual conflict within David's family, which would be patterned on David's sin (12:7–12). The sins highlighted were sexual misconduct and murder. Both appear here and set in motion the plotline developed to 20:22. David's sin is forgiven but its complications have to be resolved. Nathan also said that David's problems would come from his family, something highlighted by the abundant use of familial language through the chapter (Gunn 1978: 99). The narrator keeps a careful balance in reporting this. Throughout we are only immediately aware of what the characters perceive themselves doing. They act autonomously, without manipulation (against Propp 1993: 40), but fulfil Yahweh's stated purpose in David's punishment.

The links with David's sin in chs. 11 – 12 are more extensive than simply repeating his crimes. The presentation of events here is also important in highlighting the deep parallels that exist. Just as David used intermediaries to bring Bathsheba to himself (11:3–4), now he is the intermediary who ensures Tamar comes to Amnon (13:7). Amnon's rape of Tamar is like David's adultery with Bathsheba in that both events are the start of a much longer and more complex conflict. David's conflict was with Uriah, and it ran through the whole of 2 Sam. 11. Amnon's rape of Tamar triggers violence and rebellion that run through to 20:22, though the immediate connection is to 13:38, where Absalom's retribution against Amnon temporarily ceases while he is in exile. Although we see Tamar more clearly than Bathsheba since her speeches show her as an intelligent and resourceful woman (13:12–13, 16), she remains a minor character who plays no role after her rape. Just as we never know Bathsheba's perspectives in ch. 11, so we know nothing about Tamar after her return to Absalom's house. Further links are demonstrated when Absalom orders his men to kill Amnon (13:28–29), so he, like David, commits murder through others. The punishment for David's sin is thus closely patterned on his own actions. In spite of this, Amnon's story is darker (similarly, Gray 1998) because of the violence of Tamar's rape, something never said of David with Bathsheba.

There are also several allusions to 1 Sam. 25, where David was tempted to employ violence to achieve his own ends only to be stopped by Abigail's intervention (1 Sam. 25:18–35). Then Nabal was celebrating his sheep-shearing (1 Sam. 25:2–8), the celebration Absalom uses to kill Amnon (vv. 23–29). In addition, Absalom directed his servants to strike Amnon when his heart was merry from wine (13:28), Nabal's condition when Abigail returned from meeting David (1 Sam. 25:36), and the night before she told him what had happened and Yahweh struck him (1 Sam. 25:37–38). Tamar's speech to Amnon (vv. 12–13) also alludes to Nabal, where her references to what is disgraceful play on the root *nbl* (folly). The folly of which she speaks is not stupidity, but rather that which is unacceptable in Israel (Isa. 32:6; see Keefe 1993: 82), so the narrator assesses Amnon through Tamar (Seiler 1998: 98). This term also occurs in Gen. 34:7, Judg. 19:23–24 and 20:6, all passages referring to violent sexual abuse. Interweaving motifs from 1 Sam. 25 and 2 Sam. 11 – 12 are a crucial narrative element, as they demonstrate the reality of David's sin, but implicitly ask why no one intervenes in the way Abigail did. Sin and punishment are worked out, but in folly of the worst kind.

In addition, Alter (1999: 267–271) points to a range of allusions to Genesis, especially the Joseph story. Thus Potiphar's wife asks Joseph to lie with her (Gen. 39:12), but he refuses, paralleling Amnon's request in v. 11 and Tamar's response in vv. 12–13, though this also alludes to Dinah (Gen. 34). Before making this request, Amnon had ordered the room to be cleared (v. 9), just as Joseph had before revealing himself to his brothers

(Gen. 45:1). When Tamar is expelled from Amnon's rooms, we are told of the special robe worn by the king's daughters (v. 18), a robe paralleled only by Joseph's (Gen. 37:3). The Tamar narrative of Gen. 38 also runs in the background, since as well as the central female's shared name, the other names allude to one another along with a range of shared features such as sheep-shearing and plot parallels (Ho 1999). These allusions provide a central intertext for this narrative, suggesting different ways the situation of David's family could have been resolved but without parading an obvious moral.

Those strongly influenced by Rost (1982) tend to see the issue of succession developed since Amnon, as the oldest son, was presumably crown prince, though primogeniture is not established. Although Absalom was David's third son (2 Sam. 3:3), the second son, Chileab, is nowhere mentioned and presumed to be dead. The narrative is interpreted as showing how the older sons gradually disqualify themselves from the succession. Although this may be a subsidiary feature, it is far from explicit as compared to the theme of sin and punishment, and suffers from the weakness that Chileab's death is never mentioned. Focus on succession here imposes a framework that prevents the text's themes from adequate development and is not developed in the exegesis below (see Conroy 1978: 101–105).

Comment

Tamar's rape: 13:1–22

1. 'Afterwards' provides a clear link to preceding events, indicating that we are to read in the light of what has gone before. Although there is no explicit join to chs. 10 – 12, the narrator provides this link to ensure we observe the thematic connections. This verse is carefully structured, introducing the main characters in the order Absalom, David, Tamar and Amnon (Conroy 1978: 17, notes the inclusion formed by the same names in v. 22). Absalom is not a major figure in this section, but introducing him first suggests he will be later. Amnon is introduced last, while Tamar exists solely as Absalom's sister. We are therefore introduced to a fraternal conflict, with both brothers defined as David's sons, a conflict to be centred on Amnon's stated love of Tamar, though this is a misnomer for lust (Gordon 1986: 262).

2–6. Amnon's desire for Tamar meant that he made himself ill. As a 'virgin' (someone marriageable), she was in a special position within palace life, so any move Amnon made toward her was fraught with both political and sexual overtones (Matthews and Benjamin 1993: 178–181). A range of difficulties thus stood between Amnon and any sexual relationship with his sister. However, Amnon had a 'friend' in Jonadab, who is described as very wise. Since David's 'friend' Hushai is also a counsellor (15:32–37;

17:5–13), we should probably understand Jonadab in similar terms for Amnon: he was a confidant in the royal household's employ, an appropriate position for David's nephew. As a confidant he could see Amnon's problem and design a plot (Hill 1987: 389 points out parallels known from Egyptian texts) that addressed it, though his plan created only a context where Amnon and Tamar could be together (similarly, Fokkelman 1981: 109). The plan drew on Amnon's illness, but the narrator refrains from revealing any more. Yet, in doing this, Jonadab also elicited from Amnon information that exceeded the basic problem with Tamar. As with Bathsheba and her introduction as Uriah's wife, Amnon's response described Tamar as Absalom's sister, thus stressing the rivalry between the brothers. This is confirmed when, after her retirement to Absalom's house (v. 20), we do not hear of her again. If Jonadab was a co-conspirator in rape, he must have known that his suggestions would lead to further violence. But for the narrative, Jonadab is a means to an end, much as David's messengers were in bringing Bathsheba to him (11:4). The crucial point is that the plan was followed, so Tamar could come to Amnon and cook invalid food (see 'Notes') to aid his recovery. Jonadab's wisdom was vindicated when David enquired about Amnon's health and agreed to send Tamar to cook the food.

7–10. Tamar duly came and prepared the food, thoroughly innocent of what was taking place, though using the verb škb (to lie down) for Amnon here is fraught with innuendo. In one sense it is appropriate and follows Jonadab's advice, but its frequently euphemistic use lends an element of menace here. The narrative, so far paced quite quickly, now deliberately slows, providing detail about Tamar's cooking process while with Amnon. It suggests a continuation of Amnon's desire while indicating through a series of double entendres that there was still time for it to 'simmer' along with the cakes (Gray 1998: 44–47). Once the food was prepared, Amnon continued the act, requesting all the servants to leave and declining to take the food himself. He acted as the weak invalid, one too weak to look after himself, asking for privacy from his servants, and seemingly indicating his need of his sister's help in being fed. But this simply allowed the room to be cleared and drew Tamar into his bedroom.

11–14. Once Tamar is in the bedroom with Amnon, and with no witnesses present, there is a sudden and dramatic role reversal as Amnon seized his half-sister as she sought to feed him, before he summoned her to 'lie with him', the same euphemism used to describe David and Bathsheba (11:4). The key difference is that he seized her before making his request, something never stated of Bathsheba. Tamar refused to accede, although she was obviously in an impossible situation. Her answers in vv. 12–13 are short and staccato, continually denying Amnon's right to act like this, indicating that even if she agreed to have sex with him she would be humiliated as well as acting contrary to Israelite practice, an act of disgraceful folly from which neither could recover. She could not remove the reproach of her lost virginity and he would be known as a disgraceful fool. Instead, she attempted to find an acceptable solution, suggesting that Amnon approach David to request a marriage. Such marriages were prohibited by Lev. 18:9 and Deut. 27:22. It may be the law was not enforced then, or not within the royal family, but it could simply be a ploy to prevent the seemingly inevitable (Baldwin 1988: 248). All these options are left open, because the central concern is to show the heinous nature of Amnon's actions through a contrast with Tamar's applied wisdom. But Amnon was not dissuaded and carried out his plot, with the violence of the rape stressed by his greater power, and so he humiliated and 'laid her' (see 'Notes').

15–19. A major shift occurs, for Amnon now hates Tamar more than he loved her, stressed by the use of the root *śn'* (hate) four times. Hertzberg (1964: 324) interprets this as sexual hatred, which is probable and represents an unusual degree of psychological development. However the hatred is interpreted, it is central to the story's development. Amnon's hatred is initially manifested in his attempt to dismiss her, though again Tamar offers a cogent argument against this, suggesting that dismissing her without further action is worse than what he has already done, though how it is worse is left unsaid. Tamar may be suggesting he is effectively divorcing her (so Carlson 1964: 181, citing Deut. 22:28–29), but the verb *šlḥ* is common and one would expect other elements if divorce were meant. The more important point is the verb's echo with chs. 10 – 12, thus providing a further link between these narratives. Amnon's response is identical to v. 14, as he refused to heed her, dismissing his sister into a servant's care with the instruction that she be put out and the door bolted behind her. By this, the narrator points to their separation, its importance stressed by the note that the attendant carried out Amnon's directive. Only now are we told of Tamar's special robe signifying her status as a 'virgin', a robe that could now only mock her condition. Thus she mourned like a widow except that she had never been wed, only raped.

20–22. Absalom is reintroduced, seemingly perceiving what has taken place, since his question 'Has your brother Amnon been with you?' implies more than it says. It suggests Absalom knows what has taken place, though his words offer little real comfort, suggesting only that Tamar remain silent because Amnon is her brother and so should not be excessively upset. His focus on Amnon indicates that the narrative is primarily about fraternal conflict being worked out through their sister. Tamar, violated, lives desolate with her brother, bereaved and without family or the hope of one. David, we are told, hears about these events but does nothing about them. We are not told why, since there were obvious possibilities (Deut. 22:29 at least allows a fine), unless David believes this is his punishment being worked out in the family. But the narrator does not say this: we are merely told that David becomes furious. Absalom, however, expresses his anger by refusing to speak to Amnon. Where Amnon came to hate Tamar after raping her, Absalom now hates Amnon for the same reason. Thus the context is established for the sword to be operative in David's family, just as Nathan said (12:10).

Absalom's revenge and flight: 13:23–38

23–27. Tamar moves into the background since the primary conflict is between Amnon and Absalom. Her suffering merely brought this conflict to a head. So the story moves on two years as it describes the events surrounding Amnon's murder, an event that generates another cycle of violence. After two years, we come to a celebration of sheep-shearing (see 1 Sam. 25:2–8), a major community event representing an important stage in agricultural life. Celebrating this was natural. From the outset we are told Absalom had invited all the king's sons to his feast at Baal Hazor, a town about 20 miles north of Jerusalem, though one would not expect Amnon to attend. Hence Absalom came before David asking that he come to the feast. David could not do this, recognizing that, in spite of Absalom's protestations, he would be a burden. But in terms of courtesy he could not reject Absalom's alternative request that Amnon should come. David's knowledge of their enmity seems apparent from the question in v. 26, but protocol is followed, unless David suspected that Absalom might spare him the problem of executing his eldest son. But the narrator does not tell us this, nor if Absalom planned this as a ruse from the outset or if he took advantage of how things played out (Birch 1998: 1309). What matters is that David sent Amnon with the others. Amnon thus has no way of avoiding the events around him. As Tamar was trapped in the plan Amnon had set with Jonadab, so he is being caught in Absalom's trap.

28–29. Amnon is no longer a significant figure within the narrative structure. He is spoken about, but never speaks, and so is disempowered by the narrator. Absalom is the central figure who commands his servants to kill the drunk Amnon (cf. Esth. 1:10) at the feast. An important reversal occurs. In Tamar's rape, Amnon had ordered his lad (*na'ar*), but now he is silent before Absalom's command. Absalom's command, couched in the language of Yahweh war, encourages his lads (*na'ar*) not to fear, though Absalom is clearly like David and kills through others. But unlike David, he makes clear from the outset that he will accept full responsibility. Amnon's death is reported briefly, for the grim order was carried out. Unsurprisingly, the other sons flee immediately to Jerusalem on their mules (the royal transport of choice in spite of Lev. 19:19), though Absalom is not concerned with them.

30–34a. Somehow a report reached David before his sons' return that Absalom had killed them all, leaving no survivors. In response, David mourned for them as he had for his unnamed son in 12:16–23, tearing his garments and sitting on the ground. He was joined by his servants. Jonadab is reintroduced and again shows his 'wisdom' by arguing that David must not imagine all his sons have died, because only Amnon is dead. Although Jonadab has no special information, his counsel is based on Absalom's response to his sister's rape, suggesting that Absalom's actions should have been expected. Therefore, Jonadab tells David not to take Amnon's death to heart, repeating Absalom's phrase from when he spoke to Tamar (v. 20). It was cold comfort, but at least an accurate assessment of events. Jonadab was astute enough to realize that Absalom could flee, since by the time David responded he would be well away, though Jonadab does not indicate knowledge of where he has gone.

34b–36. Rather than focusing on Absalom's flight, the narrative recounts how David and those with him saw confirmation of Jonadab's interpretation when a watchman reported the arrival of a large body of people. They were initially unidentified until Jonadab pointed out that they were the king's sons coming, as he had said. Jonadab is a crucial figure for interpreting these events, but moves to the background as the sons arrive and weep bitterly.

37–38. Absalom also fled, but went instead to the home of his maternal grandparents in Geshur (3:3), a buffer state towards Syria. This provided him with some security, though presumably David could have acted against him had he wished. David mourned for his son, though we do not know which one, but did nothing more. Absalom spends three years in Geshur before the story advances further.

Explanation

Like 1 Sam. 27, God is never mentioned in this chapter, and yet all its hideous awfulness reflects David's punishment for his sin against Uriah. Because David's punishment was to come from his own family and beget violence and sexual abuse, it is unsurprising that those themes develop here. David's sexual abuse was linked to murder, as happens here, though this time the perpetrator of sexual abuse is the one murdered. David thus experiences the promised judgment from 12:7–12 as it begins to resolve itself in his household, though the characters in the narrative never do anything other than they themselves choose.

Although it contains two stories, they are inextricably linked while also preparing for what follows, with Jonadab crucial at both ends of the chapter. Amnon is David's son, trapped by his desire for his half-sister Tamar, which is described as 'love' but later becomes 'hate'. Driven by his inability to have her because she is a virgin (incest is not central) he adapts Jonadab's plan and then rapes and dismisses her. His violence is contrasted with Tamar's attitude, through whom the narrator interprets events for us. Yet, for all Tamar's pain and desolation, the chapter is ultimately about fraternal rivalry, possibly between David's eldest surviving sons. The fraternal conflict is hinted at in the opening verse's structure, developed in

Absalom's brooding silence (v. 22), which then erupted two years after the rape when Absalom ordered Amnon's murder at a feast at his property north of Jerusalem.

Through it all David is a bit-part player who sends Tamar to help her brother, is angry about the rape, sends Amnon to the fateful feast and mourns for his son. David sends and becomes emotional, but nothing else. Is he accepting his punishment, or is he so bound by his own sin that he cannot act? Within the chapter's artistry this is perhaps a false dichotomy. David's sons make free choices and so resolve David's punishment, and David's failure to act is both a free choice and the means of his punishment. David's sin may not have been terminal, but sin's effects linger.

2 SAMUEL 13:39 – 14:33

Translation

[39]King David's spirit ceased to go out after Absalom because he was consoled over Amnon since he was dead. [14:1]But Joab ben Zeruiah knew David's heart went out to Absalom. [2]So Joab sent to Tekoa and brought a wise woman from there. He said to her, 'Pretend to mourn and dress in mourning clothes. Do not anoint yourself with oil but be like a woman who has been mourning the dead for many days. [3]Then go to the king and speak thus to him.' Then Joab put the words in her mouth.

[4]When the woman from Tekoa came to the king, she fell on her face to the ground, did obeisance and said, 'Help, O King.' [5]The king said to her, 'What is troubling you?' She said, 'Truly, I am a widow, and my husband is dead. [6]But your maidservant had two sons. The two of them fought in the field and there was no one to separate them. Then one struck the other and killed him. [7]So, behold, the whole clan has risen against your maidservant and are saying, 'Give us the one who struck his brother that we may put him to death for the life of his brother whom he slew, and also destroy the heir.' So they would extinguish my remaining ember so as to leave my husband neither name nor remnant on the face of the earth.'

[8]The king said to the woman, 'Go to your house. I will issue a command concerning you.' [9]The woman of Tekoa said to the king, 'May the iniquity be upon me, my lord the king, and upon my father's house, but let the king and his throne be guiltless.' [10]The king said, 'Bring to me whoever speaks to you and he shall touch you no longer.' [11]She said, 'Let the king invoke Yahweh your God so the avenger of blood may not continue to ruin, so they do not destroy my son.' He said, 'As Yahweh lives, not one hair from your son's head shall fall to the ground.'

[12]Then the woman said, 'May your maidservant speak a word to my lord the king.' He said to her, 'Speak.' [13]The woman said, 'Why have you planned like this against God's people? When the king speaks thus, he convicts himself, for the king does not bring back his banished one. [14]We must die and are like water poured out on the ground, which cannot be gathered again. God does not remove life, but devises means by which the banished is not cast from him. [15]Now I have come to say this to

my lord the king, because the people made me afraid. So your maidservant thought, "Let me speak to the king. Perhaps the king will carry out his servant's word. [16]For the king will hearken to deliver his servant from the power of the man who would destroy me and my son together from God's heritage." [17]Your maidservant thought, "My lord the king's word will set me at rest," for my lord the king is like the angel of God to discern good and evil. Yahweh your God be with you!'

[18]The king responded to the woman, 'Please do not hide anything from me I ask you.' The woman said, 'Let my lord the king speak.' [19]The king said, 'Is Joab's hand with you in all this?' The woman responded, 'As your soul lives, my lord the king, there is no one who can turn to the right or the left from all that my lord the king speaks. Indeed, your servant Joab commanded me and set all these words in your maidservant's mouth. [20]Your servant Joab did this to change the course of things. But my lord is wise, like the wisdom of God's angel, to know all things on earth.'

[21]The king said to Joab, 'Behold, I have decided this. Go. Bring back the lad Absalom.' [22]Joab fell on his face to the ground, did obeisance and blessed the king. Joab said, 'Today your servant knows he has found favour in your eyes, my lord the king, since the king has granted your servant's request.' [23]Joab arose and went to Geshur and brought Absalom to Jerusalem. [24]The king said, 'Let him turn to his house, but he shall not see my face.' So Absalom turned to his house but did not see the king's face.

[25]In all Israel no man was so much praised for his beauty as Absalom. From the sole of his foot to the crown of his head there was no defect in him. [26]When he cut the hair of his head (for he cut it at the end of every year: he cut it when it was heavy on him), he weighed the hair of his head and it was two hundred shekels by royal standard. [27]Three sons were born to Absalom and one daughter named Tamar. She was a beautiful woman.

[28]Absalom lived two full years in Jerusalem, but he did not see the king's face. [29]So Absalom sent for Joab to send him to the king, but he was unwilling to come to him. He sent a second time but Joab was unwilling to come. [30]Then he said to his servants, 'Look, Joab's field is beside mine and he has barley there. Go and set it on fire.' So Absalom's servants set the field on fire. [31]Joab arose and came to Absalom at his house and said to him, 'Why have your servants set my field on fire?' [32]Absalom said to Joab, 'Behold, I sent for you, saying, "Come here that I might send you to the king, saying, 'Why have I come from Geshur? It would be better for me still to be there.'" Now then, let me see the king's face, and if there is iniquity in me let him put me to death.' [33]Joab went to the king and told him, and he summoned Absalom. He came to the king and did obeisance on his face to the ground before the king. And the king kissed Absalom.

Notes on the text

13:39. MT *wattĕkal dāwid* is impossible, since the f. verb cannot have David as its subject. 4QSam^a appears to support some LXX MSS and include *rûaḥ* and should be followed. *wattĕkal* may reflect exhaustion from longing (see

Ps. 84:2 [ET 84:3]), but more commonly means 'being finished'. *niḥam* is ambiguous and may mean either 'consoled' or 'avenged'.

14:4. With many MSS, LXX, Syr read *wattābō'* for *wayyōmer*. Lyke (1997: 22, 113) defends MT, but assumes an omission.

11. On K *ḥarbît* and Q *ḥarbat*, see GKC §75ff.

19. Many MSS offer *'îš* for *'iš*, but the latter is probably a variant of *yēš*. 4QSam^a reads *'āmâ* for *šipḥâ*, but MT is retained.

21. Many MSS read *'āsîtā*, but MT is a slightly more difficult reading since a scribe might imagine the reference is to what Joab has just done. However, the reference is prospective and is thus a decision made by David.

22. With Q and many MSS, read 'your servant'.

26. LXX has 'one hundred', but two hundred is also in 4QSam^a.

27. LXX^L has 'Maacah' for 'Tamar', coordinating the text to 1 Kgs 15:2, but this list need not be comprehensive since it is focused specifically on Tamar, and a different Absalom may be mentioned in 1 Kgs 15:2 (so McCarter 1984: 342). In any case, *bat* can also mean 'granddaughter'.

30. Some MSS have the common confusion of *lō'* for *lô*. If *lō'* were read, it would be asseverative, with little change in effect, but *lô* is retained. Read with Q *wĕhaṣṣîtûhā*. LXX and 4QSam^c have a lengthy plus here: 'Joab's servants came to him with their garments torn and said to him, 'Absalom's servants have set your field on fire.' Though accepted by McCarter (1984: 343) and Anderson (1989: 185), like other pluses in 2 Sam. 13:21–22, 27 and 34 are probably explanatory, and Campbell (2005: 127) is rightly suspicious.

31. With very many MSS and Q, read pl. 'servants'.

Form and structure

Where 2 Sam. 13 closely parallels 2 Sam. 11, this chapter is closer to 2 Sam. 12, though alluding to all of 10 – 12. The most obvious parallel is the use of a story to elicit judgment from David. Just as Nathan presented his parable (12:1–6), so the wise woman from Tekoa presented her fictional account of family conflict (14:4–20; on how this conforms to a standard cry of the weak, see Boyce 1988: 25–40). Both stories aimed to apply the judgment derived back to David. Similarly, the verb *šlḥ*, a *Leitwort* throughout chs. 10 – 12, is again prominent (six times), indicating how so much is carried on through messengers. All of this is coordinated around the key concern of Absalom's restoration, moving from David's longing for Absalom but his unwillingness to restore him, to his accepting Absalom's return but not seeing him, before their final meeting. It is the process of creating the meeting that matters, as is apparent from the fact that nothing beyond their greeting is narrated when they meet. Allusion is also made to 1 Sam. 25 through the wise woman's self-portrayal before David. Six times she calls herself a maidservant (*šipḥâ*) and twice a servant (*'āmâ*), whereas Abigail calls herself a maidservant (*šipḥâ*) twice and a servant (*'āmâ*) six times. So precise a reversal is perhaps accidental, but the trend is notable given the limited use of these words elsewhere in Samuel. Both also shift between the slightly more menial *šipḥâ* and *'āmâ* for rhetorical effect. This parallel is also seen in that both the woman (14:9) and Abigail (1 Sam. 25:24) indicate willingness to bear iniquity should David's judgment be unfavourable, as they intercede for someone guilty, something otherwise unparalleled.

But the parallels also interpret one another. Yahweh sent Nathan (12:1), but Joab sent the woman and provided her with her story (14:1–3). Nathan's parable elicited the relevant judgment so he could announce Yahweh's punishment on David. The wise woman achieves this in a more laboured way, but since the goal is to restore Absalom to Jerusalem it actually contributes to David's punishment. Likewise, the use of *šlḥ* is clustered around Joab's initial contact with the woman and Absalom's attempts to send him to David. Where Joab's use of violence following the message sent (*šlḥ*) to him by David was subtly applied (11:16–17), Absalom is openly violent in achieving his goals. It is not yet the sword of which Nathan spoke (12:10), but it prepares for Absalom's revolt in ch. 15. Finally, the comparison with Abigail is significant for its relationship to violence. Abigail's speech and actions prevented violence, but the wise woman's trigger more. Even the statement on the location of iniquity has contrast as well as parallel. Abigail was prepared to accept her husband's punishment, but thereby convinced David not to enact violence. This is her opening position. By contrast, the woman offers it only after David has ruled on her fictitious case because his position is still unclear. She uses it in preparing to claim that David is inconsistent in offering her a judgment he has not applied to himself in Absalom's case. Where the woman will be guilty of accusing the king, Abigail bears no guilt (see Hoftijzer 1970: 424–432).

The account contains several difficulties and ambiguities (see Polzin 1993: 139–143), leading some to argue for textual dislocation, with vv. 15–17 relocated after v. 8 (e.g. Anderson 1989: 185). This is because they interpret these verses as a return to a fictional story after its true nature is revealed. This lacks textual evidence, and it is possible to understand the encounter without this apparent contradiction (with Hoftijzer 1970). The woman speaks from a position of powerlessness, so it is here that her wisdom is most apparent.

Comment

The encounter with the wise woman: 13:39 – 14:20

13:39 – 14:3. Although the chapter's opening addresses the encounter between David and the woman from Tekoa, the narrator makes clear that

Joab is behind everything. David's spirit no longer goes out for Absalom, but Joab knows his king. Joab later ignores Absalom, so we must assume his concern is with David alone, and he sees Absalom's return as a means of serving his king, even if David does not recognize the need. With that background, we are told Joab arranges for a wise woman to be brought from Tekoa, presumably because it is relatively remote, on the edge of the Judean wilderness (10 miles south of Jerusalem), and David will not personally know her. Tekoa was also Amos' home town (Amos 1:1). Although the woman is wise, her message is dictated by Joab, as is her appearance as one in mourning. This does not mean she lacks wisdom and is simply Joab's tool. Rather, she is chosen because she can improvise and ensure the right outcome. The plan is simple, modelled on Nathan's approach to David. The woman must go dressed as a mourning widow with a story to elicit judgment from David, though this can hardly be described as a parable (Whitelam 1979: 130). The woman's skill is in how she achieves this.

14:4–7. Unlike Nathan, the woman approaches from a position of weakness, employing considerable care in gesture and language. That is why she prostrates herself before David and addresses him in the third person when requesting help. With David's permission, she recounts her story of fratricide where her two surviving sons have fought with one another, one being killed, a story with obvious parallels to Cain and Abel (Gen. 4:1–15; see Bergen 1996: 390; Lyke 1997: 25–89 explores this through a range of biblical accounts). First, she has to clarify her status as a widow to make clear that she depends upon her sons. It is this that creates the element of tragedy. There are echoes of Absalom and Amnon, though the underlying purpose is always masked. The law required the death penalty, and this was demanded within the clan for whom blood revenge was expected, but the woman's case suggests possible grounds for mercy rather than the letter of the law (cf. Exod. 21:12–14; Num. 35:30–34). A family's destruction could be sufficient for withholding the normal punishment (v. 7; see Deut. 25:5–10).

8–11. David's answer in v. 8 is meant to conclude the conversation, though he provides no content for his decision. Therefore, the woman's declaration about her family's guilt and the innocence of the throne enables the conversation to continue, though declaring David and his throne innocent is ironic for readers who know that David and his throne are far from that (Birch 1998: 1314). The woman employs multilayered speech, claiming to bear the guilt and show David innocent when her purpose is the opposite. David obviously desires to end the conversation, and declares that the woman must be left alone and that he will deal with anyone who goes against his order. Again this is insufficient, and the woman asks David to invoke Yahweh as an assurance of her protection so the blood redeemer will stop and her son survive. David responds by swearing by Yahweh that not one hair of the son's head will fall to the ground (see 1 Sam. 14:45, where the same language is used for Jonathan). With this done, the woman's case appears settled.

12–14. Because of the conclusion at v. 11, the woman needed permission to speak again from v. 12. So far the fictitious case has been central, and David had merely responded to it. Now the woman must delicately raise the real issue, which is the parallel with David's actions towards Absalom, though Absalom is referred to only as the one 'banished'. The parallel is inexact, and the woman notably focuses upon the position of the people as a whole because David's decision somehow affects them all. Contrary to her earlier assertion of the king's innocence, the woman now insists on David's guilt because he does not bring the banished one back. David's guilt is his inconsistency: he is prepared to grant clemency to one son guilty of fratricide but not another, since he has left Absalom banished from Jerusalem. The woman asserts that everyone suffers where judicial practice is inconsistent. The proverb (cf. Prov. 17:14) of v. 14 is perhaps deliberately obscure because of the need to draw David in rather than accuse him too directly, but is meant to be applicable. The reference to death's certainty is probably to the inevitable human condition rather than to something specific about Absalom, but identifies a key contrast, which is that death is not God's purpose. The woman comes dangerously close to noting that David deserved death for Uriah's murder but was forgiven even if death was working itself out in his family. This provides a basis for action. God does not desire to see estrangement, and neither should David.

15–17. The narrative returns to the fictitious case. These verses are thus often placed after v. 8 (see 'Form and structure'), but the woman more probably returns to the fictitious case to suggest that Absalom's position illustrates her plight. It is important to note that she has not revealed that her case is fictitious. The hint is there, but returning to the fictional case allows her to use a double entendre, since although she appears to speak about her own case, she is actually speaking of David's (Hertzberg 1964: 333). Her stated fear of the people's action would in her case refer to the blood avenger, but in reality she points to the risk of popular action unless Absalom is restored. The long quote of her supposed thoughts in vv. 15b–16 claims to provide a reason for her initial approach but actually stresses David's ability to act for Absalom, while the final flattery of v. 17 reinforces the point since the rest David can provide is for the whole nation, and his discernment is meant to see this.

18–20. David perceives what is taking place, and asks whether Joab is behind it all, placing the woman in the position of testifying in court. Although the woman employs the fawning language of the court, she confesses that Joab was behind her visit, even directing what she has said. She goes further, and points out also that Joab wanted to change the situation, though without naming Absalom directly. Joab may 'know' the king, but the one who is truly wise is the king himself.

Absalom's return to Jerusalem: 14:21–33

21–24. With her role completed, the woman disappears, and Joab as the motivating figure comes into the open. No indication is given of David's attitude to this process, and we move directly from his speaking to the woman to his encounter with Joab. Joab then receives the order he sought, to bring back Absalom, though in calling him a 'lad' (*na'ar*) David treats him either as immature or as equivalent to a servant and no more. Joab's response parallels the woman's when she approached David (14:4), and his speech is also full of court language. Whether Joab's perceptions are correct remains ambiguous. Joab believes he has found favour with David but David does not follow through on the logic of Joab's restoring Absalom. When Joab returns, there is thus surprise when Absalom is not permitted to see David. Joab leaves believing his ruse has clearly succeeded, but discovers otherwise on his return (Fokkelman 1981: 147). This may indicate some sort of house arrest, though it is unclear. However much David the father longs for his son, there is a point David the king will not cross. Absalom is in his house, and David in his, but they do not meet.

25–27. These verses are a digression, though they introduce information of subsequent importance. The digression divides Absalom's return to Jerusalem from his return to the palace. Absalom's description focuses on his beauty (cf. Song 4:7), particularly emphasizing his hair. Although the clippings' weight (approximately 4 lb) is hyperbolic, unless wet, it stresses the hair's quality. Similarly, there was no blemish on him. Good looks are a crucial element in Samuel as Saul (1 Sam. 9:1–2), Eliab (1 Sam. 16:6–7), Bathsheba (11:2) and Tamar (13:1) are all noted for their appearance, though good looks never provide security. In spite of Yahweh's advice on the matter (1 Sam. 16:7), David was also considered handsome (1 Sam. 16:12). However appearance is judged, Absalom had the appearance to attract people. He also had the blessing of a family, with three sons and a daughter. However, 2 Sam. 18:18 indicates he had no son, presumably indicating that all three boys had died. There was, therefore, only a daughter, whose beauty and name (Tamar) were constant reminders of the family conflicts. Reference to his beautiful head also prepares for his death when his head is caught in a tree (18:9), while also alluding to David's response to the woman when he asserts that 'not a hair' of her son's head will fall to the ground. For Absalom, this will be the problem.

28–33. The narrative proper now resumes, describing Absalom's frustration as he waited two years in Jerusalem without meeting his father. Displaying power's arrogance, he summoned Joab. But Joab was unwilling to act for him, apparently reasoning that restoring Absalom was enough. Twice we are told he was unwilling, matching the times Amnon was unwilling to listen to Tamar (13:14, 16). After two messengers were rejected, Absalom took a more direct approach. Again (13:27–29) Absalom commited his crimes through his servants, telling them to set Joab's barley field on fire. Absalom knew that even if Joab's primary loyalty was to David, commercial self-interest would bring him around. Joab duly came, but only to complain about Absalom's actions. Absalom was unrepentant, complaining that Joab ignored him when he wished to send Joab to the king to complain that Absalom's return from Geshur had brought no advantage. Only then did Joab agree to take Absalom's message to the king, presumably reasoning that Absalom could do more than burn a field. Although Absalom indicated willingness to suffer any appropriate penalty, he clearly knew this was hypothetical. Absalom thus came to the king, who kissed him. This may not signify reconciliation, merely a greeting. Nothing more was said, suggesting that although David and Absalom formally recognized each other, conflict remained at hand. Soon, just as Absalom bowed down to David and was kissed by him, the people would bow down to Absalom and be kissed by him (15:5).

Explanation

When reading this account, we need to remember that it is both a story in its own right and part of a larger story (2 Sam. 13 – 14), which is itself part of the story of David's sin and its punishment (2 Sam. 10 – 20), all of which is part of David's whole story. Like a succession of Russian dolls inserted inside each other, from smallest to largest, each level of the story is understood on its own terms and then integrated into the larger narrative.

Read on its own, this is the account of Absalom's exile in Geshur: ending when he is restored to Jerusalem. This reading attends to how Joab expresses loyalty to David by arranging his unstated desire for him and bringing back Absalom. Yet Joab also protects David as much as possible once David has indicated he will not see Absalom when he returns. Because David's desire is unstated, Joab has to employ an unnamed wise woman from Tekoa to act the part and tell the story that Joab set for her. Her wisdom is seen in how she can draw David along even as her double-voiced narrative also reflects on Tamar's rape and Absalom's retributive murder of Amnon in 2 Sam. 13. Yet, for all her skill, David can see Joab's hand. He has encountered such storytelling before and won't be fooled again. With the woman's role revealed she vanishes from the narrative as David meets with Joab to agree Absalom's return. But Joab does not initially know that David is unlike the father in the parable of the prodigal, and will not run to greet his son (Luke 15:20). David refuses to see him. But on Absalom's return we are told of his physical beauty. We understand what will make him attractive and yet we immediately see his ugly side in directing his servants to burn Joab's field to bring him to heel so Absalom can send him to David. Joab's loyalty has limits, and Absalom finally sees David two years after his return, five years after Amnon's murder and seven years after Tamar's rape. David kisses his son, but we know no more than this. Joab's loyalty has been costly, but father and son have the possibility of reconciliation.

But this is also part of chs. 13 – 14, and in that setting these events take on a darker hue. The narrator never indicates why David has not restored Absalom, but we know Absalom is a murderer. Killing Amnon was a calculated action, not settlement of a blood debt. Thus we see that the woman's story does not match too precisely, because her fictional sons were fighting without premeditation. Absalom has abundant premeditation, though he never does his own dirty work. Just as his servants were directed to kill Amnon, so now they burn Joab's field because Joab does not do Absalom's bidding. Absalom cannot overcome Joab's loyalty, but those loyal to Absalom are unafraid to use power for their own ends.

These events also have a context that was set by 2 Sam. 11 – 12. David's assault on Uriah through Bathsheba had been seen by Yahweh, and his punishment announced by Nathan. That punishment was patterned on David's own actions, and some of it has already appeared in ch. 13. The punishment included violence within David's family, but also to a situation where David would be assaulted as he had assaulted Uriah. Seen in that light, Absalom's attractive appearance is more threatening than hopeful, for here is one who can launch that assault, who has the character necessary to do so. And so it will be. Absalom's return prepares for his rebellion against David, dominating the next five chapters of Samuel before Sheba's rebellion. David's whole reign is thus affected by these events.

These levels are integrated within one another, and point to the fact that even Joab's loyalty, expressed in a costly way, functioned in one sense to bring the punishment Yahweh had announced. Joab chose freely, as did Absalom and David, but Yahweh's announcement continued to resolve itself through these events.

2 SAMUEL 15:1 – 16:14

Translation

[1]Later Absalom provided himself a chariot and horses and fifty men who ran before him. [2]Absalom would rise early and stand by the side of the way of the gate, and when anyone had a dispute to bring to the king for judgment, Absalom would call to him and say, 'From what city are you?', and that one would say 'From one of the tribes of Israel.' [3]Absalom would say to him, 'See, your claims are good and right, but there is no one on behalf of the king to hear you.' [4]Absalom would say, 'Oh that one would appoint me as judge in the land, and let anyone who has a dispute come to me and I would grant him justice.' [5]When one drew near to do obeisance before

him, he would put forth his hand, seize him and kiss him. [6]Thus Absalom did to all Israel who came to the king for judgment, and Absalom stole the men of Israel's allegiance.

[7]At the end of four years, Absalom said to the king, 'Please let me go to Hebron that I may fulfil a vow I made to Yahweh. [8]For your servant made a vow while I lived in Geshur in Aram, saying, "If Yahweh will indeed bring me back to Jerusalem, then I shall serve Yahweh." ' [9]The king said to him, 'Go in peace.' So he got up and went to Hebron. [10]But Absalom sent secret messengers through all the tribes in Israel, saying, 'When you hear the sound of the trumpet, then say, "Absalom has become king in Hebron." ' [11]Two hundred men who were invited went with Absalom from Jerusalem, but they travelled innocently because they did not know anything. [12]Absalom sent for Ahithophel the Gilonite, David's counsellor, from his city of Giloh while he was offering sacrifices. The conspiracy was strong because the people with Absalom continued increasing.

[13]A messenger came to David, saying, 'The people of Israel's allegiance is with Absalom.' [14]David said to all his servants with him in Jerusalem, 'Get up and let us flee, for there will be no escape for us from Absalom. Go quickly lest he overtake us quickly and bring disaster upon us and strike the city with the edge of the sword.' [15]The king's servants said to the king, 'All my lord the king chooses, your servants are ready to do.' [16]The king went out and his entire household with him, but the king left behind ten concubines to keep the house. [17]The king went out, and all the people with him, and they stopped at the most distant house.

[18]All his servants passed by him, and all the Cherethites, Pelethites and Gittites, the six hundred men who came with him from Gath, passed on before the king. [19]The king said to Ittai the Gittite, 'Why are you coming with me? Return and stay with the king, for you are foreign and also an exile from your home. [20]You came only yesterday, and shall I today make you wander with us while I go where I will? Go back and take your brothers with you; may Yahweh grant you steadfast love and faithfulness.' [21]Ittai answered the king, 'As Yahweh lives, and as my lord the king lives, surely wherever my lord the king will be, whether in death or life, there shall your servant be.' [22]David said to Ittai, 'Go and pass on.' So Ittai and all his men and all the little ones with him passed on. [23]All the land wept aloud as all the people passed by, and the king crossed the Kidron Brook, and all the people passed over on the wilderness way.

[24]Behold, Zadok and all the Levites with him were carrying the ark of the covenant of God and they set down the ark of God; and Abiathar came up until all the people finished passing out of the city. [25]The king said to Zadok, 'Take the ark of God back to the city. If I find grace in Yahweh's eyes and he brings me back, he will show me both it and his dwelling place. [26]But if he says to me, "I do not delight in you," behold, here I am, let him do to me what is right in his eyes.' [27]The king said to Zadok the priest, 'Do you see what is happening? Go back to the city in peace, you and Abiathar, with your two sons, your son Ahimaaz and Abiathar's son Jonathan. [28]See, I shall wait at the fords in the wilderness until word comes to me from you to inform me.' [29]Zadok and Abiathar returned the ark of God to Jerusalem, and they stayed there.

³⁰But David went up the ascent of the Mount of Olives, weeping as he went, his head covered and walking barefoot. All the people with him covered their heads and went up weeping as they went. ³¹It was reported to David that 'Ahithophel is among those conspiring with Absalom.' Then David said, 'Make the counsel of Ahithophel foolish, Yahweh!' ³²While David was nearing the summit where God was worshipped, behold Hushai the Archite came to meet him with his garments torn and dirt on his head. ³³David said to him, 'If you pass on with me, behold you will be a burden to me. ³⁴If you return to the city and say to Absalom, "I will be your servant, O king. I was previously servant to your father, but now I am your servant," then you can frustrate Ahithophel's counsel for me. ³⁵Are not Zadok and Abiathar the priests with you there? Every word you hear in the king's house you shall report to Zadok and Abiathar the priests. ³⁶Behold, their two sons are there with them, Zadok's son Ahimaaz and Abiathar's son Jonathan. Everything you hear you shall send to me by their hand.' ³⁷So Hushai, David's friend, entered the city just as Absalom entered Jerusalem.

^{16:1}But David passed a little beyond the summit, and there was Ziba, Mephibosheth's lad, to greet him. He had a couple of saddled asses bearing two hundred loaves, a hundred bunches of raisins, a hundred summer fruits and a skin of wine. ²The king said to Ziba, 'Why do you have these?' Ziba said, 'The asses are for the king's household to ride, the loaves and the summer fruit are for the lads to eat, and the wine is for whoever faints in the wilderness to drink.' ³The king said, 'But where is your lord's son?' Ziba said to the king, 'Behold, he has remained in Jerusalem because he thought, "Today, the house of Israel shall restore my father's kingdom to me."' ⁴The king said to Ziba, 'Behold, everything that belonged to Mephibosheth is yours.' Ziba said, 'I do obeisance; let me find favour in your eyes, my lord the king.'

⁵When King David came to Bahurim, behold a man named Shimei ben Gera from the clan of Saul's house came out from there and cursed continually as he came. ⁶He threw stones at David and all King David's servants, and all the people and all the warriors were on his right hand and his left. ⁷This is what Shimei said as he cursed, 'Get out, get out, man of bloodshed and man of Belial. ⁸Yahweh has returned on you all of the blood of Saul's house in whose place you reign, and Yahweh has given the kingdom into your son Absalom's hand. Behold, you are caught in your own evil because you are a man of blood.' ⁹Abishai ben Zeruiah said to the king, 'Why should this dead dog curse my lord the king? Let me go over and remove his head.' ¹⁰The king said, 'What do I have to do with you, you sons of Zeruiah? If he curses, and if Yahweh told him, "Curse David," then who can say, "Why are you doing this?"' ¹¹David said to Abishai and all his servants, 'Behold, my son who came forth from my loins seeks my life. How much more this Benjaminite? Leave him alone and let him curse, because Yahweh has told him to. ¹²Perhaps Yahweh will look on my iniquity and Yahweh will repay me good in place of his cursing today.' ¹³David and his men went on the road, while Shimei went alongside the parallel hillside and cursed as he went and threw stones and cast dust. ¹⁴So the king and all the people with him arrived and were faint, but he refreshed himself there.

Notes on the text

15:2. 4QSam[a] omits 'gate', but is probably tidying an awkward phrase, though McCarter (1984: 354) considers MT conflate.

4. With very many MSS, read the pl. *děbāreykā*. *rîb ûmišpāṭ* is pleonastic (Conroy 1978: 148).

6. 'Allegiance' is lit. 'heart', the sg. being used distributively. Also v. 13.

7. MT has forty years, which is improbable (but see NASB). LXX[L], Syr, Vg all read 'four'.

8. Read inf. abs. *hāšēb*.

12. Since *šlḥ* can mean 'sent for' (i.e. 'summoned'; cf. 14:29), emendation is unnecessary.

13. See note for v. 6.

15. 'My lord the king' is odd given that a group are speaking, and most LXX MSS read 'our lord the king'. But MT probably presents the words of a representative speaker, for which LXX is an attempted correction.

20. 'Yahweh grant you' restored on basis of LXX, *kai kyrios poiēsei meta sou*, the missing words having dropped out by homoioteleuton.

21. Smith (1899: 344) regards *kî 'im* as a scribal blunder, but GKC §163d indicates it can be an emphatic assurance.

23. The object marker on *midbār* is anomalous, possibly indicating that a word specifying a particular wilderness has been lost; though absent from many MSS, LXX[L] indicates the possible 'the Olive way'.

24. *wayyaṣṣiqû* is normally 'and they poured out', but the verb is used in 13:9 to mean 'dished out', and can apparently mean 'placing something' (see Fokkelman 1981: 455). NIV interprets Abiathar as offering sacrifices (similarly, Bergen 1996: 405), but the absence of an object to the verb makes this improbable.

27. David's initial question could be 'Are you not a seer?' (so NASB). Zadok is not elsewhere described like this, and the participle *rō'eh* is better understood non-technically, similar to *hinnēh* (see Hoftijzer 1971). Translation follows Anderson (1989: 201) in adding 'you and Abiathar' to clarify the switch to pl. here.

31. Read *lĕdāwid*. *higgîd* is read as a hiph. impersonal, though a hoph. would be smoother.

34. McCarter (1984: 367) defends a long plus in LXX, but MT gives good sense.

16:4. *'emṣā'* is cohortative in meaning.

12. Although several MSS support Q, and some the common emendation to *'ny*, K is retained because *'āwōn* can refer to the punishment for iniquity.

14. Some LXX MSS have David arrive at the Jordan, which 17:22 indicates is correct. But this looks like a scribal correction (similarly, Smith 1899: 349).

Form and structure

Although the previous two chapters constitute a complete narrative in their own right, they also establish the context for Absalom's revolt. This revolt dominates the narrative through to 19:43. Birch (1998: 1323; cf. Conroy 1978: 89) has argued that this section follows a chiastic structure. Modifying his proposal slightly, the following emerges:

A. David's retreat from Jerusalem, 2 Sam. 15:1 – 16:14
    B. Conflict of advisers, 2 Sam. 16:15 – 17:29
    B^1. Conflict of armies, 2 Sam. 18:1 – 19:9a [ET 19:8a]
A^1. David's return to Jerusalem, 2 Sam. 19:8b–43

Unlike the other extended chiasms (2 Sam. 5:17 – 8:18 and 21 – 24), which collect discrete narratives, this is one extended piece that also continues to develop the theme of sin and punishment announced in 12:10–12. Moreover, as Gunn (1980b) has pointed out, many points of symmetry continue into Sheba's rebellion in ch. 20. Thus, although the structure's artistry should be noted, and is highlighted by careful use of *Leitworte* such as '*ābar* throughout (Polzin 1993: 152–157), we should be aware that it remains part of a narrative rather than a significant structural block in the whole of Samuel. Koorevaar (1997: 72) has shown that Samuel has a developed structure overall that must be considered when examining component parts. It should be noted that this chiasm arises in part from the nature of the material (David's fleeing Jerusalem and later returning), and this, rather than a rhetorical goal, is significant.

This section must be interpreted on its own terms, but also with reference to the larger unit. Taken individually, it offers a carefully drawn narrative where the various elements link with each other. The origins of Absalom's revolt are laid out in 15:1–6, with its formal commencement in 15:7–12. The revolt assumes monarchy's retention (Whitelam 1979: 137): there is no return to the older tribal structures.

When word reaches him, David flees Jerusalem, and this is narrated in 15:13 – 16:14 as he moves from the city, over the Mount of Olives to Bahurim and then to the wilderness, probably the Jordan. But the narrative of David's flight, which is chronologically linked to Absalom's march on Jerusalem by synchronizing the arrival of David's friend Hushai in the city with Absalom's (15:37), is not simply reporting a retreat. As well as a march past of his forces and supporters at the edge of the city before ascending the Mount of Olives, it is arranged in a series of five encounters as David moves towards the wilderness. The first three of these (15:18–37) are with supporters (Ittai, Zadok and Abiathar and Hushai), though the second and third are interrupted by the news of Ahithophel's defection (15:30–31; see 15:12). These encounters explore through dialogue David's reawakening faith in Yahweh, a reawakening paradoxically initiated by a Philistine

(15:21). The evidence of this is demonstrated between the second and third encounters, when David prays that Yahweh overcome Ahithophel's advice. Immediately after this, David encounters Hushai and mixes faith and pragmatism, though the opportunity for these was developed in the first two encounters.

The fourth and fifth encounters (16:1–14) are geographically and socially distinguished by their occurring after David passed the summit of the Mount of Olives. More importantly, they are with Saul's associates. The first of these, with Ziba, is notable as the only encounter with no theological language, creating an ambiguity explored (but left ambiguous) in 19:25–28. Has Ziba become David's supporter, or does he grasp the opportunity for advancement? David does not seem to know, and the narrator does not tell us. The last encounter with Shimei (16:5–12) is more troubling since Shimei openly opposes and accuses David, even cursing him. David is again confronted (see 1 Sam. 24 – 26) with the troubling issue of providence's interpretation. Is he being banished, even if not for the crimes Shimei suggests? Abishai offers violence as the solution, but David has to consider Yahweh's ways in more depth, and, lacking guidance, has to allow Shimei's troubling presence.

The narrative concludes with David's arrival in the wilderness (16:13–14), but there is also the troubling note that he has left ten concubines in Jerusalem to keep the house (15:16). Their mention is important because through them Absalom will carry out a further element of Yahweh's punishment of David (12:11–12; 16:20–22). This narrative is internally complete, but requires readers to reconsider what they have already read, while simultaneously pushing forward to discover how other elements will be resolved.

Comment

Absalom's revolt begins: 15:1–12

1. After David hears of Absalom's return, attention shifts to what follows David's meeting with him. The provision of a chariot and horses in Jerusalem is a fairly pointless luxury since the terrain is not suited to chariots, but fifty runners (a private bodyguard?) also mean there is no speed advantage. The point of the exercise (cf. Adonijah in 1 Kgs 1:5) is to portray Absalom's wealth and power as a prelude to his grab for power. His move is so obvious it is surprising that David does not act immediately (see Gordon 1986: 270), but this may suggest Absalom has tapped into sources of disappointment with David's reign from the outset.

2–6. We are here given an indication of Absalom's typical actions in his claim for the throne, as he waylays people at the city's entrance before they meet David. Throughout, while feigning an interest in their context, he portrays himself as the exemplary alternative who will dispense true justice. Essentially, Absalom seeks to win Israel (the whole nation, not just the north; against Hertzberg 1964: 336) by suggesting David is too busy to dispense justice; but, given the chance, Absalom will do so. Opposition politicians know it is easier to promise than deliver, and Absalom exploits this. There may be some truth in his claims since it is hard to believe that everyone will be taken in, but he clearly exaggerates for effect. Since matters came to the king from local officials, we can imagine that some would be turned away as having insufficient grounds for appeal. Yet the woman from Tekoa shows that David did hear appeals. Interestingly, the passage presents only a single claimant, not two, as one would normally imagine in a suit. This could suggest that cases presented to the king involved the state, something that would strengthen Absalom's apparent claim of justice (so Boecker 1980: 46–47), though Absalom could have spoken to both parties. Greeting the applicant, he expresses the wish that someone appoint him to a position where he can bring about justice. The claim is pure bluster, but potentially persuasive, for, in a suit before the king, especially when a member of the royal family welcomes them so warmly, Absalom's kiss contrasts with David's cold formality in 14:33. He is cleverly ambiguous in not stating who should appoint him to this role. One might imagine David should make the appointment, but Absalom could equally suggest that the people do so. V. 6 sums this up by affirming that this is Absalom's normal practice. He thus gains extensive support, though there may have been other factors.

7–9. With Absalom's play for power revealed, the narrative switches to a conversation between David and Absalom. It presumes that relations between them have been normalized, so Absalom can request permission to visit Hebron to fulfil a vow he made should Yahweh restore him to Jerusalem. This happened at the end of four years (see 'Notes'), though whether this is four years since he returned or four years since he fled to Geshur is unclear. The former is perhaps more likely, though in either case it is a long time between the vow and its fulfilment (see Deut. 23:21). David might feel it is Joab, not Yahweh, who has ensured Absalom's return, but is apparently prepared to accept a theological reading and send him on his way. There is an ironic twist to his final words to his son, 'Go in peace,' since this is precisely what will not happen.

10–12. With permission granted, Absalom sent messengers throughout the land advising supporters of the coming coup in Hebron. Obviously, not everyone would hear the trumpets, but the point remains. How Absalom gained such support in an area that had been a bastion of support for David is unclear unless there was resentment at David's moving of the capital, and of course Absalom was born there (3:2–3). However, the support was there, and Absalom also took two hundred guests. Although they went innocently, they would appear to support him, and once the conspiracy was revealed would find it more difficult to resist Absalom in Hebron than had they been in Jerusalem (Birch 1998: 1320). More importantly, David's most trusted adviser, Ahithophel, joined the conspiracy, giving it considerable strength. The name 'Ahithophel' is not his actual name, as it means 'my brother is a fool'; though, unlike some, Chronicles does not record the original form. He may have been Bathsheba's grandfather (von Rad 1966: 184), though this is based on a common name for his son and Bathsheba's father (11:3; 23:34). The link is tenuous, and the narrator never makes it; though Bodner notes that, if the link is made, it connects the rebellion with David's sin in ch. 11 (2005: 138). However, it is better to respect the narrative's silence about Ahithophel's motivation. He is simply summoned from his home town of Giloh, about 6 miles north of Hebron (Josh. 15:51). Ahithophel's presence is an ominous sign, and much of what follows until 17:23 is an attempt to thwart him. Ahithophel's arrival is symptomatic of a larger process where Absalom's conspiracy continues to draw in support.

David's flight from Jerusalem: 15:13 – 16:14

15:13–17. David would not hear Absalom's trumpet, but events were reported to him, leading to the decision to abandon Jerusalem. This was decided immediately, and although it must have taken some time, it was a close thing, as Absalom arrived as David and his group escaped. David's urgency is apparent in his clipped commands to his servants, two imperatives urging them to movement, and the assertion that there will be no escape once Absalom has come. This is followed by another imperative and two statements describing the risk of Absalom's being quicker, where they would be defeated and Jerusalem put to the sword. Although highly defendable against external forces, Jerusalem was vulnerable to an internal foe. David's move was risky but tactically wise. The response of David's servants at least meant he had their loyalty. Thus vv. 16–17 describe David's setting out with his servants, although ten concubines were left to 'keep' the house. If they were among the concubines David took in 5:13 as women from Jerusalem, then they would have been Jebusites whose marriage to David symbolized his rule over Jerusalem, but whom he could not take with him since by his flight he effectively relinquished this position (see Hill 2006). These women became pawns in the power game between David and Absalom, as he claimed authority over Jerusalem through them, yet also provided further fulfilment of his punishment (16:20–22; cf. 20:3). With his troops, and especially his foreign mercenaries, David still had a formidable force, and he took the time to allow them to march past at the 'distant house', presumably a boundary marker at Jerusalem's limits.

18–23. From here the narrative works through David's five encounters as he moves towards the wilderness. The encounters enable the narrator to portray David more positively as one who is again prepared to submit to Yahweh's reign even as he also displays his native cunning. This is achieved by reintroducing Yahweh to the narrative. Apart from the wise woman's staged comments (14:11–20), God has neither been mentioned nor is overtly active since Solomon's renaming (12:24). Now, apart from David's encounter with Ziba (16:1–4), which retains unresolved elements, faith in Yahweh is again central, though in a wonderful irony David is reminded of this by a Philistine. The first encounter is with a group from Gath led by Ittai. His name may be Semitic and indicate some Israelite ancestry, though this is unclear, but his origin is from Gath. With him were the Cherethites and Pelethites (see 'Comment' on 8:18) supplemented by six hundred Gittites (i.e. from Gath), all of whose first loyalty was to David. The conversation with Ittai is reported at some length, as David urges Ittai to settle in Jerusalem with Absalom, whom David here refers to as 'king'. He argues that as recently arrived foreigners, and probably mercenaries, they should take the security of life in Jerusalem rather than the insecurity of travel with him. David, mentioning Yahweh for the first time since 12:22, wishes that Ittai will experience Yahweh's steadfast love (ḥesed). But this Philistine declines to take advantage of his foreign status, and pledges support to David, doing so with a Yahwistic oath of allegiance that closely echoes Ruth's to Naomi (Ruth 1:16–17). This foreigner knew better than the Israelites what Yahweh was doing, and thus pledged himself to David, the opposite of how David saw things in 1 Sam. 17:41–47. Only then did David permit his group to join him before crossing the Kidron and approaching the Mount of Olives.

24–29. David's second encounter is with the two priests Zadok and Abiathar, and some Levites with them. The priests came out with the ark of the covenant, perhaps seeing it as a military palladium (Youngblood 1992: 995). They had set it down during the march past before David instructed them to take it back. There is no sense of superstition, as if the ark's presence meant a blessing might be forced from Yahweh (cf. 1 Sam. 4:1b – 7:1). David's desire was to receive grace from Yahweh by being brought back to the city, and so sent the ark to its proper resting place. It is as if David was reshaped by the encounter with Ittai, though he also knew the matter rested with Yahweh. Nathan (12:9–12) had stated that the sword would not depart from David's house, but had made no comment on the question of whether David could be removed from the throne, so David's language is still circumspect. But faith in Yahweh does not lead to passivity, and David accordingly established an intelligence network in the city, utilizing the priests and their sons. Ostensibly, they would return to Jerusalem as faithful priests, but would in reality be David's spies. Ch. 10 showed David's using intelligence, and that is continued here. Once they had information, they would send it to 'the fords in the wilderness'. Although this must have been understood at the time, apart from their location somewhere in the wilderness of Judea, the fords are no longer known. Once everyone had passed, Zadok and Abiathar took the ark back to Jerusalem.

30–31. With the march-past finished, David and the people continued up the Mount of Olives, a feature the Gospel writers parallel to Jesus' arrival there (Luke 19:29). The group travelled in an attitude of mourning, weeping, barefoot and with their heads covered. Although David had left Jerusalem in a planned retreat, this was not a military action; it was a procession of those mourning (*Trauerprozession*, Seiler 1998: 145). The situation was aggravated by news of Ahithophel's defection. David responded with a brief prayer that Yahweh turn his advice into foolishness. This is the decisive point where David reconnected his faith with experience. He not only hoped Yahweh would act for him; he prayed he would.

32–37. The tension between divine sovereignty and human action is retained in that as soon as David reaches a summit shrine he meets Hushai, through whom David's prayer will be answered. He is described (v. 37) as 'David's friend'. Although this could describe their relationship, it more probably describes an official position, perhaps as the most trusted counsellor (see 13:3). The location may also be significant and not just a reference to where this happened. David has prayed and encountered Hushai, who will do so much to thwart Ahithophel, at a place where God is worshipped. But this also required action from David, who then convinced Hushai to return to Jerusalem to frustrate Ahithophel's advice and join his intelligence network. We are not told why, but Hushai accepted David's argument that he would be a burden if he stayed, and his most effective service would be the dangerous role of a double agent. Just as Joab gave the woman from Tekoa her message when she came to David, David now gave Hushai his. Like hers, Hushai's skill was to develop the opportunity to achieve a different purpose than might appear on the surface. Apart from frustrating Ahithophel, Hushai was also asked to pass on information from the palace through the priests, and then their sons who would bring it to David. However many were opposed to David, he still had considerable support. As Absalom arrived in the city, David was plotting his downfall, and there were just enough hints to suggest that Yahweh was attentive to David's need.

16:1–4. The fourth encounter is the first of two with Saulides, though only one of them openly claims this allegiance. The first is with Ziba, again called Mephibosheth's steward (lit. 'lad'). Since this was the role assigned to him by David (2 Sam. 9:9–11), the term may be used deliberately because he provisioned David and his group. There is uncertainty as to the number of asses he brought: *ṣemed* (couple) normally means 'a pair', but is hardly sufficient here, so we may need to understand a team of unspecified size (so Youngblood 1992: 999, though see Anderson 1989: 205). However, his provisions were significant and manifestly necessary for David's group, who apparently set off with limited supplies. There may be some uncertainty in David's question in v. 2, since it suggests Ziba is not one he expected to act like this. But Ziba is a shrewd diplomat, and carefully avoids answering David's question, addressing instead the need of David and his group. It is an act of supreme opportunism. If things go well, Ziba will be remembered; but if Absalom prospers, Ziba has lost only the provisions. With his first question ignored, David probes further in v. 3, seeking information on Mephibosheth, though, by referring to him as 'your lord's son', David shows he still regards Ziba as a supporter of Saul. Ziba's answer suggests Mephibosheth retains a fantasy that the rebellion will see him returned to the throne. Whether this is Mephibosheth's position is unclear. In 19:25–28 he claims he was slandered and, on balance, it is difficult to see how he can believe he will regain the throne. The revolt is Absalom's, and he has the popular support. His later claim of innocence is probably correct, though the narrator leaves it unresolved, so we see Ziba's opportunism. David does not assess the evidence, but simply presumes its truth, so Ziba is awarded the estate, which he flatteringly accepts.

5–12. After Ziba, the narrative approaches the wilderness as the group draw near to Bahurim (slightly east of Jerusalem and where David met Michal again in 3:16), though it is not far to Jerusalem's east. Here David encounters Shimei, a man identifying himself as a Saulide. If nothing else, the passage indicates support for Saul has not died out, though as a member of Saul's clan he may be personally aggrieved. The narrator highlights Shimei's actions in pelting David and his group with stones, dust and curses. In particular, he calls David a murderer and man of Belial (see 'Notes' on 1 Sam. 1:16), terms here largely equivalent. The reference to murder may refer to 2 Sam. 21:1–14 (Hertzberg 1964: 345). Though this is possible since the books of Samuel are not strictly chronological, it more probably refers to continued Saulide suspicion over the deaths of Abner and Ish-bosheth. Shimei claims that Yahweh has taken the kingdom from David and given it to Absalom because of his murders. The claim is important, because it again raises the question of how Yahweh is involved in the process and who can interpret events. Hushai's arrival may suggest Yahweh was acting for David in spite of his flight, but nothing is definite yet. Two responses to Shimei are possible. The sons of Zeruiah, never overly patient, follow the first, and Abishai unasked offers to decapitate Shimei. But David refuses violence, just as in his earlier encounters with Saul (1 Sam. 24:5 [ET 24:4]; 26:8–11) and suggests instead that Yahweh may have a purpose in this cursing. Until David has evidence of Yahweh's actions, he will not act. He adds that if his own son is trying to kill him, one can hardly be surprised by a Saulide's actions. But he also suggests that this may be part of the way in which Yahweh may finally show him grace because of his iniquity (see 'Notes'). The allusion shows David knew he was experiencing the punishment announced by Nathan and had to balance its reality with the hope that Yahweh might restore him.

13–14. With the encounters complete in terms of speech, David and his group continued to travel, continually pelted and cursed from the ridge by

Shimei. Their hasty flight meant they journeyed with little food and drink in spite of Ziba's provisions. When they reached their goal, presumably the Jordan (cf. 17:22), we are told they were faint ('*yp*), a word that typically refers specifically to thirst (Job 22:7; Ps. 63:2; Prov. 22:25; Isa. 29:8; Jer. 31:25), though hunger can be included (Gen. 25:29–30; Judg. 8:4–5). Tired and hungry, David could finally take some refreshment, probably drawing on Ziba's provisions.

Explanation

Ever since Nathan's announcement of David's punishment (12:10–12), the narrative has built towards this moment. The horror of Amnon's raping Tamar, Absalom's revenge killing and Joab arranging for his return to Jerusalem (chs. 13 – 14) did not complete David's punishment. They simply set the scene for this rebellion. Although rebellion is not mentioned directly in Nathan's announcement, reference to 'the sword' being rather open-ended, the fact that David was to have someone publicly engage in sexual relations with his wives ultimately refers to this. Rebellion was coming, what Yahweh announced through his prophet takes place, and David recognizes it (16:12).

But how this happens is not some form of divine remote control. We are never told why Absalom chose to rebel against David. His goals were clear, but his motives opaque. We can see his processes, however, as he stole the nation's allegiance by pretending to offer better justice than David. The irony of this theft as justice is not lost on the narrator, but the text highlights his process, waylaying supplicants before they reached David. Doing this, rather than meeting them after court, suggests he knew the falseness of his claims, though there were undoubtedly enough disappointments upon which to build his claims. Throughout 15:1–12, David remained blind and ignorant. Absalom's play for power was blatant, but David still permitted him to journey to Hebron to fulfil a supposed vow when in reality he would launch his revolt. The revolt drew in David's most trusted counsellor, Ahithophel, and grew quickly.

Yet from here there is a significant change. News of the rebellion reached David (15:13), so he quickly retreated from Jerusalem with his supporters, moving towards the wilderness of the Jordan. The move for David was geographically and theologically significant. It was in the wilderness (1 Sam. 21 – 26) that we saw David at his faithful best, and as he returns there a series of encounters see him gradually reclaiming the reality of that faith. Through his encounters with Ittai, Zadok and Abiathar, and then Hushai we see David exploring his faith, though ironically it is triggered by his encounter with Ittai, a Philistine. This exploration is seen in his refusal to take the ark and his prayer against Ahithophel (15:24–30), though this is not naive fatalism. David combines faith with action in establishing a spy network and appointing Hushai to frustrate Ahithophel. In one sense, David answers his own prayer, but in another he is astute enough to see Hushai as Yahweh's provision. This triggers the question of how to interpret providence, a question also prominent in 1 Sam. 21 – 26. The encounter with Ziba is the only one without a theological element, suggesting Ziba is more of a political opportunist than one accessing Yahweh's ways. But the final encounter with Shimei allows the opposition to voice an alternative reading of Yahweh's ways, where David is punished, though not for the sins Nathan highlighted. David might reject the basis of Shimei's charge, but knows he has to explore the question of where Yahweh is in the process.

Careful reading of the narrative brings the question of providence to the fore as the theme around which it is structured, since this encompasses Absalom's revolt as well as David's encounters. The narrative wants to model David's response as appropriate, his submitting to Yahweh's will where it is clear, waiting for further guidance where it is not, and acting decisively as the opportunity presents itself throughout. But decisive action cannot be for personal benefit, as is clear from his refusal to decapitate Shimei. Submission to Yahweh involves accepting legitimate punishment for iniquity, seeking the future Yahweh is giving, but not grasping what is not there to receive. David moves to his future in the wilderness, though in doing so goes back to his past to rediscover his roots in Yahweh.

2 SAMUEL 16:15 – 17:29

Translation

[15]Absalom and all the people, the men of Israel, came to Jerusalem, and Ahithophel was with him. [16]When Hushai the Archite, David's friend, came to Absalom, Hushai said to Absalom, 'Long live the king! Long live the king!' [17]Absalom said to Hushai, 'This is your loyalty to your friend? Why did you not go with your friend?' [18]Hushai said to Absalom, 'No, for whom Yahweh chooses (and this people and all Israel), his I shall be, and with him shall I remain. [19]So again, whom shall I serve? Should it not be before his son? As I was before your father, thus shall I be before you.'

[20]Absalom said to Ahithophel, 'Give your counsel. What should we do?' [21]Ahithophel said to Absalom, 'Go in to your father's concubines whom he left to keep the house. Then all Israel shall hear that you have made yourself odious to your father and the hands of all with you shall be strengthened.' [22]Then they pitched a tent for Absalom on the roof, and Absalom went in to his father's concubines in the sight of all Israel. [23]In those days the counsel Ahithophel gave was as if one consulted the word of God. This was how all Ahithophel's counsel was regarded by David and Absalom.

[17:1]Then Ahithophel said to Absalom, 'Let me choose twelve thousand men that I might arise and pursue David tonight. [2]I would come upon him while he is weary and discouraged, and would terrify him and all the people with him would flee. So I would strike the king alone [3]and return all the people to you. The man you seek is equivalent to the return of them all. All the people will be at peace.' [4]This advice seemed right in the eyes of Absalom and in the eyes of all the elders of Israel.

[5]Absalom said, 'Summon also Hushai the Archite, and let us hear what he also has to say.' [6]Hushai came to Absalom and Absalom said to him, 'This is what Ahithophel has said. Shall we do what he said? But if not, you speak.' [7]Hushai said to Absalom, 'The counsel that Ahithophel has given this time is not good.' [8]Hushai added, 'You know your father and his men, that they are warriors; they are enraged, like a bear robbed in the field. Your father is a man of battle: he will not spend the night with the people. [9]Look, already he will have hidden in one of the pits or some other place. When he falls on them at the outset, then whoever hears shall say, "There has been a slaughter among the people who went after Absalom." [10]For even he who is a valiant man, whose heart is like that of a lion, shall surely melt away, for all Israel knows that your father is a warrior, and valiant men are with him. [11]So my counsel is to let all Israel be gathered to you from Dan to Beersheba like the sand by the sea for multitude, and that you go into battle personally. [12]And we shall come upon him in some place where he may be found and shall fall upon him like the dew that falls on the ground and not one shall be left of him and all the men with him. [13]If he retreats to a city, then all Israel shall bear ropes to that city and we shall drag it into the valley until not even a pebble is found there.' [14]Then Absalom and all the men of Israel said, 'Hushai the Archite's counsel is better than Ahithophel's counsel,' for Yahweh had commanded to frustrate Ahithophel's good counsel so Yahweh might bring calamity on Absalom.

[15]Hushai said to Zadok and Abiathar the priests, 'Thus and so did Ahithophel counsel Absalom and Israel's elders, and thus and so did I counsel. [16]Now send quickly and report to David, saying, "Do not spend the night at the fords of the wilderness but be sure you cross over, lest the king and all the people with him be consumed."' [17]Jonathan and Ahimaaz were waiting at En Rogel, and a maid-servant would come and report to them, and they would go and report to King David, for they were not to be seen entering the city. [18]But a lad saw them and reported to Absalom. So the two of them went quickly and came to the house of a man in Bahurim with a well in his courtyard, and they went down there. [19]The woman took and spread out a covering over the well's mouth and spread grain on it so nothing was known. [20]When Absalom's servants came to the woman at the house, they said, 'Where is Ahimaaz and Jonathan?' The woman said to them, 'They crossed over the brook of water.' So they searched but did not find them, and returned to Jerusalem.

[21]After they had gone, they came up from the well and went and reported to King David. They said to David, 'Arise, cross over the water quickly, because thus and so has Ahithophel counselled against you.' [22]David arose along with all the people with him and crossed the Jordan. By dawn, there was no one left who had not crossed the Jordan.

[23]When Ahithophel saw his counsel had not been carried out, he saddled his donkey, rose and went home to his city. He organized his house, then strangled himself. So he died and was buried in his father's tomb.

[24]David reached Mahanaim; and Absalom crossed the Jordan, he and all Israel's men with him. [25]Absalom had set Amasa over the army in place of Joab. Amasa was the son of a man named Ithra the Ishmaelite who had gone to Nahash's daughter Abigal, the sister of Zeruiah, Joab's mother. [26]Israel and Absalom camped in the land of Gilead.

[27]When David reached Mahanaim, Shobi ben Nahash from Rabbah of the Ammonites, Machir ben Ammiel from Lo Debar and Barzillai the Gileadite from Rogelim [28]brought beds, basins, pottery, wheat, barley, flour, parched grain, beans, lentils, [29]honey, curds, sheep and cheese from the herd to David and the people with him to eat, for they said, 'The people are hungry, faint and thirsty in the wilderness.'

Notes on the text

16:16. Two MSS agree with LXX, reading 'Long live the king' once. But this contraction loses Hushai's loquacity when speaking to Absalom, a theme introduced here.

18. Read with Q and a number of MSS *lô* for *lō*.

20. Absalom addresses Ahithophel in the pl., perhaps seeing his representing a group of counsellors. We cannot assume Hushai is included (so Alter 1999: 294) since he is not yet within the inner circle.

23. Read with Q and many MSS *yišal 'îš*.

17:2. 'Discouraged' is lit. 'slack of hands'.

3. LXX (also ESV, NRSV) includes an extensive plus after Ahithophel's claim of returning the people. ESV renders it 'as a bride comes home to her husband. You seek the life of only one man.' Though difficult, MT can be understood (see NIV, NASU, AV) and is retained as *lectio difficilior*, understanding the initial *kĕ* as 'equivalent to' (so Fokkelman 1981: 456–457). Hushai, not Ahithophel uses similes, so one here counters their characterization.

8. McCarter (1984: 382; also Cartledge 2001: 584) supports a LXX plus 'like a sow snared in the wild', but its originality is doubtful.

11. LXX apparently read *bĕqirbām* for *baqrāb*, interpreting the root *qrb* as 'in the midst'. But this is an Aram. referring to drawing near for battle, as in Pss 55:22; 68:31; 78:9; 144:1; Eccl. 9:18; Zech. 14:3.

12. *naḥnû* is apparently an abbreviation of *'ănaḥnû*, as in Gen. 42:11; Exod. 16:7–8; Num. 32:32; Lam. 3:42. A verb would be easier (Driver 1913: 250), but is implied from the simile, so deriving one from *nwḥ* (to light upon) is unnecessary, though the verb 'to be' is implied.

13. *'ōtō* refers to David, not the city, but the two are seen as a unified whole (Fokkelman 1981: 457).

16. With many MSS read '*abrōt* (fords) for '*arbōt* (steppes). Cf. 15:28. *pen yĕbulla' lammelek* is an impersonal passive, with a dat. *lĕ* (see GKC §121a).

20. *mîkal* is generally considered corrupt, and the meaning 'brook' is doubtful, though LXX's *mikron tou hydatos* could interpret it in this way. Anderson (1989: 212) emends to 'hurried', but how this corruption occurred is difficult to see.

25. MT has Ithra as an Israelite, but LXX^A and 1 Chr. 2:17 indicate correctly that he was an Ishmaelite since the gentilic 'Israelite' is unnecessary. Many LXX MSS have Jesse for Nahash, but this is probably an exegetical correction because we expect him to be Zeruiah's father since she was David's sister. 1 Chr. 2:16 does not provide enough information to resolve the difficulties, but one could argue Zeruiah was David's half-sister, making this Nahash otherwise unknown, with Jesse marrying a woman who already had some daughters. The reading should stand, with Abigal a variant of Abigail, though not David's wife.

28. *miškāb* is collective. *qālî* (parched grain) occurs twice, as the list's seventh and tenth items. Unless some distinction is intended between grain and seeds (so NASU), it is better to follow LXX and Syr's omission, with the item accidentally copied twice.

29. *šĕpôt* is a hapax legomenon of uncertain derivation. A dairy product seems necessary in context, and cheese has the virtue of being slightly more durable and thus suitable as a supply. The alternative is that this is an idiom for the best of the cattle, but we lack evidence of 'cream' (assuming that translation) used this way (see Conroy 1978: 153).

Not everything on the list is food, but because of the list's length and focus on supplies, the narrator, presuming readers can make the necessary distinction, uses 'to eat' (see Conroy 1978: 43).

Form and structure

From David's flight, the narrative now turns to the period when Absalom was in Jerusalem preparing for the conflict of 18:1 – 19:9a [ET 19:8a]. That conflict's result is foreshadowed in Hushai and Ahithophel's conflict, a conflict running directly from 16:15 to 17:23, but which also points to the wider outcome in 17:24–29. Throughout, Absalom is a minor character. Hushai is David's palace agent, the one he met immediately after praying Yahweh would make Ahithophel's counsel folly (15:31). Ahithophel's importance is developed by the report of his counselling skills (16:21–22), and then a direct narrative comment that Ahithophel's advice is as good as asking God (16:23). Against such an adversary, Hushai's job seems impossible, as David's does if Absalom has claimed the bulk of the nation's support. Indeed, a reasonable assessment of their comparative military advice suggests Ahithophel's is vastly superior. Hushai offers bluster, but little strategy, yet Absalom and the people are persuaded by Hushai. This is so incongruous that the narrator makes a direct comment, one of crucial importance for interpreting chs. 15 – 19, which is that, to bring calamity on Absalom, Yahweh has frustrated Ahithophel's counsel (17:14). This comment not only explains why Absalom acted how he did; it also shows Yahweh's answering David's prayer. We therefore see the first glimpse of the narrative's outcome, when David will be restored to his position and Absalom defeated. Yahweh is at work, even though for large parts of the narrative he is not mentioned.

Yahweh's work both looks forward to David's restoration and looks back to his punishment announced in 12:10–12. The family conflict to which Nathan referred has been developed from 13:1, but one element has not yet been resolved. Nathan insisted that whereas David's assault on Uriah through his adultery with Bathsheba had been carried out secretly, his neighbour's assault on him would be by publicly having sex with his wives. Absalom, by accepting Ahithophel's advice to have sex with the ten concubines left to keep the palace (16:21–22), completes this final element of the punishment. Each element announced by Nathan has happened, so from this point the narrator prepares for David's return. Divine justice has been served on David, but still needs to be resolved on Absalom, though 17:14 hints what this will be.

These theological aims control the presentation of this section, though in so doing create long-recognized narrative difficulties, often leading to claims of redactional layers (see Seiler's summary, 1998: 150–163). These may be outlined as follows:

1. Absalom having sex with ten of David's concubines sits poorly with the rapid pursuit indicated by 17:24. It would have required a degree of stamina from Absalom, but would still give David extra days to escape.
2. Although Hushai's advice persuaded Absalom, 17:24 appears to suggest he followed Ahithophel's advice, but 17:23 has already reported Ahithophel's suicide because his counsel was not followed.

These problems occur only if we believe that the narrator consistently presents the material in a chronological order, but there are numerous points where Samuel is dischronologized to bring out the central theological themes (see 'Form and structure' on 1 Sam. 16:1–13). Here those themes point to both the fulfilment of David's punishment and the beginning of his return to the throne because of both 12:10–12 (punishment) and 7:3–16 (dynastic promise). It is now clear that punishment cannot supplant the dynastic promise. A plausible chronology of the narrative suggests that some events are more or less concurrent, that is Ahithophel and Hushai's conflicting advice occurs in an interlude within 16:21–22. Shortly thereafter, Absalom apparently changed his mind and employed Ahithophel's plan except that he now led the battle but lost the element of surprise. Meanwhile, Hushai informed David of Ahithophel's plan, suggesting even he did not believe his bluster would hold. Ahithophel's death is therefore narrated in advance of its occurrence relative to other events since he would have hanged himself after the defeat in the forest. His plan was frustrated more by Absalom's delay than Hushai's alternative. Nevertheless, his death is narrated now because it also allows the narrator to point out that Yahweh will give victory to David.

Comment

Conflict of advisors: 16:15 – 17:23

16:15. With David and his group reaching their unnamed destination, attention turns to Absalom. We have known since 15:37 that he was in Jerusalem, but it was first necessary to complete the account of David's flight. This section is primarily interested in Hushai and Ahithophel's conflict rather than Absalom. Absalom is the pawn played between them, and Ahithophel's importance is stressed by the verse ending with him.

16–19. Having left David in 15:37, these verses recount Hushai's arrival at the palace. The narrator mentions again that he was David's friend (see 'Comment' on 15:37), and so politically adept. He certainly reveals diplomatic skills in this section. His opening words are highly subtle. He twice proclaims 'Long live the king!' without specifying which king. Absalom takes this to refer to himself, but is somewhat suspicious. His first question in v. 17 takes 'friend' in its normal sense, suggesting Hushai was not much of a friend to David, before probing the nature of his loyalty (*ḥesed*) in the second, and asking why Hushai did not go with David. Hushai is equal to the challenge, playing the loyal civil servant, apparently loyal to the incumbent. Yet he never directly refers to the one to whom he is loyal, and the 'one chosen by Yahweh' can only be David, not Absalom. Moreover, his final statement claims only he will serve before Absalom; it never states he will serve him. Nevertheless, Absalom takes the whole speech as indicating that he is a trustworthy civil servant, loyal to the throne, not the monarch. Whereas no statement of acceptance is made, it is implied.

20–22. With Hushai established as David's spy, the narrative turns to Ahithophel. Given his reputation (v. 23), it is unsurprising that Absalom turns to Ahithophel first. The advice given, of 'going into' (a standard euphemism for sexual intercourse, though here suggesting rape) the concubines David left behind (15:16) is to make him odious to David. Although this could be intended as a public statement of David's death (albeit proleptic), it must be understood in the context of sexual relations with the wife or concubine of another man established by 3:7, 11:2–5 and

12:8–10, where this was consistently a means of attacking an enemy and claiming his power and position. Sexual congress with David's concubines effectively claimed the kingdom as a completed fact, giving the people reason to support Absalom. Ahithophel's stated reason is that Absalom would make himself odious to David, which is precisely what Absalom's claim would achieve. The narrator, though, is more interested in how this fulfils Nathan's announcement in 12:11–12, as Absalom's action is undeniably public, taking place in a tent pitched on the roof from which David had seen Bathsheba (11:2). Absalom was in breach of Lev. 18:8 and 20:11, and so was liable to the death penalty. We know David's breach of Lev. 20:10 cannot result in his own death, but Absalom has no such promise, so the moment of his apparent triumph is the point where questions about his future begin.

23. The chapter's final statement assesses Ahithophel, comparing his advice to a divine oracle. Although McKane suggests the verse equates wisdom with the oracle (1965: 55), it is rather that the oracle remains the measuring point (rightly, Gordon 1986: 279, though without Polzin's 1993: 167 implications in rejecting counsel). More importantly, it introduces a narrative tension: If Ahithophel's advice is that good, what can Hushai do about it? Yet, given the strength and weakness of his previous advice (16:20–22), even this affirmation of his effectiveness is limited slightly.

17:1–4. Having emphasized the esteem with which his advice was held, the narrator presents Ahithophel's military strategy, though as a counsellor this could only be given at Absalom's request. Because Absalom initiated the process, he could also move to Hushai. Nevertheless, the note in 16:23 insists Ahithophel's advice will be good. The plan is simple and direct. David is at his weakest point, and an immediate surgical strike that he would lead would quickly neutralize him and bring his support to Absalom. He suggests taking twelve 'thousand' men, which is perhaps a military unit from each tribe rather than a specific number, but still more men than David had (see 15:18). Crucially, he would launch the attack that night, though he still refers to David as 'the king'. Ahithophel indicates that David's death alone will bring back all the people (see 'Notes') and create the peace (perhaps through a general pardon; so Fokkelman 1981: 213) needed to establish his rule. The plan's soundness is recognized by all, though it is not yet indicated that it was the right plan.

5–6. Despite the quality of Ahithophel's advice, Absalom wanted to hear something further, perhaps because he now had two counsellors who had (seemingly) sworn themselves to him. Thus a messenger summoned Hushai. Since he was summoned, it is apparent that Hushai was not yet in the 'inner cabinet', so Absalom is giving him his opportunity. The delay in bringing Hushai is probably not great, but it provides some further respite for David (Baldwin 1988: 265), especially since Hushai must first be informed of Ahithophel's plan. V. 6 is beautifully structured, with an

alternation of verbal and nominal forms of *dbr*, highlighting the importance of what is said, but concluding with the opportunity for Hushai to
propose an alternative if he disagrees with Ahithophel. Hushai must think
quickly, but the opportunity hints that David's prayer (15:31) is being
answered.

7–10. Hushai accepts Absalom's offer, playing his role as one apparently
counselling Absalom while supporting David. Hence, he is immediately
critical of Ahithophel's plan, baldly asserting that it is not good. Although it
has seemed good to everyone else, Hushai is careful to emphasize that he is
not commenting generally on Ahithophel's advice. Although this puts him in
a dangerous position, he continues with a speech full of rhetoric but lacking
military substance. Hushai's counterproposal has two strands. Here he
stresses the dangers associated with an attack on David and his men. He
notes that David is a professional soldier, as are his men, so an attack will
suffer. This is expressed by means of the simile, creating the model by which
this mighty warrior fights, of a bear bereft of her cubs. He is sure David will
not be with the men but hidden in a pit or some other place, so the attack's
goal will not be achieved. A surgical strike killing only David is just not
possible. Finally, he suggests David may attack first, and the resulting
slaughter will mean Absalom's losing support. As he continues, his speech
becomes progressively more bombastic as there is no reason why all this
should occur, especially since Hushai carefully ignores the obvious fact that
David and his men are weak and tired. This is crucial. Ahithophel saw
that David and his men would be weak and dispirited. Hushai does nothing
to disprove it, because proof is impossible. He merely proposes a counter,
trusting David's reputation as a warrior to convince Absalom.

11–13. The second part of Hushai's speech makes his proposal. He
suggests a huge army be drawn from all Israel ('Dan to Beersheba' is a
merismus, suggesting national support; see Anderson 1989: 215), with
Absalom leading the battle. This may play on Absalom's vanity since
Ahithophel's plan did not involve Absalom, though as indicated above
('Form and structure'), Absalom may have been otherwise engaged. The
plan is simply that wherever David is found, this huge army will fall on him
'like the dew that falls on the ground', with none of David's supporters
surviving. David can have no safe haven because any city sheltering him
will be destroyed. The army will be so huge that David cannot possibly
win, though how this army will be equipped is never stated. Hushai's plan,
imagining David in situations where he cannot survive, is all rhetorical
flourish but no detail. It sounds impressive but never says how David will
be defeated, and one can argue that if his first prospect, of the army falling
upon David like the dew, were convincing, there would be no need for the
second. But unlike Ahithophel, no one is asked to oppose Hushai.

14. In purely military terms Ahithophel's plan was superior. Yet
Absalom and the men of Israel pronounced Hushai's better. Such a
statement might be seen as an indication of Absalom's own vanity except

that we have one of the comparatively rare narrative intrusions here: the narrator tells us that this turn of events was from Yahweh so that Yahweh might bring calamity on Absalom. Yahweh rarely acts directly in chs. 9 – 20, but instances like this are of obvious significance. Yahweh's act is tied to David's directions to Hushai in 15:34. David wanted to frustrate (*prr*) Ahithophel's counsel, and Yahweh has here commanded to frustrate (*prr*) it, a clear link with David's prayer of 15:31.

15–17. With his plan's success, Hushai employed David's intelligence network from 15:24–29. The process is involved, with the message passing through several hands. In vv. 15–16 the narrator recounts the specifics of this incident, with Hushai's reporting Ahithophel's plan and his own, before directing David to cross the Jordan (see 'Notes') lest disaster befall him. Given Absalom's acceptance of his plan, such haste should not be necessary, but Hushai took no chances in case someone saw through his earlier bluster. The narrator breaks this off in v. 17 to describe how messages were sent, suggesting, for a routine to have been established, a few days have passed since Absalom's arrival. The process required a message to Zadok and Abiathar reporting the events. They then sent a servant girl to En Rogel (Josh. 15:16), a spring just south of the town. She told the priests' sons, who reported to David. Jonathan and Ahimaaz could not be seen entering and leaving the town, perhaps because they were known supporters of David. This highlights the vulnerability of David's network, while providing a context where faith and ingenuity cooperate.

18–22. Unfortunately for Jonathan and Ahimaaz, the system's vulnerability was quickly exposed. A lad saw them, which forced them to hide down a supporter's well in Bahurim, Shimei's home town (16:5). Yet they were fortunate that Absalom's troops were clearly not locals or else the well's location would have been known, and the woman's ruse of covering it exposed. With this advantage, the owner's wife sent them in the wrong direction, a classical mark of underdog tricksters (see Prouser 1994). There are striking parallels with the arrival of the spies at Rahab's house in Josh. 2, suggesting a deliberate echo of those events. This could be subtly indicating the rightness of David's cause. With their escape made, the two messengers reported to David. Interestingly, they reported Ahithophel's advice, not Hushai's, suggesting it was still felt that Absalom would recognize the inherent superiority of that plan. Whichever plan was followed, once David crossed the Jordan it was much harder for Absalom to make a sudden strike because of the time involved in crossing the river with an army. Yet the note of timing is also important: David and his group did not finish crossing until daybreak, while Ahithophel planned to attack that night. Had Ahithophel's plan been carried through, David could not have escaped, but this chronological note hints again at Yahweh's involvement.

23. The end of this affair for Ahithophel came when his advice was overturned, though, as noted ('Form and structure'), it was not so much that his plan was rejected as that it had failed because of Absalom's

modifications through Hushai's intervention. The account of his suicide
has been brought forward to highlight Ahithophel's own defeat and stress
that Yahweh is still with David. Faced with Absalom's defeat (18:1–18), he
decided to return to Giloh (15:12), organize his affairs, and take his life.
This was not pique, and neither was it a noble act since the OT does not
view suicide in those terms (see 'Comment' on 1 Sam. 31:4–5). Rather,
Ahithophel recognized that with the advantage lost to David, he would be
executed once David regained control. He chose to take his life and spare
himself a humiliating trial. He did not suspect it was a divinely ordained
failure on his part (Hertzberg 1964: 353), though he was at least buried in
the family tomb. Matthew's account of Judas' death (Matt. 27:5) is
modelled on Ahithophel's.

Preparations for battle: 17:24–29

24–26. With conflict between Hushai and Ahithophel resolved, we return
to the larger conflict between David and Absalom. One's resolution
points to the other's. This section represents a transition, preparing for
the battle and its consequences in 18:1 – 19:8a [ET 19:7a]. David had
reached Mahanaim, about 30 miles north-east of the Jordan's crossing
when Absalom came with his army and crossed over. Mahanaim was Ish-
bosheth's capital (2:8), but now provided David with a strategic base for
his defence. Absalom, meanwhile, had appointed Amasa, Joab and David's
cousin, over the army, extending the rebellion's familial conflict, though
David subsequently employed Amasa (19:14 [ET 19:13]; 20:4–5). However, the contrast is only explicitly drawn between Joab and Amasa
because their conflict over the army's command drives the narrative from
this rebellion into Sheba's. The genealogical note in v. 25 is obscure (see
'Notes'), but makes clear that Amasa was as an Israelite, in spite of his
Ishmaelite heritage, possibly through an unusual type of marriage where
the woman remained in her father's household so the child's nationality
was determined through the mother (so Smith 1899: 355). More importantly, the Israelite army was now also in Gilead.
    27–29. These verses are annalistic, but delay the battle report while
pointing to David's regional support. The material list indicates David and
his troops had the necessary provisions, but also wide support for David in
the Transjordan (both Lo Debar and Rogelim were probably there). This
support base was not limited to Israelites since an Ammonite (Shobi
ben Nahash) provided for him, while Machir's earlier association with
Mephibosheth (9:4–5) might have suggested he supported Saul. Barzillai
features later (19:33–40 [ET 19:32–39] and 1 Kgs 2:7), but is probably
different from the Barzillai mentioned in 21:8. They offer support because
they recognize the people's need due to the relative lack of resources for them
in the area. Again there is a hint that things are turning in David's favour.

Explanation

This narrative, with the conflict between counsellors at its heart, treads a narrow path emphasizing both God's hidden purposes and the reality that human decisions are free and require responsibility. This enables the narrative to show that Absalom's apparent moment of triumph, where his victory is almost complete, is where David's punishment is complete and so also begins his return to the throne. The narrator thus demonstrates that David's punishment (12:10–12) does not remove the promised kingdom (7:3–16). The NT recognizes that the promise passes through David's descendants (Ps. 45:7 [ET 45:6]; Heb. 1:8) to become an unshakeable kingdom (Heb. 12:28), but the same narrow path is trod.

The importance of human decision is everywhere in this account. Absalom is fully responsible for deciding to accept Hushai's claims at face value despite his language's ambiguity. He is responsible for accepting Ahithophel's advice and raping David's concubines to indicate his break with his father and his claim of the throne. He is also responsible for rejecting Ahithophel's strategy for Hushai's, even if he finally implements one closer to Ahithophel's. Ahithophel likewise is an astute counsellor who can seize an advantage when he sees it, not only in his advice about David's concubines, but also in his military strategy. His suicide, for all its narrative elegance, is still where he accepts his choices' outcome. Hushai may be the one through whom Yahweh prevented Ahithophel's plan, but Hushai still needed to apply his rhetorical skills. David, likewise, has made decisions he implemented through Hushai and the spy network as well as the process of moving those with him as far as possible. Finally, Shobi, Machir and Barzillai freely choose to provision David and his men. No one is compelled to act against his will: each bears full responsibility for his decisions.

Yet throughout Yahweh's purposes are being fulfilled. Evidence for this can be seen in how Absalom's actions fulfil the punishment announced by Nathan (12:11b–12), and even more explicitly in the narrative aside of 17:14. It was ultimately Yahweh who determined that Ahithophel's good military strategy would not be implemented; this gave David the necessary time to get his men into the security of Mahanaim. This was also the answer to David's prayer of 15:31. Once this is recognized, other elements of Yahweh's involvement may be recognized. In having sex with David's concubines, Absalom placed himself under the death penalty. When David's spies were seen, their escape was certainly resourceful, but also hints at Yahweh's protection; and while the provisions in 17:27–29 may have come from residents of the Transjordan, they hint at Yahweh's presence with David. Yahweh's purposes are being fulfilled, so we see hints of the coming battle's outcome because Yahweh has not abandoned David. But every ounce of human commitment must still be applied, just as the two are evident throughout this narrative. It is because of this same combination that the writer to the Hebrews emphasizes that God's kingdom is unshakeable, and yet urges his readers to be sure they enter it (Heb. 12:23–29).

2 SAMUEL 18:1 – 19:9a [ET 19:8a]

Translation

¹David mustered the people with him, and appointed over them commanders of thousands and commanders of hundreds. ²David sent out the people, one-third under Joab, one-third under Joab's brother Abishai the son of Zeruiah, and one-third under Ittai the Gittite. The king said to the people, 'I myself will go forth with you.' ³But the people said, 'You shall not go forth, for if we are forced to flee, they will not care about us. If half of us die, they will not care about us. For you are worth ten thousand of us. It is better if you support us from the city.' ⁴The king said to them, 'I will do what is good in your eyes.' The king stood by the gate's side and all the people went forth in hundreds and thousands. ⁵The king commanded Joab, Abishai and Ittai, 'Be gentle for my sake with the lad Absalom.' All the people heard when the king ordered the commanders about Absalom.

⁶The people went out to the field to confront Israel, and the battle was in the Forest of Ephraim. ⁷The men of Israel were defeated there before David's servants, and the slaughter there that day was very great, twenty thousand men. ⁸The battle was scattered across the face of all the land, and the forest devoured more that day than the sword.

⁹Absalom happened to meet David's servants. Absalom was mounted on a mule, and the mule went under the thick branches of a great oak. His head was caught fast in the oak, and he was stuck between heaven and earth, while the mule which was under him continued on. ¹⁰A certain man saw it and told Joab. He said, 'Behold, I saw Absalom hanging in an oak.' ¹¹Joab said to the man who told him, 'Behold, you saw, so why didn't you strike him to the ground there? I would have given you ten pieces of silver and a belt.' ¹²The man said to Joab, 'Even if I were to receive a thousand pieces of silver, I would not put forth my hand against the king's son, for in our hearing the king commanded you, Abishai and Ittai, "For my sake, protect the lad Absalom." ¹³Otherwise, had I acted treacherously against his life (and nothing is hidden from the king), you yourself would have stood aloof.' ¹⁴Joab said, 'I will not waste time like this with you.' He took three javelins in his hand and thrust them through Absalom's heart while he was still alive in the heart of the oak. ¹⁵Then ten lads who carried Joab's kit gathered round, struck Absalom and killed him.

¹⁶Joab sounded the trumpet, and the people returned from pursuing Israel, for Joab restrained the people. ¹⁷They took Absalom and cast him in the forest into a deep pit and piled upon it a great heap of stones. All Israel fled, each man to his tent. ¹⁸Absalom had taken and erected a pillar for himself which was in the King's Valley in his lifetime, for he said, 'I have no son to keep my name in remembrance.' He named the pillar after himself, so it is called 'Absalom's Monument' to this day.

[19]Ahimaaz ben Zadok said, 'Let me run and I will announce tidings to the king, that Yahweh has released him from his enemies' power.' [20]Joab said to him, 'You shall not carry tidings today. You may carry tidings another day, but you shall not bear tidings today, for the king's son is dead.' [21]Joab said to the Cushite, 'Go. Report to the king what you have seen.' The Cushite did obeisance to Joab, then ran. [22]Ahimaaz ben Zadok continued and said to Joab, 'Whatever happens, let me also run after the Cushite.' Joab said, 'Why should you run, my son, since you will have no reward for the tidings?' [23]'Whatever happens,' he said, 'I will run.' So he said to him, 'Run.' Ahimaaz ran by way of the plain and overtook the Cushite. [24]David was sitting between the two gates and the lookout went to the gate's roof by the wall. He looked up and saw, behold, a man running on his own. [25]The lookout called and reported to the king. The king said, 'If he is on his own, there are tidings in his mouth.' He continued to run and draw near. [26]The lookout saw another man running, and the lookout called to the gate and said, 'Behold, a man running on his own.' The king said, 'This one also bears tidings.' [27]Then the lookout said, 'I see the first runner, and he runs like Ahimaaz ben Zadok.' The king said, 'He is a good man, and comes with good tidings.'

[28]Ahimaaz called out to the king, 'All is well.' He did obeisance before the king with his face to the ground and said, 'Blessed be Yahweh your God who has delivered up the men who lifted their hand against my lord the king.' [29]The king said, 'Is it well with the lad Absalom?' Ahimaaz said, 'I saw a great tumult when the king's servant Joab sent your servant, but I do not know what happened.' [30]The king said, 'Turn aside and stand here.' So he turned aside and stood still.

[31]Then, behold, the Cushite came and the Cushite said, 'Let my lord the king receive tidings, for Yahweh has freed you this day from the power of all those who rose against you.' [32]The king said to the Cushite, 'Is it well with the lad Absalom?' The Cushite said, 'May the king's enemies be like the lad, and all who rise against you for harm.' [19:1]The king was deeply moved, and went up to the chamber above the gate and wept. As he went he said, 'O my son, Absalom, my son, my son, Absalom. If only I had died in your place! O Absalom, my son, my son.'

[2]It was reported to Joab, 'Behold, the king is weeping and mourning for Absalom.' [3]So that day's victory was turned to mourning for all the people, for the people heard on that day, 'The king is grieved over his son.' [4]So the people went by stealth that day to enter the city as humiliated people who flee from battle go by stealth. [5]The king covered his face, and the king cried out with a loud voice, 'O my son, Absalom, Absalom, my son, my son.'

[6]Joab came to the king indoors and said, 'Today you have covered with shame the faces of all your servants who delivered your life today, along with the life of your sons, your daughters, the life of your wives and the life of your concubines, [7]by loving those who hate you and hating those who love you. For you have declared today that commanders and servants are nothing to you; for I know today that if Absalom was alive and all of us today were dead, then this would please you. [8]But now, rise. Go and speak to the heart of your servants, for I swear by Yahweh that if you do not go out, not a man will stay the night with you, and this calamity will be worse for you than every calamity that has come upon you since

you were a lad until now.' ⁹ᵃSo the king rose and sat in the gate. When they told all the people, 'Behold, the king is sitting in the gate,' then all the people came before the king.

Notes on the text

18:3. With two MSS and LXX, read *'attâ* for *'attâ*.

9. Most versions agree with 4QSamᵃ, reading *tlh* here and 18:10 rather than the qal passive of *ntn* (parsed as hoph. in BDB, but see GKC §53u and *DCH*). These are orthographically similar, but MT remains preferable. *'ēlâ* is either an oak or a terebinth; ESV manages to have both here.

12. Read, with Q, *lû* or possibly *lû'*. The conjunction either initiates a case unlikely to be realized (see Deut. 32:29; Judg. 8:19; 13:23; 1 Sam. 14:30; 2 Sam. 19:7 [ET 19:6]; Mic. 2:11; Ps. 81:14–17) or a wish unlikely to be granted (see Gen. 17:18; Num. 14:2; 20:3; Josh. 7:7). Read *lî* with two MSS, LXX, Syr and Tg for MT *mî*, unless with McCarter (1984: 401) *mî* is understood as an enclitic particle.

13. Many MSS and Q read *napšî* for *napšô*. If followed, it means that striking Absalom means the man dealt recklessly with his own life. K is retained, but there is little to choose.

14. The meaning of *šĕbāṭîm* is uncertain. It normally refers to clubs or rods, but here refers to a stabbing implement. It is not a spear (*ḥănît* would be used), so is a javelin or wooden dart.

16. There is a pun in that *tq'* refers both to sounding the trumpet and Joab's thrusting his javelins through Absalom. Both bring an end within the battle.

23. Read 'he said' with LXX. *kikkar* means something round, here the known shape of that section of the Jordan plain (see Gen. 13:12).

26. LXX adds 'another', a correct observation but probably a correction.

29. Some MSS include the interrogative for David's question, but this is not necessary (yet see v. 32).

19:1. EVV treat this as 18:33, starting ch. 19 in the next verse.

7 [ET 6]. Read, with Q, *lû* or possibly *lû'*. See note on 18:12.

Form and structure

Absalom's rebellion has been faltering since David sent Hushai to Jerusalem to thwart Ahithophel's advice (15:30–37). Hushai was the answer to David's prayer, though the narrator has indicated that he succeeded only because of Yahweh's intervention (17:14). The conflict between the counsellors that dominated 16:15 – 17:24 pointed to David's victory because Yahweh was acting for him, since this stage of his punishment was complete. But Absalom remained ignorant of this, and set out in pursuit

(17:25–26). Although his strategy was broadly Ahithophel's, he adopted Hushai's suggestion that he lead the army, but with Amasa as his military commander. The counsellors' conflict now works itself out in battle in the Forest of Ephraim, a site David chose and which worked to his advantage as it lacked the space for large-scale military activities, benefiting David's smaller, more mobile force.

Although the military conflict could be explored in detail, the narrative refrains from doing so, devoting only 18:6–8 to it. Instead, it focuses on David and Absalom's relationship, with the battle providing its backdrop. So the opening stresses that David wanted Absalom treated gently (18:4–5), though he could not enforce this because his troops insisted he remain in Mahanaim. After Absalom was caught in the tree, the soldier who found him refused to kill him because of David's order, though Joab showed no such scruples (18:9–16), before sounding the trumpet to end hostilities. More space is given to narrating how David heard of the battle's outcome (18:19–19:1 [ET 18:33]) and the effects of his sorrow over Absalom's death (19:2–9a [ET 19:1–8a]) than the battle itself. The monarchy is at stake, but this is a story of a divided family, and since David is Yahweh's chosen king how he coped is more important than providing endless military details. The narrator may do this to encourage Absalom's supporters to return to David since it demonstrates he was not vindictive towards his enemy (so Birch 1998: 1135), but the narrator more probably wants to show both David's strengths and weaknesses through this style of narration.

There are several links between this account and 2:11 – 3:1, the last time Israel endured civil war over the throne (similarly, Polzin 1993: 182–187). In both cases Joab and Abishai are prominent in David's army (2:18, 24; 18:2), while both battles' end is signalled by Joab's sounding the trumpet (2:28; 18:16). Previously, Abner's slaying of Joab's brother Asahel (2:19–23) triggered further violence resulting in Joab's murdering Abner (3:27) even though David was negotiating with him. This time Joab murdered Absalom (18:9–15), ignoring David's order that he be treated well. David himself was absent from both battles. Joab's violence is a problem, but David is compromised because he used Joab to murder Uriah (11:14–25). Nathan said the sword would never depart from David's house (12:10), and the narrative hints at its continuation even as Absalom is overcome. No one incident tells the whole of David's punishment, but Yahweh's word still dominates.

Comment

Absalom's death: 18:1–18

1–2a. The narrative's opening records David's preparations for battle. This indicates that he was setting the agenda, ensuring the most favourable outcome. Organizing his army into 'thousands' and 'hundreds' reflects the traditional military divisions without specifically indicating their size. Dividing the army into three equal units, each with its own commander demotes Joab, but replicates Saul's strategy at Jabesh Gilead (1 Sam. 11:11). We know Joab does not accept situations like this, and as the narrative progresses he gradually reclaims control over the whole army. Abishai and Ittai, like Absalom's commander, Amasa, are not mentioned again. The division of David's forces introduces the keyword *yād* (lit. 'hand') that runs through this narrative (18:2 [×3], 4, 12, 18–19, 28, 31). David's power is distributed, whereas Absalom's will be concentrated in his monument (18:18).

2b–5. David, like Absalom, desired to lead the army, but David was persuaded to remain in the city (presumably Mahanaim). Comparing David with ten thousand of his men colourfully suggests his death was Absalom's forces' aim, just as Ahithophel counselled in 17:2–4 (Seiler 1998: 180), though the counsel of David's men is the opposite of what Hushai suggested to Absalom (17:11; see Conroy 1978: 57). Accepting their argument, he stood by the town gate, remaining there while they marched into battle. Just as David's troops marched past while fleeing Jerusalem (15:18–23), so now they march past to the battle from which he will be restored. David's army would ordinarily have the goal of Absalom's death, except David ordered his commanders to deal gently with Absalom, a command overheard by all. David's concern was not just for Absalom. His order was for his own sake too, indicating his involvement in events. The order establishes a tension that remains unresolved until 19:8–9a [ET19:7–8a], though also explaining David's mourning at 19:1. But by accepting the men's argument that he remain, David could not control what happened to Absalom.

6–8. The battle account is remarkably brief, indicating that it is not central to the narrative. It provides the background to Absalom's death, demonstrating that Hushai's strategy of mass numbers could not bring victory. The location of 'the Forest of Ephraim' is uncertain, and though parts of it would be close to Mahanaim, it must have run across the Jordan (Josh. 17:15–17). The forest is said to fight for David and to have killed more of Absalom's men than David's forces. This probably implies that his soldiers exploited conditions, especially as the scattering of forces played into David's hands. But it is another element on David's side, one more pointer towards Yahweh's decision to restore him (Baldwin 1988: 269). As with Joab's victory over Abner (2:31), casualties are given only for Absalom's troops, a strategy that enables the narrator to stress the extent of David's victory. Although the exact size of a 'thousand' is unknown, the twenty units destroyed would probably have exceeded McCarter's estimate (1984: 405) of one hundred to two hundred and eighty men.

9. Absalom's death remains the narrative's primary concern, especially because it involves Joab's disobeying David's orders. The battle was dispensed with in three verses, but Absalom's death takes nine, to which is appended the note about his monument. Absalom obviously participated in the battle, and is the classic example of how the forest fought for David. That earlier statement prepares for Absalom's experience. Accidentally encountering some of David's men, he fled on his mule, but caught his head in an oak tree's branches (the article may indicate a well-known tree), and is colourfully described as being 'between heaven and earth' (a unique order for this word pair; Wiggins 1997: 74). Since at least Josephus (*Ant.* 7.239) it has been thought that Absalom was caught by his luxuriant hair (14:26; still defended by Youngblood 1992: 1019). 'Head' could stand by synecdoche for 'hair', but the narrator does not make this explicit (see Gordon 1986: 284–285), and his hair was unlikely to support him without his mule. Although his exact situation cannot be determined, he was unable to free himself, perhaps being knocked unconscious.

10–15. The narrative now detours to a conversation between Joab and an unnamed soldier who saw Absalom. The soldier obeyed David's command and did nothing against Absalom (though without assisting him), refusing to be tempted by Joab's bribe to kill him, even quoting back David's command given to Joab along with Abishai and Ittai. Responding to Joab's suggestion that he might have received ten pieces of silver for the killing, he claims that even if he felt the weight of a thousand pieces in his hand he would not kill Absalom. His response shows his faithfulness to David, while suggesting Joab is not entirely to be trusted since the man doubted Joab would support him if the matter came to trial. The soldier obviously countenanced such a possibility given his declaration that nothing was hidden from the king (cf. 14:17; 19:28 [ET 19:27]). But Joab's loyalty is different, and he decides to kill Absalom as the best way to protect David. The man who brought Absalom back from exile (14:1–24) will not do so this time. Instead, he thrusts three 'javelins' (see 'Notes') into Absalom, an action that begins his death, although ten of his assistants complete the task.

16–18. Absalom's death ends the battle because the conflict was between him and David. Its end was signalled by Joab's (see 2:28) sounding the trumpet to restrain his troops; unnecessary bloodshed would alienate the defeated even more, and could not be risked (Campbell 2005: 159). Lacking another leader, the Israelite levy could not continue, and the fratricidal struggle ceases. Absalom is given the burial of the accursed, something hinted at as he hung on the tree (Deut. 21:22–23), and buried away from the family tomb in a pit (see 17:9) in the forest, with only a cairn marking his presence (cf. Josh. 7:25). Meanwhile, all his troops had fled. It was an ignominious monument, one the narrator contrasts with a pillar he erected as a monument (*yād*) to himself because he had no son to carry on his name. According to 14:27 he had three sons apart from his daughter Tamar, so the assumption is that they died young (but see Seiler 1998: 177). The site of the pillar in the King's valley is unknown (not the 'Absalom's Tomb' near Jerusalem that is Hellenistic or Roman),

but is probably somewhere in the Kidron valley. Like the builders at
Babel, Absalom sought to protect his name (Gen. 11:4), but his actions
were equally futile, something stressed by Deut. 16:22's prohibition of
pillars.

David's grief over Absalom: 18:19 – 9:9a [ET 19:8a]

18:19–23. Meanwhile, David remained at the city. Naturally, he had to be
informed. It is unclear why Joab initially opposed sending Ahimaaz, unless
he felt the Cushite was more expendable should David respond as he had
with previous messengers who had brought bad news (see 1:15; 4:12).
However, those messengers implicated themselves, which is not the case
here (Anderson 1989: 226). Ahimaaz' excitement is expressed as a
theological statement: he interprets the victory as indicating that Yahweh
has freed (or vindicated, *špṭ*) David from Absalom. From his perspective,
this is good news. But Joab declined for that day, noting that the king's son
had died, although not naming Absalom directly. Instead, he directed an
unnamed Cushite (someone from the region between the first and sixth
cataracts of the Nile, probably a black African; see Lokel 2006: 525) to
report what he had seen. These may be carefully chosen words for we do
not know what the Cushite saw, though having paid his respects he began
his journey. Yet Ahimaaz continued to press for permission to go. Possibly,
Ahimaaz thought there might be some reward, whereas Joab knew that
even as a messenger of good news (in terms of the battle: *bśr* normally
refers to good tidings) he would not receive any reward (also *bśr*), a point
he makes explicit. Yet Ahimaaz' excitement about reporting eventually
persuaded Joab to grant him permission. The runners' routes were obscure.
It is generally felt that the Cushite took the direct route through the forest,
whereas Ahimaaz took the longer but easier route around it on the plain of
the Jordan, passing the Cushite and arriving first.

24–27. The narrative switches to David, seated between the city's inner
and outer gates where he saw the troops march out (18:4). The account of
the two runners parallels Jehu's approach to Jezreel (2 Kgs 9:17–20),
suggesting a traditional composition technique. The narrative carefully
reveals information only as David discovers it. Hence the lookout's first
report from the gatehouse roof is of a runner coming alone. David
reasoned a single runner signified good news (*bśr*), perhaps because there
was no sign of pursuit. Good news here would be the defeat of Absalom's
forces, but also word that Absalom was well. Then the lookout saw the
second runner, and reported this to David, who reached the same
conclusion. As the runners approached, the lookout could recognize
Ahimaaz by his distinctive running style. David thus felt more confident
of good news, attaching his positive assessment of his character to the
anticipated message. David's assessment of Ahimaaz suggests Joab's initial

opposition to sending him was well founded, but Joab could not have known that Ahimaaz would arrive before the Cushite.

28–30. With Ahimaaz identified, the narrative reports his meeting with David, with the conversation begun by Ahimaaz. His report contained only one word, *šālôm*, before his paying respects by prostrating himself before David. Ironically, *šālôm* was David's last word to Absalom (15:9), as well as what Ahithophel claimed he could bring about through his proposed strike on David (17:3). With respects paid, Ahimaaz presented a fuller, more explicitly theological report, blessing Yahweh for delivering up the men who had set themselves against David. It is a joyous claim of victory, a celebration of the outcome that is essentially that of the narrator. But Ahimaaz said nothing about Absalom, though he knew from Joab's statement in v. 20 that Absalom was dead. But the only *šālôm* that concerned David was Absalom's condition, yet in response to a direct question Ahimaaz obfuscated, as is evident from his confused speech ('nearly gibberish': Alter 1999: 309), referring only to Joab's sending him, not his desire to report (Conroy 1978:73). He claimed only to have seen confusion around Joab, but not enough to know what had happened to Absalom. No reason is given for Ahimaaz' actions, though perhaps he only now realized he could not give David the good news he desired. With this unsatisfactory response, Ahimaaz steps aside for the incoming Cushite.

18:31 – 19:1 [ET 18:33]. The Cushite focuses on the battle's result, but also refrains from commenting directly on Absalom while replicating Ahimaaz' earlier statement that Yahweh has freed (or vindicated, *špṭ*) David from all who rose against him. Like Ahimaaz, the emphasis is on good news. But David persists, asking about Absalom's welfare (*šālôm*). Although the Cushite's answer is indirect, he makes clear that Absalom is dead, but without indicating Joab's role. David responded with overwhelming grief, marked by his withdrawal from the messengers as he went to the room above the gate. He wept and repeated five times what is in Hebr. one brief word, *'my son'* (*běnî*) and Absalom's name three times, expressing the impossible wish to have died instead of him. Some criticize David here, and it is true that he is not an effective king. But as Gordon observes, 'even in times of high drama, a king may be a father' (1986: 287).

19:2–5 [ET 19:1–4]. Absalom's forces were defeated, but David had not come to terms with his death. The focus now is on what is reported to Joab and its resultant effect on the army's morale. Joab's return is passed over in silence; all that matters is that he knows of David's behaviour. V. 2 is the main statement, with vv. 3–5 essentially digressing to indicate how much David's continued and very public grief undermined the army and people's morale. Victory (see 1 Sam. 18:6–7) now became a time of mourning. Instead of a triumphant re-entry, the perfect return after their outgoing parade (18:4), they returned quietly as if they had lost the battle and were seeking to avoid further shame. Meanwhile, David covered his face in mourning, and continued to repeat Absalom's name and 'my son'.

6–9a. When the news reached Joab, he went directly to the king, though that it was indoors suggests a degree of privacy. His statement in vv. 6–8 rebukes David, and is the only rebuke David receives in the whole of Absalom's rebellion. Its urgency may be seen in the repetition of 'today' and the lack of court language, contrasting with the two messengers. David lacks the luxury of time. Joab argues, in what is the longest spoken sentence in Samuel (Fokkelman 1981: 271) that these people have been completely loyal to David, but he is failing to recognize their loyalty, and so shames them rather than providing the due honour (on dimensions of shame, see Olyan 1996: 208–211; Kruger 1998), a crucial charge. Joab stresses that these are the people who delivered David and his family. David has been lamenting 'my son', so Joab points out that because of their efforts, the lives of David's other sons, daughters, wives and concubines have been delivered, the gain far outweighing the loss. Joab extended this argument by claiming that David's actions showed him loving his enemies and hating his friends. The language is forceful, though the love–hate contrast is comparative rather than absolute (cf. Mal. 1:2–5; Matt. 6:24; Luke 14:26), suggesting David's preference is for his enemies (the contrast with Matt. 5:43–48 should not be pressed too far). Joab drives this home by claiming David's preference was for Absalom to live rather than all his troops. Ever the political realist, Joab recognizes the harm this does, and in a succession of three imperatives at the start of v. 8 [ET v. 7] directs David again to enter the gate and address his servants, or else lose all support. The use of an oath invoking Yahweh could indicate a veiled threat that Joab would claim the throne for himself (always a risk with a powerful general), but given Joab's apparent preference for the military power it is more likely simple *Realpolitik*. If David lost his traditional support, the damage caused would exceed all that had gone before. Convinced of the political necessity, David returned to the gate, a sign not only of his restoration, but also that he knew his public role as king had to prevail over his grief as a father. With that done, his supporters returned, though there is no indication of his addressing the people as Joab directed. Yet this is where David's restoration to the throne formally began, for he had a group who acknowledged him as king.

Explanation

The defeat of Absalom's main counsellor, Ahithophel, by Hushai (17:1–14) is matched by the defeat of his forces by David in the Forest of Ephraim. Although Yahweh is not mentioned throughout the battle account, Ahimaaz expresses the narrator's view; Yahweh has freed David from all his enemies (18:19). By placing this comment immediately after the narrator's own about Absalom's demise and his misguided attempt at creating a memorial for himself, we have at the story's heart the central themes it develops. Absalom's attempts at glory, whether through his appearance (14:26), subsequent grab for power and prestige (15:1–6), or deliberate attempt to make himself odious to David and claim the throne by raping his father's concubines (16:20–22), have all failed. Rather than glory, he received the ignominious burial of those accursed because they were hanged on a tree (Deut. 21:22–23, but see Gal. 3:10–14). Absalom's actions, murder and rape of David's concubines as well as treason brought him to an accursed death. Yet David has been freed from his enemies, though Ahimaaz expressing this through a forensic metaphor (špṭ may refer to an act of judgment) provides a mechanism for linking this act of deliverance to the larger narrative that has been driven by David's attack on Uriah through Bathsheba and Nathan's declaration of his punishment (12:10–12). Yahweh has vindicated David, and given him freedom once more, freedom that allows him to reclaim his lost throne, if not the glory that has gone with it. This is the narrative's central theological claim.

How this occurs is extraordinarily messy, but the narrator explores only the main characters on David's side. Absalom is silent in this chapter, even while hanging in the tree, so he is acted upon but never shown to act himself. David has been a mystery throughout Samuel in that we almost never receive insight into his emotions and motivations. Yet suddenly they come flooding through as he directs his troops to deal gently with Absalom. More than that, the long and involved process by which he discovers the battle's outcome and Absalom's death enable the narrator to show how desperately he wants his son to live. His grief invites our sympathy because it shows the struggle of both king and father. Yet if we gain new insights into David, Joab is more opaque than ever. He hears David's order but still arranges Absalom's death, yet sees the need to be circumspect in reporting this. Joab is never squeamish about killing (3:27; 11:14–21), and though earlier involved in restoring Absalom (14:1–24), recognized that Absalom alive was a continued threat. Yet he also saw the effect of David's public grief on the men and brought David to see the importance of his public role.

Why, then, does the narrative go to such lengths to explore David's dilemma as both a public and a private figure when a simple statement of victory (such as 18:6–8) could suffice? The reason possibly lies in the book's larger structure, something largely ignored by those who see 2 Sam. 9 – 20 finding its conclusion in 1 Kgs 1 – 2 rather 2 Sam. 21 – 24. In 2 Sam. 5:17 – 8:18 a chiastic structure (see 'Form and structure' on 5:17–25) focuses on David as a public figure. His role in battle and worship is public, and David is never explored as a private figure. Yet another chiastic structure follows in chs. 21 – 24 (see 'Form and structure' on 21:1–14) that is structurally similar to 5:17 – 8:18. There we explore David as the private figure, especially in 22:1 – 23:7, and his military role is scaled back. Seen in this light, this narrative opens up David as a private figure and prepares for the faith of that private figure's matching the public role. It was this disjunction that chs. 11 – 12 so vigorously exposed and it is from the pain of this outcome that the move back towards coherence between these domains begins as David begins his move back towards the throne.

2 SAMUEL 19:9b–44 [ET 19:8b–43]

Translation

[9b]Now Israel had fled, each to his tent. [10]All the people were arguing throughout all Israel's tribes, saying, 'The king delivered us from the power of our enemies, and he saved us from the power of the Philistines, but now he has fled the land because of Absalom. [11]But Absalom, whom we anointed over us, is dead in the battle. So now, why are you silent about bringing back the king?' And all Israel's word came to the king.
    [12]King David sent to the priests Zadok and Abiathar, 'Speak to Judah's elders, saying, "Why are you the last to bring the king back to his house? [13]You are my brothers; you are my bone and my flesh. Why are you the last to bring the king back?" [14]To Amasa you shall say, "Are you not my bone and my flesh? Thus may God do to me, and thus may he continue to do, if you are not commander of the army before me from now on in place of Joab."' [15]So he turned the heart of every man of Judah as one, and they sent to the king, 'Come back, you and all your servants.' [16]The king returned and came as far as the Jordan. Judah came to Gilgal to meet the king and bring the king across the Jordan.
    [17]Shimei ben Gera the Benjaminite from Bahurim hurried and came down with the men of Judah to meet King David. [18]A thousand men from Benjamin were with him. And Ziba, the lad from Saul's house, and his fifteen sons and twenty servants, rushed to the Jordan before the king. [19]They kept crossing the ford to bring the king's house across and to do what pleased him. Then Shimei ben Gera fell down before the king when Shimei had crossed the Jordan, [20]and said to the king, 'Let not my lord consider me guilty, nor remember how your servant erred on the day when my lord the king left Jerusalem, so the king takes it to heart, [21]for your servant knows I have sinned, so behold, I have come today as the first of the whole house of Joseph to come down to meet my lord the king.' [22]Abishai ben Zeruiah answered, 'Should not Shimei be put to death for this, for he cursed Yahweh's anointed?' [23]But David said, 'What do I have to do with you sons of Zeruiah, that you should today be an adversary to me? Should any man be put to death in Israel today? Do I not know today that I am king over Israel?' [24]The king said to Shimei, 'You shall not die.' And the king swore him an oath.
    [25]Mephibosheth, Saul's grandson, came down to meet the king. He had not cared for his feet nor trimmed his moustache nor washed his garments from the day the king left until the day he returned in peace. [26]When he came from Jerusalem to meet the king, the king said to him, 'Why did you not go with me, Mephibosheth?' [27]He said, 'My lord the king, my servant dealt treacherously with me, for your servant said, "I will saddle myself a donkey and mount up and go to the king, for your

servant is lame." [28]He has slandered your servant to my lord the king, but my lord the king is like the angel of God, so do what seems good to you. [29]For all my father's household was nothing but men doomed to death before my lord the king, but you have put your servant among those who eat at your table. What right do I yet have that I should cry out to the king?' [30]The king said to him, 'Why do you speak any more of these matters? I have decreed. You and Ziba shall divide the estate.' [31]Mephibosheth said to the king, 'Let him take it all since my lord the king has come to his house in peace.'

[32]Barzillai the Gileadite came down from Rogelim and passed on with the king to the Jordan to give him a send-off at the Jordan. [33]Barzillai was very old, eighty years old; he had sustained the king in his sojourn at Mahanaim because he was a very wealthy man. [34]The king said to Barzillai, 'You cross over with me and I will sustain you in Jerusalem with me.' [35]Barzillai said to the king, 'How long have I to live that I should go up with the king to Jerusalem? [36]I am eighty years old today. Can I distinguish between pleasant and unpleasant? Can your servant taste what I eat or drink? Can I yet hear the voice of singing men and singing women? Why should your servant yet be a burden to my lord the king? [37]Your servant will pass on a little across the Jordan. Why should the king grant me this recompense? [38]Please let your servant return that I may die in my city near my father and mother's grave. But here is your servant Chimham. Let him cross over with my lord the king, and let him deal with him as seems right to him.' [39]The king said, 'Chimham shall cross over with me, but I shall deal with him as seems right to you, and all you require of me I shall do for you.' [40]Then all the people crossed the Jordan, and the king crossed. The king kissed Barzillai and blessed him, and then he returned to his place. [41]The king crossed over to Gilgal, and Chimham crossed over with him, and all the people of Judah and half the people of Israel accompanied the king.

[42]Then behold, all the men of Israel came to the king and said to the king, 'Why have our brothers, the men of Judah, stolen you that they brought the king and his household over the Jordan, and all David's men with him?' [43]All the men of Judah answered the men of Israel, 'Because the king is our close relative. Why are you angry about this matter? Have we eaten at the king's expense? Has he given us any gift?' [44]The men of Israel answered the men of Judah, 'We have ten shares in the king and in David also more than you. Why have you treated us with contempt when we were first to suggest bringing the king back?' But the men of Judah's response was harsher than that of the men of Israel.

Notes on the text

Verse numbers for EVV are one less than MT throughout this chapter. All references are to MT versification, as in the trans.

9b. Two MSS and LXX[L] read 'all Israel'.

11. Following LXX (and possibly 4QSam[a]), 'all Israel's word came to the king' is placed at the end of v. 11 rather than v. 12. A copyist has skipped from one occurrence of *hammelek* to another.

12. With LXX, omit the second *'el bêtô*.

19. With Tg, read *wĕ'ābĕrû* for MT *wĕ'ābĕrâ*. The reference of the suffix on *bĕ'ābrô* is uncertain, but since later events indicate David had not crossed the Jordan, it probably refers to Shimei.

23. Questions are not always marked, so the verse's second question is noted only by context. P. L. Day (1987) interprets *śāṭān lî* forensically as 'accuser on my behalf'. While possible, the traditional interpretation is preferred.

25. Syr and some LXX MSS have 'Jonathan's son' for 'Saul's son'. While technically correct, *ben* can mean 'grandson'.

26. With a few MSS read *ka'ăšer* for *kî*. The preposition *min* before Jerusalem is implied, unless these events happened when David reached Jerusalem, but are narrated here to group his encounters. Since Samuel does not always narrate events in a strict chronology, this is possible (cf. Mark's grouping of controversy stories in Mark 2:1 – 3:6). The absence of *'br* here could argue for that possibility, but that Mephibosheth has 'come down' (*yrd*) makes it probable that this is at the Jordan since one comes down from Jerusalem.

27. With many MSS read *'el* for *'et*.

28. 'Slandered' renders the pi. of *rgl*, the same root as 'foot', a prominent word in Mephibosheth's story.

32. *'et bayyardēn* appears to be a compound reading, *'et* having been introduced for the unusual *bayyardēn*, but creating an anomalous text.

33. *bĕšîbātô* is problematic, but presumes a substantive derived from *yšb*.

41. With several MSS read *kimhām* for *kimhān*.

43. Parse *niśśē't* as a ni. inf. abs., though vocalization is odd.

Form and structure

Absalom's defeat did not result in David's return to the throne since certain obstacles remained. David needed an invitation from the tribes to become king again. The conflict this generates between Judah and the northern tribes bookends this narrative. This suggests Absalom had received such an invitation, even being anointed by them (19:11 [ET 19:10]). David had claimed Judah's throne (2:1–4) before receiving Israel's after Ish-bosheth's murder (5:1–5), and his return is closely modelled on this first accession. David invited Judah to take the lead, describing them as his bone and flesh (the phrase the men of Israel used in 5:1). Although David's message resulted in an invitation to reclaim Judah's throne, it ultimately triggered Sheba's rebellion (20:1–22) because of the conflict between north and south (19:42–44 [ET 19:41–43]). Like David's initial accession (2:1 – 5:5), there was war between north and south. Absalom's death, like Saul's, did not result in immediate national support for David. He made one play for northern support in appointing Amasa as army commander in place of Joab (19:14 [ET 19:13]), but this seems to have had little effect.

As well as approaching Judah, David negotiated three encounters that form this narrative's centrepiece. Two encounters, with Shimei and Mephibosheth, reflect on David's flight from Jerusalem (16:1–14), while the third with Barzillai reflects on his provisioning David in 17:27–29. An encounter with Mephibosheth's steward, Ziba, is mixed into that with Shimei, but largely passed over. These encounters are an important means of linking the return from Mahanaim to earlier events, causing us to reread those events in the light of these. David's prayer against Ahithophel (15:31) has been decisively answered, but his decision to see if Yahweh will bring him back to Jerusalem because he has found favour with him (15:25–26) has not. By the narrator directing readers to David's flight we are given a theological assessment of this narrative, though Yahweh is not said to have done anything in it. David is returning, though here he reaches only Gilgal, and can be magnanimous in victory, because he has found favour with Yahweh. David remains a careful politician, but his successes are not simply clever politics. The author of 1 Kgs 2:1–9 raises Shimei and Barzillai, along with Joab, in David's final instructions to Solomon.

The lack of direct reference to Yahweh not only permits reflection on David's wish in 15:25–26, but also directs readers to David's punishment (12:10–12). There Yahweh declared the sword would not depart from his house, suggesting continued violence, not just Absalom's rebellion. The reality of this is hinted at in 19:42–44 [ET 19:41–43]), so David's return is not peaceful. Although David is returning to favour, the punishment lingers.

Comment

Judah, Israel and David's reign: 19:9b–16 [ET 19:8b–15]

9b [ET 8b]. With David's having reclaimed power in Mahanaim, Israel fled, picking up the narrative thread left aside since 18:17, and using the phrase as used there. How David was informed of Absalom's death is now set aside to narrate how he began to reclaim the throne.

10–11 [ET 9–10]. Although David reclaimed power in Mahanaim, it was hardly a significant power base, as Ish-bosheth had previously discovered (2:8–10). But his position caused confusion among those who anointed Absalom, something the narrator demonstrates by citing discussion within all the tribes, not just the north. The conflict was between two historical situations and two contemporary ones introduced by 'and now' (*wĕ'attâ*). The historical points were that David had defeated their enemies, especially the Philistines, and that Absalom had died in battle. The first current issue was that David had fled the land (by entering the

Transjordan) because of Absalom, something requiring action. The second 'and now' introduces a rhetorical question against those who had not yet sought to bring David back. Historical issues are balanced by a present imperative. They had sided with Absalom as king. Given his death, could they restore David? This discussion within all Israel (north and south) is reported to David (see 'Notes').

12–14 [ET 11–13]. The narrator turns from popular conversation to those initiated by David. He took the initiative by summoning Zadok and Abiathar to bring Judah's elders to his assistance. They were not only David's 'brothers'; they are his 'bone and flesh'. The phrase signifies both kinship and covenantal relationships (see 5:1–5). David saw that his power base lay with Judah, and perhaps wished to begin in a way parallel to his previous ascent to both thrones, though there is undoubted irony in beginning from Ish-bosheth's former capital. Since Absalom launched his revolt from Hebron (15:10), Judah's support was not necessarily with David, so David might also have been re-establishing his home base. The discussion within all Israel was concluded by a rhetorical question, and David's message to Judah's elders opens and closes with a similar one. The question picks up on the intertribal discussion but modifies it, suggesting Judah was lagging when they should have been first. Covenant and kinship were spurs to action. Along with this, he also sent a message to Amasa with a rhetorical question also describing him as 'bone and flesh'. Like Joab, Amasa was David's nephew, though in a more complex way than Joab (see 'Notes' on 17:25), so kinship was clearly important. But David intended to develop this relationship; hence this more unusual phrase. This message went further, with David's placing himself under a self-curse (see 1 Sam. 25:22; 2 Sam. 3:9, 35) if he failed to appoint Amasa as permanent army commander in place of Joab. Although some personal element in his relationship with Joab might be reflected, it was politically expedient since it could rally some opponents behind him again. Both messages supported the same political aim.

9.15–16 [ET 14–15]. David's actions (Campbell 2005: 161 believes it was Amasa, but the 'he' is probably David) were enough to regain Judah's support 'as one man'. The narrator refrains from commenting on the northern tribes' attitude since their sense of alienation becomes apparent only at the chapter's end. Judah's positive response is seen when they invite David to return along with his servants, in this case all who continued to support him and not merely his household. Hence David came to the Jordan at Gilgal where he was met by the people of Judah to bring him across. Gilgal was a crucial site in Israel's move to monarchy as its place of renewal when Samuel had laid out kingship's terms (1 Sam. 11:12 – 12:25) as well as being where Israel entered the land (Josh. 3 – 4). For David, it was also a place of new beginnings. However, David remains on the east bank as the encounters with Shimei, Mephiosheth and Barzillai are recounted.

Three encounters: 19:17–41 [ET 19:16–40]

17–19a. Remaining on the east bank (see 'Notes' on 19:19), David is met by Shimei, who cursed him when he fled Jerusalem (16:5–13). With him are a 'thousand' men, probably a Benjamite military unit. Shimei's position is undoubtedly tenuous, which is why his speed in coming to the Jordan is emphasized. The presence of a significant body of men probably points to the support he can bring David. Before the encounter with Shimei is recounted, the narrative takes an interlude to refer to Mephibosheth's servant Ziba who also rushes down with his sons and servants. Since Ziba's position is resolved through the encounter with Mephibosheth, no dialogue from his meeting is provided. Rather, the focus is on his coordinating the ferrying of David's resources across the river to please David. Ziba's position as a prominent supporter of Saul might have made his position somewhat ambiguous, even though he provisioned David as he fled. The encounter with Mephibosheth also casts doubt on his claims, and knowing this might have spurred him to action. Whatever his motives, it was important that he be among the first to meet David on his return.

19b–24 [ET 18b–23]. The narrative of Shimei, again introduced by his full patronym (see 19:17 [ET 19:16]), is resumed by noting that he crossed the Jordan and prostrated himself before David. With David ascendant, Shimei must resolve the difficulties his earlier actions created. His speech to David does not confess sin, assuming his guilt to be self-evident. Instead, adopting proper court form, he twice asks for an acquittal. His obsequious speech is notable for its move from third to second person and back, initially addressing David as 'my lord' and asking David not to consider him guilty, then addressing him directly and asking him not to recall the events of 16:5–13. Resuming third person court address, before returning to the reality of his guilt he finally asks that David not take the matter to heart. As evidence of repentance he points out that he is the 'first of the house of Joseph' there to meet David. Although Joseph normally refers to Ephraim and Manasseh, it here means all the northern tribes. Shimei is the first non-Judahite to greet David, though Ziba may make a similar claim. Before David speaks, Abishai repeats his offer of 16:9, this time offering a legal basis since Shimei cursed Yahweh's anointed, language not used since David's encounters with Saul in the wilderness (1 Sam. 24:7, 11 [ET 24:6, 10]; 26:9, 11, 16, 23). David's initial response is identical to 16:10, but he adds that Abishai (and Joab) have become his adversaries (*śāṭān*; cf. Mark 8:33). Since David now knows of his restoration, he will not be vindictive, promising on oath not to execute Shimei (see 1 Sam. 11:13). But David is also driven by political expedience since his northern power base is limited. When that is resolved, he can leave Shimei's execution to Solomon (1 Kgs 2:8–9).

25–29 [ET 24–28]. David's next encounter, again east of the Jordan (see 'Notes' on 19:26), is with Mephibosheth. Before the speech, the narrator pauses to describe Mephibosheth as Saul's descendant and mentions his dishevelled appearance, with his feet untreated, his moustache untrimmed and clothes unwashed since David fled Jerusalem until his return in peace (šālôm). These are signs of mourning, though since we do not know the nature of his lameness the reference to his feet is obscure, but is more than a failure to cut his toenails (so McCarter 1984: 421). David was suspicious, even though Mephibosheth's dishevelled appearance would not indicate support for Absalom or his own purposes. David's question is direct, asking why he had not joined him. Mephibosheth's response also employs court language, describing himself as David's servant. He claims he was tricked by his servant (though Ziba is unnamed), and prevented from going in spite of attempting to prepare his donkey so he could ride with David. Because of his lameness, he could not overcome the obstacles he faced. Further, the unnamed servant slandered him before David, so the case against Mephibosheth is not as clear as David might have thought. Mephibosheth closes by saying David is like 'an angel of God', an appeal for a decision to be made, the same idiom used in 14:17, 20 (but see 1 Sam. 29:9). However, he recognizes his appeal's limits when he acknowledges the provision he has received from David (9:7) in spite of being a member of the previous ruling family. But that David will 'do what seems good' provides him with some hope.

30–31 [ET 29–30]. With this appeal made, David divides the estate between Mephibosheth and Ziba. This may be due to exasperation since he cannot make an informed decision. After all, experience with the Gibeonites in Josh. 9 showed that appearance might not tell the truth. Alternatively, David could wait to see who renounced their claim to determine the innocent party, in which case Mephibosheth would be innocent (Young-blood 1992: 1037). Mephibosheth is probably innocent, but the narrative is careful to show only what David knows, so however much we think Ziba or Mephibosheth have not received justice, readers face the same ambiguity as David over their claims. Mephibosheth's response could suggest he was happy for Ziba to have the whole estate, but was possibly an indirect way of accepting the offer, which points to David's magnanimity (cf. Gen. 23:10–16, Esth. 3:11, where apparently rejected offers are actually accepted). Mephibosheth is discretely ambiguous.

32–34 [ET 31–33]. The encounters move from those opposed to David to those whose loyalty is unclear until we reach those who are indisputably loyal. The pattern of 15:13 – 16:14, where David's encounters went from those most loyal to those most opposed to him, is thus reversed. As a wealthy farmer, Barzillai was one of a small collective who provisioned David while at Mahanaim (17:27–29). He too came to see David east of the Jordan and send him to Jerusalem. But we are introduced to a new element about Barzillai, which is his great age, eighty being an age few would have reached. David desired to reward his faithfulness by taking him to Jerusalem, where he would provide for him instead.

35–38 [ET 34–37]. Barzillai negotiates the delicate process of refusing a royal order (however politely put). Staying within the bounds of court etiquette, he cites his age as preventing him from going. Rather than refusing directly, he offers four questions, all of which point to age as a defining issue, into which key statements are mingled. The first question asks how long he has left to live, a question reinforced when he declares he is eighty. He then poses a second question of three parts, all of which indicate he could not properly enjoy court life since his senses of taste and hearing (cf. Eccl. 2:8) are dimmed with age. Court life is of limited value to him. This also is the force of the third question, which asks why he should be a burden to the king. Although he is prepared to go a little further across the Jordan, he finishes his questions by asking why he should receive such a reward, effectively declining it. Instead, he desires simply to die in his home town, since burial within the family tomb is important for someone of his social status (Matthews 1991: 128–130). These statements draw links with Ahithophel, who likewise died in his own town, though Barzillai is his mirror image (Fokkelman 1981: 308). In his place he offers Chimham, presumably a younger son though not mentioned elsewhere, to go in his place. He says David can do for him as he pleases, effectively suggesting he do for Chimham what he has offered him.

39–41 [ET 38–40]. Where Barzillai asked that David do what he thought right for Chimham, David responds that he will do for him what Barzillai wants. David is king again, but knows the importance of support. Thus the two bind themselves in faithfulness, a relationship based on trust and sealed with a kiss and a blessing that David gives to Barzillai, something not requiring an oath, unlike with Shimei. In his final directives to Solomon, David, because of Barzillai's loyalty, is concerned only with his sons, suggesting Barzillai had died by then (1 Kgs 2:7). Only now does David cross the Jordan and enter Gilgal, bringing Chimham with him. But an ominous note is sounded, because although David brought all Judah with him, only half of Israel came. David had his support from Judah, but this pointed to a renewed fracture between north and south that the early summary of his reign (5:17 – 8:18) indicates he sought to overcome.

Judah, Israel and David's reign: 19:42–44 [ET 19:41–43]

42 [ET 41]. The tensions between the tribes quickly surface once David is over the river. Although half of Israel cross with David, they appear to join the other members of the northern tribes since it is all Israel (i.e. the north, though probably only the soldiers; Seiler 1998: 200) which complains that Judah, although a brother tribe, has stolen David from them by bringing him and his household across the Jordan. The Israelites act only on what they know, and are apparently unaware that David initiated Judah's actions.

43–44 [ET 42–43]. Although Israel questions David, no response is recorded. As with Absalom's revolt, events occur without his intervention although he is aware of them. Instead, there is only Judah's answer, claiming a prior right to David on the grounds that he is a nearer kinsman to them than the rest of Israel, accepting David's terms from 19:13 [ET 19:12]. They therefore suggest the northern tribes have no basis for anger. Although their conclusion is difficult to interpret (see 'Notes'), they seemingly claim to have received no special treatment from David for leading the tribes in bringing him back. Israel's response claims 'ten shares' (*yādôt*) in David, probably referring to the number of northern tribes if Levi is scattered throughout. Whereas Judah claims a biological priority, Israel claims a numerical one. Moreover, Israel claims a chronological priority by being first to speak of restoring the king (19:11 [ET 19:10]). The bickering is pointless (reminiscent of Judg. 12:1–6), and Israel's claims receive a harsh response from Judah, indicating the depth of the north–south division. David may be back on the throne, but the end of Absalom's revolt has not healed the divisions he exploited. Instead, by reducing Israel's status relative to Judah (Olyan 1996: 211–212), David is more or less back where he began in 2:1–7.

Explanation

With Absalom's death, one might imagine David would march to Jerusalem and reclaim his throne. But matters were more complex than that. Although Absalom undoubtedly exaggerated his complaints, he must have accessed significant disquiet to mass the rebellion he did. Defeating Absalom did not mean David's immediate return.

Throughout, David's rule is characterized by political awareness. He was blind to his children, but had an otherwise sure touch, building up support among the marginalized (1 Sam. 22:2) and extending this support. The challenge here was winning back his former support without alienating continuing support. David had faced this issue before and resolved it (2 Sam. 1:1 – 5:16), which is why there are several allusions to those chapters. David remains the consummate politician.

Hence he responded to national discussion in 19:10–11 [ET 19:9–10] by inviting Judah to take the lead in restoring him while replacing Joab with Amasa as army commander. David began with Judah because they were his own tribe, though they were to lead the restoration, not claim him for themselves. Amasa's appointment, in spite of his ineptness for Absalom, kept the army's command within the family, but held out an olive branch to the rebels. It showed not retribution but David's concern with reconciliation. Reconciliation also holds together the three subsequent encounters. Shimei was a member of Saul's family and represented those opposed to David. By assuring Shimei he would not be executed for his curses

(16:5–13), David reached out to a known enemy. The encounter with Mephibosheth was with someone whose loyalty was uncertain, especially given Ziba's claims (16:1–4). Mephibosheth remains ambiguous, and David was faced with claims that he could not resolve, finally dividing Saul's estate between Mephibosheth and Ziba. Where no resolution was possible, David still sought reconciliation. Finally, his encounter with Barzillai was with a supporter, and here David could be generous. Barzillai knew he could not benefit personally and so arranged for Chimham to accompany David. David wanted to retain reconciliation, something evidenced by his offer to do that which Barzillai wanted. Yet, when David crossed the Jordan, conflict broke out between Judah and the north. Politics alone could not resolve the problems, even if they could help.

The reason for this lies in the narrative's larger theological agenda, though God is barely mentioned within it. David has found favour with Yahweh. His wish of 15:25 is being fulfilled, and the reversal of his encounters as he fled points to this. But the punishment stipulated that the sword should not depart from David (12:10–12). One rebellion could not fulfil that stern declaration, so the resolution of one conflict leads to another. Yahweh has responded to David's wish and prayer, and though David still needs to be astute, Yahweh's word still rules.

2 SAMUEL 20

Translation

¹There happened to be a man of Belial there whose name was Sheba ben Bichri, a Benjaminite. He sounded the trumpet and said:

'There is no portion for us in David,
  no inheritance for us with the son of Jesse.
Every man to his tents, O Israel.'

²All the men of Israel withdrew from David and followed Sheba ben Bichri, but the men of Judah stayed with their king from the Jordan to Jerusalem.

³David came to his house at Jerusalem. The king took the ten concubines he had left to keep the house and put them in the house of confinement and provided for them, but did not go in to them. They were confined until the day of their death, living as widows.

⁴The king said to Amasa, 'Summon the men of Judah for me within three days, and present yourself here.' ⁵Amasa went to summon Judah, but he delayed beyond the set time appointed for him. ⁶So David said to Abishai, 'Now Sheba ben Bichri will do us more harm than Absalom. Take your lord's servants and pursue him lest he find fortified cities and snatch our eyes.' ⁷Joab's men pursued him along with the Cherethites, Pelethites and all the warriors. They went from Jerusalem to pursue

Sheba ben Bichri. [8]When they were by the great stone at Gibeon, Amasa came to them. Joab was dressed in his military attire, and over it was a belt with a sheathed sword upon his waist. As he went forward, it fell out. [9]Joab said to Amasa, 'Is it well with you my brother?' Joab's right hand grasped Amasa by the beard to kiss him. [10]But Amasa was not alert to the sword that was in Joab's hand, and he struck him with it in the belly and spilled his entrails on to the ground. He did not strike him a second time, but he died.

Then Joab and his brother Abishai pursued Sheba ben Bichri. [11]One of Joab's lads took his stand beside him and said, 'Whoever favours Joab and whoever is for David let him follow Joab.' [12]Amasa lay wallowing in blood in the middle of the highway and the man saw everyone stopped. So he moved Amasa from the highway to a field and threw a garment over him when he saw all the people who came upon him stopped. [13]Once he was moved from the highway, all the people passed by after Joab to pursue Sheba ben Bichri.

[14]Sheba passed through all the tribes of Israel to Abel, even Beth Maacah, and all the Bichrites were gathered and followed him. [15]Joab's forces came and besieged him in Abel of Beth Maacah and they cast up a siege mound against the city and it stood by the rampart. All the people with Joab were battering the wall to bring it down. [16]A wise woman called from the city, 'Listen! Listen! Say to Joab, "Come here and I will speak to you."' [17]He came to her, and the woman said, 'Are you Joab?' He said, 'I am.' She said to him, 'Listen to the words of your maidservant.' He said, 'I am listening.' [18]She said, 'They used to say in former times, "Let them but ask in Abel and it will be resolved." [19]I am one of those who are peaceable and faithful in Israel, but you are seeking to kill off a city that is a mother in Israel. Why should you swallow up Yahweh's heritage?' [20]Joab answered, 'Far be it, far be it for me that I should swallow up or destroy. [21]That is not the case. But a man from the hill country of Ephraim, Sheba ben Bichri is his name, has raised his hand against the king, against David. Hand over him alone and I will leave the city.' The woman said to Joab, 'Behold, his head will be thrown to you over the wall.' [22]The woman went to all the people with her wisdom, and they cut off Sheba ben Bichri's head and threw it to Joab. Then he sounded the trumpet and they were dispersed from the city, each man to his tent. Joab returned to Jerusalem to the king.

[23]Now Joab was over all Israel's army, and Benaiah ben Jehoiada was over the Cherethites and Pelethites. [24]Adoram was over the corvée, and Jehoshaphat ben Ahilud was the recorder. [25]Sheva was secretary and Zadok and Abiathar were priests, [26]while Ira the Jairite was also David's priest.

Notes on the text

3. Some MSS read *wa'ălêhen* for *wa'ălêhem*, but gender confusion for f. pl. is common. The phrase *'almĕnût ḥayyût* is obscure, but suggests they were widows of the living (i.e. David).

6. Syr has Joab for Abishai, harmonizing this verse with the following. But if *'ădōneykā* refers to Joab, this is unnecessary (similarly, Smith 1899:

369). With a number of MSS and LXX read '*ăttâ* for '*ăttâ*. Read *yimṣā*' for *māṣā*'. The last phrase is difficult, but versional uncertainty suggests MT is correct, perhaps an obscure idiom, where the king's 'eyes' refers to royal control of fortified cities (R. W. Anderson 1990).

8. Joab's description is overloaded and awkward, but the sense is clear enough to retain MT (with Neiderhiser 1981). But see McCarter (1984: 427) for alternatives.

10. 4QSam[a] has the expected *rdpw* here. See LXX.

14. Move atnach back to *ma'ăkâ*. The MT's Berites are unknown and probably a corruption of Bichrites (so LXX[B]), who would be members of Sheba's family who entered the city with him (see Gordon 1986: 295). Sheba must thus be the sentence's unstated subject. With Q and many MSS read *wayyiqāhălû*.

15. The subject reverts to Joab's forces, though this is unmarked in MT.

18-19. The combination of qal inf. abs. for a verb (*š'l*) with pi. is unusual but not unattested. See GKC §113w. The awkwardness leads many (e.g. McCarter 1984: 428–429) to prefer LXX, though only after resolving inner-Gr. problems (see JB). But Gordon (1993) has shown MT can be retained.

20. Several MSS omit the second *ḥālîlâ*. This could indicate dittography in MT, but the number of doubled words in this section supports its originality.

23. As is common in Samuel, '*el* stands for '*al*. 'Cherethites' follows Q and versions for 'Cerites', which is a transcriptional error (though see 2 Kgs 11:4, 19).

Form and structure

The end of Absalom's revolt did not mean the end of Israel's political conflict. Indeed, the close of David's return to Jerusalem (19:42–44 [ET 19:41–43]) indicates the immediate political antecedent for this dispute was disagreement between Judah and the northern tribes over David on his return. However, the narrative also points to a larger theological purpose, which can be traced back to David's punishment from 12:10. Yahweh declared the sword would not depart from David's house and there would be continued violence throughout his reign. David chose violence in his attack on Uriah, whether that violence was expressed sexually with his wife, attempting to create a judicial fiction to justify execution or the murder itself (see 'Form and structure' on 2 Sam. 11). The bitter fruit David reaped was continued violence. Moreover, David's punishment was to be 'before the sun' (12:12), highlighting both the judicial justice of what David received and its public nature. The violence David began secretly is now publicly expressed. Sheba ben Bichri, the revolt's leader, may be a 'man of Belial' (20:1) whose own violence leads him to an unpalatable end, but he is also the means of demonstrating the enduring nature of David's punishment. 1 Kgs 1 – 2 (see 'Form and structure' on 2 Sam. 9) shows this continued in David's final days and beyond.

Sheba's rebellion is more briefly told than Absalom's, following the pattern of 1 Sam. 18:1 – 2 Sam. 5:5. That consisted of a long rivalry narrative (1 Sam. 18:1 – 2 Sam. 1:27, David and Saul) followed by a short rivalry narrative (2 Sam. 2:1 – 5:5, David and Ish-bosheth). There are notable parallels between this account and Ish-bosheth's. Most obviously, both Abner and Ish-bosheth were murdered by someone who struck them in the belly (*nkh* + *ḥōmeš*; 3:27; 4:6–7), the formula used when Joab murdered Amasa (20:10). Sheba, like Ish-bosheth (also Goliath and Saul) is beheaded (4:7; 20:22). The formula *nkh* + *ḥōmeš* also occurs when Abner killed Asahel (2:23), but nowhere else in the OT. Amasa's murder closely parallels Abner's (3:27), both being rivals killed by Joab. However, the parallels have one important limitation in that the previous deaths (save for Asahel) benefited David politically. This murder weakens David, since he appointed Amasa army commander in place of Joab to invite the northern tribes to rejoin him. Paradoxically, this further confirms David's complaint in 3:39 where he observed that the sons of Zeruiah were too harsh for him, and could only pray Yahweh would repay the evildoer. David discovered in his own experience that Yahweh does repay the evildoer, but still faced the problem of the power of the sons of Zeruiah, a power he could not break, perhaps because he had used it for his own ends (11:14–21).

As the second revolt narrative, it closely follows Absalom's. As well as the dispute in 19:42–44 [ET 19:41–43], it contains important links with the earlier story (see Gunn 1980b; Seiler 1998: 217). Thus ten concubines left by David (15:16–17) and raped by Absalom (16:22) are noted in 20:3 as the first issue addressed by David on his return to Jerusalem. Amasa's appointment (19:13–14 [ET 19:12–13]) may have gained northern support, but it meant Joab would act against him (20:10). The wise woman in Abel (20:16–22) echoes the wise woman from Tekoa (14:1–20) employed by Joab to convince David to restore Absalom after Amnon's murder, as well as Abigail in 1 Sam. 25. Slightly more subtly, both Absalom (14:23) and Joab (20:23) return from the same area to Jerusalem. These links show Sheba's revolt is part of a continuing story that has further reverberations in the final division of the kingdoms when Sheba's rallying cry (20:1) becomes that of the northern tribes against Rehoboam (1 Kgs 12:16). Unlike Saul, David has not lost the throne, because he accepts Yahweh's punishment, but David's house still suffers. With these links, both past and future, the second administrative list (20:23–26) closes off the larger narrative of chs. 9 – 20 by paralleling the earlier list from 8:15–18, while the sounding of the trumpet and scattering of the troops (20:1, 22) indicates that Sheba's rebellion is also complete.

Comment

Sheba's rebellion: 20:1–22

1–2. Sheba's rebellion is clearly linked with events at Gilgal at the end of the previous chapter. It is the outcome of those events rather than something independent, since the chapter's first word indicates Sheba was there. Sheba, somewhat unusually, is always described by his patronym. Bichri was possibly an important figure, and there is some evidence of association with Saul's family if we equate Bichri with Becorath (1 Sam. 9:1; see Hertzberg 1964: 371). Even if we cannot make this link with certainty, as a Benjaminite he was still someone whose sympathies were unlikely to be with David. He is characterized as a 'man of Belial', a phrase pointing to someone contemptible (see 'Comment' on 1 Sam. 2:12), perhaps because of his attempted secession. The narrator thus immediately warns us that he represents trouble. While at Gilgal, he sounded the trumpet (cf. Joab at 18:16 and 20:22), which here summons a withdrawal from David. Its meaning is made explicit in his poem on the northern tribes' share in David, contrasting with the declaration of 19:44 [ET 19:43]. Rather than claiming ten shares in David (a large majority), Sheba now asserts there is no value for the northern tribes in staying with him. This is reinforced in the poem's opening parallelism where both portion and inheritance in David are denied. Israel is the majority shareholder, but David is not an investment yielding any return. This leads to the poem's third line, which summons Israel to depart. Much the same ditty occurs at 1 Kgs 12:16 when the northern tribes separated from Judah. Sheba does not directly initiate rebellion. Instead, he tried to convince the northern tribes to secede from Judah whom he believed were favoured under David. The north's desertion and Judah's loyalty are political convictions, but military action is then almost inevitable (cf. 1 Kgs 12:21). There is some uncertainty about the claim that 'all Israel' abandoned David for Sheba since the subsequent narrative does not indicate significant support for him. It is therefore one of sympathies rather than actions, which is perhaps why David was concerned that this rebellion might be more damaging than Absalom's (20:6).

3. With rebellion declared, David returned to Jerusalem and put his house in order, putting the ten concubines left behind (15:16–17) and raped by Absalom (16:22) into confinement. Although harsh (though a concubine's lot was hardly desirable), it might indicate to the northern tribes a scaling down of court excesses. The concubines' situation is difficult to determine (see 'Notes'), but they were apparently treated as widows for the rest of their life, though this was a legal fiction. Reference to them is more than simply resolution of an outstanding issue from Absalom's rebellion, for their confinement echoes Abigail's words of 1 Sam. 25:29 (Polzin 1993: 197–198), while pointing forward to Joab's siege of Abel. David is back in Jerusalem (15:25), but it is not to a place of blessing.

4–7. Sheba remained David's principal concern, so Amasa was directed to raise a levy of the men of Judah and return in three days. The time was short, but David knew speed was essential and his standing army too small, especially if Israel's tribal levy had gone home. Amasa failed to complete the task in time. No reason is given for this, merely that he had tarried beyond the appointed time. Hence Abishai was sent out. David's instructions to Abishai indicate his concern, expressing the opinion that Sheba's revolt could be more damaging than Absalom's, perhaps because it threatened to divide the kingdoms. Joab was not directly included, though Abishai being told to take his lord's servants might be an oblique reference. Certainly, Joab is mentioned in v. 7, but it seems both Amasa and Abishai were now senior to him in the army, with David effectively promoting Abishai here. Yet subsequent events indicate Abishai saw their positions remaining as before. Whereas Amasa was to raise the tribal levy, Abishai was sent with the standing army (including the Cherethites and Pelethites, David's mercenary units) and commanded to pursue Sheba. David's initial strategy must have been for the army and levy jointly to pursue Sheba, but Amasa's delay meant Abishai's departing without the levy. The longer it took for the pursuit to begin, the more likely it was that Sheba might find shelter in a walled town and undermine David's national military strategy (see 'Notes').

8–10a. The narrative reverts to Amasa as he arrived at Gibeon and met the army by a large stone. Gibeon's mention provides an important link with 21:1–14, where it is again prominent, though the battle leading to Asahel's death was also here (2:13). This was a curious place for them to meet since it was about 6 miles north of Jerusalem, and outside the area of Judah's tribal levy, especially since the levy would be slower than the army. Since the levy is never mentioned, Amasa might have wandered around ineffectively, something consistent with his failure to use his numerical advantage at the Forest of Ephraim (18:6–8). More importantly, it enabled Joab to kill his adversary, which he did in a manner similar to Abner's murder (3:27), striking him in the belly. Cartledge (2001: 627) highlights several thematic parallels to Judg. 3:15–16, 20–26, though these may reflect a type scene. The irony is that when Joab saw Amasa, he addressed Amasa as a brother and asked if it was well (šālôm). In Abner's murder the narrator three times stresses Abner had left David in peace (šālôm). Although the exact details are uncertain because of textual difficulties in v. 8 (see 'Notes'), Joab seemingly contrived to allow a short sword to fall from his belt while greeting Amasa. Before reaching the ground he could have caught it with his left hand, and murdered Amasa while offering a greeting kiss. By greeting Amasa with his right hand, the normal weapon hand, he took Amasa unawares (Neiderhiser 1981: 210). One blow killed him, though the description of his wallowing in his blood suggests death itself was delayed.

10b–13. With Amasa murdered, but not removed, Joab resumed command of the army and set off with Abishai after Sheba, leaving one of his lads watching Amasa's body. When he set out, Joab summoned the troops to follow him. Joab's summons is remarkable in that he made a commitment to himself the mark of commitment to David. Abishai made no protest, apparently content to let Joab lead, but Joab was astute enough to draw support back to himself. Try as David might, Joab would not go quietly. But Amasa's body on the road was distracting the troops (see 2:13) from the call to follow Joab. But Joab was blessed with resourceful men, and when the man assigned to Amasa's body saw what was happening, he pulled the body off the road and covered it with a cloak. Unlike Absalom, Amasa was not even buried. What mattered was that the troops followed Joab to pursue Sheba.

14–15. Once Amasa is removed the narrative returns to Sheba (see 'Notes'). Joab's return to power is as important as Sheba's overthrow because Joab's presence points to the possibility of continued violence in David's house. Sheba had fled to Israel's far north. Abel, slightly west of Israel's classical northern border of Dan, is also Beth Maacah (with minor spelling variations in 1 Kgs 15:20; 2 Kgs 15:29; it is Abel Maim in 2 Chr. 16:4), about 85 miles from Gilgal, where Sheba's rebellion began. The double naming of the city is intriguing, since Beth Maacah associates it with the king of Geshur, suggesting (3:3) it was a town with a mixed heritage in Israel. On the way, Sheba summoned his kinsmen (see 'Notes'), but apparently not many more since no others are said to have joined him, and entered the city. Although it provided security, he could also be trapped there, the problem David narrowly avoided at Keilah (1 Sam. 23:6–14). Joab arrived and began siege warfare, for which he had significant experience (11:1; 12:26–31). This involved constructing a siege mound from which Joab's troops could batter the walls, seeking to create a breach while starving out those inside.

16–19. After his initial words, Sheba is not granted any further speech. He is disempowered as Amnon was at the end of ch. 13. He is discussed, but never allowed to speak himself. The climax of this occurs while Joab is besieging the city. A wise woman in the town initiated a conversation with Joab. The urgency of her summons is evident from the fact that in the eleven words of her first speech, four are imperatives and another is a cohortative, which has much the same effect. Joab must come and she must speak. The importance of her role as speaker is clear when Joab approaches since it is her speech that dominates. After confirming Joab's identity, she again uses the imperative, directing him to listen, though she is astute enough to style herself as Joab's maidservant. Joab accepts this, and she then quotes an apparently old proverb about the city's wisdom, claiming that the city's traditions knew how to resolve conflicts. As a city representative, she characterizes herself as peaceful and trustworthy, something she contrasts with Joab, whose actions were contrary to Deut.

20:10. Although she speaks about what Joab was doing, she effectively questions his motives because he not only sought to destroy a city with an important role in caring for the nation's life ('a mother in Israel'), he sought to destroy part of Yahweh's heritage. It is a telling accusation, because to do that meant Joab, and in effect David, surrendered the right to rule Yahweh's people. The woman's wisdom is demonstrated in the care of her argument.

20–22. Only now does Joab's speech come to prominence. Faced with this accusation, he responds with a repeated interjection of denial, picking up the woman's own words. Destruction of the city, or indeed Yahweh's heritage, was not his goal. All he sought was Sheba. But Joab can be careful in his rhetoric, because before requesting Sheba's handover he carefully outlines his identity as a man from the hill country of Ephraim (apparently, his place of residence since 20:1 indicates he was a Benjaminite), and then names him as Sheba before outlining his insurrection against King David. Only then does he name his terms: hand over Sheba and he will leave the city. The woman immediately offered to have Sheba beheaded and to deliver his head at that time the following day. Her statement's structure makes it seem as if it is already done, although it has not yet taken place. It is the certainty that is stressed, certainty reaching its ineluctable conclusion when the woman applies her wisdom instead to the townspeople who remove Sheba's head and throw it over to Joab. So Sheba comes to an ignominious end, like Absalom, with a focus on his head (Fokkelman 1981: 335), and there is no longer a secession movement. With Sheba's death, Joab sounds the trumpet, but instead of summoning the people to battle, it is time to disperse. David is again safe as king, but safe with Joab secure in his position back in Jerusalem.

David's administration: 20:23–26

23. This note concludes the rebellions against David, though hinting that this was not the end. But David is re-established, and the return of ordered government is evidence of this. This list does not begin with David (unlike 8:15–18), but since the previous chapters stressed he was king, it is now unnecessary to do so. It also means this list no longer claims David administered justice and equity. Too much has taken place to say that here. Pride of place now goes to Joab as army commander, as in 8:15, but Benaiah ben Jehoiada's place over the mercenary forces is highlighted. Joab's power is not as great as it was, but he remains significant. Benaiah not only gains fame as a mighty warrior (23:20–23) but also notoriety as Solomon's assassin in 1 Kgs 2.

24–26. A significant addition to this list is the mention of Adoram over the corvée, a significant change indicating the presence of forced labour in Israel. Solomon will develop this further (1 Kgs 4:6; 5:27–28

[ET 5:13–14]; 9:15, 21; 11:28; 12:18), though the actual practice went well back in Israel (Bergen 1996: 439). He is presumably the Adoniram of Solomon's administration whose policies contributed to the separation of the kingdoms that was avoided here. The rest of the list is similar to 8:16–18 (see comments there) except that Sheva is now secretary (unless these are variant names), the priests are now Zadok and Abiathar (as opposed to Ahimelech ben Abiathar, presumably the previous Abiathar's grandson) and David's priest is Ira the Jairite, not his sons. Ira (not mentioned elsewhere) is perhaps David's chaplain, though how we understand this relative to his sons' earlier role is unclear.

Explanation

Absalom's rebellion did not end revolt under David, but neither would we expect it to in the light of Nathan's announcement in 12:10–12. Reading this chapter, one could almost feel we are reading a variation on a theme, a riff with its own components but not adding anything especially new. Absalom rebelled and was defeated, Sheba rebelled and was defeated, and each in some way lost his head, even if one situation was a family revolt and the other tribal. But this does not do justice to this account's subtlety, which serves a larger purpose within Samuel than usually recognized.

It certainly provides a second rebellion against David, but also points to a third rebellion, one that has not erupted but leaves its threat across the whole of it. When David appointed Amasa and Abishai, he demoted Joab. Whether this was revenge for his actions against Absalom or simply a desire to rid himself of someone whose presence could be compromising is never said. But Joab was a survivor, and though content to serve David, he never allowed his own authority to be challenged. The narrator highlights this when David sent out Abishai with 'Joab's men' (20:7). Abishai's command is always limited, because these men's first loyalty was to Joab. Likewise, Joab had no compunction in murdering his cousin Amasa when he met him at Gibeon, before summoning the people to follow him, making loyalty to him the precondition for loyalty to David (20:11). From this point Joab commands David's forces, so when they reach Abel in the far north the wise woman there has no doubt she must bargain with Joab to save the city (20:16–19). Through their interaction the city is saved and only Sheba killed, so Joab can return to Jerusalem. His abiding power is confirmed as his name heads the list of David's officials as army commander. Sheba's rebellion is partly a story where the narrator can point to Joab's abiding threat even as it recounts the second rebellion against David. But the narrative's greater focus is still on Joab. David can never rid himself of his army commander because he is compromised by his own willingness to employ Joab's violence (11:14–21). The enduring sword is thus not only Sheba's rebellion, but also turns out to be Joab's abiding threat.

But this story does more than simply provide evidence of Yahweh's continued punishment of David. By providing links to the earlier rivalry story with Ish-bosheth where David refused to use violence to grasp power it further reflects on what kingship can be. David refused to grasp violence even when those around him employed it. Yahweh had to bring him the throne. Now David's private violence has spilled into the community as he becomes enmeshed in its ways. That his list of administrators no longer observes he ensured justice is thus significant. Likewise, Yahweh is barely mentioned here since this chapter is more about politics and grasping power. These absences point to where things have gone wrong, while subtly hinting at how David might put things right. It is to this that Samuel now turns.

2 SAMUEL 21:1-14

Translation

[1]There was a famine in the days of David for three years, year after year. So David sought Yahweh's face, and Yahweh said, 'There is bloodguilt upon Saul and his house because he put the Gibeonites to death.' [2]The king summoned the Gibeonites and talked with them. The Gibeonites were not Israelites but from the Amorite remnant. The Israelites had sworn an oath to them, but Saul sought to kill them in his zeal for the Israelites and Judah. [3]David said to the Gibeonites, 'What shall I do for you? With what shall I make atonement so you might bless Yahweh's heritage?' [4]The Gibeonites said to him, 'It is not a matter of silver and gold between us and Saul and his house, and neither is it for us to put a man to death in Israel.' He said, 'What are you saying I should do for you?' [5]They said to the king, 'For the man who consumed us and devised our extermination so we had no place within Israel's borders, [6]let seven of his sons be given to us and we will execute them before Yahweh at Gibeah of Saul, the chosen one of Yahweh.' The king said, 'I will give them.'

[7]But the king spared Mephibosheth ben Jonathan ben Saul because of the oath of Yahweh between them, between David and Jonathan ben Saul. [8]The king took two sons of Rizpah bat Aiah whom she had borne to Saul, Armoni and Mephibosheth, and five sons of Merab bat Saul whom she had borne to Adriel ben Barzillai the Meholathite, [9]and gave them into the Gibeonites' power and they executed them on the mountain before Yahweh, so the seven of them fell together. They were put to death in the opening days of harvest, at the beginning of the barley harvest.

[10]Then Rizpah bat Aiah took sackcloth and spread it for herself on the rock, from the beginning of harvest until rain fell upon them from the heavens. She did not permit a bird to rest upon them by day, nor a creature of the field by night. [11]When what Rizpah bat Aiah, Saul's concubine, was doing was reported to David, [12]he went and took the bones of Saul and the bones of Jonathan his son from the

leaders of Jabesh Gilead who had stolen them from the square of Beth Shan where the Philistines had fastened them on the day the Philistines killed Saul on Gilboa. [13]He brought up from there the bones of Saul and the bones of Jonathan his son, and they gathered the bones of those executed. [14]They buried the bones of Saul and Jonathan his son in the land of Benjamin at Zela, in the tomb of Kish his father. They did all the king commanded and, after this, God responded to prayer for the land.

Notes on the text

1. Confusion between *'el* and *'al* recurs. A pronominal suffix on *bêt* is expected, but the effect may be achieved through the following art. (see Simon 2000: 58–59).

2. The verb *'mr* normally introduces direct speech, but occasionally functions as a synonym for *dbr* (Gen. 4:8 MT).

4. A number of MSS and Q read the pl. *lānû* for *lî*. But the sg. is more probable, as the Gibeonites speak collectively.

6. A number of MSS support Q, probably a qal passive, but the meaning is not significantly different from K. Some LXX traditions read Gibeon rather than Gibeah, but evidence for this is slight, despite recent support for Wellhausen's emendation (see NRSV) by Anderson (1989: 247). The sense of hiph. *yq'* (cf. Num. 25:4) is uncertain. A range of means of execution have been proposed, including hanging and disembowelment, though it is probably related to being put out of joint (see *NIDOTTE* 3:521). Because of this, the neutral 'execution' is used.

8. Although most MT MSS have Michal, two read Merab, as does one LXX, Syr and Tg (though harmonizing, largely followed by AV). Michal probably crept into the tradition as Saul's better-known daughter, but was childless (6:23), while 1 Sam. 18:19 also lists Adriel as Merab's husband.

9. Read *šb'tm*, *hmh* and *bthlt* with Q and a number of MSS.

10. Confusion between *'el* and *'al* recurs.

11. On the passive construction, see GKC §121a.

14. The verb *'tr* (supplicate) occurs only here and 24:25 in Samuel, both in ni., providing another link between these accounts. Its only other occurrence in the Former Prophets is Judg. 13:8, but there in qal.

Form and structure

Sheba's rebellion (20:1–22) closed off the narrative of David's punishment for his sin against Uriah (11:1–27), but left open the possibility of further unrest in a way consistent with Nathan's announcement (12:10–12). But David has been punished for his sin and so continues to reign. Unlike Saul he will not lose the throne, because Yahweh's promise (7:15–16) overcomes his sin. Nevertheless, chs. 9 – 20 have shown a serious disjuncture between the public and private David, a disjuncture that is an important element within the overall structure of 5:17 – 24:25. As noted ('Form and structure' on 5:17–25), 5:17 – 8:14 forms an extended chiasm, containing two accounts of military success surrounding two accounts of David in worship. That chiasm focuses upon David as a public figure, especially in worship since both ark and temple represent the king as a national figure. This is carried over into the military accounts that stress David's achievements with Yahweh's help, but that ignore the part played by David's soldiers. It assesses the whole of David's reign, drawing on materials from across it, providing a positive judgment of it.

But David's assault on Uriah in 2 Sam. 11, his inability to resolve the problem of Amnon's rape of Tamar, Absalom's subsequent murder of him (2 Sam. 13) and Absalom and Sheba's rebellions (2 Sam. 15 – 20) show a different David. In that extended narrative David is judged negatively. This is because David's private life contradicts the public figure of 5:17 – 8:14. Yet Samuel presents David as Israel's model king, whom many later texts hold up as the basis for the messianic hope. How then can Samuel still present a positive assessment of David as a whole?

The answer is provided in chs. 21 – 24. Although often dismissed as 'The Samuel Appendix', and which even Fokkelman (1990: 11) judges as aesthetically displeasing (see Sternberg's 1987: 42 dismissive remarks), these chapters are more important than traditionally recognized (Firth 2001: 214–220). It has been noted at least since Budde (1902: 304) that these chapters are a carefully structured chiasm, but because they were generally treated as a miscellany (see Klement 2000a: 17–60) the reasons for this structure were not pursued (Childs 1979: 272). Yet this section structurally parallels 5:17 – 8:14:

A.   Famine, 21:1–14
   B.   Warrior stories, 21:15–22
      C.   A psalm, 22:1–51
      C^1. A psalm, 23:1–7
   B^1. Warrior stories, 23:8–39
A^1. Plague, 24:1–25

Apart from the outermost components, the chiasm mirrors that of 5:17 – 8:14, except now battles are reported through David's men, and the central psalms show David in worship himself, uniting his life's private and public elements. David the man has learnt what David the king knew already: that life is centred on knowing and doing Yahweh's will. The outermost elements also contribute since they show the relationship between private royal sin and national experience. Although David is responsible for only the plague, in both he seeks to resolve problems, and unlike Saul acknowledges his own sin (24:10). Klement (2000a: 165–166) has shown that each of the first three elements critiques Saul, providing movement within the chiasm, while Polzin (1993: 207–210) has noted the careful use of the numbers 3 and 7 (and multiples) throughout. Like 5:17 – 8:14, this chiasm is dischronologized in order to emphasize its key themes. Rather than being an appendix, these chapters are an intentional conclusion to Samuel (Klement 2000a: 147–149). This function can be appreciated through Samuel's major songs, so Hannah's Song (1 Sam. 2:1–10) and David's Thanksgiving (22:1–51) and Last Words (23:1–7) bookend the whole, pivoting on the lament over Jonathan and Saul (1:17–27). David brings together his public and private life in the songs, demonstrating a proper understanding of Hannah's Song and can thus be judged positively, in spite of his monstrous sin.

This reading differs from Brueggemann (1988; 1990b: 89–90) who, building on the same structural observations, argues these chapters deconstruct the high royal ideology developed in chs. 5 – 8. That a high ideology of royal power is developed in 5:17 – 8:14 is reasonable: the problem is the idea of deconstruction occurring here when much of 9 – 20 showed David cannot function as Yahweh's king when his own house was disordered. David has been deconstructed. The question is how he can be put back together. That reconstruction does not whitewash David (24:10), but does suggest a way forward where David submits to Yahweh (similarly, Birch 1998: 1355). These chapters offer something positive about David and kingship, though they are astute enough to know, like Samuel himself (1 Sam. 8:10–18), that kings are not always good news.

Because 21 – 24 includes narratives from across David's reign, efforts have been made to place these passages more precisely. It is often argued that 21:1–14 represents the first half of a story completed in 2 Sam. 9 (see 'Form and structure' there), but this remains uncertain and Frolov and Orel (1994) have cast doubt on its linguistic basis. More importantly, it follows Shimei's accusations (16:5–13), so the folly of those accusations has been demonstrated in the outcome of earlier events, though one can understand why he acted as he did. Because chronological markers have not been preserved, it is impossible to be more precise than observing that this is probably from earlier in David's reign when issues with Saul were more pressing. The literary context is more important for interpretation than a reconstructed history that exceeds the presented elements. Chavel's source-critical analysis (2003) also fails on this basis, though his analytical bases are not persuasive. The important question is therefore how to read this account. Brueggemann's (1990b: 336–338) reading is suspicious, with the narrative's claims set aside to suggest this is an account of self-serving politics. But what is self-serving for one generation may not be so for another, and this narrative carefully indicates that David responds only to an existing problem: he does not seek an opportunity to destroy Saul's family. It is a story of David's putting right Saul's sin, though ch. 24 shows he is perfectly capable of making his own mistakes.

Comment

1–2. The narrative opening is abrupt, making no attempt to connect to the previous story. Instead, we are told of a famine that lasted three years during David's reign. Because it includes events at Gibeon it must come from his time over Israel and Judah, but greater specificity is not possible (see 'Form and structure'). The threat posed by the famine is emphasized by the additional note that it ran year after year. In a society without the means to store significant amounts of food, a three-year famine was devastating. We are not told if the whole land was affected or not, but since Lev. 26:20 and Deut. 28:24 indicate that Yahweh would send famine on Israel for breach of faith, seeking Yahweh was the appropriate action. We are probably to imagine David's engaging in an extended period of cultic activity and prayer (see 12:16) to discern the famine's cause, seeking an oracle, though we cannot know where this was. In response, Yahweh points to an otherwise unknown act of Saul and his family against the Gibeonites where he tried to kill them. The Gibeonites were a Canaanite (specifically Amorite) group who continued to live within Israel after deceiving Joshua but were protected by their covenant relationship with Israel (Josh. 9:3–27). Such killing incurred bloodguilt, both as murder and breach of covenant. These require atonement (Num. 35:30–34), normally requited by the kinsman-redeemer (*gō'el*), but this had not occurred. Faced with this, David summoned the Gibeonites to seek a resolution. Before David's question can be given, the narrator recounts both why they were in Israel and the nature of Saul's crime. Motivated by zeal for Israel and Judah, Saul had ignored the covenant and tried to kill them, though details are lacking.

3–6. After the digression, v. 3 resumes with David's questions. That his concern is with bloodguilt's resolution is clear as they move through two stages. The first is general, asking what he should do for the Gibeonites. The second addresses the specifics, seeking the means of atonement for what has been done because of his concern that Israel, as Yahweh's heritage, should be blessed. In asking this second question, David uses the imperative to bless, a construction stressing the importance of it taking place. Offered a virtual blank cheque, the Gibeonite's response is a model of political cunning and understatement. They know they operate from a position of weakness, so although David has offered them the chance to name their price, they decline to do so. They state only that it is not a matter of money (prohibited by Num. 35:31) and it is not for them to put someone to death. Yet this makes clear that they want David to put someone to death. What matters is that they should not do it. David is not drawn in quite so easily, and asks for clarification. This time, they reveal their desire, but its mode of revelation is very careful. Rather than a direct claim, the whole of v. 5 restates Saul's crimes, going further by emphasizing he had sought genocide and not simply to kill some Gibeonites.

Although Gibeon's location close to Saul's city of Gibeah could indicate a political decision by Saul to improve his position, the narrator and Gibeonites refrain from making this claim, leaving it only as misplaced zeal. But calling it planned extermination makes it impossible that it was simply carrying a battle too far. As genocide, this was determined and planned. Only then do the Gibeonites make their atonement request, which was that seven men from Saul's family be given to them for execution before Yahweh at Saul's own town. It is unlikely that the seven cover all Saul's family, so it is probably a representative number pointing to completeness. Against genocide, it is deemed sufficient, though the means of execution is unclear (see 'Notes'). What matters is that the execution is before Yahweh, and thus both a public judicial act and one of ritual since Saul was Yahweh's chosen one. Gibeah would have been used for the executions because it was where the genocide was planned. David had made the offer, and so accepted their terms, declaring he would give the Gibeonites their request.

7-9. David could not give any descendant of Saul because of his covenant (here an 'oath of Yahweh') with Jonathan (1 Sam. 20:12-17; 21:1 [ET 20:42]). Because of this covenant's priority, David spared Mephibosheth. Instead, he took Armoni and another Mephibosheth, two of Saul's sons from his concubine Rizpah, along with five of Saul's grandsons born to his daughter Merab (see 'Notes') and her husband Adriel. Adriel is a descendant of Barzillai the Meholathite (i.e. from Abel Mehola), but this Barzillai is not the same as Barzillai the Gileadite mentioned in 17:27; 19:32–41 [ET 19:31–40]) since Abel Mehola is probably just west of the Jordan, and thus not in Gilead. Rizpah was previously mentioned as the (claimed) source of conflict between Abner and Ish-bosheth (3:7–10), while Merab had married Adriel after David declined to accept Saul's offer of her hand while he was attempting to kill David (1 Sam. 18:17–19). The details are sparse, the narrator adding only that the Gibeonites executed these seven men on the hill before Yahweh, so they died together. Their death's timing was important in the light of the famine since they were executed at the beginning of the barley harvest, which occurs in April. This was traditionally the first grain harvested in Israel and preceded the wheat harvest (see Ruth 1:22; 2:23). If famine was the issue, then the idea was to make atonement before anything could damage the harvest, though it is also possible that the timing was when the harvest would be brought in, not that there was one.

10. We now expect the famine to be resolved, but the narrator refrains from making this point, focusing instead on the more personal outcome of these Saulide deaths. Merab's response is not recorded, but Rizpah's is outlined in some detail. She took some rough cloth and spread it on the rock, apparently as a place to sit (unless it was a type of tent; so Alter 1999: 332), staying there from the beginning of the harvest through to the coming of the rains, possibly in the autumn unless unseasonable earlier rains are meant. While there, she protected the corpses by driving off birds during the day and wild animals at night (cf. Gen. 15:11). Since a proper burial was mandated even for criminals (Deut. 21:23; see Matthews 1991: 128), leaving them unburied disgraced them (Jer. 16:4; Amos 4:3). There may also be an allusion to David's words to Goliath (1 Sam. 17:44, 46), which would be fitting in the light of the next section. However, exposure of bodies was a common punishment for covenant breach, and Saul had broken covenant with the Gibeonites.

11–14. Rizpah's exemplary commitment to her family was reported to David, and, spurred to act, he collected Saul and Jonathan's bones from the leaders of Jabesh Gilead. They had rescued the corpses from where the Philistines had hung them at Beth Shan following Saul's death on Gilboa (1 Sam. 31:11–13) before burning them (see 'Comment' there). However, that apparently did not generate enough heat to destroy the bones, so David could collect them and bring them along with the bones of the seven who were executed. Although v. 14 states explicitly only that David buried Saul and Jonathan's bones in the family tomb, the gathering of the others' bones suggests they were also buried at the family tomb of Kish at Zela (Josh. 18:28; possibly Khirbet Salah, about 3 miles south of Gibeah) in Benjamin. Only now is God said to respond to entreaties for the land. Although the decision to execute members of Saul's family was judicially acceptable to resolve the bloodguilt, leaving the bodies exposed was not (against Smith 1899: 376). Justice for genocide could not add excessive punishment. David could respond to Yahweh and resolve the land's need, but he also needed the spur provided by Rizpah in her loyalty to her family (see Simon 2000: 77).

Explanation

The Conclusion's first narrative is undoubtedly one Western readers find strange and distant. Executing members of Saul's family to atone for Saul's sin seems cruel and barbaric, contrary to what we expect in the Bible. On the other hand, Rizpah's commitment to her family shows an exemplary dedication we might be encouraged to emulate. But responses are often culturally conditioned, and West (1997) has shown that readers from other contexts often respond in rather different ways. For all its horror, the execution of the seven Saulides actually limits violence, being much less than Saul enacted when attempting genocide against the Gibeonites. The execution's importance is that it simultaneously addressed Israel's covenant commitment to protect the Gibeonites and the bloodguilt generated by murder. This combination of elements is what permits the unusual circumstance of sons being put to death for their father's sin.

But the story's horror story should not distract from its larger function within the Samuel Conclusion. It demonstrates something 9 – 20 has not, that the king's sin is not only politically important; it profoundly affects national well-being in terms of its covenant relationship with Yahweh. Saul's sin was not isolated, impacting only himself and his victims. The whole nation was plunged into famine because of it and David's failure to put it right. Only when Yahweh brought covenant curses to bear did David enquire of him, and so discover the famine's cause. Faced with Saul's sin and its implications, he approached the Gibeonites to discover the means of atonement. Yet David would not let his own covenant relationship with Jonathan be breached, and so spared Jonathan's son Mephibosheth even as seven other Saulides were handed over for execution. The narrative carefully notes that their execution was not the point of resolution, as their bodies were left exposed in an act of further humiliation. This humiliation was too much for Rizpah, who camped on a rock and protected them, moving David to ensure a proper burial for the family. Only then did God respond to prayer for the land. David had to resolve the demands of bloodguilt, but could not demand humiliation.

As well as leading into the Conclusion, this narrative also comments on what has so far happened. David, as a public figure, could celebrate success because of Yahweh's presence with him, but also saw his family damaged because of his sin in ch. 11. David now sees that the king's sin, both Saul's and to some extent his own, damages the nation as well as oneself. An alignment between public position and private life is required, one that is prepared to put Yahweh's demands first.

2 SAMUEL 21:15–22

Translation

[15] Again there was battle between the Philistines and Israel. David went down with his servants to battle the Philistines, but David grew weary. [16] Ishbi Benob, who was among the giants' descendants, and whose spearhead weighed three hundred shekels of bronze and who was armed with a new sword, wanted to kill David, [17] but Abishai ben Zeruiah helped him, struck the Philistine and killed him. Then David's men swore to him, 'You shall not again go out with us to battle, so you do not quench Israel's lamp.'

[18] After this there was again battle with the Philistines in Gob. Sibbecai the Hushathite struck Saph who was one of the giants' descendants. [19] Again there was battle with the Philistines at Gob, and Elhanan ben Jair struck Lahmi, Goliath's brother from Gath: his spear shaft was like a weaver's beam. [20] Again there was battle at Gath, and there was a man of great stature with six fingers on each hand and six toes on each foot, twenty-four in all, who had also been born to the giant. [21] He reproached Israel, but Jonathan ben Shimei, David's brother, struck him. [22] These four were born to the giant in Gath, but they fell at David's hand and his servants' hand.

Notes on the text

16. With many MSS and Q, read 'Ishbi' as part of a proper name. K has *wyšbw*, which McCarter (1984: 448) derives from *šbh*, 'and captured him'. But on balance a personal name is preferable. Since spears were not made of bronze, *qênō* is probably 'his spearhead', though this depends on LXX, since *qayin* is a hapax legomenon. *hārāpâ* is a collective sg., hence 'the giants' rather than a proper name (so NIV). Maintaining the art. after *lĕ* in v. 20 is unusual, but note 1 Sam. 13:21. Anderson (1989: 253) claims GKC §35n as indicating a proper noun, but the parallels offered do not make this case. A link with the Rephaim as ancient giants (Gen. 14:5; Deut. 2:10–11, 20; 3:13; Josh. 12:4; 13:12; 17:15; 18:16; 1 Chr. 20:4, 6, 8) is thus preferred to the idea that these soldiers were devoted to the god Rapha (with *NIDOTTE* 3:1176; 4:676–678; against McCarter 1984: 449–450, see Youngblood 1992: 1059). 'Sword' is added from Syr and Vg. MT does not define the piece of new equipment. The second *mišqel* is in error, and should read *šeqel*.

18. 1 Chr. 20:4 has 'Gezer' for Gob (supported by McCarter 1984: 448), though LXX has Gath, anticipating vv. 19–20. Gezer has the virtue of being known, though that may make it suspect. H. G. M. Williamson (1982: 142) suspects Gezer is in the region of Gob, the Chronicler clarifying the location for his readers, so Gob should stand.

19. Apart from location, the reading follows 1 Chr. 20:5 since it can be shown that the Chronicles text form is earlier. First, *'ōrĕgîm* is inserted into the proper name of Jaare from the verse's end, where it properly refers to weavers, but remains as a clear marker of corruption at this point. Since Bethlehem and Lahmi (with direct object marker) are similar, they have probably been confused; but once Lahmi was removed, Goliath became the direct object (see Provan, Long and Longman 2003: 225).

20. Neither K *mādîn* (Midian?) nor Q *mdwn* (quarrel) is plausible. 1 Chr. 20:6 suggests *mdh* (stature), from which both K and Q could derive due to orthographic similarity (so Anderson 1989: 253).

21. For K Shimei, Q has Shimeah (so NIV). Both may be variants of Shammah (1 Sam. 16:9).

Form and structure

The Conclusion's second section is the first set of warrior stories. They are similar to the minor judges in Judg. 12:8–15, introducing a character and providing minimal detail with no theological colouring. This contrasts with the remaining stories in Samuel, which are generally notable for their narrative quality; whereas these four read like archival notes, which may be what they are. Yet because of the Conclusion's structure, the same is true for its parallel in 23:8–39, suggesting this section is less concerned with narrative form than basic details. If so, then the lack of detail is vital to their meaning.

These four stories all follow the same basic pattern, indicating Philistine conflict and concluding by noting which Israelite struck down the Philistine giant. The second and third stories (vv. 18–19) are briefest, with only these elements, while the first and fourth are slightly more detailed, including something about David. Accounts two to four also locate the skirmish. Remarkably, in accounts one and four a member of David's family, not David, kills the giant. The presence of Philistine giants, along with several common elements (see 'Comment'), has led to comparisons with 1 Sam. 17, where David killed Goliath. Yet although Goliath is called a 'champion', he is never called a 'giant' (*hārāpâ*), though his brother Lahmi (see 'Notes') is (v. 19). Where 1 Sam. 17 is full of narrative drama, these accounts refrain from developing any tension beyond David's weakness. It seems likely that full accounts would distract from this, and so details are kept to the bare minimum. Allusions to 1 Sam. 17 are important, but principally remind readers of Saul's time because of his importance for the Conclusion's first half (Klement 2000a: 165–166).

Commentators have spilled a great deal of ink on the question of who killed Goliath, something thrown up by MT of 21:19. The most common view is of a genuine contradiction where a minor hero's achievement (Elhanan) is assigned to David (see McKenzie 2000: 76). Various solutions have been offered, such as the suggestion that Elhanan was David's personal name and David a throne name (Honeyman 1948: 23–24), that there were two giants named Goliath or a variant, that Goliath represents a 'type' of giant (Hertzberg 1964: 387). But (see 'Notes') there are reasons for believing that a more original text is found in 1 Chr. 20:5, in which case Elhanan killed Goliath's brother Lahmi. The Chronicles text is often dismissed as a pious correction (so e.g. Smith 1899: 377) since 1 Sam. 17 claims David killed Goliath, but this was something equally known to Samuel's compilers, and they would have been unlikely to retain such contradictions. Rather than a contradiction, Samuel's compilers were content to indicate that David could not always lead in battle (see 18:3), and that the king's power perhaps lay more in his ability to generate commitment than in his personal achievements. There is therefore a fresh alignment of power. Where the previous narrative pointed to the damage kings do by misusing power, this set shows that the triumphant David of 5:17–25 and 8:1–14 succeeded because of Yahweh's presence and human loyalty. The king's public claims must be tempered by humility.

Comment

15–17. The opening suggests this short account follows another battle report that is not included here. That David was dealing with Philistines suggests a time early in his reign, but it is impossible to know whether this preceded 5:17–25. The conflict meant David and his forces went down from the hill country towards the coastal plain for battle, yet before we have any battle notice we are told David grew weary. Although a cognate has been used (16:14; 17:29), it is the first time David is unable to continue in combat. It is clear from 10:1 – 11:1 that David did not always go to war, but that these events are from earlier in his reign highlights his limitations throughout. David's position was weakened by a Philistine giant named Ishbi Benob (see 'Notes') who saw this as an opportunity to kill David. His ability to do so is indicated by his spear's bronze head weighing three hundred shekels (roughly 7 lb) and some new equipment, possibly a sword (see 'Notes'). His spear head was only half the weight of Goliath's one of iron (1 Sam. 17:7), but heavy enough to do considerable damage. David was helped by his nephew Abishai ben Zeruiah (see 'Comment' on 1 Sam. 26:6–7), who killed the giant. Consistent with each of these stories, we are not told how he did so. All that matters is the outcome. Hence his men swore that he should not continue to go to battle with them, lest in doing so he quench Israel's lamp. The lamp symbolism (*nēr*) is important for the Davidic monarchy (1 Kgs 11:36; 15:4; 2 Kgs 8:19; 2 Chr. 21:7), perhaps drawing on the tabernacle lamp (Lev. 24:2; 1 Sam. 3:3), but it also plays an important part in the Conclusion, recurring in 22:29 (with a spelling variant). There David claims Yahweh is his lamp, which itself further limits the men's claim here. They see David as crucial, but not necessarily as a warrior. His importance is his ability to guide the nation, again where the private and public roles come together.

18–19. Apart from the chronological note at the beginning of v. 18, the opening of the second and third battle accounts are worded identically. Conflict with the Philistines continued, with both battles occurring in Gob. This location is uncertain; but if the Chronicler's Gezer is indicative (see 'Notes'), it is north of the coastal plain, about 25 miles west of Jerusalem. Overcoming one giant was not the whole story. The first of these (Saph) is overcome by Sibbecai, who may be the Mebunnai in 23:27 (cf. 1 Chr. 11:29) from Hushah, about 4 miles south-west of Bethlehem. The second, Lahmi, is Goliath's brother (see 'Notes') and he is also linked to Goliath by possessing a spear like a weaver's beam (see 'Comment' on 1 Sam. 17:7). If this Elhanan is the same as the Elhanan ben Dodo of 23:24, then either Jair or Dodo was a prominent ancestor and the other his father, but it is impossible to know which.

20–22. The final account follows the standard pattern except for the location at Gath (see 'Comment' on 1 Sam. 21:11 [ET 21:10]), with this giant unnamed. At his introduction we are told he possessed six fingers and six toes on each foot, twenty-four digits in all. He acted like Goliath and reproached Israel (1 Sam. 17:10, 26), but was killed by another of David's nephews, Jonathan ben Shimei (see 'Notes'), who would be Jonadab's brother (13:3). An appended note says that all four giants were, like Goliath, associated with Gath, but died at the hand of David and his men. David did not actually kill them, but was associated with the victory because it was done through his men.

Explanation

These four battle notes about the Philistines and killing giants form an important element within the Samuel Conclusion. Although David acted against the Philistines (1 Sam. 17; 2 Sam. 5:17–25), here he is fallible, depending on his soldiers and family. These accounts provide an important commentary on 5:17–25. There he gained victory because of Yahweh's presence and his willingness to act as Yahweh directed. It is therefore possible to imagine a heroic David who did not struggle, for whom Yahweh's presence meant inevitable and easy victory. But that means staying content with the public claims of power, claims chs. 9 – 20 have shown to be questionable. Samuel does not deny those claims, but by showing David's weakness indicates instead the need for royal humility. David's men believe in having a king (v. 17), but public declarations must be reconciled to private reality. However great David's victories were, his soldiers knew other heroes were to be recognized. The king is not to claim glory, but to be one with his community, leading from within, recognizing others' gifts. Jesus affirms this, stressing the importance of servant leadership within the community of his disciples (Mark 10:45).

2 SAMUEL 22

Translation

[1]David spoke to Yahweh this song's words on the day Yahweh delivered him from the hand of all his enemies and from the hand of Saul. [2]He said:

> 'Yahweh is my cliff and my fortress and my deliverer,
> 3   my God, my rock in whom I take refuge,
>   my shield and the horn of my salvation,
>   my stronghold and my refuge,
>   my saviour – you save me from violence.
> [4]I call on Yahweh who is worthy to be praised
>   and am saved from my enemies.
>
> [5]'For the breakers of death encompassed me,
>   the torrents of Belial overwhelmed me,
>   [6]the cords of Sheol surrounded me,
>   the snares of death confronted me.

⁷In my distress I called upon Yahweh;
    yes, to my God I called.
 He heard my voice from his temple;
    my cry for help was in his ears.
⁸The earth reeled and rocked;
    the foundations of the heavens trembled
    and quaked because he was angry.
⁹Smoke went up from his nostrils,
    and devouring fire from his mouth;
    coals blazed out from it.
¹⁰He parted the heavens and came down;
    thick darkness was under his feet.
¹¹He rode a cherub and flew;
    he sped upon the wings of the wind.
¹²He made darkness around him his canopy,
    gathered waters, clouds of the sky.
¹³From the brightness before him
    coals of fire blazed.
¹⁴Yahweh thundered from the heavens,
    and the Most High put forth his voice.
¹⁵He sent forth arrows and scattered them,
    lightning, and he confused them.
¹⁶The channels of the sea were revealed,
    the foundations of the world exposed at Yahweh's rebuke,
    at the blast of breath from his nostrils.

¹⁷'He sent from on high: he took me;
    he drew me out from many waters;
¹⁸he delivered me from my fierce enemy,
    from those who hated me when they were stronger than me.
¹⁹They confronted me on my day of distress,
    but Yahweh was my support.
²⁰He brought me out to a broad place;
    he rescued me because he delighted in me.

²¹'Yahweh dealt with me according to my righteousness,
    according to the cleanness of my hands has he rewarded me.
²²For I have kept Yahweh's ways,
    and have not wickedly left my God.
²³For all his ordinances were before me,
    and from his statutes I did not turn aside.
²⁴I was blameless before him,
    and kept myself from iniquity.
²⁵So Yahweh has rewarded me according to my righteousness,
    according to my cleanness in his sight.

²⁶With the kind you show yourself kind;
   with the blameless you show yourself blameless.
²⁷With the pure you show yourself pure,
   but with the perverted you show yourself astute.
²⁸You save a humble people,
   but your eyes are on the haughty: you bring them down.
²⁹For you are my lamp, O Yahweh;
   yes, Yahweh illumines my darkness.
³⁰For by you I can leap a ditch;
   by my God I can jump over a wall.
³¹As for God, his ways are perfect;
   Yahweh's utterance is tested;
  he is a shield to all who seek refuge in him.

³²'For who is God apart from Yahweh,
   and who is a rock apart from our God?
³³God is my strong fortress;
   he sets the blameless in his way.
³⁴He makes my feet like those of a deer,
   and sets me on high places,
³⁵teaching my hands for battle,
   and my arms can bend a bronze bow.
³⁶You have given me your shield of victory;
   your condescension makes me great.
³⁷You enlarge my steps beneath me,
   and my ankles have not been shaken.
³⁸I pursued my enemies and destroyed them,
   and did not turn back until they were consumed.
³⁹I devoured them and shattered them so they did not rise:
   they fell under my feet.
⁴⁰You have girded me with strength for battle;
   you made those who rose against me bow down.
⁴¹You gave me my enemies' neck:
   I exterminated those who hate me.
⁴²They looked, but there was no saviour,
   to Yahweh but he did not answer them.
⁴³I pulverized them like the earth's dust;
   I crushed and stamped them down like the mud of the streets.
⁴⁴You delivered me from my people's contentions;
   you kept me as head of the nations;
  a people I have not known served me.
⁴⁵Foreigners came cringing to me;
   as soon as they hear, they obey me.
⁴⁶Foreigners languish;
   they come trembling from their fortresses.

[47]'Yahweh lives, and blessed be my rock,
   and exalted be my God, the rock of my salvation;
[48]the God who gives me vengeance,
   and brought down peoples under me,
[49]   and who brings me out from my enemies,
   and exalted me over those who rise against me;
   you rescued me from the violent.
[50]Therefore, I will laud you, O Yahweh, among the nations,
   and I will sing praise to your name.
[51]He is a tower of salvation for his king,
   and demonstrates loyalty to his anointed,
   to David and his seed for ever.'

Notes on the text

3. Vocalize *'ĕlōhê* as *'ĕlōhay* (so most EVV). NIV takes *ḥāmās* collectively, 'violent men', but the normal sense can stand (so ESV, NRSV, NASU), while allowing for the pl. in v. 49 (though Ps. 18:49 [ET 18:48] is also sg.).

8. Tg and Syr have 'mountains' for 'heavens', consistent with Ps. 18:8 [ET 18:7]. One normally speaks of mountains' foundations, but MT's unusual nature suggests originality.

9. Sometimes, as here, the preposition *bĕ* means 'from'. This is its normal sense in Ugaritic.

11. With very many MSS and Q, read *d'h* for *r'h* (see Ps. 18:11).

12. For *skwt* read *sktw* by metathesis (Youngblood 1992: 1078; see Ps. 18:12 [ET 18:11]).

23. The pl. 'ordinances' is found in Q and many MSS (see Ps. 18:23 [ET 18:22]).

25. Many MSS refer to 'cleanness of hands', conforming with v. 21 and Ps. 18:25 [ET 18:24]. But because this is a standard form, the shorter text is more likely original. Cross and Freedman (1953: 28) omit the verse because of similarities with v. 20, but lack MS support.

27. Read *ptl* with two MSS (so BDB; see Ps. 18:27 [ET 18:26]). MT *tpl* results from metathesis. *ptl* is otherwise 'to twist' (Gen. 30:8; Job 5:13; Prov. 8:8), and can be negative, but appears positive here; hence 'astute' (so NASB).

28. Vocalize *'et* as *'attā*, a defective spelling of the pronoun, since the *nota objecti* is rare in poetry.

30. The verb *rwṣ* + object is anomalous. McCarter (1984: 469) emends to *dwṣ* (a minor orthographic change, similar to v. 11; see Job 41:14) with the sense 'leap', thus paralleling *dlg*, 'jump'. In this way, *gĕdûd*, understood as something cut in and hence a defensive 'ditch', contrasts with *šûr*, 'wall'. Craigie (1983: 170) toys with *rṣṣ*, 'crush', but McCarter's solution is preferable.

34. Read 'my feet' (MT 'his feet') with many MSS and Q (see Ps. 18:34 [ET 18:33]). Read *bāmôt* for *bāmôtay*, the yod being a dittograph.

35. Lack of concord in gender and number between the verb *niḥat* and 'arms' is explicable (GKC §145o).

36. McCarter (1984: 471) treats *māgēn* as 'gift', drawing on Ugaritic *mgn*. While plausible, and the poem shows evidence of Ugaritic influence (see Cross and Freedman 1953: 24), its use of military language suggests that 'shield' is appropriate (see v. 3). Ps. 18:36 [ET 18:35] inserts 'your right hand sustains me' between the lines here, but is secondary (McCarter 1984: 460).

46. Read *ḥrg* for MT *ḥgr* (see Ps. 18:46 [ET 18:45]).

47. Vocalize *'ĕlōhê* as *'ĕlōhay* (so most EVV).

51. Read *migdôl* with many MSS and Q (see Ps. 18:51 [ET 18:50]). K *migdîl* is possible, but we probably have a closing fortress reference, balancing those in vv. 2–3, 33 (similarly, Fokkelman 1990: 394–395).

Form and structure

We now reach the Samuel Conclusion's inner segment, an element balanced by David's 'Last Words' in 23:1–7. These poems comment on David's story through personal reflection on David's life and experience. Both poems are seemingly ancient, employing archaic forms (see esp. Cross and Freedman 1953 on 2 Sam. 22), though the question of what is archaic and what is an archaism remains. Nevertheless, a date in the tenth century cannot be ruled out (allowing for updating in some spelling), and is perhaps more probable. But the key is to recognize the poem's function within Samuel's literary structure, where it provides both an inner segment of the Conclusion's chiasm and, along with 23:1–7, a boundary marker on Samuel as a whole through its parallels with Hannah's Song (1 Sam. 2:1–10; see Fokkelman 1990: 354; Simon 2000: 247–248; Watts 1992: 24). These outer poetic blocks pivot around David's lament over Saul and Jonathan in 1:18–27, with several verbal links between them. These links show the poem is not only vital for interpreting the Samuel Conclusion, but also for the structure of Samuel as a whole (Koorevaar 1997: 71). These poems witness to David's personal faith, contrasting with its public expression in 2 Sam. 6, but this testimony has wider implications.

2 Sam. 22 is virtually identical to Ps. 18, though 2 Sam. 22 has more defective spelling. Psalms occurring in multiple locations are common, even within the psalter itself. With minor variations, Ps. 14 is the same as Ps. 53, and Ps. 40:13–17 as Ps. 70, while Ps. 108 combines Pss 57:7–11 and 60:5–12. 1 Chr. 16 also draws together several psalms. This suggests that several psalm collections were made and used by different groups, with the current psalter resulting from an extensive editing process (Howard 2005: 24–29). But these texts all show evidence of editing

relevant to their current location. Hence Ps. 53 prefers Elohim, whereas Ps. 14 uses Yahweh; but this is typical of the so-called Elohistic Psalter (Pss 42 – 83), which shows a heavy preference for Elohim. Just as many hymns are rewritten for contemporary usage, so also these psalms were adapted for local liturgical conditions. It is unsurprising, therefore, to find some differences between these texts that are related to their present location, because both have had minor changes wrought for their present use (see Adam 2001: 145–203). Rather than one of these being borrowed from the other, and so to be corrected by it where variants occur (noting Tsumura's 1999: 393–397 cautions about variants), they are probably derived from a common source (tentatively 'Royal War Songs') and then integrated into their present position. Therefore, although one can recognize transcriptional errors by comparing the two, we cannot create a hybrid that may never have existed (similarly, Fokkelman 1990: 389). 2 Sam. 22 has its own textual history, separate from Ps. 18, which must be respected.

The poem can be classified as a royal thanksgiving, where three main areas of praise are bounded by an opening (vv. 2–4) and concluding (vv. 47–51) statement. Within these boundaries the poem describes a theophany (vv. 5–20) and Yahweh's reliability (vv. 21–31) before reflecting on Yahweh's actions for David (vv. 32–46). Fokkelman's strophic analysis (1990: 334–336) largely agrees with these divisions. McCann (1996: 746) notes a similar structure, while emphasizing the poem's eschatological thrust. Although some suggest the poem is composite (see Kleer 1996: 19–20), its unity has also been defended (see Adam's summary [2001: 30–36], though he opts for development), and a unified reading poem is generally more persuasive (following Kuntz 1983: 19–21). Here it is presented as David's reflection on what Yahweh has done for him, expressing his personal faith in Yahweh. This is important given the scarcity of references to Yahweh since ch. 12, whereas both this poem and 23:1–7 are thoroughly theocentric (see Watts 1992: 104). Although it is impossible to place this psalm precisely, reference to Saul suggests it is from early in David's reign, whereas 23:1–7 is clearly late. Together, they indicate that David has learned his lesson and put Yahweh back at the centre. David again knows that his achievements are only through Yahweh. This is why the poem closes with the hope of a future for David and his descendants.

Comment

Context and opening praise: 22:1–4

1. Where David was silent in 21:15–22, we now encounter his longest utterance, its length (365 words in Hebr.) emphasizing its importance for the whole book (Bergen 2003: 374–376). Although David is not mentioned directly for much of the psalm, his importance for its interpretation is stressed by his mention here and in the last line of v. 51, creating a Davidic envelope for it. David is said to have recited the song on the day Yahweh delivered him from Saul and all his enemies. We know of no single day when this was so unless it was his accession day for Israel and Judah (5:1–5), and so early in his reign. That he spoke the song could mean he was taking up an existing royal song suitable to his position rather than being the composer. However, the psalm's key theme is established here; David responds to what Yahweh has done for him. What David has done himself is less important. Yahweh's deeds are crucial.

2–4. The opening omits Ps. 18's first line with its affirmation of commitment to Yahweh, focusing instead upon Yahweh's character. The poem piles up protective epithets for Yahweh. The language of Yahweh as a 'cliff' or 'rock' is common in the Psalms ('cliff', Pss 31:4 [ET 31:3]; 42:10 [ET 42:9]; 71:3; 'rock', Pss 19:15 [ET 19:14]; 28:1; 73:26; 89:27 [ET 89:26]; 92:16 [ET 92:15]; 94:22; 144:1; see Obinwa 2006: 169–170), and typically relates to his saving power. Such language is matched by statements about Yahweh as refuge, shield or fortress, again pointing to his protective ability. Yahweh's protection is not just passive because he is also said to have delivered David, so he can be described as a 'horn of salvation'. The language of both rock and horn echoes Hannah's Song (1 Sam. 2:2, 10). There Yahweh was Hannah's rock who exalted his anointed's horn, whereas here his anointed reflects on Yahweh as the horn, or source, of power. Salvation language recurs in v. 51, pointing again to the psalm's envelope construction. As a commentary on David's experience, it echoes the times he was delivered from Saul in the wilderness (1 Sam. 23:19 – 24:22 [ET 23:19 – 24:23]; 26:1–25), while Yahweh's saving David from violence refers both to Saul's attempts on his life (18:10 – 19:24) and times where David was saved from violence himself (1 Sam. 25). David knows Yahweh is worthy of praise, because he has called on him in the past and Yahweh has acted for him.

Theophany and deliverance: 22:5–20

5–7. A time when Yahweh's saving power was summoned is recounted. The language is stereotyped, making it impossible to note a specific moment, though this is appropriate to a thanksgiving that reflects several moments of deliverance. Reference to water, and especially waves, to symbolize all that is threatening is frequent in Pss 42:8 [ET 42:7], 88:8 [ET 88:7], though waves are here paralleled to cords and snares, things that encompass someone. The breakers and snares are associated with death, with which Sheol is a natural link as the place of the dead, possibly those under divine judgment (Johnston 2002: 79–83). Association with Belial's cords (personifying that opposed to Yahweh; see Simon 2000: 221) is more unusual, though parallel constructions (Pss 41:9 [ET 41:8]; 101:3; Nah. 1:11) confirm that the emphasis is on that which is contrary to Yahweh's will. The exact distress is not stated, but its severity is emphasized. It was from this that David called upon Yahweh and had his cry heard, with the two references to the cry balanced by two references to Yahweh's hearing. Yahweh heard from his temple, which is not Jerusalem but the place where the ark was, as in 1 Sam. 1 – 3, where a temple in Shiloh is mentioned – unless the heavenly sanctuary is in mind (so Gordon 1986: 305).

8–11. Yahweh's response is described in an extended account of his coming to help, drawing on the Sinai theophany (Exod. 19:16–20; see Niehaus 1995: 302–304), a standard evocation of Yahweh's saving presence (Hab. 3:1–16; but see its subversion in Mic. 1:2–7). The language is pictorial, describing the coming of a powerful storm before which all creation trembles since the storm's power signifies Yahweh's anger against those causing his servant distress. Smoke as a sign of anger and the consuming fire point back to Sinai, while the smoke is perhaps linked to the gloomy darkness said to be under his feet as the wind appears to tear open the heavens (see Ps. 144:5; Mark 1:10). Yahweh is said to have come with these symbols of power, riding swiftly with the wind's power on a cherub, a winged angelic being (Gen. 3:24; 1 Kgs 6:23–35). However, the more immediate link is with the ark, with 1 Sam. 4:4 and 2 Sam. 6:2 referring to Yahweh as enthroned on the cherubim on the ark. These allusions also point to the threat of divine presence since both were points where failing to recognize Yahweh's holiness brought judgment.

12–16. Yahweh's coming points to the arrival of power that is both threatening and hopeful, as is evident from his impact on creation. Allusion to a storm is again clear in the gathering waters and dark storm clouds, while the coals of fire that blaze forth and the scattered arrows allude to lightning. Nothing can stand before the storm's power, so creation's bottom elements are exposed, the channels of the sea perhaps being the entrance to the underworld (McCarter 1984: 467). The powerful wind, which is merely Yahweh's breath, is greater than all creation. Yet in the midst of this coming we are told that Yahweh thundered from heaven, language evoking Hannah's Song (1 Sam. 2:10) and Yahweh's thunder that overcame the Philistines (1 Sam. 7:10). Nothing can withstand Yahweh's power when he comes.

17–20. Theophanic language is still employed, but now applied to Yahweh's actions for David. These actions, generating distress in vv. 5–6, relate to the context and create an inclusion within this section. Yahweh is said to have sent from on high and drawn David back from the power of waters threatening to overwhelm him, with the powers of death now described as his enemies. Because of Yahweh, they could not overcome David, even though they were more powerful than him. Within Samuel this points to the time in the wilderness when Saul could not catch David (1 Sam. 23 – 26), even with superior forces. Yahweh's support meant

David survived, and ultimately triumphed. This triumph is described as being led out to a broad space, contrasting with the distress of v. 7 (*ṣar*), which is lit. being 'pressed in'. Deliverance is into a place of freedom, freedom David enjoys because of Yahweh's delight in him, presumably as the man after Yahweh's heart (1 Sam. 13:14). This delight also answers David's prayer of 15:26 (Carlson 1964: 251).

Yahweh's reliability: 22:21–31

21–25. The reason for Yahweh's deliverance is now stated: David has received the reward of righteousness. Dealing with people according to their righteousness is related to the prayers of the accused in the Psalms (e.g. 7, 17, 109, 139; see Firth 2005c: 17–50). There a petitioner asks to be judged by Yahweh according to his righteousness (or innocence, Ps. 7:9 [ET 7:8]) because an accusation was false. This took place in the sanctuary as the final site for appeals (Deut. 17:8–13). The language here (perhaps also Pss 66, 138) expresses thanks because Yahweh has rendered a just judgment. The storm theophany from vv. 6–16 is left behind, but Yahweh's presence remains central. This background provides a framework for the thanksgiving's language that might otherwise seem ironic in the light of David's assault against Uriah and the resulting complications. Both righteousness and clean hands (Ps. 24:4) are associated with specific situations, not general declarations. David's claim of having kept to Yahweh's ways, and specifically those of Torah, is not a general claim but specific to the setting established in v. 1. Twice (1 Sam. 24, 26) David could have killed Saul, but twice refused. Likewise, since he refused to benefit from violence, he twice executed those who claimed to have killed on his behalf (1:11–16; 4:9–12). In Samuel the claim is that David received the reward of the kingdom because he refused to seize it. Yet even as this is highlighted, placing this poem after events concerning Uriah is an ironic reminder of what David has also done. There is a positive statement by and about David and an ironic criticism of him, criticism that knows David has been both punished and forgiven (see Hertzberg 1964: 396).

26–31. The emphasis moves from David's righteousness to Yahweh's reliability. Each line of vv. 26–27a takes a noun describing the faithful and then uses the cognate verb to show that Yahweh responds to them in the same way, though vv. 21–25 also claim he has done this for David. This suddenly ends in 27b where the focus switches to the perverted, the untrustworthy (Prov. 11:20; 17:20; 19:1; 28:6) with whom Yahweh shows himself astute (see 'Notes'). The perverted twist things one way, but Yahweh twists them back. The importance of this is emphasized when v. 28 asserts that Yahweh saves a humble people, whereas he brings down the proud (see Ps. 138:6). This offers a conceptual parallel to the previous verse in terms of Yahweh's concern for the weak, but also prepares for

vv. 29–30, which focus on what knowing Yahweh means for David. Where his men called him the 'lamp of Israel' (21:18), David now asserts that Yahweh is his lamp, shining in his darkness and enabling him to overcome his enemies' defences (see 'Notes' on v. 30). Shining light enables David to see, but with Yahweh's help defensive ditches and walls cannot restrain him. Where the previous section moved from describing Yahweh's coming in general terms and applying it to David's experience, this section begins and ends with such application. This is built around Yahweh's reliability, his character being reaffirmed as trustworthy and secure in v. 31 with the three metaphors of 'perfect in his ways', 'tested utterance' and a 'shield' all building around this central theme. David knows this from experience.

Yahweh as deliverer: 22:32–46

32–35. The poem's third section begins by describing Yahweh's nature and actions. The questions of v. 32 are rhetorical, stressing that there is no God but Yahweh, and the rock imagery points back to the opening assertions (v. 3) and forward to the double affirmation that Yahweh is a rock in the concluding praise (v. 47). The image of Yahweh as a rock (*ṣûr*) is pivotal, reflecting several texts such as Deut. 32:4, where the image points to Yahweh's justice. But the rock as a symbol of security is more evident here, and continues in Yahweh's description as a fortress, though this blends into a series of statements in vv. 33b–35 that describe his deeds. The first of these, placing the blameless in his way, echoes Yahweh's characterization in v. 31, and points to Yahweh as both protector and guide of his people. This is seen in how he sets his people in secure places (see Hab. 3:19), the reference to the hind's feet alluding both to their ability to reach otherwise inaccessible places on the mountains and David's lament over Saul and Jonathan (1:19, 25). Provision is also seen in granting the ability to use a bronze bow, probably referring to a binding on an early composite bow rather than its whole construction. There is also parallelism between the hands and the feet, suggesting Yahweh's total provision for David. Taken in the light of this section's opening claim, it is not only that Yahweh keeps David, but also that there is no other divinity of whom this can be said.

36–37. David directly addresses Yahweh, pointing to specific things he has done for him. Indeed, the balance of this section alternates between statements of what David has done and what Yahweh has done for him. The shield of victory is linked to the tower of salvation with which the psalm ends, but victory comes through Yahweh's condescension, that is, through his deeds which cannot be attributed to David's merit. This contrasts with vv. 21–25, again showing that those verses do not refer to David's character in general. Yahweh's condescension has given David victory and power (e.g. 8:1–14), something affirmed by the mention that David's steps have been enlarged, giving him freedom to act. This is not David's achievement, but Yahweh's. Reference to the shield (and bow in v. 35) links this poem with David's lament over Saul and Jonathan (1:21–22), perhaps suggesting that Yahweh's ultimate defeat of Saul has given David security.

38–39. Having described Yahweh's deeds for him, David now describes some of his own military exploits. The terminology is stereotyped, so it is difficult to point to any specific moment, but the context within Samuel points to victories such as those in 5:17–25. The crucial point is not that David has achieved these victories, but rather that he describes them in thanksgiving because they have been achieved through Yahweh.

40–42. The emphasis returns to Yahweh's actions for David in contrast to others. Yahweh has granted David strength for battle (notwithstanding 21:15), but this was matched when Yahweh gave the enemies over to David. David had claimed this to Goliath in 1 Sam. 17:45–47, in whose case the claim of extermination was not mere rhetoric, and was demonstrated again in 5:17–25. David could look to Yahweh with hope, but his enemies are ruled out from the right of appeal to Yahweh by the statements of vv. 26–28.

43. A final statement of David's acts is the concluding response to Yahweh's deeds. A series of metaphors related to treading down dust are applied to David's actions against the enemies, though the context insists this was achieved only because of what Yahweh did for him.

44–46. The section on Yahweh as deliverer closes by again pointing to what Yahweh has done for David. As is evident for much of this psalm, the claims are typical rather than specific, but receive new meaning because of their placement within Samuel. Thus when David declares that Yahweh has delivered him from his own people's contentions, the larger context suggests that reflection on the revolts of Absalom and Sheba is appropriate, though earlier events such as David's escape from Keilah (1 Sam. 23:7–14) are also relevant. That David has been kept as head of nations not only prepares for a pair of references to foreigners, but also draws on his victories in 8:1–14, though the processes through which that happened is also evidenced in 21:15–22. Hence David now reigns over a significant body of nations where foreigners come to do his bidding, such as is seen in 8:9–10. Yahweh's presence with David as deliverer and the one granting victory has thus been recognized by more than Israel alone.

Concluding praise: 22:47–51

47–49. The poem's closing section draws together the main themes of the whole. Yahweh lives and is the rock who provides security, and is therefore blessed and exalted. The double reference to the 'rock' builds on two earlier references (vv. 3, 32), though describing Yahweh as 'the rock of my salvation' also draws on Deut. 32:5, while blessing Yahweh as rock also occurs in Ps. 144:1. These themes are applied here to Yahweh as the God who gives vengeance and places peoples under David. This is not to claim that Yahweh acts simply to bring revenge, for his vengeance is related to his just rule as king (Peels 2003: 81; see Deut. 32:31–43). David can rule because Yahweh overcomes those who, like Absalom and Sheba, rise against David with violence.

50–51. The psalm concludes with David's praising Yahweh, though this praise is not restricted to Israel but is praise sung to Yahweh's name (representing his character) among the nations (Rom. 15:9). This reference alludes again to David's speech in 1 Sam. 17:45–47, where he claimed that Goliath's forthcoming defeat testified to the whole world. Israel's existence was for all creation, and therefore David's praise must be sung before the nations. That praise's content is outlined again in the final verse, which again alludes to Hannah's Song (1 Sam. 2:10) with its dual reference to Yahweh's 'king' and his 'anointed'. The terms are largely synonymous, but the combination occurs only in these two verses in Samuel, though here they are specifically focused on David and his descendants. Reference to David's descendants echoes 7:11–16 and in turn prepares for reference to David as 'anointed' in 23:1. Yahweh is described as a tower of salvation for his king, language pointing back to v. 2, while his loyalty (*ḥesed*) links to v. 26, tying the whole psalm together. The psalm's eschatological orientation is that it looks back on what Yahweh has done for David, and simultaneously waits for what he will do for his descendants in the light of 2 Sam. 7.

Explanation

This chapter forms one part of the Samuel Conclusion's centre. Its extended poetic form marks it out as important since it breaks with narrative and instead testifies to Yahweh's dependability and goodness. Here David recites the poem's words, and in so doing offers a reflective commentary on all of Samuel, a commentary that joins Hannah's Song (1 Sam. 2:1–10) and David's lament over Saul and Jonathan (2 Sam. 1:18–27) in providing the book's central themes. Power and success, especially for kings, is not found in military prowess. Rather, the king's hope (and that of his subjects) is found when the king submits to Yahweh's reign and discovers that all necessary resources are found in Yahweh. This is consistent with Samuel's farewell speech (1 Sam. 12).

Placing of these words here creates a dialogue with the rest of Samuel. Most immediately, within the balancing chiasms of 5:17 – 8:14 and 21:1 – 24:25 they comment upon David as both warrior and worshipper. The battle accounts in 5:17–25 and 8:1–14 could suggest that David was irresistible as king, although even there the theme was tempered by noting

Yahweh's presence. Similarly, the worship in 2 Sam. 6 – 7 is full of public activity, and though we have both David's dance (6:14–15) and prayer (7:18–29), the focus is on public performance rather than private faith. Yet here David offers testimony that points to Yahweh's awesome power, insisting that whatever has been achieved has happened because of Yahweh. In particular, Yahweh responded to David's cry for help and made all his power evident, power no king could overcome. There is no scope for personal aggrandisement, for all power belongs to Yahweh.

The psalm also reflects on the rest of Samuel because so many of its allusions take concrete form in David's flight from Saul and refusal to kill him and Absalom, and Sheba's rebellions against David. These allusions provide a rich tapestry against which to read the psalm and join David in his thanksgiving. That the psalm is said to reflect his deliverance from Saul and all his enemies (v. 1) encourages such a reading. Throughout his life, David has found Yahweh to be trustworthy and faithful. The heart of the psalm (vv. 21–31) reflects on this in terms of David's own righteousness, though somewhat ironically in the light of his attack on Uriah (2 Sam. 11; cf. 1 Kgs 15:5). But David does not claim perfection. Rather, he has discovered Yahweh's grace, grace that has sustained his reign through forgiveness. It is because of grace that David offers praise, even as he looks to what Yahweh will continue to do through his descendants. This hope is echoed in several texts in the OT, but comes to its fulfilment in Jesus (Matt. 1:6–17), the Son of David who submitted himself to God in ways beyond David's (Heb. 5:7–10).

2 SAMUEL 23:1–7

Translation

[1]These are David's last words:

'The oracle of David ben Jesse,
   the oracle of the man God raised up,
the anointed of the God of Jacob,
   the delight of the Songs of Israel.
[2]The Spirit of Yahweh speaks by me;
   his word is upon my tongue.
[3]The God of Israel said,
   the Rock of Israel spoke to me,
"One who rules folk justly,
   one who rules by the fear of God,
[4]is like the light of the morning as the sun rises,
   a morning with no clouds,
      as grass sprouts at the brightness after rain."

⁵For is not my house thus with God?
  For he has established an eternal covenant with me,
    ordered in all things and secured.
 Will he not cause to prosper,
    all my welfare and desire?
⁶"But Belial is like thorns:
    all of them will be thrust away,
    for they cannot be taken with the hand.
⁷But the man who touches them
    is armed with iron and the shaft of a spear,
    and they are utterly consumed with fire on the throne."'

Notes on the text

1. Read *'l* rather than *'l* with 4QSamᵃ's probable text (see Starbuck 1999: 181). McCarter (1984: 480) derives *zĕmirôt* from a root meaning 'stronghold' (see NRSV), but its attestation is debatable, whereas 'song' is well established, and none of the possibilities for 'stronghold' in *DCH* (Exod. 15:2; Isa. 12:2; Ps. 118:14) is definite. Since songs often praise Yahweh, this could be a divine title, though deliberate ambiguity is possible.

2. *rûaḥ* is normally f., but can be m., making emendation unnecessary (with Simon 2000: 275).

5. *kî lō'* could be asseverative (so Smith 1899: 382; Richardson 1971: 265; Anderson 1989: 267), but taking it as a rhetorical question leads to a similar interpretation.

6. Using Belial on its own is unusual (see 'Comment'), but subsequent plurals referring back to it means it still draws on the idiom 'sons of Belial'.

7. For *ml'* meaning 'to arm oneself', see 2 Kgs 9:24. *bašābet* is widely deleted, but Starbuck (1999: 182) makes an important link, noting how it can refer to a throne. This creates a minor inclusion with v. 1, which also points to royal terminology. Naeh (1996) draws on rabbinic literature to suggest the word is associated with destruction by heat, but this is less likely because of the gap between this text's composition and his rabbinic sources.

Form and structure

This brief poem commences the movement out from the centre of the chiasm of the Samuel Conclusion (see 'Form and structure' on 21:1–14). There are both links and distinctions with the preceding chapter, a feature typical of the different psalm groups within the psalter. Indeed, this poem also features in a Qumran Psalms collection (11QPsᵃ), so the presence of features common to the psalter's formation in 22:1 – 23:7 is unsurprising. The most obvious link between these poems is that the last verse of ch. 22

and the first verse here refer to David as anointed (*māšîaḥ*), while the concluding reference to David's offspring in 22:51 is paralleled by mention of David's house in 23:5. More surprising links in vocabulary include speaking of the worthless (*bĕlî'al*; 22:5, 23:6; left untranslated as Belial) and various pieces of military equipment. These also point to Hannah's Song (1 Sam. 2:1–10) and David's lament over Saul and Jonathan, both of which include 'anointed' (*māšîaḥ*; 1 Sam. 2:10; 2 Sam. 1:24), discussion of man/warrior (*gbr*; see Firth 2007: 79–80) and reference to military equipment. One should also note that immediately after Hannah's Song we are introduced to Eli's sons, who are 'sons of Belial' (1 Sam. 2:12). The close links both bind 22:1–51 and 23:1–7 and point to the rest of Samuel, especially the main songs, as the context for interpretation. Other links between 22:1–51 and 23:1–7 are thematic, but it is notable that allusions to 2 Sam. 7:3–17 build through ch. 22, and become explicit in 23:1–7. Yet there is also deliberate disjunction between these poems. This is established by their headings, with 22:1 pointing towards David's earlier reign, while 23:1 indicates that this poem is from the end of his life, perhaps his final public words. Hence they provide an overview of David's reign. Apart from this, we noted ('Form and structure', 21:1–14) that the first half of the Samuel Conclusion emphasized Saul, whereas the second half focuses only on David as king. The change in title flags this shift's beginning.

The poem is presented as an oracle showing considerable similarities with those of Balaam (Num. 24:3–9, 15–19), especially the use of *nĕ'um* ('oracle'; 23:1; Num. 24:3, 15; only in Ps. 36:3 and Prov. 30:1 is *nĕ'um* used of anyone speaking other than God), and links this to the oracle giver's identity. Balaam's oracles are often regarded as among the most ancient poems in the Bible (see Ashley 1993: 437–440), and it is unsurprising that this poem is usually regarded as quite ancient, possibly tenth century BC (Richardson 1971: 257), making Davidic attribution plausible (similarly, Gordon 1986: 309). This would be consistent with ch. 22, suggesting these poems were joined very early. Because the poem is cast as an oracle, it takes a prophetic form, making this not only David's personal claims, but also an announcement of Yahweh's word and David's response to it. This word is closely tied to 7:1–17 (Firth 2005b: 97–98), pointing again to how 5:17 – 8:14 and chs. 21 – 24 interpret one another. Characterizing David as a prophet contrasts with Saul (1 Sam. 10:10–13; 18:10; 19:22–24), where prophecy consisted of ecstatic experiences. By contrast, David is a prophet of the word (against Noll 1997:154).

Comment

1. The heading sets this piece off from the surrounding text. David's last words are probably not a deathbed recording but a final public statement. This heading combines with 22:1 to show that the songs at the Samuel

Conclusion's heart represent David's reflection on all his reign. The heading introduces the poem, but its content is surprising since its opening word (nĕ'um) is typically part of a prophetic oracle. As noted ('Form and structure'), the closest parallel is found in Balaam's oracles, which also employ 'oracle' (nĕ'um) at the start of successive poetic lines (Num. 24:3–4, 15–16), while identifying the speaker by name and patronym in the first line before commenting on the speaker as a man (geber). David's last words differ in having only two lines of introduction as opposed to the three of Balaam, but the parallels are otherwise close (see Starbuck 1999: 186–189). David's words are thus presented as a prophetic oracle that simultaneously looks to the past and the future. This prophetic character matches David's last words to Hannah's Song (1 Sam. 2:1–10), which, though not called an oracle (nĕ'um), is clearly prophetic. Yet David's oracle also differs from Balaam's since where Balaam claims God enables him to see, David speaks of what God has done for him as the one whom God raised up, an expression that receives further definition in that David is God's anointed, a title that, though previously associated with Saul (at 19:22 [ET 19:21] and 22:51) was applied to David. The verse's final line is enigmatic, perhaps deliberately so (see 'Notes'). As the delight of Israel's praises, David can be understood as the one Israel loves to include in her praises, such as the song in 1 Sam. 18:7. But it is also possible that Israel's praises is a divine title that parallels 'God of Jacob', in which case David is the one in whom God delights. It is unnecessary to decide between these options, because the ambiguity employed enables David to claim that both are true.

2–3a. Consistent with the prophetic form, four lines describe Yahweh's speaking through David, meaning the introduction's four lines are matched by four lines emphasizing the revealed nature of David's message. Though the lines are largely parallel, each adds depth to David and Yahweh's presentation. There is a small inclusion within the section in that the first and last lines both use *dibber* (spoke) plus a preposition with first person suffix. The opening claim is that Yahweh's Spirit speaks through David, a statement pointing to the oracle's authority while alluding to the Spirit's rushing upon him at his anointing and remaining with him in contrast to the Spirit's departure from Saul (1 Sam. 16:13–14). The second line claims Yahweh's word is on David's tongue, though 'word' (millâ) is an unusual Aram. (or at least, non-Judahite term; so Rendsburg 1988: 117–118), occurring in only Pss 19:5 [ET 19:4], 139:4 and Prov. 23:9 outside Job, where it is quite common. Even in Job it occurs only in poetic texts, but nowhere else does it refer to God's word. The third line is more general, affirming that Israel's God spoke, which is balanced by the claim that the Rock of Israel (another divine title; see 'Comment' on 22:3) had spoken to David. Hence v. 2 makes a general claim about Yahweh's speaking through David, whereas v. 3a indicates that the poem is about to announce something specific Yahweh has said. David can be understood as a prophetic vehicle for Yahweh's message, and the following text is an example of it.

The divine epithets point to Yahweh's empowering presence (his Spirit) and his strength (the Rock), with the empowering presence being something that endures. Thus the poem's authority and David as the vehicle of Yahweh's message are emphasized.

3b–4. After the build-up of the opening verses, we now receive the actual message given by Yahweh to David. It now becomes clear why this message was spoken to David rather than simply by him since it addresses the work of those who rule (*môšēl*). The first two lines effectively summon David to rule justly (*ṣādîq*) and in the fear (reverence) of God, though it is expressed indirectly. The exercise of justice was said to be integral to David's reign in 8:15, and chs. 6 – 7 showed David acting in the fear of God. But David's assault on Uriah through Bathsheba (2 Sam. 11 – 12), Tamar's rape and Amnon's murder (2 Sam. 13) and the traumas caused for the nation in the rebellions of Absalom (2 Sam. 15 – 19) and Sheba (2 Sam. 20) set this in a different light. Indeed, according to 15:1–6 a perceived lack of justice laid the groundwork for Absalom's revolt. Nevertheless, the participial form of the opening lines means that the oracle's message is not restricted to David alone, which is why it was important to insist in vv. 2–3a that Yahweh spoke both to and through David, so these words set the pattern for all rulers. A series of three lines pointing to outcomes for such rulers is attached in v. 4. The three are largely parallel, but again show some development, especially in the third line. Such a ruler is compared to sunlight (a common motif for rulers in ANE) on a clear morning and the growth of grass after the rain. Sun and rain stand as effective opposites. This is stressed by the reference to the cloudless morning in the second line, but together the three lines refer to creation's bounty. Yahweh has placed order in creation, so also a ruler who governs with equity and the fear of God brings order to a realm. Such a statement is a memory of what David was, a rebuke because of what he did and a hopeful pointer to what he and any ruler can be.

5. The oracle is broken off for a personal aside. In the light of events since 2 Sam. 11, David is no shining light for monarchy. Perhaps that is why he does not make a claim about himself. Rather, he claims that his house (*bayit*) stands in this relationship to God. This is important because although the word 'house' has occurred fifty-nine times since 2 Sam. 7, only here and 12:8–10 is it employed with the specific sense of David's dynasty. David's last words make an important link with 7:1–17, a promise explicitly described as a covenant (*běrît*). But the link with 12:8–10 is also important, because there Nathan spoke of the punishment affecting David's house. Now, because David's house stands in the relationship with God described here, we know David's punishment for his sin against Uriah has not terminated the promise (Firth 2005b: 97–98). Instead, the language of an eternal covenant is employed to insist that Yahweh's promise from 7:1–17 abides. David's house, and through it David himself, can again be kingship's model, a model applied throughout Kings. David can never be accused of apostasy (Carlson 1964: 258), and can therefore be a model for those who follow. The covenant is something God has both established for David, and also ordered and made secure in everything. It is not a covenant that can be cast aside, a point that leads into the messianic hope associated with the Davidic covenant. But hope is not restricted to the distant future, because the assurance of covenant leads to David's being sure of God's continued provision for him so that both his welfare and desire are prospered. This is not claiming that God will give David anything he wants, since David's welfare is found only in remaining in covenant. It does, however, understand that God will continue to honour the covenant.

6–7. These verses either continue the oracle (vv. 3b–4; Anderson 1989: 267) or add a wisdom comment from the poet addressing the oracle's content (del Olmo Lete 1984: 424). Either is possible, but there is no need to separate these options since the whole poem is built on David's presentation as a prophet, and wisdom material is quite common in the prophets (e.g. Jer. 9:23–24; McKane 1965: 86–93). The contrast is between the just ruler of vv. 3b–4 and wickedness, personified as 'Belial'. The personification is evident from the fact that in the noun's nine previous occurrences it always described someone as a son (1 Sam. 2:12; 10:27; 25:17), daughter (1 Sam. 1:16) or man (1 Sam. 25:25; 30:22; 2 Sam. 16:7; 20:1; 22:5) of Belial (see 'Notes'). Belial, representing worthlessness or ungodliness (AV's 'naughty person' at Prov. 6:12 is seriously misleading for modern readers), is contrasted with righteousness. The contrast is also seen in plant imagery: where the just king 'sprouts', Belial is like thorns, something painful that no hand wishes to grasp. Just as the outcome for the righteous ruler is inevitable, so also Belial's end is assured. Such embodied wickedness is rejected or, if touched upon, is done only through armed confrontation, a theme neatly highlighted in the polysemy of 'iron' and 'wood', both of which can refer to farming and military equipment (Youngblood 1992: 1084). That Belial here personifies ungodly rulers is clear from their end, in that they are utterly consumed by fire on the throne (see 'Notes'). So the oracle draws on the two-ways structure to show both how a ruler should live and the outcome for the ruler who chooses either path (cf. Ps. 1; Matt. 7:13–14). David's house may know its current position is secured through covenant (v. 5), but the warning of covenant curses for unfaithfulness lie just below the surface.

Explanation

David's last words, along with ch. 22, form the Samuel Conclusion's heart. The two are interlinked through shared vocabulary and themes that in turn provide links through 1:19–27 to Hannah's Song (1 Sam. 2:1–10). These poems form the theological framework through which Samuel tells its story of monarchy's rise and how David's house was established as the ruling dynasty. It is important that David's words are presented in the mode of prophecy (a theme the NT develops; Matt. 22:43; Acts 2:30) through reference to an oracle and the Spirit's work, so they not only reflect on David's position but also look forward to suggest the direction David's successors should take as rulers. Similar language is employed in Ps. 72, though there as a prayer for the king to conform to the pattern described here, whereas here the emphasis is upon the provision of a pattern for all rulers to follow.

Looking back, this poem assesses David as ruler. God's word to and through David is that he has attained his position because of what God has done for him. He may have finally come to national prominence, but that prominence comes only because of God's work on his behalf. The youngest son of a not particularly prominent family from Bethlehem would not normally rise to such prominence, but David has done so by God's choice. It was also important for David that he could claim to have fulfilled the words of the oracle in vv. 3b–4 to some extent, something asserted on his behalf in 8:15. Moreover, as one who had not rejected Yahweh's greater rule (unlike Saul), David could claim that his house stood in a just relationship with God and so lived under the blessing of an eternal covenant, a phrase not otherwise used of the Davidic covenant. The wider narrative knows of his appalling failures, but these are not the last word. Placed here, David's oracle is the utterance of a forgiven man.

It is because David is forgiven that this poem also looks forward. That these are David's last words shows they are late in his life; but by offering guidance for just rulers in how to practise justice (vv. 3b–4) and what they should avoid (vv. 6–7), David continues to guide those who follow him, stressing how they should conduct themselves. Given the wider context of David's story, the guidance comes with a warning; but this does not change the fact that because David's house was secure in its covenant relationship with Yahweh, David could look to his successors. Although this ultimately takes a messianic direction, we should not overlook the fact that David speaks to rulers, not just kings, so the pattern for just government is not just associated with the king individually. Yet that David is presented as the 'anointed' (v. 1) of Yahweh lends an almost inevitably messianic tone to this future hope. So the poem's language would not only be taken up by Jesus (Matt. 13:36–43); it would be used by the NT to depict him as the one who truly rules and will rule justly (1 Cor. 15:25; Rev. 11:15–18).

2 SAMUEL 23:8–39

Translation

[8]These are the names of David's mighty men. Josheb Basshebeth the Tachemonite: he was chief of the captains and brandished his spear against eight hundred whom he killed at one time.

⁹After him was Eleazar ben Dodo ben Ahohi, one of three mighty men with David when they defied the Philistines who were gathered there for battle. The Israelites withdrew, ¹⁰but he rose up and struck the Philistines until his hand was weary and clung to the sword. Yahweh wrought a great victory that day, and the people returned after him only to strip the slain.

¹¹And after him was Shammah ben Agee the Hararite. The Philistines had gathered at Lehi in a plot of a field filled with lentils, and the people fled from the Philistines. ¹²But he took his stand in the midst of the plot, defended it and struck the Philistines, and Yahweh wrought a great victory.

¹³And three of the thirty chief men went down and came at harvest time to David at the Cave of Adullam, while a Philistine troop camped in the Valley of Rephaim. ¹⁴David was then in the stronghold, while the Philistine garrison was in Bethlehem. ¹⁵David craved and said, 'Who will give me water to drink from the well at Bethlehem, which is by the gate?' ¹⁶The three mighty men broke through the Philistine camp and drew water from the well at Bethlehem, which is by the gate, and carried and brought it to David. But he would not drink it and poured it out to Yahweh. ¹⁷He said, 'Far be it from me, O Yahweh, that I should do this. Shall I drink the blood of men who went at the risk of their lives?' So he would not drink it. These things the three mighty men did.

¹⁸Abishai, the brother of Joab, the son of Zeruiah, was division chief, and he brandished his spear against three hundred whom he killed, and won renown with the Three. ¹⁹Was he not the most honoured apart from the Three? He was a commander for them, but did not attain to the Three.

²⁰Benaiah ben Jehoiada, a valiant man from Kabzeel who had done great deeds, struck two sons of Ariel of Moab. He also went down and struck a lion in the middle of a pit on a snowy day. ²¹He also struck an Egyptian man of formidable appearance, though the Egyptian had a spear in his hand. He went down to him with a club and snatched the spear from the Egyptian's hand and killed him with the spear. ²²These things Benaiah ben Jehoiada did and he won renown with the three mighty men. ²³He was more renowned than the Thirty, but did not attain to the Three, yet David appointed him to his bodyguard.

²⁴Asahel, Joab's brother was in the Thirty; Elhanan ben Dodo of Bethlehem, ²⁵Shammah the Harodite, Elika the Harodite, ²⁶Helez the Paltite, Ira ben Iqqesh the Tekoite, ²⁷Abiezer the Anathothite, Mebunnai the Hushathite, ²⁸Zalmon the Ahohite, Mahrai the Netophathite, ²⁹Heleb ben Baanah the Netophathite, Ittai ben Ribai from Gibeah of the sons of Benjamin, ³⁰Benaiah, a Pirathonite, Hiddai from the brooks of Gaash, ³¹Abi-albon the Arbathite, Azmaveth the Barhumite, ³²Elihaba the Shaalbonite, the sons of Jashen, Jonathan, ³³Shammah the Hararite, Ahiam ben Sharar the Hararite, ³⁴Eliphelet ben Ahasbai the son of the Maacathite, Eliam ben Ahithophel the Gilonite, ³⁵Hezro the Carmelite, Paarai the Arbite, ³⁶Igal ben Nathan from Zobah, Bani the Gadite, ³⁷Zelek the Ammonite, Nahrai the Beerothite who carried Joab the son of Zeruiah's kit, ³⁸Ira the Ithrite, Gareb the Ithrite, ³⁹Uriah the Hittite, thirty-seven in all.

Notes on the text

8. LXX^L suggests *šĕlōšâ*, 'Three', for *šalîšî*, perhaps 'a third part' and hence a commander of a third of the army (perhaps deriving from chariotry). However, the word's etymological connection may have moved significantly (compare 'quartermaster'), referring to a commander rather than something etymologically identifiable (see Na'aman 1988; Schley 1990). This removes the need to find the categories of the 'Three' and the 'Thirty' as consistently as many modern translations suggest (see AV and RSV), much of which is based on versions (esp. LXX^L and Syr). Moreover, *šalîšî* elsewhere refers to a senior soldier (2 Kgs 7:2, 17, 19; 9:25; 15:25), a meaning contextually suitable here. MT *'ădînô ha'eṣnô* is obscure, but unlikely to mean that Josheb was also known as Adino the Eznite (so NASU). LXX^B recognizes the problem and conflates MT with 1 Chr. 11:11, but MT is more probably a corruption of *'ôrēr 'et ḥănît* in Chronicles and two MSS. The conflict with 1 Chr. 11:11 over the number killed is difficult, but Samuel is perhaps preferred because so many references in this chapter use the root 'three' (see v. 18) that Chronicles has conformed this account to the numerical pattern.

9. Reading *dôdô* with Q and many MSS, McCarter (1984: 490) argues for a lacuna, but Simon (2000: 185) rightly defends MT.

11. Although *laḥayyâ* could mean 'to a troop' or similar (NASU, NIV), a toponym is preferable (ESV, NRSV).

13. With Q, read 'three' for K 'thirty'.

17. 'Shall I drink' is understood from context. Despite McCarter's concerns (1984: 491), the verb *šth* could have been lost, though the speech could be given in a deliberately elliptical manner to indicate David's stress.

18. K reads *šĕlîšî*, presumably 'the third (part)', perhaps of the army; while Q has *šĕlōšâ*, 'the Three'. The reading of 'the Thirty' is found in Syr and two MSS. K is retained as a 'third of the army'; hence 'division'. The final clause is omitted from some versions, but is secure in the MT.

19. Read *šĕlôšîm* with 1 Chr. 11:25 and one MS.

20. With many MSS and Q, read *ḥayil* for *ḥay*. The idiom 'son of valour' characterized Benaiah. Read 'sons of Ariel' with LXX.

21. Though *mareh* describes a quality of appearance, typically to indicate good looks (e.g. Gen. 12:11; 24:16), it can also refer to other qualities (Exod. 24:17). Since the point is the threat the Egyptian posed, 'formidable' is appropriate, and preferable to NIV's 'huge' since size is not specified. 1 Chr. 11:23's 'man of size' is interpretative rather than textual (similarly, Simon 2000: 187), perhaps drawing on traditions unknown to the writer of Samuel.

27. 1 Chr. 11:29 has Sibbecai for Mebunnai, possibly identifying this person with the warrior in 21:18.

37. With Q and many MSS, read *nōśē'*, the sg. being required.

Form and structure

The Conclusion's fifth section lists some of David's warriors, providing brief details of their exploits, paralleling 21:15–22. As there, only the essential details are given. Again the list shows that victory was not achieved through David alone. Rather, David's warriors were important contributors to it. But there is one important shift: unlike 21:15–22, Yahweh's involvement is mentioned. Both vv. 10 and 12 say that victory came from Yahweh, while David also worships Yahweh in v. 17. These comments about the source of victory and worship practices links these passages to 5:17–25 and 8:1–14, both part of the earlier chiasm assessing all of David's reign (5:17 – 8:14). This link is strengthened by reference to the Valley of Rephaim in 5:18 and 23:13. So the Conclusion and earlier summary bracket the Court Narrative to show it is not the last word on David's reign. Even though the warrior lists in the Conclusion provide evidence of the achievements of David's warriors, David himself is not portrayed negatively, as is clear from vv. 13–17, though the exact nature of the water ritual is unclear.

This passage deals principally with two main groups of David's warriors who are known as the Three and the Thirty, though the meaning of these titles is confused by the fact that some points refer to three warriors who are not part of the Three (vv. 13, 16) but are in another group. This is complicated by numerous textual problems surrounding the root *šlš*, from which both 'three' and 'thirty', but also 'captain' and 'division', derive, while Benaiah is reported as slaying three hundred. As is evident from the 'Notes', there are numerous points of uncertainty as to whether one reads 'three' or 'thirty', and textual emendation is widely practised to bring consistency to it, though this translation does so less than most. However, although the principal military groups are the Three and the Thirty, they do not constitute the whole of the list, which can be arranged as follows:

23:8	Josheb Basshebeth, chief of the captains
23:9–12	Eleazar and Shammah, members of the Three
23:13–18	Exploits of some mighty men of the Thirty
23:19–23	Abishai and Benaiah, commanders not in the Three but above the Thirty
23:24–39	Asahel to Uriah, members of the Thirty

It is thus evident that not all of David's special troops belonged to the Three or the Thirty, since Josheb Basshebeth stands above the Three, while Abishai and Benaiah rank between the Three and the Thirty. The section is set out in order of rank, though Fokkelman (1990: 300) rightly notes that military prowess does not necessarily go with rank. This structure shows that we know only of two men within the Three, as well as two whose rank stood between those groups. Yet there are at least thirty-three members in the Thirty (Jashen's sons are unnamed, but there must be at least two to be added to the thirty-one names; see 1 Chr. 11:26–47), and the text closes by noting that there were thirty-seven in all. One could arrange this information to reach the thirty-seven in several ways because of the variable of Jashen's sons, but perhaps the simplest is to allow for thirty-three members of the Thirty, and then include Eleazar and Shammah from the Three and Abishai and Benaiah from the intermediate rank, thus forming thirty-seven, all of whom are commanded by Josheb Basshebeth. Nevertheless, a precise interpretation of the thirty-seven is impossible, though once it is recognized that 'Three' and 'Thirty' are military ranks, we appreciate that there do not have to be three or thirty people holding the rank. Interpretative difficulties in vv. 32–33 further complicate the matter. These obscurities and the fact that the list of the Thirty makes no attempt at suggesting support from all Israel for David point to the list's antiquity (similarly, McCarter 1984: 501).

Perhaps the list's most surprising absence (other than passing mentions in vv. 18, 37) is Joab. Both his brothers appear (vv. 18–19, 24), but Joab does not, although he is acknowledged. Indeed, both his brothers head their respective sections. If not for the passing mention, one might conclude that Joab's importance is being undercut. However, it is more likely that those listed represent David's elite troops who comprise a special contingent within the army as a whole, of which Joab is (for the most part) its commander. Joab, like David, stands outside the list (similarly, Birch 1998: 1376). While Joab's omission is notable, more importance should be given to Uriah the Hittite's mention as the Thirty's last member. His placement is partially due to the fact that those with non-Israelite backgrounds are placed later, but may also remind readers of the Court Narrative. If Eliam ben Ahithophel (v. 34) is Bathsheba's father (and no definite connection is made), then this provides an additional link, but his placement in the list lacks any prominence. Yet Uriah's placement is emphatic, and provides further information to shape the reading of ch. 11. We now learn he was probably close to David, though that would not have stopped David from viewing him as a threat.

Comment

The senior ranks: 23:8–12

8. The listing of David's mighty men begins with an evocation of Exod. 1:1, announcing that this chapter too is to provide a list of names. The mighty men are *gibbōrîm*, a word from the same root as used to describe David in 23:1, so David is linked to them, though they remain his men. The list is headed by Josheb Basshebeth the Tachemonite (a patronym that cannot be identified) who is the chief of David's captains (see 'Notes'),

suggesting he commanded the elite corps. His name may represent a deliberate corruption, as Gr. MSS suggest a name like Ishbaal, though if there was originally a Baal compound name, the corruption is more extensive than elsewhere in Samuel (1 Chr. 11:11 and 27:2 call him Jashobeam). He is said to have slain eight hundred at one time (see 'Notes'), a remarkable feat that clearly justifies his position. This may have happened through troop deployment rather than single combat, but as commander the credit would go to him.

9–10. Immediately below Josheb Basshebeth were Eleazar and Shammah, who held rank in the Three. For Eleazar we are given his father and grandfather's names rather than his place of origin, though neither name is mentioned in Samuel. Ahohi might be a figure in 1 Chr. 8:4, which would make Eleazar a Benjaminite (similarly, Zalmon in v. 28). He joined David in defying the Philistines when the rest of the troops had withdrawn. This might be in 1 Sam. 17 (so Ackroyd 1977: 223; the root *ḥrp*, which occurs here, is prominent there; cf. 1 Chr. 11:13), but if so his main achievements occurred after David killed Goliath. However, 21:15–22 indicates a range of conflicts with the Philistines, so this event's timing is uncertain. Eleazar's achievement was to rise against overwhelming opposition and continue to oppose the Philistines even when his hand muscles were so tired they were virtually frozen on to his sword. The day's outcome (for which casualty figures are not given) was that Yahweh gave victory, repeating the theme from 5:17–25 and 8:1–14. Eleazar was David's mighty man, but Yahweh was the hero.

11–12. Joining Eleazar is Shammah ben Agee, a Hararite, a clan that cannot definitely be identified. He may be junior in rank to Eleazar within the Three since his citation is introduced in a similar manner to Eleazar's, and he is junior to Josheb Basshebeth, though the phrase may merely mean he was another member of the Three. Like Eleazar, he distinguished himself against Philistines, in his case in part of a field of lentils at Lehi (Judg. 15:14, 17), which the Philistines apparently saw as a possible food supply. He too faced a situation where the men fled; but where Eleazar rose up, Shammah stood firm. Like Eleazar, the narrative affirms that Yahweh gave the victory, again paralleling 5:17–25 and 8:1–14.

Exploits of the three warriors: 23:13–17

13–14. The actions of three warriors from the lower rank of David's elite, known as the Thirty, are now described. The Thirty were senior troops, and this anecdote illustrates their skill and bravery. As with Eleazar and Shammah, their citation arose amid conflict with the Philistines. This time, David was at Adullam (see 1 Sam. 22:1) during harvest, which was around May–June when the weather was hot and dry. Meanwhile, the Philistines were in the Valley of Rephaim (see 2 Sam. 5:18), which is also the root for the 'giants' of 21:15–22, making a further connection there. As in 5:17, David was in his stronghold (*mĕṣûdâ*), perhaps a fortified area inside the cave, with the Philistines garrisoned at Bethlehem, providing a base to move towards the Jordan valley. A Philistine advance so far into Israel makes it possible that this occurred while David was an outlaw, though it could also have been shortly before the Philistine defeat in 5:17–25. David's movement would be restricted, especially his access to Israelite lands.

15–16a. Confronted with this, David voices a desire to drink water from a well by Bethlehem's gate. It is not directly expressing thirst since the time involved in a 10-mile journey through Philistine lines hardly allows for that, but rather for free access to his territory symbolized by the water. David engendered radical loyalty, and three of his men broke through Philistine lines, implying that they fought through to Bethlehem, where they drew water from the well. Even drawing the water was risky since the gate's prominence meant it would be carefully watched. Such action was both brave and foolhardy, but shows their devotion to David.

16b–17. David will not drink the water, in spite of his men's commitment. Instead, he transforms it into worship by pouring out the water before Yahweh. No identical rite occurs in the Bible, though libations and drink offerings do exist (see Gen. 35:14; Lev. 23:13; Num. 6:15; cf. Phil. 2:17). This is a spontaneous act of giving what is of value to Yahweh, an informal expression of worship. Its meaning is seen where David declares to Yahweh that he cannot drink this water because only Yahweh is worthy of such sacrificial action. His men have not died, so their 'blood' is a metaphor for sacrificial devotion, but the risk taken is too great. David insists such devotion belongs to Yahweh. Nevertheless, the citation's closing note reminds us that this was typical of these men, whose valour and skill was recognized, although David's worship transformed it this time.

The middle ranks: 23:18–23

18–19. Before listing the Thirty, two intermediate soldiers are listed, both having featured previously. The first is Abishai, one of Zeruiah's three sons. Although introduction by patronym is usual, these three are introduced through their mother, perhaps to strengthen their links with David. But Abishai is first identified as Joab's brother, ensuring no confusion over his identity. First introduced in 1 Sam. 26:6 as David's companion in Saul's camp, he is consistently portrayed as someone willing to use violence to further David's cause, violence David has often tried, somewhat unsuccessfully, to check (2 Sam. 2:18, 24; 3:30; 16:9–12; 18:1–12). He is also an effective warrior and passionately committed to David, as seen in his defeat of the giant who attacked David in 21:15–17, another link between the Conclusion's warrior accounts. Abishai's citation is similar to Josheb Basshebeth's (v. 8; see 'Notes'), except he is said to have killed only three hundred. Again this could refer to the achievement of men under his command, but the victory is credited to him. Despite these achievements, Abishai did not attain to the rank of the Three, though he was the most honoured of those below them. The Three employed him as a troop commander, but he was not promoted to the Three.

20-23. The second intermediate soldier is Benaiah ben Jehoiada, previously mentioned as the Cherethites and Pelethites' commander in 8:18 (see 'Comment' there) and 20:23. This command was separate from the main army, though the focus here is on his own valour. He originated from Kabzeel, a town in Judah's extreme south (Josh. 15:21), though its exact site is unknown. As someone noted for many valorous deeds, it is appropriate that Benaiah's citation covers three different activities, all joined by the verb *nkh* (to strike). The first of these, striking two sons of Ariel of Moab (see 'Notes'), is obscure. 'Ariel' could mean 'lion of God', thus characterizing the opposing soldiers as men of great strength. But Ariel could be a proper name, though, if so, Ariel must have been remembered as a dangerous foe. Hertzberg (1964: 406) prefers to think of them as powerful lions. It is probably best to regard the phrase as characterizing two powerful opponents. However, lion imagery in the name Ariel joins to the citation's second element, the killing of a lion in a pit on a snowy day. Lions are always dangerous, but this one had either fallen into a storage pit or been placed there for amusement, rather like the later Roman pattern. Given Israelite society's essentially subsistence nature, the former is more likely, and the lion had to be killed so the pit could be used. The event was memorable because of snow that day. Finally, he had struck an impressive Egyptian (see 'Notes'). According to 1 Chr. 11:23, he was over 7 feet tall. Since David is not known to have fought Egypt, the Egyptian was probably a mercenary. Although armed with only a club in a possible single combat, Benaiah overpowered the Egyptian, snatched his spear and killed him. As with Abishai, these were Benaiah's typical actions, gaining him a level of renown appropriate to the Three, and above the Thirty. Nevertheless, he was not promoted to the Three, but was rewarded by David with command of his bodyguard, perhaps the Cherethites and Pelethites.

The Thirty: 23:24-39

24-29. All the senior officers are named and given a citation demonstrating the reason for their position. Following them, we have a list of the 'Thirty', though this is a rank within David's elite rather than a particular number that was required. Members of the Thirty are simply listed, with only enough details to enable a proper identification. The list begins and ends with figures known elsewhere in Samuel. Asahel was Zeruiah's third son, killed while David was king of Judah alone (2:18-23). Uriah the

Hittite was killed by David through Joab in 11:14–17 when David was king in Jerusalem. This suggests the list was constantly updated, making it unlikely that there were ever exactly Thirty. None of the others is definitely mentioned elsewhere in Samuel, so the list's arrangement, beginning with Asahel and ending with Uriah, is probably to highlight them. The list is also structured so the soldiers listed earlier tend to come from the region of Bethlehem, though care must be taken with obscure sites such as Harod (for Shammah and Elika). Helez may have come from the region of Hebron since his patronym is associated with Caleb (1 Chr. 2:47). Ira's hometown of Tekoa is a few miles south of Bethlehem on the eastern slopes of the Judean hills, and was also Amos' home (Amos 1:1). Abiezer is the first non-Judean, coming from the Benjaminite town of Anathoth, a little north of Jerusalem, from which the prophet Jeremiah would come (Jer. 1:1), though with Mebunnai (see 'Notes') we probably return to the region of Bethlehem if the village of Husha is located to its south-west. Zalmon is apparently a Benjaminite since Ahoah occurs in 1 Chr. 8:4 as a descendant of Benjamin (see Eleazar in v. 9), and Maharai's town of Netophah was also in the region of Bethlehem (Ezra 2:22; Neh. 7:26). Heleb and Ittai are given patronyms and places of origin, with Heleb joining Maharai in coming from Netophah, while Ittai's Benjaminite origin is specified to distinguish him from Ittai the Gittite (2 Sam. 15:19–23).

30–37. The list begins to include warriors from across Israel and some of non-Israelite origin, indicating the gradual spread of David's influence. The mode of listing continues as before. Benaiah comes from Pirathon in Ephraim, about 10 miles south-west of Shechem, also the home of Abdon (Judg. 12:15). Hiddai's home by the brooks of Gaash is in a similar region, apparently near Mount Gaash, which is close to Joshua's burial place (Judg. 2:9). Abi Albon may come from the region of Beth Arabah, placing his home on the Judah–Benjamin border, but this is uncertain. Azmaveth came from Bahurim, just north-east of Jerusalem, a town that supported David while he fled from Absalom (2 Sam. 16:5; 17:18). Elihaba may come from Shaalbin (Josh. 19:41–42), part of Dan's original allocation. The list may have some damage as the names of Jashen's sons are not provided and no information is given about Jonathan. Variants resolving this may be attempts to resolve a difficulty, and it is better to consider the possibility that an evolving list used different methods of identification. Another Shammah is mentioned, who, like the member of the Three (v. 11), was a Hararite. It is possible that Ahiam should also be so identified, though the spelling is different. Eliphelet and Eliam join Heleb and Ittai (v. 29) in having both patronym and place of origin. Eliphelet is from Maacah, either the Aramean kingdom (the home of Absalom's mother, 2 Sam. 10:6) or a clan in southern Judah (1 Chr. 4:19). Eliam is the son of David's counsellor, Ahithophel (2 Sam. 15:12; 17:23), and comes from Giloh, a town in Judah's southern hills (Josh. 15:51). He may be Bathsheba's father (11:3), but the link is never definitively made. Hezri is another from Judah if the Carmel here is the town in the Negeb, though Paarai's description as an Arbite cannot be identified. If Eliphelet is Judean, then Igal is the first foreigner mentioned, coming from Zobah, a kingdom David defeated in 8:3–12. Bani, a Gadite, is identified only by tribe. If Eliphelet is from Judah, Bani is the first from east of the Jordan. He is followed by Zelek from Ammon, a people across the Jordan whom David had subjugated (8:12), who also triggered the war in 10:1–14 and 12:26–31. Naharai is from Beeroth, the home town of Ish-bosheth's killers (2 Sam. 4:3–12). He became Joab's kit-bearer, suggesting David's support came even from areas closely associated with Saul. Both Ira and Gareb are Ithrites, possibly descendants of Canaanite peoples. The list closes with Uriah the Hittite, the best-known member, principally because David murdered him. Here he shows the extent of David's support, while throwing a dark shadow across the whole list. On the meaning of the claim that there were thirty-seven in all, see 'Form and structure'.

Explanation

While David was still an outlaw, he developed a group of men around him. They were not initially powerful, but were made up from those distressed and disenfranchised under Saul (1 Sam. 22:2). The list's geographic structure, especially within the Thirty, suggests it reaches back to that time. If so, Klement (2000a: 195) is right to point from this list to Hannah's Song (1 Sam. 2:1–10). Hannah spoke of the reversal of fortunes, where the powerful are broken and the weak made powerful with Yahweh's help. The list illustrates this, demonstrating that Yahweh, in fulfilling his promise of kingship through David, transforms both individuals and societies. It is also important to note that this section twice points to Yahweh's giving victory, tying the Conclusion to 5:17–25. Hence the Samuel Conclusion simultaneously points to the book's beginning and the start of David's reign while looking in hope at what Yahweh will continue to do.

Although the focus is on Yahweh's achievements, this passage is also aware that Yahweh's work was carried out through his servants. As such, the bravery of the heroes who receive citations is noted, yet simultaneously relativized by David's worship when the anonymous three bring him water from Bethlehem. Human endeavour is vital, but submission to Yahweh is more important still. The importance of this submission is illustrated through the list of the Thirty, and in particular that the first and last members of the list died pointlessly. Asahel's death was simple hubris, for he failed to see that pursuing Abner (2:18–23) was unnecessary. Loyalty to Yahweh and king did not justify folly. But Uriah's closing mention is more important, for this simple act of naming a soldier again evokes David's sin. The penalty for David's sin has been paid, but though Hannah's Song is a source of rejoicing for the weak, it continues to warn the powerful, a warning David and his descendants need to heed.

2 SAMUEL 24

Translation

[1]Again Yahweh's anger burned against Israel, and he incited David against them, saying, 'Go, count Israel and Judah.' [2]The king said to Joab, the army commander who was with him, 'Go about through all Israel's tribes from Dan to Beersheba and register the people that I might know their number.'

[3]Joab said to the king, 'May Yahweh your God add to the people about a hundred times as many as they are while the eyes of my lord the king still see. But why does my lord the king delight in this thing?' [4]But the king's word prevailed over Joab and the army commanders. Joab went out with the army commanders from the king's presence to register the people of Israel. [5]They crossed the Jordan and began at Aroer, and from the city which is in the middle of the Gad valley, then to Jazer. [6]They came to Gilead and to the land of Tahtim Hodshi, then to Dan, Iyyon and around to Sidon, [7]and came to the fortress of Tyre and all the Hivite and Canaanite cities; and they went out to the Negeb of Judah, Beersheba. [8]When they had roved through all the land, at the end of nine months and twenty days, they entered Jerusalem. [9]Joab gave the count of the people registered to the king: in Israel there were eight hundred thousand valiant men drawing the sword, and five hundred thousand men of Judah.

[10]But David's heart struck him after numbering the people. David said to Yahweh, 'I have sinned greatly in what I have done. But now, Yahweh, please remove your servant's iniquity because I have acted very foolishly.' [11]David rose in the morning, and Yahweh's word came to the prophet Gad, David's seer, saying, [12]'Go, and say to David, "Thus has Yahweh said, 'I am offering you three things. Choose for yourself one of them and I will do it to you.'"' [13]Gad came to David and reported to him. He said to him, 'Shall seven years of famine in your land, or three months of fleeing from before your foes while they pursue you, or three days of pestilence in your land come upon you? Now consider and see what answer I shall take back to him who sent me.' [14]David said to Gad, 'I am greatly distressed. Let us fall into Yahweh's hand because his compassion is great. But let me not fall into human hands.'

[15]Then Yahweh sent a pestilence in Israel from the morning to the appointed time, and seventy thousand of the people from Dan to Beersheba died. [16]When the angel of Jerusalem put forth his hand to destroy it, Yahweh relented concerning the calamity and said to the angel who was destroying many people, 'It is enough; restrain your hand.' The angel of Yahweh was by Araunah the Jebusite's threshing floor. [17]When David saw the angel who was striking down the people, he said to Yahweh, 'Behold, I have sinned; I have acted iniquitously. But these sheep, what have they done? Please let your hand be against me and against my father's house.'

¹⁸Gad came to David at that time and said to him, 'Go up, erect an altar to Yahweh on Araunah the Jebusite's threshing floor.' ¹⁹David went up according to Gad's word, as Yahweh commanded. ²⁰Araunah looked down and saw the king and his servants approaching him, so Araunah went out and did obeisance before the king with his face to the ground. ²¹Araunah said, 'Why has my lord the king come to his servant?' David said, 'To buy the threshing floor from you to build an altar to Yahweh, so the plague may be restrained from the people.' ²²Araunah said to David, 'Let my lord the king take and offer up what seems good in his eyes. See: the oxen for the burnt offering, and the sledges and ox-yokes for wood. ²³Araunah gives everything, O king, to the king.' Araunah said to the king, 'May Yahweh your God accept you.' ²⁴The king said to Araunah, 'No, I shall surely buy it from you for a price. I will not offer up to Yahweh my God burnt offerings which cost me nothing.' David purchased the threshing floor and the oxen for fifty shekels of silver. ²⁵David built there an altar to Yahweh and offered up burnt offerings and peace offerings. Yahweh was supplicated for the land and the plague was restrained from Israel.

Notes on the text

1. On the syntax, see Koorevaar 1995.

2. The shift from the sg. *šûṭ* to the pl. *piqdû* has led to various harmonizations. But Joab's position as army commander meant a personal directive to him could be expressed in the pl. because of the group he took with him.

4. *'el* is here interchangeable with *'al*. One might expect *milipnê* rather than *lipnê*, as per the versions, but outward movement is perhaps suggested by *ys'*, and the versions correct to the expected form.

5. With LXX, read *wyḥlw* for MT *wyḥnw* since Aroer is the commencement point. Similarly, read *wmn* for *ymyn* since a reference to the south plays no role.

6. Tahtim Hodshi is odd, and probably defective. However, the main alternatives (summarized by McCarter 1984: 504–505) are problematic. The suggestion that it refers to the Hittites of Kadesh is unlikely since Kadesh on the Orontes is too far north and Kadesh in Naphtali too far south. 'Below Mount Hermon' fits geographically, but the required confusion between *š* and *m* is difficult to justify. A toponym between Gilead and Dan is needed, and Tahtim Hodshi is reluctantly treated as such (similarly, Simon 2000: 103) since it is better to admit uncertainty than accept unconvincing emendations. As MT stands, *y'n* is a proper noun, but is better read as a defective spelling of Iyyon (*'yn*), the current reading caused by metathesis (see Fokkelman 1990: 398).

13. 1 Chr. 21:12's (see LXX) three years of famine is probably a copying error standardizing the punishments around the number 3.

14. Read *raḥămāyw* with Q.

16. *'el* is here interchangeable with *'al*. Araunah may be a title rather than a name, since he is here 'the Araunah', though this is also possible for names. The name is non-Israelite, and its spelling varies, becoming 'Ornan' in Chronicles, indicating uncertainty about its representation, making proposed etymologies insecure.

17. The second *wayyōmer* is resumptive, and thus not represented in translation.

23. *hammelek* is omitted by most versions, and a few MSS, but is retained as a courtly vocative.

Form and structure

Balancing 21:1–14, the Conclusion's closing account is another plague narrative. The link between them is emphasized by use of 'again' at the outset, though it is unclear that the two were ever a single unit. As before, David must find the mechanism for ameliorating Yahweh's anger, but the crucial difference is that this time the sin is his own. Nevertheless, the narrative's peculiarity is not that David both sins and confesses his sin, since this also occurs in 2 Sam. 11 – 12. Rather, it is that David was incited by Yahweh; yet, in spite of this, when Gad directed him to choose his punishment, he committed himself and the people into Yahweh's hands because of his compassion. Complicating this is the uncertainty about what David's sin was. Num. 1 and 26 record censuses taken to determine numbers available for military service, so a census as such was not sinful (for taxation, see Exod. 30:11–16; 38:25–26), and there is nothing here to suggest that this census required the payment of the ransom noted in Exod. 30:13 (against Hertzberg 1964: 411–412). A clue may be provided in Joab's route to gather this information, since it seems to follow the nation's maximal boundaries. If so, Israel may not have been on a war footing and David's sin may be seeking to usurp Yahweh's authority over Israelite kings by initiating this when it is not needed, even when incited by Yahweh (Klement 2000a: 174–178). That both David and Israel are affected shows how closely intertwined king is with nation.

The plague this generated is resolved by neither his initial confession (v. 10), nor his second (v. 17), though both play their part. Rather, resolution comes when David purchases Araunah's threshing floor to build an altar to Yahweh. Only once that is completed and offerings made is Yahweh supplicated. This allows us, with Schenker (1982: 33–35), to read the narrative as a whole rather than a composite. Although Chronicles develops this, making explicit that this was where the temple site was (linking it to Isaac's near-sacrifice in Gen. 22), such concerns remain inchoate here. There is nothing here, nor in 1 Kgs 8, linking the temple's construction with this site, so 1 Chr. 21:1 – 22:5 may offer the story's first interpretation (so Schenker 1982: ii). We cannot therefore import themes from Chronicles since that narrative has a different goal, though that account is still an important guide for interpreting the Samuel text. The important analogy is with the earlier plague account. In 21:14, after Yahweh was appeased at Gibeah (following Rizpah's intervention), he responded to prayer for the land and removed the famine. Here David must initiate proper worship to supplicate Yahweh. Sacrifice and prayer are bound together in both accounts. Similarly, David must respond to Yahweh's directives. In 21:1 he sought and received an oracle outlining the famine's cause in order to resolve the problem, while here Gad, to negotiate a resolution, approaches him with Yahweh's command (24:18–19). These parallels point to the story's goal within Samuel, showing how David worked out the king's role as one under Yahweh but with freedom within that to determine how the king should function.

Comment

The census: 24:1–9

1. That Yahweh's anger burned against Israel again presumes an earlier time against which to read this narrative. Although the Conclusion's connection is to 21:1–15, there is no reference to anger there. The last reference to divine anger was 6:7, when Uzzah grasped the ark and was struck down. There Yahweh's anger was kindled by a failure to follow correct cultic practice, and something similar may be present here, though nothing else suggests a link to 2 Sam. 6. Although this chapter's events are unique, their context is not. The close link between people and king is also suggested in that although Yahweh's anger was against Israel, he incited David against them, commanding him to count (*mnh*) Israel and Judah. Israel and Judah's inclusion indicates the period of the united kingdom (see 5:1–5), though it is probable that the reference to Israel covers the whole nation since all are subsequently afflicted. The troubling issue for many is that Yahweh incites David to do something he later has to confess is sinful. 1 Chr. 21:1 may offer a solution if we translate it as 'Satan incited David...' (e.g. NIV), but this requires *śāṭān* to be a proper noun referring to the figure the NT knows also as the devil (Rev. 12:9; 20:2), which, according to Cartledge (2001: 697), is a blatant contradiction. But in Hebr. *śāṭān* can simply mean 'an adversary' (Num. 22:22; 1 Sam. 29:4; 2 Sam. 19:23 [ET 19:22]; Ps. 109:6 [ET 109:5]), and if so-interpreted in Chronicles, may be a circumlocution for 'God'. The same noun (with the art.) in Job 1 – 2 refers to a member of Yahweh's heavenly court (the devil's advocate, one might say), and seems to function similarly in Zech. 3:1–2. The *śāṭān* in those texts is not independent of Yahweh, for he does only what Yahweh permits; so Chronicles may mean much the same as Samuel. A better approach considers the analogy of Job 1 – 2 where

Yahweh is ultimately responsible for Job's suffering. From the perspective of both Job and this chapter, nothing falls outside Yahweh's control, but humans are still fully responsible (see 2 Cor. 12:7). As readers we know something crucial that is hidden from the human characters (see Fokkelman 1990: 310; Simon 2000: 113).

2. Following the incitement, we move immediately to David's directing Joab. Joab is described as the army (*ḥayil*) commander, a term distinguishing him from those mentioned in 23:8–39. Joab was with David, as befits his role, but represents the army since David's directives involve them (see 'Notes'). Joab is directed to traverse the whole of Israel's territory ('from Dan to Beersheba' being shorthand for this) and register the people. Given that Hebr. narrative is generally fond of repeating verbal roots, the fact that two different words for numbering the people are used (*pqd*, *spr*) and that neither was used by Yahweh in v. 1 (*mnh*) may be significant, though they overlap to some extent. However, other than 1 Kgs 20:25 and 1 Chr. 27:24 (which alludes to this event), the qal of *mnh* is not used for a military muster, but refers to a general count (Gen. 13:16; Num. 23:10; 2 Kgs 12:11 [ET 12:10]; Ps. 90:12; Isa. 65:12). But *pqd* is often used in military contexts, notably in the wilderness traditions (Num. 1:3, 19, 44; 26:63–64; cf. Josh. 8:10; 1 Sam. 11:8; 13:15; 2 Sam. 18:1; 2 Kgs 3:6) for registering those available for battle. Finally, *spr* is not used militarily, but represents record-keeping for subsequent action (Lev. 15:13, 28; 23:15; 25:8; 2 Chr. 2:1, 16 [ET 2:2, 17]). David may exceed Yahweh's directive in seeking both to count Israel and Judah and formally register them for military and taxation purposes. One must not overstate this, because *mnh* and *spr* can be synonymous (Gen. 13:16; Num. 23:10; 1 Kgs 3:8), and other synonyms for counting are available (*ḥšb*, *kss*), but varying the terms is suggestive, especially if David's stated reason for the census is to know the number, a number that v. 9 relates to military service. The terms used in Joab's report match David's, so he precisely fulfils David's command, whereas David's fulfilment of Yahweh's directive is interpretative.

3–4. Joab's response is a surprising expression of faith. Generally, such expressions seem foreign to him given his propensity to violence (3:27; 11:14–17; 18:10–15). It is not unprecedented (10:12), though court protocol might require him to express his concerns like this. Joab's position is that David does not need a count, hinting that a census may be dangerous. A census's danger may be implied by Exod. 30:12, which links counting (*pqd*) with plague (*negep–deber* is used in vv. 13, 15, but see vv. 21, 25), though only by providing a mechanism for preventing plague. Joab does not directly counter David (unlike 19:1–8), but his closing question has that effect. We do not hear David's response, but that David's position prevailed over both Joab and the army commanders shows Joab's position was widely held. Accordingly, Joab and the commanders left to begin the registration (*pqd*) of the people of Israel, though since the count ultimately distinguished Judah from Israel, 'Israel' here refers to the whole nation.

5–7. Their itinerary is briefly outlined, though it cannot be fully reconstructed (see 'Notes'). Leaving Jerusalem, they crossed the Jordan to begin their registration at Aroer. This cannot be the Negeb town where David sent spoil (1 Sam. 30:28), and must be the town just north of the Arnon (Deut. 4:48; modern Arair) unless Num. 32:34 indicates that Gad built a town with the same name further north. This is less likely, so Joab's team began the process in the extreme south-east of Israelite territory. From there they went north to an unknown city in Gad and then to Jazer, about 12 miles south of Mahanaim before going further north within Gilead. The journey took them to Dan and across the Jordan's headwaters to Iyyon (see 'Notes'), as they headed slightly further north to reach the coast at Sidon, before moving south to Tyre. The journey from Gilead took Joab's group outside Israelite territory as they would have gone through Geshur and Maacah into southern Lebanon, though David had subjugated these regions (see 8:3–14, though no Edomite territory is reflected here). That the registration covered other peoples is made explicit by Joab's group entering Hivite and Canaanite cities. Little is known about the Hivites other than that they were a native people of the land (Gen. 10:17), though the Gibeonites are given this label in Josh. 9:7. Since 'Canaanite' is a generalizing term we cannot be too specific, but Joab's group probably headed south into the land, ultimately reaching the far south in the Negeb at Beersheba. Whatever their personal misgivings, Joab's group followed David's instructions precisely.

8–9. The exact completion of David's command is confirmed by noting they had gone through all the land, the verb *šûṭ* (rove) matching David's directive (v. 2). After nine months and twenty days, they returned to report to David at Jerusalem. The matching of vocabulary with v. 2 is further emphasized as Joab gave the number (*spr*) of those registered (*pqd*), with a division made between Israel and Judah. Since Israel's men are described as those who drew the sword, it is clear that the registration considered military availability. Taken at face value, the numbers for both Israel (eight hundred thousand) and Judah (five hundred thousand) are very high, but as elsewhere (see 'Comment' on 1 Sam. 4:2), a 'thousand' probably refers to the largest of Israel's military units, though they probably had considerably less in them than a thousand. The numbers in 1 Chr. 21:5 are quite different (Josephus is different again), suggesting the exact tradition of the numbers may not have been passed down unless there is deliberate hyperbole (Fouts 1997: 382), though the numbers involved are always large.

Confession and punishment: 24:10–17

10. Only subtle hints have been given that David has erred, but the element of sin now comes to the fore. Because he had numbered (*spr*) the people, David's heart struck him, echoing his refusal to kill Saul (1 Sam. 24:6

[ET 24:5]). The phrase indicates an awareness of guilt, particularly guilt where David has nearly transgressed the boundaries of behaviour appropriate for one anointed by Yahweh, though exactly what he did wrong is never indicated beyond the hint in vv. 2 and 9 that he exceeded Yahweh's command, attempting to work something to his own military advantage. The depth of David's awareness of sin is marked, as in prayer he acknowledged his sin (*ḥṭ'*) and asked that his iniquity (*'wn*) be removed. The language is reminiscent of Ps. 51:4 [ET 51:2] in its use of terms for sin (Carlson 1964: 207 also highlights 2 Sam. 12:13), though David adds that he has acted very foolishly. Readers of the text in English might connect this to Nabal (1 Sam. 25), but a different root is used here for folly (*skl*). The other person in Samuel said to have been very foolish was Saul when he failed to wait for Samuel before making his offering (1 Sam. 13:13) and also when confessing to David (1 Sam. 26:21). In each of these, Saul had transgressed the boundaries of what was appropriate for Yahweh's anointed, so this theme both introduces David's confession and provides its point of closure. 1 Sam. 12 provided clear limits to the king's powers and rights, and David effectively confesses that he has transgressed them.

11–14. David apparently waited the night for Yahweh's response, so that (like 7:4) word came back with a prophet in the morning. The prophet this time is Gad, last mentioned at David's stronghold in 1 Sam. 22:5. Gad is called David's seer, a prophetic label not previously used in Samuel. As David's seer he fulfilled a court role, as did Nathan (7:1–17; 12:1–15a; see Schenker 1982: 31–32), but the crucial point is that Yahweh's word came to him. Yahweh's directive to Gad was to announce to David that Yahweh was offering a choice of three things that could befall the king. David needed to choose from them so Yahweh would do it, a choice without analogy in the OT. Yahweh's initial message is not fully reported, so the narrator can delay announcing the choices until Gad comes to David. None is desirable, though they are more or less equivalent in effect. The first and third options are national in impact since the first is for seven years of famine and the last for three days of pestilence. Seven years of famine (see 'Notes') would exceed the three years brought on by Saul's sin (21:1), though plague is something new. Taken at face value, the middle option (David being pursued by his enemies for three months) might be considered as personal to David, but such a pursuit would ravage the whole country. Each option affects both David and the nation, consistent with the fact that Yahweh's anger has been kindled against the nation through David (v. 1; similarly, Simon 2000: 143). The pressure on David is to make an immediate decision. He effectively chooses not to decide and leaves the matter to Yahweh, his distress perhaps making the choice impossible. What he will not accept is falling into human hands, effectively ruling out the second option, but is prepared to commit both himself and the people to Yahweh on the basis of Yahweh's great compassion. The interaction between king and people continues, because David is clear that the whole nation should fall into Yahweh's power, but he should not fall into the power of his enemies. David is not avoiding personal suffering, because his own flight would be destructive for the nation. Rather, at both the corporate and personal level he chooses Yahweh, but otherwise leaves open the option of either famine or pestilence.

15–16. The choice having been passed across, Yahweh chose three days of pestilence. It started in the morning, presumably from when the choices were presented to David, and ran until the appointed time (mô'ēd), though what this time might be is unclear. The pestilence did not run for three days because Yahweh relented as it approached Jerusalem. LXX interprets mô'ēd as the midday meal, but Gordon (1986: 320) is rightly sceptical. It is better to understand the appointed time as indicating that the pestilence could have run for the full three days in order to appreciate that Yahweh relented. However long it ran, seventy thousand were killed. 'Thousand' in v. 9 probably means a military unit; and if that is so here, then David's military strength was reduced by seventy such units (similarly, Youngblood 1992: 1100). An angel (introduced in v. 16) was apparently the means by which the pestilence was sent, though only when the pestilence was about to be released on Jerusalem did Yahweh relent and the angel was commanded to cease. This creates an intriguing parallel with 1 Sam. 15:10 and 29, though the effect is again to stress that the statement about Yahweh's not relenting (1 Sam. 15:29) is not an ontological declaration about Yahweh's nature but rather relates to the certainty of Saul's rejection as king. It is not that Yahweh is incapable of relenting, but that in that instance a limit had been reached. Such a limit had not been reached with David, so the angel could be commanded to drop the hand pictured as reaching out against Jerusalem. The close relationship between Yahweh and the angel is stressed by the fact that the angel is then named as the angel of Yahweh, a label that consistently indicates the presence of Yahweh (Gen. 16:7–14; Exod. 32:34; Judg. 2:1–4; 6:20–23; see Dyrness 1979: 41–42). However picturesque the language of the angel might be, it was still Yahweh who acted. The point where the command was given to the angel to stop was when he reached the threshing floor (a place for threshing harvested grain) of the Jebusite Araunah (see 'Notes'). A non-Israelite, he had remained in Jerusalem after its capture by David and appears to have been a man of some wealth who was prepared to continue to work with David.

17. This section is bounded by David's two confessions and the development between them. The second confession occurs when David sees the angel who is striking the people. This suggests the angel was still active and David's prayer either preceded or was simultaneous with Yahweh's command to the angel to stop. The order of presentation is vital because it foregrounds Yahweh's mercy, while acknowledging the role of David's confession. As before, David speaks of both his 'sin' (ht') and his 'iniquity' ('wn), but distinguishes himself from the people whom he styles as sheep.

Although portraying a monarch's people as sheep is a common ANE theme, it takes on special resonance in the light of David's earlier profession (1 Sam. 16:11; 17:34). Just as he rescued his father's flocks (1 Sam. 17:34–37), so he must now rescue his people. The grasping David of 2 Sam. 11 must again become the giving David who understands his role as his people's guardian; and just as he previously faced the wrath of both lion and bear, now he must face that of Yahweh. A parallel may be drawn with Exod. 32:30–35, where Moses interceded for the people, though there the innocent Moses could not prevent a plague, whereas here the guilty David does (Schenker 1982: 36).

David mediates reconciliation: 24:18–25

18–19. The significance of Araunah's mention becomes clear only as Gad re-enters the narrative. As with David's first confession, his second also leads to Gad's involvement (Fokkelman 1990: 317). Gad directs David to go up and establish an altar on Araunah's threshing floor where the angel stopped. No reason is given for this, though the narrator indicates the angel acts as Yahweh's messenger. David now does as Yahweh has commanded through Gad, an important contrast with v. 2, where David introduced small changes to Yahweh's command. Once more he is a king operating under Yahweh's authority.

20–23. David again operates under Yahweh's authority, but must still resolve the question of how to fulfil the command he received. To record this, the narrator focuses on Araunah and his perspective when he saw David and his attendants approaching, something he could do because of the threshing floor's height. Araunah does not know about Yahweh's command, but is astute enough to know he must pay his king proper respect. Therefore, he prostrates himself before asking in appropriate court language (see 9:6) why David has come. David's directive had said that he should establish an altar to Yahweh, but had not indicated how this was to happen. Responding to Araunah, David focuses first on purchasing the threshing floor before indicating that this is so he can build an altar to Yahweh. To this he adds the note that the altar's erection is the mechanism for restraining the plague, something Gad had not said, though it was a reasonable deduction. This placed Araunah in an awkward position. One could hardly stand in the king's way or negotiate a good price. Indeed, one might expect the land to be seized, possibly why he offers the land and everything necessary for the sacrifice as a gift to David, though he might only have thought of a temporary worship site (see 1 Sam. 6:14). Araunah also expresses the wish that Yahweh accept David. The unequal negotiating positions make this land purchase somewhat different from that of Abraham in Gen. 23, weakening the parallels suggested by McDonough (1999).

24–25. David's confession made him recognize that he could not simply take from his people, whether Israelite or resident foreigner. That is not the role of Israel's king. Hence David declined Araunah's offer and insisted he would pay in full on the principle that a sacrifice must be costly (see 2 Cor. 8:1–15) since worship that costs nothing is hardly worthy of the name. Accordingly, David paid fifty shekels of silver (a little over a pound in weight: Chronicles has six hundred shekels of gold, presumably for the surrounding area) for the threshing floor, which in context was presumably a fair price. There, exactly as Yahweh had commanded, David built an altar where he offered up burnt offerings and peace offerings. The burnt offering (Lev. 1) is associated with making atonement (Lev. 1:4), while the peace offering (Lev. 3) was a mechanism for inviting one's community to share in worship. Plurals are used for both, indicating that David was not stingy in this act of worship. We are probably to understand that David not only addressed his own need for atonement but that he also saw the need as king to do so for the whole community. Since Yahweh's anger was directed against Israel (v. 1), it is only right that the story's concluding note be that Yahweh was now supplicated for the land and the plague restrained. David's confession had brought a national reprieve, but now because he had faithfully done as Yahweh had commanded, the whole nation was restored in its relationship with Yahweh. What David achieved in the light of Saul's sin (21:14) he here achieves for himself, an entirely appropriate place to end the books of Samuel.

Explanation

For modern readers, and no doubt many ancient ones, this is one of the most perplexing narratives in Samuel, if not the OT as a whole. It induces levels of confusion because it insists that Yahweh was angry with Israel and so incited David to take a census that was so sinful it merited extreme punishment, though why it was sinful can only be implied. More curiously, David could even choose his own punishment, though he had already confessed his sin (v. 10). Moreover, even though Yahweh had stilled the angel who was bringing plague and David had confessed again, David still had to negotiate the purchase of a threshing floor as the site for sacrifices. Yahweh was only then supplicated and the plague restrained. What is a narrative like this doing here, not only rounding off the Conclusion, but also ending the books of Samuel?

Consideration of that question requires that some matters stay shrouded in mystery. We are never told why Yahweh was angry with Israel, and in spite of the links with 21:1–14 we cannot simply read from one to the other. The Samuel Conclusion may be structured as a chiasm, but is read sequentially. A sequential reading is not only aware of the Conclusion; it is aware of Samuel as a whole. Read against this background, we appreciate that Israel has transgressed boundaries of covenant, though we do not know how. Where Saul's sin brought famine, David's brings plague. But, as with the famine (21:1–14), David must work towards a resolution. There is an important balance here: Israel is to be punished, but by working this through inciting David, Yahweh also provides a means by which that punishment's full effects can be ameliorated. Punishment is not avoided, but its full effects are not felt, notwithstanding the loss of life in the pestilence. There is a close analogy with 2 Sam. 11 – 12: sin results in punishment, but Yahweh does not allow punishment to reach its full potential.

For David the narrative demonstrates that he is a king who understands the monarch's role in Israel, although he is also tempted to abuse power. The census appears to be determining military status, possibly in a way that exceeds Yahweh's directive. David could still be grasping, but he also realized that the king finally had to submit to Yahweh. His repentance in v. 10 is a step beyond ch. 12, because here David initiates the process, and Gad's role is merely to announce the punishment options. Even from here David could go further, for although Yahweh's mercy was there, he still had to work out how that should be applied, even down to details like purchasing Araunah's threshing floor. There he committed himself to worship, through sacrifice that made atonement, and shared with the community. The nation's future security was discovered in this act, where Yahweh was merciful, but David was fully committed to worship and to leading his people in it. This was what David had done in 6:17–18, but his worship is also reminiscent of Hannah's in 1 Sam. 1. For both, Yahweh was the problem, but Yahweh was also the solution. The difference is that although Hannah saw an immediate resolution through Samuel's birth, she also looked forward to Yahweh's king as the one through whom Yahweh's reign would be expressed (2:10). David here embodies this, pointing the way forward for the nation and the kings who will follow, and ultimately to Jesus as the one whose sacrifice truly draws all to himself (John 12:32). Samuel thus closes by reminding us of where it began, but also by pointing beyond itself. For all its perplexity, we can imagine no better ending.

BIBLIOGRAPHY

COMMENTARIES ON 1 AND 2 SAMUEL

Ackroyd, P. R. (1971), *The First Book of Samuel*, CBC, Cambridge: Cambridge
    University Press.
—— (1977), *The Second Book of Samuel*, CBC, Cambridge: Cambridge
    University Press.
Alter, R. (1999), *The David Story: A Translation with Commentary of 1 and
    2 Samuel*, New York: Norton.
Anderson, A. A. (1989), *2 Samuel*, WBC, Dallas: Word.
Arnold, B. T. (2003), *1 & 2 Samuel*, NIVAC, Grand Rapids: Zondervan.
Baldwin, J. G. (1988), *1 and 2 Samuel: An Introduction and Commentary*,
    TOTC, Leicester: IVP.
Bergen, R. D. (1996), *1, 2 Samuel*, NAC, Nashville: Broadman & Holman.
Birch, B. C. (1998), 'The First and Second Books of Samuel', in L. E. Keck (ed.),
    The New Interpreter's Bible, Nashville: Abingdon, 2:947–1383.
Brueggemann, W. (1990b), *First and Second Samuel*, Interpretation, Louisville:
    John Knox.
Budde, K. (1902), *Die Bücher Samuel erklärt*, Tübingen: Mohr.
Cartledge, T. W. (2001), *1 and 2 Samuel*, SHBC, Macon: Smyth & Helwys.
Campbell, A. F. (2003), *1 Samuel*, FOTL, Grand Rapids: Eerdmans.
—— (2005), *2 Samuel*, FOTL, Grand Rapids: Eerdmans.
Davis, D. R. (2000), *1 Samuel: Looking on the Heart*, FOB, Fearn: Christian
    Focus.
—— (2001), *2 Samuel: Out of Every Adversity*, FOB, Fearn: Christian Focus.
Evans, M. J. (2000), *1 and 2 Samuel*, NIBCOT, Peabody: Hendrickson.
—— (2004), *The Message of Samuel: Personalities, Potential, Power and
    Politics*, BST, Leicester: IVP.
Goldingay, J. (2000), *Men Behaving Badly*, Carlisle: Paternoster.
Gordon, R. P. (1986), *I & II Samuel: A Commentary*, Grand Rapids: Zondervan.
Hentschel, G. (1994), '1 Samuel', in J. Scharbert and G. Hentschel, *Rut,
    1 Samuel*, NEchtB, Würzburg: Echter Verlag.
Hertzberg, H. W. (1964), *I & II Samuel: A Commentary*, OTL, London: SCM.
Jobling, D. (1998), *1 Samuel*, Berit Olam, Collegeville: Liturgical.
Keil, C. F., and F. Delitzsch, (1956), *Biblical Commentary on the Books of
    Samuel*, Grand Rapids: Eerdmans.
Klein, R. W. (1983), *1 Samuel*, WBC, Waco: Word.
Mauchline, J. (1971), *1 and 2 Samuel*, NCB, London: Marshall, Morgan &
    Scott.

McCarter, P. K., Jr. (1980a), *1 Samuel: A New Translation with Notes and Commentary*, AB, Garden City: Doubleday.
—— (1984), *II Samuel: A New Translation with Notes and Commentary*, AB, Garden City: Doubleday.
McKane, W. (1963), *I & II Samuel: Introduction and Commentary*, TBC, London: SCM.
Mowvley, H. (1998), *1 & 2 Samuel*, TPBC, Oxford: Bible Reading Fellowship.
Peterson, E. (1999), *First and Second Samuel*, IBS, Louisville: Westminster John Knox.
Philbek, B. F., Jr. (1970), '1–2 Samuel', in C. J. Allen (ed.), *The Broadman Bible Commentary* 3:1–145.
Robinson, G. (1993), *Let us Be Like the Nations: A Commentary on the Books of 1 and 2 Samuel*, ITC, Edinburgh: Handsel.
Smith, H. P. (1899), *A Critical and Exegetical Commentary on the Books of Samuel*, ICC, Edinburgh: T. & T. Clark.
Stoebe, H. J. (1973), *Das erste Buch Samuelis*, KAT, Gütersloh: Gerd Mohn.
Tsumura, D. T. (2007), *The First Book of Samuel*, NICOT, Grand Rapids: Eerdmans.
Van Zyl, A. H. (1988, 1989), *1 Samuël*, 2 vols., POT, Nijkerk: G. F. Callenbach BV.
Youngblood, R. F. (1992), '1, 2 Samuel', in F. E. Gaebelein (ed.), *The Expositor's Bible Commentary*, Grand Rapids: Zondervan, 3:551–1104.

OTHER WORKS

Ackerman, J. S. (1990), 'Knowing Good and Evil: A Literary Analysis of the Court History in 2 Samuel 9–20 and 1 Kings 1–2', *JBL* 109:41–60.
Ackerman, S. (2002), 'The Personal Is Political: Covenantal and Affectionate Love ('āhēb 'āhăbâ) in the Hebrew Bible', *VT* 52:437–458.
Ackroyd, P. R. (1981), 'The Succession Narrative (so-called)', *Int* 35:383–396.
Adam, K.-P. (2001), *Der Königliche Held: Die Entsprechung von kämpfendem God und kämpfendem König in Psalm 18*, Neukirchen-Vluyn: Neukirchener Verlag.
—— (2007), *Saul und David in der judäischen Geschichtsschreibung*, Tübingen: Mohr Siebeck.
Ahlström, G. W. (1984), 'The Travels of the Ark: A Religio-Political Composition', *JNES* 43:141–149.
Albrektson, B. (1977), 'Some Observations on Two Oracular Passages in 1 Sam', *ASTI* 11:1–10.
Allen, L. C. (1999), '1 & 2 Chronicles', in L. E. Keck (ed.), *The New Interpreter's Bible*, Nashville: Abingdon, 3:297–659.
Alter, R. (1981), *The Art of Biblical Narrative*, New York: Basic.
—— (1985), *The Art of Biblical Poetry*, Edinburgh: T. & T. Clark.
Althann, R. (1981), '1 Sam 13:1: A Poetic Couplet', *Bib* 62:241–246.

—— (1984), 'Northwest Semitic Notes on Some Texts in1 Samuel', *JNSL* 12:27–34.

Altpeter, G. (1982), 'II Sam 12, 1–15a: Eine strukturalistische Analyse', *TZ* 38:46–52.

Amit, Y. (1994), ' "Am I Not More to You Than Ten Sons?" (1 Samuel 1:8): Male and Female Interpretations', in Brenner 1994: 68–76.

—— (2006), 'The Delicate Balance in the Image of Saul and Its Place in the Deuteronomistic History', in Ehrlich and White 2006: 71–79.

Anderson, B. W. (1996), 'When God Repents', *BRev* 12.3:21, 44.

—— (1999), *Contours of Old Testament Theology*, Minneapolis: Fortress.

Anderson, R. W., Jr. (1990), ' "And He Grasp Away Our Eye": A Note on II Sam 20:6', *ZAW* 102:392–306.

Angert-Quilter, T., and L. Wall (2001), 'The Spirit-Wife at Endor', *JSOT* 92:55–72.

Arnold, B. T. (1989), 'The Amalekite's Report of Saul's Death: Political Intrigue or Incompatible Sources?', *JETS* 32:289–298.

—— (2004), 'A Pre-Deuteronomistc Bicolon in 1 Samuel 12:21?', *JBL* 123.1:137–142.

Arnold, P. M., S. J. (1990), *Gibeah: The Search for a Biblical City*, Sheffield: Sheffield Academic Press.

Ashley, T. R. (1993), *The Book of Numbers*, NICOT, Grand Rapids: Eerdmans.

Aster, S. Z. (2003), 'What Was Doeg the Edomite's Title? Textual Emendation versus a Comparative Approach', *JBL* 122:353–361.

Auffret, P. (1995), 'Et d'un trône de gloire il les fait heriter: Etude structurelle du cantique d'Anne', *OTE* 8:223–240.

Auld, A. G. (1994), *Kings without Privilege: David and Moses in the Story of the Bible's Kings*, Edinburgh: T. & T. Clark.

—— (2004), *Samuel at the Threshold: Selected Works of Graeme Auld*, Aldershot: Ashgate.

Avioz, M. (2005a), 'Could Saul Rule Forever? A New Look at 1 Samuel 13:13–14', *JHS* 5, art. 16.

—— (2005b), *Nathan's Oracle (2 Samuel 7), and Its Interpreters*, Bern: Peter Lang.

Báez-Camargo, G. (1980), 'Biblical Archaeology Helps the Translator', *TBT* 3.1:318–322.

Bailey, R. C. (1990), *David in Love and War: The Pursuit of Power in 2 Samuel 10–12*, Sheffield: JSOT Press.

—— (1995), 'The Redemption of Yahweh: A Literary Critical Function of the Songs of Hannah and David', *BibInt* 3:215–230.

Balentine, S. E. (1993), *Prayer in the Hebrew Bible: The Drama of Divine–Human Dialogue*, Minneapolis: Fortress.

Bar-Efrat, S. (1989), *Narrative Art in the Bible*, Sheffield: Almond.

Barnett, R. D. (1990), 'Six Fingers and Six Toes: Polydactylism in the Ancient World', *BAR* 16.3:46–51.

Barr, J. (1968), *Comparative Philology and the Text of the Old Testament*, Oxford: Oxford University Press.

Barrick, W. B. (1997), 'Saul's Demise, David's Lament and Custer's Last Stand', *JSOT* 73:25–41.

Bartelmus, R. (1987), 'Tempus als Strukturprinzip: Anmerkungen zur stilistischen und teologischer Relevanz des Tempusgebrauchs im "Lied der Hanna" (1 Sam 2:1–10)', *BZ* 31:15–35.

Becker-Spörl, S. (1992), *'Und Hanna betete und sie sprach . . .' Literarische Untersuchungen zu 1 Sam 2:1–10*, Tübingen: Francke.

Begg, C. T. (1982), 'The Reading *shbty (km)* in Deut 29,9 and 2 Sam 7,7', *ETL* 58:87–105.

———(1988), 'The Re-Reading in 2 Sam 7,7: Some Remarks', *RB* 95:551–558.

Begin, M. (1992), 'The Prophet Samuel and King Saul', *JBQ* 20:225–233.

Bellefontaine, E. (1987), 'Customary Law and Chieftanship: Judicial Aspects of 2 Samuel 14:4–21', *JSOT* 38:47–72.

ben-Barak, Z. (1979), 'The Mizpah Covenant (1 Sam 10:25) – The Source of the Israelite Monarchic Covenant', *ZAW* 91:30–43.

———(1981), 'Meribaal and the System of Land Grants in Ancient Israel', *Bib* 62:73–91.

Bentzen, A. (1948), 'The Cultic Use of the Story of the Ark in Samuel', *JBL* 67:37–53.

Bergen, R. D. (2003), 'Authorial Intent and the Spoken Word: A Discourse Critical Analysis of Speech Acts in Accounts of Israel's United Monarchy (1 Sam 1–1 Kings 11)', in D. M. Howard and M. A. Grisanti (eds.), *Giving the Sense: Understanding and Using Old Testament Historical Texts*, Grand Rapids: Kregel, 360–379.

Berges, U. (1990), *Die Verwerfung Sauls*, Würzburg: Echter Verlag.

Bergh, R. H. van den (2008), 'Deadly Traits: A Narratological Analysis of Character in 2 Samuel 11', *OTE* 21.1:180–192.

Berlin, A. (1982), 'Characterization in Biblical Narrative: David's Wives', *JSOT* 23:69–85.

Bettenzoli, G. (1986a), 'Samuel und das Problem des Königtums: Die Tradition von Gilgal', *BZ* 30:222–236.

———(1986b), 'Samuel und Saul in der geschichtlicher und theologischer Auffassung', *ZAW* 98:338–351.

Beuken, W. A. M. (1978), '1 Samuel 28: The Prophet as "Hammer of Witches"', *JSOT* 6:3–17.

Bezuidenhout, L. C. (1997), 'Voorstellungs van Batseba: Intertekstualiteit in literêre kuns, beeldende kuns en werklikheid', *HTS* 53:529–542.

Biddle, M. E. (2002), 'Ancestral Motifs in 1 Samuel 25: Intertextuality and Characterization', *JBL* 121:617–638.

Bietenhard, S. (1999), 'Michal und die Frau am Fenster: Ein Beitrag zur Motiv-und Redaktionsgeschichte von II Sam 6,16.20–23', *TZ* 55:3–25.

Bimson, J. J. (ed.) (1995), *Illustrated Encyclopedia of Bible Places*, Leicester: IVP.

Bimson, J. J., P. Kane, J. H. Paterson, D. J. Wiseman and D. R. W. Wood (eds.) (1995), *New Bible Atlas*, Leicester: IVP.

Biran, A. (1983), '"And David Sent Spoils ... to the Elders in Aroer" (1 Samuel 30:26–28)', *BAR* 9.2:28–37.

Birch, B. C. (1976), *The Rise of the Israelite Monarchy: The Growth and Development of 1 Samuel 7–15*, Missoula: Scholar's Press.

Blenkinsopp, J. (1969), 'Kiriath-Jearim and the Ark', *JBL* 88:143–156.

—— (2002), 'Saul and the Mistress of the Spirits', in A. G. Hunter and P. R. Davies (eds.), *Sense and Sensitivity: Essays on Reading the Bible in Memory of Robert P. Carroll*, London: Sheffield Academic Press, 40–61.

Blomberg, C. L. (2005), *Contagious Holiness: Jesus' Meals with Sinners*, Leicester: Apollos.

Bodner, K. (2001), 'Nathan: Prophet, Politician and Novelist?', *JSOT* 95:43–54.

—— (2002), 'Is Joab a Reader-Response Critic?', *JSOT* 27:19–35.

—— (2003), 'Eliab and the Deuteronomist', *JSOT* 28:55–71.

—— (2004), 'Layers of Ambiguity in 2 Samuel 11, 1', *ETL* 80:102–111.

—— (2005), *David Observed: A King in the Eyes of his Court*, Sheffield: Phoenix.

Boecker, H. J. (1969), *Die Beurteilung der Anfänge des Königtums in den deuteronomistischen Abschnitten des 1. Samuelbuches: Ein Beitrag zum Problem des "deuteronomistischen Geschichtswerks"*, Neukirchen-Vluyn: Neukirchener Verlag.

—— (1980), *Law and the Administration of Justice in the Old Testament and Ancient East*, London: SPCK.

Botha, P. J. (1986), '2 Samuel 7 against the Background of Ancient Near-Eastern Memorial Inscriptions', in van Wyk 1986: 62–78.

Boyce, R. N. (1988), *The Cry to God in the Old Testament*, Atlanta: Scholars Press.

Branch, R. G. (2005), 'Rizpah: An Activist in Nation Building. An Analysis of 2 Samuel 21:1–14', *JSem* 14:74–94.

Braun, R. (1986), *1 Chronicles*, WBC, Word: Waco.

Brenner, A. (ed.) (1994), *A Feminist Companion to Samuel and Kings*, Sheffield: Sheffield Academic Press.

Brettler, M. (1997), 'The Composition of 1 Samuel 1–2', *JBL* 116:601–612.

Bright, J. (1980), *A History of Israel*, 3rd ed., London: SCM.

Brown, J. K. (2007), *Scripture as Communication: Introducing Biblical Hermeneutics*, Grand Rapids: Baker Academic.

Brueggemann, W. (1985), *David's Truth in Israel's Imagination & Memory*, Philadelphia: Fortress.

—— (1988), '2 Samuel 21–24: An Appendix of Deconstruction', *CBQ* 50:383–397; repr. in Brueggemann 1992: 235–251.

—— (1989), 'Narrative Intentionality in 1 Samuel 29', *JSOT* 43:21–35.

—— (1990a), '1 Samuel: A Sense of Beginning', *ZAW* 102:33–48; repr. in Brueggemann 1992: 219–234.

—— (1990c), *Power, Providence and Personality: Biblical Insight into Life and Ministry*, Louisville: Westminster John Knox.

—— (1992), *Old Testament Theology: Essays on Structure, Theme and Text*, ed. P. D. Miller, Minneapolis: Fortress.

—— (1993), 'Narrative Coherence and Theological Intentionality in 1 Samuel 18', *CBQ* 55:225–243.

—— (2002), *Ichabod Toward Home: The Journey of God's Glory*, Grand Rapids: Eerdmans.

Cahill, J. (2004), 'Jerusalem in David and Solomon's Time', *BAR* 30.6:20–31, 62–63.

Calderone, P. J. (1966), *Dynastic Oracle and Suzerainty Treaty: 2 Samuel 7, 8–16*, Manila: Loyola House of Studies.

Camp, C. V. (1981), 'The Wise Woman of 2 Samuel: A Role Model for Women in Early Israel', *CBQ* 43:14–29.

Campbell, A. F. (1975), *The Ark Narrative (1 Sam 4–6; 2 Sam 6): A Form Critical and Traditio-Historical Study*, SBLDS 16, Missoula: Scholar's Press.

—— (1979), 'Yahweh and the Ark: A Case Study in Narrative', *JBL* 98:31–43.

—— (1986), 'From Philistine to Throne (1 Samuel 16:14–18:16)', *AusBR* 34:35–41.

—— (1991), 'Past History and Present Text: The Clash of Critical and Post-Critical Approaches to Biblical Text', *AusBR* 39:1–18.

—— (2002), 'The Storyteller's Role: Reported Story and Biblical Text', *CBQ* 64:427–441.

Carlson, R. A. (1964), *David the Chosen King: A Traditio-Historical Approach to the Second Book of Samuel*, Uppsala: Almqvist & Wiksells Boktryckeri.

Cartledge, T. W. (1989), 'Were Nazirite Vows Unconditional?', *CBQ* 51:409–422.

Ceresko, A. R. (1985), 'A Rhetorical Analysis of David's "Boast" (1 Sam 17:34–37): Some Reflections on Method', *CBQ* 47:58–74.

—— (2001), 'The Identity of "The Blind and the Lame" *('iwwer upisseah)* in 2 Samuel 5:8b', *CBQ* 63.1:23–30.

Chavel, S. (2003), 'Compositry and Creativity in 2 Samuel 21:1–14', *JBL* 122:23–52.

Childs, B. S. (1979), *Introduction to the Old Testament as Scripture*, London: SCM.

Chisholm, R. B., Jr. (1998), *From Exegesis to Exposition: A Practical Guide to Using Biblical Hebrew*, Grand Rapids: Baker.

Claasen, W. T. (1980), '1 Sam 3:19 – A Case of Context and Semantics', *JNSL* 8:1–9.

Clements, R. E. (1967), *Abraham and David: Genesis 15 and its Meaning for Israelite Tradition*, London: SCM.

—— (1989), 'The Messianic Hope in the Old Testament', *JSOT* 43:3–19.

Clines, D. J. A., and T. C. Eskanazi (eds.) (1991), *Telling Queen Michal's Story: An Experiment in Comparative Interpretation*, Sheffield: JSOT Press.

Coats, G. W. (1981), 'Parable, Fable and Anecdote: Storytelling in the Succession Narrative', *Int* 35:368–382.

—— (1986), 'II Samuel 12:1–7a', *Int* 40:170–175.

Cogan, M. (1995), 'The Road to Endor', in Wright et al. 1995: 319–326.

Coggins, R. (1991), 'On Kings and Disguises', *JSOT* 50:55–62.

Cohen, K. I. (1994), 'King Saul: A Bungler from the Beginning', *BRev* 10.5:34–39, 56–57.

Cohen, M. (2001), 'II Sam 24 ou l'histoire d'un décret royal avorté', *ZAW* 113:17–40.

Cole, D. (1980), 'How Water Tunnels Worked', *BAR* 6.2:8–29.

Collins, N. L. (1991), 'The Start of the Pre-Exilic Calendar Day of David and the Amalekites: A Note on 1 Samuel xxx 17', *VT* 41:203–210.

Conroy, C. C. (1978), *Absalom Absalom! Narrative and Language in 2 Sam 13–20*, Rome: Pontifical Biblical Institute.

Cook, E. M. (1994), '1 Samuel xx 26–xxi 5 According to 4QSam[b]', *VT* 44:442–454.

Cook, S. L. (1994), 'The Text and Philology of 1 Samuel XIII 20–1', *VT* 44:250–254.

Couffignal, R. (1998), 'Le Récit du règne de Saül (1 Samuel 9–31)', *ETR* 88:3–20.

Coxon, P. W. (1981), 'A Note on "Bathsheba" in 2 Sam 12:1–6', *Bib* 62:247–250.

Craig, K. M., Jr. (1993), 'The Characterization of God in 2 Samuel 7:1–17', *Semeia* 63:159–176.

—— (1994), 'Rhetorical Aspects of Questions Answered with Silence in 1 Samuel 14:37 and 28:6', *CBQ* 56:221–239.

Craigie, P. C. (1983), *Psalms 1–50*, WBC, Waco: Word.

Cross, F. M., Jr. (1973), *Canaanite Myth and Hebrew Epic*, Cambridge, Mass.: Harvard.

Cross, F. M., Jr., and D. N. Freedman (1953), 'A Royal Song of Thanksgiving: II Samuel 22 = Psalm 18, *JBL* 72:15–34.

Cryer, F. H. (1985), 'David's Rise to Power and the Death of Abner: An Analysis of 1 Samuel xxvi 14–16 and its Redaction-Critical Implications', *VT* 35:385–394.

Curtis, A. (ed.) (2007), *Oxford Bible Atlas*, 4th ed., Oxford: Oxford University Press.

Cushman, B. W. (2003), 'The Politics of the Royal Harem and the Case of Bat-Sheba', *JSOT* 30:327–343.

Dahood, M., A. Magnante and L. Provera (1980), 'Instrumental *lamedh* in II Samuel 3,34', *Bib* 61:261.

Danin, A. (1979), 'Do You Know Where the Ibexes Give Birth?', *BAR* 5:50–51.

Daube, D. (1998), 'Absalom and the Ideal King', *VT* 48:315–325.

Davies, P. R. (1977), 'The History of the Ark in the Books of Samuel', *JNSL* 5:9–18.

Day, J. (1993), 'Bedan, Abdon or Barak in 1 Samuel xii 11?', *VT* 43:261–264.

Day, P. L. (1987), 'Abishai the śāṭān in 2 Samuel 19:17–24', *CBQ* 49:543–547.

De Tarragon, J.-M. (1979), 'David et l'arche: II Samuel VI', *RB* 86:514–523.

Deboys, D. E. (1989), '1 Samuel xxix 6', *VT* 39:214–219.

Deist, F. (1992), 'Coincidence as a Motif of Divine Intervention in 1 Samuel 9', *OTE* 6:7–18.

Delcor, M. (1964), 'Yahweh et Dagon', *VT* 14:138–140.

Dickson, C. (2006), 'Is There a King in Israel? Exploring Foil Characterization in 2 Samuel 18–19', *SABJT* 15:63–72.

Dietrich, W. (1972), *Prophetie und Geschichte*, Göttingen: Vandenhoeck & Ruprecht.

—— (1996), 'Die Erzäluhngen von David und Goliath in 1 Sam 17', *ZAW* 108:172–191.

Dietrich, W., and T. Naumann, (2000), 'The David–Saul Narrative', in Knoppers and McConville 2000: 276–318.

Dragga, S. (1987), 'In the Shadow of the Judge: The Failure of Saul', *JSOT* 38:39–46.

Driver, S. R. (1913), *Notes on the Hebrew Text and Topography of the Books of Samuel*, Oxford: Clarendon.

Dumbrell, W. J. (1985), *Covenant and Creation*, Carlisle: Paternoster.

Dyrness, W. (1979), *Themes in Old Testament Theology*, Downers Grove: IVP.

Eaton, M. R. (1994), 'Some Instances of Flyting in the Hebrew Bible', *JSOT* 61:3–14.

Eberhart, C. (2002), 'Beobachtungen zum Verbrennungsritus bei Schlachtopfer und Gemeinschafts-Schlachtopfer', *Bib* 83:88–96.

Edelman, D. V. (1984), 'Saul's Rescue of Jabesh-Gilead (1 Samuel 11:1–11): Sorting Story from History', *ZAW* 96:195–209.

—— (1986), 'Saul's Battle against Amaleq (1 Sam 15)', *JSOT* 35:71–83.

—— (1988), 'The Authenticity of 2 Sam 1:26 in the Lament over Saul and Jonathan', *SJOT* 1:66–75.

—— (1991), *King Saul in the Historiography of Judah*, Sheffield: JSOT Press.

Edenburg, C. (1998), 'How (Not) to Murder a King: Variations on a Theme in 1 Sam 24; 26', *SJOT* 12:64–85.

Ehrlich, C. S., and M. C. White (2006), *Saul in Story and Tradition*, Tübingen: Mohr Siebeck.

Eissfeldt, O. (1965), *The Old Testament: An Introduction*, Oxford: Blackwell.

Epsztein, L. (1986), *Social Justice in the Ancient Near East and the People of the Bible*, London: SCM.

Eslinger, L. M. (1983), 'Viewpoints and Points of View in 1 Samuel 8–12', *JSOT* 26:61–76.

—— (1985), *Kingship of God in Crisis: A Close Reading of 1 Samuel 1–12*, Sheffield: Almond.

—— (1986), 'A Change of Heart: 1 Samuel 16', in Eslinger and Taylor 1986: 341–361.

—— (1994), *House of God or House of David: The Rhetoric of 2 Samuel 7*, Sheffield, JSOT Press.

Eslinger, L. M., and G. Taylor (eds.) (1986), *Ascribe to the Lord: Biblical and Other Studies in Memory of Peter C. Craigie*, Sheffield: JSOT Press.

Exum, J. C., and S. D. Moore (eds.) (1998), *Biblical Studies / Cultural Studies: The Third Sheffield Colloquium*, Sheffield: Sheffield Academic Press.

Eybers, I. H. (1978), *A Geography of Biblical Israel and its Surroundings; with Maps*, 2nd ed., Pretoria: NGBK.

Faust, A. (2006), 'Settlement Patterns and State Formation in Southern Samaria and the Archaeology of Saul', in Ehrlich and White 2006: 14–38.

Fenton, T. L. (1997), 'Deuteronomistic Advocacy of the nâbî: 1 Samuel ix 9 and Questions of Israelite Prophecy', *VT* 47:23–42.

Fincke, A. (2001), *The Samuel Scroll from Qumran: 4QSam^a Restored and Compared to the Septuagint and 4QSam^c*, Leiden: Brill.

Finkelstein, I. (2002), 'The Philistines in the Bible: A Late Monarchic Perspective', *JSOT* 27.2:131–167.

Firth, D. G. (1999), 'Psalms of Testimony', *OTE* 12.3:440–454.

—— (2001), 'Shining the Lamp: The Rhetoric of 2 Samuel 5–24', *TynB* 52.2:203–224.

—— (2003), '*Parallelismus Membrorum* in Prose Narrative: The Function of Repetition in 1 Samuel 5–6', *OTE* 15.3:647–656.

—— (2005a), 'Play It Again Sam: The Poetics of Narrative Repetition in 1 Samuel 1–7', *TynB* 56.2:1–17.

—— (2005b), 'Speech Acts and Covenant in 2 Samuel 7:1–17', in J. A. Grant and A. I. Wilson (eds.), *The God of Covenant: Biblical, Theological and Contemporary Perspectives*, Leicester: Apollos, 79–99.

—— (2005c), *Surrendering Retribution in the Psalms: Responses to Violence in the Individual Complaints*, Milton Keynes: Paternoster.

—— (2005d), ' "That the World May Know." Narrative Poetics in 1 Samuel 16–17', in M. Parsons (ed.), *Text and Task: Scripture and Mission*, Milton Keynes: Paternoster, 20–32.

—— (2006), 'Testimonies True (?) and False (?) in 1 Samuel 21–22', *SABJT* 15:20–27.

—— (2007), 'The Accession Narrative (1 Samuel 27 – 2 Samuel 1)', *TynB* 58.1:61–82.

—— (2008), 'David and Uriah with an Occasional Appearance by Uriah's Wife: Reading and Re-Reading 2 Samuel 11', *OTE* 21.2:310–328.

Fischer, A. (1989), 'David und Bathseba: Ein literarkritischer und motivgeschichtler Beitrag zu II Sam 11', *ZAW* 101:50–59.

Fischer, S. (2001), '1 Samuel 28: The Woman at Endor – Who Is She and What Does She See?', *OTE* 14:26–46.

Flanagan, J. W. (1972), 'Court History or Succession Document? A Study of 2 Samuel 9–20 and 1 Kings 1–2', *JBL* 92:172–181.

—— (1983), 'Social Transformation and Ritual in 2 Samuel 6', in C. L. Meyers and M. O'Connor (eds.), *The Word of the Lord Shall Go Forth: Festschrift for D. N. Freedman*, Winona Lake: Eisenbrauns, 361–372.

Fokkelman, J. P. (1981), *Narrative Art and Poetry in the Books of Samuel: A Full Interpretation Based on Stylistic and Structural Analyses*. Vol. 1: *King David (II Sam. 9–20 & I Kings 1–2)*, Assen: van Gorcum.

—— (1984), 'A Lie Born of Truth, Too Weak to Contain It: A Structural Reading of 2 Sam 1:1–16', *OTS* 23:39–55.

—— (1986), *Narrative Art and Poetry in the Books of Samuel: A Full Interpretation Based on Stylistic and Structural Analyses*. Vol. 2: *The Crossing Fates (I Sam. 13–31 & II Sam. 1)*, Assen: van Gorcum.

—— (1989), 'Saul and David: Crossed Fates', *BRev* 5.3:20–32.

—— (1990), *Narrative Art and Poetry in the Books of Samuel: A Full Interpretation Based on Stylistic and Structural Analyses*. Vol. 3: *Throne and City (II Sam. 2–8 & 21–24)*, Assen: van Gorcum.

—— (1993), *Narrative Art and Poetry in the Books of Samuel: A Full Interpretation Based on Stylistic and Structural Analyses*. Vol. 4: *Vow and Desire (I Sam. 1–12)*, Assen: van Gorcum.

Fontaine, C. (1986), 'The Bearing of Wisdom and the Shape of 2 Samuel 11–12 and 1 Kings 3', *JSOT* 34:61–77.

Foresti, F. (1984), *The Rejection of Saul in the Perspective of the Deuteronomistic School*, Rome: Edizioni del Teresanum.

Fouts, D. M. (1992), 'Added Support for Reading "70 Men" in 1 Samuel vi 19', *VT* 42:394.

—— (1997), 'A Defense of the Hyperbolic Interpretation of Large Numbers in the Old Testament', *JETS* 40:377–387.

Fretheim, T. (1985), 'Divine Foreknowledge, Divine Constancy and the Rejection of Saul's Kingship', *CBQ* 47:595–602.

Frisch, A. (1996), ' "For I Feared the People and I Yielded to Them" (1 Sam 15, 24) – Is Saul's Guilt Attenuated or Intensified?', *ZAW* 108:98–104.

—— (2004), ' "And David Perceived" (2 Samuel 5,2): A Direct Insight into David's Soul and its Meaning in Context', *SJOT* 18.1:77–92.

Fritz, V. (1976), 'Die Deutungen des Königtums Sauls in den Überlieferungen von siener Entstehung 1 Sam 9–11', *ZAW* 88:346–362.

Frolov, S. (2002), 'Succession Narrative: A "Document" or a Phantom?', *JBL* 121:81–104.

—— (2007a), 'Bedan: A Riddle in Context', *JBL* 126:164–167.

—— (2007b), 'The Semiotics of Covert Action in 1 Samuel 9–10', *JSOT* 31.4:429–450.

Frolov, S., and V. Orel (1994), 'On the Meaning of 2 Sam 9, 1', *BN* 73:31–32.

—— (1994), 'Notes on 1 Samuel', *BN* 74:15–24.

—— (1995), 'A Nameless City', *JBQ* 23:252–256.

—— (1996), 'Was the Lad a Lad? On the Interpretation of 1 Sam 1:24', *BN* 81:5–7.

—— (1999), 'David in Jerusalem', *ZAW* 111:609–615.

Garsiel, M. (1983), *The First Book of Samuel: A Literary Study of Comparative Structures, Analogies and Parallels*, Jerusalem: Rubin Mass.

—— (1993), 'The Story of David and Bathsheba: A Different Approach', *CBQ* 55:244–262.

Geoghegan, J. C. (2003), ' "Until This Day" and the Preexilic Redaction of the Deuteronomistic History', *JBL* 122:201–227.

George, M. K. (1999), 'Constructing Identity in 1 Samuel 17', *BibInt* 7:389–412.

—— (2002a), 'Fluid Stability in 2 Samuel 7', *CBQ*, 64:17–36.

—— (2002b), 'Yhwh's Own Heart', *CBQ* 64:442–459.

Gerbrandt, G. E. (1986), *Kingship According to the Deuteronomistic History*, Atlanta: Scholar's Press.

Geyer, J. B. (1981), 'Mice and Rites in 1 Samuel v–vi', *VT* 31:293–304.

Geyer, M. L. (1987), 'Stopping the Juggernaut: A Close Reading of 2 Samuel 20:13–22', *USQR* 41:33–42.

Gitay, Y. (1992), 'Reflections on the Poetics of the Samuel Narrative: The Question of the Ark Narrative', *CBQ* 54:221–230.

Gnuse, R. K. (1981), 'Dreams and their Theological Significance in the Biblical Tradition', *CurTM* 8:166–171.

—— (1984), *The Dream Theophany of Samuel: Its Structure in Relation to Ancient Near Eastern Dreams and Its Theological Significance*, Lanham: University of America Press.

—— (1998), 'Spilt Water – Tales of David (2 Sam 23,13–17) and Alexander (Arrian, *Anabasis of Alexander* 6.26.1–3)', *SJOT* 12:232–248.

Gordon, R. P. (1980), 'David's Rise and Saul's Demise: Narrative Analogy in 1 Samuel 24–26', *TynB* 31:37–64.

—— (1984), *1 & 2 Samuel*, Sheffield: JSOT Press.

—— (1990), 'Word-Play and Verse Order in 1 Samuel xxiv 5–8', *VT* 40:139–144.

—— (1993), 'The Variable Wisdom of Abel: The MT and Versions at 2 Samuel xx 18–19', *VT* 43:215–226.

—— (1994), 'Who Made the Kingmaker? Reflections on Samuel and the Institution of the Monarchy', in Millard et al. 1994: 255–270.

Görg, M. (1991), 'Ittai aus Gat', *BN* 60:20–23.

Grant, J. J. M. (1997), '2 Samuel 23:1–7', *Int* 51:415–418.

Gray, M. (1998), 'Amnon: A Chip off the Old Block? Rhetorical Strategy in 2 Samuel 13:7–15: The Rape of Tamar and the Humiliation of the Poor', *JSOT* 77:39–54.

Green, B. (2003a), 'Enacting Imaginatively the Unthinkable: 1 Samuel 25 and the Story of Saul', *BibInt* 11:1–23.

—— (2003b), *How Are the Mighty Fallen? A Dialogical Study of King Saul in 1 Samuel*, London: Sheffield Academic Press.

—— (2003c), *King Saul's Asking*, Collegeville: Liturgical.

Grisanti, M. A. (1999), 'The Davidic Covenant', *TMSJ* 10:233–250.

Grønbaek, J. (1971), *Die Geschichte vom Aufstieg Davids (1. Sam. 15–2. Sam. 5): Tradition und Komposition*, Copenhagen: Prostant apud Munksgaard.

Groom, S. (2003), *Linguistic Analysis of Biblical Hebrew*, Carlisle: Paternoster.

Gunn, D. M. (1978), *The Story of King David: Genre and Interpretation*, Sheffield: JSOT Press.

—— (1980a), *The Fate of King Saul: An Interpretation of a Biblical Story*, Sheffield: JSOT Press.

—— (1980b), 'From Jerusalem to the Jordan and Back: Symmetry in 2 Samuel xv–xx', *VT* 30:109–113.

—— (ed.) (1991), *Narrative and Novella in Samuel: Studies by Hugo Gressman and Other Scholars 1906–1923*, Sheffield: Almond.

Gunn, D. M., and D. N. Fewell (1993), *Narrative in the Hebrew Bible*, Oxford: Oxford University Press.

Habel, N. C. (1965), 'The Form and Significance of the Call Narratives', *ZAW* 77:297–323.

Haelewyck, J.-C. (1994), 'Le Meurtre d'Asaël, une peripetie de la bataille de Gabaon', *ZAW* 106:27–39.

—— (1995a), 'David a-t-il régné du vivant de Saül? Etude litéraire et historique de II Sm 2,1–11', *RTL* 26:165–184.

—— (1995b), 'La Mort d'Abner: 2 Sam 3,31–39', *RB* 102:161–192.

—— (1997), 'L'Assassinat d'Ishbaal (2 Samuel IV 1–12)', *VT* 47.2:145–153.

Hagan, H. (1979), 'Deception as Motif and Theme in 2 Sam 9–20', *Bib* 60:301–326.

Hagelia, H. (1994), *Numbering the Stars: A Phraseological Analysis of Genesis 15*, Stockholm: Almqvist & Wiksell.

Halpern, B. (2001), *David's Secret Demons: Messiah, Murderer, Traitor, King*, Grand Rapids: Eerdmans.

Hamilton, M. W. (2006), 'The Creation of Saul's Royal Body: Reflections on 1 Samuel 8–10', in Ehrlich and White 2006: 139–155.

Hanson, K. C. (1996), 'When the King Crosses the Line: Royal Deviance and Restitution in Levantine Ideologies', *BTB* 26:11–25.

Harris, S. L. (1981), '1 Samuel viii 7–8', *VT* 31:79–80.

Hawk, L. D. (1996), 'Saul as Sacrifice: The Tragedy of Israel's First Monarch', *BRev* 12.6:20–25, 56.

Hebert, E. D. (1994), '2 Samuel v 6: An Interpretative Crux Reconsidered in the Light of 4QSam^a', *VT* 44.3:340–348.

Heimerdinger, J.-M. (1999), *Topic, Focus and Foreground in Ancient Hebrew Narratives*, Sheffield: Sheffield Academic Press.

Hill, A. E. (1987), 'A Jonadab Connection in the Absalom Conspiracy?', *JETS* 30:387–390.

—— (2006), 'On David's "Taking" and "Leaving" Concubines: (2 Samuel 5:13, 15:16)', *JBL* 125.1:129–139.

Ho, C. Y. S. (1999), 'The Stories of the Family Troubles of Judah and David: A Study of Their Literary Links', *VT* 49:514–531.

Hoerth, A. J., G. L. Mattingly and E. M. Yamauchi (eds.) (1994), *Peoples of the Old Testament World*, Grand Rapids: Baker.

Hoftijzer, J. (1970), 'David and the Tekoite Woman', *VT* 20:419–444.

——— (1971), 'A Peculiar Question: A Note on 2 Sam 15:27', *VT* 21:606–609.

Holloway, S. W. (1987), 'Distaff, Crutch or Chain Gang: The Curse of the House of Joab in 2 Samuel iii 29', *VT* 37.3:370–375.

Holloway, S. W., and L. K. Handy (eds.) (1995), *The Pitcher Is Broken: Memorial Essays for Gösta W. Ahlström*, Sheffield: Sheffield Academic Press.

Holter, K. S. (1989), 'Was Philistine Dagon a Fish-God? Some New Questions and an Old Answer', *SJOT* 1:142–147.

Honeyman, A. M. (1948), 'The Evidence for Regnal Names among the Hebrews', *JBL* 67:13–25.

Howard, D. M. (1989), 'The Transfer of Power from Saul to David in 1 Sam 16:13–14', *JETS* 32:473–483.

——— (2005), 'The Psalms and Current Study', in P. S. Johnston and D. G. Firth (eds.), *Interpreting the Psalms: Issues and Approaches*, Apollos: Leicester, 23–40.

Hubbard, R. L. (1984), 'The Hebrew Root *PG‘* as a Legal Term', *JETS* 27:129–133.

Humphreys, W. L. (1980), 'The Rise and Fall of King Saul: A Study of an Ancient Narrative Stratum in 1 Samuel', *JSOT* 18:74–90.

Hunter, J. H. (1991), 'Deconstruction and the Old Testament: An Evaluation of "Context" with Reference to 1 Samuel 9:2', *OTE* 4:362–372.

Hurowitz, V. A. (1994), 'Eli's Adjuration of Samuel (1 Samuel iii 17–18), in the Light of a "Diviner's Protocol" from Mari (AEM I/1, 1)', *VT* 44:483–498.

Hutter, M. (1983), 'Religionsgeschichtliche Erwägungen zu *'lhym* in 1 Sam 28,13', *BN* 21:32–36.

Hyman, R. T. (1995), 'The Power of Persuasions: Judah, Abigail and Hushai', *JBQ* 23:9–16.

Isser, S. (2003), *The Sword of Goliath: David in Heroic Literature*, Atlanta: SBL.

Jacobson, H. (1992), 'The Judge Bedan (1 Samuel xii 11)', *VT* 42:123–124.

——— (1994), 'Bedan and Barak Reconsidered', *VT* 44:108–109.

Jagt, K. A. van der (1996), 'What Did Saul Eat when He First Met Samuel? Light from Anthropology on Biblical Texts', *BT* 47:226–230.

Janzen, J. G. (1983), ' "Samuel Opened the Doors of the House of Yahweh" (1 Samuel 3:15)', *JSOT* 26:89–96.

Jarrell, R. H. (2002), 'The Birth Narrative as Female Counterpart to Covenant', *JSOT* 97:3–18.

Jensen, H. L. (1992), 'Desire, Rivalry and Collective Violence in the "Succession Narrative" ', *JSOT* 55:39–59.

Jobling, D. (1986a), *The Sense of Biblical Narrative: Structural Analyses in the Hebrew Bible*, Sheffield: Sheffield Academic Press.

────── (1986b), *The Sense of Biblical Narrative: Structural Analyses in the Hebrew Bible II*, Sheffield: JSOT Press.

────── (2000), 'What, if Anything, Is 1 Samuel?', in Knoppers and McConville 2000: 601–614.

Johnston, P. S. (2002), *Shades of Sheol: Death and Afterlife in the Old Testament*, Leicester: Apollos.

Jones, G. H. (1990), *The Nathan Narratives*, Sheffield: JSOT Press.

Kaiser, O. (1986), 'Some Observations on the Succession Narrative', in van Wyk 1986: 130–147.

────── (1988), 'Beobachtungen zur sogennanten Thronnachfolgungeerzählung Davids', *ETL* 64:5–20.

Kalimi, I. (2001), 'A Transmission of Tradition: The Number of Jesse's Sons', *TZ* 57:1–9.

Kallai, Z. (1996), 'Samuel in Qumrān: Expansion of a Historiographical Pattern (4QSamᵃ)', *RB* 103:581–591.

Kammerer, S. (1997), 'Die missratenen Söhne Samuels', *BN* 88:226–230.

Kapelrud, A. S. (1988), 'The Covenant as Agreement', *SJOT* 1:30–38.

Katzoff, L. (1985), 'The Hamsin and the Rain', *DD* 13:184–187.

Kaufmann, A. S. (1988), 'Fixing the Site of the Tabernacle at Shiloh', *BAR* 14.6:46–52.

Kearney, P. J. (1973), 'The Role of the Gibeonites in the Deuteronomic History', *CBQ* 35:1–19.

Keefe, A. A. (1993), 'Rapes of Women / Wars of Men', *Semeia* 61:79–97.

Kellermann, D. (1990), 'Die Geschichte von David und Goliath im Lichte der Endokrinologie', *ZAW* 102:344–357.

Kempinski, A. (1981), 'Is Tel Masos an Amalekite Settlement?', *BAR* 7.3:52–53.

Kent, G. (2008), 'Repetition as Narrative Tactic in 1 Samuel 28', PhD diss., Cliff College.

Kessler, J. (2000), 'Sexuality and Politics: The Motif of the Displaced Husband in the Books of Samuel', *CBQ* 62:409–423.

Keys, G. (1996), *The Wages of Sin: A Reappraisal of the 'Succession Narrative'*, Sheffield: Sheffield Academic Press.

Kim, E. K. (1984), 'A Study of the Rapid Change of Mood in the Lament Psalms, with a Special Inquiry into the Impetus for its Expression', PhD diss., Union Theological Seminary.

Kleer, M. (1996), *'Der liebliche Sänger der Psalmen Israels.' Untersuchungen zu David als Dicther und Beter der Psalmen*, Bodenheim: Philo Verlagsgesellschaft.

Klein, L. R. (1994), 'Hannah: Marginalized Victim and Social Redeemer', in Brenner 1994: 77–92.

Klein, R. W. (2004), 'The Last Words of David', *CurTM* 31:15–23.

Kleiner, M. (1995), *Saul in Endor, Wahrsagung oder Totenbeschworung?: Eine synchrone und diachrone Untersuchung zu 1 Samuel 28*, Leipzig: Benno.

Klement, H. H. (2000a), *2 Samuel 21–24: Context, Structure and Meaning in the Samuel Conclusion*, Bern: Peter Lang.

Klement, H. H. (2000b), 'David und "Hiram von Tyrus" – Zum Unterschied von literarischer und chronologischer Sequenz in Biblischer Historiographie', *JET* 14:5–33.

Kleven, T. (1992), 'Hebrew Style in 2 Samuel 6', *JETS* 35:299–314.

——— (1994a), 'Up the Waterspout: How David's General Joab Got inside Jerusalem', *BAR* 20.4:34–35.

——— (1994b), 'The Use of *snr* in Ugaritic and 2 Samuel v8: Hebrew Usage and Comparative Philiology', *VT* 44:195–204.

Knight, D. A. (1985), 'Moral Values and Literary Traditions: The Case of the Succession Narrative', *Semeia* 34:7–23.

Knoppers, G. N. (2000), 'Introduction', in Knoppers and McConville 2000: 1–18.

——— (2006), 'Israel's First King and "the Kingdom of YHWH in the Hands of the Sons of David." The Place of the Saulide Monarchy in the Chronicler's Historiography', in Ehrlich and White 2006: 187–213.

Knoppers, G. N., and J. G. McConville (2000), *Reconsidering Israel and Judah: Recent Studies on the Deuteronomistic History*, Winona Lake: Eisenbrauns.

Kooij, A. van der (1992), 'The Story of David and Goliath: The Early History of its Text', *ETL* 68:118–131.

Koorevaar, H.-J. (1995), ' "Gott" oder "man" (jemand), "Satan" oder "ein Gegner." Die Übersetzung der Präfixkonjugation dritte Person maskulin Singular in 2 Sam 24,1 und der Begriff "Satan" in 1 Chr 21, auf grund eines Vergleiches dieser parallelen Texte miteinander', *Fund* 3:224–235.

——— (1997), 'De macrostructuur van het boek Samuël en de theologische implicaties daarvan', *AcT* 17:56–86.

Kraus, H.-J. (1988), *Psalms 1–59: A Commentary*, Minneapolis: Augsburg.

Krause, M. (1983), 'II Sam 11:4 und das Konzeptionsoptimum', *ZAW* 95:434–437.

Kreuzer, S. (1996), ' "Saul war noch zwei Jahre König…" Textgeschichtlich, literarische und historische Beobachtungen zu 1 Sam 13,1', *BZ* 40:263–270.

——— (2006), 'Saul – Not Always – at War: A New Perspective on the Rise of Kingship in Israel', in Ehrlich and White 2006: 39–58.

Kruger, P. A. (1998), ' "Liminality" in 2 Samuel 19:1–9: A Short Note', *JNSL* 24:195–199.

Kruze, H. (1985), 'David's Covenant', *VT* 35.1 139–164.

Kuntz, J. K. (1983), 'Psalm 18: A Rhetorical-Critical Analysis', *JSOT* 26:3–31.

Laato, A. (1997), 'Second Samuel 7 and Ancient Near Eastern Royal Ideology', *CBQ* 59:244–269.

Lang, B. (1988), 'Afterlife – Ancient Israel's Changing Vision of the World Beyond', *BRev* 4.1:12–23.

Lasine, S. (1989), 'Judicial Narratives and the Ethics of Reading: The Reader as Judge of the Dispute between Mephibosheth and Ziba', *HS* 30:49–69.

Lawlor, J. I. (1982), 'Theology and Art in the Narrative of the Ammonite War (2 Samuel 10–12)', *GTJ* 3:193–205.

Lawton, R. B. (1989), '1 Samuel 18: David, Merob and Michal', *CBQ* 51:423–425.

—— (1993), 'Saul, Jonathan and the "Son of Jesse"', *JSOT* 58:35–46.

Layton, S. C. (1993), 'A Chain Gang in 2 Samuel 3:29: A Rejoinder', *VT* 39.1:81–86.

Lehmann, K.-P. (1991), 'Prophetie und Königsmacht in Israel: Exegetische Anmerkungen zu den Erzäluhngen über Saul's Königtum in Israel (1 Sam 8–15)', *TK* 14.2:25–42.

Leithart, P. J. (2001), 'Nabal and his Wine', *JBL* 120:525–527.

—— (2002), 'David's Threat to Nabal: How a Little Vulgarity Got the Point Across', *BRev* 18.5:18–23:59.

Lemos, T. M. (2006), 'Shame and Mutilation of Enemies in the Hebrew Bible', *JBL* 125.2:225–241.

Lescow, T. (2002), 'Die Komposition der Tamar-Erzählung II Sam 13, 1–22', *ZAW* 114:110–111.

Leuchter, M. (2005), 'A King Like All the Nations: The Composition of 1 Samuel 8, 11–19', *ZAW* 117:543–558.

Levenson, J. D. (1985), 'A Technical Meaning for *n'm* in the Hebrew Bible', *VT* 35:61–67.

Lewis, P. E. (2007), 'Is There a Parallel between 1 Samuel 3 and the Sixth Chapter of the Egyptian Book of the Dead?', *JSOT* 31.3:365–376.

Lewis, T. J. (1985), 'The Songs of Hannah and Deborah: HDL-II ("Growing Plump")', *JBL* 104:105–108.

—— (1991), 'The Ancestral Estate (*nḥlt 'lhym*) in 2 Samuel 14:16', *JBL* 110:597–612.

—— (1994), 'The Textual History of the Song of Hannah: 1 Samuel ii 1–10', *VT* 44:18–46.

Licht, J. (1989), 'The Hebrew Bible Contains the Oldest Surviving History', *BRev* 5.6:22–25, 38.

Linafelt, T. (1992), 'Taking Women in Samuel: Readers/ Responses/ Responsibility', in D. N. Fewell (ed.) (1992), *Reading Between Texts: Intertextuality and the Hebrew Bible*, Louisville: Westminster John Knox, 99–114.

Lipinski, E. (1974), 'NAGID, der Kronprinz', *VT* 24:497–499.

Loader, J. A. (2000), 'Das Haus Elis und das Haus Davids: Wie Gott sein Wort zürucknehmen kann', *HTS* 56:492–505.

—— (2005), 'Emptied Life – Death as the Reverse of Life in Ancient Israel', *OTE* 18.3:703–721.

Lokel, P. (2006), 'Previously Unstoried Lives: The Case of Old Testament Cush and its Relevance to Africa', *OTE* 19:525–537.

Long, B. O. (1987), 'Framing Repetitions in Biblical Historiography', *JBL* 106:385–399.

Long, V. P. (1989), *The Reign and Rejection of King Saul: A Case for Literary and Theological Coherence*, Missoula: Scholar's Press.

—— (1993), 'Interpolation or Characterization: How Are we to Understand Saul's Two Confessions?', *Presb* 19:49–53.

—— (1994), 'How Did Saul Become King? Literary Reading and Historical Reconstruction', in Millard et al. 1994: 271–284.

Longman, T., III (1983), '1 Sam 12:16–19: Divine Omnipotence or Covenant Curse?', *WJT* 45:168–171.

Longman, T., III, and D. G. Reid (1995), *God Is a Warrior*, Grand Rapids: Zondervan.

Lust, J. (1983), 'The Story of David and Goliath in Hebrew and Greek', *ETL* 59:5–25.

Lyke, L. L. (1997), *King David with the Wise Woman of Tekoa: The Resonance of Tradition in Parabolic Narrative*, Sheffield: Sheffield Academic Press.

McCann, J. C., Jr. (1996), 'Psalms', in L. E. Keck (ed.), *The New Interpreter's Bible*, Nashville: Abingdon, 4:641–1280.

McCarter, P. K., Jr. (1980b), 'The Apology of David', *JBL* 99:489–504.

—— (1981), ' "Plots, True or False": The Succession Narrative as Court Apologetic', *Int* 35:355–367.

—— (2000), 'The Apology of David', in Knoppers and McConville 2000: 260–275.

McCarthy, D. J. (1965), '2 Samuel 7 and the Structure of the Deuteronomic History', *JBL* 84.2:131–138.

McConville, J. G. (1993), *Judgment and Promise: An Interpretation of the Book of Jeremiah*, Leicester: Apollos.

—— (2002), *Deuteronomy*, AOTC, Leicester: Apollos.

McCormick, C. M. (2006), 'From Box to Throne: The Development of the Ark in DtrH and P', in Ehrlich and White 2006: 175–186.

McDonough, S. M. (1999), ' "And David Was Old, Advanced in Years": 2 Sam xxiv 18–25, 1 Kings 1, and Genesis xxiii–xxiv', *VT* 49:128–131.

McKane, W. (1965), *Prophets and Wise Men*, London: SCM.

McKenzie, S. L. (2000), *King David: A Biography*, New York: Oxford University Press.

—— (2006), 'Saul in the Deuteronomistic History', in Ehrlich and White 2006: 59–70.

Malul, M. (2003), '*lĕdabbēr baššelî* (2 Sam 3:27), "to Talk Peace" ', *JHS* 4, art. 30.

March, W. E. (1981), 'II Samuel 7:1–17', *Int* 35:397–400.

Margalith, O. (1983), 'The Meaning of '*plym* in 1 Samuel v–vi', *VT* 33:339–341.

Martin, J. A. (1984a), 'The Literary Quality of 1 and 2 Samuel', *BSac* 141:131–145.

—— (1984b), 'The Structure of 1 and 2 Samuel', *BSac* 141:28–42.

—— (1984c), 'The Text of 1 and 2 Samuel', *BSac* 141:209–222.

—— (1984d), 'The Theology of Samuel', *BSac* 141:303–314.

Mastin, B. A. (2003), 'The Role of Abigail in 1 Samuel 25', *AUSS* 41:45–53.

Matthews, V. H. (1991), *Manners and Customs in the Bible: An Illustrated Guide to Daily Life in Bible Times*, rev. ed., Peabody: Hendrickson.

Matthews, V. H., and D. C. Benjamin (1992), 'From Village to Tribe', *TBT* 30:235–239.

—— (1993), *Social World of Ancient Israel: 1250–587 BCE*, Peabody: Hendrickson.

May, H. G. (ed.) (1974), *Oxford Bible Atlas*, 2nd ed., London: Oxford University Press.

Mayes, A. D. H. (1978), 'The Rise of the Israelite Monarchy', *ZAW* 90:1–19.

—— (1986), 'The Gibeonites as a Historical and Theological Problem in the Old Testament', *PIBA* 10:13–24.

Mays, J. L. (1986), 'The David of the Psalms', *Int* 40:143–155.

Meadows, J. N. (1975), 'A Traditio-Historical Study of II Samuel 9–20, I Kings 1–2', PhD diss., Southern Baptist Theological Seminary.

Meier, S. A. (2006), 'The Sword. From Saul to David', in Ehrlich and White 2006: 156–174.

Mendelsohn, I. (1956), 'Samuel's Denunciation of Kingship in Light of the Akkadian Documents from Ugarit', *BASOR* 143:17–22.

Mettinger, T. N. D. (1976), *King and Messiah: The Civil and Sacral Legitimation of the Israelite Kings*, Lund: CWK Gleerup.

Meyers, C. (1995), 'An Ethnoarchaeological Analysis of Hannah's Sacrifice', in Wright et al. 1995: 77–91.

—— (1996), 'The Hannah Narrative in Feminist Perspective', in J. E. Wright and V. H. Matthews (eds.) (1996), *Go to the Land I will Show You: Studies in Honour of Dwight S. Young*, Winona Lake: Eisenbrauns, 117–126.

Millard, A. R. (1986–7), 'Archaeology and the World of the Bible', *BAIAS* 6:46–48.

Millard, A. R., J. K. Hoffmeier and D. W. Baker (eds.) (1994), *Faith, Tradition and History: Old Testament Historiography in Its Near Eastern Context*, Winona Lake: Eisenbrauns.

Miller, P. D., Jr. (1994), *They Cried to the Lord: The Form and Function of Biblical Prayer*, Minneapolis: Fortress.

Miller, P. D., Jr., and J. J. M. Roberts (1977), *The Hand of the Lord: A Reassessment of the 'Ark Narrative' of 1 Samuel*, Baltimore: Johns Hopkins University Press.

Miscall, P. D. (1979), 'Literary Unity in Old Testament Narrative', *Semeia* 15:27–44.

—— (1986), *1 Samuel: A Literary Reading*, Bloomington: Indiana University Press.

Moberley, R. W. L. (1998), 'God Is Not a Human That He Should Repent (Numbers 23:19 & 1 Samuel 15:29)', in T. K. Beal and T. Linafelt (eds.), *God in the Fray: A Tribute to Walter Brueggemann*, Minneapolis: Fortress, 112–123.

Mobley, G. (2006), 'Glimpses of the Heroic Saul', in Ehrlich and White 2006: 80–87.

Moenikes, A. (1995), *Die gründsatzliche Ablehung des Königtums in der Hebräischen Bibel: Ein Beitrag zur Religionsgeschichte in des Alten Israel*, Weinheim; Beltz Athenäum.

Mommer, P. (1991), *Samuel: Geschichte und Überlieferung*, Neukirchen-Vluyn: Neukirchener Verlag.

Muhly, J. D. (1982), 'How Iron Technology Changed the Ancient World – And Gave the Philistines a Military Edge', *BAR* 8.6:40–54.

Muntingh, L. M. (1986), 'The Role of Joab in the Succession Narrative', in van Wyk 1986: 202–217.

Muraoka, T. (1996), '1 Sam 1, 15 Again', *Bib* 77:98–99.

Murray, D. F. (1987), 'Once Again *'t 'chd mkl shbty ysr'l* in II Samuel 7:7', *RB* 94:389–396.

—— (1990), *'mqwm* and the Future of Israel in 2 Samuel vii 10', *VT* 40:298–320.

—— (1998), *Divine Prerogative and Royal Pretension: Pragmatics, Poetics and Polemics in a Narrative Sequence about David (2 Samuel 5,17–7,29)*, Sheffield: Sheffield Academic Press.

Na'aman, N. (1988), 'The List of David's Officers (*šālîšîm*)', *VT* 38:71–79.

—— (1992), 'The Pre-Deuteronomistic Story of King Saul and Its Historical Significance', *CBQ* 54:638–658.

—— (1998), 'Ittai the Gittite', *BN* 94:22–25.

Naeh, S. (1996), 'A New Suggestion Regarding 2 Samuel xxiii 7', *VT* 46:260–265.

Nahum, Y. ben (1991), 'What Ailed the Son of Kish (1 Sam 10:10–12, 19:24)?', *JBQ* 19:244–249.

Neiderhiser, E. A. (1979–80), 'One More Proposal for 1 Samuel 13:1', *HS* 20.21:44–46.

—— (1981), '2 Samuel 20:8–10: A Note for a Commentary', *JETS* 24:209–211.

Nelson, R. (1981), *The Double Redaction of the Deuteronomistic History*, Sheffield: JSOT Press.

—— (1991), 'The Role of the Priesthood in the Deuteronomistic History', *Congress Volume 1989*, VTSup 43, Leiden: Brill.

Nicol, G. G. (1988), 'Bathsheba, a Clever Woman?', *ExpTim* 99:360–363.

—— (1997), 'The Alleged Rape of Bathsheba: Some Observations on Ambiguity in Biblical Narrative', *JSOT* 73:43–54.

—— (1998), 'David, Abigail and Bathsheba, Nabal and Uriah: Transformations within a Triangle', *SJOT* 12:130–145.

Niehaus, J. J. (1995), *God at Sinai: Covenant and Theophany in the Bible and Ancient Near East*, Grand Rapids: Zondervan.

Nihan, C. L. (1998), 'L'Injustice des fils de Samuel, au tournant d'une époque', *BN* 94:26–32.

—— (2003), '1 Samuel 28 and the Condemnation of Necromancy in Persian Yehud', in T. E. Klutz (ed.), *Magic in the Biblical World: From the Rod of Aaron to the Ring of Solomon*, London: Sheffield Academic Press, 23–54.

—— (2006), 'Saul among the Prophets (1 Sam 10:10–12 and 19:18–24): The Reworking of Saul's Figure in the Context of the Debate on

"Charismatic Prophecy" in the Persian Era', in Ehrlich and White 2006: 88–118.

Nissinen, M. (1998), *Homoeroticism in the Biblical World*, Minneapolis: Fortress.

——— (1999), 'Die Liebe von David und Jonathan als Frage der modernen Exegese', *Bib* 80:250–263.

Noll, K. L. (1997), *The Faces of David*, Sheffield: Sheffield Academic Press.

——— (2007), 'Deuteronomistic History or Deuteronomic Debate? (A Thought Experiment)', *JSOT* 31:311–345.

North, R. (1982), 'David's Rise: Sacral, Military or Psychiatric?', *Bib* 63:524–544.

Noth, M. (1960), *The History of Israel*, 2nd ed., London: Adam & Charles Black.

——— (1981), *The Deuteronomistic History*, Sheffield: JSOT Press.

O'Day, G. (1985), 'Singing Woman's Song: A Hermeneutic of Liberation', *CurTM* 12:203–210.

O'Rourke Boyle, M. (2001), 'The Law of the Heart: The Death of a Fool (1 Samuel 25)', *JBL* 120:401–427.

Obinwa, I. M. C. (2006), *Yahweh My Refuge: A Critical Analysis of Psalm 71*, Frankfurt am Main: Peter Lang.

Oeming, M. (1994), 'Die Eroberung Jerusalems durch David in deuteronomistischer und chronistischer Darstellung (II Sam 5, 6–9 und I Chr 11,4–8): Ein Beitrag zur *narrativen Theologie* der beiden Geschichtswerke', *ZAW* 106:404–420.

Olmo Lete, G. del (1984), 'David's Farewell Oracle (2 Sam 23, 1–7): A Literary Analysis', *VT* 34:414–437.

Olyan, S. M. (1996), 'Honor, Shame, and Covenant Relations in Ancient Israel and its Environment', *JBL* 115:201–218.

——— (1998), 'Anyone Blind or Lame Shall Not Enter the House: On the Interpretation of Second Samuel 5:8b', *CBQ* 60:218–227.

Orel, V. (1998), 'The Great Fall of Dagon', *ZAW* 110:427–432.

Peels, H. G. L. (2003), *Shadow Sides: God in the Old Testament*, Carlisle: Paternoster.

Perdue, L. G. (1984), ' "Is There Anyone Left of the House of Saul": Ambiguity and the Characterization of David in the Succession Narrative', *JSOT* 30:67–84.

Petersen, D. L. (1981), *The Roles of Israel's Prophets*, Sheffield: JSOT Press.

Petter, D. (2004), 'Foregrounding the 'ēšet 'ûriyyâ haḥittî in II Samuel xi–xii', *VT* 54:403–407.

Phillips, G. (2006), 'The Priestly Right of the Prophet Samuel?', *SABJT* 15:101–112.

Piggott, S. M. (1998), '1 Samuel 28 – Saul and the Not So Wicked Witch of Endor', *RevExp* 95:435–444.

——— (2002), 'Wives, Witches and Wise Women: Prophetic Heralds of Kingship in 1 and 2 Samuel', *RevExp* 99:145–174.

Pisano, S. (1984), *Additions or Omissions in the Books of Samuel: The Significant Pluses and Minuses in the Massoretic, LXX and Qumran Texts*, Göttingen: Vandenhoeck & Ruprecht.

Pleins, J. D. (1992), 'Son Slayers and their Sons', *CBQ* 54:29–38.

Plöger, O. (2000), 'Speech and Prayer in the Deuteronomistc and the Chronicler's Histories', in Knoppers and McConville 2000: 31–46.

Polzin, R. (1980), *Moses and the Deuteronomist*, Bloomington: University of Indiana Press.

——— (1988), 'On Taking Renewal Seriously', in Eslinger and Taylor 1986: 493–507.

——— (1989), *Samuel and the Deuteronomist: A Literary Interpretation of the Deuteronomic History*. Pt. 2: *1 Samuel*, Bloomington: University of Indiana Press.

——— (1993), *David and the Deuteronomist: A Literary Interpretation of the Deuteronomic History*. Pt. 3: *2 Samuel*, Bloomington: University of Indiana Press.

Propp, W. H. (1993), 'Kinship in 2 Samuel 13', *CBQ* 55:39–53.

——— (1998), 'Was Samuel a Nazirite?', *BRev* 14.4:2.

Prouser, O. H. (1994), 'The Truth about Women and Lying', *JSOT* 61:15–28.

——— (1998), 'Clothes Maketh the Man: Keys to Meaning in the Stories of Saul and David', *BRev* 14.1:22–27.

Provan, I., V. P. Long and T. Longman III (2003), *A Biblical History of Israel*, Louisville: Westminster John Knox.

Pyper, H. S. (1993), 'The Enticement to Re-Read: Repetition as Parody in 2 Samuel', *BibInt* 1:153–166.

Rad, G. von (1966), *The Problem of the Hexateuch and Other Essays*, Edinburgh: Oliver & Boyd.

——— (1991), *Holy War in Ancient Israel*, Grand Rapids: Eerdmans.

Ratner, R. (1987), 'Three Bulls or One? A Reappraisal of 1 Samuel 1:24', *Bib* 68:98–102.

Rebera, B. A. (1989), ' "He Got Up" – Or Did He? (1 Samuel 20:25)', *BT* 40:212–218.

Reich, R., and E. Shukron (1999), 'Light at the End of the Tunnel', *BAR* 25.1:22–33, 72.

Reinhartz, A. (1993), 'Anonymity and Character in the Books of Samuel', *Semeia* 63:117–141.

Reis, P. T. (1994), 'Collusion at Nob: A New Reading of 1 Samuel 21–22', *JSOT* 61:59–73.

——— (1997), 'Eating the Blood: Saul and the Witch of Endor', *JSOT* 73:3–23.

——— (2006), 'Killing the Messenger: David's Policy or Politics?', *JSOT* 31.2:167–191.

Rendsburg, G. A. (1988), 'The Northern Origin of "The Last Words of David" (2 Sam 23:1–7)', *Bib* 69:113–121.

——— (1989), 'Additional Notes on "The Last Words of David" (2 Sam 23:1–7)', *Bib* 70:403–408.

———— (1999), 'Confused Language as a Deliberate Device in Biblical Hebrew Narrative', *JHS*, vol. 2. Available online at <http://www.arts.ualberta.ca/JHS/index.htm>.

Rendtorff, R. (1993), *Canon and Theology: Overtures to an Old Testament Theology*, Minneapolis: Fortress.

Rezetko, R. (2007), *Source and Revision in the Narratives of David's Transfer of the Ark: Text, Language, and Story in 2 Samuel 6 and 1 Chronicles 13, 15–16*, London: T. & T. Clark.

Richardson, H. N. (1971), 'The Last Words of David: Some Notes on 2 Samuel 23:1–7', *JBL* 90:257–266.

Rinquest, L. (2006), 'Necromancing Samuel: Saul Asks Witch Which? A Narrative Perspective on 1 Samuel 28', *SABJT* 15:37–42.

Roberts, J. J. M. (1999), 'The Legal Basis for Saul's Slaughter of the Priests of Nob', *JNSL* 25.1:21–29.

Römer, T. C. (ed.) (2000), *The Future of the Deuteronomistic History*, Leuven: Peeters.

Rooy, H. F. van (1986), 'Nathan's Promise and the Succession History', in van Wyk 1986: 321–338.

Rosenberg, J. (1989), 'The Institutional Matrix of Treachery in 2 Samuel 11', *Semeia* 46:103–116.

Rost, L. (1982), *The Succession to the Throne of David*, Sheffield: Almond.

Roth, W. (1978), 'You Are the Man: Structural Interaction in 2 Samuel 10–12', *Semeia* 8:1–13.

Rowley, H. H. (1956), *The Faith of Israel: Aspects of Old Testament Thought*, London: SCM.

Rudman, D. (2000), 'The Commissioning Stories of Saul and David as Theological Allegory', *VT* 50:519–530.

———— (2001), 'Why Was Saul Rejected? A Reassessment of 1 Samuel 9–15', *ScrB* 31:101–107.

Sagi, A. (1994), 'The Punishment of Amalek in Jewish Tradition: Coping with a Moral Problem', *HTR* 87:323–346.

Sanders, P. (2004), 'So May God Do to Me!', *Bib* 85:91–98.

Scheffler, E. (2006), 'The Politics of the (Deuteronomistic) David and Jesus', *OTE* 19:950–967.

Schenker, A. (1982), *Der Mächtige im Schmelzofen des Mitleids*, Fribourg: Universitätsverlag; Göttingen: Vandenhoeck & Ruprecht.

———— (1989), 'Gelübde im Alten Testament: Unbeachtete Aspekte', *VT* 39:87–91.

Schipper, J. (2003), ' "Why Do You Still Speak of Your Affairs?" Polyphony in Mephibosheth's Exchanges with David in 2 Samuel', *VT* 53:344–351.

———— (2007), 'Did David Overinterpret Nathan's Parable in 2 Samuel 12:1–6?', *JBL* 126:383–391.

Schley, D. G. (1990), 'The *šālîšîm*: Officers or Special Three-Man Squads?', *VT* 40:321–326.

Schmidt, B. B. (1995), 'The "Witch of Endor", 1 Samuel 28, and Ancient Near Eastern Necromancy', in M. W. Meyer and P. A. Mirecki (eds.), *Ancient Magic and Ritual Power*, Leiden: Brill, 111–129.

Schmitt, H.-C. (1992), 'Das sogenannte vorprophetische Berufsschema: Zur "geistigen Heimat" des Berufungsformulars von Ex 3,9–12, Jdc 6,11–24 und 1 Sam 9,1–10:16', *ZAW* 104:202–216.

Schniedewind, W. M. (1999), *Society and the Promise to David: The Reception History of 2 Samuel 7:1–17*, Oxford: Oxford University Press.

Scholz, S. (2004), 'Gender, Class, and Androcentric Compliance in the Rapes of Enslaved Women in the Hebrew Bible', *Lectio Difficilior* 1. Available online at <http://www.lectio.unibe.ch/04_1/Scholz.Enslaved.htm>.

Schroer, S., and T. Staubli (1996), 'Saul, David und Jonathan – eine Dreieckgeschichte? Ein Beitrag zum Thema "Homosexualität im Ersten Testament"', *BK* 51:15–22.

Schrunk, K.-D. (1983), 'David's "Schlupfwinkel" in Juda', *VT* 33:110–113.

Schüngel-Straumann, H. (1981), 'Kritik am Königtum im Alten Testament', *BK* 36:194–200.

Schwartz, R. M. (1991), 'Adultery in the House of David: The Meta-Narrative of Biblical Scholarship and the Narratives of the Bible', *Semeia* 54:35–55.

Seger, J. D. (1984), 'The Location of Biblical Ziklag', *BA* 47:47–53.

Seidl, T. (1986), 'David statt Saul: Göttliche Legitimation und menschliche Kompetenz des Königs als Motive der Redaktion von 1 Sam 16–18', *ZAW* 98:39–55.

Seiler, S. (1998), *Die Geschichte von der Thronfolge Davids (2 Sam 9–20; 1 Kön 1–2): Untersuchungen zur Literarkritik und Tendenz*, Berlin: Walter de Gruyter.

Selman, M. J. (1994), *1 Chronicles*, TOTC, Leicester: IVP.

Seters, J. van (2000), 'The Deuteronomist from Joshua to Samuel', in Knoppers and McConville 2000: 204–239.

Shalom Brooks, S. (1996), 'Saul and the Samson Narrative', *JSOT* 76:19–25.

——— (2005), *Saul and the Monarchy: A New Look*, Aldershot: Ashgate.

Shanks, H. (1985), 'The City of David after Five Years of Digging', *BAR* 11.6:22–38.

——— (1999a), 'I Climbed Warren's Shaft (but Joab Never Did)', *BAR* 25.6:30–35.

——— (1999b), 'New Life for an Old Theory', *BAR* 25.1:6, 60, 72.

Shaviv, S. (1984), '*nābî* and *nāgîd* in 1 Samuel ix 1–x 16', *VT* 34:108–113.

Shea, W. H. (1987), 'A Possible Biblical Connection for the Beth Shemesh Ostracon', *AUSS* 25:257–266.

——— (1990a), 'Further Light on the Beth Shemesh Ostracon', *AUSS* 28:115–125.

——— (1990b), 'Further Light on the Biblical Connection of the Beth Shemesh Ostracon', *AUSS* 28:115–125.

——— (1990c), 'The 'Izbet Sartah Ostracon', *AUSS* 28:59–86.

Sheriffs, D. C. T. (1979), 'The Phrases *ina IGI DN* and *lipnēy yhwh* in Treaty and Covenant Texts', *JNSL* 7:55–68.

Simon, L. T. (2000), *Identity and Identification: An Exegetical and Theological Study of 2 Sam 21–24*, Rome: Gregorian University.

Ska, J.-L. (1990), *Our Fathers Have Told Us: An Introduction to the Analysis of Hebrew Narratives*, Rome: Pontifical Biblical Institute.

Smelik, K. A. D. (1989), 'The Ark Narrative Reconsidered', *OTS* 25:128–144.

—— (1992), 'Hidden Messages in the Ark Narrative: An Analysis of I Samuel iv–vi and II Samuel vi', in idem, *Converting the Past: Studies in Ancient Israelite and Moabite Historiography*, Leiden: Brill, 35–58.

Smend, R. (2000), 'The Law and the Nations: A Contribution to the Deuteronomistic Tradition History', in Knoppers and McConville 2000: 95–110.

Smith, J. (1990), 'The Discourse Structure of the Rape of Tamar (2 Samuel 13:1–22), *VE* 20:21–42.

Snyman, G. (1994), 'Old Testament Theology: Fabulous Dreams of the Other Side of Time and Space', *OTE* 7:453–465.

Spero, S. (1991), 'An Elegy of David, to Teach the Sons of Judah the Bow', *JBQ* 19:155–163.

Spina, F. A. (1991), 'A Prophet's "Pregnant Pause": Samuel's Silence in the Ark Narrative (1 Sam 4:1–7:2', *HBT* 13.1:59–73.

—— (1994), 'Eli's Seat: The Transition from Priest to Prophet in 1 Samuel 1–4', *JSOT* 62:67–75.

Starbuck, S. R. A. (1999), *Court Oracles in the Psalms: The So-Called Royal Psalms in Their Ancient Near Eastern Context*, Atlanta: Society of Biblical Literature.

Stein, P. (1997), ' "Und man berichtete Saul . . . " text- und literarkritische Untersuchungen zu 1. Samuelis 24 und 26', *BN* 40:46–66.

Stern, P. D. (1989), '1 Samuel 15: Towards an Ancient View of the War-Herem', *UF* 21:413–420.

Sternberg, M. (1985), *The Poetics of Biblical Narrative*, Bloomington: Indiana University Press.

Stirrup, A. (2000), ' "Why Has Yahweh Defeated Us Today Before the Philistines?" The Question of the Ark Narrative', *TynB* 51:81–100.

Stoebe, H. J. (1986), 'David und Uria: Überlegungen zur Überlieterung von 2 Sam 11', *Bib* 67:388–396.

—— (1989), 'Überlegungen zur Exegese historischer Texte – dargestellt am den Samuelisbüchern', *TZ* 45:290–314.

Thompson, J. A. (1974), 'The Significance of the Verb *Love* in the David–Jonathan Narratives in 1 Samuel', *VT* 24:334–338.

Toorn, K. van der (1993), 'Saul and the Rise of Israelite State Religion', *VT* 43:519–542.

Toorn, K. van der, and C. Houtman (1994), 'David and the Ark', *JBL* 113:209–231.

Tov, E. (1986), 'The David and Goliath Saga', *BRev* 2.4:34–41.

Trible, P. (1978), *God and the Rhetoric of Sexuality*, Philadelphia: Fortress.

Tsevat, M. (1987), 'Die Namengebung Samuels und die Substitutionstheorie', *ZAW* 99:250–254.

Tsumura, D. T. (1992), '*ḥămôr leḥem* (1 Samuel xvi 20)', *VT* 42:412–414.

———(1995), 'Bedan, a Copyist's Error?', *VT* 45:122–123.

———(1999), 'Scribal Errors or Phonetic Spellings: Samuel as an Aural Text', *VT* 49:390–411.

Tur-Sinai, N. H. (1951), 'The Ark of God at Beit Shemesh (1 Samuel VI) and Peres Uzza (2 Samuel VI, 1 Chronicles XIII)', *VT* 4.1:275–286.

Ulrich, E. C., Jr. (1978), *The Qumran Text of Samuel and Josephus*, Missoula: Scholar's Press.

Ulshöfer, H. K. (1977), 'Nathan's Opposition to David's Intention to Build a Temple in the Light of Selected Ancient Near Eastern Texts', PhD diss., Boston University Graduate School.

Vanderhooft, D. (1999), 'Dwelling Beneath the Sacred Place: A Proposal for Reading 2 Samuel 7:10', *JBL* 118:625–633.

Vanderkam, J. C. (1980), 'Davidic Complicity in the Deaths of Abner and Eshbaal: A Historical and Redactional Study', *JBL* 99:521–539.

Vannoy, J. R. (1978), *Covenant Renewal at Gilgal: A Study of 1 Samuel 11:14–12:25*, Cherry Hill: Mack.

Vargon, S. (1996), 'The Blind and the Lame', *VT* 46:498–514.

Vaux, R. de (1965), *Ancient Israel: Its Life and Institutions*, 2nd ed., London: Darton Longman & Todd.

Veijola, T. (1975), *Die Ewige Dynastie: David und die Entstehung seiner Dynastie nach der deuteronomistischen Darstellung*, Helsinki: Suomalainen Tiedeakatemia.

———(1984), 'David in Keila', *RB* 91:51–87.

———(2000), 'Solomon: Bathsheba's Firstborn', in Knoppers and McConville 2000: 340–357.

Vorster, W. S. (1986), 'Readers, Readings and the Succession Narrative: An Essay on Reception Criticism', in van Wyk 1986: 339–353.

Walters, S. D. (1988), 'Hannah and Anna: The Greek and Hebrew Texts of 1 Samuel 1', *JBL* 107:385–412.

Waltke, B. K. (1988), 'The Phenomenon of Conditionality within Unconditional Covenants', in A. Gileadi (ed.), *Israel's Apostasy and Restoration: Essays in Honor of Roland K. Harrison*, Grand Rapids: Baker, 123–139.

———(1991), 'Superscripts, Postscripts, or Both', *JBL* 110:583–596.

Walton, J. H. (2007), *Ancient Near Eastern Thought and the Old Testament: Introducing the Conceptual World of the Hebrew Bible*, Nottingham: Apollos.

Watson, W. G. E. (1985), 'The Structure of 1 Sam 3', *BZ* 29:90–93.

———(1986), *Classical Hebrew Poetry: A Guide to its Techniques*, 2nd ed., Sheffield: Sheffield Academic Press.

Watts, J. W. (1992), *Psalms and Story: Inset Hymns in Hebrew Narrative*, Sheffield: JSOT.

Webb, N. (2006), '1 Samuel 17:55: "Abner, Whose Son Is That Young Man?" – A Response to Saul's Amnesia', *SABJT* 15:10–19.

Weinfeld, M. (1972), *Deuteronomy and the Deuteronomic School*, Oxford: Clarendon.

Weippert, H. (2000), '"Histories" and "History": Promise and Fulfilment in the Deuteronomistic Historical Work', in Knoppers and McConville 2000: 47–61.

Weiss, R. (1976), 'La Main du Seigneur sera contre vous et contre vos pères (1 Samuel XII, 15)', *RB* 83:51–54.

Wenham, G. J. (1975), 'Were David's Sons Priests?', *ZAW* 87:79–82.

Wenham, J. W. (1967), 'Large Numbers in the Old Testament', *TynB* 18:19–53.

Wénin, A., 'Le Discours de Jonathan à David (1 S 20, 12–16), et outré notes (2, 20; 9, 24; 15,9)', *Bib* 64:1–19.

Wesselius, J. W. (1990), 'Joab's Death and the Central Theme of the Succession Narrative (2 Samuel ix 1–1 Kings ii)', *VT* 40:336–351.

——— (1991), 'De wijze vrouwen in 2 Samuel 14 en 20', *NTT* 45:89–100.

West, G. (1997), 'Reading on the Boundaries: Reading 2 Samuel 21:1–14 with Rizpah', *Scr* 63:527–537.

Wharton, J. A. (1981), 'A Plausible Tale: Story and Theology in II Samuel 9–20, I Kings 1–2', *Int* 35:341–354.

White, E. (2007), 'Michal the Misinterpreted', *JSOT* 31.4:451–464.

White, M. C. (2006), 'Saul and Jonathan in 1 Samuel 1 and 14', in Ehrlich and White 2006: 119–138.

Whitelam, K. (1979), *The Just King: Monarchial Judicial Authority in Ancient Israel*, Sheffield: JSOT Press.

Whybray, R. N. (1968), *The Succession Narrative: A Study of II Sam 9–20 and 1 Kings 1 and 2*, London: SCM.

Wicke, D. W. (1986), 'The Structure of 1 Samuel 3: Another View', *BZ* 30:256–258.

Wiggins, S. A. (1993), 'Old Testament Dagan in the Light of Ugarit', *VT* 43:268–274.

——— (1997), 'Between Heaven and Earth: Absalom's Dilemma', *JNSL* 23:73–81.

Wilkinson, J. (1977), 'The Philistine Epidemic of 1 Samuel 5 and 6', *ExpTim* 88:137–141.

Williams, J. G. (1994), 'Sacrifice and the Beginnings of Kingship', *Semeia* 67:73–92.

Williamson, H. G. M. (1982), *1 and 2 Chronicles*, NCBC, Grand Rapids: Eerdmans; London: Marshall, Morgan & Scott.

Williamson, P. R. (2007), *Sealed with an Oath: Covenant in God's Unfolding Purpose*, Nottingham: Apollos.

Willis, J. T. (1971), 'An Anti-Elide Narrative Tradition from a Prophetic Circle at the Ramah Sanctuary', *JBL* 90:288–308.

Wittenberg, G. H. (1986), 'Ideology Critique and the Succession Narrative', in van Wyk 1986: 354–379.

Wolde, E. van (2003), 'In Words and Pictures: The Sun in 2 Samuel 12:7–12', *BibInt* 11:259–278.

Wolff, H. W. (2000), 'The Kerygma of the Deuteronomistic Historical Work', in Knoppers and McConville 2000: 62–94.

Wong, G. C. I. (1997), 'Who Loved Whom? A Note on 1 Samuel xvi 21', *VT* 47:554–556.

Wozniak, J. (1983), 'Drei verschiedene literarische Beschreibungen des bundes zwischen Jonathan und David', *BZ* 27:213–218.

Wright, C. J. H. (1990), *God's People in God's Land: Family, Land and Property in the Old Testament*, Carlisle: Paternoster.

—— (2004), *Old Testament Ethics for the People of God*, Leicester: IVP.

—— (2006), *The Mission of God: Unlocking the Bible's Grand Narrative*, Nottingham: IVP.

Wright, D. P. (2002), 'Music and Dance in 2 Samuel 6', *JBL* 121:201–225.

Wright, D. P., D. N. Freedman and A. Hurvitz (eds.) (1995), *Pomegranates and Golden Bells: Studies in Jewish, Biblical and Near Eastern Ritual, Law and Literature in Honor of Jacob Milgrom*, Winona Lake: Eisenbrauns.

Wright, J. W. (1993), 'The Innocence of David in 1 Chronicles 21', *JSOT* 60:87–105.

Wyatt, N. (1990), 'David's Census and the Tripartite Theory', *VT* 40:352–360.

—— (1995), 'Jonathan's Adventure and a Philological Conundrum', *PEQ* 127:62–69.

Wyk, W. C. van (ed.) (1986), *Studies in the Succession Narrative*, OTWSA Proceedings 1984 and 1985.

Yee, G. A. (1988a), 'The Anatomy of Biblical Parody: The Dirge Form in 2 Samuel 1 and Isaiah 14', *CBQ* 50:565–586.

—— (1988b), ' "Fraught with Background," Literary Ambiguity in II Samuel 11', *Int* 42:240–253.

Zapf, D. L. (1984), 'How Are the Mighty Fallen! A Study of 2 Samuel 1:17–27', *GTJ* 5:95–126.

Zehnder, M. (1998), 'Exegetische Beobachtungen zu den David-Jonathan-Geschichten', *Bib* 79:153–179.

Ziegler, Y. (2007), ' "So Shall God Do . . . ": Variations of an Oath Formula and Its Literary Meaning', *JBL* 126:59–81.

Zwickel, W. (1994), 'Dagon's abgeschlagener Kopf (1 Samuel v 3–4)', *VT* 44:239–249.

Zyl, A. H. van (1982), 'Die teologie van 'n naam', *NGTT* 23:317–319.

—— (1984), '1 Sam 1:2–2:11 – A Life World Lament of Affliction', *JNSL* 12:151–161.

—— (1998), 'Jy was baie na aan my hart (2 Sam 1:26)', *SK* 19:664–675.

Zyl, D. C. van (1993), 'Hannah's Share, Once More 1 Samuel 1:5', *OTE* 6:364–366.

INDEX OF REFERENCES TO
SCRIPTURE AND RELATED
LITERATURE

INDEX OF AUTHORS

INDEX OF SUBJECTS